MW00800354

WAIS–IV, WMS–IV, AND ACS

WAIS–IV, WMS–IV, AND ACS

Advanced Clinical Interpretation

Edited by

JAMES A. HOLDNACK
LISA WHIPPLE DROZDICK
LAWRENCE G. WEISS
Pearson Assessment, San Antonio, Texas, USA

GRANT L. IVERSON
University of British Columbia, Vancouver, Canada

AMSTERDAM • BOSTON • HEIDELBERG • LONDON
NEW YORK • OXFORD • PARIS • SAN DIEGO
SAN FRANCISCO • SINGAPORE • SYDNEY • TOKYO
Academic Press is an imprint of Elsevier

Academic Press is an imprint of Elsevier
32 Jamestown Road, London NW1 7BY, UK
225 Wyman Street, Waltham, MA 02451, USA
525 B Street, Suite 1800, San Diego, CA 92101-4495, USA

This book is printed on acid-free paper. ∞

Copyright © 2013 Elsevier Inc. All rights reserved

No part of this publication may be reproduced, stored in a retrieval system or
transmitted in any form or by any means electronic, mechanical, photocopying,
recording or otherwise without the prior written permission of the publisher.

Permissions may be sought directly from Elsevier's Science & Technology Rights
Department in Oxford, UK: phone (+44) (0) 1865 843830; fax (+44) (0) 1865 853333;
email: permissions@elsevier.com. Alternatively, visit the Science and Technology Books
website at www.elsevierdirect.com/rights for further information.

Notice
No responsibility is assumed by the publisher for any injury and/or damage to persons
or property as a matter of products liability, negligence or otherwise, or from any use
or operation of any methods, products, instructions or ideas contained in the material
herein. Because of rapid advances in the medical sciences, in particular, independent
verification of diagnoses and drug dosages should be made.

British Library Cataloguing-in-Publication Data
A catalogue record for this book is available from the British Library

Library of Congress Cataloging-in-Publication Data
A catalog record for this book is available from the Library of Congress

ISBN: 978-0-12-386934-0

For information on all Academic Press publications
visit our website at www.store.elsevier.com

Typeset by MPS Limited, Chennai, India
www.adi-mps.com

Printed and bound in United States of America

13 14 15 16 10 9 8 7 6 5 4 3 2 1

Working together
to grow libraries in
developing countries

www.elsevier.com • www.bookaid.org

CONTENTS

7. Assessing Performance Validity with the ACS   331

JAMES A. HOLDNACK, SCOTT MILLIS, GLENN J. LARRABEE AND GRANT L. IVERSON

8. Assessing Social Cognition Using the ACS for WAIS–IV and WMS–IV   367

YANA SUCHY AND JAMES A HOLDNACK

9. Assessing Cognition in Older Adults with the WAIS–IV, WMS–IV, and ACS   407

LISA WHIPPLE DROZDICK, JAMES A. HOLDNACK, TIMOTHY SALTHOUSE
AND C. MUNRO CULLUM

10. Using the WAIS–IV/WMS–IV/ACS Following Moderate-Severe Traumatic Brain Injury   485

GRANT L. IVERSON, JAMES A. HOLDNACK AND RAEL T. LANGE

11. Assessing Individuals with Psychiatric and Developmental Disorders   545

GERALD GOLDSTEIN, HOWARD OAKES, DAVID LOVEJOY AND JAMES A. HOLDNACK

Appendices containing Tables for chapters 2, 5 & 6 are available online at:
http://booksite.elsevier.com/9780123869340.

List of Contributors

Brian L. Brooks Alberta Children's Hospital and University of Calgary, Calgary, Alberta, Canada

Gordon J. Chelune University of Utah, Salt Lake City, Utah, USA

C. Munro Cullum UT Southwestern Medical Center, Dallas, Texas, USA

Lisa Whipple Drozdick Pearson Assessment, San Antonio, Texas, USA

Gerald Goldstein VA Pittsburgh Healthcare System, Pittsburgh, Pennsylvania, USA

James A. Holdnack Pearson Assessment, San Antonio, Texas, USA

Grant L. Iverson Department of Physical Medicine and Rehabilitation, Harvard Medical School; and Red Sox Foundation and Massachusetts General Hospital Home Base Program, Boston, Massachusetts, USA

Rael T. Lange Defense and Veterans Brain Injury Center, Walter Reed National Military Medical Center, Bethesda, Maryland, USA; and Department of Psychiatry, University of British Columbia, Vancouver, British Columbia, Canada

Glenn J. Larrabee Independent Practice, Sarasota, Florida, USA

David Lovejoy Hartford Hospital, West Hartford, Connecticut, USA, and The University of Connecticut School of Medicine, Farmington, Connecticut, USA

Scott Millis Wayne State University School of Medicine, Detroit, Michigan, USA

Howard Oakes Hartford Hospital, West Hartford, Connecticut, USA, and The University of Connecticut School of Medicine, Farmington, Connecticut, USA

Timothy Salthouse University of Virginia, Charlottesville, Virginia, USA

Mike R. Schoenberg University of South Florida College of Medicine, Tampa, Florida, USA

Yana Suchy University of Utah, Salt Lake City, Utah, USA

Sarah Tartar Hartford Hospital, Hartford, Connecticut, USA

Lawrence G. Weiss Pearson Assessment, San Antonio, Texas, USA

Xiaobin Zhou Pearson Assessment, San Antonio, Texas, USA

Preface

The publication of the Wechsler Adult Intelligence Scale—Fourth Edition (WAIS—IV: Wechsler, 2008) and Wechsler Memory Scale—Fourth Edition (WMS—IV: Wechsler, 2009) continue the tradition of psychometric and theoretical evolution of the Wechsler scales. The field of psychology has become increasingly sophisticated and the questions facing clinicians are complex, requiring new tools and approaches to evaluating different aspects of cognition. As more cases in court require scientific evidence of a clinician's interpretation, greater psychometric knowledge and validation of results is required. The introduction of the Advanced Clinical Solutions for WAIS—IV and WMS—IV (ACS: Pearson, 2009) reflects the evolution of the field. The data often presented post-publication in scientific journals and reports is now developed and validated within a test publication. This book provides additional data for the WAIS—IV, WMS—IV, and ACS to assist clinicians performing evaluations with complex clinical questions. Each chapter introduces a topic, provides extensive data on that area, applies the data in multiple case studies, and summarizes the key learning points. Early chapters focus on methodological and psychometric issues, while later chapters illustrate the use of the tools and measures in specific clinical populations. It is hoped that the information in this book will serve not only clinicians, but also the clients with complex clinical presentations with whom they work.

The book begins with an overview of the WAIS—IV, WMS—IV, ACS, and WMS—IV Flexible Approach (Pearson, 2009). Holdnack, Drozdick, Zhou, and Weiss provide a detailed overview of the instruments, and information on the cognitive abilities required to complete the tasks is described. The joint factor structure of the WAIS—IV/WMS—IV and normative data for new indexes are also presented. The ACS scores, procedures, and subtests are introduced, including: additional index scores and measures of learning and memory errors; external and embedded suboptimal effort tools to identify examinees that may be putting forth inadequate effort; demographic norms and the Test of Premorbid Functioning (TOPF) designed to determine if a patient's current test performance is expected or represents a decline from a previous level of ability; serial assessment tools to evaluate change in cognitive abilities over time; and measures of social cognition and executive functioning. The combination of the WAIS—IV, WMS—IV, and ACS provides a comprehensive and robust assessment, enabling the evaluation of specific hypotheses about a patient's cognitive functioning.

Multivariate base rates for the WAIS–IV, WMS–IV, and combined WAIS–IV and WMS–IV are presented in Chapter 2. In routine practice, clinicians use multiple measures of cognition, often across multiple cognitive domains. However, using a large battery of tests will increase the probability that an individual will have one or more low scores in healthy adults and older adults. Brooks, Iverson, and Holdnack present normative data enabling the clinician to interpret scores obtained from a battery of tests. The use of multivariate base rates can improve the diagnostic accuracy of the WAIS–IV and WMS–IV. Numerous base rate tables are provided as appendices to this chapter.

Cognitive variability in healthy controls is discussed by Oakes, Lovejoy, Tarter, and Holdnack in Chapter 3. Most individuals have strengths and weaknesses in their abilities. This is reflected in large differences between highest and lowest obtained scores. This variability is greater in individuals of with above-average intelligence or in individuals having one or more isolated very high scores. Given the commonly observed significant differences in healthy controls, it may be difficult to determine if strengths and weaknesses are strongly associated with a pathological process. Normative data presented in this chapter enables the clinician to identify normal and atypical variability.

The relationship between demographic and background characteristics and performance on cognitive measures is well researched and documented. Sex, education, and ethnicity have been identified as factors that need to be considered when interpreting performance on cognitive tests. In Chapter 4, Holdnack and Weiss provide a review of the relationship between these variables and the recent editions of the WAIS and WMS, and describe the utility of and difficulty using demographically adjusted norms. Demographic adjustments are used to identify changes in cognitive functioning from an estimated premorbid functioning level and thus may not be appropriate in all cases, particularly for individuals with chronic psychiatric, developmental, medical, or neurological conditions or for individuals whose background characteristics are not consistent with his or her demographic group.

The process of predicting premorbid functioning through the use of the TOPF and OPIE–IV is discussed in Chapter 5 by Schoenberg, Lange, Holdnack, and Iverson. The estimation of premorbid cognitive functioning is an important component of neuropsychological evaluations following brain injury, acquired neurological problems, or dementia. Statistical approaches for estimating premorbid cognitive functioning involve demographic models, current performance models, and combined demographic and performance models. The TOPF and the OPIE–IV were developed to estimate premorbid functioning based on the WAIS–IV. The TOPF also provides estimates of WMS–IV indexes. In addition, prediction of WASI–II performance is provided in

Chapter 5. Each model presented is described in detail, including the strengths and weaknesses of that approach.

Psychologists frequently conduct multiple evaluations across time on the same individual to determine if cognitive functioning has improved, remained stable, or declined from an established baseline evaluation. This is frequently done to track progress following an injury or intervention or to document decline in a neurological or psychiatric condition. However, improvement in scores may occur due to statistical or personal reasons unrelated to true changes in cognition, such as regression to the mean, practice effects, or situational factors such as motivation. In Chapter 6, Holdnack, Drozdick, Iverson, and Chelune discuss the issues around changes in cognitive scores over time and present regression-based reliable change methodologies that describe serial assessment while reducing the impact of measurement error, regression to the mean, and practice effects. Measures to assess change across time or across editions of WAIS and WMS are presented.

In Chapter 7, Holdnack, Millis, Larrabee, and Iverson describe the impact of response bias on the measurement of cognitive functioning. Response bias is a process by which an examinee intentionally or unintentionally responds to test items to present themselves as cognitively impaired. When response bias is present, the results of the test are no longer an accurate assessment of the examinee's ability. This chapter illustrates the use of external and embedded measures from the ACS and the WAIS–IV/WMS–IV to identify response bias.

The social cognition measures of the ACS are described in Chapter 8. Many clinical populations, including patients diagnosed with neurological, psychiatric, and developmental disorders, as well as patients suffering traumatic brain injury, have impairments in components of social cognition. Suchy and Holdnack describe the current state of research on social cognition and the application of the ACS Social Perception test in a variety of clinical populations.

The WAIS–IV and WMS–IV are commonly used in the assessment of older adults. In Chapter 9, Drozdick, Holdnack, Salthouse, and Cullum provide an overview of normal cognitive aging and the differential assessments used to differentiate pathological changes in cognitive functioning from normal aging. Many of the tools developed for the WAIS–IV, WMS–IV, ACS, and Texas Functional Living Scales (TFLS) may be used in the neurocognitive assessment of older adults. WAIS–IV and WMS–IV index and subtest scores for normally aging adults, and for individuals with Alzheimer disease or MCI, are presented. In addition, the performance of these groups using demographically adjusted norms is presented, and OPIE and TOPF prediction equations were calculated for older adults. Variability measures and multivariate base rates are also examined with older adults.

Individuals with traumatic brain injury (TBI) are frequently referred for evaluations. Many of the tools developed for ACS are particularly relevant in this population, including serial assessment, premorbid ability estimation, and suboptimal effort, due to the complex nature of the injuries and frequent involvement of outside agencies in evaluations (e.g., court, disability). In Chapter 10, Iverson, Holdnack, and Lange discuss the use of the WAIS–IV, WMS–IV, and ACS with patients with TBI. This chapter describes the use of these tools in depth by providing studies contrasting normally developing individuals and individuals with TBI. Although there is considerable variability in the short- and long-term outcomes for individuals who sustain a moderate to severe TBIs, many will experience permanent cognitive deficits.

In Chapter 11, Goldstein, Oakes, Lovejoy, and Holdnack describe the use of the WAIS–IV, WMS–IV, and ACS in populations of psychiatric and developmental disorders, specifically in individuals with schizophrenia and autism. Individuals with major psychiatric and developmental disorders have a variety of cognitive impairments that impact their daily functioning. Cognitive functioning in schizophrenia is associated with a number of important outcomes, including the ability to benefit from work training programs and interventions focused on improving instrumental activities of daily living. Appropriate assessment of cognitive skills is important for appropriate treatment planning.

We would like to thank individuals who contributed to this volume including: Dr. Helen Carlson, Lonna Mitchell, and Emily Tam for populating the Tables in Chapter 2, Dr. Shawnda Lanting and Yana Pogrebetsky for cross-checking values in Chapter 2, Megan Wright for assistance with a literature review and tables for Chapter 10, and Jennifer Bernardo for assistance with manuscript preparation on several chapters. The editors would also like to thank Pearson for supporting this project and permission to use the WAIS–IV standardization data and manual content for portions of this book. Nikki Levy, publisher at Academic Press, provided encouragement and direction to the editors throughout this project. As with our other Wechsler books, her efforts played an integral part in this volume's completion. Our sincere appreciation also goes to Senior Developmental Editor Barbara Makinster for their assistance in preparing the final manuscript for publication. To all of our authors, many of whom served on the WAIS–IV and WMS–IV Advisory Panel, your valuable contributions to the understanding and assessment of intelligence continue even beyond the publication of the WAIS–IV.

James A. Holdnack
Lisa Whipple Drozdick
Larry G. Weiss
Grant L. Iverson

Overview of the WAIS–IV/ WMS–IV/ACS

Lisa Whipple Drozdick, James A. Holdnack, Lawrence G. Weiss and Xiaobin Zhou

Pearson Assessment, San Antonio, Texas, USA

INTRODUCTION

The Wechsler Adult Intelligence Scale–Fourth Edition (WAIS–IV: Wechsler, 2008) and the Wechsler Memory Scale–Fourth Edition (WMS–IV: Wechsler, 2009), combined with other measures, are frequently used in comprehensive evaluations. This book is about best practices in using these instruments together, and introduces advanced clinical solutions specific to neuropsychological evaluations. The Advanced Clinical Solutions for WAIS–IV and WMS–IV (ACS: Pearson, 2009) and the WMS–IV Flexible Approach (WMS–IV Flex: Pearson, 2010) expand the constructs assessed across the two instruments for use with specific neurodiagnostic questions.

This chapter assumes the reader has basic knowledge of WAIS–IV and WMS–IV subtests, administration, and general interpretative strategies. Detailed descriptions of the subtests and composites are available elsewhere (see Coalson, Raiford, Saklofske, & Weiss, 2010; Drozdick, Wahlstrom, Zhu, & Weiss, 2011; Wechsler, 2008, 2009). This chapter presents a more in-depth overview of the constructs measured by the WAIS–IV and WMS–IV, goes beyond the numbers to explore cognitive factors that influence performance on each of the major clinical domains assessed, and introduces more advanced procedures not found in the WAIS–IV and WMS–IV administration and technical manuals. Following this high level presentation of the instruments,

WAIS-IV, WMS-IV, and ACS.
DOI: http://dx.doi.org/10.1016/B978-0-12-386934-0.00001-8 © 2013 Elsevier Inc. All rights reserved.

information on the joint factor structure of the combined instruments is described. The chapter concludes with descriptions of ACS and WMS–IV Flex.

WAIS–IV CONTENT AND APPROACH TO DEVELOPMENT

In a continuation of the evolution of the Wechsler model, the WAIS–IV index scores are the primary focus of clinical interpretation. This is a shift from the original Wechsler model of intelligence, which was based on a two-part structure comprised of the Verbal Intelligence Quotient (VIQ) and Performance Intelligence Quotient (PIQ). The current Wechsler factor model includes four factors: Verbal Comprehension, Perceptual Reasoning, Working Memory, and Processing Speed. The shift in focus to more specific factor-based indexes began in 1991 when the WISC–III introduced four factor-based index scores as an optional alternative to the traditional VIQ/PIQ structure; the WAIS–III followed suit in 1997. In 2003, the WISC–IV dropped VIQ and PIQ, eliminating them from the test in favor of the four factor-based structures presented in WISC–III. In addition, the name of the Freedom from Distractibility Index was changed to the Working Memory Index to reflect the increasing understanding of the construct. The name of the Perceptual Organization Index was changed to the Perceptual Reasoning Index to accurately describe the increased focus on perceptual reasoning among the newly created perceptual subtests, and clinical interpretation was focused on the four index scores. The WAIS–IV adopted the four-factor model in 2008, completing the transformation of the Wechsler series of tests.

To be fair to Dr. Wechsler's legacy, his model has always included subtests which measure working memory and processing speed, just not in the current index structure reflected in WAIS–IV. These measures were included in the VIQ and PIQ structures depending on whether the stimuli and response processes were verbal or visual–perceptual, respectively. Contemporary researchers have developed well-articulated theories about the underlying neurocognitive processes tapped by these tasks and their relation to intelligence. Original Wechsler subtests such as Arithmetic and Digit Span are now understood as measures of working memory; and Coding, or Digit Symbol as it was originally named, is now understood as a measure of cognitive processing speed. As more was learned about the importance of these constructs in the expression of intelligent behavior, the Wechsler tests adapted by disentangling these constructs from other skills included in the VIQ and PIQ. New tasks such as Letter Number Sequencing and

Cancellation were added to expand the assessment of working memory and processing speed, respectively. Also, Digit Span was significantly revised in WAIS–IV to include digit sequencing items to improve the assessment of working memory based on our current understanding of that construct.

Similarly, several long-standing Wechsler subtests are believed to be related to fluid reasoning (i.e., Similarities, Block Design). Subsequently, new subtests have been developed to measure this construct more directly such as Matrix Reasoning (which first appeared in WISC–III and was subsequently included in WISC–IV, WAIS–III, and WAIS–IV), Picture Concepts (which first appeared in WISC–IV and then was added to WPPSI–III), and Figure Weights and Visual Puzzles which debuted in the WAIS–IV.

Without Dr. Wechsler's far-reaching clinical insights, the field of intellectual assessment would not be where it is today. However, the WAIS–IV is a different test then the one that Dr. Wechsler introduced, one that builds upon multiple modern theories of cognitive neuroscience and is informed by ongoing clinical and neuropsychological research.

WAIS–IV INDEX SCORES AND STRUCTURE

Figure 1.1 presents a visual model of the WAIS–IV. The composite scores, comprised of the four index scores and Full Scale Intelligence Quotient (FSIQ), are presented in ovals and are the primary focus of interpretation. The subtests are listed below the index in which they are

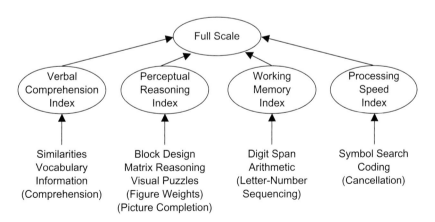

FIGURE 1.1   **WAIS–IV Factor Model.**

included. Parentheses are used to differentiate supplemental subtests from the core subtests used to derive index scores.

Verbal Comprehension Index

The Verbal Comprehension Index (VCI) reflects an individual's ability to comprehend verbal stimuli, reason with semantic material, and communicate thoughts and ideas with words. Such abilities are imperative for intelligent functioning in modern society. As shown in Figure 1.1, the VCI consists of the Similarities (SI), Vocabulary (VC), and Information (IN) subtests. The Comprehension (CO) subtest is supplemental. All VCI subtests are well-known and researched measures of verbal comprehension.

Perceptual Reasoning Index

The Perceptual Reasoning Index (PRI) measures fluid reasoning along with some perceptual organization. Required WAIS–IV subtests are Block Design (BD), Matrix Reasoning (MR), and Visual Puzzles (VP). The Figure Weights (FW) subtest is supplemental. Block Design and MR are well-known measures of visual–spatial organization and fluid reasoning, respectively.

Two subtests are new to WAIS–IV: Visual Puzzles and Figure Weights. Visual Puzzles measures the ability to analyze and synthesize abstract, nonverbal, visual material. Successful performance requires the ability to maintain a visual image in mind temporarily while mentally rotating, inverting, and otherwise manipulating that image and matching the resulting percept to a visual target. It also requires the integration of multiple related cognitive processes including visual perception, simultaneous processing, working memory, spatial visualization, spatial manipulation, and visuoconstruction abilities. Figure Weights measures quantitative and analogical reasoning. Quantitative reasoning tasks can involve fluid reasoning processes expressed as mathematical processes, emphasizing either inductive or deductive logic. Although the solution to each FW item can be expressed with algebraic equations, there is no task requirement to do so, eliminating the demand for acquired knowledge of advanced mathematical equations. Figure Weights involve working memory, but it is reduced relative to typical quantitative tasks (e.g., mental arithmetic) through the continual visual presentation of items in a stimulus book that allows the patient to refresh stimuli held in working memory while solving the problem.

Working Memory Index

The Working Memory Index (WMI) measures attention, concentration, and working memory. The WMI consists of two primary subtests, Digit Span (DS) and Arithmetic (AR), and the supplemental Letter-Number Sequencing (LN). The DS subtest includes three tasks: Digit Span Forward (DSF), Digit Span Backward (DSB), and the new Digit Span Sequencing (DSS). DSF measures short-term memory, not working memory. DSB and DSS measure auditory working memory. The current reformulation of the AR subtest represents a substantial transformation from previous editions and is a much improved measure of working memory. Compared to its predecessors, the WAIS–IV AR subtest contains reduced verbiage in the word problems, fewer items with time bonuses, and simpler numerical calculations with more steps, reducing the pull of mathematical skill and increasing the activation of working memory.

Processing Speed Index

The Processing Speed Index (PSI) measures the speed of mental processing, using visual stimuli and graphomotor skills, and is related to the efficient use of other cognitive abilities. A weakness in simple visual scanning and tracking may leave a patient less time and mental energy for the complex task of understanding new material. The PSI includes the core Coding (CD) and Symbol Search (SS) subtests and the supplemental Cancellation (CA) subtest. Cancellation is similar to previously developed cancellation tasks designed to measure processing speed, visual selective attention, vigilance, perceptual speed, and visual–motor ability (Bate, Mathias, & Crawford, 2001; Geldmacher, Fritsch, & Riedel, 2000; Sattler, 2008; Wojciulik, Husain, Clarke, & Driver, 2001). Cancellation tasks have been used extensively in neuropsychological settings as measures of visual neglect, response inhibition, and motor perseveration (Adair, Na, Schwartz, & Heilman, 1998; Geldmacher et al., 2000; Lezak, Howieson, & Loring, 2004; Na, Adair, Kang, Chung, Lee, & Heilman, 1999). Relative to the WISC–IV version of CA, a decision-making component was added in the WAIS–IV to place more complex cognitive demands on examinees. The patient must simultaneously discriminate both the color and the shape of the stimuli and inhibit responding when only one of the two features is present.

General Ability Index

The General Ability Index (GAI) summarizes performance on the VCI and PRI in a single number. These two indexes are traditionally thought to contain the most highly 'g'-loaded subtests within WAIS–IV. As discussed later however, AR has moved up considerably in the ranking of g-loadings, but is not included in GAI. The WAIS–IV GAI excludes the contributions of the WMI and PSI to intelligence. Clearly, GAI and FSIQ can lead to different impressions of a patient's overall ability when there is variability across the four indexes.

The GAI was first developed for use with WISC–III in ability-achievement discrepancy analyses (Prifitera, Weiss, & Saklofske, 1998) because many students with learning disability (LD) exhibit cognitive processing deficits in working memory and processing speed concomitant with their learning disabilities. This pattern can result in lower FSIQ scores for individuals with LD, and consequently smaller discrepancies with achievement, thus making it less likely that he or she will be identified as underachieving and in need of services. Thus, use of GAI as a measure of global intelligence for comparisons with other abilities impacted by lower performance on working memory and processing speed, such as achievement, is often a more appropriate comparison with those constructs than FSIQ.

Other uses for the GAI have since been identified. For example, GAI may be an appropriate estimate of overall ability when physical or sensory disorders invalidate performance on the working memory or processing speed tasks, or both. Another possible use is in approximating the pre-injury cognitive status and memory abilities of patients with traumatic brain injury. All discrepancies between the WAIS–IV and WMS–IV utilize the GAI in place of the FSIQ. Memory impairment is often compromised in the same clinical conditions where low WMI and PSI scores are observed (e.g., moderate-to-severe traumatic brain injury: TBI). Similar to the differences observed in LD evaluations, when FSIQ is lower due to comparatively low WMI and PSI scores, it is more difficult to find differences between intellectual functioning and memory functioning. The VCI and PRI tend to be less affected in clinical disorders in which memory functioning is also impacted. The use of GAI allows the practitioner to better identify memory deficits in patients with concomitant PSI and/or WMI deficits.

Prifitera, Saklofske and Weiss (2005) suggest that some practitioners may prefer the GAI as an alternative way of summarizing overall ability. This suggestion has led to an increasing number of psychological evaluations in which the GAI is described as a better estimate of overall ability than FSIQ whenever the WMI or PSI scores are significantly lower than the VCI or PRI scores. As subsequently clarified, this is not what the authors intended (Prifitera, Saklofske, & Weiss, 2008). The GAI should be considered a better estimate of intelligence than FSIQ only when there are sound clinical reasons to exclude WMI and PSI, such as invalid administration due to lack of effort, sensory or physical impairments, or disturbance of the testing session. Working memory and processing speed are essential components of a comprehensive assessment of intelligence, and excluding them from the estimate of overall intelligence simply because the patient's abilities in those areas are relative weaknesses is poor practice. Such practice will result in unrealistically high estimates of intelligence for these patients, possibly excluding them from needed services and creating unrealistic employment expectations. The GAI can be a vital comparison measure in an evaluation when described correctly; however, it is not the best estimate of overall intelligence because it suffers from construct underrepresentation.

Cognitive Proficiency Index

The Cognitive Proficiency Index (CPI) summarizes performance on the working memory and processing speed indices of the WAIS–IV in a single score. The CPI represents a set of functions whose common element is the proficiency with which one processes certain types of cognitive information. Proficient processing, through quick visual speed and good mental control, facilitates fluid reasoning and the acquisition of new material by reducing the cognitive demands of novel or higher order tasks (Weiss, Saklofske, Prifitera, & Holdnack, 2006). In other words, efficient cognitive processing facilitates learning and problem-solving by "freeing up" cognitive resources for more advanced, higher level skills.

The WAIS–IV CPI excludes the contributions of verbal comprehension and perceptual reasoning to intelligence. Thus, CPI and GAI can provide different views into a patient's cognitive abilities when there is significant variability across the relevant index scores. Both views are sometimes necessary to form a complete picture of an individual's strengths and weaknesses that is not distorted by combining a set of diverse abilities into a single overall score. Rather than reporting GAI as the best estimate of overall ability when the profile of abilities is diverse, it is sometimes better practice to describe both the GAI and CPI in the psychological evaluation. Norms tables for the WAIS–IV CPI are provided in Weiss, Saklofske, Coalson and Raiford (2010).

ISSUES IN SUMMARIZING OVERALL ABILITY

The FSIQ has strong explanatory and predictive power at the group and individual level. Still, the use of an overall summary score may mask individual differences among the broad domains of general ability, especially in patients with neuropsychological deficits where the focus of clinical attention is not prediction but diagnosis of underlying cognitive deficits. For this reason, the relevance of reporting IQ scores has been questioned (Fiorello et al., 2007). Yet, other researchers suggest that FSIQ may be an equally valid measure of general ability for individuals or groups having highly variable index scores as for those having consistent index scores (Daniel, 2007) and that there may be no difference in the predictive validity of FSIQ for low-scatter and high-scatter groups (Watkins, Glutting, & Lei, 2007).

FSIQ is an especially strong predictor of educational attainment, occupational level, memory functioning, and school achievement (Wechsler, 2008, 2009). FSIQ and achievement, for example, correlate strongly, typically around 0.70. This means that FSIQ explains about half the variance in achievement. There is no known variable or collection of variables that comes close to fully accounting for the other half. Beyond the relationship with achievement, there is considerable ecological and criterion validity for the use of an overall estimate of general intelligence in a variety of areas related to success in life including pre-employment testing and predicting job performance (Gottfredson, 1997, 1998; Kuncel, Hezlett, & Ones, 2004). Thus, when the focus of clinical attention is prediction then FSIQ is often the most potent predictor. When the focus is clinical diagnosis of pathology then the index scores are often more informative.

Unlike every other Wechsler interpretative system that has been written, we discuss FSIQ last, rather than first. This is not to devalue the explanatory and predictive power of the FSIQ, but to emphasize the descriptive clinical power of the WAIS–IV Indexes and to place FSIQ in its proper role of providing a relevant backdrop against which the index scores are evaluated. This is consistent with our position that the first line of clinical interpretation rests with the index scores.

A POSSIBLE FIFTH FACTOR

Several studies have explored the WAIS–IV factor model. Benson, Hulac and Kranzler (2010) argued for the superiority of a five-factor model in which Matrix Reasoning, Figure Weights, and Arithmetic loaded on a fifth factor termed Fluid Reasoning. Ward, Bergman and Herbert (2011) proposed a modification of the WAIS–IV four factor model in which residual factors were formed for visual–spatial reasoning (BD, VP, and PC) and quantitative reasoning (FW and AR). Ward and colleagues argued that this modified model was theoretically consistent yet superior to the original WAIS–IV model, but that there was no compelling statistical reason to prefer the Benson et al. (2010)

five-factor model over the modified four-factor model. Weiss, Keith, Chen, and Zhu (2013a) tested a five-factor model in which quantitative reasoning (AR and FW) was defined as a narrow ability subsumed under the fluid reasoning factor (MR, FW, and AR). Weiss et al. found that although the fit was slightly better for this model, it was excellent for both the four and five factor models. They extended previous findings by demonstrating full measurement invariance between normal and clinical samples for both models. The above studies included the supplemental subtests, which is clearly best practice for model definition but often of limited utility to practitioners who have administered only the core subtests. Using only core WAIS–IV subtests, Lichtenberger and Kaufman (2009) proposed a five-factor model in which the fluid factor consists of MR and AR (without FW that is supplemental).

These WAIS–IV studies should be interpreted in light of the literature on the WISC–IV factor structure because the two tests have the same conceptual model, albeit with a couple of different subtests. Extant research on WISC–IV factor structure contains a similar set of findings as WAIS–IV: both four- and five-factor models emerge as good fits to the data, and the fifth factor is often characterized as fluid reasoning; although complicated by the interpretation of Arithmetic as fluid or quantitative reasoning (Bodin, Pardini, Burns, & Stevens, 2009; Chen, Keith, Chen, & Chang, 2009; Chen, Keith, Weiss, Zhu, & Li, 2010; Chen, & Zhu, 2012; Keith, Fine, Taub, Reynolds, Kranzler, 2006; Lecerf, Rossier, Favez, Reverte, & Coleaux, 2010; Weiss, Keith, Chen, & Zhu, 2013b).

It is interesting to observe how the g-loadings of Wechsler subtests shift as the composition of subtests shifts with each new edition of the test. While it has been axiomatic for decades that VC and BD are the most highly g-loaded subtests on the Wechsler scales, AR now emerges as one of the three highest g-loading subtests in WAIS–IV studies, even ranking first in some studies. Arithmetic is clearly a factorially complex, multiply determined task that requires the integration of several cognitive abilities including verbal conceptualization, working memory, and numerical reasoning; and perhaps the integrative task demands are what make the AR subtest partly fluid in nature. At the same time, the numerical stimuli of the AR task logically invokes interpretations based partly on quantitative reasoning, considered as a subtype of fluid reasoning in the Cattell, Horn, Carroll (CHC) model of intelligence (Carroll, 1993).

While the clinical interpretation of a possible fifth factor requires further research, the main point for clinicians to keep in mind is that when patients present large discrepancies between the subtests that compose the PR or WM indexes, there is some empirical support for interpreting these patterns. When the BD and VP scores hang together separately from MR and FW, consider interpretations based on visual–spatial organization versus fluid reasoning. When AR is aberrant within the WMI but hangs together with FW, consider interpretations based on quantitative reasoning versus working memory.

WAIS–IV: GOING BEYOND THE NUMBERS

Cognitive Influences on VCI

Although the VCI includes tasks that require prior knowledge of certain words and information, it would be a mistake to interpret this index only as a measure of words and facts taught in school. Clearly, some base knowledge of words must be assumed in order to measure verbal reasoning; after all, one could not measure verbal reasoning without using words. Barring an unusually limiting environment, performance on these tasks reflects a person's ability to grasp verbally presented facts typically available in the world around them, to reason with semantic constructs, and to express their reasoning with words. VCI measures crystallized knowledge, the breadth and depth of a person's acquired knowledge of a culture, and the effective application of this knowledge. This store of primarily verbal or language-based knowledge may represent abilities developed largely through the investment of other abilities during educational and general life experience (McGrew & Flanagan, 1998, p. 20).

A low score on VCI may reflect low verbal comprehension or expression ability, a lack of opportunity to develop particular verbal abilities, or some kind of "interference" that compromises the acquisition or expression of abilities (e.g., traumatic brain injury, mild cognitive impairment, aphasia, epilepsy). Prior to making an interpretation of low verbal ability, the psychologist should ask: was the required knowledge acquired but cannot be recalled (for several possible reasons) or was it never acquired in the first place? One useful methodology for addressing this issue is the "recognition paradigm." All of the WAIS–IV verbal comprehension subtests require free recall of verbal information, which is a much more difficult cognitive task than cued recall or recognition. Some individuals may answer incorrectly because they could not retrieve information from long-term storage even though they know the information. In these cases, the information may be more readily recalled if a clue is given or the correct information can be selected from a set of possible answers. This can be observed in everyday situations when someone struggles to recall the name of a colleague. However, recall improves when additional clues are provided, such as the university he or she is from or the initial letter-sound of his or her name. Moreover, when a possible name is suggested, a recognition task, it is instantly recognized as correct or incorrect. In these situations, it may be instructive to consider the patient's responses to a verbal recognition task such as the Peabody Picture Vocabulary Test–Fourth edition (PPVT–IV: Dunn & Dunn, 2007). The comparison between Vocabulary and PPVT performance informs the examiner if the patient has the knowledge, but either has difficulty expressing it or accessing it. If memory problems are suspected (e.g., accessing learned material), the clinician can consider additional memory assessment with a memory test such as the California Verbal Learning Test–Second Edition (Delis, Kramer, Kaplan, & Ober, 2000); or the WMS–IV that requires the patient to learn information and recall it immediately, or following cues recall or recognize the information after a delay. This provides an empirical evaluation of whether an examinee's responses were a function of lack of encoding (i.e., poor performance on all recall and recognition measures) or lack of access to knowledge previously learned and stored in the semantic lexicon (i.e., poor performance on recall in contrast to good performance on recognition). Clearly, this makes a critical difference in interpretation and is one reason we describe intelligence test scores in terms of current functioning rather than immutable capacity.

In neurological, psychiatric, or developmental disorders, in which language functioning has been compromised or has not developed normally, VCI results may represent difficulties with language functioning; rather than low intellectual ability. The WAIS–IV verbal subtests place significant demands on expressive language functioning. Poor expressive language skills can result in lower scores on these tests. Each subtest requires varying demands on expressive language functioning (e.g., one word vs. multiple sentence responses). Variability across subtests may be a reflection of expressive language difficulties. As noted earlier, expressive language problems can be evaluated using recognition verbal tests. Receptive language skills are also significantly related to VCI performance. Patients with receptive language impairments will achieve low scores on VCI. Acquired deficits in receptive language function can compromise VCI performance. When low VCI scores are obtained and expressive and/or receptive language impairments are suspected, further evaluation of general language skills can clarify if low VCI performance relates to low verbal intellectual functioning or impaired language functioning.

Cognitive Influences on PRI

Although it would seem ideal to assess fluid reasoning alone without tapping other domains of cognition, this is patently impossible. Reasoning must take place on some subject. Just as verbal reasoning cannot be assessed without invoking verbal stimuli and therefore some base of crystallized knowledge, non-verbal fluid reasoning cannot occur in a sterile vacuum (Weiss et al., 2010). Once any type of stimulus is presented, other factors come into play. For example, matrix analogy tasks are frequently described as pure measures of fluid reasoning; however, the task involves multiple cognitive skills, including visuoperceptual skills, attention, visual discrimination, fluid reasoning, and the ability to articulate a response verbally or motorically (i.e., pointing). Factor analytic studies demonstrate that each subtest loads primarily on one factor; however, there are often minor loadings on other factors. Indeed, it may be the successful integration of multiple cognitive processes to solve a novel problem that is the essence of fluid reasoning.

In neurological, developmental, or medical conditions in which visual processes are significantly affected, the PRI index may not be a good measure of intellectual ability. Brain injury affecting a patient's visual field or producing visual neglect syndrome, will affect the patient's ability to accurately process visual information but not necessarily impair their ability to reason. The PRI will also be compromised in disorders affecting the spatial processing (e.g., Turner's Syndrome: Kesler et al., 2004; Messina et al., 2007). Although the tasks in PRI require attention to visual detail, these measures are not significantly affected by disorders of sustained attention such as Attention Deficit Hyperactivity Disorder (ADHD: Wechsler, 2008). The PRI index can be affected by motor problems due to the motor demands of the BD subtest. Clinicians may consider using alternate subtest substitution (e.g., Picture Completion or Figure Weights) when testing patients with known motor difficulties.

Cognitive Influences on WMI

Working memory is the ability to hold information in mind temporarily while performing some operation on or manipulation with that information, or engaging in an interfering task and then accurately reproducing the updated information or correctly acting on it. Working memory can be thought of as mental control (an executive process) involving reasonably higher-order tasks (rather than rote tasks), and it presumes attention and concentration. As described by Jonides, Lacey, & Nee (2005), *"Working memory is a system that can store a small amount of information briefly, keeping that information quickly accessible and available for transformation by rules and strategies, while updating it frequently"* (p. 2).

Baddeley (2003) developed the seminal model of the working memory system. He proposes a *phonological loop* and a *visual–spatial sketchpad* in which verbal and visual stimuli respectively are stored and refreshed, and a *central executive* that controls attention directed toward these sources. A fourth component known as the *episodic buffer* was subsequently included in this model. This buffer is assumed to be attentionally controlled by the central executive and to be accessible to conscious awareness. Baddeley regards the episodic buffer as a crucial feature of the capacity of working memory to act as a global workspace that is accessed by conscious awareness. When working memory requires information from long-term storage, it may be "downloaded" into the episodic buffer rather than simply activated within long-term memory (Baddeley, 2003).

Models of working memory and their neural underpinnings are still being actively researched and refined, and the associated terminology will continue to evolve for some time. The term *registration* is used herein to convey the process by which stimuli are taken in and maintained in immediate memory. Capacity for registering information in immediate memory can be measured by the length of the person's immediate forward span. *Mental manipulation* implies updating or transforming information active in immediate memory. This can be as simple as rehearsal and chunking of information to keep it active or continuously refreshing the contents of the storage buffer based on new input, or it may involve abstract manipulation of the stored content. The precise point in this process at which working memory resources are invoked is debatable. For example, although attending to, storing, and repeating a license plate number may appear only to involve short-term memory, the role of working memory may enter the picture when there is interference from other sources, a mnemonic is employed to assist in remembering the alphanumeric characters, or the observer is also asked to recall the type of car. Thus, these processes may be more of a continuum as the point at which one moves from passive registration of auditory stimuli to active strategies for maintenance is not always clear.

Employed adults with serious deficits in working memory may have considerable difficulties at work. In addition, mental arithmetic tasks are frequently required in real life situations. For example, estimating driving time, halving a casserole recipe, determining the value of a 30% off coupon at a clothing store, determining the value of a 20% tip on a restaurant bill, making change, and exchanging currencies between US or Canadian Dollars, Euros, or Pesos all require mental arithmetic. A weakness in working memory may make the processing of complex information more time consuming and tax the individual's mental energies more quickly compared to co-workers; perhaps contributing to more frequent errors on a variety of job-related tasks that require sustained attention and concentration. Adults with auditory working memory disorders may experience difficulty jotting down notes of key points in a business meeting while continuing to attend to the meeting, keeping in mind the next point they want to make in a business negotiation or sales-call while listening to the other party, shifting attention to return a phone call after being interrupted by the boss, or sustaining concentration to complete a monthly budget report without being distracted by routine emails, as well as employing good judgment to shift tasks when an email arrives with a red flag signifying that it is urgent. Executive function system deficits in planning, organization, and the ability to shift cognitive sets should be evaluated in individuals with working memory difficulties. In addition, psychologists should be alert to the social and behavioral consequences of mental fatigue and work stress that can ensue from these disorders, and carefully assess the level of social support and emotional resiliency possessed by the patient. Such issues might be considered in return-to-work evaluations.

For young adults in school who have not learned grade level skills related to arithmetic calculation and mathematical operations, or any adults with a history of primary mathematical disability, the Arithmetic subtest may not be an accurate indication of working memory. The Arithmetic subtest assesses a complex set of cognitive skills and abilities and a low score may have several appropriate interpretations depending on the clinical context. For example, a patient with low scores on all three subtests is more likely to have a problem with WM than a patient who earns average or above average scores on DS and LN but below average scores on AR. In the latter instance, the issue may be more one of not having learned the required arithmetic skills or having a specific learning difficulty related to arithmetic. Alternatively, a patient who earns a higher score on AR than DS or LN may be one for whom arithmetic is highly developed; for example, an individual for whom mathematics is well grounded in work life (e.g., an accountant, math teacher, actuary). For this reason, it may be helpful to administer all three WM subtests whenever there is a question about either WM or arithmetic skills and to consider administering WMS–IV visual working memory subtests. A serious deficit in working memory cannot only create difficulties at work and in daily functioning, but may also have major implications for the academic lives of young adults in school or vocational training programs.

The WAIS–IV working memory tasks also require the processing of auditory and linguistic information. Patients with significant auditory acuity problems may experience difficulty on the working memory subtests because they did not accurately hear the stimuli. This is a particular concern with older adult populations in which hearing loss is common. Patients with language impairments will also have difficulty performing these tests. The Arithmetic subtest requires intact receptive language skills and often cross-loads on the VCI. When auditory or language problems are present, the WMI may not represent working memory functioning but rather reflect the deficits in these other cognitive domains. When auditory processing or language deficits are present, the clinician may choose to use the WMS–IV visual working memory measures to assess this construct.

Cognitive Influences on PSI

Performance on PSI subtests may be influenced by short-term visual memory, attention, visual scanning and tracking, visual discrimination, or visual–motor coordination. Patients may complete fewer items on this task if they present with fine motor difficulties due to neurological, medical, psychiatric, or developmental disorders (e.g., stroke, chronic alcoholism, medication side effects) but this does not necessarily imply a problem with processing speed. Additionally, an individual with obsessive-compulsive traits may earn lower scores, not due to a processing speed deficit but rather due to a specific response style. Moreover, an individual with mania who rushes through these tasks will likely make sufficient errors and obtain lower scores on the PSI subtests and index. Again, this may not be due to an underlying processing speed deficit but rather a behavioral correlate (i.e., impulsivity) of a psychiatric disorder. It is important to include behavioral observations and ensure that the findings from the WAIS–IV corroborate or are supported by the complete clinical picture.

Processing speed is theoretically important to both the acquisition and expression of intelligence. From a neurodevelopmental perspective, there are large and obvious age-related trends in processing speed that are accompanied by age-related changes in the number of transient connections to the central nervous system and increases in myelination. Several investigators have found that measures of infant processing speed predict later IQ scores (e.g., Dougherty & Haith, 1997) and WAIS–IV PSI scores are potentially sensitive to neurological disorders such as epilepsy (Wechsler, 2008).

Thus, speed of mental processing is more than simply doing a task at a faster or slower rate but in itself is a key cognitive and individual differences variable. There is consistent evidence that both simple and choice reaction time correlate about 0.20 or slightly higher with scores from intelligence tests while inspection time, hypothesized by some to be a measure of the rate that information is processed, correlates about 0.40 with intelligence test scores (see Deary, 2001; Deary & Stough, 1996). The significant role of mental speed has been implicated in studies of cognition and aging. Salthouse (1996a,b; 2000a,b) has argued that the decline observed in general mental ability with age is mainly due to a slowing of mental processing speed. In fact, removing the effects of mental speed on intelligence test scores removes the largest effects that have been linked to age.

In contrast to reaction time measures, the PSI subtests included in the WAIS–IV are relatively simple visual scanning tasks for most patients. However, it would be a mistake to think of the PSI as a measure of simple clerical functions that are not relevant or related to intellectual functioning. Although PSI is listed last in representations of Wechsler factor structures as a matter of convention, it frequently emerges third in most factor analyses and accounts for greater variance in intelligence than does the working memory factor. In match-controlled clinical group studies with the WAIS–IV, the PSI was observed to have the largest effect sizes among the four index scores in the traumatic brain injury, Alzheimer, autism, Asperger's, ADHD, and depression groups, although the effect size for the depression group was small (Wechsler, 2008). In most cases, one or more other index scores were a close second in terms of effect sizes. The PRI had the next highest effect size for the TBI group. The VCI had the next highest effect size for the autism group. The WMI had the next highest effect size for the ADHD group. Although these studies are instructive with regard to the possible interplay among cognitive functions in specific disorders, practitioners are discouraged from considering these profiles as diagnostic markers and encouraged to complete clinical evaluations based on test results combined with history and background factors.

As operationally defined in WAIS–IV, the PSI indicates the rapidity with which a patient processes simple or routine visual information without making errors of either omission or commission. Many novel learning tasks involve information processing that is both routine (such as reading a policy memo at work) and complex (such as determining the impact of the memo on one's job function). When speed of processing information is at least in the average range or a relative strength for a patient, this may facilitate both reasoning and the acquisition of new information. Slowness in the speed of processing routine information taxes the working memory structures because information fades from short-term storage before it is fully processed (Weiss et al., 2010). This may make the task of comprehending and integrating novel information more time-consuming and consequently more difficult. It may be hypothesized that working adults with processing speed deficits learn less material in the same amount of time or take longer to learn the same amount of material compared to co-workers without processing speed deficits. These individuals mentally tire more easily at work because of the additional cognitive effort required to perform routine tasks, perhaps leading to more frequent paper work errors, job stress, poor job evaluations, and job failures. As the years pass, these individuals are likely to spend less time on mentally demanding tasks involving new learning thus leading to smaller stores of newly crystallized job knowledge over time relative to colleagues, and possibly stalled or derailed career paths. This may be mitigated by non-cognitive factors such as a strong drive to task mastery (i.e., motivation) resulting in the individual working longer and harder to achieve success. As described, slow processing speed taxes the entire cognitive network and has wide-ranging effects on other cognitive processes that are observable outside the testing room and have important consequences in the lives of patients. In summary, processing speed interacts in a critical way with other higher-order cognitive functions and may impact general cognitive functioning, new learning, and everyday performance (Weiss et al., 2010).

WAIS–IV AS A NEUROPSYCHOLOGICAL INSTRUMENT

The WAIS–IV was primarily designed as a measure of intellectual ability. However, the WAIS has a long history of use as a neuropsychological instrument as well. The identification of an individual's cognitive strengths and weaknesses is an inherent aspect of neuropsychological assessment and is incorporated into the WAIS–IV through the inclusion of the individual indexes and index comparisons. Historically, the various Wechsler scales have been used to provide a global level of ability to which performance on other measures were compared. In addition, the indexes and subtests have been used as measures of specific cognitive domains and abilities, respectively. The increasing emphasis on clean factor-derived indexes, instead of modality-driven factors, reflects the growing importance of assessing cognitive abilities across multiple domains. While the four-factor model described in the WAIS–IV manual reflects the index structure, Benson et al. (2010) describe the subtest alignment utilizing five broad factors of the Cattell-Horn-Carroll (CHC) theory, further establishing the utility of the WAIS–IV in measuring cognitive strengths and weaknesses. Cullum and Larabee (2010) provide a thorough review of the use of the WAIS scales in neuropsychology, including detailed information on the changes from WAIS–III to WAIS–IV.

A recent initial study (McCrea & Robinson, 2011) utilizing the WAIS–IV in five neurological patients provides preliminary support for the underlying neurological processes involved in the three new subtests on the WAIS–IV: Visual Puzzles, Figure Weights, and Cancellation. In addition, Fallows and Hilsabeck (2012) examined the new WAIS–IV Visual Puzzles task and found that it correlated highly with measures of visuospatial reasoning, verbal learning and recall, mental flexibility, processing speed, and naming. These correlations suggest that Visual Puzzles is not a pure measure of visuoperceptual reasoning; it requires additional abilities. However, the majority of evidence on the underlying processes is derived from studies involving earlier versions of the WAIS. Twelve subtests in the WAIS–IV were previously included in the WAIS–III and although some content has been modified or updated, the subtests are largely unchanged. Brief reviews of the research conducted with WAIS–III in brain injury and neuroimaging are warranted.

Studies of Predecessor Versions Related to Brain Injury

There is a long history of using the WAIS to assess patients with mild or moderate-to-severe brain injury, beginning with the publication of the original WAIS. Originally, the performance discrepancy between the VIQ and the PIQ was the focus of investigation; however, although discrepancies were observed in patients with TBI, they were not significantly greater than those observed in non-clinical controls (Hawkins, Plehn, & Borgaro, 2002). The introduction of the four indexes in the WAIS–III allowed for the comparison of index strengths and weaknesses across clinical groups and non-clinical controls. The most consistent finding in TBI comparisons is lower scores on the processing speed index and subtests (Axelrod, Fichtenberg, Liethen, Czarnota, & Stucky, 2001; Fisher, Ledbetter, Cohen, Marmor, & Tulsky, 2000; Kennedy, Clement, & Curtiss, 2003). Clement, Kennedy, and Curtiss (2003) examined the performance of military patients with TBI and found relatively stable performance on the verbal comprehension index and subtests. Increasing differences were observed across domains with smaller performance differences on the perceptual organization domain, greater differences observed on the freedom from distractibility (working memory) domain, and the greatest differences on the processing speed domain. Finally, differences between FSIQ and GAI differentiate patients with neurocognitive disorders from non-clinical controls; patients with neurocognitive disorder have higher GAI than FSIQ scores (Harrison, DeLisle, & Parker, 2008).

At the subtest level, processing speed and working memory subtests tend to display the largest differences between patients with TBI and non-clinical controls. Donders, Tulsky and Zhu (2001) examined the performance of Letter-Number Sequencing, Symbol Search, and Matrix Reasoning, new tasks on the WAIS–III, and found that both LNS and SS were significantly different between groups but MR was not significantly different. Sanchez-Carrion, Fernandez-Espejo, Junque, Falcon,

Bargallo and Roig (2008) examined the working memory index and subtests and found significantly poorer performance in patients with severe TBI on Digits Backward, Letter-Number Sequencing, and the WAIS–III WMI. Interestingly, specific behaviors have also been found to differentiate performance of patients with TBI from non-clinical controls. Wilde, Boake and Sherer (2000) found that patients with TBI produced a greater number of broken configurations on the BD subtest than non-clinical controls; moreover, patients with right craniotomies had higher rates than those with left or no craniotomies.

WMS–IV CONTENT AND APPROACH TO DEVELOPMENT

The Wechsler Memory Scale–Fourth Edition (WMS–IV) is a significant update from the previous edition. The current edition presents a simpler, more streamlined assessment of memory functioning. The development of the WMS–IV began with a review of the research literature and the psychometric properties of each WMS–III subtest and index, including usability, clinical applicability, cultural and gender bias, reliability and stability, score range and distribution, and clinical utility. In addition, surveys of WMS–III users were conducted to evaluate current administration and scoring difficulties, and an expert panel of researchers was formed to provide guidance and evaluation of the WMS–IV development and research plans, as well as its usability and clinical utility. Detailed information on the modifications and improvements to the content, psychometric properties, and clinical utility are provided in the WMS–IV Technical Manual. A brief description of the major changes is provided here.

Memory testing is increasingly being used in older adults, producing a unique challenge to examiners balancing the need for comprehensive assessment and the need to focus assessments within a reasonable testing time for older patients. To address the specific needs of older adults, two separate batteries were developed for the WMS–IV, one for adults and one for older adults. Administration time for the older adult battery is shorter than for the adult battery. In addition, several subtests included in the adult battery were not included in the older adult battery and the content was modified for the verbal subtests across batteries. Finally, the CVLT–II can be substituted for Verbal Paired Associates subtest in the Verbal Memory Index, shortening administration time for examiners utilizing both assessments.

As mentioned, the index structure was simplified to focus assessment on more comprehensive, stable indexes. Supplemental indexes were moved to the ACS; the General Memory Index was dropped; and recognition memory was removed from the Delayed Memory Index. In addition to the changes to the index structure, several subtests were modified, overlap of subtests with the WAIS–IV was reduced, the working memory index was focused on the visual modality to complement the WAIS–IV verbal working memory index, and the impact of guessing on visual memory was reduced. The new visual memory index more accurately measures visual memory, including spatial memory and memory for visual details. Finally, several new scores were developed for the WMS–IV. Process scores were added to provide more in-depth evaluation of memory processes and contrast scaled scores were developed, based on a method introduced by Holdnack (2007) and introduced in the NEPSY–II, to provide normative data on comparison scores.

WMS–IV INDEX STRUCTURE

Figure 1.2 presents a visual model of the WMS–IV Adult battery. The five index scores are presented in ovals and are the primary focus of the interpretation. Subtests may be included in multiple indexes; the subtests are listed within one index in which they are included. If they are included in a second index, an arrow indicates the second index. Figure 1.3 presents a visual model of the WMS–IV Older Adult battery. Four index scores are available for the Older Adult battery; Spatial Addition is not included in the Older Adult battery so the Visual Working Memory Index is not available.

Auditory Memory Index

The Auditory Memory Index (AMI) reflects an individual's ability to listen to information presented orally, encode it and repeat it immediately, and recall it after a 20–30 minute delay. The subtests within the

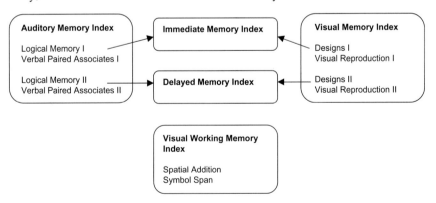

FIGURE 1.2 **WMS–IV Adult Battery Structure.**

index assess memory for semantically and sequentially related and unrelated information, and multi-trial and single-trial learning. The AMI consists of the immediate and delayed conditions of Logical Memory (LM) and Verbal Paired Associates (VPA).

CVLT–II scores may be substituted for VPA scores in deriving the AMI. CVLT–II, like VPA, is a list-learning task and measures auditory verbal memory. CVLT–II may be preferred for individuals who have difficulty understanding the task requirements of pairing unrelated words.

There are several differences between the subtests comprising AMI across the batteries. Verbal Paired Associates has fewer word pairs in the Older Adult battery, 10 as opposed to 14 in the Adult battery. The fewer number of words improve the floor of the test in older adults, while the longer list ensured adequate ceiling in younger adults. Also, with older adults, a shorter story is used in LM and is repeated to help improve the floor. The changes across batteries improve the subtest level scaling and overall functioning of the subtests and the AMI.

Visual Memory Index

The Visual Memory Index (VMI) reflects an individual's ability to register, encode, and retrieve visual and spatial information, and to reconstruct it immediately and following a 20–30 minute delay. The subtests within the index assess memory for visual detail, spatial relations, and single-trial learning. Recall of spatial locations is also assessed in the Adult battery but is not directly measured in the Older Adult battery. The VMI consists of the immediate and delayed conditions of Visual Reproduction and Designs in the Adult battery and of the immediate and delayed conditions of Visual Reproduction in the Older Adult battery.

The subtest differences in the composition of the VMI across batteries need to be accounted for in administration and interpretation of results. The Designs (DE) subtest was designed for the WMS–IV Visual

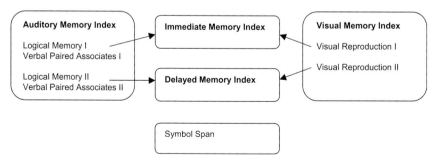

FIGURE 1.3   **WMS–IV Older Adult Battery Structure.**

Memory domain and is not included in the Older Adult battery due to an inadequate floor in the older age groups. Although recall of spatial relations is required in Visual Reproduction (VR), Designs more directly measures spatial memory. Therefore, spatial memory has a greater influence on the Adult battery. Moreover, VR requires a motor response, and although the scoring system was modified from the WMS–III to directly relate scores to memory functioning, motor ability may influence results. Both DE and VR require reconstruction of the visual stimuli presented; however, DE uses a recognition format while VR is free recall. As previously mentioned, recognition tasks are typically easier than free recall tasks and this should be considered if scores are disparate across DE and VR. It is important to note that the guess factor in DE is lower than that observed in many visual memory tasks (e.g., 50% guess rate for Faces in the WMS–III).

Immediate Memory Index

The Immediate Memory Index (IMI) measures the ability to recall information presented orally and visually immediately after the presentation of the stimuli. It includes the immediate recall conditions for each of the primary subtests, Visual Reproduction, Verbal Paired Associates, Logical Memory, and Designs in the Adult battery; and Visual Reproduction, Verbal Paired Associates, and Logical Memory in the Older Adult battery.

There are differences in the subtest composition of the IMI across batteries. The IMI has an equal number of verbal and visual subtests in the Adult battery and therefore is not influenced more heavily by one modality. However, on the Older Adult battery the IMI is more weighted to auditory memory difficulties than visual memory problems. There are also large differences within the subtests comprising the index. The subtests included in the IMI include measures of different modalities of memory, different response requirements (e.g., verbal, motor), multi-trial and single-trial learning, encoding and recall of related and unrelated stimuli, and encoding and recall of spatial and visual detail memory. Moreover, the CVLT–II may be substituted for VPA scores changing the specific skills assessed within the index. Interpretation of the specific aspects of memory functioning will differ between the Adult battery and the Older Adult battery and within each battery based on the scores comprising the IMI.

Delayed Memory Index

The Delayed Memory Index (DMI) assesses the ability to recall visual and verbal information following a 20- to 30-minute delay. It is composed of the delayed recall conditions for each of the primary sub-tests, Visual Reproduction, Verbal Paired Associates, Logical Memory, and Designs in the Adult battery; and Visual Reproduction, Verbal Paired Associates, and Logical Memory in the Older Adult battery.

There are differences in the subtest composition of the DMI across batteries. Just like described for the IMI, the DMI has an equal number of verbal and visual subtests in the Adult battery and therefore is not influenced more heavily by one modality. However, on the Older Adult battery the DMI is more weighted to auditory memory difficulties than visual memory problems. There are also large subtest differences within the DMI. The subtests included in the DMI include measures of differ-ent modalities of memory, different response requirements (e.g., verbal, motor), recall of related and unrelated stimuli, and recall of spatial and visual detail memory. Moreover, the CVLT–II may be substituted for VPA scores changing the specific skills assessed within the index. Interpretation of the specific aspects of memory functioning will differ between the Adult battery and the Older Adult battery and within each battery based on the scores comprising the DMI.

It is important to note that performance on the DMI is directly affected by the initial encoding ability observed on the IMI. Inherently, delayed recall is limited by the amount of information encoded during the immediate learning and recall of the information. Delayed memory ability needs to be considered within the context of initial memory functioning.

Visual Working Memory Index

The Visual Working Memory Index (VWMI) measures visuospatial working memory span and mental manipulation of visual details and spatial information. It is derived from the Spatial Addition and Symbol Span scaled scores; it is not available in the Older Adult battery because Spatial Addition is not included in the Older Adult battery.

WMS–IV: GOING BEYOND THE NUMBERS

Cognitive Influences on Auditory Memory Index

The AMI is not a pure measure of verbal memory; performance can be influenced by abilities other than verbal memory. In order to deter-mine whether a low AMI score can be attributed to difficulties with auditory memory functioning, other factors that influence performance need to be considered. Because the AMI is a language-based index, any disturbance in language functioning is likely to impact scores. Some additional problems that influence performance on the AMI include auditory acuity deficits, receptive or expressive language difficulties, problems with attention or executive functioning, and poor working memory. Some of these difficulties can be determined by examining performance across the subtests within the AMI.

Adequate performance on LM requires the examinee to pay attention to the examiner, to listen to and process moderately complex sentences (receptive language), and to recall and verbally express what was learned (expressive language) both immediately and following a 20–30 minute delay. In addition to language and memory skills, LM requires auditory working memory to actively process information to improve effective storage and retrieval. Additionally, auditory attention, hearing acuity, and articulation may influence results on this subtest.

VPA requires the examinee to pay attention to the examiner, to listen to and process unrelated word pairs (receptive language), and to recall and verbally express what was learned (expressive language) both immediately and following a 20–30 minute delay. Experience and familiarity with the words in the pairs will help with recall; novel words are more difficult to learn and recall. Although the words on VPA are at the first- to third-grade level, individuals with significant language problems or who are not native English speakers may experience difficulty encoding and retrieving the words. The expressive and receptive language demands, single-word pairs versus complex sentences, are lower on VPA than on LM. Like LM, VPA requires auditory working memory to actively process information to improve effective storage and retrieval. Additionally, auditory attention, hearing acuity, and articulation may influence results on this subtest.

There are some unique attributes of each task that may help identify specific problems. First, LM involves recall of sequential information presented in a logical framework. This may assist recall as recall of some details may trigger recall of other details in the story. Alternately, VPA involves the recall of mostly unrelated words. Four word pairs are easier and involve related words but the majority of words are unrelated. Examinees that perform better on LM may benefit from the logical structure of the information. Second, VPA involves cued recall; the examinee is provided with one of the word pairs and asked to recall the second word. This cue may make recall easier. Third, VPA stimuli are repeated four times whereas for most adults, LM stories are not repeated; one story is repeated in the Older Adult battery. Additionally, on VPA, examinees are reminded of the correct answer when they miss an item during the learning trials. Examinees who perform better on VPA may be benefitting from the additional learning, corrective feedback, and/or recall cues. Finally, some aspects of executive functioning may play a role in performance on VPA. In addition to memory and verbal ability, the examinee must understand the task of pairing two unassociated words; examinees with very concrete thinking may have difficulty with comprehending the task, not with verbal memory.

Cognitive Influences on Visual Memory Index

Just like that described for the AMI, the VMI is not a pure measure of visual memory. In order to determine whether a low VMI score can be attributed to difficulties with visual memory functioning, other factors that influence performance need to be considered. Because the VMI requires processing of visual information, any disturbance in visual functioning, including visual–spatial processing and visual perceptual reasoning, is likely to impact scores. Some additional problems that influence performance on the VMI include visual acuity deficits, visual–spatial processing difficulties, problems with attention or executive functioning, and poor working memory. Due to the brief exposure time of the stimuli, processing speed and attention may also impact performance. Some of these difficulties can be determined by assessing performance across the subtests within the VMI.

Visual Reproduction requires the examinee to pay attention to the visual stimuli for 10 seconds, evaluate the specific details and the relative spatial relationship among the elements of the design, visually scan the page to ensure all the salient pieces of information are encoded, process the visual–perceptual and visual–spatial features in working memory until it is stored into long-term memory, and produce the images using integrated visual–motor ability. Moreover, elements of the designs may be verbalized by the examinee (e.g., flags, boxes, circles, dots), making language ability contribute to performance. Finally, executive functioning may play a role in organizing and encoding the visual information efficiently and in aiding the planning required for responding.

Designs require the examinee to pay attention to the visual stimuli for 10 seconds, evaluate the design details and location of each detail within the 4-by-4 grid, visually scan the page to ensure all the salient pieces of information are encoded, process the visual–perceptual and visual–spatial information in working memory until it is consolidated into long-term memory, and reproduce the image using cards. Unlike VR, verbalization is unlikely to facilitate encoding and retrieval of the visual–spatial information due to the number of designs within and across items and the timed exposure. However, location information may be verbally encoded if an examinee labels the grid spaces logically (e.g., A2, A4, C3). Therefore, verbal abilities should not strongly influence performance on this test, particularly on the recall of visual details.

Executive functioning may also play a role in VR as the examinee's ability to organize and encode the visual information efficiently may improve performance.

Cognitive Influences on Visual Working Memory Index

The VWMI is influenced by cognitive abilities outside of visual working memory. Although a low score on the VWMI may indicate difficulty with visual working memory, other cognitive problems may influence performance and need to be considered. Because the VWMI requires processing of visual–spatial information, any visual functioning difficulties will affect performance. Some additional problems that influence performance on the VWMI include visual acuity deficits, visual–spatial processing impairments, severe attention or executive functioning problems, and poor cognitive processing speed.

Spatial Addition (SA) requires the examinee to pay attention to the examiner, comprehend the task directions, quickly scan and encode the exact locations of the dots on each stimulus page, mentally compare the locations across stimuli, inhibit encoding of red dot locations, and produce a response by placing cards in the grid. Impairments in processing speed, attention, and executive functioning may result in difficulty with the task. Although this subtest is difficult to verbalize, good verbal skills may facilitate comprehension and retention of the subtest rules.

Symbol Span (SSP) required the examinee to attend to the visual stimuli, quickly scan and encode the visual and sequential information, and select the correct stimuli from an array in the correct sequence. Visual attention may impact performance, particularly attention to visual details. The stimuli on SSP are difficult to verbalize; therefore, language functioning is not likely to affect performance.

Cognitive Influences on Intermediate Memory Index and Delayed Memory Index

Although low scores on the Immediate and Delayed Memory Indexes indicate difficulties with memory functioning, other cognitive problems may influence performance on these measures and need to be considered when interpreting the results. These problems include auditory or visual acuity deficits, attention or executive functioning problems, language impairment, poor working memory or processing speed, and visual–spatial processing impairment. Any cognitive ability that is required to complete tasks on the AMI or VMI contributes to performance on the IMI and DMI.

JOINT FACTOR STRUCTURE OF THE WAIS–IV AND WMS–IV

The co-norming of WAIS–IV and WMS–IV makes it possible to explore the joint factor structure of the two batteries. Similar joint factor analytic studies have been published for the WAIS-R and WMS-R (Bowden, Carstairs, & Shores, 1999) and the WAIS–III and WMS–III (Tulsky & Price, 2003). Tulsky and Price (2003) completed an extensive evaluation of the joint factor structure of the WAIS–III and WMS–III. They reported that a six-factor model of Verbal Comprehension, Perceptual Organization, Processing Speed, Working Memory, Visual Memory, and Auditory Memory, was best supported by the data. Model specification errors were observed when immediate and delayed memory factors were evaluated; additionally, Faces was observed to have a poor fit on any factor. The model fit was best when subtests were allowed to load on multiple factors, specifically Arithmetic, Spatial Span, Picture Arrangement, and Visual Reproduction (Tulsky & Price, 2003).

Holdnack, Zhou, Larrabee, Millis and Salthouse (2011) evaluated the joint factor structure of the WAIS–IV and WMS–IV. In that study, both five- and seven-factor models produced similar statistical results. The five-factor model consisted of a hierarchical general factor, Verbal Comprehension, Perceptual Reasoning, Working Memory, Processing Speed, and Memory. The seven-factor model did not include a hierarchical general ability factor but was comprised of Verbal Comprehension, Perceptual Reasoning, Auditory Working Memory, Visual Working Memory, Processing Speed, Auditory Memory, and Visual Memory. The five-factor model required more subtest cross-loadings to achieve best statistical fit compared to the seven-factor model. The primary difference between the two models is the emergence of modality specific factors in the seven-factor versus the five-factor model. Also, the seven-factor model produces model specification errors when a general hierarchical factor is included. The factor analysis reported by Holdnack et al. (2011) used only the delayed memory measures from the WMS–IV to avoid model specification error that can occur due to the statistical dependency between immediate and delayed memory tests.

In this chapter, we present the five- and seven-factor models, including the immediate and delayed memory tests. The purpose is to evaluate the impact on model fit when immediate memory measures are included in the analysis. There will be no attempt to identify separate immediate and delayed memory factors because this will yield model specification errors. In the current analysis, the error terms of the immediate and delayed subtests will be allowed to correlate to account for their statistical dependence.

Participants for this study included 900 healthy people between 16 and 69 years of age, from the WAIS–IV/WMS–IV standardization sample. All participants were administered both the WAIS–IV and the WMS–IV adult battery. The 10 age-adjusted scaled scores of the primary subtests from the WAIS–IV (Vocabulary, Information, Similarities, Digit Span, Arithmetic, Block Design, Matrix Reasoning, Visual Puzzles, Coding, and Symbol Search), and the age-adjusted scaled scores of the 10 primary subtests from the WMS–IV (Logical Memory I & II, Verbal Paired Associates I & II, Visual Reproduction I & II, Spatial Addition, and Symbol Span) were included in this analysis.

Confirmatory Factor Analysis was used to identify the best latent factor structure of the 20 WAIS–IV/WMS–IV subtests. Multiple goodness-of-fit measures were used to evaluate various factor models including: likelihood-ratio chi-square, rescaled chi-square statistics (χ^2/df), adjusted goodness-of-fit index (AGFI; Jöreskog & Sörbom, 1993), Steiger's (1990) root mean squared error of approximation (RMSEA), standardized root-mean-square residual (SRMSR), Tucker–Lewis non-normed fit index (TLI; Tucker & Lewis, 1973), and Schwarz's bayesian information criterion (BIC). Each of the statistical approaches evaluates components of the factor model to determine the best statistical fit to the data.

The base models evaluated in this CFA are presented in Table 1.1. The first model is a five-factor hierarchical model including general factor and five second level factors (Verbal Comprehension, Perceptual Reasoning, Working Memory, Processing Speed, and Memory). In addition to the cross-loadings listed in Table A1.1, three variations of cross-loadings were also evaluated using CFA. The first model includes the additional cross-loadings of Designs and Symbol Span with Perceptual Reasoning. The second model adds Matrix Reasoning cross-loading on Working Memory to the first model. The third model incorporates, to the base model, the cross-loadings of Logical Memory I & II on Verbal Comprehension, Matrix Reasoning on Working Memory, and Symbol Span on Memory. The fit statistics for these models are presented in Table 1.2. Figure 1.3 shows the best fit of all the models. This version of the five-factor model has RMSEA values <0.05, AGFI = 0.94, and CFI and TLI > 0.95 indicating a very good fit to the data. Holdnack et al. (2011) reported $\chi^2 = 278.60$, AGFI = 0.95, RMSEA = 0.047, SRMSR = 0.030, CFI = 0.97, and TLI = 0.96 for the same five-factor model that did not include immediate memory measures. Inclusion of immediate memory measures improves model fit and provides empirical support for these tests as loading on a general memory factor.

The second base model presented in Table 1.1 is a seven-factor non-hierarchical model comprised of Verbal Comprehension, Perceptual Reasoning, Auditory Working Memory, Visual Working Memory, Processing Speed, Auditory Working Memory, and Visual Working

TABLE 1.1   Model Specifications for Confirmatory Analysis with Immediate Memory Subtests (Base Models)

Model	Factor	Variables
1	Verbal	Vocabulary, Similarities, Information
(Five-factor hierarchical)	Perceptual	Block Design, Visual Puzzles, Matrix Reasoning
	Processing Speed	Coding, Symbol Search
	Working Memory	Arithmetic[1], Digit Span, Symbol Span, Spatial Addition[2]
	Memory	Logical Memory I & II, Verbal Paired Associates I & II, Designs I & II, Visual Reproduction I & II[3]
2	Verbal	Vocabulary, Similarities, Information
(Seven-factor non-hierarchical)	Perceptual	Block Design, Visual Puzzles, Matrix Reasoning
	Processing Speed	Coding, Symbol Search
	Auditory Working Memory	Arithmetic[1], Digit Span
	Visual Working Memory	Symbol Span, Spatial Addition[2]
	Auditory Memory	Logical Memory I & II, Verbal Paired Associates I & II
	Visual Memory	Designs I & II, Visual Reproduction I & II

[1]*Arithmetic cross-loads on Verbal Comprehension.*
[2]*Spatial Addition cross-loads on Perceptual Reasoning.*
[3]*Visual Reproduction Immediate and Delayed cross-load on Perceptual Reasoning.*
Errors are allowed to correlate between the immediate and delayed tasks.

TABLE 1.2   Confirmatory Factor Analysis Statistics with WAIS–IV and WMS–IV subtests for Models Including Immediate Memory Subtests

Model	χ^2	df	χ^2/df	AGFI	RMSEA	SRMSR	CFI	TLI	SBC
1 base	541.76	157	3.45	0.92	0.052	0.044	0.96	0.96	902.29
1.1	465.30	154	3.02	0.93	0.047	0.039	0.97	0.96	846.23
1.2	418.50	153	2.74	0.94	0.044	0.037	0.97	0.96	806.24
1.3	386.12	153	2.52	0.94	0.041	0.037	0.98	0.97	773.85
2 base	342.06	143	2.39	0.94	0.039	0.029	0.98	0.97	797.82
2.2	317.48	141	2.25	0.95	0.037	0.028	0.98	0.98	786.84

Copyright 2009 by Pearson, Inc. Reproduced with permission. All rights reserved.

Memory. Holdnack et al. (2011) reported that allowing cross-loading of Visual Reproduction on Perceptual Reasoning in addition to Arithmetic cross-loading on Verbal Comprehension and Spatial Addition cross-loading on Perceptual Reasoning did not yield improved model fit. Inclusion of immediate memory measures may further strengthen the factor structure through the addition of more measures on specific memory factors; potentially eliminate the need for any subtest cross-loadings. Table 1.2 presents the results of the seven-factor CFA results. Model 2.1, which allows cross-loadings for Arithmetic and Spatial Span, fits the data better than any other model, including the five-factor model. By comparison, the CFA using immediate memory measures was very similar to the results reported for the analysis using delayed memory only: $\chi^2 = 237.56$, AGFI = 0.94, RMSEA = 0.046, RMSR = 0.027, CFI = 0.98, and TLI = 0.96 (Holdnack et al., 2011).

The results of this CFA confirm that both five- and seven-factor models provide a good fit to joint factor structure of the WAIS–IV/WMS–IV. Inclusion of immediate and delayed memory measures in the analysis yields similar, albeit slightly improved, fit statistics compared to using only delayed memory measures. The slight improvement in model fit may be due to a lack of independence between immediate and delayed memory measures; however, the results of both analyses are very consistent. Additionally, the fit statistics for the seven-factor model are better than those reported by Tulsky and Price (2003) for the best six-factor model (e.g., CFI = 0.96, TLI = 0.96, AGFI = 0.93, RMSEA = 0.045). Therefore, the addition of measures of visual working memory appears to improve the overall measurement model. Figures 1.4 and 1.5 show the latent factor model and subtest factor loadings for the five- and seven-factor models, respectively.

Although the seven-factors presented in the model have few cross-loadings, this does not indicate that there is not considerable overlap in performance on these measures. That is, the factors are correlated with one another and some indexes will correlate more highly than others. Table 1.3 presents correlations between the seven factors. The Perceptual Reasoning factor correlates highly with both Visual Working Memory and Visual Memory. Having better perceptual reasoning abilities may yield better performance on visual based memory tests, or *vice versa*. Visual Memory and Visual Working Memory are highly correlated. This high correlation is not surprising given the high degree of overlap in the stimuli and methodology used. The primary difference between the tasks relates to how much and how long visual information must be retained and accessed in memory. Both Visual Working Memory and Perceptual Reasoning have consistently high correlations with other factors, suggesting that these skills are important in overall cognitive functioning.

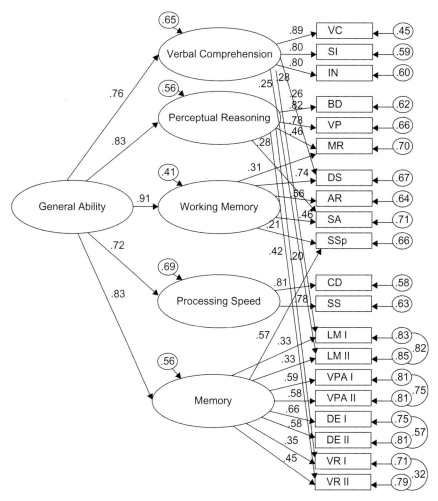

FIGURE 1.4   **Five-Factor Model of WAIS–IV/WMS–IV Subtests.** Note: VC = Vocabulary, SI = Similarities, IN = Information, BD = Block Design, VP = Visual Puzzles, MR = Matrix Reasoning, DS = Digit Span, AR = Arithmetic, CD = Coding, SS = Symbol Search, SA = Spatial Addition, SSp = Symbol Span, LM I = Logical Memory Immediate, LM II = Logical Memory Delayed, VPA I = Verbal Paired Associates Immediate, VPA II = Verbal Paired Associates Delayed, DE I = Designs Immediate, DE II = Designs Delayed, VR I = Visual Reproduction Immediate, VR II = Visual Reproduction Delayed.

The clinical implications of the CFA are that the five- and seven-factor models are equally valid models for interpreting WAIS–IV/WMS–IV data. In the four-factor model, modality specific working memory and memory measures are not considered separately; rather,

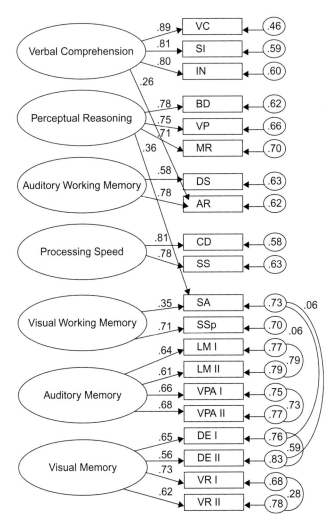

FIGURE 1.5 Seven-Factor Model of WAIS–IV/WMS–IV Subtests. Note: VC = Vocabulary, SI = Similarities, IN = Information, BD = Block Design, VP = Visual Puzzles, MR = Matrix Reasoning, DS = Digit Span, AR = Arithmetic, CD = Coding, SS = Symbol Search, SA = Spatial Addition, SSp = Symbol Span, LM I = Logical Memory Immediate, LM II = Logical Memory Delayed, VPA I = Verbal Paired Associates Immediate, VPA II = Verbal Paired Associates Delayed, DE I = Designs Immediate, DE II = Designs Delayed, VR I = Visual Reproduction Immediate, VR II = Visual Reproduction Delayed.

general factors for each construct are indicated. The implication for interpreting the WMS–IV based on these results is a focus on the Immediate and Delayed Memory Indexes, which are composed of

TABLE 1.3   Factor Correlations Seven-Factor Model

Factors	VC	PR	PS	AWM	VWM	AM
PR	0.72					
PS	0.48	0.67				
AWM	0.69	0.76	0.68			
VWM	0.71	0.88	0.71	0.87		
AM	0.71	0.61	0.53	0.69	0.83	
VM	0.62	0.89	0.61	0.67	0.99	0.77

Note: VC = Verbal Comprehension, PR = Perceptual Reasoning, PS = Processing Speed,
AWM = Auditory Working Memory, VWM = Visual Working Memory, AM = Auditory Memory,
VM = Visual Memory.

measures from each of the auditory and visual memory subtests. When looking at the combined WAIS–IV and WMS–IV, administering only one working memory index (e.g., WAIS–IV WMI or WMS–IV VWMI) is required because they provide similar estimates of working memory functioning. Alternately, a general memory index and working memory index can be used. The additional sixth factor (e.g., hierarchical general factor) is represented by the WAIS–IV Full-Scale IQ. In the five-factor model, FSIQ would also be evaluated to provide additional information in regard to overall cognitive functioning. The five-factor model requires an additional focus on evaluating subtest level variability to account for the influence of multiple cognitive skills on memory and working memory subtests. The clinician will need to evaluate the reason for a particularly low subtest score (e.g., poor memory functioning vs. poor visual–spatial abilities).

The seven-factor model, although more complex in terms of the number of index scores evaluated, does not require significant additional evaluation of subtest variability. Although two subtests cross-load, the influence of these cross-loadings may be examined at the index level with the application of contrast scores (Wechsler, 2009). There is a very high correlation between the visual working memory and visual memory indexes due to significant similarities in content and methodology. Additionally, better visual working memory facilitates encoding of information into long-term memory stores. In clinical populations, where deficits in delayed memory relative to working memory are present, these indexes may dissociate. When using the seven-factor model, the index scores and relevant contrast scores are the primary level of interpretation.

ADDITIONAL WAIS–IV AND WMS–IV INDEX SCORES

The factor analytic studies suggest additional factors may be useful for analyzing combined WAIS–IV/WMS–IV data. Traditionally, indexes have been derived for each battery separately. However, because the WAIS–IV and WMS–IV are co-normed, it is possible to derive index scores from subtests across the two batteries. Based on the five-factor model, general memory and working memory indexes are indicated. Another factor analytic study indicates that a quantitative index from subtests on the WAIS–IV (Weiss et al., 2013a) can be identified. Additionally, the Spatial Addition test has a high degree of correlation with measures of math reasoning and computation and measures aspects of quantitative reasoning (Wechsler, 2009). Finally, conceptually based indexes for the WMS–IV to assess retrieval and retention at the index level, can be derived.

General Memory Index

A WMS–IV General Memory Index (GMI) was developed consistent with the five-factor model. For adolescents and adults aged 16–69 (i.e., WMS–IV Adult battery) the GMI is computed by summing the scaled scores for LM I, LM II, VPA I, VPA II, VR I, VR II, DE I and DE II. For older adults aged 65–90 (i.e., WMS–IV Older Adult battery) the GMI is computed by summing the scaled scores for LM I, LM II, VPA I, VPA II, VR I, and VR II. The GMI is a complex measure that includes immediate, delayed, auditory, and visual memory measures. Like WAIS–IV FSIQ, it can provide an overall picture of the patient's memory functioning. The sum of scaled scores to standard score conversion for adolescents and adults aged 16–69 and adults aged 65–90 are presented in Tables 1.4 and 1.5, respectively.

Working Memory Index

A combined WAIS–IV/WMS–IV Working Memory Index (CWMI) was developed consistent with the five-factor model. This index is available for ages 16–69 (i.e., WMS–IV Adult battery). The CWMI is computed by summing the WAIS–IV/WMS–IV AR, DS, SA and SSp subtest scaled scores. The CWMI is a complex measure that includes auditory, visual, working memory and quantitative processing measures. Like the GMI, it can provide an overall picture of the patient's working memory functioning. The sum of scaled scores to standard score conversion for adolescents and adults aged 16–69 are presented in Table 1.4.

TABLE 1.4 Sum of Scaled Scores to Index Score for Adult Battery Ages 16–69

Index	Retention	Retrieval	Quantitative	General Memory	Working Memory
55	<21	<20	<8	<31	<14
56			8	31	14
57	21	20	9	32	15
58			10	33	16
59					
60		21		34	
61	22	22	11	35	17
62		23	12	36	
63			13	37	
64	23			38	19
65		24		39–40	
66	24		14	41	
67		25		42	20
68	25			43	
69	26	26	15	44	
70				45	21
71	27	27	16	46	
72				47	22
73	28			48	
74		28	17	49	23
75	29			50	
76			18	51–52	24
77	30	29		53	25
78			19	54–55	
79		30		56	26
80	31		20	57	27
81				58	28
82	32	31	21	59–60	29
83				61	

(Continued)

TABLE 1.4 (Continued)

Index	Retention	Retrieval	Quantitative	General Memory	Working Memory
84	33	32	22	62	30
85				63	31
86		33	23	64	32
87	34		24	65–66	
88				67	33
89	35	34	25	68	34
90		35		69	
91	36		26	70	35
92				71	
93	37	36	27	72	36
94		37		73	37
95	38	38	28	74–75	
96				76	38
97	39	38	29	77	
98				78	39
99		39	30	79	
100	40			80–81	40
101		40	31	82	41
102	41			83	
103		41	32	84	42
104				85–86	43
105	42	42	33	87	
106		43		88	44
107	43		34	89	45
108		44		90	
109		45		91	46
110	44		35	92	47
111		46		93	
112	45		36	94	48

(*Continued*)

TABLE 1.4 (Continued)

Index	Retention	Retrieval	Quantitative	General Memory	Working Memory
113		47		95–96	49
114			37	97	
115	46			98	50
116		48	38	99	
117	47		39	100	51
118		49		101	
119	48		40	102	52
120	49	50		103	
121			41	104	53
122					
123	50	51	42	105	54
124					
125	51	52	43	106	55
126		53		107	
127	52	54	44	108	56
128				109	
129	53	55	45	110	57
130					
131	54			111	
132		56	46	112	58
133	55			113	
134		57	47		59
135	56	58		114	
136		59		115	60
137	57	60	48	116	61
138	58			117	62
139					63
140				118	
141					

(*Continued*)

TABLE 1.4   (Continued)

Index	Retention	Retrieval	Quantitative	General Memory	Working Memory
142	59	61	49		64
143	60	62	50	119	65
144	61			120	
145	>61	>62	>50	>120	>65

Copyright 2009 Pearson, Inc. Reproduced with permission. All rights reserved.

Quantitative Reasoning Index

A combined WAIS–IV/WMS–IV Quantitative Reasoning Index (QRI) was developed using measures that correlate highly with math performance and are conceptually associated with quantitative reasoning. The Arithmetic subtest requires examinees to perform mathematical operations and computations in working memory. The Figure Weights subtest tests the examinee's ability to reason using numeric-symbolic associations. The Spatial Addition subtest measures the examinees ability to add and subtract spatial locations in working memory, tapping spatial aspects of mental arithmetic. Spatial Addition was designed specifically as a visual analog of the WAIS–IV Arithmetic subtest. The subtests show similarities in how they function. Both tests correlate highly with math performance and both have split-loadings in factor analysis with more complex reasoning factors (i.e., Arithmetic with VCI and Spatial Addition with PRI).

In addition to quantitative reasoning, this index is heavily influenced by working memory skills. QRI is calculated by summing the scaled scores for AR, FW, and SA. It is available for adolescents and adults aged 16–69. The sum of scaled scores to standard score conversions are presented in Table 1.4.

Retrieval Index

The WMS–IV Retrieval Index assesses the patient's overall relationship between free recall and recognition memory. Low scores on this index indicate very good recognition skills compared to free recall. In the context of low delayed memory functioning, this would indicate impairment in retrieving information from long-term memory. High scores indicate low recognition scores compared to free recall. The WMS–IV Retrieval Index is derived by summing the delayed free recall versus recognition contrast scores for LM, VPA, VR, and DE for

TABLE 1.5 Sum of Scaled Scores to Index Score for Older Adult Battery Ages 65–90

Index	Retention	Retrieval	General Memory	Working Memory
55	<13	<13	<22	<12
56		13	22	
57	13		23	
58		14	24	
59			25	
60				12
61	14			
62		15	26	
63			27	
64	15		28	13
65			29	
66		16	30	
67		17	31	14
68	16		32	
69		18	33	15
70	17			
71	18	19	34	16
72	19			
73		20	35	17
74	20		36	
75			37	18
76		21	38	
77	21		39	19
78		22	40	
79	22			20
80			41	21
81		23	42	
82	23		43	22
83		24	44	

(*Continued*)

TABLE 1.5   (Continued)

Index	Retention	Retrieval	General Memory	Working Memory
84	24		45	23
85			46	
86	25	25		24
87			47	
88	26	26	48	25
89			49	
90			50	
91	27	27	51–52	26
92			53	
93	28		54	27
94		28	55	
95			56	28
96	29	29	57	
97			58	29
98	30		59	
99		30	60	30
100			61	
101	31		62	31
102		31	63	
103	32		64	
104			65	32
105		32	66	
106	33		67	33
107		33		
108			68	34
109		34	69	
110	34		70	35
111				
112		35	71	36

(*Continued*)

TABLE 1.5 (Continued)

Index	Retention	Retrieval	General Memory	Working Memory
113	35		72	
114			73	37
115		36	74	
116	36		75	38
117		37	76	
118	37	38		39
119			77	
120	38		78	
121		39	79	40
122		40	80	
123	39	41		41
124			81	
125			82	
126	40	42	83	42
127			84	
128		43	85	
129	41			
130		44	86	43
131	42			
132		45	87	44
133	43			
134			88	
135				45
136	44	46	89	
137				46
138	45			
139		47	90	
140			91	47
141	46			
142		48		48
143	47		92	
144				
145	>47	>48	>92	>48

Copyright 2009 Pearson, Inc. Reproduced with permission. All rights reserved.

adolescents and adults aged 16–69 and for LM, VPA, and VR for older adults aged 65–90. This is a complex retrieval measure being comprised of both visual and auditory memory measures. The sum of scaled scores to standard score conversions for adolescents and adults aged 16–69 and for adults aged 65–90 are presented in Tables 1.4 and 1.5, respectively.

Retention Index

The WMS–IV Retention Index assesses the patient's overall relationship between immediate and delayed memory. High scores on this index indicate very good retention of information from immediate to delayed recall. Low scores indicate a high rate of forgetting from immediate to delayed recall. In the context of low delayed memory functioning, this would indicate significantly impaired long-term memory functioning. The WMS–IV Retention Index is derived by summing the immediate recall versus delayed contrast scores for LM, VPA, VR, and DE for adolescents and adults aged 16–69 and for LM, VPA, and VR for older adults aged 65–90. This is a complex retention measure being comprised of both visual and auditory memory measures. The sum of scaled scores to standard score conversions for adolescents and adults aged 16–69 and adults aged 65–90 are presented in Tables 1.4 and 1.5, respectively.

ADVANCED CLINICAL SOLUTIONS FOR WAIS–IV AND WMS–IV

The ACS was published following the WAIS–IV and WMS–IV to provide examiners with a variety of tools to use in specific clinical situations. It is unlikely that all of the tools would be appropriate for a single case but each tool would be essential in some cases. The processes, additional scores, and additional instruments included in the ACS complete the assessment array necessary for assessing adolescents and adults with the WAIS–IV and WMS–IV. The ACS includes additional scores for the WMS–IV, measures of and normative data for suboptimal effort, serial assessment scores for WAIS–IV and WMS–IV (including cross edition serial assessments), demographically adjusted subtest and index norms for WAIS–IV and WMS–IV, measures for predicting premorbid IQ and memory functioning, and measures of social cognition.

Additional Scores for WMS–IV

For general evaluations, the scores provided in the WAIS–IV and WMS–IV are sufficient to answer the clinical question for a specific client. The WAIS–IV and WMS–IV include subtest, index, and contrast scores, and key process scores for a wide array of cognitive domains. However, some evaluations may require more in-depth examination of specific memory abilities. The ACS provides additional index- and subtest-level scores and contrast scores for examiners needing more information on the memory processes involved in performance on the WMS–IV. Only one additional score is provided for WAIS–IV: Cancellation Commission Errors. Scores are presented as scaled scores or cumulative percentages based on raw score range and distribution in non-clinical populations. All the normative data for the ACS additional scores are provided in the *ACS Administration and Scoring Manual*.

Index Scores

The ACS provides additional WMS–IV index scores that break down and describe memory functioning. The additional memory indexes are based on scores obtained during the WMS–IV assessment; they do not require additional testing. However, some of the indexes require that the optional recognition trials and DE process scores on the WMS–IV be administered or derived. The additional ACS indexes are: Auditory Immediate, Auditory Delayed, Auditory Recognition, Visual Immediate, Visual Delayed, Visual Recognition, Designs Spatial, and Designs Content. For the Older Adult battery, only the Auditory Immediate, Auditory Delayed, and Auditory Recognition Indexes can be derived. Index-level contrast scaled scores are also available with the ACS.

The Auditory Immediate Index (AII) measures the ability to encode and recall orally presented information immediately after the presentation of the stimuli. It includes scores from the immediate conditions of LM and VPA. CVLT–II Trials 1–5 may be substituted for VPA I to obtain this index score. The AII reflects an examinee's immediate memory for both semantically and sequentially related and unrelated verbal information learned across single and multiple learning trials.

The Auditory Delayed Index (ADI) measures the ability to recall orally presented information following a 20–30 minute delay after presentation of the stimuli. It includes scores from the delayed recall conditions of LM and VPA. CVLT–II Long-Delay may be substituted for VPA II to obtain this index score. The ADI reflects an examinee's delayed free and cued recall for both semantically and sequentially related and unrelated verbal information learned across single and multiple learning trials.

The Auditory Recognition Index (ARI) measures the retrieval of auditory information through recognition of orally presented information following a 20–30 minute delay. It includes scores from the delayed recognition conditions of LM and VPA. The ARI is derived from the age-adjusted cumulative percentages. The ARI reflects an examinee's delayed recognition memory for both semantically and sequentially related and unrelated verbal information learned across both single and multiple learning trials.

The Visual Immediate Index (VII) measures the ability to encode, recall, and recognize visually presented information immediately after the stimulus is presented. It includes scores from the immediate conditions of DE and VR. It is only available for the Adult battery. The VII reflects an examinee's immediate memory for visual details, the relationship among the visual details, and spatial locations learned in single learning trials.

The Visual Delayed Index (VDI) measures the ability to recall visually presented information following a 20–30 minute delay after presentation of the stimuli. It includes scores from the delayed conditions of DE and VR, and is only available for the Adult battery. The VDI reflects an examinee's delayed recall and recognition memory for visual details, the relationship among the visual details, and spatial locations learned in single learning trials.

The Visual Recognition Index (VRI) measures the ability to encode and recognize visually presented information following a 20–30 minute delay. It includes scores from the recognition conditions of DE and VR. The VRI is derived from the age-adjusted cumulative percentages. The VRI reflects an examinee's delayed recognition memory for visual details, the relationship among the visual details, and spatial locations.

The Designs Spatial Index (DSI) measures the ability to encode and recall spatial information immediately and following a 20–30 minute delay. It includes the location scores from Designs I and Designs II. The DSI is the most robust measure of spatial memory provided with the WMS–IV, particularly for use in comparisons.

The Designs Content Index (DCI) measures the ability to encode and recognize visual details immediately after presentation and following a 20–30 minute delay. The DCI provides a robust measure of memory for visual detail and is particularly helpful in comparisons with other aspects of visual memory.

Index Contrast Scores

The WMS–IV provides contrast scores for most subtests with immediate and delayed conditions or recall and recognition tasks. Additionally, several index level contrast scaled scores are provided. Contrast scaled scores adjust one score (i.e., the dependent score) based on the examinee's performance on another variable (i.e., the control variable) to allow the examiner to examine performance on one skill within the context of a second, typically higher-level skill (e.g., recall vs. recognition). Contrast scaled scores use a scaled score metric (e.g., mean of 10 and a standard deviation of 3) for score comparisons within or between subtests or indexes. For example, the DE Immediate Recall versus Delayed Recall Contrast Scaled Score describes the examinee's ability to recall a set of newly-learned designs following a delay, in the context of his or her ability to initially learn and encode the information (e.g., delayed recall adjusted for immediate recall). The new score represents the examinee's performance on delayed memory in comparison to individuals of similar immediate memory ability. It is important to note that contrast scaled scores are used to interpret scores in relation to similar ability peers; they do not replace subtest scaled scores and should not be substituted for subtest scores in reports or to compute index scores. Detailed information on the methodology, derivation, and interpretation of the contrast scaled scores is provided in the WMS–IV Technical Manual (Wechsler, 2008) and other sources (Drozdick, Holdnack, & Hilsabeck, 2011; Holdnack, 2007; Holdnack & Drozdick, 2010).

Five new index-level contrast scores are provided in the ACS to compare the additional indexes: Auditory Immediate Index versus Auditory Delayed Index, Auditory Recognition Index versus Auditory Delayed Index, Visual Immediate Index versus Visual Delayed Index, Visual Recognition Index versus Visual Delayed Index, and Designs Spatial Index versus Designs Content Index. All five contrast scores are available for the Adult battery; however, only the two auditory index contrast scales scores are available in the Older Adult battery.

Logical Memory Additional Scores

Several process scores for LM are included in the ACS. The first group of LM scores describes performance on a single story. Typically, two stories are administered during LM; however, sometimes one story may be invalid due to administration errors or other reasons, or an examiner may want to limit testing time and administer only one of the stories. Moreover, performance within a story can be reviewed even when both stories are administered. The ACS provides individual story norms for the recall and recognition trials of each story, including the first and second recall of Story A in the Older Adult battery. The single-story norms should be interpreted with caution due to the limited amount of data in the single sample of behavior on which the score is based. Score reliabilities are lower for the single story scores than those reported for the LM scores obtained with multiple stories. Story level norms are provided for each story for immediate recall and delayed recall and recognition. Recall scores produce scaled scores while the recognition scores are converted to cumulative percentages.

In addition to the single story norms, several contrast scores are available to compare performance within a story. The LM I Story A First Recall versus Story A Second Recall Contrast Scaled Score describes performance on the second immediate recall of Story A, controlling for the initial level of encoding observed in the initial recall. This provides information on the learning improvement for story recall following repetition. Low scores suggest that the examinee did not benefit from the repetition of the story to the same degree as others with similar single-trial recall ability. This might suggest that repetition of material alone will not improve performance. A second set of contrast scores describes the examinee's performance on delayed recall within the context of the examinee's immediate encoding and recall ability. This is similar to the overall LM Immediate versus Delayed Recall contrast scaled score.

A third type of score quantifying the use of memory cues during LM delayed recall is provided in the ACS. On occasion, an examinee reports that they cannot recall a story. The examiner will provide a memory cue to elicit the recall of further information. The examiner can note the use of prompts to facilitate retrieval from long-term memory stores. A cumulative percentage is provided for the number of cues required during LM delayed recall. Unusually high numbers of prompts may suggest difficulties with long-term retrieval of verbal information. Interpretation of this score requires observation of the response to cueing: an examinee showing good recall following a cue may have some difficulty with accessing encoded information. Alternately, poor recall following a cue may suggest more significant problems with retrieval or poor encoding of verbal material into long-term memory. Administration of recognition trials may help clarify the problem as good scores on recognition suggest good encoding of material. Table 1.6 lists the LM additional scores provided in the ACS.

Verbal Paired Associates Additional Scores

VPA provides a wealth of detailed information on VPA performance through ACS additional scores. The ACS scores for VPA include error scores, process scores, and contrast scaled scores. Table 1.7 lists the VPA additional scores provided in the ACS, by score type.

Memory errors represent a breakdown in encoding and learning of material and/or in retrieval of learned information. Cognitive skills outside of memory can influence these errors. Memory errors are complex and multiple sources of information are required to confirm hypotheses about the influence of other cognitive functions on memory functioning when high rates of memory errors are observed. The ACS VPA error scores can help elucidate memory process strengths and weaknesses.

TABLE 1.6   ACS Additional Logical Memory Scores, by Type of Score

Single-Story Scores	Contrast Scaled Scores	Process Scores
LM I Story A First Recall Scaled Score	LM I Story A First Recall vs. Story A Second Recall	LM II Cue Given Cumulative Percentage
LM I Story A Second Recall Scaled Score	LM Story A First Recall vs. Story A Delayed Recall	
LM I Story A Scaled Score	LM Story B Immediate Recall vs. Delayed Recall	
LM I Story B Scaled Score	LM Story C Immediate Recall vs. Delayed Recall	
LM I Story C Scaled Score		
LM II Story A Scaled Score		
LM II Story B Scaled Score		
LM II Story C Scaled Score		
LM II Story A Recognition Cumulative Percentage		
LM II Story B Recognition Cumulative Percentage		
LM II Story C Recognition Cumulative Percentage		

When used with WAIS–IV, a more comprehensive picture of cognitive influences on performance can be realized.

Several error scores are included in the ACS: intra-list and extra-list intrusion errors, total intrusion errors, false positives, and repetition errors. Intrusion errors are specific to the immediate and delayed recall trials. Intra-list intrusions are errors in which the examinee provides a word included in one of the word pairs but associates it with the wrong word. They are relatively common among typically developing individuals because they reflect good encoding of the individual words but poor encoding of the association between words. A modest number of intra-list errors is expected during initial learning trials with fewer errors occurring as the learning trials continue. High rates of intra-list errors across trials are unusual and suggest significant difficulty with associative memory. Alternately, the examinee may recall a novel word, unrelated to the word pairs. This extra-list intrusion indicates poor encoding of the words in the word pairs. Examination of specific intrusions provided by the examinee can be important. Semantic errors (e.g., a response with a high degree of similarity to a target word) are relatively common, while intrusions of novel, unrelated words are a more

TABLE 1.7   ACS Additional Verbal Paired Associates Scores, by Type of Score

Error Scores	Process Scores	Contrast Scaled Scores
VPA I Extra-List Intrusions Cumulative Percentage	VPA I Recall A Scaled Score	VPA I Recall A vs. Recall D
VPA I Intra-List Intrusions Cumulative Percentage	VPA I Recall D Scaled Score	VPA I Easy Items vs. Hard Items
VPA I Intrusions Scaled Score	VPA I Easy Items Scaled Score	
VPA II Extra-List Intrusions Cumulative Percentage	VPA I Hard Items Scaled Score	
VPA II Intra-List Intrusions Cumulative Percentage	VPA II Easy Items Cumulative Percentage	
VPA II Intrusions Cumulative Percentage	VPA II Hard Items Cumulative Percentage	
VPA II Recognition False Positives Cumulative Percentage	VPA II Recognition Easy Items Cumulative Percentage	
VPA II Word Recall Intrusions Cumulative Percentage	VPA II Recognition Hard Items Cumulative Percentage	
VPA II Word Recall Repetitions Cumulative Percentage	VPA II Recognition Hits Cumulative Percentage	
	VPA II Recognition Discriminability Cumulative Percentage	

serious type of memory error as they represent a breakdown in the encoding and retrieval of both the verbal information and associations. Finally, the ACS provides a score for the total number of intrusions, obtained by summing the total number of intra-list and extra-list errors for either VPA I or VPA II. Interpreting the total intrusion score must take into account the type and severity of memory errors (e.g., extra-list and intra-list) made.

The ACS also examines errors on VPA II Recognition and Word Recall. For VPA II Recognition, false positives, an incorrect response in which the examinee identifies an incorrect word pair as one of the target word pairs, are evaluated. Low rates of false positives are common in typically developing adults. However, medium to high rates of false positives may suggest poor recognition of information or poor monitoring of responding (e.g., poor discrimination of response choices or poor attention). The type of errors made by the examinee may be meaningful (e.g., incorrect associations, incorrect words) and provide insight into errors.

For VPA II Word Recall, intrusion and repetition errors are tabulated; no association errors are examined because the examinee does not pair the words on this recall task. Intrusion errors are not split into types on this task; however, it may be helpful to examine whether the intrusions are semantically related or novel words. When the examinee repeats the same word without self-correcting it is a repetition error and it is related to an examinee's ability to filter out redundant information or self-monitor their responses. Errors on free recall indicate problems with learning, encoding, retrieval, or self-monitoring of memory functions. Multiple error scores can provide data on the consistency and type of an examinee's memory difficulties.

Process scores describe a specific aspect of memory performance, providing detailed information on memory performance. Different process scores are available for each condition. For the recall conditions, Recall A, Recall D, Easy Items, and Hard Items are evaluated. Only Easy Items and Hard Items are evaluated in the delayed condition. Easy Items, Hard Items, Hit Rate, and Discriminability are presented for the Recognition trial.

The two recall trial process scores: VPA I Recall A and VPA I Recall D, provide information on learning. VPA I Recall A describes encoding of verbal information following a single exposure. Comparing this score to various LM I performance provides effects of the organization of presented material on memory functioning. VPA I Recall D describes the amount of information encoded and retrieved following four presentations of word pairs. This can be compared to VPA Recall A to provide an estimate of learning curve or to quantify the change in memory functioning associated with repeating information.

In developing VPA, four word pairs were designed to be "easy." For these items, the word pairs are semantically related (e.g., boy–girl). Research demonstrated a relatively low level of association for the pairs to prevent examinees from getting points for simply guessing a word associated with the initial word (see Pearson, 2010). The remaining word pairs were designed to be "hard," by using word pairs that are semantically unrelated. The easy items scores measure recall of semantically-related items. These items have a previous association in long-term semantic memory that should facilitate encoding and retrieval of those items. Low scores on easy items scores may indicate more severe difficulties because the examinee is not benefitting from the semantic relationship of the items. The difficult items scores are a more direct measure of verbal associative learning than the easy items scores. Because the difficult items have no semantic relationship, there is no previous association in semantic memory to facilitate encoding and retrieval. Comparing performance on easy and difficult items provides information on the degree to which existing semantic associations facilitate encoding and retrieval of verbal associations.

The process scores for the recognition condition further breakdown the ability to recognize learned information and provide insight on encoding versus retrieval problems. Easy and difficult items on the recognition trial measure encoding for semantically related and unrelated word pairs. Low scores on easy items are unusual in healthy controls and likely reflect a significant problem with encoding semantically related items after multiple exposures. Alternately, low scores on difficult items may indicate difficulties learning new associations. Comparisons between easy and hard items can also be revealing. If easy items are within the normal range, a low difficult items score may suggest a specific problem with novel associative learning; however, if both easy and difficult item scores are low, there is likely a general deficit in associative learning. Hit rate reflects the number of correctly identified target word-pairs. A high hit rate score indicates good recognition of correct information, not necessarily good recognition overall. Low scores indicate poor encoding of the target information. On the other hand, Discriminability evenly weights the ability to accurately classify targets and distracters. This score limits the influence of response bias on the yes/no recognition trials and helps to identify difficulties with recognition. Low scores on discriminability indicate problems recognizing learned associations and suggest encoding difficulty. If differences are observed between the recognition condition score and the Discriminability score, the examinee may have exhibited a response bias.

Several contrast scaled scores compare performance on the ACS additional VPA scores. The VPA I Recall A versus Recall D contrast scaled score estimates learning slope across the VPA I learning trials. It describes performance on Recall D given performance on Recall A and reflects the amount of improvement in performance due to repeating the information. Low scores indicate that the examinee's performance does not improve following repetition of the information. High scores indicate significantly improved performance following repeated exposure over single exposure.

The VPA I Easy Items versus Hard Items contrast scaled score describes the ability to learn novel verbal associations controlling for the ability to learn semantically related verbal associations. Low scores indicate unexpectedly low ability to recall novel associations given the ability to recall semantically related items and may represent a breakdown in verbal memory functioning that is masked in the total score by the examinee performing well on the easy items. A high score indicates better than expected performance on the novel associations considering recall of semantically related items. Interpretation of this contrast scaled score will require evaluation of the item-level performance.

Visual Reproduction Scores

The ACS provides error, process, and contrast scores for the VR subtest. Two error scores are provided: VR I and VR II Additional Design Elements. An additional design element in VR is an intrusion, in VR they are visual details added to the designs by the examinee during recall that was not present in the original design. High numbers of additional design elements may indicate difficulty monitoring recall of visual details for accuracy, impairment of visual–perceptual processing, or poor recall of visual information. Results from other visual–perceptual, executive functioning, or memory measures, or other sources of information can help clarify the underlying difficulty.

Two process scores are included in the ACS: VR I and VR II Average Completion Time. These scores enable the clinician to evaluate the influence of response speed on performance. Examinees who draw very quickly run the risk of losing points due to careless mistakes, while very slow examinees may lose points for forgetting specific design details due to the length of time from exposure to drawing a specific element. Conversely, speed may not be related to memory performance but to issues with processing speed or impulsivity. Outliers may impact the average completion time and should be considered (e.g., a long completion time for one design among relatively fast completion times). High scores indicate much faster response time than expected while low scores indicate a slower-than-expected drawing time.

Finally, two additional contrast scaled scores are available on the ACS: VR I Average Completion Time versus Immediate Recall and VR II Average Completion Time versus Delayed Recall. These scores describe memory performance in relation to how quickly the designs were drawn. This score should only be used when the performance is likely to have been affected by the speed at which the examinee drew the designs. Low scores indicate poor memory scores given the speed at which the examinee completed the designs; high scores indicate relatively good memory performance given the speed at which the examinee completed the designs. Table 1.8 lists the VR additional scores provided in the ACS, by score types.

TABLE 1.8   ACS Additional VR Scores, by Type of Score

Error Scores	Process Scores	Contrast Scaled Scores
VR I Additional Design Elements Cumulative Percentage	VR I Average Completion Time Scaled Score	VR I Average Completion Time vs. Immediate Recall
VR II Additional Design Elements Cumulative Percentage	VR II Average Completion Time Scaled Score	VR II Average Completion Time vs. Delayed Recall

Designs Scores

One additional score is provided in ACS for DE, DE Rule Violations. It is the number of items on which the examinee violates a rule by placing more cards in the memory grid than required. This type of error is fairly unusual because the examiner indicates how many cards are required for each item. Low scores may not necessarily reflect a memory error but a lapse in attention during instructions, poor comprehension of the task, or poor monitoring of responses.

Suboptimal Effort

Every cognitive assessment requires effort on the part of the examinee. Fluctuating or poor effort can result in lowered scores unrelated to actual deficits. Assessment of effort is increasingly included in clinical evaluations, particularly in those in which poor performance may benefit the examinee. Assessing effort can be difficult because many factors can influence effort, including medications, fatigue, motivation, and depression or other psychological disorders. Multiple sources of information are required to determine and validate if an individual is giving suboptimal effort. The ACS includes a new measure of effort, Word Choice, and normative and comparative information on embedded measures of effort in the WAIS–IV and the WMS–IV.

Measures

The Word Choice subtest is a forced choice memory test. Examinees are read and shown a list of 50 words, and then asked to select the word they heard from two choices. Typically, developing individuals obtain nearly perfect scores. Information on chance performance by an examinee is provided as well as performance data from multiple clinical samples, including simulator (i.e., individuals asked to feign poor performance) and no stimulus groups (i.e., individuals who were never shown the words). An examinee's performance can be compared to these data to determine if his or her performance is worse than performance observed in true clinical populations.

In addition to Word Choice, several embedded effort scores from the WAIS–IV and WMS–IV can be calculated and compared to performance by clinical groups. The embedded effort measures are WAIS–IV Reliable Digit Span (sum of the number of digits in the longest span correctly recalled on both trials of an item on both Digit Span Forward and Digit Span Backward), WMS–IV Logical Memory II Recognition, WMS–IV Verbal Paired Associates II Recognition, and WMS–IV Visual Reproduction II Recognition.

Scores

In the ACS, the Word Choice and embedded effort measures scores for an individual are compared to the base rates of performance in a mixed clinical population, individual clinical populations of interest such as traumatic brain injury, simulators, and no stimulus exposure (i.e., random guessing) groups. The base rates of unexpectedly low performance utilize scores across the five validity indicators, rather than individual effort scores to decrease the likelihood of a misclassification based on minimal data. The base rate tables provide frequency information for different cut-off criteria including the 2%, 5%, 10%, 15%, and 25%, obtained in the mixed clinical sample. These different base rates provide information on the frequency with which a specific clinical group obtains multiple scores below the specified cut-off criteria.

Most members of clinical populations perform adequately on effort measures (Arnett & Franzen, 1997; Ashendorf, Constantinou, & McCaffrey, 2004; Gierok, Dickson, & Cole, 2005; Macciocchi, Seel, Alderson, & Godsall, 2006), with the exception of severely impaired individuals such as those with dementia and intellectual disability (Frazier, Youngstrom, Naugle, Haggerty, & Busch, 2007; Milanovich, Axelrod, & Millis, 1996; Tombaugh, 1997). Effort measures may not be particularly useful or indicative of effort in these severely impaired populations. For examinee's whose performance on multiple effort measures is lower than that observed in most clinical populations and for the clinical sample for which they may be a member, then there is the potential that the performance of the examinee may not have put forth sufficient effort or may be exaggerating deficits.

Interpretation

Caution should be exercised when interpreting the suboptimal effort measures; they were not designed to diagnosis malingering. Moreover, they do not measure full range of effort (e.g., suboptimal to average effort to superior effort). The ACS suboptimal effort measures identify examinees whose performance on the Word Choice and embedded validity measures is unexpectedly low given his or her clinical characteristics. They may suggest that effort given by the examinee was atypically low or indicative of exaggeration but they should be used in conjunction with other information to make appropriate clinical decisions and diagnoses. For more information on the development, use, application, and interpretation of the ACS suboptimal effort measures, see Chapter 7.

SERIAL ASSESSMENT WITH WAIS–IV AND WMS–IV

In clinical and research settings, individuals are routinely re-evaluated with the same instruments. Typically, this is done to determine if a change in ability has occurred as part of an ongoing disease process (e.g., dementia) or following treatment or intervention. However, a number of statistical and personal effects need to be accounted for before a change in performance can be attributed to a change in actual ability. Scores on re-evaluation need to be considered within this context in order to avoid incorrect interpretation of changes in scores on re-test. The ACS serial assessment scores are adjusted for the statistical and person effects known to influence retest scores in normally developing individuals. Use of these scores greatly increases the likelihood of correctly interpreting the relation between changes in scores and actual changes in ability. Regression-based serial assessment scores are provided for the WAIS–IV core and WMS–IV primary subtest and composite scores. For more detailed information on the development, appropriate use, application, and interpretation of serial assessment scores, see Chapter 6 (Serial Assessment).

Demographically Adjusted Norms

Standard norms compare an individual's performance to a group of peers, typically same-age peers. When the purpose of the evaluation is to evaluate the examinee in relation to the general population, standard norms are the most appropriate and psychometrically robust method of comparison. However, some clinical questions require the examiner to determine whether an examinee has experienced a change in functioning, or to compare the examinee to individuals with similar background characteristics (e.g., education level). For these types of evaluations, demographically adjusted norms may be appropriate.

Demographically adjusted norms compare an individual's performance to individuals with similar background characteristics (e.g., education level). The ACS applies demographic adjustments (i.e., education only, full demographics) to the standard age-adjusted WAIS–IV and WMS–IV subtest and composite scores. See Chapter 4 (Demographic Adjustments) for detailed information on the development of the ACS demographically adjusted norms, their use, applicability, and interpretation.

Test of Premorbid Functioning (TOPF)

Clinicians are frequently asked to determine if an examinee's current functioning is lower than their functioning prior to an injury or onset of neurological disease process. Current performance does not provide information on how current performance related to prior ability. For example, low performance on a current assessment does not indicate a decline because the examinee may have had low ability prior to the injury. For most individuals, testing was not completed prior to these injuries and the examiner is required to estimate the examinee's prior functioning. Historically, an individual's background characteristics (e.g., education, occupation) were used to estimate premorbid ability. However, this approach is prone to error due to estimation error and bias. Modern approaches to estimating premorbid functioning involve statistical approaches to providing estimates of ability based on current performance on tasks that are known to be minimally affected by cognitive change, at least in individuals with mild to moderate impairment, or on demographic comparisons.

The Test of Premorbid Functioning (TOPF) was developed for the ACS to estimate an individual's premorbid WAIS–IV and WMS–IV scores. The TOPF is a reading task in which the examinee reads aloud words that have irregular grapheme-to-phoneme translation. It is a revision of the Wechsler Test of Adult Reading (WTAR: Pearson, 2001) and shares methodology and some content with the National Adult Reading Test (NART: Nelson, 1982), the American Version of the National Adult Reading Test (AMNART: Grober & Sliwinski, 1991), and the North American Adult Reading Test (NAART: Blair & Spreen, 1989). This type of reading task is less affected by cognitive disease processes and injury than other measures of intellectual and memory functioning.

The TOPF can be used alone or in conjunction with demographic characteristics to provide estimates of premorbid ability. Demographic variables relate to cognitive and memory ability and predict premorbid ability without additional cognitive functioning measures, such as the TOPF. The ACS provides premorbid estimates of the WAIS–IV and WMS–IV subtest and index scores using TOPF alone, demographic variables alone, and TOPF and demographics together. Chapter 5 (Predicting Premorbid Ability) provides detailed information on the relationship between demographics and performance on intellectual and memory tests, and the development, use, and interpretation of ACS premorbid estimations.

Social Perception

Social cognition skills are required to appropriately interact with others in personal, vocational, and educational settings. Social cognition encompasses a wide variety of skills, including affect recognition, facial memory and recognition, appropriate interpretation of affect and prosody, and theory of mind. Neurological, psychiatric, and developmental conditions (e.g., Autistic Disorder, Schizophrenia) often impact social ability or include them as diagnostic criteria. Deficits in social cognition directly impact an examinee's ability to function in most environments. In addition to specific deficits in social cognition, general cognitive deficits often produce difficulties in aspects of social cognition.

Three social cognition subtests were developed for ACS to measure aspects of social cognition, including facial affect recognition, recognition and identification of affect from prosody, ability to verbalize a speaker's intent, face recognition, and recall of names and pertinent information. Each subtest measures different clinical aspects of social cognition and can be used independently or in combination. The Social Perception subtests provide information on some basic processes involved in social cognition. A detailed review of the assessment of social cognition and the development, use, and interpretation of the ACS Social Perception measures is provided in Chapter 8 (Assessing Social Cognition).

Social Perception

Social Perception measures comprehension of social communication, including facial affect recognition and naming, affect recognition from prosody and facial expressions, and affect recognition from prosody and interaction between people. Three tasks comprise Social Perception: Affect Naming, Prosody-Face Matching, and Prosody-Pair Matching. In Affect Naming, the examinee is shown photographs of faces and selects an emotion from a card to describe the affect demonstrated in the photograph. In Prosody-Face Matching, the examinee hears an audio-recorded statement and selects one face from four choices that matches the emotion expressed in the recording. In Prosody-Pair Matching, the examinee hears an audio-recorded statement and selects one photograph of interacting pairs of individuals from four choices that matches the meaning of the speaker's statement. For Prosody-Face Matching and Prosody-Pair Matching, the statement content may not match the emotion expressed. This intentional lack of matching allows for better measurement of more subtle forms of communication, such as sarcasm. Available scores assess the examinee's overall performance, as well as the individual skills measured within and across the three tasks.

Faces

The Faces subtest measures immediate and delayed recall of faces. Early learning trials require facial discrimination and recognition as well as spatial memory. The examinee is shown a grid with photographs of various faces in some of the cells for 10 seconds. Following removal of the stimulus, the examinee selects faces from a set of cards and places the cards in the grid from memory. Three learning trials are used in the immediate recall condition and a delayed recall task is administered 20–30 minutes following exposure.

Names

The Names subtest measures visual–verbal association for faces and names and activities, and incidental recall of facial expressions. It requires the ability to recall proper names and semantic information when provided a visual cue. The examinee is shown a series of photographs of children in a variety of affective states. For each photograph, the examiner is told the name of the child and an activity in which the child participates. The examinee is then shown each photograph and asked to recall the child's name and activity. Three learning trials are used to teach the examinee the photos, names, activities, and associations. In addition to long-term memory for proper names and semantic information, the delayed recall trial measures incidental learning of affective states. On delayed recall, neutral faces of the children are shown to the examinee and he or she is asked to recall the emotion expressed by the child in the learning trials.

WMS–IV FLEXIBLE APPROACH

The WMS–IV Flexible Approach (WMS–IV Flex) is the most recent addition to the array of products associated with the WAIS–IV and WMS–IV. It provides alternate measures and index scores for the WMS–IV using the subtests included in the original publication, the ACS, and/or new subtests designed for the WMS–IV Flex. These alternate indexes either require less administration time or incorporate the new subtests. The availability of multiple indexes increases the flexibility of the WMS–IV and its utility in assessments for different clinical populations, referral questions, and examinee needs. For most assessments, it is recommended that the standard WMS–IV be used as it provides a highly reliable assessment of core memory functions, including measures of immediate and delayed memory, auditory and visual memory, visual working memory, and free recall, cued, and recognition memory. In addition, results from the WMS–IV can be directly compared to results obtained with WAIS–IV. The subtests and alternate indexes provided in the WMS–IV Flex are designed to assist in tailoring assessments for examinees who require a shorter battery or alternate measures of memory.

The subtests and alternate indexes of the WMS–IV Flex also allow the substitution of supplemental visual memory measures for primary subtests in the WMS–IV indexes, similar to the CVLT–II substitution allowed in the Verbal Memory Index in the WMS–IV. For all of the alternate indexes, the examiner must utilize clinical judgment in selecting the most appropriate battery for each examinee. The use of the alternate indexes in place of WMS–IV indexes does limit the utility of the memory indexes, most markedly in relation to comparisons with the WAIS–IV. Alternate indexes are not compared to performance on WAIS–IV. Also, substitution of subtests into the indexes will change the interpretation of those indexes. For example, the WMS–IV Flex visual memory subtests involve auditory–visual association measures, while the WMS–IV visual memory subtests primarily measure visual memory. The composition of the index needs to be considered when interpreting results.

Alternate Subtests

Two alternate visual memory subtests are included in the WMS–IV Flex: Logos and Names. Logos measures immediate and delayed recall memory for visual–verbal associations. The examinee is shown either eight or 16 logos one at a time. With the presentation of each logo, the examinee is told the name of the company associated with each logo. Each name is a nonsense word. Following the presentation of the logos, the examinee is told the name of a logo and asked to select the logo from six choices. The logo–name pairs are presented three across three learning trials. A delayed trial is given following a 20–30 minute delay. The Names subtest is from the ACS and described in detail previously. It measures immediate and delayed face–name association memory.

Alternate Indexes

The WMS–IV Flexible Approach offers several subtest combinations that yield Immediate, Delayed, Visual, and Auditory Memory Index scores. These subtest combinations include combinations of subtests from the WMS–IV and the WMS–IV Flex. The new indexes included in the WMS–IV Flex emphasize reduced administration time, reduced motor requirements, or the assessment visual–verbal association memory. None of the WMS–IV Flex alternate indexes should be substituted for WMS–IV indexes in comparisons to WAIS–IV.

One shorter alternative battery, LMVR, was developed to provide a brief assessment for older adults. LMVR consists of LM and Visual Reproduction (VR) from the WMS–IV and provides Immediate, Delayed, Auditory, and Visual Memory Indexes. The second group of alternate subtest combinations utilizes the WMS–IV Flex subtests. VRLO includes

VR from the WMS–IV and Logos (LO) from the WMS–IV Flex. This combination provides a visual index with multiple indicators of visual memory but is not a pure measure of visual memory. Only Visual Immediate and Visual Delayed Indexes are available on VRLO due to the lack of an auditory memory subtest in the short battery. LONA includes the LO and Names (NA) subtests to create alternate auditory–visual indexes (immediate, delayed, and total). The new Auditory–Visual Memory Index (AVMI) is included in this battery and measures aspects of auditory and visual learning and memory, and assesses immediate, delayed, and overall memory functioning. This configuration explicitly measures auditory–visual association memory and is not as direct a measure of visual memory functioning as the visual indexes obtained in WMS–IV. However, it may be useful as a general memory screener because it quickly taps visual and auditory learning and recall.

CASE STUDIES

CASE STUDY 1

Mr. J. is a 62-year-old, African-American, married male. He presented to his family physician with concerns regarding his attention and memory functioning. Over the past year, Mr. J.'s wife has noticed a significant change in his cognitive functioning. He has become forgetful for recent events and has forgotten to pay bills on several occasions. Currently, she is managing the family finances and general household management. Mr. J. retired from his job as a laboratory technician at a local hospital 9 months ago after having difficulties learning new procedures at work. Mr. J. also reports a significant change in his ability to remember and reports that he cannot think as clearly as he has in the past. Physically, Mr. J. is generally healthy; although he takes medication for high cholesterol, and he has poorly controlled hypertension.

Mr. J.'s family physician referred him for a neurological evaluation. The neurologist observed mildly decreased mental status. An MRI of his brain revealed evidence of white matter damage interpreted as reflecting small vessel ischemic changes. Mr. J. was referred for neuropsychological assessment to evaluate for decline in cognitive functioning. As part of the neuropsychological evaluation, the clinician administered the WAIS–IV and WMS–IV. The results of these tests are presented in Table 1.9.

Mr. J.'s performance on the WAIS–IV was in the average range for all of the indexes. Among the four core index scores, his best performance was on WMI which was significantly better than VCI and PSI ($p < 0.05$). Although these indexes were significantly different from one

TABLE 1.9 WAIS–IV and WMS–IV Scores for Mr. J

WAIS–IV Index	Score	%ile	WMS–IV Index	Score	%ile
Verbal Comprehension	95	37	Auditory Memory	62	1
Perceptual Reasoning	102	55	Visual Memory	84	14
Working Memory Index	105	63	Visual Working Memory	97	42
Processing Speed	102	55	Immediate Memory	78	7
Full Scale IQ	98	45	Delayed Memory	61	<1
General Ability Index	98	45	General Memory Index	69	2
WAIS–IV Subtest			**WMS–IV Subtest**		
Similarities	12	84	Logical Memory I	4	2
Vocabulary	9	37	Logical Memory II	2	<1
Information	6	9	Verbal Paired Associates I	5	5
Block Design	8	25	Verbal Paired Associates II	4	2
Matrix Reasoning	12	84	Designs I	10	50
Visual Puzzles	11	63	Designs II	7	16
Digit Span	11	63	Visual Reproduction I	8	25
Arithmetic	11	63	Visual Reproduction II	4	2
Symbol Search	7	16	Spatial Addition	15	95
Coding	10	50	Symbol Span	4	2

another, the frequency of the difference is fairly common in the standardization sample (i.e., 20.6% and 18.4%, respectively). Subtest level performance ranged from low average to high average. His performance was notable for a relative weakness on the Information subtest ($p < 0.05$, base rate 5–10%).

The WMS–IV BCSE results were in the low range (<5%, 5th percentile). This indicates rather significant deficits in general cognitive status. He performed poorly on executive functioning, memory, and processing speed measures. Mr. J. showed considerable variability in his WMS–IV performance. His VWMI, like his WAIS–IV WMI, was in the average range. Immediate memory functioning was in the borderline range and delayed performance was extremely low. Auditory memory was in the extremely low range and visual memory was low average. The Retrieval Index (87, 19 percentile) was in the low average range indicating that recognition memory is not better than free recall. The Retention Index (61, <1 percentile) was in the extremely low range indicating a high degree of forgetting. Similarly, the immediate versus delayed contrast score (SS = 2) was in the extremely low range, confirming poor retention of information from immediate to delayed recall. The Visual Working Memory versus Visual Memory index contrast score was in the low average range (SS = 6, 9th percentile) indicating lower than expected visual memory functioning compared to visual working memory.

Subtest performance was quite variable ranging from extremely low to superior. Among immediate memory measures, Designs I was a significant strength and Logical Memory I was a significant weakness. Delayed memory functioning was notable for a strength in Designs II. All recognition trials were in the extremely low range (≤2nd percentile), with the exception of VR II Recognition subtest comparisons which were in the borderline to low average range (SS = 4 to 7). This indicates a significant loss of information from immediate to delayed recall for each subtest. Visual working memory subtests were significantly different from one another with Spatial Addition being significantly higher than Symbol Span.

The WMS–IV test results indicate significant deficits in long-term memory functioning and overall cognitive status. Presenting information in a recognition format does not help his ability to recall information indicating encoding rather than retrieval impairment. Visual working memory skills were quite variable with spatial better than visual detail working memory.

The comparison between the WAIS–IV and WMS–IV enables the clinician to identify specific deficits in memory functioning relative to general cognitive functioning. Table 1.10 presents the WAIS–IV/WMS–IV contrast scores. The GAI is significantly better than all memory measures; however, visual working memory is consistent with GAI. In particular, IMI, AMI, and DMI are very low compared to GAI (SS = 4, 2nd percentile, SS = 1, <1st percentile, and SS = 1, <1st percentile, respectively). Auditory memory is significantly lower than expected compared to VCI (SS = 1, <1st percentile) and WMI (SS = 1, <1st percentile). Visual Memory is significantly lower than PRI (SS = 5, 5th percentile) and GAI (22 = 6, 9th percentile). Visual working memory is consistent with WAIS–IV indexes.

The WAIS–IV and WMS–IV results indicate that Mr. J. has average intellectual abilities and intact working memory. In the context of these average abilities, he has rather deficient memory functioning, particularly auditory and delayed memory. He has rather severe problems with memory encoding and retention of information over time. Based on the overall presenting symptoms, test results, and collateral interviews, Mr. J. was diagnosed with Mild Cognitive Impairment. Follow-up assessment was recommended in 12 months.

TABLE 1.10   WAIS–IV versus WMS–IV Contrast Scores for Mr. J

Contrast Scaled Scores	Score 1	Score 2	Contrast Scaled Score
General Ability Index vs. Auditory Memory Index	98	62	2
General Ability Index vs. Visual Memory Index	98	84	6
General Ability Index vs. Visual Working Memory Index	98	97	10
General Ability Index vs. Immediate Memory Index	98	78	4
General Ability Index vs. Delayed Memory Index	98	61	1
Verbal Comprehension Index vs. Auditory Memory Index	95	62	1
Perceptual Reasoning Index vs. Visual Memory Index	102	84	5
Perceptual Reasoning Index vs. Visual Working Memory Index	102	97	9
Working Memory Index vs. Auditory Memory Index	105	62	1
Working Memory Index vs. Visual Working Memory Index	105	97	8

CASE STUDY 2

Mr. H. is a 16-year-old, Hispanic, male who has a long-term history of right temporal lobe epilepsy. Seizures began when he was 9 years of age and he has been treated with anti-seizure medication since that time. His seizures have been managed but not completely controlled. Over the past year, his seizures have increased in intensity and frequency. Multiple medication adjustments and changes have not yielded satisfactory improvement in his condition. Due to the frequency of his seizures, he has missed a significant amount of school time. He has received some in home education services; however, the frequency of the seizure activity has limited his ability to maintain focus and energy on his schoolwork. After consulting with a neurosurgeon, the family decided that temporal lobectomy surgery was the best option to improve his medical status and improve his quality of life. The family was aware of the potential risks of the surgery; however, the potential benefits outweighed the potential disadvantages.

TABLE 1.11 WAIS–IV/WMS–IV Scores for Mr. H

WAIS–IV Index	Score	%ile	WMS–IV Index	Score	%ile
Verbal Comprehension	85	16	Auditory Memory	109	73
Perceptual Reasoning	79	8	Visual Memory	86	18
Working Memory Index	80	9	Visual Working Memory	83	13
Processing Speed	79	8	Immediate Memory	102	55
Full Scale IQ	77	6	Delayed Memory	93	32
General Ability	80	9	General Memory	97	42
Combined Working Memory	80	8	Quantitative	80	8
WAIS–IV Subtest			**WMS–IV Subtest**		
Similarities	7	16	Logical Memory I	12	75
Vocabulary	7	16	Logical Memory II	10	50
Information	8	25	Verbal Paired Associates I	12	75
Block Design	7	16	Verbal Paired Associates II	12	75
Matrix Reasoning	6	9	Designs I	10	50
Visual Puzzles	6	9	Designs II	7	16
Digit Span	6	9	Visual Reproduction I	7	16
Arithmetic	7	16	Visual Reproduction II	7	16
Symbol Search	6	9	Spatial Addition	5	5
Coding	6	9	Symbol Span	9	37

Mr. H. has a long history of academic difficulties related to his seizure disorder. He has frequently missed school and even when he has been able to attend regularly his learning is somewhat diminished. He has difficulty in most subjects, with math his weakest subject. He also has some psychiatric issues related to depression, social anxiety, and poor social skills. Mr. H. is classified as a student with a physical impairment enabling him to receive some special education services.

Mr. H. underwent neurosurgery for temporal lobectomy 3 months ago. The surgery was successful and he experienced a good recovery. His seizures are now well controlled with medication. His mood is improved and his parents observe that he seems to have better attention and more cognitive stamina. Neuropsychological evaluation was recommended post surgery to evaluate cognitive functioning and to help aid in educational planning. The results of the WAIS–IV and WMS–IV are presented in Table 1.11.

The WAIS–IV results indicate borderline to low average general cognitive functioning. Mr. H.'s best performance was observed on the VCI index; however, there was no significant variability in WAIS–IV functioning indicating consistency across complex cognitive functions. Subtest performance ranged from borderline to average. There were no significant strengths or weaknesses among WAIS–IV subtests.

WMS–IV scores were borderline to low average. General memory functioning was in the average range. The Auditory Memory Index was average and visual memory was low average. Visual memory was unexpectedly lower than auditory memory (contrast SS = 6, 9th percentile). Immediate memory and delayed memory functioning were both in the average range; however, delayed memory was lower than expected compared to immediate memory (contrast SS = 7, 16th percentile). Visual working memory was low average. Visual memory functioning was consistent with visual working memory (contrast SS = 10, 50th percentile). At the index level, Mr. H. shows a weakness in visual and delayed memory functioning.

WMS–IV subtest performance ranged from borderline to high average. Mr. H.'s performance was notable for a strength in delayed Verbal Paired Associates and a weakness in immediate Visual Reproduction. Spatial Addition was significantly lower than Symbol Span. Process measures indicate that delayed memory for visual detailed is higher than memory for spatial information (contrast SS = 13, 75th percentile). Memory functioning is characterized by a weakness in visual memory, particularly spatial memory functioning. Spatial working memory is a relative weakness compared to working memory for visual details.

WAIS–IV/WMS–IV combined index scores were in the low average range for both working memory and quantitative reasoning. Table 1.12 presents WAIS–IV/WMS–IV index contrast scores. The results indicate that Visual Memory and Visual Working Memory are consistent with WAIS–IV GAI and PRI. Auditory memory is a significant strength compared to GAI, VCI, and WMI. Immediate memory is also a strength compared to GAI. The results indicate that Mr. H. has borderline to low average cognitive functioning with a relative strength in auditory memory.

Because Mr. H. had long-standing difficulties with social relationships, the ACS: Social Perception test was administered as part of this evaluation. This test evaluates the examinee's ability to understand facial and auditory expressions of emotion. Mr. H. performed in the borderline range on Affect Naming (SS = 5, 5th percentile). He performed in the average range on Prosody (SS = 8, 25th percentile) and Pairs (SS = 11, 75th percentile). His overall level of performance on this test was unusually low (SS = 6, 9th percentile). These results indicate that Mr. H. has difficulty reading facial expressions of emotion. He

TABLE 1.12 WAIS−IV/WMS−IV Contrast Scores for Mr. H

Contrast Scaled Scores	Score 1	Score 2	Contrast Scaled Score
General Ability Index vs. Auditory Memory Index	80	109	14
General Ability Index vs. Visual Memory Index	80	86	10
General Ability Index vs. Visual Working Memory Index	80	83	9
General Ability Index vs. Immediate Memory Index	80	102	14
General Ability Index vs. Delayed Memory Index	80	93	10
Verbal Comprehension Index vs. Auditory Memory Index	85	109	14
Perceptual Reasoning Index vs. Visual Memory Index	79	86	10
Perceptual Reasoning Index vs. Visual Working Memory Index	79	83	10
Working Memory Index vs. Auditory Memory Index	80	109	14
Working Memory Index vs. Visual Working Memory Index	80	83	9

reads facial expressions better when getting both auditory (i.e., prosody) and facial cues, with his best performance when he has more social cues (i.e., body language, prosody, and facial expressions). Compared to his general cognitive functioning (i.e., WAIS−IV GAI), his Social Perception total score is in the average range (contrast SS = 8, 25th percentile). His social perception is not significantly worse than his overall intellectual functioning; however, he has some strengths and weakness in that domain which can inform intervention.

Based on these results, the school developed an education plan that focused on Mr. H.'s strengths in verbal memory. Additionally, he participated in a social skills group that focused on recognizing and responding to emotional expressions. He is also exploring vocational training options. Overall, his quality of life significantly improved and consequently dramatic improvements were observed in his mood and energy level.

SUMMARY

The WAIS–IV is a comprehensive battery assessing general and specific cognitive functioning in adolescents and adults. The WAIS–IV is comprised of 10 subtests that measure verbal, perceptual, auditory working memory, and visual–perceptual processing speed. Factor analytic studies support the four-factor model of Verbal Comprehension, Perceptual Reasoning, Working Memory, and Processing Speed with additional factors such as Fluid and Quantitative Reasoning also being supported. While the WAIS–IV indexes measure specific constructs, they are also influenced by additional cognitive abilities. Deficits in expressive or receptive language skills, memory impairments, auditory acuity, visual processing, attention, and executive functions can influence WAIS–IV performance to varying degrees. It is important to consider that patients with neurological, developmental, and psychiatric conditions may have deficits in basic cognitive skills that affect their performance on the WAIS–IV.

The WMS–IV is a battery of tests designed to measure multiple components of memory functioning. The WMS–IV assesses visual working memory, immediate and delayed memory, and auditory and visual memory. More specific aspects of memory including verbal learning, free recall, recognition, associative learning, and memory for spatial locations and visual details are assessed. Using specific score comparisons (e.g., contrast scores), deficits associated with rapid forgetting, poor memory encoding, or difficulties retrieving information from memory can be identified. Visual Working Memory is a new index in the Wechsler family of tests. In this index, working memory for both spatial and visual details is assessed. The WMS–IV uniquely enables the clinician to differentiate spatial from visual detail aspects of memory. Like the WAIS–IV, WMS–IV subtests are complex tasks measuring multiple abilities not just memory functioning. Patients with neurological, developmental, and psychiatric conditions may have verbal, visual, attention, executive functioning, or deficits in other basic skills that can negatively impact WMS–IV performance.

The power of the combined WAIS–IV/WMS–IV is derived from the co-norming of the tests. Sophisticated statistical comparisons can be derived when tests are co-normed. Joint factor analysis of the batteries indicates that five- or seven-factors fit the data very well. The expansion of the construct coverage of the combined battery yields a better factor model than either test alone or compared to the predecessor editions. WAIS–IV and WMS–IV scores can be compared using a variety of statistical techniques enabling the evaluation of specific hypotheses about cognitive functioning.

The ACS expands the construct coverage of the WAIS–IV and WMS–IV and provides statistical tools for sophisticated evaluation of WAIS–IV and WMS–IV performance. The ACS includes additional scores for the WMS–IV that assess rate of learning, visual and verbal memory errors, and additional indexes to refine memory assessment. The ACS suboptimal effort tools use external and embedded measures to identify examinees that may be putting forth inadequate effort. Demographic norms and the Test of Premorbid Functioning (TOPF) are statistical measurement tools designed to determine if a patient's current test performance is expected or represents a decline from a previous level of ability. Clinicians can also use the serial assessment tools to identify a significant change in cognitive abilities over time. Finally, the ACS provides additional construct coverage with tests measuring social cognition and executive functioning.

The WAIS–IV/WMS–IV/ACS is a comprehensive assessment system designed to enable clinicians to evaluate specific hypotheses about a patient's cognitive functioning. The system is designed to allow the use of as much or as little of the batteries as is needed to answer a specific hypotheses. In order to effectively use this system, the clinician must understand the purpose and applicability of the tools available in these tests batteries. The remainder of this book is devoted to that purpose.

KEY LEARNING

- The WAIS–IV is comprised of 10 core subtests and five supplemental subtests. Four indexes, Verbal Comprehension, Perceptual Reasoning, Working Memory Index, and Processing Speed, and Full-Scale IQ are included.
- Additional WAIS–IV Indexes available include General Ability (VCI and PRI) and Cognitive Proficiency (WMI and PSI). Research indicates an additional Fluid Reasoning or Quantitative Reasoning Index may also fit the WAIS–IV data. Primary level of interpretation for the WAIS–IV is the four core indexes and FSIQ.
- While each index measures a specific aspect of cognitive functioning, multiple other abilities also affect performance. Verbal Comprehension can be affected by expressive and/or receptive language impairment, auditory processing difficulties, or memory impairment. Perceptual Reasoning can be affected by deficits in primary visuo-perceptual or spatial skills, visual attention, and visual working memory. Working Memory can be affected by deficits in brief focused attention, math skills, receptive language functioning,

and auditory processing. Processing Speed can be affected by motor impairment or visual–perceptual impairment.

- The WMS–IV Adult battery is comprised of four core memory subtests, each with an immediate, delayed, and recognition trial and two subtests measuring visual working memory. The WMS–IV Older Adult battery has three of the four memory tests and one of the visual working memory tests. There are five core WMS–IV indexes: Immediate, Delayed, Auditory, Visual, and Visual Working Memory. The WMS–IV visual memory and visual working memory measures allow the clinician to differentiate spatial from visual detail recall.
- The WMS–IV indexes primarily measure memory functioning; however, performance on each index is influenced by additional cognitive skills. Language, visual–perceptual skills, attention, auditory processing, and fine-motor skills can affect WMS–IV performance.
- The WAIS–IV and WMS–IV were co-normed and have no overlapping content. Joint factor analyses indicate five- or seven-factors best define the combined battery. The seven-factor model includes: Verbal Comprehension, Perceptual Reasoning, Auditory Working Memory, Visual Working Memory, Processing Speed, Auditory Memory, and Visual Memory.
- New factors for WMS–IV and combined WAIS–IV/WMS–IV have been developed. These new indexes are Quantitative Reasoning, Combined Working Memory, General Memory, Retention, and Retrieval. The ACS for WAIS–IV and WMS–IV provides additional tools for evaluating cognitive functioning as well as statistical procedures for sophisticated evaluation of WAIS–IV and WMS–IV scores.
- ACS extra scores provide additional measures for WAIS–IV CA, WMS–IV VPA, VR, DE, and VPA. The additional scores measure memory errors, learning curve, easy versus hard items on VPA, individual story performance for LM, and rule violations for DE. There are also additional indexes for WMS–IV including immediate, delayed, and delayed recognition for auditory and visual memory and a spatial and content index for Designs.
- ACS Test of Premorbid Functioning is a reading test used to estimate premorbid intellectual and memory functions. The TOPF enables users to choose from three models: TOPF only, Demographics only, or combined TOPF and Demographics. Complex or simple demographic data can be used. TOPF is co-normed with WAIS–IV and WMS–IV; therefore, sophisticated statistical analysis can be performed to compare predicted premorbid and actual WAIS–IV

and WMS–IV functioning. The purpose of the TOPF is to identify loss of cognitive functioning.

- ACS Demographic norms allow examiners to adjust index and scaled scores by education or by education, sex, and ethnicity. Adjusting scores allows clinicians to determine if a patient's score is relatively high or low compared to individuals with a similar background. The purpose of demographic norms is to identify loss in cognitive functioning.
- The ACS serial assessment provides statistical data for comparing two assessments over time to identify loss or gain in cognitive functioning.
- ACS suboptimal effort uses a forced choice memory paradigm along with reliable digit span, logical memory recognition, VPA recognition, and VR recognition to identify unexpectedly low performance. The purpose is to identify individuals that may be simulating cognitive impairment.
- The ACS social cognition measures evaluate facial affect recognition, prosody, body language, face memory, and face-name associations.
- The ACS executive functioning measures include the Trail-Making Test and Verbal Fluency from the D-KEFS.
- The WMS–IV Flex allows for a shortened WMS–IV assessment.

References

Adair, J. C., Na, D. L., Schwartz, R. L., & Heilman, K. M. (1998). Analysis of primary and secondary influences on spatial neglect. *Brain and Cognition, 37*(3), 351–367.

Arnett, P. A., & Franzen, M. D. (1997). Performance of substance abusers with memory deficits on measures of malingering. *Archives of Clinical Neuropsychology, 12*(5), 513–518.

Ashendorf, L., Constantinou, M., & McCaffrey, R. J. (2004). The effect of depression and anxiety on the TOMM in community-dwelling older adults. *Archives of Clinical Neuropsychology, 19*(1), 125–130.

Axelrod, B. N., Fichtenberg, N. L., Liethen, P. C., Czarnota, M. A., & Stucky, K. (2001). Performance characteristics of postacute and traumatic brain injury patients on the WAIS–III and WMS–III. *The Clinical Neuropsychologist, 15*(4), 516–520.

Baddeley, A. (2003). Working memory: Looking back and looking forward. *Nature Reviews/Neuroscience, 4*(10), 829–839.

Bate, A. J., Mathias, J. L., & Crawford, J. R. (2001). Performance on the test of everyday attention and standard tests of attention following sever traumatic brain injury. *The Clinical Neuropsychologist, 15*, 405–422.

Benson, N., Hulac, D. M., & Kranzler, J. H. (2010). Independent examination of Wechsler adult intelligence scale–fourth edition (WAIS–IV): What does the WAIS–IV measure? *Psychological Assessment, 22*(1), 121–130.

Blair, J. R., & Spreen, O. (1989). Predicting premorbid IQ: A revision of the national adult reading test. *The Clinical Neuropsychologist, 3*, 129–136.

Bodin, D., Pardini, D. A., Burns, T. G., & Stevens, A. B. (2009). Higher order factor structure of the WISC-IV in a clinical neuropsychological sample. *Child Neuropsychology, 15*(5), 417–424.

Bowden, S. C., Carstairs, J. R., & Shores, E. A. (1999). Confirmatory factor analysis of combined Wechsler adult intelligence scale–revised and Wechsler memory scale–revised scores in a healthy community sample. *Psychological Assessment, 11*(3), 339–344.

Carroll, J. B. (1993). *Human cognitive abilities: A survey of factor analytic studies.* New York: Cambridge University Press.

Chen, H., Keith, T., Chen, Y., & Chang, B. (2009). What does the WISC-IV measure? Validation of the scoring and CHC-based interpretative approaches. *Journal of Research in Education Sciences, 54*(3), 85–108.

Chen, H., Keith, T., Weiss, L., Zhu, J., & Li, Y. (2010). Testing for multigroup invariance of second-order WISC-IV structure across China, Hong Kong, Macau, and Taiwan. *Personality and Individual Differences, 49*(7), 677–682.

Chen, H., & Zhu, J. (2012). Measurement invariance of WISC-IV across normative and clinical samples. *Personality and Individual Differences, 52*(2), 161–166.

Coalson, D. L., Raiford, S. E., Saklofske, D. H., & Weiss, L. G. (2010). WAIS–IV: Advanced assessment of intelligence. In L. G. Weiss, D. H. Saklofske, D. Coalson, & S. E. Raiford (Eds.), WAIS–IV clinical use and interpretation: Scientist–practitioner perspectives. San Diego: Elsevier Science.

Cullum, C. M., & Larrabee, G. J. (2010). WAIS–IV use in neuropsychological assessment. In L. G. Weiss, D. H. Saklofske, D. Coalson, & S. E. Raiford (Eds.), *WAIS–IV clinical use and interpretation: Scientist–practitioner perspectives.* San Diego: Elsevier Science.

Daniel, M. H. (2007). "Scatter" and the construct validity of FSIQ: Comment on Fiorello et al. (2007). *Applied Neuropsychology, 14*(4), 291–295.

Deary, I. J. (2001). *Intelligence: A very short introduction.* Oxford: Oxford University Press.

Deary, I. J., & Stough, C. (1996). Intelligence and inspection time: Achievements, prospects, and problems. *American Psychologist, 51*(6), 599–608.

Delis, D., Kramer, J., Kaplan, E., & Ober, B. (2000). *Manual for the California verbal learning test–second edition.* San Antonio: Pearson.

Donders, J., Tulsky, D. S., & Zhu, J. (2001). Criterion validity of new WAIS–III subtest scores after traumatic brain injury. *Journal of the International Neuropsychological Society, 7*(7), 892–898.

Dougherty, T. M., & Haith, M. (1997). Infant expectations and reaction times as predictors of childhood speed of processing and IQ. *Developmental Psychology, 33*(1), 146–155.

Drozdick, L. W., Holdnack, J. A., & Hilsabeck, R. (2011). *Essentials of WMS–IV assessment.* Hoboken, NJ: John Wiley & Sons, Inc..

Drozdick, L. W., Wahlstrom, D., Zhu, J., & Weiss, L. G. (2011). The Wechsler adult intelligence scale–fourth edition (WAIS–IV) and Wechsler memory scale–fourth edition (WMS–IV). In D. P. Flanagan, & P. L. Harrison (Eds.), *Contemporary intellectual assessment–third edition* (pp. 197–223). New York: Guilford Press.

Dunn, L. M., & Dunn, D. M. (2007). Peabody picture vocabulary test–fourth edition. Minneapolis, MN: Pearson.

Fallows, R. R., & Hilsabeck, R. C. (2012). WAIS–IV visual puzzles in a mixed clinical sample. *The Clinical Neuropsychologist, 26*(6), 942–950.

Fiorello, C. A., Hale, J. B., Holdnack, J. A., Kavanagh, J. A., Terrell, J., & Long, L. (2007). Interpreting intelligence test results for children with disabilities: Is global intelligence relevant? *Applied Neuropsychology, 14*(1), 2–12.

Fisher, D. C., Ledbetter, M. F., Cohen, N. J., Marmor, D., & Tulsky, D. S. (2000). WAIS–III and WMS–III profiles of mildly to severely brain-injured patients. *Applied Neuropsychology: Adult, 7*(3), 126–132.

Frazier, T. W., Youngstrom, E. A., Naugle, R. I., Haggerty, K. A., & Busch, R. M. (2007). The latent structure of cognitive symptom exaggeration on the Victoria symptom validity test. *Archives of Clinical Neuropsychology, 22*(2), 197–211.

Geldmacher, D. S., Fritsch, T., & Riedel, T. M. (2000). Effects of stimulus properties and age on random-array letter cancellation tasks. *Aging, Neuropsychology, and Cognition, 7*(3), 194−204.

Gierok, S. D., Dickson, A. L., & Cole, J. A. (2005). Performance of forensic and non-forensic adult psychiatric inpatients on the test of memory malingering. *Archives of Clinical Neuropsychology, 20*(6), 755−760.

Gottfredson, L. S. (1997). Why g matters: The complexity of everyday life. *Intelligence, 24*(1), 79−132.

Gottfredson, L. S. (1998). The general intelligence factor. *Scientific American Presents, 9*(4), 24−29.

Grober, E., & Sliwinski, M. (1991). Development and validation of a model for estimating premorbid verbal intelligence in the elderly. *Journal of Clinical and Experimental Neuropsychology, 13*(6), 933−949.

Harrison, A. G., DeLisle, M. M., & Parker, K. C. H. (2008). An investigation of the general abilities index in a group of diagnostically mixed patients. *Journal of Psychoeducational Assessment, 26*(3), 247−259.

Hawkins, K. A., Plehn, K., & Borgaro, S. (2002). Verbal IQ−performance IQ differentials in traumatic brain injury samples. *Archives of Clinical Neuropsychology, 17*(1), 49−56.

Holdnack, J. (2007). A new method for comparing performance on two cognitive variables: WMS−III general memory performance controlling for WAIS−III General Ability Index. Presented at the thirty-fifth Annual Meeting of the International Neuropsychological Society, Portland, OR.

Holdnack, J. A., & Drozdick, L. W. (2010). Using WAIS−IV with WMS−IV. In L. G. Weiss, D. H. Saklofske, D. L. Coalson, & S. E. Raiford (Eds.), *WAIS−IV: Advanced in the assessment of intelligence* (Vol. 1, pp. 237−283). London, Burlington, San Diego: Academic Press.

Holdnack, J. A., Zhou, X., Larrabee, G. J., Millis, S. R., & Salthouse, T. A. (2011). Confirmatory factor analysis of the WAIS−IV/WMS−IV. *Assessment, 18*(2), 178−191.

Jonides, J., Lacey, S. C., & Nee, D. E. (2005). Process of working memory in mind and brain. *Current Directions in Psychological Science, 14*(1), 2−5.

Jöreskog, K. G., & Sörbom, D. (1993). *LISREL 8: User's reference guide.* Chicago: Scientific Software International.

Keith, T. Z., Fine, J. G., Taub, G., Reynolds, M. R., & Kranzler, J. H. (2006). Higher order, multi-sample, confirmatory factor analysis of the Wechsler intelligence scale for children−fourth edition: What does it measure? *School Psychology Review, 35*(1), 108−127.

Kennedy, J. E., Clement, P. F., & Curtiss, G. (2003). WAIS−III processing speed index scores after TBI: The influence of working memory, psychomotor speed and perceptual processing. *The Clinical Neuropsychologist, 17*(3), 303−307.

Kesler, S. R., Haberecht, M. F., Menon, V., Warsofsky, I. S., Dyer-Friedman, J., Neely, E. K., & Reiss, A. L. (2004). Functional neuroanatomy of spatial orientation processing in turner syndrome. *Cerebral Cortex, 14*(2), 174−180.

Kuncel, N. R., Hezlett, S. A., & Ones, D. S. (2004). Academic performance, career potential, creativity, and job performance: Can one construct predict them all? *Journal of Personality and Social Psychology, 86*(1), 148−161.

Lichtenberger, E., & Kaufman, A. S. (2009). *Essentials of WAIS−IV assessment.* New York: Wiley.

Lecerf, T., Rossier, J., Favez, N., Reverte, I., & Coleaux, L. (2010). The four versus alternative six factor structure of the French WISC-IV: Comparisons using confirmatory factor analyses. *Swiss Journal of Psychology, 69*(4), 221−232.

Lezak, M. D., Howieson, D. B., & Loring, D. W. (with Hannay, H. J. & Fischer, J. S.) (2004). *Neuropsychological assessment,* 4th ed. New York: Oxford University Press.

Macciocchi, S. N., Seel, R. T., Alderson, A., & Godsall, R. (2006). Victoria symptom validity test performance in acute severe traumatic brain injury: Implications for test interpretation. *Archives of Clinical Neuropsychology, 21*(5), 395–404.

McCrea, S. M., & Robinson, T. P. (2011). Visual puzzles, figure weights, and cancellation: Some preliminary hypotheses on the functional and neural substrates of these three new WAIS–IV subtests. *International Scholarly Research Network Neurology, 2011*, 1–19.

McGrew, K., & Flanagan, D. P. (1998). *The intelligence test desk reference (ITDR) Gf–Gc cross-battery assessment*. Boston: Allyn and Bacon.

Messina, M. F., Zirilli, G., Civa, R., Rulli, I., Salzano, G., Aversa, T., & Valenzise, M. (2007). Neurocognitive profile in turner's syndrome is not affected by growth impairment. *Journal of Pediatric Endocrinology and Metabolism, 20*(6), 677–684.

Milanovich, J. R., Axelrod, B. N., & Millis, S. R. (1996). Validation of the simulation index–revised with a mixed clinical population. *Archives of Clinical Neuropsychology, 11*(1), 53–59.

Na, D. L., Adair, J. C., Kang, Y., Chung, C. S., Lee, K. H., & Heilman, K. M. (1999). Motor perseverative behavior on a line cancellation task. *Neurology, 52*(8), 1569–1576.

Nelson, H. E. (1982). *National adult reading test*. Windsor: NFER-Nelson.

Pearson (2001). *Wechsler test of adult reading*. San Antonio, TX: Pearson Education.

Pearson (2009). *Advanced clinical solutions for use with WAIS–IV and WMS–IV*. San Antonio: Pearson Education.

Pearson (2010). *Manual for the Wechsler memory scale–fourth edition flexible approach*. San Antonio, TX: Pearson Education.

Prifitera, A., Saklofske, D. H., & Weiss, L. G. (2005). WISC-IV clinical use and interpretation: Scientist–practitioner perspectives. San Diego: Academic Press.

Prifitera, A., Saklofske, D. H., & Weiss, L. G. (2008). WISC–IV clinical assessment and intervention, second edition. San Diego: Academic Press.

Prifitera, A., Weiss, L. G., & Saklofske, D. H. (1998). The WISC–III in context. In A. Prifitera, & D. H. Saklofske (Eds.), *WISC–III clinical use and interpretation: Scientist–practitioner perspectives* (pp. 1–38). San Diego: Academic Press.

Salthouse, T. A. (1996a). Constraints on theories of cognitive aging. *Psychonomic Bulletin and Review, 3*(3), 287–299.

Salthouse, T. A. (1996b). The processing speed theory of adult age differences in cognition. *Psychological Review, 103*(3), 403–428.

Salthouse, T. A. (2000a). Pressing issues in cognitive aging. In D. C. Park, & N. Schwarz (Eds.), *Cognitive Aging: A Primer* (pp. 43–54). Philadelphia: Psychology Press.

Salthouse, T. A. (2000b). Steps toward the explanation of adult age differences in cognition. In T. J. Perfect, & E. A. Maylor (Eds.), *Models of cognitive aging* (pp. 19–49). New York: Oxford University Press.

Sanchez-Carrion, R., Fernandez-Espejo, D., Junque, C., Falcon, C., Bargallo, N., & Roig, T., et al. (2008). A longitudinal fMRI study of working memory in severe TBI patients with diffuse axonal injury. *Neuroimage, 43*(3), 421–429.

Sattler, J. M. (2008). *Resource guide to accompany assessment of children: Cognitive foundations* (5th ed.). San Diego, CA: JM Sattler.

Steiger, J. H. (1990). Structural model evaluation and modification: An interval estimation approach. *Multivariate Behavioral Research, 25*(2), 173–180.

Tombaugh, T. N. (1997). The test of memory malingering (TOMM): Normative data from cognitively intact and cognitively impaired individuals. *Psychological Assessment, 9*(3), 260–268.

Tucker, L. R., & Lewis, C. (1973). A reliability coefficient for maximum likelihood factor analysis. *Psychometrika, 38*(1), 1–10.

Tulsky, D. S., & Price, L. R. (2003). The joint WAIS–III and WMS–III factor structure: Development and cross-validation of a six-factor model of cognitive functioning. *Psychological Assessment*, *15*(2), 149–162.

Ward, L. C., Bergman, M. A., & Herbert, K. R. (2011). WAIS–IV subtest covariance structure: Conceptual and statistical considerations. *Psychological Assessment*, *24*(2), 328–340.

Watkins, M. W., Glutting, J. J., & Lei, P. W. (2007). Validity of the full-scale IQ when there is significant variability among WISC–III and WISC-IV factor scores. *Applied Neuropsychology: Adult*, *14*(1), 13–20.

Wechsler, D. (2008). Wechsler adult intelligence scale–fourth edition. San Antonio: Pearson.

Wechsler, D. (2009). Wechsler memory scale–fourth edition. San Antonio: Pearson.

Weiss, L. G., Keith, T. Z., Chen, H., & Zhu, J. (2013a). WAIS–IV: Clinical validation of the four- and five-factor interpretive approaches. *Journal of Psychoeducational Assessment*, in press.

Weiss, L. G., Keith, T. Z., Chen, H., & Zhu, J. (2013b). WISC-IV: Clinical validation of the four- and five-factor interpretive approaches. *Journal of Psychoeducational Assessment*, in press.

Weiss, L. G., Saklofske, D. H., Coalson, D., & Raiford, S. E. (2010). Theoretical, empirical, and clinical foundations of the WAIS–IV index scores. In L. G. Weiss, D. H. Saklofske, D. Coalson, & S. E. Raiford (Eds.), *WAIS–IV:* Clinical use and interpretation: Scientist–practitioner perspectives. San Diego: Academic Press.

Weiss, L. G., Saklofske, D. H., Prifitera, A., & Holdnack, J. A. (2006). *WISC–IV: Advanced clinical interpretation*. San Diego: Academic Press.

Wilde, M. C., Boake, C., & Sherer, M. (2000). Wechsler adult intelligence scale-revised block design broken configuration errors in nonpenetrating traumatic brain injury. *Applied Neuropsychology: Adult*, *7*(4), 208–214.

Wojciulik, E., Husain, M., Clarke, K., & Driver, J. (2001). Spatial working memory deficit in unilateral neglect. *Neuropsycholgia*, *39*(4), 390–**396**.

2

Understanding and Using Multivariate Base Rates with the WAIS–IV/WMS–IV

Brian L. Brooks*, Grant L. Iverson** and James A. Holdnack***

*Alberta Children's Hospital and University of Calgary, Calgary, Alberta, Canada **Harvard Medical School, Boston, Massachusetts, USA ***Pearson Assessment, San Antonio, Texas, USA

INTRODUCTION

Psychologists have developed, studied, validated, and refined the methodology for assessing cognition. Psychologists are well suited to measure and quantify cognitive impairment that may occur in patients with developmental, acquired, or degenerative disorders. In the process of measuring and quantifying cognitive impairment, clinicians often give a large battery of tests that are designed to tap into different cognitive domains. Even a brief screen of cognitive abilities involves the administration of several tests. Psychologists must interpret a large amount of information in light of the patient's history, collaborative medical or health information, academic or employment information, and/or subjective complaints. Summarizing and interpreting a large amount of test information is an evolving skill set for clinicians.

As a profession, we have been trained and conditioned to rely heavily on the bell curve when interpreting cognitive test performance. Applying the properties of the bell curve to an assessment involving many individual tests can result in a fundamental misunderstanding

WAIS-IV, WMS-IV, and ACS.
DOI: http://dx.doi.org/10.1016/B978-0-12-386934-0.00002-X

© 2013 Elsevier Inc. All rights reserved.

and misinterpretation of low scores. When interpreting cognitive data, clinicians should keep in mind that it is normal for healthy children, adults, and older adults to have some variability in their cognitive abilities. In fact, it would be considered very uncommon for a person to have all of their scores on a test battery fall at the same level (e.g., having no more than a one standard deviation spread between the highest and lowest scores is found in only 0.3% of healthy adults on the Wechsler Adult Intelligence Scale–Fourth Edition (WAIS–IV: Wechsler, 2008), Table B.6, Administration and Scoring Manual). Chapter 3 discusses issues of cognitive variability in detail, providing normative data for expected levels of subtest and index score variability.

In addition to normal test score scatter, it is also normal for healthy children, adults, and older adults to obtain some low scores, particularly when multiple tests are administered. Two fundamental assumptions relating to test scores can lead to errors in clinical judgment. The first is a belief that if a person is "normal" then *all* of his or her scores should be "normal." The second is a belief that an "abnormal" test score is synonymous with atypicality, particularly brain injury. The clinical inference derived from a percentile rank is a relatively accurate indicator of a person's level of functioning on each test in *isolation*, but not when all tests are considered *simultaneously*. Put simply, only 5% of healthy adults will obtain a scaled score of five or lower on the Logical Memory subtest of the Wechsler Memory Scale–Fourth Edition (WMS–IV: Wechsler, 2009). However, if a practitioner administers the entire WMS–IV, and interprets the eight primary memory scores, then 29% of healthy adults will obtain one or more scores at or below the fifth percentile. In other words, the normative distributional properties of the bell curve are accurate for one test—*but not for multiple tests*. Thus, clinicians must guard against the incorrect inference that obtaining a low test score is necessarily unusual when multiple tests are considered simultaneously. The likelihood of obtaining low scores, when several scores are administered and interpreted, is referred to herein as multivariate base rates (i.e., also referred to as the "base rates of low scores" or the "prevalence of low scores").

This chapter examines the psychometric principles associated with multivariate base rates and presents clinically useful tables for interpreting performance on the WAIS–IV and WMS–IV batteries. This is an expansion of Brooks, Iverson and Holdnack (2011), which commented on the multivariate base rates for the full WAIS–IV/WMS–IV. The goal of this chapter is to improve the clinical usefulness and diagnostic accuracy of the WAIS–IV and WMS–IV through the use of base-rate information.

RESEARCH ON MULTIVARIATE BASE RATES

Research on multivariate base rates has illustrated and emphasized that when healthy people complete a battery of tests, a substantial minority will obtain one or more low scores (Axelrod & Wall, 2007; Binder, Iverson, & Brooks, 2009; Brooks, 2010, 2011; Brooks et al., 2011; Brooks, Iverson, Holdnack & Feldman, 2008; Brooks, Iverson, Lanting, Horton, & Reynolds, 2012; Brooks, Iverson, & White, 2007; Brooks, Strauss, Sherman, Iverson, & Slick, 2009; Crawford, Garthwaite, & Gault, 2007; Heaton, Grant, & Matthews, 1991; Heaton, Miller, Taylor, & Grant, 2004; Ingraham & Aiken, 1996; Iverson & Brooks, 2011; Iverson, Brooks, & Holdnack, 2008a; Iverson, Brooks, White, & Stern, 2008b; Palmer, Boone, Lesser, & Wohl, 1998; Schretlen, Testa, Winicki, Pearlson, & Gordon, 2008). This extensive line of research has provided clinicians with information for interpreting test performance in children, adults, and older adults on several large batteries of co-normed neuropsychological tests, including the Children's Memory Scale (CMS: Brooks, Iverson, Sherman, & Holdnack, 2009), the NEPSY–Second Edition (NEPSY–II: Brooks, Sherman, & Iverson, 2010), the Expanded Halstead–Reitan Neuropsychological Battery (EHRNB: see Table 4 in Binder et al., 2009; see Figure 9 in Heaton et al., 2004), the Neuropsychological Assessment Battery (NAB: Brooks et al., 2007; Brooks, Iverson, & White, 2009; Iverson & Brooks, 2011; Iverson et al., 2008b), the Test of Verbal Conceptualization and Fluency (TVCF: Brooks et al., 2012), the Wechsler Intelligence Scale for Children–Fourth Edition (WISC–IV: Brooks, 2010, 2011), the Wechsler Adult Intelligence Scale–Third Edition/Wechsler Memory Scale–Third Edition co-normed battery (WAIS–III/WMS–III: Iverson et al., 2008a), and the Wechsler Adult Intelligence Scale–Fourth Edition/Wechsler Memory Scale–Fourth Edition co-normed battery (WAIS–IV/WMS–IV: Brooks et al., 2011).

Using multivariate base rates can reduce the potential for misdiagnosis (and missed diagnosis) of *cognitive impairment*. For example, let's assume that a clinician interprets test scores that are more than 1.5 standard deviations below the mean as being representative of acquired memory impairment, such as amnestic mild cognitive impairment (MCI). Using this criterion, 26% of the *healthy* older adults from the WMS–III standardization sample had one or more subtest scores in this range (i.e., using the cut-off of ≤5th percentile; Brooks et al., 2008). In a follow-up study, healthy older adults were compared to patients with possible or probable Alzheimer's disease on three memory tests (Logical Memory, Word List, and Visual Reproduction), and new psychometric criteria for memory impairment were developed (Brooks,

Iverson, Feldman, & Holdnack, 2009). These three subtests produce eight scaled scores (i.e., Logical Memory I, Visual Reproduction I, Word List I Total Recall, Logical Memory II, Visual Reproduction II, Word List II Total Recall, Visual Reproduction Recognition, and Word List Recognition). When considering the entire sample of healthy older adults, having six or more scores ≤16th percentile (i.e., scaled score of seven or lower) occurred in only 6.0%, and having three or more memory scores ≤5th percentile (i.e., scaled score of 5 or lower) was found in only 5.1%. In other words, if a clinician or researcher wants to fix the false positive rate at 5% on memory testing, you cannot use a scaled score of five if multiple tests are administered. Brooks and colleagues (2009) applied operational criteria for memory impairment, using a multivariate base rate approach, which resulted in only 6% of healthy older adults but 94.1% of the Alzheimer's sample being classified as having probable memory impairment. These studies using the WMS–III provide preliminary evidence that knowing the base rates of low scores can improve diagnostic accuracy and substantially reduce false positives (e.g., 6% vs. 26%).

It is the thesis of this chapter that understanding the prevalence of low scores can potentially lead to improvement in the clinical usefulness and diagnostic accuracy of cognitive assessment. That is, it should help clinicians to reduce false positives and false negatives by supplementing current interpretive methods and clinical judgment with base-rate data. The following section describes five principles of multivariate base rates (Brooks et al., 2009; Brooks & Iverson, 2012; Iverson & Brooks, 2011; Iverson, Brooks, & Holdnack, 2012), with many examples derived from the WAIS–IV and WMS–IV batteries.

FIVE PSYCHOMETRIC PRINCIPLES FOR MULTIVARIATE BASE RATES

This section discusses five psychometric principles to consider when evaluating a person for cognitive impairment. The discussion of these principles has been previously presented (Brooks et al., 2009; Brooks & Iverson, 2012; Iverson & Brooks, 2011; Iverson et al., 2012), but an overview is warranted for this chapter. The principles presented include an understanding that low scores are common across all batteries of cognitive tests (Principle 1), that there is an inverse relation between the number of low scores and the cut-off score used (Principle 2), that the number of low scores obtained increases with the number of tests administered and interpreted (Principle 3), that the number of low scores vary by demographic groups (Principle 4), and that ability level (e.g., intelligence) impacts the rate of obtained low scores (Principle 5). An understanding of these psychometric principles is invaluable for any clinician. Moreover, it is important for clinicians to consider and apply these principles when interpreting a battery of neuropsychological tests. For the most part, examples to support these principles will be derived from the WAIS–IV and WMS–IV tables that are presented later in this chapter. Following the discussion of these five principles, several tables will be presented for various combinations of WAIS–IV and WMS–IV subtests (refer to Tables A2.1–A2.29 in the Appendix at: http://booksite.elsevier.com/9780123869340). These look-up tables provide ready-to-use information on the prevalence of low scores for the interpretation of most combinations of WAIS–IV and WMS–IV tests.

Principle 1: Low Scores are Common across All Test Batteries

When healthy people are administered a battery of tests (i.e., any battery, fixed or flexible, brief or extensive, pediatric or adult), it is common for them to obtain some low scores (Axelrod & Wall, 2007; Binder et al., 2009; Brooks, 2010, 2011; Brooks et al., 2007, 2008, 2009, 2011, 2012; Crawford et al., 2007; Heaton et al., 1991; Heaton et al., 2004; Ingraham & Aiken, 1996; Iverson & Brooks, 2011; Iverson et al., 2008a, 2008b; Iverson et al., 2012; Palmer et al., 1998; Schretlen et al., 2008). This is because there is a substantial amount of intraindividual variability in cognitive test scores obtained from healthy people. This variability can arise from situational factors, longstanding weaknesses or both. Figure 2.1 illustrates the first principle that low scores are common across test batteries, with no battery being immune to this principle. This figure presents the prevalence of scores (i.e., using the 16th percentile as a cut-off score) in healthy adults on the Neuropsychological Assessment Battery (NAB: Stern & White, 2003), the Expanded Halstead-Reitan Neuropsychological Battery (E-HRNB: Heaton et al., 2004), the combination of the Wechsler Adult Intelligence Scale–Third Edition (WAIS–III: Wechsler, 1997a) and Wechsler Memory Scale–Third Edition (WMS–III: Wechsler, 1997b), and the combination of the Wechsler Adult Intelligence Scale–Fourth Edition (WAIS–IV: Wechsler, 2008) and the Wechsler Memory Scale–Fourth Edition (WMS–IV: Wechsler, 2009). As seen in Figure 2.1, the majority of healthy adults have two or more scores falling below 1SD from the mean on all four of these different batteries. A substantial minority has five or more low scores, and even as many as one out of four have seven or more low scores on these batteries. Regardless which test battery is administered and interpreted, it is important to keep in mind that having some low scores is considered "common."

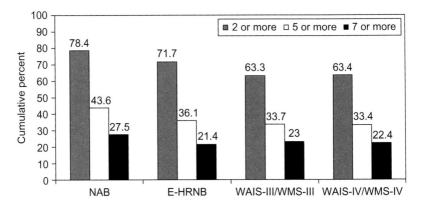

FIGURE 2.1 **Low scores on different adult batteries (percentages of healthy adults with low scores; 1 SD cut-off).** NAB = Neuropsychological Assessment Battery (36 scores); E-HRNB = Expanded Halstead-Reitan Neuropsychological Battery (25 scores); WAIS–III/WMS–III = Wechsler Adult Intelligence Scale – III and Wechsler Memory Scale–III (20 scores); and WAIS–IV/WMS–IV = Wechsler Adult Intelligence Scale–IV and Wechsler Memory Scale–IV (20 scores). Bars represent percent of healthy adults from standardization samples who had (a) 2 or more, (b) 5 or more, or (c) 7 or more scores below the 16th percentile (i.e., T < 40 or SS < 7), with the exception of WAIS–IV/WMS–IV which used the cut-off of "at or below" the 16th percentile.

Principle 2: The Number of Low Scores Depends on Where You Set Your Cut-off Score

If you ask psychologists for the cut-off score used to determine cognitive impairment, you will likely receive different answers. Some psychologists have fixed and consistent definitions of low scores (e.g., 1 SD below the mean, 5th percentile, or 2 SDs below the mean), whereas other psychologists might vary their definition based on the characteristics of the examinee. For example, a psychologist might determine that a low average score for a highly educated person with very superior intelligence could be a significant decline in functioning. On the other hand, a low average score in a person who has a long-standing history of borderline intelligence and supportive employment may produce an expected level of performance. In reality, there is no universal agreement on the definition of a low score, and clinical interpretation of test performance depends on patient characteristics. Both approaches have strengths and weaknesses, psychometrically. The key is to carefully define the psychometric strengths and limitations of the specific approach taken for interpreting psychological tests.

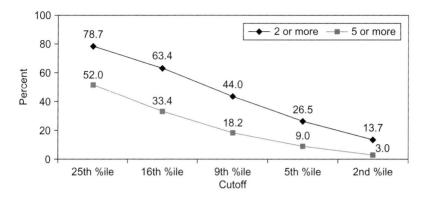

FIGURE 2.2   Number of low WAIS–IV/WMS–IV scores depends on the cut-off score used (percentages of healthy adults with low scores). SD = Standard Deviation. The 20 primary standard scores from the WAIS–IV/WMS–IV were considered. Each data point represents the percent of healthy adults (ages 16–69 years) from the WAIS–WMS–IV standardization sample who had (a) 2 or more or (b) 5 or more scores ≤25th percentile, ≤16th percentile, ≤10th percentile, ≤5th percentile, or ≤2nd percentile.

Selecting a cut-off score for test interpretation requires a balance between sensitivity and specificity. Higher cut-off scores (i.e., closer to the mean) are more likely to identify those who have cognitive problems (improved sensitivity), but they are also more likely to include those who do not have cognitive problems (reduced specificity and increased false positives). On the other hand, lower cut-off scores (i.e., further away from the mean) are less likely to identify those with cognitive problems (reduced sensitivity and increased false negatives, especially in higher functioning people), but are also less likely to include those who do not have cognitive problems (improved specificity). Some clinicians may consider the balance of sensitivity and specificity when interpreting a single score, but fail to consider this balance when interpreting multiple scores.

Using data from the WAIS–IV/WMS–IV as an example, Figure 2.2 illustrates the percentage of healthy people who obtain low scores based on five different cut-off scores: 25th percentile, 16th percentile, 10th percentile, 5th percentile, and 2nd percentile. As the cut-off score gets progressively lower (i.e., further away from the mean), the number of healthy people who would be incorrectly identified (i.e., higher specificity/fewer false positives) as having cognitive problems declines. For example, having five or more low scores on the WAIS–IV/WMS–IV would be found in 52% of healthy people when using the 25th percentile as the cut-off score, but only 3% when using the 2nd percentile as the cut-off score.

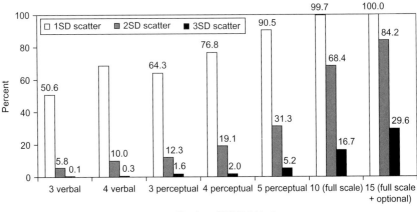

FIGURE 2.3   **Amount of test-score scatter depends on the number of tests administered and interpreted (percentages of healthy adults with different ranges of scatter).** SD = standard deviation. 3 Verbal = 3 core Verbal Comprehension subtests; 4 Verbal = 3 core Verbal Comprehension subtests plus the Comprehension subtest; 3 Perceptual = 3 core Perceptual Reasoning subtests; 4 Perceptual = 3 core Perceptual Reasoning subtests plus Figure Weights; 5 Perceptual = 3 core Perceptual Reasoning subtests plus Figure Weights and Picture Completion. Data adapted from Table B.6 in the WAIS–IV Administration and Scoring Manual.

Principle 3: The Number of Low Scores Depends on the Number of Tests Administered and Interpreted

Psychologists have an immense repertoire of cognitive tests at their disposal. Assessments can range from brief cognitive screening evaluations to more comprehensive testing with large batteries. Regardless of the approach taken in any assessment (brief, extensive, or somewhere in the middle), psychological evaluations often consist of several tests, yielding numerous scores, and requiring interpretation simultaneously.

Figure 2.3 demonstrates that increased numbers of tests within a battery will result in a greater amount of subtest scatter. Although test-score scatter may not be the specific reason for some low scores across a battery, it should be acknowledged that some scores will fall below cut-off scores as a result of scatter. Consider, for example, the prevalence of a two standard deviation difference between the lowest and highest subtest scores on the WAIS–IV. When only three verbal subtests are considered, it is uncommon (5.8%) for people in the healthy standardization sample to have a two standard deviation difference between the lowest and highest scores. However, when considering the 10 primary subtests or all 15 subtests (10 primary plus 5 supplemental),

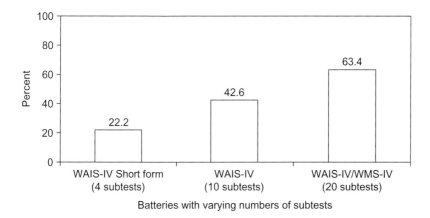

FIGURE 2.4 **Number of low scores depends on the number of tests administered and interpreted (percentages of healthy adults with two or more subtest scores 16th percentile).** WAIS–IV short form is comprised of Vocabulary, Similarities, Matrix Reasoning, and Block Design. WAIS–IV is comprised of the 10 core subtests. WAIS–IV/WMS–IV is comprised of the 20 core subtests.

the prevalence of two standard deviations between lowest and highest subtest scores increases to 68% and 84%, respectively. Even a three standard deviation difference between lowest and highest, a finding that is very uncommon when considering just the verbal or just the perceptual tests, occurs in a substantial minority of healthy adults when considering 10 or 15 subtests from the WAIS–IV. A three SD difference between highest and lowest scores occurs in 16.7% when considering the 10 primary subtests and 29.6% when considering the 15 subtests.

Figure 2.4 illustrates the principle that increasing the number of tests will increase the likelihood of low scores. In this example, increasing numbers of subtests (i.e., 4, 10, 20) from the WAIS–IV and WMS–IV batteries are examined for the prevalence of low scores. With a four-subtest version of the WAIS–IV (i.e., Vocabulary, Similarities, Matrix Reasoning, and Block Design), 22% of healthy adults will have two or more scores at least one standard deviation below the mean. On the full WAIS–IV, which contains 10 subtests, 43% of healthy adults will have two or more scores at least one standard deviation below the mean. And finally, on the 20 subtests from the full WAIS–IV/WMS–IV battery, 63% of healthy adults will have two or more scores at least one standard deviation below the mean. These examples illustrate that as the number of tests increase, the prevalence of low scores also increases. Regardless of which cut-off score is used (i.e., 25th, 16th, 9th, 5th, or 2nd percentiles), the expected number of low scores increases with lengthier test batteries.

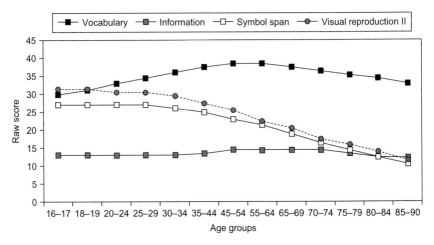

FIGURE 2.5   **Performance across healthy adult age groups on selected measures of verbal knowledge, visual working memory, and visual memory.** Values represent raw scores needed to obtain a scaled score of 10 (50th percentile). If a range was presented in the manual, then the middle of the range was selected. Values for the WAIS–IV Vocabulary and Information were obtained from Table A.1 in the WAIS–IV Administration and Scoring Manual. Values for the WMS–IV Spatial Span and Visual Reproduction were derived from Table D.1 in the WMS–IV Administration and Scoring Manual.

Principle 4: The Number of Low Scores Varies by Demographic Characteristics of the Examinee

Many cognitive abilities vary by demographic characteristics, including age, gender, ethnicity and level of education (Beatty, Mold, & Gontkovsky, 2003; Collaer & Nelson, 2002; Donders, Zhu, & Tulsky, 2001; Geary, Saults, Liu, & Hoard, 2000; Herlitz, Nilsson, & Backman, 1997; Norman, Evans, Miller, & Heaton, 2000; Voyer, Voyer, & Bryden, 1995). As a result of demographic-based differences in performance on cognitive testing, many test publishers provide demographically-adjusted normative data. Consider, for example, the impact of age on performance on selected WAIS–IV and WMS–IV measures (Figure 2.5). For this figure, the mean raw score for each age group is presented for four different measures. On a measure of verbal knowledge, such as Vocabulary, performance increases slightly throughout adulthood, peaks around 45–65 years of age, and then declines again slightly. On another measure of verbal knowledge, Information, performance remains relatively consistent from age 16 to 90 years. In contrast, performance on measures of working memory (Symbol Span) and visual memory (Visual Reproduction II) steadily decline as the age of sample increases.

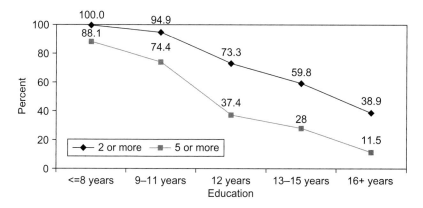

FIGURE 2.6 **Low scores are more common in healthy people with fewer years of education (cut-off ≤16th percentile).** Analyses included all 20 primary subtest scores from the WAIS–IV/WMS–IV in adults between 16–69 years.

Level of education is another important variable to consider when interpreting cognitive test results (Heaton et al., 2004; Heaton, Taylor, & Manly, 2003; Ivnik, Makec, Smith, Tangolos, & Peterson, 1996; Morgan et al., 2007; Rosselli & Ardila, 2003; Ryan et al., 2005). Many cognitive measures have education-adjusted normative scores. And, it is also true that there are differences in the prevalence of low scores on batteries of tests across levels of education. Figure 2.6, for example, illustrates how common it is to have subtest scores on the WAIS–IV/WMS–IV battery of tests fall at least one standard deviation below the mean by level of education. In healthy adults with eight or fewer years of education, 100% have at least two low scores on the WAIS–IV/ WMS–IV and 88% have five or more low scores. When considering those with 16 or more years of education, the prevalence of low scores is much lower than in those with high school education. However, even in those with 16 + years, having five or more scores (out of 20) fall at or below the 16th percentile is found in 11.5% of healthy adults, and 39% of these highly educated people have two or more scaled scores of 7 or less.

Principle 5: The Number of Low Scores Varies by Level of Intelligence

Cognitive abilities are related to intellectual functioning (Horton, 1999; Steinberg, Bieliauskas, Smith, & Ivnik, 2005; Steinberg, Bieliauskas, Smith, Ivnik, & Malec, 2005; Tremont, Hoffman, Scott, & Adams, 1998; Warner, Ernst, Townes, Peel, & Preston, 1987). With the

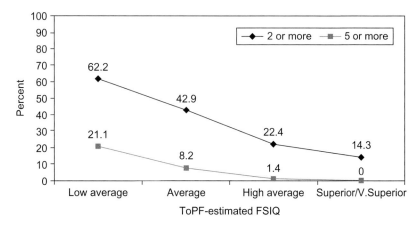

FIGURE 2.7   **Low WMS–IV scores depend on level of estimated intelligence (cutoff ≤16th percentile; percentages of healthy adults with low scores).** ToPF = Test of Premorbid Functioning with simple demographics. Analyses included the eight primary memory scores from the WMS–IV for healthy adults between 16–69 years (Logical Memory, Verbal Paired Associates, Visual Reproduction, and Designs).

WAIS–IV and WMS–IV, correlations between the FSIQ and the five WMS–IV index scores range from $r = 0.57$ (AMI) to $r = 0.71$ (VWMI) (Wechsler, 2009). As a result of significant and often large correlations between intelligence and cognitive domains, people with below-average intellectual abilities have more low scores on cognitive tests than people with above average intelligence.

Figure 2.7 illustrates the difference in multivariate base rates based on level of intellectual functioning. For example, one in five healthy adults with low average estimated intellectual abilities (i.e., TOPF with simple demographics estimated FSIQ) have five or more WMS–IV scores at least one standard deviation below the mean. However, having five or more WMS–IV scores at or below the 16th percentile is extremely uncommon in healthy adults with high average estimated intellectual abilities (1.4%), and was not found in any of the healthy adults with superior or very superior estimated intellectual abilities (0%) in the standardization sample. Regardless of which cut-off score is used or the number of low scores considered, there is a gradual decline in the prevalence of low scores across increasing levels of intellectual abilities. When interpreting multivariate base rates, it is very important to consider the prevalence of low scores based on level of intelligence. Using education- or demographically-adjusted norms will not remove the effect of intelligence on the base rate of low scores.

MULTIVARIATE BASE RATES FOR THE WAIS–IV AND WMS–IV

With the publication of the Wechsler Adult Intelligence Scale–Fourth Edition (WAIS–IV: Wechsler, 2008) and the Wechsler Memory Scales–Fourth Edition (WMS–IV: Wechsler, 2009), new information on the prevalence of low scores is needed to facilitate the advanced clinical interpretation of performance on these batteries. Some basic multivariate information for the full WAIS–IV/WMS–IV battery has been published (Brooks et al., 2011). Tables A2.1–A2.29 in the Appendix provide multivariate base rates for the WAIS–IV and WMS–IV. To use these tables properly, clinicians need to find the correct table with the exact tests being interpreted (i.e., tests cannot be substituted), they need to select the most appropriate comparison group (i.e., intellectual level, years of education, and/or age group), and determine which cut-off score is the most suitable for interpretation of the prevalence of low scores. To illustrate the clinical application of the multivariate base rates tables, six case examples are presented in Tables 2.1 and 2.2.

As seen in the case examples of Tables 2.1 and 2.2, base rate analyses can at times, be very helpful for a better understanding of how common or uncommon it is to get certain patterns of low scores. It is a serious interpretive mistake to apply the logic of the bell curve to the interpretation of isolated low scores across a battery of tests. For example, the probability of obtaining one subtest scaled score of 6 or lower on the WAIS–IV or WMS–IV is not 9%. In fact, it is *common* for healthy adults of average estimated intelligence to obtain one unusually low score (i.e., SS = 6 or lower) on the WAIS–IV (BR = 41.7%; see Table A2.14) and the WMS–IV (BR = 43.9%; see Table A2.16). If a clinician decided to interpret a scaled score of 5 or lower on one or more WMS–IV delayed memory subtests (see Table A2.27) as the psychometric criterion for acquired memory impairment, then the false positive rate would not be 5%, as predicted by the bell curve. Rather, it would be 33.7% for those with estimated below average intelligence, 22.2% for those with average intelligence, 10.8% for those with high average intelligence, and 9.1% for those with superior intelligence. Obviously, it would be a serious mistake to assume there is only a 5% chance of obtaining a WMS–IV delayed memory subtest scaled score of 5. The base rate tables in the appendices are designed to supplement, not replace, clinical judgment. These base rate tables can be used to strengthen the scientific underpinnings of clinical judgment.

TABLE 2.1   WAIS–IV and WMS–IV Performance in Six Case Examples

	Case 1	Case 2	Case 3	Case 4	Case 5	Case 6
Diagnosis	Dep/Pain	FTD	Mod TBI	Dep/Anx	ADHD/TBI	MS
Age	57	63	26	19	26	45
Gender	M	F	F	F	M	M
Education	16	14	16	13	10	16
Race	Asian	White	White	White	White	White
Litigation/Disability Evaluation	No	No	No	No	No	No
ACS Effort Scores >25%ile	5/5	2/4	5/5	5/5	5/5	4/5
ToPF-Simple Predicted FSIQ	116	102	108	NA	NA	107
WAIS–IV Index Scores						
Full Scale IQ	116	99	107	104	89	98
Verbal Comprehension Index	114	72	112	112	85	102
Perceptual Reasoning Index	107	109	111	96	109	111
Working Memory Index	114	122	83	97	92	77
Processing Speed Index	120	102	100	100	76	94
WAIS–IV Subtest Scores						
Vocabulary	15	5	12	12	7	14
Information	13	6	11	16	6	7
Similarities	10	4	14	9	9	10
Block Design	13	7	10	9	10	9
Visual Puzzles	10	14	14	10	13	15
Matrix Reasoning	11	14	12	9	12	12
Digit Span	6	17	6	7	9	8
Arithmetic	19	11	8	12	8	4
Coding	14	11	9	7	6	11
Symbol Search	13	10	11	13	5	7
WAIS–IV Supplementary Subtest Scores						
Letter Number Sequencing	8	11	8	8	7	6
Cancellation	7	12	10	10	6	9

(Continued)

TABLE 2.1   (Continued)

	Case 1	Case 2	Case 3	Case 4	Case 5	Case 6
WMS–IV Index Scores						
Visual Working Memory Index	103	103	103	123	85	106
Auditory Memory Index	100	67	113	102	88	81
Visual Memory Index	115	90	103	98	87	104
Immediate Memory Index	103	75	113	107	87	87
Delayed Memory Index	114	78	107	94	84	94
WMS–IV Subtest Scores						
Spatial Addition	12	15	11	15	9	12
Symbol Span	9	6	10	13	6	10
Logical Memory I	7	2	16	12	4	7
Verbal Paired Associates I	12	5	9	10	12	6
Visual Reproduction I	12	9	14	11	9	11
Designs I	11	9	9	11	8	9
Logical Memory II	7	4	16	10	5	7
Verbal Paired Associates II	14	7	8	10	11	7
Visual Reproduction II	14	9	10	6	9	11
Designs II	13	7	10	11	6	12

CONCLUSIONS

Psychologists and neuropsychologists do not interpret cognitive tests in isolation. In virtually all clinical situations, multiple tests are administered and then interpreted in an integrated fashion. Over the past few years, however, practitioners have relied heavily on the immutable characteristics of the bell curve—and often unwittingly applied the logic of a single test score to a battery of tests. Put simply, when a client obtains a test score at the 5th percentile, the psychologist is tempted to believe that only 5% of healthy people would have that particular score (or a lower score). This is true when considering one test score from a normative sample that conforms to the bell curve. However, when considering a battery of tests the interpretive context changes dramatically. Having one or more scores at or below the 7th percentile (T < 35) occurs in 59.4% of healthy adults when considering

TABLE 2.2   Prevalence rates of Low WAIS–IV and WMS–IV Scores in Six Case Examples

	Cut-off Scores				
Case #1: Recurrent Depression and Chronic Pain (Ed = 16; Predicted IQ = 116)	≤25th %ile	≤16th %ile	≤9th %ile	≤5th %ile	≤2nd %ile
Number of Low Age-Adjusted Index scores (10 Indexes)	0	0	0	0	0
Prevalence Rate in Total Sample (Table A2.1)	38.0	52.9	69.6	79.4	89.8
Prevalence Rate in Same Education (Table A2.1)	63.7	77.8	91.9	94.4	98.7
Prevalence Rate in Same TOPF-predicted FSIQ (Table A2.1)	66.7	78.9	93.2	95.2	97.3
Number of Low Age-Adjusted Subtest scores (20 Subtests)	3	3	1	0	0
Prevalence Rate in Total Sample (Table A2.2)	70.3	51.6	61.1	57.1	74.5
Prevalence Rate in Same Education (Table A2.2)	44.0	25.2*	38.0	78.2	89.3
Prevalence Rate in Same TOPF-predicted FSIQ (Table A2.2)	37.4	21.1*	35.4	79.6	89.8
Number of Low Working Memory Scores (DS, AR, LNS)	2	1	1	0	0
Prevalence Rate in Total Sample (Table A2.21)	27.2	31.8	19.7	90.2	96.9
Prevalence Rate in Same Education (Table A2.22)	8.8*	12.1	5.4	99.2	99.6
Prevalence Rate in Same TOPF-predicted FSIQ (Table A2.21)	2.5*	6.4	3.2	100.0	100.0
Number of Low WMS-IV Subtest Scores (8 scores)	2	2	0	0	0
Prevalence Rate in Total Sample (Table A2.16)	57.1	43.0	56.8	70.6	82.3

(*Continued*)

TABLE 2.2 (Continued)

	Cut-off Scores				
Prevalence Rate in Same Education (Table A2.16)	36.3	22.8	75.9	84.4	93.2
Prevalence Rate in Same TOPF-predicted FSIQ (Table A2.16)	35.4	**22.4***	76.9	85.0	91.2

Summary of Case #1: Considering the 10 index scores derived from the WAIS–IV and WMS–IV, the patient did not have a single below average score. This is normal for people with university degrees and above average intelligence. Across the 20 primary subtest scores, he had three scores at or below the 16th percentile. This pattern occurs in approximately 20–25% of health adults with university degrees or above average intelligence. He had two verbal working memory subtest scores that were below average (≤25th percentile). This is uncommon in people with university degrees (i.e., base rate (BR) = 8.8%) and rare in people with above average intelligence (BR = 2.5%). Considering the eight primary memory subtests, he obtained two scores ≤16th percentile—a pattern that occurs in 22.4% of people with estimated high average intelligence. Overall, he appears to have lower than expected scores on some tests involving auditory attention, working memory, and memory (DS, LNS, LMI, and LMII).

Case #2: Frontotemporal Dementia (Ed = 14; Predicted IQ = 102)	≤25th %ile	≤16th %ile	≤9th %ile	≤5th %ile	≤2nd %ile
Number of Low Age-Adjusted Index scores (10 Indexes)	5	4	4	3	1
Prevalence Rate in Total Sample (Table A2.1)	22.6	17.9	9.8	8.1	10.2
Prevalence Rate in Same Education (Table A2.1)	16.9	14.2	7.3	6.5	7.3
Prevalence Rate in Same TOPF-predicted FSIQ (Table A2.1)	17.7	12.5	**4.4***	4.4	5.8
Number of Low Age-Adjusted Subtest scores (20 Subtests)	10	10	7	5	3
Prevalence Rate in Total Sample (Table A2.2)	23.0	12.6	11.1	9.0	7.4
Prevalence Rate in Same Education (Table A2.2)	17.2	8.0	8.0	6.5	5.0
Prevalence Rate in Same TOPF-predicted FSIQ (Table A2.2)	17.7	**7.1***	6.5	5.0	4.0
Number of Low WMS-IV Subtest Scores (8 scores)	5	5	3	3	2

(Continued)

TABLE 2.2   (Continued)

Case #2: Frontotemporal Dementia (Ed = 14; Predicted IQ = 102)	≤25th %ile	≤16th %ile	≤9th %ile	≤5th %ile	≤2nd %ile
Prevalence Rate in Total Sample (Table A2.16)	17.6	10.2	13.9	7.2	8.7
Prevalence Rate in Same Education (Table A2.16)	15.5	9.1	13.2	5.7	7.9
Prevalence Rate in Same TOPF-predicted FSIQ (Table A2.16)	15.5	8.2*	12.6	6.1	7.3

Summary of Case #2: Considering the 10 index scores from the WAIS–IV and WMS–IV, the patient had four scores below the 10th percentile. This is very uncommon, occurring in only 4.4% of healthy adults with estimated average intellectual abilities. Across the 20 primary subtest scores, he had 10 scores ≤16th percentile; this is an uncommon finding in healthy adults with estimated average intelligence (BR = 7.1%). Considering the eight memory subtests from the WMS–IV, he obtained five scores that were ≤16th percentile (BR = 8.2%). Overall, he shows evidence of impairment in verbal intellectual abilities and verbal learning and memory.

Case #3: Moderate TBI 2 Years Post Injury (Ed = 16; Predicted IQ = 108)	≤25th %ile	≤16th %ile	≤9th %ile	≤5th %ile	≤2nd %ile
Number of Low Age-Adjusted Index scores (10 Indexes)	1	1	0	0	0
Prevalence Rate in Total Sample (Table A2.1)	62.0	47.1	69.6	79.4	89.8
Prevalence Rate in Same Education (Table A2.1)	36.3	22.2*	91.9	94.4	98.7
Prevalence Rate in Same TOPF-predicted FSIQ (Table A2.1)	63.5	44.3*	73.3	84.6	94.2
Number of Low Age-Adjusted Subtest scores (20 Subtests)	3	1	1	0	0
Prevalence Rate in Total Sample (Table A2.2)	70.3	77.8	61.1*	57.1	74.5
Prevalence Rate in Same Education (Table A2.2)	44.0	58.1	38.0*	78.2	89.3
Prevalence Rate in Same TOPF-predicted FSIQ (Table A2.2)	74.9	82.5	62.4*	58.2	78.7

(Continued)

TABLE 2.2   (Continued)

Case #3: Moderate TBI 2 Years Post Injury (Ed = 16; Predicted IQ = 108)	≤25th %ile	≤16th %ile	≤9th %ile	≤5th %ile	≤2nd %ile
Number of Low Working Memory Scores (DS, AR, LNS)	3	1	1	0	0
Prevalence Rate in Total Sample (Table A2.21)	13.7	31.8	19.7	90.2	96.9
Prevalence Rate in Same Education (Table A2.22)	2.9*	28.2	5.4	93.3	99.6
Prevalence Rate in Same TOPF-predicted FSIQ (Table A2.21)	9.0*	12.1	15.9	99.2	98.5
Number of Low WMS-IV Subtest Scores (8 scores)	1	0	0	0	0
Prevalence Rate in Total Sample (Table A2.16)	73.9	42.7	56.8	70.6	82.3
Prevalence Rate in Same Education (Table A2.16)	58.6	63.3	75.9	84.4	93.2
Prevalence Rate in Same TOPF-predicted FSIQ (Table A2.16)	76.4	40.4	56.1	70.9	84.1

Summary of Case #3: Considering the 10 index scores from the WAIS–IV and WMS–IV, the patient had only one score ≤16th percentile. Having one or more scores in this range occurs in 44.3% of adults with estimated average intellectual abilities and 22.2% of those with university degrees. Across the 20 primary subtest scores, she had one score below the 10th percentile. Having one or more scores below the 10th percentile, when considering all 20, is common in healthy adults. Considering the three verbal working memory scores, she obtained all three at or below the 25th percentile. This is a very uncommon finding in people with estimated average intelligence (BR = 9.0% and people with university degrees (BR = 2.9%). Overall, her scores were broadly normal in most cognitive domains. However, her performance on tests of auditory attention and working memory was much lower than expected.

Case #4: Depression and Anxiety (Ed = 13)	≤25th %ile	≤16th %ile	≤9th %ile	≤5th %ile	≤2nd %ile
Number of Low Age-Adjusted Subtest scores (20 Subtests)	3	3	1	0	0
Prevalence Rate in Total Sample (Table A2.2)	70.3	51.6	61.1	57.1	74.5
Prevalence Rate in Same Education (Table A2.2)	69.7*	49.4	56.7*	64.0	79.7

(*Continued*)

TABLE 2.2   (Continued)

Case #4: Depression and Anxiety (Ed = 13)	≤25th %ile	≤16th %ile	≤9th %ile	≤5th %ile	≤2nd %ile
Number of Low Working Memory Scores (DS, AR, LNS)	2	1	0	0	0
Prevalence Rate in Total Sample (Table A2.21)	27.2	31.8	80.3	90.2	96.9
Prevalence Rate in Same Education (Table A2.22)	21.4	24.4*	86.5	93.6	98.9
Number of Low WMS-IV Subtest Scores (8 scores)	1	1	1	0	0
Prevalence Rate in Total Sample (Table A2.16)	73.9	57.3	43.2	70.6	82.3
Prevalence Rate in Same Education (Table A2.16)	71.7	52.8	38.5	74.0	82.6
Number of Low WMS-IV Delayed Memory Scores (4 scores)	1	1	1	0	0
Prevalence Rate in Total Sample (Table A2.27)	59.1	50.2	33.9	77.9	86.8
Prevalence Rate in Same Education (Table A2.28)	57.7	46.6	30.8*	82.7	88.7

Summary of Case #4: Considering the 10 index scores from the WAIS–IV and WMS–IV, she did not have a single below average score. Across the 20 primary subtest scores, she had three scores ≤25th percentile and one score ≤10th percentile. This is common in healthy adults and adults with 13–15 years of education. Having one verbal working memory score ≤16th percentile (BR = 24.4%) and one delayed memory score below the 10th percentile (BR = 30.8%) is relatively common in healthy adults with 13–15 years of education. Overall, she performed reasonably well across this battery of cognitive tests. Improvement in her mental health might be associated with some concomitant improvement in her cognitive functioning.

Case #5: ADHD and Moderate Traumatic Brain Injury (Ed = 10)	≤25th %ile	≤16th %ile	≤9th %ile	≤5th %ile	≤2nd %ile
Number of Low Age-Adjusted Index scores (10 Indexes)	8	4	1	1	0
Prevalence Rate in Total Sample (Table A2.1)	10.1	17.9	30.4	20.6*	89.8
Prevalence Rate in Same Education (Table A2.1)	34.6*	52.6*	66.7	57.7*	65.4

(Continued)

TABLE 2.2   (Continued)

Case #5: ADHD and Moderate Traumatic Brain Injury (Ed = 10)	≤25th %ile	≤16th %ile	≤9th %ile	≤5th %ile	≤2nd %ile
Number of Low Age-Adjusted Subtest scores (20 Subtests)	10	8	7	3	1
Prevalence Rate in Total Sample (Table A2.2)	23.0	18.9	11.1	17.3	25.5
Prevalence Rate in Same Education (Table A2.2)	57.7	50.0	30.8*	51.3	57.7
Number of Low Working Memory Scores (DS, AR, LNS)	2	1	0	0	0
Prevalence Rate in Total Sample (Table A2.21)	27.2	31.8	80.3	90.2	96.9
Prevalence Rate in Same Education (Table A2.22)	61.5	66.7	57.7	75.6	87.2
Number of Low Processing Speed Scores (CD, SS, CAN)	3	3	3	1	0
Prevalence Rate in Total Sample (Table A2.23)	11.7	5.5	2.2	12.8	94.7
Prevalence Rate in Same Education (Table A2.24)	26.9	12.8	6.4*	25.6	89.7
Number of Low WMS-IV Subtest Scores (8 scores)	4	3	3	2	1
Prevalence Rate in Total Sample (Table A2.16)	29.8	27.9	13.9*	15.5	17.7
Prevalence Rate in Same Education (Table A2.16)	55.7	57.0	36.7*	39.2	38.0

Summary of Case #5: Considering the 10 index scores from the WAIS–IV and WMS–IV, he had eight scores ≤25th percentile and four scores ≤16th percentile, which is common in adults with 9–11 years of education (BR = 34.6% and 52.6%, respectively). Across the 20 primary subtest scores, he had seven scores below the 10th percentile. This, too, is common in adults with 9–11 years of education (BR = 30.8). Of those seven low scores, three of them were in the Processing Speed domain. Having three processing speed scores below the 10th percentile is an uncommon finding in adults with 9–11 years of education (BR = 6.4%). Having three out of eight WMS–IV memory scores below the 10th percentile is uncommon in the general population (BR = 13.9%) but common in adults with 9–11 years of education (BR = 36.7%). Overall, his performance on memory testing was lower than expected for the general population, but not unusual for people with 9–11 years of education. His performance on tests of processing speed was much lower than expected for people who do not graduate from high school.

(Continued)

TABLE 2.2   (Continued)

Case #6: Multiple Sclerosis (Ed = 16; Predicted IQ = 107)	≤25th %ile	≤16th %ile	≤9th %ile	≤5th %ile	≤2nd %ile
Number of Low Age-Adjusted Index scores (10 Indexes)	3	2	1	0	0
Prevalence Rate in Total Sample (Table A2.1)	36.4	30.2	30.4	79.4	89.8
Prevalence Rate in Same Education (Table A2.1)	15.0	9.4*	8.1	94.4	98.7
Prevalence Rate in Same TOPF-predicted FSIQ (Table A2.1)	32.6	26.1*	26.7	84.6	94.2
Number of Low Age-Adjusted Subtest scores (20 Subtests)	8	7	2	1	1
Prevalence Rate in Total Sample (Table A2.2)	32.0	22.4	44.0	42.9	25.5
Prevalence Rate in Same Education (Table A2.2)	10.7	4.7*	19.7	21.8	10.7
Prevalence Rate in Same TOPF-predicted FSIQ (Table A2.2)	28.0	18.2*	43.6	41.8	21.3
Number of Low Working Memory Scores (DS, AR, LNS)	3	2	2	1	1
Prevalence Rate in Total Sample (Table A2.21)	13.7	13.7	6.3	9.8	3.1
Prevalence Rate in Same Education (Table A2.22)	2.9	0.8	<0.4	0.8	<0.4
Prevalence Rate in Same TOPF-predicted FSIQ (Table A2.21)	9.0	8.8	2.3*	6.7	1.5
Number of Low Processing Speed Scores (CD, SS, CAN)	1	1	0	0	0
Prevalence Rate in Total Sample (Table A2.23)	52.7	36.3	78.6	87.1	94.7
Prevalence Rate in Same Education (Table A2.24)	37.2	24.7*	89.5	93.7	98.7
Prevalence Rate in Same TOPF-predicted FSIQ (Table A2.23)	51.2	31.9*	82.0	91.6	96.9

(*Continued*)

TABLE 2.2   (Continued)

Case #6: Multiple Sclerosis (Ed = 16; Predicted IQ = 107)	≤25th %ile	≤16th %ile	≤9th %ile	≤5th %ile	≤2nd %ile
Number of Low WMS-IV Subtest Scores (8 scores)	4	4	1	0	0
Prevalence Rate in Total Sample (Table A2.16)	29.8	17.8*	43.2	70.6	82.3
Prevalence Rate in Same Education (Table A2.16)	13.5	**6.3***	12.7	84.4	93.2
Prevalence Rate in Same TOPF-predicted FSIQ (Table A2.16)	28.7	**16.5***	43.9	70.9	84.1

Summary of Case #6: Considering the 10 index scores from the WAIS–IV and WMS–IV, he had two scores ≤16th percentile. This is relatively common in people with average estimated intelligence (BR = 26.1%) but uncommon in people with university degrees (BR = 9.4%). Across the 20 primary subtest scores, he had seven scores ≤16th percentile. This is relatively uncommon in people with average estimated intelligence (BR = 18.2%) and rare in people with university degrees (BR = 4.7%). In the working memory domain, he had two scores below the 10th percentile; this is rare in people with average estimated intelligence (BR = 2.3%). Having one below average score in the processing speed domain is relatively common in adults with average intelligence and those with university degrees. However, having four out of eight memory scores that are below average is uncommon in adults with average intelligence (BR = 16.5%) and rare in adults with university degrees (BR = 6.3%). Overall, he performed much lower than expected on tests of auditory working memory and verbal learning and memory.

Note: Bold asterisked scores indicate entries of particular interest for interpretation.

25 scores from the Expanded HRNB (Binder et al., 2009). Having one or more scores at or below the 5th percentile occurs in 70.2% when considering the 36 primary T-scores from the NAB (Iverson et al., 2008b), 43.3% when considering the 20 primary subtest scores from the combined WAIS–III/WMS–III (Binder et al., 2009; Iverson, Brooks, & Holdnack, 2009), 43% when considering the 20 primary subtest scores from the WAIS–IV/WMS–IV, 27% when considering the 10 primary scores from the WAIS–IV, and 29% of healthy adults when considering the eight primary memory scores from the WMS–IV.

As part of the interpretive procedure for a battery of tests, the psychologist must use his or her clinical judgment to consider all of the test scores simultaneously when interpreting the patient's performance. Although one or more low scores might be suggestive of an acquired impairment, it is important to consider that having inter-subtest variability and obtaining low scores might be "normal" for that particular person. Obtaining low scores might be attributable to measurement error (broadly defined), normative sample characteristics (i.e., having healthy people, rather than clinical groups, at the lower end of the distribution), longstanding weaknesses in certain areas, fluctuations in motivation and effort, psychological interference, and other situational factors such as inattentiveness, fatigue, or minor illness (Binder et al., 2009).

This chapter presented five psychometric principles to consider when interpreting multiple test scores. Low scores are common across all batteries of tests (Principle 1), there is an inverse relation between the number of low scores and the cut-off score used (Principle 2), the number of low scores obtained increases with the number of tests administered and interpreted (Principle 3), the number of low scores can change depending on the demographic characteristics of a sample (Principle 4), and different levels of intellectual functioning are inherently going to have different rates of low scores (Principle 5). With this information, clinicians are better able to guard against over-interpreting an isolated low score. By presenting clinically-useful tables for the WAIS–IV and WMS–IV, clinicians are able to supplement test interpretation with multivariate base rates.

Multivariate base rates can be used to determine if a person's profile (i.e., the number of low scores) is broadly normal or uncommon in healthy people. In other words, it could be expected that an individual with longstanding low intellectual functioning would have multiple low scores on the WAIS–IV/WMS–IV, which could be considered "broadly normal" for that person in terms of his or her level of functioning and have always been areas of identified weakness.[1] For example, in healthy adults with low average intelligence, having four WAIS–IV/WMS–IV index scores at or below the 16th percentile is considered common (i.e., this is found in 42% of healthy adults with TOPF with simple demographics predicted FSIQ = 80–89). That is, these low scores might not reflect a *change* in cognitive functioning due to injury or disease. In contrast, an individual suffering an acquired brain injury may have more low scores than expected as a consequence of the injury or other factors that may need to be considered. The presence of more low scores than would be expected in healthy people is not necessarily diagnostic of a specific clinical condition such as dementia

---

[1]It is important to consider that identifying some low scores as being "common" in healthy people does not negate the possibility that the low scores could reflect a cognitive weakness for that person. For example, it may be "common" for a person with 10 years of education to have one or more scores at or below the 2nd percentile (found in 34% of healthy Adults with 9–11 years of education), but that does not mean that this person does not have a longstanding cognitive weakness in that particular domain.

or a brain injury. Instead, it indicates that the number of low scores obtained is atypical in healthy people. It is incumbent on the clinician to determine if the low scores reflect the consequences of injury or disease, or if other factors (e.g., level of effort, medications, other medical conditions, normal variability) fully or partially account for the number of obtained low scores. Ultimately, multivariate base rates are used as another tool to supplement, but not replace, clinical judgment when simultaneously interpreting numerous cognitive test scores.

KEY LEARNING

- A single low score does not necessarily represent a decline in cognitive ability; obtaining multiple low scores is common in some healthy adults.
- The probability of obtaining a low score when administering one test is consistent with the Gaussian normal distribution, that is, 5% of individuals will obtain a scaled score of 5 or less, or index score of 75 or less on any single measure. In the context of administering multiple cognitive tests, the likelihood of obtaining one low score increases significantly (e.g., 29% for full WMS—IV). Sensitivity/ specificity of a test is directly related to the cut-score used to define a low score. The number of low scores obtained is directly related to the cut-offs used, the number of tests administered, demographic characteristics, and intellectual ability.
- Multivariate base rate data is specifically used to evaluate whether or not the examinee has experienced a decline in cognitive status. Obtaining more low scores than is expected for the individual's education or premorbid intellectual functioning may signal such a decline; however, other factors (e.g., motivation, fatigue) may also account for obtained results.
- Using multivariate base rates does not replace other forms of clinical interpretation, that is, the clinician should still evaluate the strengths and weaknesses of performance within a cognitive profile, overall cognitive functioning, and cognitive functioning within the context of presenting symptoms. Multivariate base rates are not intended for diagnosing developmental conditions such as intellectual deficiency or language disorder, and should be used in conjunction with clinical judgment and all other clinical information.
- Multivariate base rate tables can be used to improve diagnostic accuracy.

The Appendix containing tables for Chapter 2 can be found online at: http://booksite.elsevier.com/9780123869340

References

Axelrod, B. N., & Wall, J. R. (2007). Expectancy of impaired neuropsychological test scores in a non-clinical sample. *International Journal of Neuroscience, 117*(11), 1591–1602.

Beatty, W. W., Mold, J. W., & Gontkovsky, S. T. (2003). RBANS performance: Influences of sex and education. *Journal of Clinical and Experimental Neuropsychology, 25*(8), 1065–1069.

Binder, L. M., Iverson, G. L., & Brooks, B. L. (2009). To err is human: "Abnormal" neuropsychological scores and variability are common in healthy adults. *Archives of Clinical Neuropsychology, 24*, 31–46.

Brooks, B. L. (2010). Seeing the forest for the trees: Prevalence of low scores on the Wechsler intelligence scale for children–fourth edition (WISC–IV). *Psychological Assessment, 22*(3), 650–656.

Brooks, B. L. (2011). A study of low scores in Canadian children and adolescents on the Wechsler intelligence scale for children–fourth edition (WISC–IV). *Child Neuropsychology, 17*(3), 281–289.

Brooks, B. L., Holdnack, J. A., & Iverson, G. L. (2011). Advanced clinical interpretation of the WAIS–IV and WMS–IV: Prevalence of low scores varies by level of intelligence and years of education. *Assessment, 18*, 156–167.

Brooks, B. L., & Iverson, G. L. (2012). Improving accuracy when identifying cognitive impairment in pediatric neuropsychological assessments. In E. M. S. Sherman, & B. L. Brooks (Eds.), *Pediatric Forensic Neuropsychology* (pp. 66–88). New York: Oxford University Press.

Brooks, B. L., Iverson, G. L., Feldman, H. H., & Holdnack, J. A. (2009). Minimizing misdiagnosis: Psychometric criteria for possible or probable memory impairment. *Dementia and Geriatric Cognitive Disorders, 27*(5), 439–450.

Brooks, B. L., Iverson, G. L., Holdnack, J. A., & Feldman, H. H. (2008). Potential for misclassification of mild cognitive impairment: A study of memory scores on the Wechsler memory scale-III in healthy older adults. *Journal of the International Neuropsychological Society, 14*(3), 463–478.

Brooks, B. L., Iverson, G. L., Lanting, S. C., Horton, A. M., & Reynolds, C. R. (2012). Improving test interpretation for detecting executive dysfunction in adults and older adults: Prevalence of low scores on the test of verbal conceptualization and fluency. *Applied Neuropsychology, 19*(1), 61–70.

Brooks, B. L., Iverson, G. L., Sherman, E. M. S., & Holdnack, J. A. (2009). Healthy children and adolescents obtain some low scores across a battery of memory tests. *Journal of the International Neuropsychological Society, 15*(4), 613–617.

Brooks, B. L., Iverson, G. L., & White, T. (2007). Substantial risk of "Accidental MCI" in healthy older adults: Base rates of low memory scores in neuropsychological assessment. *Journal of the International Neuropsychological Society, 13*(3), 490–500.

Brooks, B. L., Iverson, G. L., & White, T. (2009). Advanced interpretation of the neuropsychological assessment battery (NAB) with older adults: Base rate analyses, discrepancy scores, and interpreting change. *Archives of Clinical Neuropsychology, 24*(7), 647–657.

Brooks, B. L., Sherman, E. M. S., & Iverson, G. L. (2010). Healthy children get some low scores too: Prevalence of low scores on the NEPSY-II in pre-schoolers, children, and adolescents. *Archives of Clinical Neuropsychology, 25*, 182–190.

Brooks, B. L., Strauss, E., Sherman, E. M. S., Iverson, G. L., & Slick, D. J. (2009). Developments in neuropsychological assessment: Refining psychometric and clinical interpretive methods. *Canadian Psychology, 50*(3), 196–209.

Collaer, M. L., & Nelson, J. D. (2002). Large visuospatial sex difference in line judgment: Possible role of attentional factors. *Brain and Cognition, 49*(1), 1–12.

Crawford, J. R., Garthwaite, P. H., & Gault, C. B. (2007). Estimating the percentage of the population with abnormally low scores (or abnormally large score differences) on standardized neuropsychological test batteries: A generic method with applications. *Neuropsychology, 21*(4), 419–430.

Donders, J., Zhu, J., & Tulsky, D. (2001). Factor index score patterns in the WAIS-III standardization sample. *Assessment, 8*(2), 193–203.

Geary, D. C., Saults, S. J., Liu, F., & Hoard, M. K. (2000). Sex differences in spatial cognition, computational fluency, and arithmetical reasoning. *Journal of Experimental and Child Psychology, 77*(4), 337–353.

Heaton, R. K., Grant, I., & Matthews, C. G. (1991). *Comprehensive norms for an extended Halstead-Reitan battery: Demographic corrections, research findings, and clinical applications.* Odessa, FL: Psychological Assessment Resources, Inc.

Heaton, R. K., Miller, S. W., Taylor, M. J., & Grant, I. (2004). *Revised comprehensive norms for an expanded Halstead-Reitan battery: Demographically adjusted neuropsychological norms for African American and Caucasian adults professional manual.* Lutz, FL: Psychological Assessment Resources.

Heaton, R. K., Taylor, M. J., & Manly, J. (2003). Demographic effects and use of demographically corrected norms with the WAIS-III and WMS-III. In D. S. Tulsky, D. H. Saklofske, G. J. Chelune, R. K. Heaton, R. J. Ivnik, R. Bornstein, A. Prifitera, & M. Ledbetter (Eds.), *Clinical Interpretation of the WAIS-III and WMS-III* (pp. 183–210). San Diego, CA: Academic Press.

Herlitz, A., Nilsson, L. G., & Backman, L. (1997). Gender differences in episodic memory. *Memory & Cognition, 25*(6), 801–811.

Horton, A. M., Jr. (1999). Above-average intelligence and neuropsychological test score performance. *International Journal of Neuroscience, 99*(1–4), 221–231.

Ingraham, L. J., & Aiken, C. B. (1996). An empirical approach to determining criteria for abnormality in test batteries with multiple measures. *Neuropsychology, 10*, 120–124.

Iverson, G. L., & Brooks, B. L. (2011). Improving accuracy for identifying cognitive impairment. In M. R. Schoenberg, & J. G. Scott (Eds.), *The black book of neuropsychology: A syndrome–based approach* (pp. 923–950). New York: Springer.

Iverson, G. L., Brooks, B. L., & Holdnack, J. A. (2009). *Low scores across the WAIS-III/WMS-III vary by education & intelligence.* Paper presented at the thirty-seventh annual meeting of the international neuropsychological society, Atlanta, GA.

Iverson, G. L., Brooks, B. L., & Holdnack, J. A. (2012). Evidence-based neuropsychological assessment following work-related injury. In S. S. Bush, & G. L. Iverson (Eds.), *Neuropsychological assessment of workplace injuries.* New York: Guilford Press.

Iverson, G. L., Brooks, B. L., & Holdnack, J. A. (2008a). Misdiagnosis of cognitive impairment in forensic neuropsychology. In R. L. Heilbronner (Ed.), *Neuropsychology in the courtroom: Expert analysis of reports and testimony* (pp. 243–266). New York: Guilford Press.

Iverson, G. L., Brooks, B. L., White, T., & Stern, R. A. (2008b). Neuropsychological assessment battery (NAB): Introduction and advanced interpretation. In A. M. Horton, Jr., & D. Wedding (Eds.), *The neuropsychology handbook* (3rd ed., pp. 279–343). New York: Springer Publishing Inc.

Ivnik, R. J., Makec, J. F., Smith, G. E., Tangolos, E. G., & Peterson, R. C. (1996). Neuropsychological tests' norms above age 55: COWAT, BNT, MAE Token, WRAT-R Reading, AMNART, STROOP, TMT, and JLO. *The Clinical Neuropsychologist, 10*, 262–278.

Morgan, E. E., Woods, S. P., Scott, J. C., Childers, M., Beck, J. M., & Ellis, R. J., et al. (2007). Predictive validity of demographically adjusted normative standards for the HIV dementia scale. *Journal of Clinical Experimental Neuropsychology, 30*, 83–90.

Norman, M. A., Evans, J. D., Miller, W. S., & Heaton, R. K. (2000). Demographically corrected norms for the California verbal learning test. *Journal of Clinical and Experimental Neuropsychology, 22*(1), 80–94.

Palmer, B. W., Boone, K. B., Lesser, I. M., & Wohl, M. A. (1998). Base rates of "impaired" neuropsychological test performance among healthy older adults. *Archives of Clinical Neuropsychology, 13*(6), 503–511.

Rosselli, M., & Ardila, A. (2003). The impact of culture and education on non-verbal neuropsychological measurements: A critical review. *Brain Cognition, 52*(3), 326–333.

Ryan, E. L., Baird, R., Mindt, M. R., Byrd, D., Monzones, J., & Bank, S. M. (2005). Neuropsychological impairment in racial/ethnic minorities with HIV infection and low literacy levels: Effects of education and reading level in participant characterization. *Journal of International Neuropsychological Society, 11*(7), 889–898.

Schretlen, D. J., Testa, S. M., Winicki, J. M., Pearlson, G. D., & Gordon, B. (2008). Frequency and bases of abnormal performance by healthy adults on neuropsychological testing. *Journal of the International Neuropsychological Society, 14*(3), 436–445.

Steinberg, B. A., Bieliauskas, L. A., Smith, G. E., & Ivnik, R. J. (2005). Mayo's older americans normative studies: Age- and IQ-adjusted norms for the trail-making test, the stroop test, and mae controlled oral word association test. *Clinical Neuropsychology, 19* (3–4), 329–377.

Steinberg, B. A., Bieliauskas, L. A., Smith, G. E., Ivnik, R. J., & Malec, J. F. (2005). Mayo's older Americans normative studies: Age- and IQ-adjusted norms for the auditory verbal learning test and the visual spatial learning test. *Clinical Neuropsychology, 19*(3–4), 464–523.

Stern, R. A., & White, T. (2003). *Neuropsychological assessment battery.* Lutz, FL: Psychological Assessment Resources.

Tremont, G., Hoffman, R. G., Scott, J. G., & Adams, R. L. (1998). Effect of intellectual level on neuropsychological test performance: A response to Dodrill (1997). *The Clinical Neuropsychologist, 12,* 560–567.

Voyer, D., Voyer, S., & Bryden, M. P. (1995). Magnitude of sex differences in spatial abilities: A meta-analysis and consideration of critical variables. *Psychological Bulletin, 117* (2), 250–270.

Warner, M. H., Ernst, J., Townes, B. D., Peel, J., & Preston, M. (1987). Relationships between IQ and neuropsychological measures in neuropsychiatric populations: Within-laboratory and cross-cultural replications using WAIS and WAIS-R. *Journal of Clinical and Experimental Neuropsychology, 9*(5), 545–562.

Wechsler, D. (1997a). *Wechsler adult intelligence scale–third edition.* San Antonio, TX: Psychological Corporation.

Wechsler, D. (1997b). *Wechsler memory scale–third edition.* San Antonio, TX: The Psychological Corporation.

Wechsler, D. (2008). *Wechsler adult intelligence scale–fourth edition.* San Antonio, TX: Pearson.

Wechsler, D. (2009). *Wechsler memory scale–fourth edition.* San Antonio, TX: Pearson.

Understanding Index and Subtest Scatter in Healthy Adults

Howard Oakes*, David Lovejoy*, Sarah Tartar*
and James A. Holdnack**

*Hartford Hospital, Hartford, Connecticut, USA **Pearson Assessment,
San Antonio, Texas, USA

INTRODUCTION

Clinicians frequently compare performance between tests and subtests in order to determine if a patient exhibits significant strengths or weaknesses in his or her cognitive functioning as part of psychological, psychoeducational, and neuropsychological evaluations. In such evaluations, the clinician may have specific hypotheses related to the presenting condition or referral question such as: *"Is academic achievement significantly different from intellectual ability?" "Is memory functioning impaired relative to general cognitive ability?" "Is there a significant difference between verbal and visual–perceptual abilities?"* or *"Is there a difference between visual and auditory memory functioning?"* Or, in some cases, the examiner does not have an *a priori* hypothesis about which cognitive functions may be relative strengths or weaknesses and explores all possible comparisons. This process frequently involves numerous pairwise comparisons or a comparison of a specific measure versus an average or global indicator of a specific ability (e.g., VCI (Verbal Comprehension Index) versus the average of all WAIS–IV indexes or WMS–IV Auditory Memory vs. WAIS–IV General Ability Index).

WAIS-IV, WMS-IV, and ACS.
DOI: http://dx.doi.org/10.1016/B978-0-12-386934-0.00003-1

© 2013 Elsevier Inc. All rights reserved.

When variability is observed, the clinician often interprets those results in light of the presenting problems and diagnostic considerations.

The practice of interpreting test scatter or the relative differences among and between various scores associated with psychometric tests is steeped in a rich historical and clinical tradition. The interpretation of test scatter has historically been used as a tool to help in determining the presence of cognitive abnormality and to aid in developing hypotheses about an individual's pattern of cognitive strengths and weaknesses (Kaufman & Lichtenberger, 2006; Lezak, Howieson, & Loring, 2004; Sattler & Ryan, 2009). Statistical investigations into determining normal and abnormal levels of test scatter on certain Wechsler tests date back more than 40 years (Kaufman, 1976). However, these early investigations were related primarily to the cognitive performance of children on the WISC−R. Some of the earliest scatter norms for the WAIS−R were published approximately 10 years later (Matarazzo, Daniel, Prifitera, & Herman, 1988; Matarazzo & Herman, 1985). Since these initial investigations into the base rates of test scatter, a significant literature has developed in relation to the investigation of test score variability in normal and clinical populations (see Chapter 2 for a discussion of how this literature applies to the WAIS−IV/WMS−IV).

A high degree of variability among cognitive skills, or specific types of variability, are thought to be associated with specific clinical populations or are considered a general indicator of abnormal brain functioning. Given the large quantity of pairwise comparisons that could be made in a battery of tests, the probability of a type 1 error is inflated relative to the specific significance level used to identify differences between two test scores (i.e., a p value of 0.05 applied only to a single comparison not to multiple comparisons). This is a similar issue to the multivariate base rate problem described in Chapter 2. In order to determine if variability is atypical, the clinician must first understand the base rate of variability in healthy controls.

Some clinicians apply interpretive strategies that may lead to greater vulnerability to either false positive or false negative errors. For example, it is common for clinicians to interpret "large" amounts of apparent subtest scatter as an abnormal finding. It appears that some clinicians enter an evaluation with a misguided *a priori* hypothesis that there should be general consistency (e.g., minimal variability) across subtest and index scores. Additionally, variability in cognitive functions is not necessarily consistent across all examinees. The contributory factors to this variability may include examinee factors (age, sex, education, ethnicity, and overall level of intellectual functioning) and examination factors (the number of tests administered, the cut-off scores used to determine abnormality, level of reliability, and the intercorrelation between and among tests). For example, it would be difficult for clinicians to know how much variability would be expected for patients with 16 years of education versus those with 9–11 years of education. In order to effectively evaluate scatter in a battery of tests, the clinician needs statistical data to determine when variability is atypical.

This chapter addresses the interpretation of relative differences among index scores and among subtests within and between WAIS–IV and WMS–IV batteries. The chapter builds upon the foundational information presented in Chapter 2 of this book that broadly addresses the use of multivariate base rates in understanding and interpreting WAIS–IV and WMS–IV data. The present chapter is designed to emphasize practical and evidence-based approaches to interpreting subtest scatter that: (a) echo many of the basic principles put forth in Chapter 2, (b) presents normative tables to aid with the interpretation of test scatter, and (c) provide case study examples that emphasize the integration of clinical data with base rate principles in a fashion consistent with evidence-based practices.

BASIC CONCEPTS

This section addresses some of the basic concepts that clinicians should be aware of as they enter into the process of test scatter interpretation. Some of these concepts are fairly clear such as the definition of scatter. Other concepts such as the nature of "abnormality" and the "clinical context" of the testing raise philosophical questions about the way in which tests are interpreted and urge the clinician to think more broadly about the complexities of scatter interpretation.

The authors of this chapter espouse an evidence-based interpretive process in relation to test scatter interpretation. As with any set of tests administered in a clinical setting, a final interpretation of the tests reflects a blending of a clinician's understanding of the psychometric properties associated with the tests, external research related to the condition of interest or the setting of interest, and the clinical circumstances and presentation of the individual at hand (APA, 2005; Iverson, Brooks & Holdnack, 2012). The integration of clinical experience and expertise with empirical research related to a test or tests is the essence of evidence-based medicine and psychological assessment/treatment. The application of multivariate base rate analyses covered in earlier chapters and presented through the tables within this chapter can help to supplement and enhance clinical decision making in an evidence-based fashion. Employing such methods can help the clinician to better understand the potential empirical strengths and weaknesses of a clinical interpretive strategy pertaining to test scatter. Further, with the use of actual normative data, the subjective nature of test scatter interpretation can be reduced, resulting in less idiosyncratic interpretations.

Conceptually, the discussion of cognitive variability in this chapter focuses on the use of variability as a diagnostic indicator of a clinical condition or as an indication of brain dysfunction. However, variability, even in normal subjects, may represent strengths and weaknesses in cognitive functioning. For example, when verbal abilities are significantly lower than perceptual abilities, this is an indication that the individual may have some difficulties with verbal tasks in their daily living depending on the level of performance. This difference does not necessarily implicate some impairment or dysfunction in dominant hemisphere functioning; rather, it may be just a normal variation of cognitive strengths and weaknesses. Few "healthy" individuals will have perfectly equivalent cognitive abilities across multiple domains. Variations in test performance may reflect "real" strengths and weaknesses observed in other settings or may reflect the effects of the test environment, lapses in attention, or waxing and waning of effort throughout a long assessment. All factors must be considered when evaluating whether or not variability is meaningful in terms of actual abilities and the diagnostic implications of observed variations in test performance.

A Definition of Scatter

To briefly review for the purposes of this chapter, test scatter associated with the WAIS–IV and WMS–IV can be conceptualized in two broad fashions. First, test scatter can be defined as the difference between two test scores, such as the highest and lowest subtest scores or a pair of index scores that are of interest. It can also be defined as the degree of overall variability among multiple tests or the difference of each score from the average performance of the measures within the set of scores in question. The standard deviation of scores around the average level of performance is the calculation used to measure general profile variability. Discussion of intra-test scatter is beyond the scope of this chapter but can be an important component of test interpretation in general.

Basic Empirical Challenges When Interpreting Multiple Tests and Test Scatter

Crawford, Gault and Garthwaite (2007) offer an excellent description of the challenges associated with the interpretation of test scores when multiple tests are administered. If a single test is administered as part of an evaluation and that test yields a single score, the clinician's normative adjustment and associated interpretation may be fairly straightforward. That is, the score is compared to a normative sample and an understanding is derived as to where that individual's score falls in relation to demographically similar others. A decision is then made as to whether that score is abnormally low or not, in comparison to the normative group. Indeed, outside of brief cognitive tests such as the Mini Mental Status Examination (Folstein, Folstein & McHugh, 1975), it is rare for a neuropsychologist or psychologist to administer, score, and interpret a single test as the entirety of an evaluation. For instance, the administration of the WAIS–IV and/or WMS–IV alone results in the potential interpretation of over two dozen subtests and more than fifty associated scores from those subtests. Therefore, if we know that when multiple tests are administered there is an increased probability of a healthy person obtaining some low scores, and that most healthy people have cognitive strengths and weaknesses, then how do we differentiate normal from abnormal test scatter?

Knowing the prevalence or base rates of low or abnormal scores across tests in normal populations and in clinical populations (i.e., multivariate base rates) can be informative, as the clinician struggles with the interpretation of test scatter. The primary interpretive message conveyed in Chapter 2 is that having some "low" scores is statistically common for the average individual. The actual number of low scores obtained by an examinee can depend upon a number of important variables including: (a) how one actually defines a low score, (b) demographic variables (e.g., age, sex, education and ethnicity), (c) the person's overall level of intellectual functioning, (d) the actual number of tests administered, and (e) the level of intercorrelation between and among tests. Each of these variables should be considered as one develops an interpretive strategy to address an examinee's test scatter.

Cognitive Abnormality and Test Scatter

How one defines abnormal and/or impaired performance on cognitive tests can differ widely from clinician to clinician (Garb & Schramke, 1996). For instance, something as simple as differences in the cut score a clinician uses to identify abnormal or impaired performance (e.g., using a cut score at the 5th percentile as opposed to a cut score at the 10th percentile) may result in significant interpretive differences regarding abnormality or impairment. Adjustment of cut scores in a more stringent direction can result in more false negative errors whereas adjustment in a more liberal direction can result in more false positive errors. Rather than employing a strict cut score for every test battery interpretation, some clinicians may also use a more flexible exploratory approach to scatter interpretation, examining multiple cut scores to test hypotheses based on clinical context, and considering research related to the population of interest, prior to arriving at a conclusion about the presence and nature of any abnormality or impairment.

The authors of this chapter have seen many clinical instances in which base rate information was never gathered, was ignored or was disregarded by clinicians during an analysis of test scatter. It is argued that a clinician should at the very least, consider available base rate information during hypothesis development related to test scatter, even if the final clinical decision is swayed more by other aspects of an examinee's clinical presentation or other case-related variables. This would reflect the true spirit of an evidence-based approach to test interpretation. Some of the authors' examples of more commonly observed instances in which clinicians have not examined base rate data in their interpretive process are listed below:

- Determining differences exist between subtest scores that are not significantly different.
- Determining if differences between scores are statistically significant, without following up on the base rate occurrence of such differences in the normal population (mistaking statistical for clinical significance).
- Determining that because of someone's education or overall IQ that test scatter is abnormal, without following up on the rate of occurrences of such differences in the population of interest.
- Determining that because of someone's occupation that test scatter is abnormal, without following up on the rate of occurrences of such differences in the population of interest.
- Qualitatively interpreting test scatter without reference to statistical significance or ascertaining whether base rate information is available.
- Associating a "pattern" of scatter to a specific diagnosis in the absence of empirical data to support this conclusion.
- Extrapolating conclusions regarding differences across separate tests without available data (particularly with tests that are not normally distributed).

Cognitive Abnormality versus Interpretation of Intraindividual Strengths and Weaknesses

Much of this chapter addresses an interpretive process geared toward distinguishing normal versus abnormal test scatter and/or test performance. The clinician engaged in such an interpretive process may be interested in determining and/or documenting the cognitive impact of a clinical condition, in terms of cognitive abnormality. Conditions of interest may include neurodevelopmental conditions, psychiatric conditions, or neurologic conditions that have a known impact on cognitive functioning. To determine whether or not the condition of interest is associated with abnormal variability across a group of tests, the clinician must first determine whether or not the observed variability across the tests breaches known thresholds for abnormality. The clinician may then comment as to whether the observed abnormality across tests is consistent with the cognitive abnormalities associated with the condition of interest. The clinician needs to consider that research studies of specific clinical conditions present aggregate data and therefore the results are not necessarily characteristic of all individuals with the condition of interest. Not only does this apply to the level of performance but also the relative performance between measures of interest. Most notably, the mean difference between measures in a profile of tests is not likely to be large enough to accurately differentiate members of one clinical group from members of the general population.

It must also be recognized that there is no conceptual reason to assume that variability in cognitive functioning will be intrinsic to all clinical conditions, and across the specific cognitive measure being utilized. In some cases, a *lack of variability* within a construct may be more indicative of a clinical condition than variability in that functioning (e.g., memory functioning in dementia and intellectual functioning in those with intellectual disability). Therefore, the expectation that variability is the rule for all clinical groups can mislead clinical judgment. The interpretive process by which a clinician characterizes abnormal test scatter as consistent with a particular condition differs from stating that low scores are diagnostic of a specific condition, or indicative of a decline in functioning. That is, a diagnostic statement such as *"The test scatter indicates a diagnosis of Traumatic Brain Injury"* is substantially different from the statement *"The test scatter is consistent with cognitive variability associated with Traumatic Brain Injury."* Like all cognitive tests, the WAIS–IV and WMS–IV batteries have not been shown to have sufficient diagnostic classification rates (i.e., sensitivity, specificity, positive predictive power, and negative predictive power) to be utilized in isolation to diagnose specific neurodevelopmental, psychiatric, and neurologic conditions. Even in conditions such as Intellectual Disability that rely heavily upon cognitive data for a diagnosis, intellectual functioning is paired with information related to adaptive functioning and clinical presentation for establishment of a diagnosis.

In addition to the identification of cognitive abnormality, test scatter can also be used to characterize an individual's cognitive strengths and weaknesses. As mentioned earlier in this chapter and in other chapters associated with this book, the average person presents with a range of personal cognitive strengths and cognitive weaknesses. The evaluation of subtest scatter can be helpful with the characterization of an individual's cognitive strengths and weaknesses. Indeed, such interpretations may occur within the overall context of normal-range variability across administered tests. At this point, there remains no clear consensus on defining relative strengths or weakness. However, a statistically significant difference between scores should be present as a basis for beginning such interpretations.

The Problem of Overlapping Distributions and the Interpretation of Scatter

It would be ideal for simplicity's sake to take a narrow black or white view in relation to the statistical classification of typical versus atypical test scatter. However, clinicians are often forced to operate in a decisional gray zone defined by the intersection or overlap of distributions representing potential normal functionality (i.e., a distribution of scores associated with the test performance of a normal group) and potential abnormal functionality (i.e., a distribution of scores associated with the test performance of a clinical group). Simply put, some healthy people have large inter-test variability or high-low scatter and some clinical patients have low inter-test variability and low scatter. Moreover, some "healthy" adults have cognitive weaknesses and some clinical patients have relative cognitive weaknesses (pre-existing and/or acquired), but might not have any cognitive impairments.

PATTERNS OF COGNITIVE VARIABILITY IN HEALTHY ADULTS

The standardization samples for the WAIS–IV provide data regarding the expected variability in cognitive performance in the general population. These samples provide the normative data for the tests themselves; subsequently, these samples can provide normative data for measures of variability. The calculation for each variability measure is detailed in the WAIS–IV manual. Tables of normative data for multiple measures of cognitive variability are provided and factors that either increase or decrease variability are evaluated. Examples of using the computations and normative data are presented.

Conceptualizing Highest and Lowest Scores

Chapter 2 illustrated that when a battery of tests are administered it is common for healthy adults to have one or more low scores. Similarly, it would be expected that the same individuals would have one or more high scores. Applying the concept of *regression to the mean*—which is a statistical phenomenon whereby individuals scoring higher or lower than the mean have a tendency to perform closer to the mean on subsequent tests—it would be expected that individuals would have relative high and low scores that vary around their personal mean performance and by the mean performance of the normative group as a whole. Regression to the mean reflects the imperfect correlation between tests, imperfect test reliability, and/or normal fluctuations in performance on cognitive testing.

The WAIS–IV and WMS–IV norms yield a mean of 100 and a standard deviation of 15 for indexes, and means and standard deviations of 10 and three for subtests. While these are the mean scores for the overall group, individuals within the normative sample can be higher or lower than the populations mean score. The average level of performance for any individual is best described by the Full-Scale IQ because this score is composed of all the core measures in the battery. If normal healthy adults do not show any variability in cognitive functioning, then the highest obtained score for any individual would equal their lowest obtained score, and both would equal their mean performance. This can be demonstrated by evaluating each person's highest score and lowest score and determining what is the average of all for each person. Based on the norms of the test, these scores should both be 100 for indexes and 10 for subtests.

In the WAIS–IV normative sample, the average highest index score is 110.4 with a standard deviation of 13.9. This means that nearly half the normative sample will have at least one index of 110 or greater. Only 23.7% of healthy adults have an index score of 100 or less as his or her best performance. Stated differently, three out of four healthy adults will have at least one index that is greater than 100. For subtests, the highest average attained score for adults in the normative sample is 13.5 with a standard deviation of 2.7. Only 13% of adults had 10 or less as their highest subtest score. Because at least 50% of examinees have at least one score in the high average range, an examinee's highest score will not represent their overall ability. The highest obtained score should not create an expectation about how well an individual should do on other measures within the battery. Additionally, high scores may be related to overall observed variability within a profile. It is important to consider that having at least one score above the mean is typical and it is very unusual for examinees in the normative sample to have a low average score as their highest level of performance.

Because most individuals have at least one score above the mean, it is a mathematical certainty that most will also have one score below the mean. The average lowest achieved index score on the WAIS–IV is 90.0 (SD = 12.3) and the average lowest achieved subtest score is 6.8 (SD = 2.2). In the normative sample, 89% of examinees have at least one scaled score below 10 on the WAIS–IV subtests and 75% have at least one index below a score of 100. If the average highest subtest scaled score is about 13 and the average lowest score is about seven, most examinees should have about a six point difference between their highest and lowest subtest scores and 20 points between their highest and lowest index scores (e.g., $110 - 90 = 20$). Statistically, using the normative data, the actual average difference between highest and lowest subtest and index scores is 6.6 and 20.4, respectively. Most examinees in the standardization sample (85%) had a difference of at least 5 points between their highest and lowest subtest scaled scores and approximately 90% have highest versus lowest index score differences of 10 points. A 10 point difference is statistically significant at the $p < 0.15$ level for any pairwise comparison for most ages; for example, VCI versus PRI (Perceptual Reasoning Index), VCI versus WMI (Working Memory Index). The base rate for a 10 point discrepancy between any two indexes varies between 22 and 28% depending on the scores compared, revealing a dramatically different base rate for individual index comparisons than for the highest versus lowest index scores. The difference of 6.6 scaled score points between highest and lowest subtest scaled scores is statistically significant at the $p < 0.05$ level for any pairwise comparison; for example, Block Design versus Vocabulary, Block Design versus Digit Span, Vocabulary versus Similarities. These results indicate that a healthy adult will have at least one statistically significant difference between a pair of indexes and/or subtests. The base rate for any specific comparison will be much lower than the base rate for the highest versus lowest difference. This discrepancy in base rates represents the impact of univariate versus multivariate base rates of difference scores.

Evaluating Overall Performance Variability

Another method for determining profile variability involves computing the standard deviation of the subtest scores around the mean subtest scores, and the standard deviation of the index scores around the mean index performance. This value represents not the extreme of variability but the *average variability* within the profile. The average standard deviation among WAIS–IV core subtests is about two scaled score points, and for index scores it is about 9 points. Stated differently, on average, subtests vary from the mean subtest scores by about 2 points and index scores vary from the mean index score by about 9 points. For most individuals, scaled scores will range ± 2 points from their mean performance (i.e., if the mean is eight, most scores will be between six and 10) and at the index level their index standard scores will vary ± 9 points from their average index score (i.e., if the mean is 90 most index scores will fall between 81 and 99). In the standardization sample, 85% of examinees have average subtest standard deviation variability of 1.5 subtest scaled scores and five index standard score points, or larger. No subject had a standard deviation of zero nor did any examinee have a highest versus lowest discrepancy of zero for either indexes or subtests. Therefore, some variability is typical of healthy controls and for most subjects a "high" degree of variability is normal.

Normative Data

In this chapter, new normative data are presented for highest score, lowest score, the difference between the highest and lowest score, and standard deviation scores from the examinee's own mean. These norms are presented on the same metric as the ability-based normative data for subtests and indexes. These norms can be used to identify greater or less than expected variability. Tables 3.1 and 3.2 provide normative data for these variability indicators for WAIS–IV subtests and indexes, respectively.

These tables are used to identify atypical profile variability or profile suppression (i.e., unusually low "highest" and "lowest" scores). For example, an examinee with a 10-point difference between his highest and lowest subtest scores has a highest versus lowest scaled score of five, indicating that only 5% of the standardization sample had a larger difference between highest and lowest scores. As seen in Table 3.1, it is considered normal (i.e., average, scaled scores = 8–12) for people to have their lowest WAIS–IV subtest score between six and eight, their highest score between 12 and 15, and their high-low subtest difference score range from 5 to 8.

To calculate the standard deviation of the subtests, the mean of the core subtest scaled scores must be identified by adding up the 10 subtest scaled scores and dividing by 10. The standard deviation is obtained by subtracting each subtest scaled score from the mean scaled score, computing the square of each subtest versus mean difference, summing the total of the squared difference scores, dividing the sum by nine, and computing the square root of that value. For an examinee

TABLE 3.1 Scaled Score Conversions for Indicators of WAIS–IV Subtest Variability

Scaled Score	Highest versus Lowest	Standard Deviation	Lowest Score	Highest Score
1	>15	>4.34		<5
2	14–15	3.98–4.33		5
3	12–13	3.66–3.97	1	6
4	11	3.35–3.65	2	7–8
5	10	3.10–3.34	3	9
6	–	2.87–3.09	4	10
7	9	2.62–2.86	5	11
8	8	2.38–2.61	–	12
9	7	2.17–2.37	6	13
10	–	2.00–2.16	7	–
11	6	1.78–1.99	–	14
12	5	1.60–1.77	8	15
13	–	1.43–1.59	9	16
14	4	1.32–1.42	10	17
15	–	1.16–1.31	–	18
16	3	0.99–1.15	11	–
17	2	0.94–0.98	12	19
18	1	0.84–0.93	–	
19	0	<0.84	>12	

Note: These norms are based on the 10 core WAIS–ICV subtests.
Copyright 2009 by Pearson, Inc. Reproduced with permission. All rights reserved.

with the subtest scaled scores of 6, 9, 10, 5, 8, 11, 9, 7, 10, and 12, the standard deviation is calculated using the steps listed below:

Step 1: sum the scaled scores,
$6 + 9 + 10 + 5 + 8 + 11 + 9 + 7 + 10 + 12 = 87$
Step 2: divide the sum by 10, $87/10 = 8.7$
Step 3: subtract each subtest score from the mean, $(6 - 8.7 = -2.7)$, $(9 - 8.7 = 0.3)$, $(10 - 8.7 = 1.3)$, $(5 - 8.7 = -3.7)$, $(8 - 8.7 = -0.7)$, $(11 - 8.7 = 2.3)$, $(9 - 8.7 = 0.3)$, $(7 - 8.7 = -1.7)$, $(10 - 8.7 = 1.3)$, $(12 - 8.7 = 3.3)$.
Step 4: square the differences, $(-2.7)^2 = 7.29$, $(0.3)^2 = 0.09$, $(1.3)^2 = 1.69$, $(-3.7)^2 = 4.81$, $(-0.7)^2 = 0.49$, $(2.3)^2 = 5.29$, $(0.3)^2 = 0.09$, $(-1.7)^2 = 2.89$, $(1.3)^2 = 1.69$, $(3.3)^2 = 10.89$

TABLE 3.2   Scaled Score Conversions for Indicators of WAIS−IV Index Variability

Scaled Score	Highest versus Lowest	Standard Deviation	Lowest Score	Highest Score
1	>53	> 22.96	<53	<63
2	47−53	21.38−22.96	53−55	63−70
3	44−46	19.55−21.37	56−60	71−76
4	41−43	17.63−19.54	61−67	77−83
5	36−40	15.90−17.62	68−71	84−89
6	32−35	14.17−15.89	72−75	90−94
7	28−31	12.57−14.16	76−80	95−99
8	25−27	10.86−12.56	81−83	100−104
9	22−24	9.38−10.85	84−88	105−108
10	18−21	7.94−9.37	89−92	109−113
11	15−17	6.60−7.93	93−96	114−117
12	13−14	5.50−6.59	97−100	118−122
13	10−12	4.55−5.49	101−104	123−126
14	9	3.70−4.54	105−107	127−131
15	7−8	2.89−3.69	108−111	132−134
16	5−6	2.22−2.88	112−114	135−138
17	4	1.83−2.21	115−117	139−141
18	3	1.50−1.82	118−119	142−146
19	<3	<1.82	>119	>146

Note: These norms are based on four core WAIS−IV Indexes.
Copyright 2009 by Pearson, Inc. Reproduced with permission. All rights reserved.

Step 5: sum the squares,
7.29 + 0.09 + 1.69 + 4.81 + 0.49 + 5.29 + 0.09 + 2.89 + 1.69 + 10.89 = 35.22
Step 6: divide the sum of squares by 9, 35.22/9 = 3.91
Step 7: calculate the square root of the average sum of squares, $\sqrt{3.91} = 1.98$
Step 8: obtain scaled score from Table 3.1, 1.98 = 11
Step 9: WAIS−IV technical manual, using standard Wechsler metrics a scaled score of 11 is a percentile rank of 63 and is in the average range.

This is the method for calculating the standard deviation of the profile. In another case, an examinee may have a subtest standard deviation of 2.83 that would be equal to a scaled score of seven indicating that their profile variability is at the 16th percentile. The interpretation for variability measures is that a high scaled score indicates low variability and a low scaled score indicates a high degree of variability. Low scores on these measures always indicate inconsistent (i.e., high variability) cognitive abilities, while high scores indicate very consistent (i.e., low variability) cognitive abilities.

The same process can be applied to deriving normative variability data for WAIS–IV Indexes. For example, a difference between the highest and lowest index of 19 points (SS = 10) would be considered average cognitive variability, while a difference of 33 points (SS = 6) would indicate a greater than expected degree of cognitive variability or low consistency in performance. Similarly, an index standard deviation of nine (SS = 10) would be considered average while a score of 16 (SS = 5) would indicate borderline level of cognitive consistency or a higher than expected level of cognitive variability.

In addition to normative data for consistency measures, Tables 3.1 and 3.2 provide information comparing the examinee's highest and lowest scores to the standardization sample. If the highest obtained score is low compared to the general population, the examinee shows a *suppressed profile* which means that the highest score is unusually low and therefore the examinee will likely have generally low scores. The lowest obtained score indicates if the examinee's worst performance is unusual compared to the general population, suggesting an usually low performance. For example, if an examinee's highest subtest scaled score is 10, this yields a scaled score of six, which is in the low average range in the normative sample, an unusual finding. Only 9% of the normative sample had a highest score on the WAIS–IV that was lower than 10. This is in contrast to the typical interpretation of a scaled score of 10, which indicates an average ability level. Similarly, if the examinees *lowest* score is a 10, that would indicate a very good performance (SS = 14), which is in the high average range. The examinees lowest score is better than 91% of the general population.

The same analysis was also performed for the 10 subtests scaled scores and five indexes of the WMS–IV Adult battery and the seven subtest scaled scores and four indexes of the WMS–IV Older Adult battery. The average highest obtained score on the WMS–IV Adult battery was 13.5 for the subtests and 110 for the indexes. The average difference between highest and lowest scores was approximately 7 points for the subtests and 17 points for the indexes. For older adults, the average difference between highest and lowest scores was 5.5 for the subtests and 7.5 for the indexes. These are smaller discrepancies than were observed for the WAIS–IV and WMS–IV adult battery which may be related to the reduced number of scores on the older adult battery. Normative data for the WMS–IV Adult and Older Adult battery are provided in

Tables 3.3–3.6. Normative data for variability in the combined WAIS–IV/WMS–IV sample are in Tables 3.7–3.10 for the adult and older adult batteries. The average highest score in the combined battery was 14.5 for subtests with an average highest versus lowest subtest score difference of 8.5 scaled score points. The average highest index score in the combined battery was 115 and the average difference between the highest and lowest index scores was 28 points. When more scores are included in the battery, the discrepancy between highest and lowest scores is larger. Also, when there are a large number of scores, it is very unusual for a healthy control not to obtain at least one subtest scaled score of 10 or more.

TABLE 3.3 Scaled Score Conversions for Indicators of WMS–IV Adult Battery Subtest Variability

Scaled Score	Highest versus Lowest	Standard deviation	Lowest Score	Highest Score
1	>15	>4.74	–	>6
2	15	4.32–4.74	–	6
3	13–14	4.14–4.31	1	7
4	12	3.79–4.13	–	8
5	11	3.41–3.78	2	9
6	10	3.07–3.40	3	10
7	9	2.87–3.06	4	11
8	8	2.53–2.86	5	12
9	–	2.30–2.52	6	13
10	7	2.06–2.29	7	–
11	6	1.84–2.05	–	14
12	5	1.64–1.83	8	15
13	–	1.48–1.63	9	16
14	4	1.29–1.47	10	17
15	–	1.17–1.28	11	–
16	3	1.07–1.16	–	18
17	–	0.95–1.06	12	19
18	–	0.84–0.94	–	–
19	<3	<0.84	13	–

Note: These norms are based on the 10 core subtests of the WMS–IV Adult battery.
Copyright 2009 by Pearson, Inc. Reproduced with permission. All rights reserved.

TABLE 3.4 Scaled Score Conversions for Indicators of WMS–IV Adult Battery Index Variability

Scaled Score	Highest versus Lowest	Standard Deviation	Lowest Score	Highest Score
1	>50	>19.14	<54	<69
2	48–50	18.94–19.14	54–57	69–73
3	44–47	17.23–18.93	58–62	74–77
4	38–43	14.95–17.22	63–65	78–82
5	35–37	13.55–14.94	66–69	83–87
6	30–34	11.72–13.54	70–74	88–93
7	26–29	10.26–11.71	75–80	94–97
8	22–25	8.57–10.25	81–84	98–102
9	19–21	7.42–8.56	85–88	103–107
10	16–18	6.30–7.41	89–93	108–112
11	13–15	5.22–6.29	94–97	113–116
12	11–12	4.39–5.21	98–102	117–122
13	9–10	3.61–4.38	103–106	123–125
14	8	3.03–3.60	107–111	126–129
15	6–7	2.41–3.02	112–115	130–132
16	5	1.95–2.40	116–118	133–134
17	4	1.58–1.94	119–121	135–139
18	3	1.14–1.57	122–123	140–148
19	<3	<1.14	>123	>148

Note: These norms are based on the five core index scores of the WMS–IV Adult battery.
Copyright 2009 by Pearson, Inc. Reproduced with permission. All rights reserved.

Factors Associated with Greater or Lesser Performance Variability

The results presented in the previous section are based on the entire standardization sample. However, there is reason to believe that score variability would not be consistent across all groups or ability levels. For instance, if an examinee's highest subtest scaled score is seven then the biggest discrepancy between the highest and lowest score possible is only 6 points, which would be considered an average degree of variability on the WAIS–IV. Factors related to profile variability can be evaluated in a number of ways. Background variables, such as

TABLE 3.5   Scaled Score Conversions for Indicators of WMS–IV Older Adult
Battery Subtest Variability

Scaled Score	Highest versus Lowest	Standard Deviation	Lowest Score	Highest Score
1	>12	>4.73	–	>6
2	12	4.36–4.72	1	6
3	11	3.93–4.35	–	7
4	10	3.51–3.92	2	8
5	9	3.21–3.50	3	9
6	–	3.00–3.20	–	–
7	8	2.73–2.99	4	10
8	7	2.43–2.72	5	11
9	6	2.14–2.42	6	12
10	–	1.90–2.13	7	13
11	5	1.68–1.89	8	14
12	4	1.46–1.67	9	–
13	–	1.27–1.45	10	15
14	3	1.11–1.26	–	16
15	–	0.95–1.10	11	17
16	2	0.90–0.94	12	–
17	–	0.76–0.89	–	18
18	–	0.70–0.75	13	–
19	<2	<0.70	>13	19

Note: These norms are based on the seven core subtest of the WMS–IV older adult battery.
Copyright 2009 by Pearson, Inc. Reproduced with permission. All rights reserved.

education level, can be correlated with score variability measures.
Additionally, ability level measures can be correlated with profile variability, and variability measures can be compared in clinical groups.
Table 3.11 presents correlation coefficients for age, education, and highest performance level with measures of WAIS–IV performance
variability.

There is a statistically significant relationship between age, education level and measures of performance variability. Education also significantly correlates with the highest and lowest obtained index and subtest scores (Tables 3.12 and 3.13). While the correlation between age and

TABLE 3.6   Scaled Score Conversions for Indicators of WMS–IV Older Adult Battery Index Variability

Scaled Score	Highest versus Lowest	Standard Deviation	Lowest Score	Highest Score
1	>28	> 14.00	<55	<69
2	24–28	12.10–14.00	55	69
3	21–23	10.69–12.09	56–62	70–74
4	19–20	9.61–10.68	63–68	75–77
5	17–18	8.62–9.60	69–74	78–81
6	15–16	7.51–8.61	75–77	82–86
7	13–14	6.51–7.50	78–82	87–92
8	11–12	5.51–6.50	83–88	93–96
9	9–10	4.58–5.50	89–93	97–101
10	7–8	3.61–4.57	94–99	102–106
11	6	3.00–3.60	100–102	107–111
12	5	2.31–2.99	103–108	112–116
13	4	2.00–2.30	109–112	117–121
14	3	1.52–1.99	113–117	122–126
15	2	1.00–1.51	118–122	127–132
16	1	0.58–0.99	123–127	133–136
17	–	–	128–130	137–139
18	0	<0.58	131–134	140–141
19	–	–	>134	>141

Note: These norms are based on the four core Indexes of the WMS–IV older adult battery.
Copyright 2009 by Pearson, Inc. Reproduced with permission. All rights reserved.

variability is statistically significant, the relationship is very small. Education level has a moderate association with both variability and overall ability. The subtest and index highest scores have significant correlations with variability and are generally larger than the education effects. Based on these correlations, the level of performance variability is primarily associated with the examinees highest score (i.e., education is related to both variability and highest score so the effects of education are likely due to the impact on highest achieved score). The negative correlation indicates that the higher the highest score, the greater the variability (e.g., variability scores are scaled so lower scores equal more variability).

TABLE 3.7 Scaled Score Conversions for Indicators of Combined WAIS–IV/ WMS–IV Adult Battery Subtest Variability

Scaled Score	Highest versus Lowest	Standard Deviation	Lowest Score	Highest Score
1	>15	>4.34	–	<8
2	–	3.99–4.34	–	–
3	15	3.70–3.98	1	8
4	14	3.42–3.69	–	9
5	13	3.21–3.41	2	10
6	12	2.91–3.20	3	11
7	11	2.72–2.90	4	12
8	10	2.51–2.71	–	13
9	9	2.35–2.50	5	14
10	–	2.18–2.34	6	–
11	8	2.02–2.17	–	15
12	7	1.87–2.01	7	16
13	–	1.76–1.86	8	17
14	6	1.62–1.75	9	18
15	–	1.50–1.61	–	–
16	5	1.36–1.49	10	19
17	–	1.29–1.35	11	–
18	4	1.15–1.28	–	–
19	<4	<1.15	<11	–

Note: These norms are based on the 20 core subtests of the combined WAIS–IV and WMS–IV adult batteries.
Copyright 2009 by Pearson, Inc. Reproduced with permission. All rights reserved.

The WMS–IV data show similar effects for age, education, and highest score on test variability. In general, the highest obtained score has a significant effect on profile variability; therefore, adjusting the variability scores by the highest score may yield better results and more accurately represent performance variability.

Performance Variability in Other Samples

Most of the clinical data related to performance variability is presented later in this book in the chapters devoted to various clinical

TABLE 3.8 Scaled Score Conversions for Indicators of Combined WAIS−IV/WMS−IV Adult Battery Index Variability

Scaled Score	Highest versus Lowest	Standard Deviation	Lowest Score	Highest Score
1	>62	>20.24	<54	<75
2	55−62	19.69−20.24	54−56	75−80
3	53−54	17.22−19.68	57−59	81−85
4	49−52	15.74−17.21	60−63	86−90
5	45−48	14.44−15.73	64−67	91−95
6	40−44	13.34−14.43	68−71	96−99
7	37−39	11.90−13.33	72−76	100−103
8	33−36	10.72−11.89	77−80	104−108
9	30−32	9.65−10.71	81−84	109−112
10	27−29	8.64−9.64	85−88	113−117
11	24−26	7.65−8.63	89−92	118−122
12	21−23	6.74−7.64	93−96	123−126
13	18−20	5.97−6.73	97−100	127−130
14	16−17	5.34−5.96	101−103	131−133
15	14−15	4.65−5.33	104−108	134−135
16	12−13	3.90−4.64	109−111	136−138
17	10−11	3.70−3.89	112−115	139−142
18	9	3.21−3.69	116	143−148
19	<9	<3.21	>116	>148

These norms are based on the nine core indexes of the combined WAIS−IV and WMS−IV adult batteries.
Copyright 2009 by Pearson, Inc. Reproduced with permission. All rights reserved.

conditions. In this section, variability data is presented for borderline, mild, and moderate intellectual disability; gifted; and left and right temporal lobectomy groups. The first four groups show the effect of general intellectual ability level on variability measures. Temporal lobectomy groups would be expected to have domains of spared and impaired cognitive functions, which should result in greater than normal performance variability. Variability data for Alzheimer's disease, mild cognitive impairment, moderate to severe traumatic brain injury, schizophrenia, autism, and Asperger's disorder are presented in Chapters 9 (Assessing Cognition in Older Adults with the WAIS−IV,

TABLE 3.9   Scaled Score Conversions for Indicators of Combined WAIS−IV/
WMS−IV Older Adult Battery Subtest Variability

Scaled Score	Highest versus Lowest	Standard Deviation	Lowest Score	Highest Score
1	>14	>4.63	−	<8
2	14	4.02−4.63	−	−
3	13	3.56−4.01	1	8
4	12	3.38−3.55	−	9
5	11	3.07−3.37	2	10
6	−	2.87−3.06	3	11
7	10	2.66−2.86	4	−
8	9	2.48−2.65	5	12
9	−	2.28−2.47	−	13
10	8	2.12−2.27	6	14
11	7	1.97−2.11	7	15
12	−	1.77−1.96	8	−
13	6	1.64−1.76	−	16
14	5	1.53−1.63	9	17
15	−	1.38−1.52	10	18
16	4	1.28−1.37	−	−
17	−	1.20−1.27	11	19
18	−	1.05−1.19	−	−
19	<4	<1.05	>11	−

These norms are based on the 17 core subtests of the WAIS−IV and WMS−IV older adult batteries.
Copyright 2009 by Pearson, Inc. Reproduced with permission. All rights reserved.

WMS−IV, and ACS), 10 (Using the WAIS−IV/WMS−IV/ACS
Following Moderate-Severe Traumatic Brain Injury), and 11 (Assessing
Individual's with Psychiatric and Developmental Disorders). Table 3.14
presents descriptive statistics for the WAIS−IV, WMS−IV, and combined WAIS−IV/WMS−IV variability measures for the gifted and clinical samples. WMS−IV data is not available for the Gifted or Borderline
samples.

Gifted examinees show superior performance on the highest and
lowest obtained WAIS−IV subtest and index scores, which is consistent
with their classification as having superior cognitive abilities.
Variability indicators (e.g., subtest/index highest vs. lowest score and

TABLE 3.10 Scaled Score Conversions for Indicators of Combined WAIS−IV/ WMS−IV Older Adult Battery Index Variability

Scaled Score	Highest versus Lowest	Standard Deviation	Lowest Score	Highest Score
1	>62	>25.62	<55	<77
2	60−62	24.10−25.62	55	77−80
3	53−59	18.43−24.09	56−59	81−84
4	45−52	16.34−18.42	60−62	85−88
5	40−44	13.98−16.33	63−67	89−92
6	37−39	12.64−13.97	68−72	93−96
7	33−36	11.42−12.63	73−76	97−101
8	29−32	10.26−11.41	77−80	102−104
9	26−28	9.03−10.25	81−85	105−109
10	23−25	8.11−9.02	86−89	110−115
11	21−22	7.32−8.10	90−93	116−119
12	18−20	6.36−7.31	94−97	120−122
13	15−17	5.31−6.35	98−100	123−126
14	13−14	4.57−5.30	101−104	127−132
15	11−12	3.92−4.56	105−107	133−135
16	10	3.67−3.91	108−110	136−137
17	9	3.37−3.66	111−112	138
18	8	3.15−3.36	113−114	139
19	<8	<3.15	>114	>139

Note: These norms are based on the eight core indexes of the WAIS−IV and WMS−IV older adult batteries.
Copyright 2009 by Pearson, Inc. Reproduced with permission. All rights reserved.

subtest/index standard deviation), in this group, were in the average range (e.g., SS = 8.4 to 8.6); however, they had the most performance variability of all the samples (recall that lower scaled scores indicate more variability). The borderline, mild, and moderate intellectual disability samples have very low highest and lowest scores, which is consistent with their low cognitive functioning. Observe that as intellectual disability increases, profile consistency increases (e.g., highest vs. lowest WAIS−IV subtests variability SS = 12.8, 13.1, and 15.3 for borderline, mild, and moderate intellectual disability, respectively) or in other

TABLE 3.11   Correlation of Age, Education, and Subtest/Index Highest Scores with WAIS–IV Variability Measure Scaled Scores

WAIS–IV Variability	Age	Education	Subtest Highest	Index Highest
Subtest high vs. low	**0.06**	−0.08	**−0.62**	–
Subtest standard deviation	**0.07**	−0.08	**−0.59**	–
Subtest highest	0.03	**0.41**	–	–
Subtest lowest	0.02	**0.45**	**0.64**	–
Index high vs. low	**0.06**	−0.05	–	**−0.49**
Index standard deviation	**0.07**	−0.05	–	**−0.49**
Index highest	0.03	**0.44**	–	–
Index lowest	0.01	**0.47**	–	**0.74**

Note: Statistically significant correlations ($p < 0.05$) are in bold.
Copyright 2009 by Pearson, Inc. Reproduced with permission. All rights reserved.

TABLE 3.12   Correlation of Age, Education, and Subtest/Index Highest Scores with WMS–IV Adult Battery Variability Measure Scaled Scores

WMS–IV Variability	Age	Education	Subtest Highest	Index Highest
Subtest high vs. low	**0.21**	− 0.04	**− 0.41**	–
Subtest standard deviation	**0.10**	0.02	**− 0.35**	–
Subtest highest	0.08	**0.30**	–	–
Subtest lowest	0.10	**0.35**	**0.59**	–
Index high vs. low	**0.17**	− 0.05	–	**− 0.32**
Index standard deviation	**0.11**	− 0.03	–	**− 0.31**
Index highest	0.03	**0.37**	–	–
Index lowest	0.06	**0.34**	–	**0.78**

Note: Statistically significant correlations ($p < 0.05$) are in bold.
Copyright 2009 by Pearson, Inc. Reproduced with permission. All rights reserved.

words variability decreases. Because of their low ability, these performance profiles are suppressed, resulting in low variability. On the WAIS–IV, the left and right lobectomy groups have low average (e.g., SS <8 on subtest highest and lowest scores) highest and lowest scores and average variability (e.g., SS >7 and <12 on highest vs. lowest and standard deviation measures). The results combining the WAIS–IV and WMS–IV are similar to those for the WAIS–IV alone; however, there is

TABLE 3.13   Correlation of Age, Education, and Subtest/Index Highest Scores with WMS–IV Older Adult Battery Variability Measure Scaled Scores

WMS–IV Variability	Age	Education	Subtest Highest Score	Index Highest Score
Subtest high vs. low	0.05	0.04	**− 0.36**	–
Subtest standard deviation	0.06	0.05	**− 0.35**	–
Subtest highest	0.03	**0.33**	–	–
Subtest lowest	0.03	**0.31**	**0.64**	–
Index high vs. low	**0.33**	− 0.09	–	**− 0.29**
Index standard deviation	**0.26**	− 0.13	–	**− 0.28**
Index highest	0.09	**0.39**	–	–
Index lowest	0.07	**0.33**	–	**0.84**

Note: Statistically significant correlations ($p < 0.05$) are in bold
Copyright 2009 by Pearson, Inc. Reproduced with permission. All rights reserved.

TABLE 3.14   WAIS–IV/WMS–IV Variability Measures in Gifted and Clinical Samples

Variability Measures	Gifted	Borderline IQ	Mild Intellectual Deficiency	Moderate Intellectual Deficiency	Left Temporal Lobectomy	Right Temporal Lobectomy
WAIS–IV Subtest High vs. Low	8.5 (2.4)	12.8 (3.2)	13.1 (2.4)	15.3 (1.6)	10.2 (2.7)	10.4 (3.5)
WAIS–IV Subtest Standard Deviation	8.6 (2.7)	13.0 (3.5)	13.5 (2.5)	15.7 (2.0)	9.7 (2.6)	10.7 (3.4)
WAIS–IV Subtest Highest Score	14.8 (1.7)	4.8 (1.5)	3.1 (1.4)	1.5 (0.8)	7.3 (3.1)	8.1 (3.4)
WAIS–IV Subtest Lowest Score	14.2 (2.4)	5.8 (1.7)	3.7 (1.0)	3.1 (0.4)	6.9 (2.2)	7.9 (2.7)

(Continued)

TABLE 3.14 (Continued)

Variability Measures	Gifted	Borderline IQ	Mild Intellectual Deficiency	Moderate Intellectual Deficiency	Left Temporal Lobectomy	Right Temporal Lobectomy
WAIS–IV Index High vs. Low	8.6 (2.8)	11.4 (3.1)	11.9 (2.3)	14.6 (2.7)	9.7 (2.3)	10.4 (3.4)
WAIS–IV Index Standard Deviation	8.4 (2.8)	11.7 (3.0)	12.0 (2.4)	14.7 (2.7)	9.8 (2.0)	10.6 (3.3)
WAIS–IV Index Highest Score	15.0 (2.1)	5.0 (1.6)	2.8 (1.4)	1.6 (1.0)	7.7 (2.7)	7.9 (3.0)
WAIS–IV Index Lowest Score	14.4 (2.5)	5.0 (1.7)	2.6 (1.4)	1.6 (1.0)	7.3 (3.1)	7.9 (2.5)
WMS–IV Subtest High vs. Low	–	–	10.1 (3.1)	14.0 (3.5)	9.8 (2.4)	10.5 (2.9)
WMS–IV Subtest Standard Deviation	–	–	9.9 (3.1)	13.5 (3.6)	8.8 (2.6)	10.2 (3.0)
WMS–IV Subtest Highest Score	–	–	4.2 (2.1)	2.0 (1.6)	7.2 (2.7)	7.1 (2.4)
WMS–IV Subtest Lowest Score	–	–	3.6 (1.2)	3.2 (0.7)	6.9 (2.8)	7.4 (3.1)
WMS–IV Index High vs. Low	–	–	9.8 (2.9)	13.1 (3.5)	8.9 (4.8)	9.9 (3.5)
WMS–IV Index Standard Deviation	–	–	9.6 (2.8)	12.8 (3.5)	8.2 (4.3)	9.5 (3.0)

(Continued)

TABLE 3.14   (Continued)

Variability Measures	Gifted	Borderline IQ	Mild Intellectual Deficiency	Moderate Intellectual Deficiency	Left Temporal Lobectomy	Right Temporal Lobectomy
WMS–IV Index Highest Score	–	–	3.0 (1.9)	1.3 (0.9)	8.0 (3.4)	7.3 (3.1)
WMS–IV Index Lowest Score	–	–	2.4 (1.6)	1.3 (1.0)	6.5 (3.5)	6.9 (3.0)
WAIS–IV/ WMS–IV Subtest High vs. Low	–	–	12.0 (2.9)	16.1 (3.3)	10.0 (2.5)	10.6 (2.8)
WAIS–IV/ WMS–IV Subtest Standard Deviation	–	–	11.9 (2.7)	15.6 (3.2)	8.6 (3.1)	10.2 (2.8)
WAIS–IV/ WMS–IV Subtest Highest Score	–	–	3.7 (1.8)	1.6 (1.5)	7.6 (2.7)	7.9 (3.3)
WAIS–IV/ WMS–IV Subtest Lowest Score	–	–	4.3 (0.6)	3.0 (0.0)	7.1 (3.3)	7.9 (3.5)
WAIS–IV/ WMS–IV Index High vs. Low	–	–	11.2 (2.7)	13.9 (2.8)	8.1 (3.4)	9.8 (2.7)
WAIS–IV/ WMS–IV Index Standard Deviation	–	–	11.3 (3.0)	13.8 (2.9)	8.2 (3.2)	9.9 (2.7)
WAIS–IV/ WMS–IV Index Highest Score	–	–	2.4 (1.2)	1.2 (0.6)	8.1 (3.0)	7.9 (3.2)

(Continued)

WAIS-IV, WMS-IV, AND ACS

TABLE 3.14   (Continued)

Variability Measures	Gifted	Borderline IQ	Mild Intellectual Deficiency	Moderate Intellectual Deficiency	Left Temporal Lobectomy	Right Temporal Lobectomy
WAIS–IV/ WMS–IV Index Lowest Score	–	–	2.4 (1.5)	1.1 (0.3)	6.9 (3.4)	7.6 (3.3)

Note: Variability scores expressed in scaled score units where high scores indicate consistent performance among measures and low scores indicate a high degree of cognitive variability.
Copyright 2009 by Pearson, Inc. Reproduced with permission. All rights reserved.

more variability in the left temporal lobectomy group when both batteries are considered together. The right and left temporal lobectomy profiles are somewhat suppressed due to low average "highest" scores.

These results strongly suggest that examinees with low "highest" scores will show *reduced performance variability*. The reduced performance variability is illustrated by high scaled scores on the highest versus lowest and standard deviation variability measures. In many clinical groups, the highest score will be low compared to normal controls and subsequently they will show *less score variability*. These results run contrary to the belief that clinical samples should show more variability in cognitive functioning than healthy controls. Therefore, to accurately evaluate profile variability in clinical samples, it is important to control for low "highest" scores.

Variability by Highest Score

Profile variability is significantly correlated with the person's highest obtained subtest and index score. Thus, gifted individuals show more performance variability than other samples. In contrast, intellectually impaired groups show less cognitive variability than healthy controls. Applying basic mathematic principles, it is easy to understand why having a low "highest" score would limit the amount of variability that could be observed. If the highest score is an eight, then the maximum highest versus lowest difference is 7 points, which is in the average range. Tables 3.15–3.24 provide normative data by highest score level.

The normative data clearly illustrate the effect of the highest achieved score in profile variability. On the WAIS–IV subtests, for individuals having a highest score in the 16–19 range, the average difference between highest and lowest scores is 8.5 scaled score points. By comparison, if the highest score is in the 10–11 range, the average

TABLE 3.15 WAIS–IV Subtest Variability Measures Scaled Scores by Highest Subtest Standard Score

	Highest vs. Lowest Subtest Scaled Score by Highest Score						Subtest Standard Deviation by Highest Score					
Scaled Score	<8*	8–9	10–11	12–13	14–15	16–19	<8*	8–9	10–11	12–13	14–15	16–19
1	—	—	>9	>10	>11	>15	>2.30	>2.70	>3.26	>3.17	>3.94	>5.09
2	—	—	—	10	—	—	2.13–2.30	2.53–2.70	2.94–3.26	3.09–3.17	3.78–3.94	4.74–5.09
3	—	8	9	—	11	15	2.01–2.12	2.50–2.52	2.66–2.93	2.98–3.08	3.46–3.77	4.24–4.73
4	—	—	8	9	—	13–14	1.87–2.00	2.37–2.49	2.47–2.65	2.88–2.97	3.33–3.45	3.87–4.23
5	6	7	—	—	10	12	1.84–1.86	2.20–2.36	2.33–2.46	2.74–2.87	3.05–3.32	3.63–3.86
6	—	—	7	8	9	—	1.66–1.83	2.00–2.19	2.22–2.31	2.51–2.73	2.83–3.04	3.29–3.62
7	—	6	—	—	—	11	1.60–1.65	1.85–1.99	2.08–2.21	2.36–2.50	2.63–2.82	3.13–3.28
8	5	—	—	7	8	10	1.48–1.59	1.70–1.84	1.95–2.07	2.21–2.34	2.45–2.62	2.95–3.12
9	—	5	6	—	—	9	1.43–1.47	1.57–1.69	1.79–1.94	2.06–2.20	2.28–2.44	2.72–2.94
10	4	—	—	6	7	—	1.37–1.42	1.43–1.56	1.65–1.78	1.90–2.05	2.11–2.27	2.54–2.71
11	—	4	5	—	6	8	1.25–1.36	1.34–1.42	1.52–1.64	1.75–1.89	1.91–2.10	2.32–2.53
12	—	—	—	5	—	7	1.08–1.24	1.25–1.33	1.42–1.51	1.60–1.74	1.75–1.90	2.13–2.32
13	3	—	—	—	5	—	1.03–1.07	1.15–1.24	1.27–1.41	1.45–1.59	1.64–1.74	1.91–2.12
14	—	3	4	4	—	6	0.94–1.02	0.99–1.14	1.15–1.26	1.34–1.44	1.45–1.63	1.77–1.90
15	2	—	—	—	4	5	0.79–0.93	0.95–0.98	1.03–1.14	1.18–1.33	1.29–1.44	1.63–1.76
16	—	—	3	—	—	—	0.70–0.78	0.92–0.94	0.95–1.02	1.07–1.17	1.17–1.28	1.49–1.62
17	1	2	—	3	3	—	0.63–0.69	0.82–0.91	0.84–0.94	0.95–1.06	1.06–1.16	1.35–1.48
18	—	1	—	—	—	4	0.60–0.62	0.67–0.81	0.72–0.83	0.92–0.94	1.03–1.05	1.25–1.34
19	0	0	<3	<3	<3	<4	<0.60	<0.67	<0.72	<0.92	<1.03	<1.25

*No one in the normative sample achieved a highest scaled score of less than three and only 3.9% had highest scores less than eight.

Note: Column headers represent the examinees highest obtained subtest score.

Copyright 2009 by Pearson, Inc. Reproduced with permission. All rights reserved.

TABLE 3.16 WAIS–IV Index Variability Measures Scaled Scores by Highest Index Standard Score

	Highest vs. Lowest Index Score by Highest Score						Index Standard Deviation By Highest Score					
Scaled Score	<90*	90–99	100–109	110–119	120–129	>129	<90*	90–99	100–109	110–119	120–129	>129
1	>30	>38	>40	>55	>62	>72	>14.00	>18.00	>18.25	>26.08	>27.98	>29.94
2	30	34–38	40	44–55	50–61	72	13.78–14.00	17.15–18.00	17.33–18.25	20.04–26.08	22.96–27.98	23.07–29.94
3	29	30–33	35–39	41–43	46–49	52–71	13.33–13.77	15.42–17.14	15.85–17.32	18.46–20.03	21.49–22.95	22.59–23.06
4	28	27–29	33–34	38–40	43–45	47–51	12.29–13.32	13.34–15.41	14.55–15.84	16.88–18.45	19.81–21.48	21.38–22.58
5	26–27	25–26	30–32	36–37	41–42	46	11.18–12.28	12.40–13.33	13.23–14.54	15.31–16.87	17.42–19.80	19.74–21.37
6	22–25	23–24	27–29	32–35	36–40	42–45	10.02–11.17	10.89–12.39	12.12–13.22	14.01–15.30	15.88–17.41	18.79–19.73
7	19–21	21–22	24–26	28–31	33–35	40–41	8.43–10.01	10.13–10.88	10.47–12.11	12.63–14.00	14.25–15.87	17.39–18.78
8	17–18	18–20	21–23	25–27	30–32	37–39	7.59–8.42	9.25–10.12	9.29–10.46	10.87–12.62	13.23–14.24	16.08–17.38
9	15–16	16–17	19–20	22–24	27–29	33–36	6.60–7.58	8.06–9.24	8.25–9.28	9.57–10.86	12.04–13.22	14.48–16.07
10	13–14	14–15	16–18	19–21	24–26	29–32	5.89–6.59	6.95–8.05	6.98–8.24	8.30–9.56	10.75–12.03	12.97–14.47
11	11–12	12–13	13–15	16–18	21–23	26–28	4.86–5.88	5.38–6.94	5.68–6.97	7.07–8.29	9.42–10.74	11.35–12.98
12	9–10	10–11	11–12	14–15	18–20	24–25	4.08–4.85	4.49–5.37	4.79–5.67	5.91–7.06	7.87–9.41	10.21–11.34
13	8	9	9–10	12–13	16–17	21–23	3.40–4.07	3.94–4.48	4.04–4.78	5.07–5.90	6.70–7.86	9.03–10.20
14	6–7	7–8	8	10–11	13–15	17–20	2.94–3.39	3.16–3.92	3.46–4.03	4.24–5.06	5.74–6.69	7.68–9.02
15	5	6	6–7	8–9	11–12	14–16	2.22–2.93	2.35–3.15	2.65–3.45	3.40–4.23	4.92–5.73	6.08–7.67
16	4	5	5	7	8–10	13	1.91–2.21	2.03–2.34	2.06–2.64	2.87–3.39	3.56–4.91	5.32–6.07
17	3	3–4	3–4	5–6	6–7	11–12	1.29–1.90	1.29–2.02	1.50–2.05	1.83–2.86	2.16–3.55	4.00–5.31
18	1–2	2	2	4	5	8–10	1.26–1.28	1.26–1.28	1.26–1.49	1.49–1.82	1.84–2.15	3.83–3.99
19	0	0–1	0–1	<4	<5	<8	<1.26	<1.26	<1.26	<1.49	<1.84	<3.83

*Only 7% of the normative sample had highest index scores less than 90.

Note: Column headers represent highest obtained index score.

Copyright 2009 by Pearson, Inc. Reproduced with permission. All rights reserved.

TABLE 3.17 WMS–IV Adult Battery Subtest Variability Measures Scaled Scores by Highest Subtest Scaled Score

Scaled Score	Highest vs. Lowest Subtest Scaled Score by Highest Score						Subtest Standard Deviation By Highest Score					
	<8*	8–9*	10–11	12–13	14–15	16–19	<8*	8–9*	10–11	12–13	14–15	16–19
1					>13	>16	>2.83	>3.45	>3.69	>4.22	>4.34	>5.7
2				12		16	2.63–2.83	3.15–3.45	3.40–3.69	4.14–4.21	4.31–4.33	5.21–5.69
3			10		13	15	2.46–2.62	2.84–3.14	3.36–3.39	3.78–4.13	4.13–4.30	4.74–5.20
4				11	12		2.33–2.45	2.63–2.83	3.27–3.35	3.41–3.77	3.68–4.12	4.30–4.73
5		8	9	10	11	13–14	2.07–2.32	2.46–2.62	2.80–3.26	3.06–3.40	3.41–3.67	4.06–4.29
6	6		8	9	10	12	2.00–2.06	2.33–2.45	2.55–2.79	2.90–3.05	3.13–3.40	3.74–4.05
7		7			9	11	1.89–1.99	2.07–2.32	2.37–2.54	2.60–2.89	2.85–3.12	3.35–3.73
8			7	8		10	1.57–1.88	2.02–2.06	2.22–2.36	2.42–2.59	2.62–2.84	2.91–3.34
9	5	6	6	7	8	9	1.45–1.56	1.83–2.01	2.02–2.21	2.17–2.41	2.35–2.61	2.73–2.90
10		5			7	8	1.34–1.44	1.71–1.82	1.87–2.01	1.99–2.16	2.17–2.34	2.49–2.72
11	4		5	6	6		1.29–1.33	1.57–1.70	1.62–1.86	1.79–1.98	1.91–2.16	2.30–2.48
12				5		7	1.15–1.28	1.43–1.56	1.48–1.61	1.64–1.78	1.71–1.90	1.99–2.29
13		4	4		5	6	1.10–1.14	1.26–1.42	1.26–1.47	1.49–1.64	1.51–1.70	1.78–1.98
14	3			4			0.95–0.99	1.20–1.25	1.20–1.25	1.29–1.48	1.35–1.50	1.64–1.77
15		3	3		4	5	0.89–0.94	1.10–1.19	1.14–1.19	1.16–1.28	1.20–1.34	1.48–1.63
16	2			3			0.73–0.88	0.97–0.99	0.97–1.13	1.06–1.15	1.08–1.19	1.40–1.47
17		2	2		3	4	0.67–0.72	0.73–0.96	0.73–0.96	0.84–1.05	0.99–1.07	1.37–1.39
18	1							0.67–0.72	0.67–0.72	0.78–0.83	0.95–0.98	1.35–1.36
19	0	<2	<2	<3	<3	<4	<0.67	<0.67	<0.67	<0.77	<0.95	<1.35

*Only 1.4% of the normative sample had highest scores <8 and only 9.6% had scores between 8–9.

Note: Column headers represent the examinees highest obtained subtest score.

Copyright 2009 by Pearson, Inc. Reproduced with permission. All rights reserved.

TABLE 3.18 WMS–IV Adult Battery Index Variability Measures Scaled Scores by Highest Index Standard Score

Scaled Score	Highest vs. Lowest Index Score by Highest Score						Index Standard Deviation By Highest Score					
	<90*	90–99	100–109	110–119	120–129	>129	<90*	90–99	100–109	110–119	120–129	>129
1	>30	>38	>50	>50	>50	>50	>15.05	>16.00	>18.93	>18.93	>19.49	>19.49
2	28–30	38	46–50	49–50	49–50	50	12.90–15.05	15.58–16.00	18.27–18.92	18.74–18.93	19.43–19.49	19.43–19.42
3	27	29–37	38–45	45–48	46–48	49	11.72–12.89	14.92–15.57	15.06–18.26	17.53–18.73	19.14–19.42	19.14–19.42
4	23–26	28	34–37	39–44	43–45	45–48	9.44–11.71	11.74–14.91	12.90–15.05	15.19–17.52	17.23–19.13	18.56–19.13
5	21–22	26–27	30–33	36–38	38–42	40–44	8.59–9.43	10.33–11.73	11.72–12.89	14.13–15.18	14.95–17.22	16.09–18.55
6	20	23–25	26–29	32–35	35–37	38–39	8.02–8.58	9.31–10.32	10.50–11.71	12.30–14.12	13.35–14.94	14.71–16.08
7	18–19	20–22	23–25	27–31	31–34	34–37	6.88–8.01	8.05–9.30	9.36–10.49	10.76–12.29	11.72–13.34	13.85–14.70
8	15–17	18–19	20–22	23–26	27–30	32–33	5.89–6.87	6.98–8.04	7.83–9.35	9.24–10.75	10.69–11.71	12.34–13.84
9	14	15–17	18–19	20–22	22–26	28–30	5.36–5.88	5.81–6.97	7.06–7.82	7.95–9.23	8.79–10.68	10.94–12.33
10	12–13	12–14	15–17	17–19	19–21	23–27	4.51–5.35	4.92–5.80	5.98–7.05	6.83–7.94	7.64–8.78	9.10–10.93
11	10–11	11	13–14	14–16	16–18	19–22	3.96–4.50	4.56–4.91	5.17–5.97	5.54–6.82	6.61–7.63	7.60–9.09
12	9	9–10	11–12	12–13	13–15	17–18	3.39–3.95	3.65–4.55	4.15–5.16	4.83–5.53	5.55–6.60	6.91–7.59
13	8	8	9–10	11	11–12	15–16	3.11–3.38	3.16–3.64	3.36–4.14	4.04–4.82	4.55–5.54	6.06–6.90
14	6–7	6–7	6–8	9–10	9–10	14	2.49–3.10	2.49–3.15	2.59–3.35	3.63–4.03	3.56–4.54	5.07–6.05
15	5	5	5	7–8	7–8	12–13	1.95–2.48	1.95–2.48	1.95–2.58	3.08–3.62	2.79–3.55	4.71–5.06
16	4	4	4	6	6	11	1.82–1.94	1.82–1.94	1.82–1.94	2.28–3.07	2.39–2.78	4.64–4.70
17	3	3	3	5	5	8–10	1.14–1.81	1.14–1.81	1.14–1.81	1.92–2.27	2.24–2.38	3.21–4.63
18	–	–	–	4	4	7	1.10–1.13	1.10–1.13	1.10–1.13	1.49–1.91	1.82–2.23	2.23–3.20
19	<3	<3	<3	<4	<4	<7	<1.10	<1.10	<1.10	<1.49	<1.82	<2.23

*Only 8.3% of the normative sample had a highest index score below 90.

Note: Column headers represent highest obtained index score.

Copyright 2009 by Pearson, Inc. Reproduced with permission. All rights reserved.

TABLE 3.19 WMS–IV Older Adult Battery Subtest Variability Measures Scaled Scores by Highest Index Standard Score

	Highest vs. Lowest Subtest Scaled Score by Highest Score						Subtest Standard Deviation By Highest Score					
Scaled Score	<8*	8–9	10–11	12–13	14–15	16–19	<8*	8–9	10–11	12–13	14–15	16–19
1	–	–	10	12	13–14	14–18	>3.30	>3.30	>3.64	>4.36	>4.73	>4.80
2	–	8	–	–	12	–	3.03–3.30	3.03–3.30	3.36–3.64	3.94–4.36	3.99–4.73	4.39–4.80
3	–	–	9	11	11	13	2.76–3.02	2.76–3.02	3.25–3.35	3.83–3.93	3.71–3.98	4.25–4.38
4	–	7	–	10	10	12	2.71–2.75	2.71–2.75	3.22–3.24	3.53–3.82	3.55–3.70	3.99–4.24
5	–	–	8	9	–	11	2.62–2.70	2.62–2.70	2.81–3.21	3.21–3.52	3.27–3.54	3.95–3.98
6	6	–	–	8	9	10	2.41–2.61	2.41–2.61	2.51–2.80	2.97–3.20	3.02–3.26	3.34–3.94
7	–	6	7	–	8	9	2.29–2.40	2.29–2.40	2.43–2.50	2.71–2.96	2.85–3.01	3.21–3.33
8	–	–	6	7	–	–	2.04–2.28	2.04–2.28	2.14–2.42	2.37–2.70	2.61–2.84	3.04–3.20
9	5	5	–	6	7	8	1.90–2.03	1.90–2.03	1.91–2.13	2.12–2.36	2.27–2.60	2.67–3.03
10	–	–	5	–	6	7	1.62–1.89	1.62–1.89	1.77–1.90	1.77–2.11	2.08–2.26	2.41–2.66
11	4	4	–	5	5	6	1.35–1.61	1.35–1.61	1.53–1.76	1.57–1.76	1.81–2.07	2.12–2.40
12	3	–	4	4	–	–	1.27–1.34	1.27–1.34	1.38–1.52	1.40–1.56	1.62–1.80	1.90–2.11
13	2	3	3	–	4	5	1.07–1.26	1.07–1.26	1.13–1.37	1.25–1.39	1.46–1.61	1.72–1.89
14	–	–	–	3	–	4	0.90–1.06	0.90–1.06	0.98–1.12	1.07–1.24	1.35–1.45	1.38–1.71
15	1	2	2	–	3	3	0.85–0.89	0.85–0.89	0.90–0.97	0.90–1.06	1.11–1.34	1.29–1.37
16	0	–	–	2	–	–	0.79–0.84	0.79–0.84	0.79–0.89	0.79–0.89	0.98–1.10	1.15–1.28
17	–	1	1	–	–	–	0.76–0.78	0.76–0.78	0.76–0.78	0.76–0.78	0.95–0.97	1.07–1.14
18	–	0	0	1	2	2	0.69–0.75	0.69–0.75	0.69–0.75	0.69–0.75	0.90–0.94	0.97–1.06
19	–	–	–	0	<2	<2	<0.69	<0.69	<0.69	<0.69	<0.90	<0.97

*Only 1.4% of the normative sample had highest scores below 8.

Note: Column headers represent the examinees highest obtained subtest score.

Copyright 2009 by Pearson, Inc. Reproduced with permission. All rights reserved.

TABLE 3.20 WMS–IV Older Adult Battery Index Variability Measures Scaled Scores by Highest Index Standard Score

Scaled Score	Highest vs. Lowest Index Score by Highest Score						Index Standard Deviation By Highest Score					
	<90	90–99	100–109	110–119	120–129	>129	<90	90–99	100–109	110–119	120–129	>129
1	>24	>24	>24	>24	>28	>28	>12.10	>12.10	>12.10	>12.10	>14.00	>14.00
2	21–24	21–24	21–24	23–24	26–28	26–28	10.44–12.10	10.44–12.10	10.69–12.10	10.69–12.10	13.59–14.00	13.59–14.00
3	19–20	19–20	19–20	20–22	23–25	23–25	10.07–10.43	10.07–10.43	10.44–10.68	10.44–10.68	12.10–13.58	12.10–13.58
4	17–18	17–18	17–18	18–19	21–22	21–22	9.31–10.06	9.31–10.06	9.31–10.43	10.07–10.43	11.37–12.09	11.37–12.09
5	15–16	15–16	15–16	16–17	19–20	19–20	8.72–9.30	8.33–9.30	8.33–9.30	8.74–10.06	10.54–11.36	10.54–11.36
6	14	14	14	14–15	17–18	17–18	7.37–8.71	6.93–8.32	7.09–8.32	7.23–8.73	8.74–10.53	8.97–10.53
7	12–13	12–13	12–13	13	15–16	16	6.11–7.36	6.43–7.08	6.43–7.08	6.43–7.22	7.55–8.73	8.50–8.96
8	10–11	11	11	11–12	13–14	15	4.93–6.10	5.20–6.42	5.20–6.42	5.57–6.42	6.66–7.54	7.55–8.49
9	8–9	9–10	9–10	10	11–12	12–14	4.00–4.92	4.36–5.19	4.36–5.19	4.93–5.56	5.51–6.65	6.35–7.54
10	7	7–8	7–8	8–9	9–10	10–11	3.21–3.99	3.51–4.35	3.51–4.35	4.16–4.92	4.73–5.50	5.29–6.34
11	5–6	6	6	6–7	7–8	8–9	2.65–3.20	3.06–3.50	3.06–3.78	3.06–4.15	3.21–4.72	3.79–5.28
12	4	5	5	5	5–6	6–7	2.00–2.64	2.31–3.05	2.31–3.05	2.52–3.05	2.65–3.20	3.06–3.78
13	3	4	4	4	4	5	1.53–1.99	2.00–2.30	2.00–2.30	2.08–2.51	2.08–2.64	2.65–3.05
14	2	3	3	3	3	4	1.15–1.52	1.53–1.99	1.53–1.99	2.00–2.07	2.00–2.07	2.08–2.64
15	–	2	2	2	2	–	1.00–1.14	1.00–1.52	1.15–1.52	1.15–1.99	1.15–1.99	2.00–2.07
16	1	1	1	1	1	3	58–0.99	0.58–0.99	1.00–1.14	1.00–1.14	1.00–1.14	1.53–1.99
17	0	0	0	–	0	2	0–0.57	<0.58	0.58–0.99	0.58–0.99	0.58–0.99	1.00–1.52
18	–	–	–	0	–	1	–	–	<0.58	<0.58	<0.58	0.58–0.99
19	–	–	–	–	–	0	–	–	–	–	–	<0.58

Note: Column headers represent highest obtained index score.
Copyright 2009 by Pearson, Inc. Reproduced with permission. All rights reserved.

TABLE 3.21 WAIS–IV/WMS–IV Adult Battery Combined Subtest Variability Measures Scaled Scores by Highest Subtest Standard Score

Scaled Score	Highest vs. Lowest Subtest Scaled Score by Highest Score						Subtest Standard Deviation By Highest Score					
	<8*	8–9*	10–11	12–13	14–15	16–19	6–7*	8–9*	10–11	12–13	14–15	16–19
1	—	—	—	—	14	>16	>2.38	>2.58	>3.10	>3.48	>3.48	>4.69
2	—	—	—	—	—	16	2.26–2.38	2.51–2.58	3.06–3.10	3.47–3.48	3.44–3.48	4.59–4.69
3	—	—	—	12	13	—	2.17–2.25	2.43–2.50	3.02–3.05	3.30–3.46	3.41–3.43	4.19–4.58
4	—	—	—	—	12	15	2.03–2.16	2.27–2.42	2.77–3.01	2.92–3.29	3.22–3.40	3.80–4.18
5	—	8	10	11	11	14	1.90–2.02	2.11–2.26	2.68–2.76	2.82–2.91	2.99–3.21	3.49–3.79
6	6	—	—	10	—	13	1.78–1.89	1.98–2.10	2.46–2.67	2.60–2.81	2.83–2.98	3.35–3.48
7	—	7	9	—	10	12	1.65–1.77	1.85–1.97	2.30–2.45	2.48–2.59	2.62–2.82	3.04–3.34
8	—	6	8	9	—	11	1.53–1.64	1.73–1.84	2.14–2.29	2.33–2.47	2.48–2.61	2.78–3.03
9	5	—	—	8	9	—	1.38–1.52	1.60–1.72	2.05–2.13	2.19–2.32	2.34–2.47	2.63–2.77
10	—	—	7	—	8	10	1.20–1.37	1.40–1.59	1.93–2.04	2.02–2.18	2.18–2.33	2.47–2.62
11	—	5	—	7	—	9	1.14–1.19	1.32–1.39	1.82–1.92	1.92–2.01	2.03–2.17	2.31–2.46
12	—	—	6	—	7	—	1.09–1.13	1.30–1.31	1.70–1.81	1.78–1.91	1.90–2.02	2.12–2.30
13	4	—	—	6	—	8	1.11–1.12	1.29–1.30	1.64–1.69	1.69–1.77	1.80–1.89	1.99–2.11
14	—	—	—	—	6	7	0.99–1.10	1.25–1.28	1.45–1.63	1.59–1.68	1.75–1.79	1.83–1.98
15	—	4	5	5	—	—	0.85–0.98	1.22–1.24	1.34–1.44	1.49–1.58	1.66–1.74	1.62–1.82
16	3	—	—	—	5	6	—	1.13–1.21	1.22–1.33	1.41–1.48	1.54–1.65	1.53–1.61
17	—	—	4	—	—	5	<0.85	0.99–1.13	1.13–1.21	1.29–1.40	1.47–1.53	1.50–1.52
18	2	3	—	4	—	—	—	<0.99	0.99–1.13	1.15–1.28	1.30–1.46	1.42–1.49
19	<2	<3	<4	<4	<5	<5	—	—	<0.99	<1.15	<1.31	<1.42

*Only 0.3% of normative sample had highest scores below eight and 3.4% had highest scores between 8–9.

Note: Column headers represent the examinees highest obtained subtest score.

Copyright 2009 by Pearson, Inc. Reproduced with permission. All rights reserved.

TABLE 3.22 WAIS–IV/WMS–IV Adult Battery Combined Index Variability Measures Scaled Scores by Highest Index Standard Score

Scaled Score	Highest vs. Lowest Index Score by Highest Score						Index Standard Deviation By Highest Score					
	<90*	90–99	100–109	110–119	120–129	>129	<90*	90–99	100–109	110–119	120–129	>129
1	>30	>40	>52	>52	>58	>72	>9.94	>14.92	>17.21	>17.21	>18.77	>22.53
2	30	40	50–52	50–52	53–58	72	9.24–9.94	14.01–14.92	16.71–17.21	16.71–17.21	17.41–18.76	21.51–22.53
3	28–29	39	47–49	48–49	50–52	63–71	8.93–9.23	13.36–14.00	15.84–16.70	16.48–16.70	16.67–17.40	20.78–21.50
4	27	38	44–46	44–47	47–49	59–62	8.60–8.92	12.29–13.35	13.80–15.83	14.81–16.47	15.00–16.66	20.19–20.79
5	26	33–37	38–43	41–43	45–46	54–58	8.45–8.59	11.69–12.28	12.67–13.79	13.96–14.80	14.58–14.99	17.38–20.18
6	24–25	30–32	34–37	39–40	42–44	52–53	8.28–8.44	10.02–11.68	11.62–12.66	12.85–13.95	13.75–14.57	16.12–17.37
7	23	28–29	32–33	36–38	39–41	48–51	8.16–8.29	9.34–10.01	10.39–11.61	11.88–12.84	12.81–13.74	14.92–16.11
8	22	26–27	29–31	33–35	36–38	42–47	7.51–8.17	8.87–9.33	9.35–10.38	10.69–11.87	11.66–12.80	13.63–14.91
9	20–21	24–25	25–28	29–32	33–35	36–41	6.82–7.52	7.89–8.86	8.39–9.34	9.48–10.68	10.46–11.65	11.63–13.62
10	19	22–23	23–24	26–28	30–32	33–35	6.30–6.84	7.15–7.88	7.42–8.38	8.41–9.47	9.89–10.45	10.42–11.62
11	18	20–21	20–22	23–25	28–29	30–32	5.61–6.29	6.21–7.14	6.67–7.41	7.63–8.40	8.89–9.88	9.54–10.41
12	16–17	18–19	18–19	21–22	26–27	27–29	5.41–5.60	5.41–6.20	6.06–6.66	6.76–7.63	8.32–8.88	8.77–9.53
13	14–15	14–17	17	18–20	23–25	25–26	4.56–5.40	4.56–5.40	5.40–6.05	6.00–6.75	7.28–8.31	8.01–8.76
14	12–13	12–13	15–16	17	20–22	23–24	4.14–4.55	4.14–4.55	4.85–5.39	5.53–5.99	6.62–7.27	7.27–8.00
15	11	11	12–14	15–16	17–19	21–22	3.89–4.13	3.89–4.13	4.08–4.84	5.15–5.52	5.95–6.61	6.27–7.26
16	10	10	11	13–14	14–16	20	3.76–3.88	3.76–3.88	3.72–4.07	4.68–5.14	5.27–5.94	5.87–6.26
17	9	9	10	10–12	10–13	17–19	2.91–3.75	2.91–3.75	3.42–3.71	4.12–4.67	4.12–5.26	5.74–5.86
18	8	8	9	9	9	16	1.92–2.90	1.92–2.90	3.22–3.41	3.22–4.11	3.22–4.11	5.46–5.73
19	<8	<8	<9	<9	<9	<16	<1.92	<1.92	<3.23	<3.22	<3.22	<5.46

*Only 3% of the normative sample had highest index scores less than 90.

Note: Column headers represent highest obtained index score.

Copyright 2009 by Pearson, Inc. Reproduced with permission. All rights reserved.

TABLE 3.23 WAIS–IV/WMS–IV Older Adult Battery Combined Subtest Variability Measures Scaled Scores by Highest Subtest Standard Score

	Highest vs. Lowest Subtest Scaled Score by Highest Score						Subtest Standard Deviation By Highest Score					
Scaled Score	<8*	8–9*	10–11	12–13	14–15	16–19	<8*	8–9*	10–11	12–13	14–15	16–19
1	–	–	–	–	–	>16	>3.5	>3.5	>3.5	>3.5	>4.34	>4.63
2	–	–	–	–	14	16	3.06–3.50	3.06–3.50	3.06–3.50	3.06–3.50	3.97–4.34	4.34–4.63
3	–	–	10	12	13	14–15	2.80–3.05	2.80–3.05	2.80–3.05	3.02–3.05	3.55–3.96	4.00–4.33
4	–	–	9	11	12	–	2.68–2.79	2.68–2.79	2.68–2.79	2.92–3.01	3.07–3.54	3.68–3.99
5	–	–	–	10	11	13	2.52–2.67	2.52–2.67	2.52–2.67	2.80–2.91	2.96–3.06	3.52–3.67
6	–	8	–	–	10	12	2.37–2.51	2.37–2.51	2.37–2.51	2.59–2.79	2.76–2.95	3.33–3.51
7	–	–	8	9	–	11	2.24–2.36	2.24–2.36	2.24–2.36	2.47–2.58	2.64–2.75	3.07–3.32
8	6	–	–	–	9	–	2.07–2.23	2.07–2.23	2.07–2.23	2.30–2.46	2.47–2.63	2.87–3.06
9	–	7	7	8	–	10	1.89–2.06	1.89–2.06	1.89–2.06	2.16–2.29	2.28–2.46	2.62–2.86
10	–	6	–	7	8	9	1.70–1.88	1.70–1.88	1.70–1.88	2.03–2.15	2.14–2.27	2.47–2.61
11	5	–	6	–	7	–	1.59–1.69	1.59–1.69	1.63–1.69	1.82–2.02	2.03–2.13	2.30–2.46
12	–	5	–	6	–	8	1.41–1.58	1.41–1.58	1.53–1.62	1.69–1.81	1.86–2.02	2.15–2.29
13	–	–	5	–	6	7	1.20–1.40	1.20–1.40	1.45–1.52	1.60–1.68	1.73–1.85	1.99–2.14
14	4	–	–	5	–	–	1.09–1.19	1.09–1.19	1.31–1.44	1.45–1.59	1.56–1.72	1.82–1.98
15	–	4	–	–	5	6	1.05–1.08	1.05–1.08	1.28–1.30	1.31–1.44	1.50–1.55	1.65–1.81
16	3	–	4	4	4	–	0.99–1.04	0.99–1.04	1.24–1.29	1.24–1.30	1.24–1.49	1.63–1.64
17	–	3	–	–	–	5	0.89–0.98	0.89–0.98	1.17–1.23	1.17–1.23	1.17–1.23	1.55–1.62
18	2	2	3	3	3	4	–	–	1.05–1.16	1.05–1.16	1.05–1.16	1.41–1.54
19	0–1	0–1	0–2	0–2	0–2	0–3	<0.89	<0.89	<1.05	<1.05	<1.05	<1.41

*Only 0.4% of the normative sample had highest scores below 8 and 4.4% had highest scores between 8 and 9.

Note: Column headers represent the examinees highest obtained subtest score.

Copyright 2009 by Pearson, Inc. Reproduced with permission. All rights reserved.

TABLE 3.24 WAIS–IV/WMS–IV Older Adult Battery Combined Index Variability Measures Scaled Scores by Highest Index Standard Score

Scaled Score	Highest vs. Lowest Index Score by Highest Score						Index Standard Deviation By Highest Score					
	<90*	90–99	100–109	110–119	120–129	>129	<90*	90–99	100–109	110–119	120–129	>129
1	>35	>40	>45	>62	>69	>69	>12.19	>15.19	>16.83	>23.46	>23.46	>23.46
2	33–35	39–40	43–45	51–62	64–69	64–69	11.90–12.19	14.00–15.19	14.38–16.83	23.00–23.45	23.00–23.45	23.00–23.45
3	30–32	36–38	41–42	43–50	54–63	59–63	11.64–11.89	13.29–13.99	13.82–14.37	17.44–22.99	18.34–22.99	22.34–22.99
4	28–29	34–35	38–40	40–42	50–53	55–58	10.79–11.63	11.89–13.28	13.45–13.81	16.34–17.43	17.35–18.33	19.77–22.33
5	25–27	31–33	36–37	38–39	43–49	50–54	10.26–10.78	11.63–11.88	12.83–13.44	14.78–16.33	16.36–17.34	18.44–19.76
6	24	29–30	32–35	36–37	39–42	45–49	9.96–10.25	10.62–11.62	11.10–12.82	12.89–14.77	14.99–16.35	17.59–18.43
7	23	27–28	27–31	31–35	37–38	40–44	8.91–9.95	9.35–10.61	9.88–11.09	11.69–12.88	13.43–14.98	15.57–17.58
8	22	23–26	25–26	29–30	32–36	37–39	7.98–8.90	7.98–9.34	8.77–9.87	10.45–11.68	11.35–13.42	13.38–15.56
9	21	21–22	22–24	26–28	28–31	35–36	6.92–7.97	7.05–7.97	8.08–8.76	9.56–10.44	10.28–11.34	12.35–13.37
10	19–20	19–20	19–21	24–25	25–27	33–34	5.61–6.91	6.61–7.04	7.06–8.07	8.26–9.55	9.64–10.27	11.15–12.34
11	16–18	16–18	16–18	21–23	23–24	28–32	5.13–5.60	5.61–6.60	6.03–7.05	7.30–8.25	8.62–9.63	10.09–11.14
12	13–15	13–15	13–15	17–20	21–22	24–27	3.91–5.12	5.13–5.60	4.88–6.02	6.23–7.29	7.80–8.61	9.21–10.08
13	11–12	11–12	11–12	15–16	19–20	23	3.54–3.90	3.91–5.12	3.99–4.87	5.29–6.22	7.21–7.79	8.79–9.20
14	10	10	10	12–14	16–18	22	3.30–3.53	3.54–3.90	3.54–3.98	4.71–5.28	6.30–7.20	7.49–8.78
15	9	9	9	10–11	13–15	21	2.97–3.29	3.30–3.53	3.30–3.53	3.68–4.70	4.31–6.29	7.39–7.48
16	6–8	6–8	6–8	6–9	9–12	18–20	2.39–2.96	2.97–3.29	2.97–3.29	2.97–3.67	4.23–4.30	7.14–7.38
17	5	5	5	5	6–8	16–17	2.07–2.38	2.39–2.96	2.39–2.96	2.39–2.96	2.51–4.22	6.99–7.13
18	4	4	4	4	5	14–15	1.50–2.06	2.07–2.38	2.07–2.38	2.07–2.38	2.41–2.50	4.58–6.88
19	<4	<4	<4	<4	<5	<14	<1.50	<2.07	<2.07	<2.07	<2.41	<5.58

*Only 4.1% of the normative sample had highest scores below 90.

Note: Column headers represent highest obtained index score.

Copyright 2009 by Pearson, Inc. Reproduced with permission. All rights reserved.

difference between highest and lowest scores is 6 points. It is important to recognize that because most healthy adults do not have a score below eight as their highest score, it is not possible to develop normative data for lower levels of ability (e.g., highest subtest scores <6). The normative data indicate that having a highest score of less than eight is an unusual finding. In examinees with very low highest scores, it is not practical to try to determine if the level of variability is atypical because their profile is so suppressed, it may not be possible to clearly identify atypicality.

Table 3.25 presents WAIS–IV/WMS–IV variability scores controlling for highest subtest or index scores in the additional samples. When controlling for the highest obtained subtest or index score, the gifted sample does not show more variability than is typical; rather their profile indicates an average degree of variability. However, controlling for their ability level does result in variability scaled scores that are higher than the unadjusted scaled scores. Therefore, considering their high ability, the gifted individuals show much less variability than when ability level is not considered. Low ability subjects, (e.g., borderline and mild intellectual disability) have an average degree of variability when accounting for their suppressed WAIS–IV profile. The moderate intellectual disability group shows less variability than is expected; however, this may be due to difficulties estimating variability when the person's highest score is very low. The left and right temporal lobectomy samples have average variability on the WAIS–IV even after controlling for their low average "highest" score. In general, the WAIS–IV results did not suggest a high degree of cognitive variability even after controlling for profile suppression. In contrast, the results for the WMS–IV indicate more variability in memory functioning when controlling for profile suppression. The mild intellectual disability group had low average WMS–IV variability scores, while, the moderate intellectual disability group had average variability. The left temporal lobectomy group had low average variability scores indicating more variability than is expected given their highest scores on the WMS–IV. The right temporal lobectomy group did show more variability on memory scores when controlling for highest score; however, the variability was in the average range. A similar pattern of results was observed across the group for the combined WAIS–IV/WMS–IV; although, the right temporal lobectomy group showed more profile variability when both batteries were considered together.

Using normative data enables the clinician to better identify typical versus atypical variability in cognitive functioning, relative to healthy adults in the normative sample. Not surprisingly, individuals with general cognitive impairment show very little cognitive variability, because they have pervasive deficits in cognition. Individuals with high

TABLE 3.25 WAIS–IV/WMS–IV Variability Measures by Highest Score in Gifted and Clinical Samples

Variability Measures	Gifted	Borderline IQ	Mild Intellectual Deficiency	Moderate Intellectual Deficiency	Left Temporal Lobectomy	Right Temporal Lobectomy
WAIS–IV subtest high vs. low	11.0 (2.5)	9.8 (3.5)	9.3 (3.0)	12.2 (2.3)	8.3 (2.5)	9.3 (3.6)
WAIS–IV subtest standard deviation	11.2 (2.8)	9.8 (3.8)	9.5 (3.3)	12.7 (2.7)	8.0 (2.2)	9.5 (3.2)
WAIS–IV index high vs. low	11.2 (2.8)	10.0 (3.5)	10.9 (2.7)	13.0 (2.2)	8.0 (2.3)	9.5 (3.2)
WAIS–IV index standard deviation	11.1 (2.9)	9.8 (3.5)	10.2 (2.8)	13.5 (3.3)	9.0 (2.0)	9.8 (3.3)
WMS–IV subtest high vs. low	—	—	7.7 (2.9)	11.3 (4.1)	8.8 (2.9)	9.3 (3.4)
WMS–IV subtest standard deviation	—	—	7.2 (3.2)	10.7 (4.5)	7.4 (3.5)	9.1 (3.4)
WMS–IV index high vs. low	—	—	7.0 (3.5)	10.5 (4.8)	7.2 (4.9)	8.7 (3.0)
WMS–IV index standard deviation	—	—	7.2 (3.2)	10.8 (4.6)	7.0 (4.7)	8.8 (3.0)
WAIS–IV/WMS–IV subtest high vs. low	—	—	6.8 (2.5)	11.4 (4.0)	8.5 (3.0)	8.6 (3.2)
WAIS–IV/WMS–IV subtest standard deviation	—	—	7.0 (2.2)	9.7 (3.6)	7.6 (3.0)	8.7 (2.7)
WAIS–IV/WMS–IV index high vs. low	—	—	7.0 (4.2)	10.1 (5.0)	6.9 (3.7)	8.0 (3.2)
WAIS–IV/WMS–IV index standard deviation	—	—	7.2 (4.4)	9.8 (5.1)	7.1 (3.4)	8.4 (3.4)

Copyright 2009 by Pearson, Inc. Reproduced with permission. All rights reserved.

intellectual ability show more variability in their performance than individuals with average function. Controlling for the highest obtained scores enables the clinician to identify typical versus atypical variability for individuals with low cognitive functioning. In the current samples, this was best exemplified in memory rather than intellectual functioning. These measures evaluate overall cognitive variability; however, clinicians often have a hypothesis regarding a comparison between specific cognitive functions (e.g., verbal vs. visual−perceptual skills). The normative data presented here are based on the largest possible difference in a cognitive profile (e.g., highest vs. lowest, which is most likely to yield a statistically significant difference). This data also provides the examiner with *an estimate* of the atypicality of any pairwise comparison even when they are not the highest versus lowest scores (e.g., Vocabulary vs. Block Design or Working Memory vs. Perceptual Reasoning). This is only an estimate of the atypicality because variability between two variables is affected by the correlation between the measures. Therefore, some comparisons may yield lower expected differences between the scores.

Pairwise Comparison of WAIS−IV Indexes

Clinicians frequently compare specific pairs of variables to determine if a patient has an unusual cognitive profile. For example, many clinical populations have relatively low Processing Speed Index scores compared to Verbal Comprehension or Perceptual Reasoning. As previously shown, the size of a discrepancy between two variables will be constrained by the level of performance on the variables being compared. For many clinical groups, the patient will have VCI or PRI below the mean and sometimes even low average or less. In order to identify differences between variables, it will be necessary to control for the ability level on at least one of the variables in the comparison. Tables 3.26−3.31 provide normative data for specific WAIS−IV index comparisons.

Table 3.26 presents normative data for VCI minus PRI stratified by VCI ability level. In this table, a negative value indicates that the PRI index score is higher than the VCI score. Therefore, a low scaled score on this measure indicates that VCI is greater than PRI by a greater than expected level. For examinees with VCI scores in the 80−89 range, a difference of 12 points with VCI > PRI is equal to a scaled score of five. Only five percent of examinees with VCI scores in the 80−89 range have VCI > PRI by that amount. In contrast, for examinees with VCI scores in the 110−119 range, a VCI > PRI difference of 26 points is required to obtain a scaled score of five. There is substantially more

TABLE 5.16 WAIS-IV Verbal Comprehension versus Perceptual Reasoning by Verbal Comprehension Level Conversion Table

	Verbal Comprehension Minus Perceptual Reasoning						
Scaled Score	<70	70–79	80–89	90–99	100–109	110–119	>119
1	>15	>20	>24	>27	>29	>39	>43
2	13–15	16–20	21–24	26–27	27–29	38	42–43
3	12	15	16–20	19–25	25–26	35–37	41
4	11	12–14	14–15	17–18	23–24	28–34	37–40
5	8–10	7–11	12–13	14–16	19–22	26–27	34–36
6	6–7	3–6	7–11	11–13	15–18	22–25	29–33
7	3–5	1–2	4–6	8–10	12–14	18–21	25–28
8	–3–2	–3– 0	0–3	4–7	8–11	12–17	20–24
9	–6– –4	–7– –4	–4– –1	1–3	4–7	8–11	16–19
10	–10– –7	–9– –8	–7– –5	–3– 0	–1– 3	3–7	10–15
11	–14– –11	–14– –10	–11– –8	–7– –4	–4– –2	–1– 2	6–9
12	–18– –15	–16– –15	–15– –12	–12– –8	–7– –5	–5– –2	0–5
13	–22– –19	–20– –17	–19– –16	–16– –13	–13– –8	–9– –6	–4– –1
14	–26– –23	–24– –21	–22– –20	–20– –17	–17– –14	–13– –10	–8– –5
15	–27	–31– –25	–28– –23	–24– –21	–21– –18	–19– –14	–11– –9
16	–28	–37– –32	–30– –29	–28– –25	–27– –22	–21– –20	–13– –12
17	–37– –29	–38– –36	–36– –31	–31– –29	–28	–26– –22	–15– –14
18	–40– –38	–45– –39	–46– –37	–39– –32	–29	–27	–18– –16
19	<–40	<–45	<–46	<–39	<–29	<–27	<–18

Note: Column headers are Verbal Comprehension Index score ranges.

Copyright 2009 by Pearson, Inc. Reproduced with permission. All rights reserved.

TABLE 3.27 WAIS–IV Verbal Comprehension versus Working Memory by Verbal Comprehension Level Conversion Table

	Verbal Comprehension Minus Working Memory						
Scaled Score	<70	70–79	80–89	90–99	100–109	110–119	>119
1	>15	>16	>23	>27	>32	>40	>43
2	14–15	16	21–23	25–27	31–32	36–40	42–43
3	12–13	14–15	18–20	22–24	24–30	32–35	39–41
4	11	9–13	13–14	18–21	20–23	28–31	35–38
5	10	7–8	11–12	15–17	18–19	24–27	32–34
6	8–9	5–6	7–10	10–14	14–17	20–23	27–31
7	6	2–4	4–6	7–9	10–13	16–19	22–26
8	2–5	−4–−1	0–3	3–6	7–9	12–15	18–21
9	−3–1	−7–−5	−3–−1	1–2	5–6	8–11	14–17
10	−9–−4	−10–−8	−7–−4	−4–0	0–4	3–7	11–13
11	−12–−10	−12–−11	−10–−8	−7–−5	−3–−1	−1–2	7–10
12	−14–−13	−16–−13	−14–−11	−11–−8	−8–−4	−5–−2	4–6
13	−18–−15	−17	−17–−15	−15–−12	−12–−9	−8–−6	1–3
14	−20–−19	−19–−18	−21–−18	−21–−16	−18–−13	−13–−9	−5–0
15	−22–−21	−25–−20	−27–−22	−26–−22	−23–−19	−18–−14	−13–−6
16	−28–−23	−28–−26	−32–−28	−29–−27	−26–−24	−21–−19	−14
17	−33–−29	−33–−29	−37–−33	−32–−30	−30–−27	−27–−22	−17–−15
18	−37–−34	−37–−34	−43–−38	−35–−33	−37–−31	−29–−28	−24–−18
19	<−37	<−37	<−43	<−35	<−37	<−29	<−25

Note: Column headers are Verbal Comprehension Index score ranges.

TABLE 3.28 WAIS–IV Verbal Comprehension versus Processing Speed by Verbal Comprehension Level Conversion Table

	Verbal Comprehension Minus Processing Speed						
Scaled Score	<70	70–79	80–89	90–99	100–109	110–119	>119
1	>20	>21	>29	>30	>34	>53	>53
2	19–20	20–21	23–29	25–30	33–34	43–53	50–53
3	18	19	20–22	23–24	29–32	38–42	47–49
4	16–17	12–18	13–19	20–22	26–28	34–37	44–46
5	12–15	8–11	9–12	16–19	22–25	28–33	42–43
6	8–11	4–7	5–8	11–15	17–21	24–27	35–41
7	5–7	−1–3	2–4	7–10	13–16	20–23	30–34
8	1–4	−4− −2	−3− −1	3–6	8–12	15–19	26–29
9	−4− 0	−9− −5	−7− −4	−2− 2	5–7	11–14	21–25
10	−11− −5	−14− −10	−11− −8	−6− −3	0–4	7–10	16–20
11	−16− −10	−18− −15	−15− −12	−10− −7	−5− −1	2–6	11–15
12	−24− −17	−25− −19	−19− −16	−15− −11	−9− −6	−3− 1	7–10
13	−34− −25	−30− −26	−24− −20	−20− −16	−14− −10	−7− −4	3–6
14	−40− −35	−33− −31	−28− −25	−26− −21	−18− −15	−10− −8	−4− 2
15	−43− −41	−37− −34	−34− −29	−29− −27	−24− −19	−14− −11	−7− −5
16	−56− −44	−42− −38	−40− −35	−34− −30	−29− −25	−20− −15	−9− −8
17	−63− −57	−44− −43	−42− −41	−37− −35	−33− −30	−25− −21	−12− −10
18	—	−46− −45	−44− −43	−39− −38	−35− −34	−27− −26	−18− −13
19	< −63	< −46	< −44	< −39	< −35	< −27	< −18

Note: Column headers are Verbal Comprehension Index score ranges.

Copyright 2009 by Pearson, Inc. Reproduced with permission. All rights reserved.

TABLE 3.29 WAIS–IV Perceptual Reasoning versus Working Memory by Perceptual Reasoning Level Conversion Table

Scaled Score	Perceptual Reasoning Minus Working Memory						
	<70	70–79	80–89	90–99	100–109	110–119	>119
1	>15	>17	>21	>27	>32	>40	>43
2	14–15	17	18–21	24–27	31–32	38–40	40–43
3	12–13	13–16	16–17	21–23	28–30	34–37	37–39
4	11	11–12	13–15	16–20	23–27	31–33	36
5	9–10	9–10	12	13–15	18–22	25–30	31–35
6	6–8	5–8	9–11	10–12	14–17	22–24	27–30
7	5	2–4	5–8	5–9	11–13	17–21	24–26
8	3–4	−2–1	1–4	2–4	8–10	13–16	19–23
9	−1–2	−6– −3	−4– 0	−1– 1	4–7	10–12	14–18
10	−4– −2	−9– −7	−8– −5	−5– −2	0–3	5–9	11–13
11	−8– −5	−12– −10	−11– −9	−8– −6	−4– −1	1–4	8–10
12	−13– −9	−16– −13	−15– −12	−12– −9	−9– −5	−4– 0	5–7
13	−18– −14	−20– −17	−20– −16	−17– −13	−12– −10	−9– −5	0–4
14	−22– −19	−21	−24– −21	−22– −18	−17– −13	−14– −10	−6– −1
15	−23	−25– −22	−32– −25	−25– −23	−21– −18	−17– −15	−14– −7
16	−28– −24	−28– −26	−35– −33	−28– −26	−25– −22	−20– −18	−17– −15
17	−32– −29	−33– −29	−37– −36	−32– −29	−32– −26	−23– −21	−19– −18
18	−33	−37– −34	−39– −38	−37– −33	−35– −33	−26– −24	−20
19	< −33	< −37	< −39	< −37	< −35	< −26	< −20

Note: Column headers are Perceptual Reasoning Index score ranges.

Copyright 2009 by Pearson, Inc. Reproduced with permission. All rights reserved.

TABLE 5.30 WAIS–IV Perceptual Reasoning versus Processing Speed by Perceptual Reasoning Level Conversion Table

Scaled Score	Perceptual Reasoning Minus Processing Speed						
	<70	70–79	80–89	90–99	100–109	110–119	>119
1	>20	>24	>24	>24	>34	>37	>47
2	19–20	22–24	22–24	22–24	33–34	37	46–47
3	18	19–21	19–21	20–21	29–32	34–36	44–45
4	16–17	14–18	15–18	17–19	24–28	31–33	41–43
5	13–15	9–13	11–14	15–16	21–23	27–30	38–40
6	7–12	5–8	7–10	11–14	17–20	23–26	33–37
7	5–6	1–4	3–6	6–10	13–16	19–22	29–32
8	4	−4–0	−1–2	2–5	8–12	14–18	25–28
9	−2–−3	−7–−5	−5–−2	−2–1	3–7	11–13	21–24
10	−5–−3	−10–−8	−8–−6	−7–−3	0–2	7–10	15–20
11	−8–−6	−15–−11	−12–−9	−10–−8	−5–−1	2–6	10–14
12	−14–−9	−21–−16	−16–−13	−15–−11	−9–−6	−2–1	6–9
13	−19–−15	−26–−22	−21–−17	−21–−16	−14–−10	−7–−3	1–5
14	−26–−20	−34–−27	−26–−22	−25–−22	−17–−15	−11–−8	−4–−0
15	−33–−27	−36–−35	−30–−27	−28–−26	−22–−18	−17–−12	−10–−5
16	−38–−34	−43–−37	−36–−31	−31–−29	−26–−23	−21–−18	−12–−11
17	−42–−39	−45–−44	−42–−37	−36–−32	−31–−27	−24–−22	−14–−13
18	−43	−52–−46	−47–−43	−42–−37	−33–−32	−25	−20–−15
19	<−43	<−52	<−47	<−42	<−33	<−25	<−20

Note: Column headers are Perceptual Reasoning Index score ranges.
Copyright 2009 by Pearson, Inc. Reproduced with permission. All rights reserved.

TABLE 3.31   WAIS–IV Working Memory versus Processing Speed by Working Memory Level Conversion Table

Scaled Score	Working Memory Minus Processing Speed						
	<70	70–79	80–89	90–99	100–109	110–119	>119
1	>15	>25	>27	>27	>34	>43	>48
2	14–15	25	25–27	25–26	32–34	41–43	48
3	12–13	19–24	21–24	23–24	29–31	35–40	43–47
4	10–11	17–18	18–20	19–22	24–28	30–34	42
5	8–9	10–16	12–17	16–18	21–23	27–29	39–41
6	5–7	6–9	8–11	13–15	16–20	25–26	34–38
7	1–4	1–5	4–7	8–12	10–15	19–24	30–33
8	−2−−0	−2−−0	0–3	5–7	6–9	15–18	26–29
9	−6−−3	−7−−3	−5−−1	0–4	2–5	12–14	22–25
10	−10−−7	−12−−8	−8−−6	−3−−1	−2−1	6–11	15–21
11	−13−−11	−19−−13	−12−−9	−8−−4	−6−−3	3–5	9–14
12	−16−−14	−23−−20	−16−−13	−13−−9	−11−−7	0–2	6–8
13	−19−−17	−28−−24	−21−−17	−17−−14	−15−−12	−6−−1	2–5
14	−25−−20	−34−−29	−25−−22	−23−−18	−19−−16	−11−−7	−2−−1
15	−31−−26	−40−−35	−28−−26	−28−−24	−25−−20	−13−−12	−7−−3
16	−36−−32	−46−−41	−36−−29	−34−−29	−30−−26	−16−−14	−9−−8
17	−42−−35	−49−−47	−44−−37	−38−−35	−33−−31	−21−−17	−12−−10
18	<−43	−50	−46−−45	−40−−39	−35−−34	−28−−22	−15−−13
19	<−43	<−50	<−46	<−40	<−35	<−28	<−15

Note: Column headers are Working Memory Index score ranges.

TABLE 3.32 WAIS–IV Index Comparison Scores by Ability Level in Gifted and Clinical Samples

Variability Measures	Gifted	Borderline IQ	Mild Intellectual Deficiency	Moderate Intellectual Deficiency	Left Temporal Lobectomy	Right Temporal Lobectomy
WAIS–IV VCI Minus PRI	10.6 (2.8)	7.4 (2.5)	7.5 (2.8)	7.4 (1.9)	10.7 (2.2)	9.0 (2.6)
WAIS–IV VCI Minus WMI	11.5 (2.8)	7.2 (2.8)	7.2 (2.1)	7.6 (1.6)	10.4 (3.0)	9.3 (1.3)
WAIS–IV VCI Minus PSI	10.1 (3.0)	8.3 (3.1)	7.6 (2.7)	8.0 (1.7)	11.0 (2.9)	8.2 (3.5)
WAIS–IV PRI Minus WMI	12.8 (3.2)	7.7 (2.9)	7.2 (2.9)	8.1 (1.5)	8.8 (2.0)	9.6 (2.1)
WAIS–IV PRI Minus PSI	10.9 (3.0)	9.3 (2.4)	8.0 (2.7)	8.9 (1.6)	10.1 (2.9)	8.4 (3.7)
WAIS–IV WMI Minus PSI	10.4 (3.2)	9.6 (2.6)	8.1 (3.1)	8.4 (1.5)	10.4 (2.4)	7.9 (3.3)

Copyright 2009 by Pearson, Inc. Reproduced with permission. All rights reserved.

variability in the high ability group than in lower ability groups. Additionally, having a low VCI score limits the degree to which VCI can be greater than PRI.

At the other end of the spectrum, a high scaled score indicates lower VCI compared to PRI than is expected. For individuals with VCI in the 80–89 range, a PRI score that is 23 points higher yields a scaled score of 15 (i.e., 95th percentile). For examinees with VCI in the 110–119 range, a PRI score that is 14 points higher than VCI is at the 95th percentile. High scores are interpreted as better than expected PRI versus VCI. Overall, this data illustrates that healthy controls have a high degree of performance variability when comparing VCI and PRI, particularly in high ability subjects.

Table 3.32 provides WAIS–IV Index comparison data by ability level for the gifted and clinical samples. The gifted sample shows relatively consistent performance between WAIS–IV Index measures. The PRI versus WMI index comparison is high average, suggesting a tendency for gifted subjects to have higher WMI versus PRI scores. In low ability samples, the borderline intellectual functioning sample had low average

VCI versus PRI and VCI versus WMI scaled scores suggesting slightly better VCI than other abilities, except processing speed. In general, PSI was consistent with other cognitive skills. In the intellectually disabled groups, VCI was slightly higher than PRI and WMI and also PSI in the mild group. Otherwise, PSI is consistent with other cognitive skills. Keeping in mind that at low levels of VCI ability, very small differences in VCI versus other index scores will yield scores in the low average range, the absolute difference between VCI and PRI can be small and still indicate a modest degree of unexpected performance. In the left and right temporal lobectomy groups, the groups showed average consistency among the index scores with the exception of lower PSI versus PRI in the right temporal lobectomy sample.

INTERPRETATION OF PROFILE SCATTER

General Considerations

Binder and Binder (2011) recommended a systematic interpretive strategy to understanding subtest scatter in the context of base rate information and characteristics of the test battery employed. These authors suggest that subtest scatter should be interpreted taking into account several factors.

- Consider "absolute" scatter, or the variability of the entire normative sample. Clinical interpretation of WAIS–IV scores should be done with an awareness of the high frequencies of large amounts of scatter in the standardization sample. The mean variability in the WAIS–IV normative sample in terms of absolute scatter (defined as the range between highest and lowest subtest score) across the 10 core subtests was 6.6 points, (SD = 2.1, median six). Eighty-five percent of individuals in the standardization sample had a difference of at least 5 points between their highest and lowest subtests. Thus, scatter is common.
- Consider the frequency of low scores in the normative sample. Using a binomial distribution, Igraham and Aiken (1996) predicted that 49% of healthy individuals would produce at least two scores that fell greater than 1 SD below the population mean if administered a battery of 10 cognitive measures. Schretlen, Testa, Winicki, Pearlson and Gordon (2008) found that 35.7% of normal individuals did in fact obtain two or more impaired scores when the 1 SD cut-off for impairment was applied. A limitation of the binomial model is the tendency to overestimate how many individuals will produce one or more abnormal scores, and will under-estimate how many will produce two or more abnormal scores (Crawford et al., 2007;

Schretlen et al., 2008). See Chapter 2 for additional discussion of multivariate base rates and their applications.

- Consider scatter adjusted for the highest subtest score to more accurately identify performance variability. The highest score has a significant effect on profile variability. Binder and Binder (2011) demonstrated that scatter was most robustly correlated with the highest subtest score for the 10 core subtests ($r = 0.62$, $r = 0.63$ when all 15 subtests were administered). Therefore, adjusting the variability scores by highest score may yield better results and more accurately represent performance variability.
- Consider the reliability of subtest discrepancies (Glass, Ryan & Charter, 2010). Practitioners often have reason to generate *a priori* hypotheses about potential patterns of strengths and weaknesses on subtest and index scores based on the presenting problem, known medical history, or other information. Such hypotheses will allow for more meaningful interpretation of statistically significant differences between index scores, and the base rates of those differences.
- Consider the clinical context in which the individual presents including educational and occupational history. The integration of clinical experience and expertise with empirical research related to a test or tests is the essence of evidence-based medicine and psychological assessment/treatment. For example, consider the clinical scenario in which an individual being evaluated based on reports of cognitive problems of unknown etiology will include the examinee's history. In this case, the individual is a high school graduate with no history of serious illness or TBI. All index scores obtained are in the average range, with the lowest index score (WMI) of 100 and the highest (VCI) of 112. In this scenario, there is nothing statistically significant regarding the degree of scatter present, and the practitioner might reasonably conclude that this profile falls within the normal range and is generally consistent with the demographic information provided. Alternatively, consider an adjusted scenario: a 25-year-old high school graduate presenting with this pattern and reporting significant decline in her ability to mentally manipulate information and reporting significant persistent headache pain related to a fall resulting in brain injury several years ago. The test scores still indicate a profile of normal cognitive abilities compared to the general population. This does not indicate an absence of a decline in function; rather, it indicates that her cognitive functions as measured by the WAIS–IV are relatively intact, and to identify a loss in ability, additional procedures may be necessary. On the other hand, if her highest score was VCI = 112 and her PSI = 80, the difference would be quite unusual—suggesting significant variability in cognitive functioning. Such a difference in

cognitive functions could be associated with the effects of a significant brain injury or other factors may have influenced these results. The test scores do not indicate the presence or absence of disease but indicate overall ability and variability in functioning. The clinician uses this information in conjunction with the presenting problems and medical history to determine if there is a pathological process affecting cognitive functioning.

- Variability is not necessarily an indication of pathology; variability might not be more common in clinical populations. In some cases, a high degree of consistency is expected when the patient population is known to have deficits in specific cognitive domains (e.g., people with intellectual disability will have consistently low IQ scores). Variability will therefore be a function of the constructs measured and the degree to which measured abilities are differentially affected in a particular clinical group. In most cases, clinical groups have *suppressed profiles* making it difficult to identify unusual levels of variability. Therefore, the *a priori* hypothesis that a patient will show greater than expected variability needs to be carefully considered; because that presupposition will be incorrect in many cases.

Interpreting Variability

Evaluating variability in general cognitive functioning follows the general principle for interpreting the WAIS–IV more generally. The process of evaluating variability in cognitive functioning is supplementary to established procedures for interpreting WAIS–IV results. The primary level of interpretation recommended for the WAIS–IV is the four core index scores. The first stage of determining if profile variability is present—to calculate variability scores and apply normative data to determine if the scores are atypical.

The highest and lowest WAIS–IV index scores are identified. Use Table 3.2 to obtain the highest and lowest normative scaled scores. If the highest obtained index score is low (e.g., use highest obtained index to scaled score conversion Table 3.2 and the scaled score is 7 or less), then the overall cognitive profile is considered suppressed due to low cognitive ability. When the highest index scaled score is very low (e.g., 5 or less), it may not be possible to statistically show that cognitive variability is present. The interpretation then reflects general cognitive impairment. The lowest obtained score indicates if the patient shows very low ability in some domains. It is possible, although unusual, to have a higher "lowest" obtained scaled score than a 'highest' obtained scaled score (e.g., in Table 3.2 if the lowest WAIS–IV index was 84 and the highest index was 98 or highest scaled score of nine and lowest scaled score of 7). This would indicate very low levels of variability in the cognitive profile given that the lowest and highest scores need to be quite similar to attain this outcome. The combination of low "highest" and low "lowest" obtained scaled scores is the most likely pattern in clinical samples, particularly those with moderate to severe cognitive impairment. Calculate the highest versus lowest index score. Using Table 3.16, identify the column associated with the highest obtained index score (e.g., use the actual age adjusted index score and not the normed highest scaled score from Table 3.2) and locate the calculated difference score. The scaled score for this difference is located in the far left column of the table. Interpret the scaled score using standard Wechsler classification nomenclature (e.g., low average, borderline, extremely low). If the score is considered low (e.g., 7 or less), then this score is interpreted as "Mr. X. shows greater than expected variability between his best and worst performance on measures of general intellectual functioning." High scores (e.g., 13 or higher) represent very consistent performance on measures of general cognitive functioning at the extremes of performance. This scaled score does not represent overall profile variability, only variability at the extremes of performance.

Calculate the standard deviation of the index scores as described earlier in this chapter (e.g., using the example provided for scaled scores substitute index scores). Use the highest obtained index score (i.e., use the actual age adjusted index score and not the normed highest index score from Table 3.2) and Table 3.16 to obtain the scaled score for the standard deviation of index scores. If the score is considered low (e.g., 7 or less), the results are interpreted as "Mr. X. shows greater than expected variability in general cognitive functioning than is expected." Likewise, if the score is high (e.g., 13 or higher), the result is interpreted as "Mr. X. shows a greater than expected consistency in his performance on measures of general cognitive functioning." Note, the interpretation can reflect normal levels of variability or unusually higher or low variability; *however, the interpretation does not suggest a specific pathological process is present.*

Variability in Specific Measures of Cognitive Ability

After the clinician identifies a presence or absence of atypical variability in general cognitive ability, he or she may have hypotheses about the relationship between specific cognitive skills. These hypotheses relate to comparisons between pairs of WAIS–IV indexes. In cases of cognitive decline or loss of cognitive functioning, the clinician may compare VCI to other index scores such as WMI and PSI as an indicator of "hold" versus "don't hold" cognitive functions. These verbal intellectual abilities may be more resistant to cognitive decline than those requiring more active attention and processing speed. Similarly, the clinician may test hypotheses about strengths and weaknesses in "crystallized" versus "fluid" reasoning skills.

The WAIS–IV administration manual provides statistics regarding comparisons between two indexes, in terms of statistical significance and base rates. Base rates of the differences can also be evaluated by overall ability level. This chapter provides the clinician with the ability to evaluate specific comparisons between two indexes controlling for the ability level on the measure of interest. *The clinician should identify the specific comparisons they wish to evaluate rather than calculating all possible comparisons. This will reduce the chances of making a Type I error that is more likely to occur as the number of comparisons increase.*

After the clinician identifies the comparisons of interest, for example VCI versus WMI and VCI versus PSI, he or she calculates the difference between each of the pairs. If, VCI = 95, WMI = 88, and PSI = 72, then the differences of interest would be +7 (VCI–WMI) and +23 (VCI–PSI). Using Table 3.27, identify the column associated with the VCI score of 95 (e.g., 90–99) and find the value of the difference in that column. Obtain the scaled score associated the VCI–WMI difference, which in this example is 7. Similarly, using Table 3.28, the clinician identifies the scaled score associated with difference between VCI and PSI as a 3. Interpret the scaled score using standard Wechsler classification nomenclature (e.g., low average, borderline, extremely low). As with all Wechsler scaled scores, a value of seven is associated with the 16th percentile and a 3 is at the first percentile. The values in this example suggest low average to highly unusual levels of variability between the comparisons in question.

The clinician interprets the results stating that "Mr. X. shows low average variability between VCI and WMI" and "Mr. X. shows highly unusual variability between VCI and PSI." The clinician uses this information in the context of a broader evaluation to provide evidence for the presence of absence of a specific cognitive deficit; though, the differences in abilities in, and of themselves, do not necessarily indicate pathology. In other situations, the results may show less variability between specific comparisons than is expected (e.g., scaled score of 13 or more). The results indicate an above average degree of cognitive consistency between the specific abilities that may or may not have any clinical significance but argues for an absence of variability in these cognitive skills.

Variability in General Cognitive Ability Using WAIS–IV Subtests

The highest and lowest WAIS–IV subtest scores are identified. Use Table 3.1 to obtain the highest and lowest subtest scaled scores. If the highest obtained score is low (e.g., 7 or less), then the overall cognitive profile is considered suppressed due to low cognitive ability. When the highest score is very low (e.g., 5 or less), it may not be possible to statistically show that cognitive variability is present. The interpretation should reflect general cognitive impairment. The lowest obtained score indicates if the patient shows very low ability in some domains. The combination of low "highest" and low "lowest" obtained scaled scores is often seen in clinical samples with general cognitive impairment.

Calculate the highest versus lowest subtest score. Using Table 3.15, identify the column associated with the highest obtained subtest score and locate the calculated difference score. The scaled score for this difference is located in the far left column of the table. Interpret the scaled score using standard Wechsler classification nomenclature (e.g., low average, borderline, extremely low). If the score is considered low (e.g., 7 or less), then this score is interpreted as "Mr. X. shows more cognitive variability between his best and worst performance than is expected on measures of general intellectual functioning." High scores (e.g., 13 or higher) represent very consistent performance on measures of general cognitive functioning at the extremes of performance.

Calculate the standard deviation of the subtest scores as described earlier in this chapter. Use the highest obtained score scaled score and Table 3.15 to obtain the scaled score associated with the standard deviation of subtest scores. If the standard deviation scaled score is considered low (e.g., 7 or less), the results are interpreted as "Mr. X. shows greater than expected variability in general cognitive functioning." Likewise, if the score is high (e.g., 13 or higher), the result is interpreted as "Mr. X. shows a greater than expected consistency in his general cognitive functioning." Note, the interpretation can reflect normal levels of variability or unusually high or low variability; however, the interpretation does not suggest a specific pathological process is present.

Variability in Memory Functioning Using WMS–IV Index and Subtest Scores

The procedure outlined for identifying significant variability on the WAIS–IV can be applied to evaluating general memory functioning on the WMS–IV. The first step is to identify variability among WMS–IV index scores. Use Table 3.4 for patients completing the full adult version and Table 3.6 for patients completing the older adult version of the WMS–IV to obtain highest and lowest index scores. Calculate the difference between the highest and lowest obtained index scores, and compute the standard deviation of index scores using the computations presented earlier in the chapter for WAIS–IV indexes. Remember that the denominator for the index scores varies depending on the number of indexes in the equation such that for five indexes, the denominator is 4 and for four indexes the denominator is 3.

Obtain the scaled scores for overall index variability using either Table 3.18 for the full adult battery or Table 3.20 for the older adult battery. If the highest versus lowest difference score is considered low (e. g., 7 or less), then this score is interpreted as "Mr. X. shows greater than expected variability between his best and worst performance on measures general memory functioning." High scores (e.g., 13 or higher) represent very consistent memory performance. If the standard deviation of the index scores is considered low (e.g., 7 or less), the results are interpreted as "Mr. X. shows greater than expected variability in general memory functioning." Likewise, if the score is high (e.g., 13 or higher), the result is interpreted as "Mr. X. shows a greater than expected consistency in his memory functioning."

Variability in WMS–IV subtest performance follows the same process outlined for WAIS–IV subtests. Use either Table 3.3 or 3.5, for the full or older adult battery, respectively, to obtain the highest and lowest attained memory subtest scores and Tables 3.17 or 3.19 for the full or older adult battery respectively, for subtest highest versus lowest and standard deviation measures. When calculating subtest standard deviations, the denominator will be different for the full and older adult batteries. The results are interpreted in the same manner as the WAIS–IV subtest variability indicators except that general memory functioning replaces general cognitive ability in the interpretative statement.

Variability in Combined Ability and Memory Functioning Using WAIS–IV and WMS–IV Index and Subtests

The procedure outlined for identifying significant variability in general cognitive ability and memory functioning individually can be applied to evaluating combined general ability and memory functioning, when both the WAIS–IV and WMS–IV have been administered. The first step is to identify variability among combined WAIS–IV/WMS–IV index scores. Use Table 3.8 for patients completing the full adult version and Table 3.10 for patients completing the older adult version of the WMS–IV to obtain highest and lowest index scores. Calculate the difference between the highest and lowest obtained index scores (the highest scores may be within the WAIS–IV, WMS–IV, or between the WAIS–IV and WMS–IV) and compute the standard deviation of index scores using the computations presented previously. Remember that the denominator for the index scores varies depending on the number of indexes in the equation such that for nine indexes, the denominator is 8 and for eight indexes the denominator is 7.

Obtain the scaled scores for overall index variability using either Table 3.22 for the full adult battery or Table 3.24 for the older adult battery. If the highest versus lowest difference score is considered low (e.g., 7 or less), then this score is interpreted as "Mr. X. shows greater than expected variability between his best and worst performance on combined measures of general ability and memory." High scores (e.g., 13 or higher) represent very consistent combined ability and memory performance. If the standard deviation of the index scores is considered low (e.g., 7 or less), the results are interpreted as "Mr. X. shows greater than expected variability in combined general ability and memory functioning." Likewise, if the score is high (e.g., 13 or higher), the result is interpreted as "Mr. X. shows a greater than expected consistency in his combined ability and memory functioning."

Variability in combined WAIS–IV/WMS–IV subtest performance follows the same process outlined for WAIS–IV and WMS–IV subtests individually. Use Tables 3.7 or 3.9 (for full or older adult batteries, respectively) to obtain the highest and lowest attained combined ability and memory scores and Tables 3.21 or 3.23 (for full or older adult batteries, respectively) for combined highest versus lowest subtests and subtest standard deviation measures. The results are interpreted in the same manner as the individual WAIS–IV and WMS–IV subtest variability indicators, except that combined ability and memory functioning replaces general cognitive ability or memory functioning in the interpretative statement.

CASE STUDIES

CASE STUDY 1

Mr. L. is a 40-year-old, white male, with 18 years of education suffering from systemic lupus erythematosus. Within the past few months, he experienced an increase in cognitive symptoms, specifically related to problems with attention and concentration. MRI results indicated the presence of two new small periventricular brain lesions. The WAIS–IV was administered as part of a larger battery and the results are presented in Table 3.33. This profile will be discussed in terms of the new methods for interpreting variability, and whether or not this variability might be clinically meaningful.

ANALYSIS OF WAIS–IV INDEX SCORE VARIABILITY Standardized normative data is available for each of these data points: Highest score, lowest score, difference score, and standard deviation scores, and may be used to identify greater than expected variability. Earlier in the chapter, Tables 3.3 and 3.4 presented normative data for these indices of variability. Table 3.3 provides normative data for indicators of subtest variability, and Table 3.34 provides normative data for index level variability indicators.

According to the traditional evaluation of pairwise differences in WAIS–IV index performance, the examinee shows significant

TABLE 3.33　WAIS–IV Core Subtest and Index Scores for Mr. L.

WAIS–IV Index	Score	%ile
Verbal Comprehension	103	58
Perceptual Reasoning	121	92
Working Memory Index	111	77
Processing Speed	89	23
WAIS–IV Subtest		
Similarities	9	37
Vocabulary	13	84
Information	10	50
Block Design	14	91
Matrix Reasoning	13	84
Visual Puzzles	14	91
Digit Span	14	91
Arithmetic	10	50
Symbol Search	6	9
Coding	10	50

TABLE 3.34　Standard WAIS–IV Index Comparisons Statistics for Mr. L.

Comparison	Score 1	Score 2	Difference	Critical Value	Significant	Base Rate
VCI–PRI	103	121	−18	8.81	Y	9.1
VCI–WMI	103	111	−8	8.81	N	27.5
VCI–PSI	103	89	14	12.12	Y	19
PRI –WMI	121	111	10	9.29	Y	23.7
PRI–PSI	121	89	32	12.47	Y	2
WMI–PSI	111	89	22	12.47	Y	8.3
FSIQ–GAI	108	113	−5	6.58	N	17.6

differences between PSI and VCI, PRI, and WMI, as well as between PRI and VCI and WMI. Based on this information, it would be reasonable to conclude that there is significant scatter among index scores with some differences being both significant and rare ($p < 0.05$, base rate = 2%). According to Table 3.2, the highest score of 121 (PRI) is in the high average range (SS = 12, 75th percentile) and his lowest score of 89 is in the average range (SS = 10, 50th percentile). The highest score indicates that he would not show a suppressed profile (as is seen in global cognitive impairment) so it may be possible to detect variability in his cognitive functions; likewise, this high score is likely to be associated with more variability in normal controls as well.

Applying the general indicators of WAIS–IV index variability presented earlier in the chapter (i.e., highest vs. lowest index score), reveals that a difference of 32 points (PRI−PSI = 121−89) is in the low average range (Table 3.2, scaled score = 6) regarding consistency in performance when compared to the normative sample. Thus, while the specific pairwise discrepancy (PRI−PSI) was very unusual in the normative sample (<2%), the presence of a 32 point high-low index score difference (when considering all index comparisons simultaneously) is at the 9th percentile. In other words, 9% of the normative sample will show a 32-point or more difference between their highest and lowest index scores. The index standard deviation is calculated below:

Step 1: compute the mean: $103 + 121 + 111 + 89 = 424$, $424/4 = 106$.
Step 2: subtract each index from the mean: $103 - 106 = -3$,
$121 - 106 = 15$, $111 - 106 = 5$, $89 - 106 = -17$.
Step 3: square the index differences: $-3 \times -3 = 9$, $15 \times 15 = 225$,
$5 \times 5 = 25$, $-17 \times -17 = 289$.
Step 4: sum the squares: $9 + 225 + 25 + 289 = 548$.
Step 5: divide the sum of squares by the number of indexes minus 1:
$548/3 = 182.67$
Step 6: calculate the square root of average sum of squares:
$\sqrt{182.67} = 13.51$

The normative data in Table 3.2 indicates that Mr. L. shows a low average (SS = 7, 16th percentile) degree of consistency in general cognitive functioning. He has a modest degree of variability in his general cognitive functioning. These measures generally confirm the interpretation of the standard pairwise comparisons that variability in general cognitive functioning is present.

ANALYSIS OF SCALED SCORE VARIABILITY Inter-subtest scatter reflects the variability of an individual's scaled scores across subtests and has been considered to be potentially diagnostically significant. Multiple approaches to quantifying scatter have been proposed (Schinka & Vanderploeg, 1997); for this discussion, two methods will be reviewed. First, the simple difference between the examinee's lowest and highest scaled scores. Second, comparing each subtest with the mean subtest scaled score. For this profile, the examinee obtained a lowest scaled score of six on Symbol Search, and a highest scaled score of 14 on several subtests (Block Design, Visual Puzzles, and Digit Span). Before further analysis, comparison of these highest and lowest scores with Table 3.1 allows for normative comparison. The lowest scaled score obtained results in a scaled score of nine, indicating that this is within the expected range of lowest scores and not abnormally low. Similarly, the highest scaled score of 14 results in a scaled score of 11. This information suggests that neither the lowest or highest obtained scaled score were abnormally low; therefore, the overall profile is in the average range and there is no evidence of profile suppression (e.g., unusually low highest and lowest scores).

Based on the simple difference method of subtest scatter, the current profile has a range of 8 points between the lowest and highest score. When compared to the normative sample, this corresponds to a scaled score of 8—indicating an average degree of variability in general intellectual functioning when comparing highest and lowest scores. The standard deviation of the subtests is 2.71 (see steps for calculating earlier in this chapter) and is considered low average range (SS = 7, 16th percentile). At the subtest level, there is a modest degree of overall variability in general cognitive ability.

Table 3.35 shows standard comparison data for WAIS–IV subtests using the pairwise difference of each subtest from the overall mean of subtests. For this patient the mean scaled score was 11.3. Based on the individual subtest to mean comparisons, only Symbol Span (base rate 2–5%) is atypically low compared to the average of all the tests.

Thus, the clinician might interpret this to reflect a relative weakness in Symbol Span relative to other subtests. However, the standard

TABLE 3.35   WAIS–IV Subtest Comparisons for Mr. L.

Comparison	Scale Score	Mean	Difference	Squared Difference	Base Rate (%)
Similarities	9	11.3	2.7	7.29	15–25
Vocabulary	13	11.3	− 2.3	5.29	>25
Information	10	11.3	2.7	7.29	>25
Block Design	14	11.3	1.7	2.89	15–25
Matrix Reasoning	13	11.3	1.7	2.89	>25
Visual Puzzles	14	11.3	− 1.3	1.69	15–25
Digit Span	14	11.3	− 5.3	28.09	15–25
Arithmetic	10	11.3	2.7	7.29	>25
Symbol Search	6	11.3	− 1.3	1.69	>2–5
Coding	10	11.3	− 1.3	1.69	>25

deviation of the subtests is low average, which suggests a more general variability in intellectual functioning than just a single weakness in Symbol Span. Therefore, there is some variability in intellectual functioning across domains identified by the overall standard deviation of subtest scores.

CONTROLLING FOR HIGHEST OBTAINED SCORE The highest obtained score has a significant effect on profile variability; therefore, adjusting the variability scores by highest score may yield results that more accurately represent performance variability. The patient's highest index score is 121. Using Table 3.16, the highest versus lowest index score difference of 32 is in the average range when controlling for the highest obtained score. The index standard deviation of 13.51 is also in the average range for individuals with a highest score in the 120–129 range. These results indicate relatively consistent general cognitive functioning when controlling for his highest ability. The modest variability reported earlier is more consistent with having a relatively high, "highest" index score than with having atypical variability in intellectual functioning. The subtest highest versus lowest score of 8 points and the subtest standard deviation are in the average range (Table 3.15, SS = 8), when considering the subtest highest scaled score of 14. The results indicate consistent performance on measures of general cognitive ability. These results do not obviate the need to consider individual strengths and weaknesses but indicates that the overall profile variability is not atypical for an individual with similar highest index and subtest scores.

For specific comparisons between index scores, the data in Table 3.33 indicate strength in visual perceptual skills and a weakness in processing speed based on all possible pairwise comparisons. For a more accurate assessment of variability between specific abilities, the clinician had developed hypotheses about expected cognitive functioning. Given that the patient was reporting a decline in cognitive functioning, the examiner expected more decline in variables related to attention and processing speed versus cognitive skills that are less affected by cognitive decline. Additionally, given that the patient worked as a mechanical engineer, the clinician hypothesized that perceptual reasoning skills may be the best indicator of general cognitive functioning. The specific comparisons of PRI versus WMI and PSI were thought to be useful indicators of cognitive decline for this patient. The obtained differences were 10 and 32 points, respectively. Using Tables 3.29 and 3.30, these differences were associated with scaled scores of 11 (63rd percentile) and 7 (16th percentile), respectively. The difference between PRI and WMI was in the average range and the difference between PRI and PSI was in the low average range. The latter suggests that processing speed is somewhat inconsistent from perceptual reasoning when controlling for the high level of perceptual reasoning ability.

CASE STUDY 1 VARIABILITY SUMMARY Although initial review of this examinee's profile appeared notable for significant variability across both index scores and individual subtests, closer review of the data using available normative comparisons for scatter do not support the conclusion that this profile contains an abnormal degree of scatter. Further, when base rates are considered, this degree of variability across subtests occurs in 25% of the normative sample. Therefore, the scatter identified in this profile's scores does not cross a threshold for significant variability when normative comparisons are applied, nor is this degree of variability unusual in the normative sample. When controlling for the patient's highest index and subtest performance, all the overall profile variability measures were in the average range.

Specific weaknesses were identified in Symbol Span and Processing Speed but the overall profile indicates an atypical degree variability. The patient's complaints of difficulties with cognition may be related to low processing speed scores. The fact that overall cognitive variability is not present does not preclude the presence of real changes in cognitive functioning; however, this clinical question may be best answered by comparing pre-morbid levels of cognition (Chapter 5, Predicting Premorbid Ability for WAIS–IV, WMS–IV and WASI–II) rather than using variability within a test battery to make that determination.

CASE STUDY 2

Mrs. S. is a 54-year-old, white female, with 12 years of education. Mrs. S. presents with complaints of attention, concentration, and memory problems. The WAIS–IV and WMS–IV were administered as part of a battery of cognitive tests and the results are presented in Table 3.36. Based on her reported history, Mild Cognitive Impairment (MCI) versus normal aging is the primary differential diagnosis. The clinician used the WAIS–IV/WMS–IV data to test specific hypotheses about Mrs. S.'s current cognitive functioning: (a) Does the profile demonstrate impairment on memory scores (particularly delayed recall)? (b) If overall memory impairment is not present, does the profile demonstrate a significant discrepancy between memory scores and other index scores? (c) If not, is there significant variability at the subtest level that would suggest abnormality?

ANALYSIS OF INDEX SCORE VARIABILITY Applying standard comparison data to the WAIS–IV results, the largest difference between the WAIS–IV Index scores was 13 (PSI vs. WMI) which was statistically significant and relatively less common (base rate = 19%) in the

TABLE 3.36 WAIS–IV/WMS–IV Core Subtest and Index Scores for Mrs. S

WAIS–IV Scores			WMS–IV Scores		
Index	Score	%ile	Index	Score	%ile
Verbal Comprehension	95	58	Auditory Memory	84	25
Perceptual Reasoning	96	92	Visual Memory	82	79
Working Memory Index	89	77	Visual Working Memory	91	87
Processing Speed	102	23	Immediate Memory	80	50
			Delayed Memory	81	55
Subtest			Subtest		
Similarities	9	37	Logical Memory I	9	37
Vocabulary	10	84	Logical Memory II	8	25
Information	8	50	Verbal Paired Associates I	6	16
Block Design	7	91	Verbal Paired Associates II	6	37
Matrix Reasoning	9	84	Designs I	6	95
Visual Puzzles	12	91	Designs II	9	91
Digit Span	8	91	Visual Reproduction I	7	37
Arithmetic	8	50	Visual Reproduction II	10	50
Symbol Search	11	9	Spatial Addition	8	95
Coding	10	50	Symbol Span	9	63

normative sample. These results suggest a weakness in working memory relative to processing speed. However, when considering that this is the highest versus lowest difference among all WAIS–IV indexes, using Table 3.2 the difference of 13 is equivalent to a scaled score of 12 (75th percentile) which is in the high average range. At the extremes of performance, she shows less than expected variability in general cognitive functioning. The standard deviation of the WAIS–IV indexes is 5.3, which is equivalent to a scaled score of 13 (75th percentile). This indicates that there is less than expected overall variability in her general cognitive functioning. The highest obtained score of 102 is equal to a scaled score of eight (75th percentile) and the lowest obtained score of 89 is equivalent to a scaled score of 10 (50th percentile) indicating that this is an unusual profile with the lowest scaled exceeding the highest obtained score. The profile is not suppressed but shows a high degree of consistency between the highest and lowest score.

On the WMS–IV, the largest difference between indexes was between VWMI (91) and IMI (80) with a discrepancy of 11 points.

Table 3.4 indicates that a WMS−IV index score discrepancy of 11 is consistent with a scaled score of 12 (75th percentile). Similarly, the index standard deviation of 4.4 is a scaled score of 12 (75th percentile), which indicates a high degree of consistency in memory functioning. The highest Index score of 91 produced a scaled score of six and the low score of AMI = 80 equates to a scaled score of seven. These results suggest a suppressed memory profile. With unexpectedly low highest and lowest scores, Memory functioning is below expected levels of performance. Subtest level performance was similar to index performance with greater than expected consistency in memory performance for highest versus lowest (SS = 12) and the standard deviation (SS = 13). The highest observed score was low average (SS = 7) but the lowest achieved scores was in the average range (SS = 9). This is an unusual finding suggesting very consistent memory skills in which the highest score is somewhat suppressed and the low score is similar to the highest score. Taken together, the index and subtest scores indicate below expected memory skills that are not severely impaired but consistently low.

When combined WAIS−IV/WMS−IV scores are combined, a similar pattern emerges. The overall profile is somewhat suppressed with the highest achieved index (SS = 7) and subtest in the average range. The lowest scores were in the average range for indexes (SS = 8) and subtests (SS = 10). Variability measures were in the high average range for subtests (SS = 13) and in the average to high average range for standard deviation and highest versus lowest (SS = 10 and 12, respectively). The results indicate lower than expected ability level across both intellectual and memory functioning, but not a severe level of impairment (e.g. lowest scores are average). When controlling for the highest obtained score, the results were essentially the same.

CASE STUDY 2 VARIABILITY SUMMARY Mrs. S.'s highest obtained scores on the WAIS−IV and WMS−IV were low yielding a suppressed profile. The lowest obtained score was in the average range, which indicates that she does not exhibit severe cognitive impairments. Mrs. S. shows a high degree of consistency in intellectual and memory functioning, even when the two batteries are combined. WAIS−IV scores are consistently higher than WMS−IV memory scores, excluding visual working memory. However, because the entire profile is somewhat suppressed, variability measures do not identify these scores as being unusually different. The overall suppression of the profile identifies this as an atypical performance but not due to extreme variability. Whether or not the scores here represent a mild degree of cognitive impairment needs to be evaluated with additional procedures such as demographic normative adjustments (see Chapter 4, Demographic Adjustments to

WAIS–IV/WMS–IV Norms) or estimated premorbid abilities (see Chapter 5, Predicting Premorbid Ability for WAIS–IV, WMS–IV and WASI–II).

SUMMARY

Healthy adults show considerable variability in performance across the WAIS–IV, WMS–IV, and combined batteries. Most individuals have strengths and weaknesses in their abilities that are reflected in large differences between their highest and lowest obtained scores. Variability in performance is greater in people with above average or superior intellectual ability. Variability is so common in healthy controls, it would be expected that most individuals would have at least one pairwise comparison that is both statistically significant and has a relatively low base rate. Additionally, most healthy controls will have at least one score above the mean and one below the mean. Observed discrepancies, despite commonly occurring, can represent true strengths and weaknesses but may not necessarily be diagnostic of an acquired cognitive impairment.

In contrast, some clinical samples show less, not more, variability than healthy adults. This runs counter to longstanding clinical lore that variability in performance is more common in people with cognitive impairment. Many individuals diagnosed with cognitive impairment, show suppressed profiles where the difference between the highest and lowest scores is too small to be significantly different. Therefore, for some clinical samples, the most appropriate hypothesis about cognitive variability is that there will be average or above average consistency (e.g., less variability) in performance, particularly on tasks related to their impairment. The clinician needs to have strong evidence that profile variability is diagnostic of a specific condition to apply a diagnostic rule that employs variability as one of the criteria.

Using normative data for general indicators of profile variability (e.g., highest vs. lowest and standard deviation of scores) controls for high false positive rates associated with performing multiple, pairwise comparisons. Furthermore, controlling for the highest level of performance can prevent misattribution of variability to a pathological process when the level of variability is common for individuals of high ability. Also, it allows for the identification of atypical variability in individuals with low overall ability. Applying global indicators of cognitive variability does not obviate the need to evaluate specific pairwise comparisons to best describe the patient's cognitive strengths and weaknesses or to develop diagnostic hypotheses, and/or possible intervention or accommodation strategies. Rather, the data provide an overall indication of variability in cognitive functions that helps the clinician to interpret significant individual pairwise comparisons in an appropriate context.

KEY LEARNING

- Healthy adults have cognitive strengths and weaknesses. Variability in test performance is common. When administered and battery of tests, significant differences between pairs of measures occurs frequently in healthy controls. Healthy controls exhibit cognitive strengths and weaknesses.
- On the WAIS–IV, the average highest obtained index score is not 100 but 111 and the highest obtained scaled score is not 10 but 13.5, on average, indicating that most healthy controls will have at least one score in the high average range.
- On the WAIS–IV, the average lowest obtained index score is 91 not 100 and the lowest obtained scaled score is seven and not 10, on average, indicating that most healthy controls will have at least one low score. In addition, the means for an individual test do not set the upper and lower expectations for performance in a battery of tests.
- On the WAIS–IV, the mean difference between highest and lowest scores is about 19.5 points for indexes and 6.5 points for subtests. It is common to have two index scores that are more than 1.2 standard deviation units apart and for two subtests that are more than two standard deviations apart. This average level discrepancy is substantially larger than the discrepancies required for significance in pairwise comparisons.
- The average standard deviation among the WAIS–IV index scores is between eight and nine index score points, and the average SD among the subtests is greater than two scaled score points. That means that 68% of an individual's scores will be roughly ±8.5 index and ±2 scaled scores from the average of his or her performance (e.g., if the mean of the person's index scores is 100 then most of his or her scores will be between 91.5 and 108.5; if a person's average scaled score is 10 then most of his or her scaled scores will be between 8 and 12).
- The WMS–IV data are very similar to the WAIS–IV when using the adult battery; however, the older adult battery shows some modest differences in highest, lowest, and discrepancy scores.
- The normed scaled scores provided in this chapter for variability measures are scaled such that a low degree of variability (e.g., high level of consistency) yields a scaled score above 10. A high degree

of variability (e.g., low levels of consistency) yields a scaled score below 10.

- Variability in test performance is correlated with education level, age, and highest and lowest obtained scores. Education effects are related to general ability effects and age effects are quite small and not clinically meaningful. Highest and lowest performance are also correlated, such that controlling for the highest obtained score will provide the best model for adjusting variability scores.

- Variability is a function of the number of tests administered. The greater the number of tests, the more likely it is that a significant discrepancy would be observed between two measures. Using combined WAIS–IV/WMS–IV tables can help control for using a large set of variables.

- Gifted individuals have more cognitive variability than individuals with varying levels of intellectual impairment when the highest obtained score is not controlled. When the highest score is not controlled, individuals with intellectual disability show a high degree of consistency in their cognitive impairment, as would be expected; controlling for ability level results in consistency measures being in the average range for these groups, except for the moderate intellectual impairment group. Therefore, variability is not necessarily diagnostic of cognitive impairment. Cognitive impairment can be present in individuals showing very consistent performance in a domain associated with the diagnosis in question.

- Clinical samples often show a suppressed profile. That is, their highest obtained score is below average – making it difficult to statistically identify variability in highest and lowest performance. Controlling for highest score may help in some cases, but when the highest scores are quite low; these patients do not show significant variability due to range restriction.

- In some cases, variability in cognitive functioning should be considered not consistent with a specific diagnosis. For example, a high degree of variability in intellectual functioning would not be expected in individuals with intellectual disability. Similarly, patients diagnosed with dementia will likely have consistently low scores on memory tests.

- In order to use atypical variability as a diagnostic criterion, there must be strong research evidence for variability in the diagnostic group in question. Most clinical studies present aggregate data for the clinical group. For example, if a *sample of patients* with traumatic brain injury have, as a group, average processing speed scores lower than verbal abilities, that does not mean that every patient with traumatic brain injury had a lower processing speed score compared to his or her verbal abilities. Aggregate data showing variability in

groups of patients does not necessarily provide sufficient information for making diagnostic conclusions about individual patients. Often, the level of discrepancy between scores is insufficient for making diagnostic conclusions as healthy individuals will also show variability in cognitive performance that in research studies is masked in aggregate data (e.g., group means).
- Multiple indicators of profile variability are presented in this chapter. The clinician can use these indicators to identify suppressed profiles, cognitive profiles that are variable but consistent with high ability, or true variability associated with extremes in cognitive performance (i.e., that is highest vs. lowest performance) or general variability in cognitive performance (i.e., standard deviation of scores).

References

American Psychological Association (APA) (2005). Policy statement on evidence-based practice in psychology. Retrieved 01.03.12 from <www.apa.org/practice/resources/ evidence/evidence-based-statement.pdf>.

Binder, L. M., & Binder, A. L. (2011). Relative subtest scatter in the WAIS–IV standardization sample. *The Clinical Neuropsychologist, 25*, 62–71.

Crawford, J. R., Gault, C. B., & Garthwaite, P. H. (2007). Estimating the percentage of the population with abnormally low scores (or abnormally large score differences) on standardized neuropsychological tests batteries: A generic method with applications. *Neuropsychology, 21*, 419–430.

Folstein, M. F., Folstein, S. E., & McHugh, P. R. (1975). "Mini-mental state". A practical method for grading the cognitive state of patients for the clinician. *Journal of Psychiatric Research, 12*, 189–198.

Garb, H. N., & Schramke, C. J. (1996). Judgment research and neuropsychological assessment: A narrative review and meta-analysis. *Psychological Bulletin, 120*, 140–153.

Glass, L. A., Ryan, J. J., & Charter, R. A. (2010). Discrepancy score reliabilities in the WAIS–IV standardization sample. *Journal of Psychoeducational Assessment, 28*, 201–208.

Igraham, L. J., & Aiken, C. B. (1996). An empirical approach to determining criteria for abnormality in test batteries with multiple measures. *Neuropsychology, 10*, 120–124.

Iverson, G. L., Brooks, B. L., & Holdnack, J. A. (2012). Evidence-based neuropsychological assessment following work-related injury. In S. S. Bush, & G. L. Iverson (Eds.), *Neuropsychological assessment of work-related injuries*. New York: The Guilford Press.

Kaufman, A. S. (1976). A new approach to the interpretation of test scatter on the WISC-R. *Journal of Learning Disabilities, 9*, 160–168.

Kaufman, A. S., & Lichtenberger, E. O. (2006). *Assessing adolescent and adult intelligence* (3rd ed.). Hoboken, NJ: Wiley.

Lezak, M. D., Howieson, D. B., & Loring, D. W. (2004). *Neuropsychological assessment* (4th ed.). New York: Oxford University Press.

Matarazzo, J. D., Daniel, M. H., Prifitera, A., & Herman, D. O. (1988). Inter-subtest scatter in the WAIS-R standardization sample. *Journal of Clinical Psychology, 44*, 940–950.

Matarazzo, J. D., & Herman, D. O. (1985). Clinical uses of the WAIS-R: Base rates of differences between VIQ and PIQ in the WAIS-R standardization sample. In B. B. Wolman (Ed.), *Handbook of intelligence: Theories, measurements and applications* (pp. 899–932). New York: John Wiley.

Sattler, J. M., & Ryan, J. J. (2009). *Assessment with the WAIS–IV*. La Mesa, CA: Jerome M. Sattler, Publisher.

Schinka, J. A., & Vanderploeg, R. D. (1997). Profile clusters in the WAIS-R standardization sample. *Journal of the International Neuropsychological Society, 3*, 120–127.

Schretlen, D. J., Testa, S. M., Winicki, J. M., Pearlson, G. D., & Gordon, B. (2008). Frequency and bases of abnormal performance by healthy adults on neuropsychological testing. *Journal of the International Neuropsychological Society, 14*, 436–445.

Further Reading

Brooks, B. L., Holdnack, J. A., & Iverson, G. L. (2011). Advanced clinical interpretation of WAIS–IV and WMS–IV: Prevalence of low scores varies by level of intelligence and years of education. *Assessment, 18*, 156–167.

4

Demographic Adjustments to WAIS–IV/WMS–IV Norms

James A. Holdnack and Larry G. Weiss

Pearson Assessment, San Antonio, Texas, USA

INTRODUCTION

Clinicians frequently evaluate patients from diverse socioeconomic and cultural backgrounds. When evaluating patients from minority or economically disadvantaged environments, the clinician needs to consider the extent to which cultural, educational, financial, and other environmental factors, such as access to healthcare, impact performance on cognitive tests. An accurate diagnosis requires the clinician to discern the degree to which an achieved low score represents the effects of a disease process rather than the impact of cultural, educational, and economic factors. Similarly, the extent to which a high level of educational achievement and financial status impact test performance should also be considered, particularly in the presence of possible cognitive loss or decline where average scores may indicate a loss of function. In these evaluations, the clinician attempts to determine if an achieved score represents an *expected* level of performance for that *individual* based on his or her background characteristics.

Standardized scores describe the rank order of an examinee's performance in comparison to individuals of similar age; however, the standardized score does not indicate whether the level of performance is atypical for individuals with similar background characteristics. A very low score reflects low cognitive functioning currently; however, it may not represent an unexpectedly low score in an examinee with a long history of low cognitive ability. Therefore, scores need to be

WAIS-IV, WMS-IV, and ACS.
DOI: http://dx.doi.org/10.1016/B978-0-12-386934-0.00004-3

© 2013 Elsevier Inc. All rights reserved.

evaluated within the context of the individual's background. If an examinee obtains a score of 90, it may represent a good, average, or poor performance for that person. For example, in a healthy examinee with 8 years of education and a history of low but stable occupational and educational performance, a score of 90 may be considered within expected limits. However, in an examinee with 21 years of education employed in a highly intellectual field, a score of 90 might represent an unexpectedly low performance. The difficulty of interpreting performance is compounded by the fact that cognitive skills vary considerably in the degree to which background factors impact test performance. Therefore, *expected* level of performance cannot accurately be determined without statistical data. At the extremes of a distribution (e.g., very high and very low education levels), the clinician can roughly estimate whether a score appears to be unexpectedly high or low; however, as background parameters approach the median it becomes increasingly difficult to accurately determine the level of expected performance. The use of demographic variables to estimate abilities improves the accuracy of estimation. It is important to note that interpreting an examinee's performance relative to their background characteristics is done *only* to identify an unexpected level of performance; that is to determine if a change has occurred from an estimated prior level of ability. Comparing a patient's performance to individuals with similar background characteristics should not be used to determine his or her ability to adequately function in general societal contexts or in place of standard scores in evaluating current performance (e.g., special education evaluations, disability due to chronic medical or psychiatric condition).

Ideally, current performance data is compared to previous results (i.e., serial assessment). In the absence of previous test data, the clinician can evaluate the current level of performance in relation to the expected performance given the patient's psychosocial history. An unexpectedly low score *potentially* represents a decline in cognitive functioning. In this situation, the clinical hypothesis involves a general or specific *loss* in cognitive functioning such as: *Does the patient have a significant loss in memory; Is there a loss in cognitive functioning following a moderate traumatic brain injury; or Is the patient's verbal ability impaired following cerebrovascular accident?* While it may be possible to determine if a patient's performance is higher than expected, clinical hypotheses rarely evaluate improved cognition without conducting serial assessments (see Chapter 6). Understanding the extent to which background factors relate to cognitive functioning is necessary for accurate application and interpretation of demographically adjusted data.

BACKGROUND FACTORS ASSOCIATED WITH TEST PERFORMANCE

Multiple independent and inter-related factors influence obtained test scores. An innumerable number of potential factors may influence test performance. The ability to detect changes in brain function in patients via changes in cognition is key in determining which variables to include in demographic adjustments. For example, if gender results in significantly higher scores for one group or another, this difference in performance could mask a change in functioning or result in mis-identification of impairment when none is present. Specifically, if men are superior at visual−perceptual functioning compared to women, then the normative data based on combined male−female performance will yield higher scores for men. Subsequently, if men have an average or low average score using population norms, this *could* represent lower than expected performance. The degree that such differences may mask unexpectedly low performance depends on the effect size of the difference. The larger the effect size, the greater the clinical implications for accurately identifying cognitive deficits. The ACS demographic adjusted norms incorporate three demographic variables that have been used in research and clinical practice for decades: sex, education, and race/ethnicity (Heaton, Grant, & Matthews 1991). The relationship of each variable with WAIS−IV and WMS−IV performance will be briefly reviewed.

Sex Effects

Research comparing cognitive performance between men and women has identified differences in multiple domains. There is no consistent sex advantage in general cognition; in some areas, men outperform women, and in others, women outperform men. There is a large body of research on gender differences not only in cognition but also in brain morphology and function. While sex differences are observed on many tasks, not all differences are relevant to the current discussion. This chapter focuses on sex differences that could impact interpretation of results in neuropsychological assessments.

In general, men outperform women on tests of general cognitive functioning, perceptual reasoning, working memory (Heaton, Taylor, & Manly, 2003; van der Sluis et al., 2006) and verbal reasoning (Heaton et al., 2003). Women perform better than men on processing speed (Camarata & Woodcock, 2006; Heaton et al., 2003; Longman, Saklofske, & Fung, 2007; van der Sluis et al., 2006). These results are important for the WAIS−IV, as these skills are core to the WAIS−IV measurement model. Within these broad domains, specific abilities can yield similar or quite different results. For example, men outperform women on perceptual reasoning tests, mental rotation tasks (Herlitz, Airaksinen, & Nordstrom, 1999), and spatial processing (Gur et al., 2012); however, women are better at face detection (McBain, Norton, & Chen, 2010). Men score higher on verbal reasoning measures, but women are better at verbal productivity (Herlitz et al., 1999). On working memory tasks, some research shows an advantage for men on verbal working memory (Heaton et al., 2003) while other studies show better visual spatial working memory but not verbal working memory (Lejbak, Crossley, & Vrbancic, 2011). Women are faster on measures of cognitive processing speed but men are faster on simple motor and sensorimotor speed tasks (Gur et al., 2012). General statements about superior functioning for one sex over the other do not apply to all skills within a domain. Therefore, the degree to which tests within domain measure different aspects of the construct in question impacts the degree and type of sex effects observed.

Differences in cognitive skills relevant to the WAIS–IV do not necessarily apply to the WMS–IV. The WMS–IV assesses auditory and visual, episodic, declarative memory functions. Research generally shows that women outperform men on many but not all types of memory functions. Women outperform men (Ragland, Coleman, Gur, Glahn, & Gur, 2000; Trahan & Quintana, 1990; Weirich, Hoffmann, Meissner, Heinz, & Bengner, 2011) and girls outperform boys (Gur et al., 2012; Kramer, Delis, Kaplan, O'Donnell, & Prifitera, 1997) on verbal learning tasks. Women show a particular advantage in the acquisition of new information rather than in maintaining acquired information (Krueger & Salthouse, 2010). The female verbal memory advantage may be related to differences in the pattern of blood flow in the temporal lobes of women versus men (Ragland et al., 2000). While single word verbal learning tasks show consistent female advantage, another verbal learning paradigm, verbal paired associates, does not demonstrate the same advantage for women (Trahan & Quintana, 1990). On visual memory tasks, inconsistent gender effects are identified with no gender effects observed on memory for visuospatial information and abstract objects (Herlitz et al., 1999; Trahan & Quintana, 1990), and females outperforming men on memory for concrete, nameable objects (Herlitz et al., 1999) and memory for faces (Lewin, Wolgers, & Herlitz, 2001). On the WMS–III, women performed significantly better than men on all the auditory and visual memory indexes (Heaton et al., 2003).

Table 4.1 presents descriptive statistics for women and men on the core WAIS–IV indexes and subtests. Performance was significantly different between men and women on all WAIS–IV index scores with a male advantage for VCI, PRI, and WMI; and a female advantage on

TABLE 4.1 WAIS—IV Core Index and Subtest Mean Scores, by Sex

Score	Male		Female		Between Group Differences	
	Mean	SD	Mean	SD	Effect Size	p
Verbal Comprehension Index	101.8	15.4	98.4	14.5	0.23	<0.001
Perceptual Reasoning Index	101.8	15.6	98.3	14.2	0.24	<0.001
Working Memory Index	101.8	15.5	98.4	14.3	0.23	<0.001
Processing Speed Index	97.7	14.5	102.1	15.1	−0.30	<0.001
Full Scale IQ	101.2	15.3	98.9	14.6	0.15	<0.001
Vocabulary	10.1	3.1	10.0	2.9	0.05	>0.05
Similarities	10.2	2.9	9.9	2.9	0.11	<0.05
Information	10.7	3.2	9.4	2.8	0.45	<0.001
Block Design	10.5	3.1	9.6	2.9	0.28	<0.001
Matrix Reasoning	10.2	3.2	10.0	3.0	0.07	>0.05
Visual Puzzles	10.4	3.2	9.7	2.8	0.25	<0.001
Digit Span	10.2	3.1	9.9	3.0	0.08	>0.05
Arithmetic	10.5	3.1	9.6	2.8	0.32	<0.001
Coding	9.4	2.9	10.5	3.0	−0.39	<0.001
Symbol Search	9.8	3.1	10.3	3.1	−0.15	<0.001

Copyright 2008 by Pearson, Inc. Reproduced with permission. All rights reserved.

PSI. The effect sizes are small ranging from 0.15 (FSIQ) to −0.30 (PSI). Greater variability is observed in sex differences at the subtest level. On VCI measures, scores on Similarities and Information were significantly higher for males than female but no difference was observed on Vocabulary. PRI subtests show a significant advantage for males on Block Design and Visual Puzzles but not on Matrix Reasoning. Auditory working memory (WMI) scores show a male advantage on Arithmetic but not on Digit Span. Women obtain significantly higher scores on both PSI subtests with the greatest difference observed on Coding compared to Symbol Search. While statistically significant differences are observed between men and women on WAIS—IV index and subtest scores, the small effect sizes indicate limited clinical significance of the differences. At the index level, the largest effect of −0.3, a difference of 5 standard score points, is similar to the standard error of measurement for most indexes. At the subtest level, the largest effect is −0.39 or about 1 scaled score difference. This is also within the standard error of measurement for these measures.

Table 4.2 provides descriptive statistics for male versus female performance on the WMS–IV. Women show significantly higher scores on Immediate, Delayed, and Auditory Memory indexes and men obtain higher Visual Working Memory index scores. There was no gender difference observed on the Visual Memory Index. These results differ from those observed on the WMS–III for Visual Memory (Wechsler, 2007), likely due to the composition of the index. On the WMS–III, the visual memory measures included face recognition and verbal–visual

TABLE 4.2 WMS–IV Core Index and Subtest Mean Scores, by Sex

Score	Male		Female		Between Group Differences	
	Mean	SD	Mean	SD	Effect Size	p
Immediate Memory Index	99.1	14.7	101.0	15.1	−0.13	<0.05
Delayed Memory Index	99.0	15.1	101.0	14.8	−0.13	<0.05
Auditory Memory Index	98.2	14.8	101.7	15.0	−0.24	<0.001
Visual Memory Index	100.5	15.3	99.8	14.6	0.05	>0.05
Visual Working Memory Index	101.3	15.4	98.8	14.7	0.17	<0.05
Logical Memory I	9.8	3.1	10.2	2.9	−0.16	<0.01
Logical Memory II	9.6	3.1	10.3	2.9	−0.25	<0.001
Verbal Paired Associates I	9.7	2.9	10.3	3.1	−0.19	<0.001
Verbal Paired Associates II	9.7	3.0	10.3	3.1	−0.19	<0.01
Visual Reproduction I	10.2	3.1	10.0	3.0	0.06	>0.05
Visual Reproduction II	10.2	3.2	9.9	2.9	0.10	>0.05
Designs I	10.0	3.0	10.1	3.0	−0.03	>0.05
Designs I Content	9.9	3.1	10.2	3.0	−0.09	>0.05
Designs I Spatial	10.2	3.1	9.8	2.9	0.12	>0.05
Designs II	10.1	3.0	10.0	3.0	0.03	>0.05
Designs II Content	9.9	3.0	10.1	3.0	−0.08	>0.05
Designs II Spatial	10.4	3.0	9.6	2.9	0.27	<0.05
Spatial Addition	10.2	3.1	9.8	2.9	0.14	<0.05
Symbol Span	10.1	3.0	10.0	3.0	0.04	>0.05

Copyright 2009 by Pearson, Inc. Reproduced with permission. All rights reserved.

association memory; on WMS–IV the visual memory measures require memory for visual detail and visual–spatial memory. The effect sizes for index level differences are quite small on WMS–IV, ranging from −0.24 (Auditory Memory Index) to 0.17 (Visual Working Memory Index). At the subtest level, women obtained higher scores on Logical Memory and Verbal Paired Associates immediate and delayed recall. Men obtained higher scores on delayed memory for spatial locations and spatial working memory. Men did not show an advantage on memory or working memory for visual details. The effect sizes on WMS–IV subtests range from −0.25 (Logical Memory II) to 0.27 (Spatial Addition). The small effect sizes for WMS–IV indexes and subtests indicate little clinical relevance for the differences since there is considerable performance overlap between men and women. Both the WAIS–IV and WMS–IV show only small differences between men and women, therefore, there are no gender-specific norms. However, sex based normative adjustments are provided in the ACS for both the WAIS–IV and WMS–IV as part of fully adjusted normative scores.

Education Effects

The effects of education on cognitive test performances have been well studied. Education has a complex relationship with cognitive test performance, particularly in clinical populations. The relationship between education and performance is likely bi-directional with good cognitive ability likely impacting educational attainment and educational attainment improving performance on cognitive instruments. The influence of education is highly variable across abilities, creating different profiles across educational levels. The expression of clinical disorders, particularly dementia, is also likely to be impacted by educational attainment. Each of these relations will be discussed in more depth.

Research evaluating the effects of education on cognitive test performance identifies significant advantages to individuals with greater educational attainment. The relationship between educational attainment and cognitive test performance is complex. Individuals with greater educational attainment are exposed to more test taking situations, may learn better test taking skills, and are exposed to more information than those with less education. These factors provide a test-taking and content exposure advantage (e.g., vocabulary) as a function of education level. Therefore, education provides an advantage to test-takers that may not necessarily relate to better cognitive abilities but rather is the outcome of greater educational experiences.

Given that general ability influences both educational attainment and test performance, individuals with high cognitive ability will perform well on cognitive tests and will be likely to obtain more education. Therefore, adjusting scores for education level will unintentionally partial out variance related to cognitive ability, not just the effects of educational background. This is an important issue. If education effects on cognitive tests *only* represent the inherent abilities of the individual and the normative data are adjusted for education level, the sensitivity of the test is reduced. However, if education effects result in better or worse test performance due to non-ability factors, then a failure to adjust normative data may mask true differences in ability on the construct in question. If a highly educated person sustains a traumatic brain injury, and age-adjusted normative data is used, it might be difficult to accurately identify and quantify the person's cognitive deficits. This is because the person's prior education could have two influences on performance: (a) many pre-injury test scores were likely above the normative mean, and (b) following injury the person might simply be better equipped to perform well in a cognitive testing situation. Conversely, if an individual with low educational attainment sustains an injury, using education adjusted scores *could* mask the severity of the deficits in cognitive functioning due to the injury since ability has an impact on educational attainment.

While the impact of education on test performance is well-documented, additional benefits of educational exposure must be considered in the context of clinical evaluations. In particular, clinicians must consider that levels of education may affect the *development* and *expression* of cognitive disorders such as dementia (Murray et al., 2011). In older adults, education correlates with cognitive performance even after controlling for other background variables (Jefferson, et al., 2011). Low levels of education may be a risk factor for the development of dementia in later life, although, this is an inconsistent finding (Sharp & Gatz, 2011). In healthy older adults, higher education is associated with increased cortical thickness which may buffer the expression of cognitive impairment in patients with dementia (Liu et al., 2012) and the positive impact of education may be greater than the negative impact of neuropathology on cognitive functioning (Murray et al., 2011). Beyond the impact on cognition, education has an overall positive impact on health and longevity that is not explained by differences in socioeconomic advantages (Baker et al., 2011). While most of the research on education effects is based on healthy elderly and dementia patients, the same principle of education affecting the development and expression of cognitive impairment likely applies to other clinical groups as well, such as traumatic brain injury. The sensitivity of a test to brain dysfunction is likely affected by education.

The relationship of education and specific cognitive measures varies considerably (Dori & Chelune, 2004; Tombaugh, Kozak, & Rees, 1999).

The degree to which educational attainment correlates with cognitive test performance is proportional to the degree to which the test correlates with general cognitive ability; tests with low correlations with general ability have lower correlations with education (Heaton et al., 2003). Since cognitive tests correlate at different levels with educational attainment, the rates at which specific cognitive profiles are observed vary considerably by education level (Dori & Chelune, 2004). For example, in individuals with higher education levels, large discrepancies between verbal scores (which tend to be high) and visual−perceptual abilities are much more common than in individuals with lower education levels (Dori & Chelune, 2004). Education level also impacts variability in performance across serial assessments in healthy adults (Pearson, 2009), although education does not reduce the rate of cognitive loss associated with dementia (Zahodne et al., 2011). In a single assessment, variability within a profile that is consistent with the examinee's education level could be mistaken as indicative of cognitive dysfunction if education is not considered. In serial assessment, controlling for education level can improve the sensitivity to changes in functioning (see Chapter 6).

High education levels can mask cognitive difficulties in patient populations, reducing the sensitivity of the tests in these populations. Similarly, low education levels can result in misidentification of cognitively healthy individuals as cognitively impaired. When education effects are not taken into consideration, over 30% of healthy adults with fewer than 12 years of education would be identified as memory impaired on the WMS−III (Heaton et al., 2003). On a battery of neuropsychological tests, healthy adults with low education levels perform in the impaired range on multiple measures, a performance that gives the appearance of global cognitive impairment (Belzunces dos Santos, de Souza Silva Tudesco, Caboclo, & Yacubian, 2011). Considering the impact of education on test performance can improve the specificity to low, but normal, cognitive functioning.

It has been argued that education level correlates with cognitive test performance in normally developing, healthy, individuals but not in clinical populations (Reitan & Wolfson, 1996). Therefore, adjusting scores for education level would only reduce the sensitivity of neuropsychological tests to brain injury. However, education is correlated with test performance in patient populations for many cognitive tests (Boone, Victor, Wen, Ranzani, & Ponton, 2007) and in some cases, education level is more highly correlated with cognitive performance in patient populations than in healthy controls (Randolph, Lansing, Ivnik, Cullum, & Hermann, 1999). Education does result in performance differences within a variety of clinical populations. Therefore, on tests where scores correlate with education, it is important for clinicians to consider the examinees education level when determining if a patient's score appears unexpectedly low. However, it is difficult for clinicians to know the correlation between a specific test and education level without statistical data.

Table 4.3 presents WAIS–IV index and subtest data by education level. Direct comparisons between two adjacent education levels, 12 years and 13–15 years of education, and between the extremes of the distribution, 8 or fewer years and more than 18 years, are provided. The overall distribution of mean scores across education levels illustrates the relationship between education and specific cognitive skills. Given the large sample sizes, even small differences between groups will yield statistically significant results; therefore, to get a better sense of the impact of education on test performance effect sizes should be evaluated.

The range of scores varies across education levels by index and subtest. At the index level, Verbal Comprehension shows the largest score variance ranges from 81.3 to 115.5. The difference between the highest and lowest education levels produces an effect size of −2.69. This is a very large effect size and indicates that education level will have a very big impact on the expression of impairment at the extremes of the distribution. For example, someone with more than 18 years of education would need to lose over 30 points on average to obtain a score 1 standard deviation below the mean; however, the mean for individuals with 8 or fewer years of education is already below 1 standard deviation below the mean. In the middle of the distribution, the difference between a high school diploma and some college produces a moderate effect for Verbal Comprehension, −0.5. The difference between adjacent groups is less extreme and the effect of adjusting scores is much smaller than the impact observed when comparing performances at the extremes. Finally, for groups near the mean in the standardization sample, such as the 13–15 year group, education adjustments will yield no interpretable difference in performance from traditional standard scores. Therefore, education-adjusted norms will be less useful in these groups.

Of the remaining index scores, the smallest range of scores is observed on Processing Speed (89.3 to 105.7). The effect size between the extreme groups is −0.97, still large but a smaller impact on the expression of loss of cognitive functioning than VCI. Additionally, note that for the high education group, there is a 10-point discrepancy between VCI and PSI with VCI being much higher than PSI. In the lowest education sample, the opposite pattern is observed. These naturally occurring differences in cognitive profiles can cloud the interpretation of differences in index performance (i.e., large VCI vs. PSI split indicative of brain injury). For the comparison of groups in the middle of the

TABLE 4.3 WAIS–IV Core Index and Subtest Mean Scores, by Education Level

| | Education Level (By Years) | | | | | | | | | | | | | | Group Differences | | | |
| | 8 or Less | | 9–11 | | 12 | | 13–15 | | 16 | | 17–18 | | More than 18 | | 12 vs. 13–15 | | Vs. More than 18 | |
Score	Mean	SD	Mean	SD	Mean	SD	Mean	SD	Mean	SD	Mean	SD	Mean	SD	Effect Size	p	Effect Size	p
Verbal Comprehension Index	81.3	13	86.7	13.9	95.2	12.8	101.6	12.5	108	12.8	110.9	11.8	115.5	11.3	−0.5	<0.001	−2.69	<0.001
Perceptual Reasoning Index	86.5	12.3	89.7	13.6	97.4	14.8	100.4	14.2	104.4	15.1	106.5	14.2	106.1	14.3	−0.2	<0.01	−1.56	<0.001
Working Memory Index	84.3	12.5	88.7	14	97	14	100.8	14.1	106	14.2	107.4	12.9	109.5	13	−0.3	<0.001	−2.00	<0.001
Processing Speed Index	89.3	17.3	90.7	15.3	98.3	14.7	101.2	14	104	14.5	106.1	13.8	105.7	15	−0.2	<0.05	−0.97	<0.001
Full Scale IQ	82	12.6	86.4	13.8	96.2	13.7	101.4	13.1	107.1	14	107.1	14	111.7	12.5	−0.4	<0.001	−2.36	<0.001
Vocabulary	6.5	2.2	7.4	2.6	9.1	2.6	10.5	2.6	11.6	2.7	12.3	2.6	13.1	2.3	−0.5	<0.001	−2.98	<0.001
Similarities	6.9	2.9	7.9	2.9	9.3	2.6	10.1	2.5	11.3	2.4	11.7	2.5	12.7	2.1	−0.3	<0.001	−2.11	<0.001
Information	6.7	2.6	7.6	2.8	9.1	2.7	10.3	2.8	11.6	2.8	12	2.6	12.6	2.6	−0.4	<0.001	−2.26	<0.001
Block Design	7.9	2.9	8.4	2.8	9.6	3	10.1	2.9	10.8	3.1	11.1	2.9	10.6	3.1	−0.1	>0.05	−0.94	<0.001
Matrix Reasoning	7.4	2.5	8	2.9	9.5	3.1	10.2	2.9	11.1	3.1	11.6	3	12.2	3	−0.2	>0.05	−1.86	<0.001
Visual Puzzles	7.9	2.4	8.4	2.7	9.7	3.1	10.1	3	10.6	3.2	10.9	3	10.6	2.9	−0.2	>0.05	−1.08	<0.001
Digit Span	7.5	2.9	8.3	3.1	9.7	2.9	10.1	2.9	11.1	3	11.1	2.7	11.5	3.1	−0.2	>0.05	−1.37	<0.001
Arithmetic	7	2.2	7.8	2.5	9.3	2.7	10.2	2.8	11.1	2.9	11.6	2.7	12	2.5	−0.3	<0.001	−2.19	<0.001
Coding	7.7	3.2	8	3	9.6	2.9	10.3	2.9	10.8	2.9	11.4	2.7	11.6	3.2	−0.2	<0.01	−1.23	<0.001
Symbol Search	8.3	3.8	8.6	3.3	9.7	3	10.2	2.9	10.7	3.1	10.9	2.9	10.9	2.9	−0.1	>0.05	−0.69	<0.001

Note: Sample size 0–8 years = 220, 9–11 years = 243, 12 years = 647, 13–15 years = 553, 16 years = 267, 17–18 years = 297, more than 18 years = 43.
Copyright 2008 by Pearson, Inc. Reproduced with permission. All rights reserved.

distribution, the effect size for PSI is only 0.20 suggesting very small performance changes between adjacent groups.

Another important characteristic of education effects on cognitive variables is that the relationship is not typically linear across education levels. In particular, observe that score change is smaller for most measures from 16 years to greater than 18 years than between other points in the distribution. A linear model would require the scores to be higher than they actually are at the higher education levels. Similarly, at the lower end of the distribution, a linear model would require lower scores than were actually obtained. In addition to score change, the standard deviation of scores is not necessarily the same across education groups. For VCI, scores become less variable as education increases. What is not illustrated in Table 4.3 is the skew of the distribution that can also change in meaningful ways across education level (e.g., from positive to negative skew). Traditional regression models, even non-linear models, do not control for changes in variability or skew across the regression line. To properly model education effect, novel norming techniques are required.

At the subtest level, Vocabulary shows the largest range between the lowest and highest educational groups, more than any other variable on the WAIS–IV ($d = -2.98$). Clearly, education effects play an important role on this test. Also, individuals of high ability tend to score highest on these tests; therefore, they will need to lose a great deal of function in this skill to show a deficit. Vocabulary, and VCI more generally, are considered resistant to decline; therefore, a patient needs to lose a lot more function on these tests in order to be considered deficient. In other words, the rate of cognitive decline is slower on these tasks early in a progressive decline and scores tend to be higher than those on other skills in highly educated patients. Therefore, Vocabulary and VCI will remain higher than other cognitive skills. Adjusting for education will have the most profound effect on these scores. On the other hand, Symbol Search shows the smallest differences of any score on the WAIS–IV. Therefore, education adjustments will have only a small effect on observed results for Symbol Search.

Table 4.4 presents descriptive statistics for the WMS–IV, by education level. Among WMS–IV Indexes, the Visual Working Memory index has the largest difference between the highest and lowest education groups ($d = -1.67$). While this difference is not as large as seen for Verbal Comprehension, it is similar to the WAIS–IV Perceptual Reasoning Index. Education shows the smallest effect on the WMS–IV Delayed Memory Index ($d = -0.89$) which is similar to the WAIS–IV Processing Speed Index effect size. At the subtest level, the largest education effect is observed on Spatial Addition ($d = -1.47$) and the smallest effect size is on Visual Reproduction II ($d = -0.49$). Adjacent education groups show small differences with the biggest differences

TABLE 4.4 WMS–IV Core Index and Subtest Mean Scores, by Education Level

| Score | Education Level (By Years) | | | | | | | | | | | | | | Group Differences | | | |
| | 8 or Less | | 9–11 | | 12 | | 13–15 | | 16 | | 17–18 | | More than 18 | | 12 vs. 13–15 | | 8 or Less vs. More than 18 | |
	Mean	SD	Mean	SD	Mean	SD	Mean	SD	Mean	SD	Mean	SD	Mean	SD	Effect Size	p	Effect Size	p
Immediate Memory Index	88.8	15.2	90.8	14.6	97.5	14.1	100.9	15.2	103.7	14.1	106.5	13.5	109.7	10.1	−0.27	<0.05	−1.45	<0.001
Delayed Memory Index	91.7	17.5	91.8	14.7	98	14.1	100.1	14.9	103.2	14.1	106.2	14.4	106.6	12.4	−0.15	>0.05	−0.89	<0.001
Auditory Memory Index	91.5	17	92.5	14	97.7	14.7	100.5	14.4	103.1	13.9	106.1	14.9	107.1	12.7	−0.20	>0.05	−0.96	<0.001
Visual Memory Index	91.2	15.9	92.2	15.2	98.3	14.7	100.2	14.7	102.8	14.7	105.4	12.9	106.5	13.2	−0.14	>0.05	−0.99	<0.001
Visual Working Memory Index	85.2	13.5	86.9	14.7	97.4	13.7	99.6	15	103.8	14	107.9	12.5	108.6	17.2	−0.14	>0.05	−1.67	<0.001
Logical Memory I	8.2	3.4	8.5	3	9.6	2.9	10.1	2.8	10.6	2.8	11.1	2.9	11.1	2.5	−0.18	>0.05	−0.90	<0.001
Logical Memory II	8.7	3.7	8.8	2.9	9.6	3.1	10.1	2.9	10.3	2.8	11	3	10.9	2.6	−0.16	>0.05	−0.62	<0.01

(Continued)

TABLE 4.4 (Continued)

| | Education Level (By Years) | | | | | | | | | | | | | | Group Differences | | | |
| | 8 or Less | | 9–11 | | 12 | | 13–15 | | 16 | | 17–18 | | More than 18 | | 12 vs. 13–15 | | 8 or Less vs. More than 18 | |
Score	Mean	SD	Mean	SD	Mean	SD	Mean	SD	Mean	SD	Mean	SD	Mean	SD	Effect Size	p	Effect Size	p
Verbal Paired Associates I	8.7	3	8.9	2.7	9.6	2.9	10.1	3	10.6	3	11	3.1	11.6	3	−0.19	>0.05	−0.96	<0.001
Verbal Paired Associates II	8.6	3.1	8.8	2.9	9.6	3	10	3	10.7	2.9	11	3	11.2	2.8	−0.12	>0.05	−0.84	<0.01
Visual Reproduction I	8.3	3.3	8.6	3.1	9.6	3.1	10.1	3	10.7	3.1	11	2.4	11.4	2.3	−0.16	>0.05	−1.00	<0.001
Visual Reproduction II	9	3.6	8.7	3.1	9.7	2.9	10	2.9	10.5	3	10.8	2.8	10.7	2.7	−0.11	>0.05	−0.49	>0.05
Designs I	7.5	2.5	8.1	2.8	9.8	2.9	10.2	3.1	10.5	2.7	10.7	2.9	10.8	2.9	−0.14	>0.05	−1.25	<0.01
Designs II	8.5	1.9	8.4	2.8	9.9	2.9	9.9	2.9	10.3	2.9	11	3.2	10.8	3.4	0.01	>0.05	−1.02	>0.05
Spatial Addition	7.2	2.4	7.9	2.7	9.5	2.8	10	3	10.8	2.8	11.6	2.7	11.2	3.8	−0.14	>0.05	−1.47	<0.001
Symbol Span	8.1	3.1	8.2	3	9.7	2.8	10	2.9	10.6	2.9	11.1	2.8	11.7	2.9	−0.13	>0.05	−1.16	<0.001

Note: Sample size 0–8 years = 149 (69), 9–11 years = 167 (91), 12 years = 438 (247), 13–15 years = 348 (238), 16 years = 172 (123), 17–18 years = 215 (142), more than 18 years = 30 (16), spatial addition and design memory in parentheses.

Copyright 2009 by Pearson, Inc. Reproduced with permission. All rights reserved.

occurring between 9–11 years versus 12 years of education, the same groups as observed on the WAIS–IV.

The findings for the education effects on the WAIS–IV and WMS–IV suggest that high levels of education may mask acquired impairments in cognitive functioning because patients need to lose a lot of ability before their performance reaches an impaired range. Similarly, those with very low levels of education may appear to be impaired without having lost any functioning. When age-adjusted standard scores are used, patients may show deficits in domains such as memory and processing speed, since these are less impacted by education and are susceptible to the effects of brain injury, but appear to have relatively intact verbal, perceptual, and working memory abilities, tasks related to education. If education adjusted norms are applied, the sensitivity and specificity should improve for patients at the ends of the distribution but have less impact on patients with average levels of educational attainment.

Tables 4.5 and 4.6 contain subtest scaled score to T-score conversions for Vocabulary and Visual Reproduction I, respectively. These tables are used by the ACS scoring assistant to convert subtest scaled scores to education-adjusted T-scores and illustrate the degree that scores are adjusted for education level. For Vocabulary, large adjustments in relative performance can be observed at the extremes of the distribution. Examinees with low education levels obtaining low average scaled scores of 6 and 7, obtain education adjusted scores in the average range. In individuals with more than 18 years of education, average scores of 8–10 are adjusted to be in the mild/moderate to mild impairment range. Visual Reproduction, however, yields much less dramatic adjustments even at the extremes of the distribution. Scaled scores of 10 remain average across all education levels. Scaled scores of 8 become low average for examinees with more than 16 years of education. For individuals with an average level of education (i.e., 12, 13–15 years), scores are not adjusted dramatically and for most variables do not change the interpretation of the scaled score.

Of all background characteristics, education is the most strongly associated with test performance. Specifically, individuals at the extreme ends of the distribution may obtain low or high scores due to education effects. These effects may mask deficits or create an impression of impairment in healthy individuals.

Race/Ethnicity Effects

Racial/ethnic differences in test performance occur on cognitive tests in healthy control (Manly, 2005) and clinical populations (Boone et al.,

TABLE 4.5 Scaled Score to Education Adjusted T-Score Conversion Table for Vocabulary

	Education Level (In Years)						
VC SS	0–8	9–11	12	13–15	16	17–18	>18
1	18	15	10	10	10	10	10
2	26	22	16	13	10	10	10
3	32	28	22	18	14	10	10
4	38	35	28	23	19	15	10
5	43	40	33	28	24	20	15
6	49	45	38	33	28	25	20
7	53	49	42	37	32	29	25
8	57	53	47	41	37	34	30
9	61	56	50	45	41	38	34
10	65	60	54	49	45	41	38
11	69	63	57	52	48	45	42
12	73	66	61	56	51	49	46
13	77	69	65	60	55	53	50
14	80	73	69	64	59	57	54
15	84	77	73	67	62	61	57
16	88	81	77	71	66	64	61
17	90	85	81	75	70	68	65
18	90	90	85	79	74	72	69
19	90	90	89	83	79	76	74

Copyright 2008 by Pearson, Inc. Reproduced with permission. All rights reserved.

2007). When considering the differences between racial/ethnic groups, there are a number of issues to consider. A detailed discussion of all the issues related to racial/ethnic group differences is beyond the scope of this chapter. Comprehensive reviews are provided in Weiss et al. (2006) and Weiss, Chen, Harris, Holdnack, & Saklofske (2010). Although not all issues are discussed here, some important aspects will be addressed.

A common misperception suggests that cognitive tests contain significant item bias that produces the differences observed between ethnic/racial groups. However, the application of modern statistical methods is used to identify and eliminate such items. Demographics, such as race,

TABLE 4.6 Scaled Score to Education Adjusted T-Score Conversion Table for Visual Reproduction I

	Education Level (In Years)						
VR II SS	0–8	9–11	12	13–15	16	17–18	>18
1	26	22	21	21	20	19	16
2	29	26	24	24	23	21	19
3	32	29	27	27	26	24	22
4	35	33	30	30	28	26	25
5	38	36	33	33	31	30	29
6	41	40	37	36	34	33	32
7	44	44	40	40	38	37	36
8	47	47	44	43	41	40	40
9	50	50	48	47	44	44	44
10	54	54	51	50	48	48	48
11	57	57	55	54	52	52	52
12	59	59	59	57	56	56	56
13	62	62	62	60	59	59	59
14	65	65	65	63	62	62	62
15	68	68	68	65	64	64	64
16	70	70	70	68	67	67	67
17	73	73	73	71	70	70	70
18	76	76	76	74	73	73	73
19	79	79	79	77	76	76	76

Copyright 2009 by Pearson, Inc. Reproduced with permission. All rights reserved.

ethnicity, and educational level, are proxy variables for a host of interacting and potentially additive environmental factors that more directly influence the development, maintenance and decline of cognitive abilities across the life span. Ethnic/racial differences can be diminished by controlling for some of these environmental factors.

Cognition is malleable, to an extent, by environmental factors that mediate opportunities for cognitive growth and maintenance of cognitive abilities and the effects of these factors may be cumulative across the life span. Enriching, stimulating environments enhance cognitive development and the maintenance of cognitive abilities; whereas impoverishing environments inhibit that growth. Further, the factors that inhibit cognitive enrichment interact with each other, such that the presence of one factor makes the occurrence of other inhibitory factors more probable. The negative effects of cognitively impoverishing environments interact over the course of a lifetime such that the impact worsens with age. At the same time, historical patterns of immigration and racism limit opportunities for quality education, occupational advancement, and access to quality health care, thereby impoverishing the cognitive developmental trajectories of generations of cultural and linguistic minority groups. When the background environmental factors are considered, racial/ethnic differences are significantly reduced.

For adults ages 20 to 90 administered the WAIS–IV, race or ethnicity explains 15 and 11% of the variance in FSIQ score differences in the African-American/White (AA/W) and Hispanic/White (H/W) comparisons, respectively. In contrast, education, occupation, income, region and gender account for 35.1% of the variance in these score differences, respectively. After controlling for this second set of variables, race or ethnicity explain 9.2 and 3.8% of the variance in AA/W and H/W score differences, respectively.

For adolescents ages 16 to 19 administered the WAIS–IV, race or ethnicity explains 5.4 and 12% of the variance in FSIQ score differences in the AA/W and H/W comparisons, respectively. In contrast, parent education, occupation, income, region, and gender account for 22.5 and 29.3% of the variance, respectively. After controlling for this second set of variables, race or ethnicity explain only 1.5 and 1.9% of the variance in AA/W and H/W score differences, respectively.

As elaborated by Weiss and colleagues (2006, 2010), data supports the thesis that observed score differences among demographic groups are not due to race or ethnicity, but to powerful environmental factors that underlie those differences. One would then expect the differences to diminish as the effects of historical racism slowly abate over generations, and as patterns of immigration and acculturation among Hispanics shift over time. Weiss et al. (2010) examined this issue by segmenting the WAIS–IV standardization sample into five birth cohorts and testing the demographic differences. There was a strong trend toward decreasing score differences with younger cohorts. As shown in Table 4.7, the score differences are reduced for younger ages. Racial and ethnic differences in IQ have been reduced by more than half a standard deviation between 1917 and 1991, a reduction only partially explained by increases in educational attainment across the generations.

Cognitive test performance relates to a number of different socioeconomic status (SES) factors, such as rates of premature births or prenatal health care, exposure to violent crime, and quality of education (McDaniel, 2006). Parent occupation and education level, and early

TABLE 4.7   WAIS–IV Mean FSIQ Difference Scores between Racial/Ethnic Groups, by Birth Cohort

	Birth Cohort				
Groups	1917–1942 (Ages 65–90)	1943–1962 (Ages 45–64)	1963–1977 (Ages 30–44)	1978–1987 (Ages 20–29)	1988–1991 (Ages 16–19)
AA/White	19.3	17.2	13.1	13.4	10
Hispanic/ White	17.9	13.62	14.2	7.3	9.3

Note: Ages shown are at time of standardization testing in 2007.
Copyright 2008 by Pearson, Inc. Reproduced with permission. All rights reserved.

educational experiences also relate to cognitive test scores and vary among ethnic groups (Byrd et al., 2006). Historically, significant monetary differences invested in the education of minority children versus white children significantly impacted the educational experiences of older African-Americans (Lucas et al., 2005). Therefore, the attained education level in older African-Americans may not be equivalent to the educational experiences of whites at the same level. However, African-Americans are a heterogeneous group and the degree to which they have experienced economic, health, occupational, or educational disadvantage varies. While it is important to consider racial/ethnic differences when interpreting test scores, considering the background of the individual is also important in making appropriate clinical decisions.

A failure to consider racial/ethnic group differences can result in misinterpretation of obtained test scores. Specifically, misinterpretations can occur when applying age only adjusted norms to identify cognitive deficits indicative of acquired brain injury or cognitive decline. When standard norms are applied, 15 to 20% of healthy Hispanics and up to 35% of healthy African-Americans may be misidentified as having general cognitive or memory dysfunction compared to 10–14% of Whites (Heaton et al., 2003). Tables 4.8 and 4.9 present WAIS–IV and WMS–IV descriptive data by racial/ethnic groups. In addition, comparison data is provided for White *vs.* African-American differences. The effect sizes for WAIS–IV indexes range from 0.8 (WMI, PSI) to 1.1 (PRI, FSIQ) and from 0.6 (Digit Span) to 1.1 (Block Design) for WAIS–IV subtests. The effect sizes for WMS–IV indexes range from 0.6 (AMI, VMI, DMI) to 0.7 (IMI, VWMI) and from 0.4 (VPA I and II, VR II) to 0.7 (LM I and II, SA, SY) for subtests.

In general, WAIS–IV shows large effect sizes and WMS–IV shows moderate differences between Whites and African-Americans.

TABLE 4.8   WAIS–IV Core Index and Subtest Mean Scores, by Ethnicity

	White		African-American		Hispanic		Asian		White vs. African-American	
Score	Mean	SD	Mean	SD	Mean	SD	Mean	SD	Effect Size	p
Verbal Comprehension Index	102.9	14.2	90.5	15	90.9	15.4	103.6	15.5	0.9	<0.001
Perceptual Reasoning Index	103	14.5	87.5	13	93.7	14.1	104.5	15.4	1.1	<0.001
Working Memory Index	102.9	14.1	91.5	14.7	90.2	14.8	104.6	15.2	0.8	<0.001
Processing Speed Index	102.4	14.5	90.6	15.5	95.7	15.1	107.4	16.1	0.8	<0.001
Full Scale IQ	103.4	14	87.7	14.4	91.1	14.5	106.1	15.5	1.1	<0.001
Vocabulary	10.6	2.8	8.4	3.1	8.2	3.1	11	3.6	0.8	<0.001
Similarities	10.5	2.7	8.4	2.9	8.4	2.9	10.4	2.7	0.8	<0.001
Information	10.5	3	8.1	2.9	8.5	3.2	10.7	2.9	0.8	<0.001
Block Design	10.6	2.9	7.6	2.6	9.1	2.8	11	3.3	1.1	<0.001
Matrix Reasoning	10.6	3	8.2	3.1	8.7	3.1	11	2.8	0.8	<0.001
Visual Puzzles	10.5	3.1	7.9	2.4	9	2.8	10.3	2.8	0.9	<0.001
Digit Span	10.5	2.9	8.8	3.1	8.3	3.1	10.8	3	0.6	<0.001
Arithmetic	10.6	2.9	8.2	2.7	8.3	2.7	11	3.2	0.8	<0.001
Coding	10.5	2.9	8.3	3.1	9	3	11.7	3.5	0.7	<0.001
Symbol Span	10.4	3	8.3	3.2	9.4	3.3	11.1	3.3	0.7	<0.001

Note: Sample Size White = 1355, African-American = 400, Hispanic = 399, Asian = 60.
Copyright 2008 by Pearson, Inc. Reproduced with permission. All rights reserved.

Subsequently, a failure to account for ethnic group differences could mask cognitive symptoms in whites or suggest cognitive impairment in healthy African-Americans.

Next to education level, race/ethnicity has the most impact on observed test performance. Studies indicate that Hispanics and African-Americans are at higher risk for misidentification of cognitive impairment in the absence of a disease process. The average performance of Whites and Asians is slightly higher than the overall population that potentially can affect the sensitivity of the WAIS–IV and

TABLE 4.9 WMS–IV Core Index and Subtest Scores, by Ethnicity

Score	White Mean	SD	African-American Mean	SD	Hispanic Mean	SD	Asian Mean	SD	White vs. African-American ES	p
Immediate Memory	101.9	14.9	91.3	14.7	94.6	14.6	104.4	14	0.7	<0.001
Delayed Memory	101.4	14.8	92.1	15.4	96.4	15.2	105	13.8	0.6	<0.001
Auditory Memory	101.9	14.9	92.5	14.8	96.1	15.5	101.1	13.8	0.6	<0.001
Visual Memory	101	14.7	92.5	15.2	96.2	14.3	107.9	14.7	0.6	<0.001
Visual Working Memory Index	102.1	14.6	91	15.5	95.6	14.9	108.2	15.8	0.7	<0.001
Logical Memory I	10.4	2.9	8.5	2.9	9	3.3	9.9	2.7	0.7	<0.001
Logical Memory II	10.4	3	8.5	2.9	9.3	3.3	9.9	2.7	0.7	<0.001
Verbal Paired Associates I	10.2	3	9	2.9	9.6	3	10.4	2.8	0.4	<0.001
Verbal Paired Associates II	10.2	3	9	3.3	9.5	3	10.6	2.9	0.4	<0.001
Visual Reproduction I	10.3	3	8.6	3.1	9.1	3	11.2	2.6	0.6	<0.001
Visual Reproduction II	10.1	3	9	3	9.6	3.2	10.8	2.7	0.4	<0.001
Designs I	10.3	3	8.7	2.9	9.2	2.9	11.7	2.7	0.5	<0.001
Designs II	10.2	3	8.9	2.6	9.5	2.7	12.1	3.3	0.5	<0.001
Spatial Addition	10.3	3	8.4	2.9	9.5	3	11.8	3.2	0.7	<0.001
Symbol Span	10.4	2.9	8.4	2.9	8.9	3.1	10.5	3.1	0.7	<0.001

Note: Sample Size White = 933 (503), African-American = 259 (174), Hispanic = 264 (206), Asian = 39 (30), spatial addition and designs in parentheses.
Copyright 2009 by Pearson, Inc. Reproduced with permission. All rights reserved.

WMS–IV in identifying cognitive deficits in these groups. Normative adjustments using race/ethnicity may improve the sensitivity and specificity of the tests in clinical application.

DEMOGRAPHIC ADJUSTMENTS TO NORMS

Given the extensive body of research demonstrating differences on cognitive tests by education, sex, and ethnicity, neuropsychological studies have proposed developing alternate norms for subgroups of examinees. Karzmark, Heaton, Grant, and Matthews (1984) applied multiple regression techniques to adjust normative data on the Halstead-Reitan Neuropsychological Battery Average Impairment Index to account for the significant correlations with education, sex, and ethnicity. Additionally, educational adjustments exist for Trail Making Tests A and B (Tombaugh, 2004), CVLT (Norman, Evans, Miller, & Heaton, 2000), PASAT (Gonzalez, 2006), and the Boston Naming Test (Heaton, Avitable, Grant, & Matthews, 1999). Ethnicity adjustments exist for the Stroop test (Moering, Schinka, Mortimer, & Graves, 2004), Symbol Digit Modalities Test (Gonzalez et al., 2007), CVLT (Norman et al., 2000), WAIS–R/WMS–R (Lucas et al., 2005), and the PASAT (Gonzalez et al., 2006). Ethnicity adjusted normative data improves diagnosis of dementia among older African Americans (Lucas et al., 2005). Full demographic corrections (i.e., education, gender, and ethnicity) were developed for the WAIS–R (Heaton et al., 1991) and the WAIS–III/WMS–III (Taylor & Heaton, 2001). The development and use of demographic adjustments has been researched for several decades.

Even though research has demonstrated the utility of demographic norms, no consensus exists about the clinical application of demographic adjustments. Reitan and Wolfson (1996) argue that it is not appropriate to make demographic adjustments in the evaluation of patients with brain injury because it makes the test less sensitive to the effects of the injury. Unadjusted raw scores (e.g., not even age adjustments) show greater cognitive impairment in clinical populations compared to using demographic adjustments (Golden & van den Broek, 1998). Both, adjusted and unadjusted scores can equally identify focal lesions (Golden & van den Broek, 1998). Alternatively, Bernard (1989) found that unadjusted scores over-classify healthy Whites with low education levels, Hispanics, and African-Americans as cognitively impaired. The neuropsychological evaluation of educationally and ethnically diverse populations is a complex issue (Brickman, Cabo, & Manly, 2006).

There are clear advantages to using demographic adjustments to normative data. When evaluating individuals with low educational attainment or ethnic/racial minorities, using only age-adjusted or raw scores decreases the specificity of cognitive tests in identifying brain injury or dysfunction (Heaton et al., 1999, 2003; Norman et al., 2000). Also, when evaluating individuals with high levels of educational attainment, demographically adjusted norms improve diagnostic sensitivity (Morgan et al., 2008). While, demographic adjustments to norms show good sensitivity and specificity for a number of clinical populations (Taylor & Heaton, 2001), their primary advantage is improving diagnostic specificity for minorities (Manly, 2005) and examinees with low education levels (Heaton et al., 1999).

Although there are advantages to adjusting norms for ethnic group differences, there are also disadvantages. Adjusted scores may be misunderstood or inappropriately applied. There is no scientific method for identifying an individual's race or ethnicity (e.g., these are primarily social/political constructs) and the background/social forces for which race/ethnicity serve as a "proxy" are not completely understood (Manly, 2005). Using race-based adjustments can result in examinees not getting needed services because their adjusted scores are higher and may fall above an established cut-off (Manly & Echemendia, 2007). Applying adjustments for racial/ethnic group membership, fails to account for the underlying cultural, health, and educational factors that produce disparities in test performance. Therefore, the adjustments do not necessarily represent characteristics of the individual but rather represent general characteristics of the group (Manly, 2005; Manly & Echemendia, 2007). It is important to consider that within groups (e.g., ethnic, education, or sex) variability is greater than between group variability. The clinician must be clear about the rationale for using demographic adjustments to norms and the impact that such adjustments can have on the outcomes of an evaluation.

When to Use Demographic Adjustments

As a clinician, the decision about whether or not to use demographically adjusted norms depends primarily on the decisions or conclusions that need to be made. For example, if the purpose of the evaluation is to determine the examinees functioning relative to the general population (e.g., ability to work in any capacity, to live independently, or to understand social conventions; capacity to consent to treatment, etc.), then using standard age-adjusted norms is appropriate. If the evaluation requires a decision regarding the examinees ability to function in a specific environment (e.g., *"Can the examinee return to his job as a physician?"*) then demographic adjustments may be appropriate. If the primary purpose of the evaluation is to identify cognitive deficits that may indicate brain dysfunction or decline in cognitive functioning, using demographic adjustments is appropriate. However, it would be inappropriate to use demographic norms to diagnose mental retardation or learning disability because these disorders are diagnosed relative to the general population (e.g., someone is not "learning disabled" compared to other Caucasians or compared to other people with Master's Degrees).

In order to appropriately use demographic adjustments, the clinician should understand how the adjustments change the scores. In other words, how does the examinee's relative rank order on the test change with adjustments and what are the consequences of reporting lower or higher scores for that individual. Note that because scores change metrics from standard scaled scores to T-scores, it is important for comparative purposes to evaluate the percentile rank changes after demographic adjustments. Adjustments made near the middle of the distribution (e.g., education levels 12, 13–15) result in very small rank order changes, particularly on memory measures. Substantially larger effects are observed at the extremes, which include Asians and Whites with high education levels, and Hispanics and African-Americans with low education levels. For high ability groups, demographic adjustments always return a lower score (i.e., percentile rank and distance from the mean) compared to the standard age-adjusted norms. For lower ability groups, the adjusted scores will always be higher (i.e., percentile rank and distance from the mean) than the standard age-adjusted scores.

If having a low score results in some benefit (e.g., eligibility for some service, or receiving medical treatment), the potential exists that using demographic adjustments may deny those benefits to the examinee. This potential negative consequence should not completely influence the decision to use demographic adjustments; however, the clinician needs to be very clear about the appropriateness and rationale for their use. Similarly, adjusting a score higher can also have a negative consequence other than denial of a benefit. For example, in death penalty cases, having a higher score can influence the decision to pursue the death penalty instead of a lesser sentence, a great consequence to the individual. Clearly, the onus is on the clinician to demonstrate that comparing the examinee to individuals of a similar background is appropriate. In other words, is an examinee with historically low cognitive ability compared to the general population (e.g., low educational attainment, low IQ scores on testing) more culpable than someone with higher education who has an average IQ compared to the general population but whose demographic adjusted scores are in the low range of cognitive ability. The consequences for the individual and for society in general must be considered. If the purpose of the evaluation is to answer a question about a *change* in cognitive functioning, then the use of demographic norms is easily defended, if not then the examiner needs to have a sound rationale for adjusting the normative data.

Development of Demographic Adjustment to Norms

Many statistical models have been applied to developing adjustments to normative data. Primarily, regression based models are used (Karzmark et al., 1984; Heaton et al., 2003). There are clear advantages to using regression techniques, as long as the correct model is applied and it is consistent with the underlying assumptions of the relationship between the background and cognitive variables being adjusted. The primary assumption made during the development of the WAIS–IV and WMS–IV demographic adjustments was that higher education is associated with better or equal cognitive skills than lower levels of education, across all groups. In other words, there is no theoretical reason to assume that African-American males with a high level of education have *worse* cognitive skills than African-American males with an average degree of education. While the assumption may seem obvious, sampling artifacts can produce unexpected findings and some regression techniques will follow the sample data, yielding unexpected results. Additionally, the assumptions of equal variances (i.e., homoscedasticity) and equal skew across the regression line were assumed to not always hold true. When these conditions are false, the regression method systematically makes errors in the adjustment of scores along the regression line. Therefore, inferential norming techniques were applied to the derivation of the WAIS–IV and WMS–IV demographic adjustments.

The demographic adjustments are derived from the WAIS–IV and WMS–IV normative samples and an additional oversample of individuals with low and high education levels, and minorities. The oversampling is important because the standardization sample may not include sufficient cases for estimating the ability of certain groups (e.g., Hispanics with 17–18 years of education).

All interactions were evaluated (e.g., age by education, education by sex, education by sex by ethnicity) to determine the most appropriate model for adjusting the normative data. Given that education only norms were required as part of the WAIS–IV/WMS–IV project, education adjustments were developed prior to adjusting for sex and ethnicity. Education level is segmented into seven bands: 8 years or less, 9 to 11 years, 12 years, 13 to 15 years, 16 years, 17 to 18 years, and over 18 years. For full demographic adjustments, the sample is divided into groups as follows: White male, White female, African-American male, African-American female, Hispanic male, Hispanic female, Asian-male and Asian female. These samples are not stratified by census but include higher percentages of examinees from lower and higher education groups and more ethnic minorities.

Derivation of Education Subtest Adjusted T-Scores

The WAIS–IV and WMS–IV demographic adjustments are derived using inferential norming (Gorsuch, 2003; Roid, 2003; Wilkins, Rolfhus, Weiss, & Zhu, 2005). Various moments (means [M], standard deviations [SD], and skewness) of each age-adjusted subtest scaled score were calculated for each education group. The moments are plotted across education level, and various polynomial regressions ranging from linear to

4th degree polynomials were fit to the moment data. Functions for each score moment were selected based on consistency with underlying theoretical expectations and the pattern of improved cognitive skills with education level observed in the sample. For each subtest, the functions are used to derive estimates of the population moments. The estimated moments are used to generate theoretical distributions for each of the reported normative education groups, yielding mid-point percentiles for each age-adjusted scaled score within education group. The mid-point percentiles are converted to T-scores, using z-normalization, with a mean of 50, a standard deviation of 10, and a range of 10–90. The progression of standard scores within and across education groups is examined, and minor irregularities are eliminated by smoothing.

Derivation of Index Scores

The subtest adjusted T-scores were summed for each of the WAIS–IV and WMS–IV index scores. The data on these sums of T-scores demonstrated a high degree of similarity across education within each of the indexes. An analysis of variance revealed no statistically significant variation by education group in the mean scores for indexes. Consequently, the education groups were combined to construct the tables of index T-score equivalents of sums of subtest T-scores.

For each scale, the distribution of the sum of scaled scores was converted to a scale with a mean of 50 and a standard deviation of 10. This conversion was accomplished by preparing a cumulative frequency distribution of the actual sum of subtest T-scores, calculating mid-point percentiles, and for each index and using z-normalization calculating the appropriate index score equivalent for the sum of subtest T-scores. Successive adjustments were based on visual inspection of the distributions while attempting to keep the means and standard deviations of the scales close to 50 and 10.

Derivation of Full Demographic (Education, Sex, Ethnicity) Subtest and Index Adjusted T-Scores

Inferential norming was also used to derive the full-demographic adjustments. For full-demographic adjustments, the education adjusted T-scores for each subtest are used to derive the moments for each normative group (e.g., male vs. female). Regression functions for each score moment are selected based on consistency with observed associations between the demographic variables and the subtest scores, the pattern of curves observed in the normative sample, and the underlying theoretical model for education effects. For each subtest, the functions were used to derive estimates of the population moments. The estimated moments were then used to generate theoretical distributions for each of the reported normative sex by education groups, yielding percentiles for each sex by education-adjusted T-score. These percentiles were converted to T-scores with a mean of 50, a standard deviation of 10, and a range of 10–90. The progression of standard scores within and across sex by education groups was then examined, and minor irregularities were eliminated by smoothing. The first step of creating sex by education norms accounts for the interaction between sex and education. The final full-demographic adjustments are made using the education by sex adjusted scores.

Functions for the four ethnic groups are derived using the sex by education-adjusted subtest T-scores. Functions for each score moment are selected based on consistency with observed associations between the demographic variables and the subtest scores, the pattern of curves observed in the normative sample, and the theoretical model of education effects. Scores are converted to fully adjusted T-scores using the procedure described previously. Finally, an additional evaluation of the distributions by education, sex, and ethnicity was done to ensure any interactions were accounted for in the final norms. Index scores are derived using the same procedure applied for the derivation of education index scores.

Table 4.10 presents full demographic-adjusted WAIS–IV Index scores by racial/ethnic group. Application of full-demographic adjustments yields no differences between the groups. The use of full demographic adjustments will increase the rank order of the scores in African-American and Hispanic groups to be equivalent to Whites and Asians. This does not necessarily make the scores more or less appropriate than education only corrections; however, the specificity of the scores for identifying brain injury and loss of cognitive functioning should improve when applied to these groups.

Intercorrelation of WAIS–IV/WMS–IV Full Demographically Adjusted Scores

Adjusting scores by demographic variables changes the relationship between scores both within and between test batteries. A detailed presentation of this phenomenon is presented in the Advanced Clinical Solutions Clinical and Interpretation Manual (Pearson, 2009). For the purposes of this chapter, it is important to have a general sense of the change in the relationship between variables of interest. In general, the correlations among WAIS–IV subtests and indexes are lower after applying demographic corrections. The correlations among WAIS–IV age-adjusted verbal subtests range from 0.64 to 0.74; however, applying full demographic adjustments reduces that range to 0.50 to 0.63. The WAIS–IV Index correlations range from 0.45 to 0.86 but only from 0.29 to 0.81 for fully adjusted T-scores. Increased variability among the

TABLE 4.10 WAIS–IV Core Index and Subtest Education and Full Demographically Adjusted Scores, by Ethnicity

Score	White Mean	White SD	African-American Mean	African-American SD	Hispanic Mean	Hispanic SD	Asian Mean	Asian SD	White Vs. African-American Effect Size	p
Verbal Comprehension Index	49.8	9.8	50	10.1	50	10.2	50.6	9.9	0	>0.05
Perceptual Reasoning Index	50	10.1	50.1	10	50	10	50.4	11	0	>0.05
Working Memory Index	49.7	9.9	50.1	9.9	49.9	10.2	51.5	9.4	0	>0.05
Processing Speed Index	49.9	10	49.9	9.9	50.2	9.8	50.5	10.1	0	>0.05
Full Scale IQ	49.8	9.8	50	10.3	50.1	10.2	50.9	10.2	0	>0.05

Note: Sample Size White = 1355, African-American = 400, Hispanic = 399, Asian = 60.
Copyright 2009 by Pearson, Inc. Reproduced with permission. All rights reserved.

WAIS–IV subtests and indexes should be expected when using demographically adjusted scores.

For the WMS–IV, the correlations are lower when demographic norms are applied although differences are smaller than those observed for the WAIS–IV. Age-adjusted verbal memory subtest correlations range from 0.37 to 0.87 and for full demographic adjustments the range is from 0.36 to 0.84. The age-adjusted index correlations range from 0.48 to 0.87 and from 0.39 to 0.85 for full demographic adjustments. Correlations between the WAIS–IV and WMS–IV are also lower when applying demographic adjustments. For age-adjusted indexes, the correlations range from 0.40 to 0.71, while the range is from 0.30 to 0.61 for full demographic adjustments. Clinicians should expect more dissociation among memory measures and between intellectual and memory functioning when using demographically adjusted norms. Greater variability does not indicate pathology but is a direct consequence of lower between test correlations (see Chapter 3, which discusses Variability in WAIS–IV/WMS–IV test scores).

The practical implication, however, is that when using demographically-adjusted norms a clinician is somewhat more likely to see greater variability between index scores. Index difference scores are often used to support an inference of acquired cognitive impairment. The clinician simply needs to be aware, however, that some of this difference, when using demographically-adjusted norms, results from how controlling variance attributable to demographic variables reduces the correlation between indexes—thus it is in part a psychometric factor that needs to be considered.

Clinical Application

Clinical data applying demographically adjusted norms is found throughout this text. In each chapter that addresses a specific clinical sample, tables comparing patients with both matched controls and a random sample of low and high education healthy controls are presented. Using matched control studies only does not illustrate the impact of demographically adjusted norms given that both the clinical group and the matched controls have scores adjusted by a constant value; therefore, the effect sizes will be very similar between using standard norms and demographically adjusted norms. Comparing clinical groups to random cases of low and high education normal controls provides a better illustration for the clinician of how the scores will enable them to identify patients from low functioning healthy individuals or to individuals with very high levels of functioning. This model better approximates the clients often seen in practice and enables a better comparison on which to make decisions about using demographic adjustments.

Caveats in Using Demographic Adjustments to Norms

The use of demographic norms requires that certain assumptions are true. The primary assumption is that the individual's demographic background is representative of their personal experiences and is a good estimate of their pre-morbid ability. There are no hard and fast rules that can be applied to answer this question; however, there are some factors to consider. The first consideration is whether or not the examinee's education level reflects their ability or not. In cases where the examinee has a chronic medical, neurological, or psychiatric condition, their education level may have been disrupted by the condition itself. Individuals with chronic epilepsy from childhood, a history of brain tumors and treatment during childhood, or any chronic disease that may have limited their ability to attend or benefit from schooling may not have reached their full academic potential. Some psychiatric conditions, such as schizophrenia, have initial onset of symptoms in adolescence and can have a negative impact on educational attainment. Similarly, individuals with learning disabilities may never achieve academically at a level consistent with their cognitive abilities. In these and similar situations, the examiner must consider if the attained level of education is a good proxy for a patient's pre-morbid intellectual functioning.

The second consideration is whether or not to use adjustments for race/ethnicity. As stated previously, racial/ethnic status cannot be determined by any scientific means and it may not be possible to accurately classify an individual client. The clinician will need to use the examinee's own conceptualization of their race/ethnicity. The clinician will also need to determine if the individual's background is representative of the factors that can result in cognitive differences between groups. In other words, if the examinee grew up in a wealthy neighborhood, with highly educated parents, attended good schools, and is also Hispanic, do the adjustments made to the normative data accurately reflect the individual's background? It was hypothesized that socioeconomic disadvantage, health care disparities, poor educational experiences, and other potential discriminatory factors may account for the between group differences but if none of these factors is present for a specific individual, does it make sense to adjust for ethnicity? There is no simple answer to this question and in some cases it may be yes (e.g., level of acculturation in the family generally may be low, affecting language development, effects of racism limiting opportunities) or in some cases no (e.g., background is not inconsistent with other non-minority groups). The clinician must use his or her judgment as to when it is appropriate to adjust for racial/ethnic differences.

The final consideration for using demographic norms is related to whether the application will really make a difference or not. If the examinee has 13 years of education, the normative adjustments will be negligible so does it make sense to adjust the scores or not? In some cases, the answer may still be yes, if the other background factors will have an impact (e.g., African-American, female, 13 years of education) and the question concerns a change in cognitive status. In other cases, it may not be helpful even when looking at a change in function. Despite the fact that the changes may or may not be large, the best approach to using demographic norms is to be consistent. If there is a question of cognitive change, then use either the education or demographic adjustments. If a patient's background is not consistent with some of the group factors that might result in between racial/ethnic group differences, then use education only adjustments. The clinician needs to be able to rationally defend his or her choice and to apply the correct norms and interpretation to answer the specific referral questions.

CASE STUDIES

CASE STUDY 1

APPROPRIATE USE OF DEMOGRAPHIC ADJUSTMENTS Mr. F. is a 59-year-old, Hispanic, married man, who completed 9 years of education. Mr. F. has suffered from Parkinson's disease for over 15 years with increasing motor symptoms but relatively intact cognition. He is ambulatory with a walker as long as he takes his medication as prescribed. Mr. F. was formerly employed as an auto mechanic for over 30 years but has not been able to work the past 7—8 years. He has been able to care for himself at home; however, within the past year, his family has observed a decline in his memory functioning and reasoning skills. The family is concerned about his capacity to remain at home alone and potential safety issues. His wife is still employed and cannot be home with her husband during the day. Mr. F. has been forgetting to take his medicine despite using a pill box and his wife calling home to remind him. He has lost weight and the family fears he is not remembering to eat during the day. Mr. F. was referred for neuropsychological evaluation to determine if there has been a significant change in memory functioning and to determine if there are early signs of dementia.

The WAIS—IV and WMS—IV were administered as part of a neuropsychological battery. Mr. F. was medicated for the evaluation but still showed characteristic signs of Parkinsonism including: resting tremor, rigidity, festinating gate, and masked facies. He had obvious difficulty initiating behavior but showed no signs of impaired mental status. Tests involving motor control were performed slowly and with difficulty. On the Brief Cognitive Status Exam (BCSE), his orientation, memory, and language were within normal limits. He showed slight processing speed and cognitive control weaknesses. His overall score of 47 was average for his age and education.

Table 4.11 presents Mr. F.'s WAIS—IV age-adjusted and demographically adjusted scores. His age-adjusted FSIQ of 74 (4th percentile) is in the borderline range of functioning. His index scores indicate deficient processing speed and working memory abilities. Verbal Comprehension is low average, while Perceptual Reasoning is in the average range. Clearly, there are significant strengths and weaknesses in this profile with some scores impaired while others are intact. Using age-adjusted scores, Verbal Comprehension is significantly lower than Perceptual Reasoning, and Working Memory and Processing Speed are significantly lower than Verbal Comprehension. While some of the scores are impaired and there is variability in the profile, does this represent a decline in functioning or are results consistent with Mr. F.'s background?

When demographic adjustments are applied, Mr. F.'s FSIQ is in the low average range. His Perceptual Reasoning Index is above average and is a relative strength compared to the Verbal Comprehension Index; however, Verbal Comprehension is average for his background. Working Memory and Processing Speed Index scores are in the impaired range even after controlling for demographic characteristics.

TABLE 4.11   Mr. F.'s Age-Adjusted and Full Demographic Adjusted WAIS–IV Scores

Score	Age Adjusted		Full Demographic Adjusted		
	Score	Percentile Rank	T-Score	Percentile Rank	Qualitative Descriptor
Verbal Comprehension Index	83	13	49	46	Average
Perceptual Reasoning Index	96	39	55	69	Above Average
Working Memory Index	66	1	35	7	Mild Impairment
Processing Speed Index	56	0.2	31	3	Mild to Moderate Impairment
Full Scale IQ	74	4	42	21	Low Average
General Ability Index	88	21	52	58	Average
Vocabulary	6	9	49	46	Average
Similarities	3	1	35	7	Mild Impairment
Information	12	75	63	90	Above Average
Block Design	6	9	42	21	Low Average
Matrix Reasoning	8	25	53	62	Average
Visual Puzzles	14	91	68	96	Above Average
Digit Span	3	1	36	8	Mild Impairment
Arithmetic	5	5	38	12	Mild Impairment
Symbol Search	3	1	35	7	Mild Impairment
Coding	1	<1	28	1	Moderate Impairment

At the subtest level, Mr. F. shows variability in Verbal Comprehension and Perceptual Reasoning domains. In the Verbal domain, he demonstrated good recall for long-term information and average vocabulary skills; he exhibited a weakness in verbal conceptual reasoning. Perceptual Reasoning is notable for good visual construction skills and mental rotation in the absence of any motor demands. Mr. F.'s Block Design performance was clearly hampered by motor initiation and control problems. Processing speed and working memory are significant weaknesses.

TABLE 4.12 Mr. F.'s Age-Adjusted and Full Demographic Adjusted WMS–IV Scores

	Age Adjusted		Full Demographic Adjusted		
Score	Score	Percentile Rank	T-Score	Percentile Rank	Qualitative Descriptor
Auditory Memory	91	27	50	50	Average
Visual Memory	81	10	43	24	Low Average
Immediate Memory	78	7	43	24	Low Average
Delayed Memory	90	25	49	46	Average
Logical Memory I	8	25	50	50	Average
Logical Memory II	9	37	51	54	Average
Verbal Paired Associates I	10	50	54	66	Average
Verbal Paired Associates II	7	16	44	27	Low Average
Designs I	8	25	50	50	Average
Designs II	10	50	56	73	Above Average
Visual Reproduction I	1	<1	27	1	Moderate Impairment
Visual Reproduction II	8	25	46	35	Average

WMS–IV standard and full demographically adjusted index and subtest scores are displayed in Table 4.12. Mr. F.'s age-adjusted index scores indicate borderline immediate recall and low average visual memory with average scores on auditory and delayed memory. Demographic adjustments show Mr. F. has low average to average memory functioning for his background. Using demographic adjustments, visual memory is significantly lower than auditory memory but the base rate is not atypical (>25%). Immediate and delayed memory scores are not significantly different from one another.

WMS–IV verbal memory subtests are generally in the average range for immediate learning and recall. His long-term cued recall for verbal associations was in the low average range that is the borderline range for his level of immediate recall on that subtest. His delayed recognition for verbal associations was average; indicating low average cued recall (contrast score) or a retrieval problem for verbally associated material. Visual memory subtest performance was remarkable for the impact of motor issues. On Designs, the examiner assisted in placing the cards in the grid but on Visual Reproduction Mr. F. struggled to draw the designs.

All scores were average except for immediate visual reproduction; which appeared to be an issue with drawing more than recall. His raw score on delayed and copy drawings were very similar to immediate recall. His copy score was also in the deficient range. Subtest memory scores were all in the average range when demographic norms were applied except for Visual Reproduction I and Verbal Paired Associates II. None of the verbal subtests are significantly different from one another when demographic norms are applied. The Designs subtest scores are significantly better than Visual Reproduction scores; and Visual Reproduction I is lower than Visual Reproduction II. Differences in visual memory functioning relate to motor skills rather than visual memory impairment. Recognition memory scores, which are not demographically adjusted, were in the borderline to high average range. A borderline score was obtained on Designs Delayed Recognition but was more likely related to inattention than memory impairment.

These test results suggest some cognitive limitations in working memory and declarative memory. Declarative memory deficits appear to be related to retrieval rather than encoding issues. Motor impairments affect performance on many of the tests making it difficult to assess the degree to which processing speed may be impaired. On non-motor based processing speed measures (BCSE mental control and inhibition), he showed lower than expected scores but not significantly impaired scores. Some degree of cognitive slowing appears to be present. The overall clinical picture does not indicate dementia; however, cognitive deficits associated with Parkinsonism in combination with increasing age are affecting his daily functioning. The family worked with the hospital social worker to arrange day programming for Mr. F. Re-evaluation in 6–9 months is recommended to track cognitive changes.

CASE STUDY 2

INAPPROPRIATE USE OF DEMOGRAPHIC ADJUSTMENTS Ms. J. is a 22-year-old, single, African-American female, referred for a disability evaluation subsequent to chronic seizure disorder. Ms. J. had been living at home with her parents and working part-time as a cashier in a clothing store. Historically, her medication has reduced but not completely controlled her seizures. Approximately 9–10 months ago, her rate of seizures increased to 4–5 times per week, interfering with her ability to work and keeping her primarily at home. Medication changes did not improve her seizure rate. About 6 months ago, she experienced a prolonged seizure episode (status epilepticus) requiring emergency hospitalization. She was successfully treated but her seizures are still not well controlled.

Ms. J. attempted to return to work 3 months ago. However, she frequently missed time from work and her employer was not able to accommodate her absences. She has obtained employment in other businesses but she was unable to maintain work on a regular part-time basis. Her parents report that she seems to fatigue easily and has problems with memory and concentration. Ms. J.'s neurologist recommended that she apply for social security disability, even though she would prefer to work. As part of the disability evaluation, she was referred for psychological assessment to document her current level of cognitive functioning.

Ms. J. has suffered from generalized seizure disorder since she was 11 years of age. Prior to the onset of her seizures, she was consistently a top student in her classes. After her seizures, she had difficulty keeping up in her classes due to frequent absences and medication side-effects. She did not require special education courses but accommodations were made for her medical condition. She graduated high school at the age of 19. She grew up in a wealthy suburban neighborhood. Her father has a Ph.D. in chemical engineering and founded his own business. Her mother has a master's degree in speech therapy and worked in a local hospital.

The psychologist administered the WAIS–IV and WMS–IV as part of the disability evaluation. The results of the WAIS–IV are presented in Table 4.13. Her performance on the WAIS–IV was consistently in the low average range. Her FSIQ (83) was at the 13th percentile and there were no significant differences among the WAIS–IV indexes. WAIS–IV subtests ranged from borderline (Coding = 5) to Average (Vocabulary, Information, and Visual Puzzles = 9). No scores were significantly different. The age-adjusted scores consistently place her cognitive skills in the low average range. Her basic vocabulary and general knowledge were average.

The psychologist applied demographically adjusted norms to determine if there was a change in cognitive functioning. She applied full demographic adjustments (Sex = female, Education = 12 years, Ethnicity = African-American) to the WAIS–IV data. The demographic adjusted index scores are all in the average range except for the Processing Speed Index which was low average. Processing Speed was significantly lower than her Verbal Comprehension and Perceptual Reasoning Index scores. Working Memory was significantly lower than Perceptual Reasoning, but the base rate occurs relatively commonly (BR = 28.9%).

The WAIS–IV subtests ranged from mild impairment (Coding = 35) to above average (Information, Visual Puzzles = 57). In the verbal domains, Similarities was significantly lower than Vocabulary and Information. Perceptual Reasoning subtests show significantly lower Matrix Reasoning compared to Visual Puzzles. No differences occurred on Working Memory measures. For Processing Speed, Symbol Search was significantly higher than Coding.

TABLE 4.13   Ms. J.'s Age-Adjusted and Full Demographic Adjusted WAIS–IV Scores

| | Age Adjusted | | Full Demographic Adjusted | | |
Score	Score	Percentile Rank	T-Score	Percentile Rank	Qualitative Descriptor
Verbal Comprehension Index	89	23	51	54	Average
Perceptual Reasoning Index	88	21	53	62	Average
Working Memory Index	86	18	47	38	Average
Processing Speed Index	81	10	40	16	Low Average
Full Scale IQ	83	13	48	42	Average
General Ability Index	87	19	52	58	Average
Vocabulary	9	37	54	66	Average
Similarities	6	9	42	21	Low Average
Information	9	37	57	76	Above Average
Block Design	8	25	53	62	Average
Matrix Reasoning	7	16	47	38	Average
Visual Puzzles	9	37	57	76	Above Average
Digit Span	7	16	43	24	Low Average
Arithmetic	8	25	51	54	Average
Coding	5	5	35	7	Mild Impairment
Symbol Search	8	25	47	38	Average

The WMS–IV data is presented in Table 4.14. The age-adjusted scores range from borderline to low average. Delayed Memory is higher than Immediate Memory (contrast score = 13). Visual Working Memory is consistent with general memory functioning. WMS–IV subtest scores range from the deficient to average range. Her performance is consistent across verbal memory subtests. On visual memory, she exhibited a weakness on Visual Reproduction I and a significant strength on Designs II. Using the WAIS–IV GAI (87), all memory scores are significantly lower than general cognitive functioning (using either predicted difference or contrast score method). Most of the comparisons are in the low average range (e.g., contrast score = 7); however, immediate memory is in the borderline range given her general ability (contrast score = 5).

TABLE 4.14 Ms. J.'s Age-Adjusted and Full Demographic Adjusted WMS–IV Scores

Score	Age Adjusted		Full Demographic Adjusted		
	Score	Percentile Rank	T-Score	Percentile Rank	Qualitative Descriptor
Auditory Memory	82	12	42	21	Low Average
Visual Memory	80	9	40	16	Low Average
Immediate Memory	73	4	36	8	Mild Impairment
Delayed Memory	80	9	42	21	Low Average
Visual Working Memory	80	9	42	21	Low Average
Logical Memory I	7	16	43	24	Low Average
Logical Memory II	7	16	43	24	Low Average
Verbal Paired Associates I	8	25	47	38	Average
Verbal Paired Associates II	6	9	41	18	Low Average
Designs I	6	9	40	16	Low Average
Designs II	11	63	60	84	Above Average
Visual Reproduction I	3	1	32	4	Mild to Moderate Impairment
Visual Reproduction II	6	9	39	14	Mild Impairment
Spatial Addition	7	16	46	35	Average
Symbol Span	6	9	41	18	Low Average

Application of demographic-adjusted norms resulted in an increase in percentile rank across all measures; however, level of functioning did not change significantly. Most of the memory scores were in the low average range. Immediate memory was in the mild impairment range. WMS–IV subtests range from the mild to moderate impairment to above average range. All memory index scores were significantly lower than WAIS–IV GAI. The psychologist interpreted the memory testing as indicative of mild memory impairments compared to intellectual functioning, particularly on free recall for visual information.

Based on the demographically adjusted norms, the psychologist concluded that Ms. J. had average intellectual abilities and in some areas above average cognitive functioning. Based on her significantly lower processing speed, working memory, and general memory functioning, the clinician inferred that she probably had some brain injury caused by the recent seizure event. This might affect her ability to work in a job requiring memory or quickly processing information but overall, her intellectual functioning would not preclude her from working. The psychologist also recommended that she might consider some vocational training or a 2-year college program.

The Case Study 2 example is proposed as a misuse of demographically adjusted norms. Why would this be a misapplication? There is a clear significant medical event which potentially could result in a change in brain functioning. The examinee wants to work and the demographic adjustments indicate that she is functioning in the average range on most intellectual skills. In fact, she has above average skills in some domains that perhaps warrant more educational investment.

The fundamental question when applying demographic adjustments to norms is *"do these variables accurately represent the patients pre-morbid intellectual ability?"* In this case, does female gender accurately represent the client's pre-morbid state? The answer would be yes. Is 12 years of education an accurate estimate of her pre-morbid ability? The answer is likely to be no because her ability to function in school and her ability to reach her potential was severely limited by her medical condition which also likely had a significant influence on her brain development. Based on her family history of high educational attainment, 12 years of education may have been the lower bounds of her potential. Does ethnicity equal African-American accurately reflect her pre-morbid abilities? The answer could be yes but it is probably no. As stated earlier in this chapter, a myriad of psychosocial factors likely related to the quality of education, access to appropriate healthcare, and socioeconomic status, may impact the test performance of African-Americans. Ms. J.'s background suggests she may not have experienced problems in these areas to the same degree as other African-Americans. The most appropriate scores to interpret in this case are probably age-adjusted normative scores. In that context, the clinician can determine how she is functioning on testing relative to people her age. These age adjusted scores reflect: (a) the developmental trajectory of her cognitive functioning in the context of a chronic seizure disorder, and (b) the possible adverse effects of her recent status epilepticus. The age-adjusted scores can be used to see if her cognition improves, remains stable, or worsens in the future.

Out of interest, if one wanted to see how her current scores relate to how she might have developed, in *the absence of a longstanding seizure disorder*, the best demographic adjustment to use for her might be 16 years of education with no adjustments for sex and ethnicity. Table 4.15 illustrates the changes in WAIS–IV performance when that model is applied.

TABLE 4.15   Ms. J.'s Age-Adjusted and Education Adjusted WAIS–IV Scores

	Age Adjusted		Education Adjusted		
Score	Score	Percentile Rank	T-Score	Percentile Rank	Qualitative Descriptor
Verbal Comprehension Index	89	23	33	5	Mild to Moderate Impairment
Perceptual Reasoning Index	88	21	39	14	Mild Impairment
Working Memory Index	86	18	35	7	Mild Impairment
Processing Speed Index	81	10	34	6	Mild to Moderate Impairment
Full Scale IQ	83	13	32	4	Mild to Moderate Impairment
General Ability Index	87	19	34	6	Mild to Moderate Impairment
Vocabulary	9	37	41	18	Low Average
Similarities	6	9	29	2	Moderate Impairment
Information	9	37	40	16	Low Average
Block Design	8	25	40	16	Low Average
Matrix Reasoning	7	16	37	10	Mild Impairment
Visual Puzzles	9	37	46	35	Average
Digit Span	7	16	35	7	Mild Impairment
Arithmetic	8	25	39	14	Mild Impairment
Coding	5	5	30	2	Mild to Moderate Impairment
Symbol Search	8	25	40	16	Low Average

Applying the education only adjustments changes the results dramatically. Where previously, scores were mostly average the scores are now mostly in the impaired to low average range. Does this suggest that she had a precipitous drop in cognitive functioning subsequent to the severe seizure event? Possibly, but more than likely, her cognitive functioning has been compromised over a long period of time due to the impact of the seizures and treatment during critical periods of brain development. There may be an additional impact of the status epilepticus but it may not be possible to determine any causality between the event and her current level of functioning. Conceptually, if one considers her broader background, Ms. J. is an individual who has experienced a significant compromise to her intellectual functioning as a consequence of a chronic neurological condition. In chronic medical, psychiatric, and developmental disorders that directly affect the examinees ability to complete their education, education level is not a good proxy for pre-morbid ability. This is why in the previous case, the adjustments were appropriate. The patient's Parkinsonism did not affect his educational attainment therefore demographic adjustments were appropriate even though he had a chronic neurological condition. In the present case, age adjusted normative data are most appropriate.

The other issue with applying demographically adjusted norms in this case relates to applying the results to daily functioning. Demographic norms are not designed to infer how the person will function in the general community, in a job, or in an academic setting. For example, if an individual with 8 years of education scores a 90 on FSIQ, their education-adjusted score will be in the above average range. An individual with 18 years of education with an FSIQ of 105 will be in the low average range. Would you predict the individual with above average education-adjusted scores to be more successful in an academic environment that the individual with the low average score? Of course not, one examinee has already shown difficulty in school and the other success by their level of educational attainment. Education adjusted scores tell you how the individual compares to people who had similar difficulty or success with educational attainment. So to infer adequate cognitive capacity for job or academic success based on educational adjustments is an inappropriate use of those scores. The scores that should be applied are the age-adjusted scores.

SUMMARY

The significant relationship between cognitive test performance and background characteristics of the individual is well established. In particular, sex, education, and ethnicity have been identified as factors that need to be considered when interpreting performance on cognitive tests. Sex differences in cognitive functioning are typically very small with gender advantages observed in both directions (i.e., males perform better on some tests while females perform better on others). Education effects occur due to exposure to more information, better test-taking skills, and more training in basic skills such as reading and writing. Educational attainment is also affected by cognitive ability; therefore, individuals with better pre-morbid skills often attain more education. Racial/ethnic group differences exist due to socioeconomic and sociopolitical differences that impact education quality, attainment, medical access, socioeconomic status, and other background factors that affect test performance. The differences are not due to how the tests are constructed or item/test bias. It is difficult to measure all the factors that produce racial/ethnic group differences, particularly the interaction of multiple complex forces, therefore race/ethnicity serves as a proxy for these effects.

The WAIS–IV shows large effects for education level, particularly when comparing the extremes of the education distribution. Sex effects on the WAIS–IV are small and ethnic group effects are moderate to large. The impact of demographic factors is significantly smaller for the WMS–IV. Applying demographic adjustments to normative data for the WAIS–IV and WMS–IV will have the greatest impact on WAIS–IV scores, particularly for patients at the ends of the demographic distribution (i.e., 8 years of education or 18 years of education). Therefore, the most clinical significance will be observed in patients at the extremes of the distribution.

The concept and clinical practice of adjusting normative data for demographics has been debated for decades. While there is no consensus about the application of such normative adjustments, many clinicians routinely use this methodology as part of neuropsychological practice. The purpose of using demographic adjustments is to *identify a change* in cognitive functioning from a pre-morbid level. Given that stated goal, it is very important to ascertain if the demographic adjustments are a good estimate of the patient's pre-morbid functioning. Demographic adjustments are not appropriate for use in individual's suffering chronic psychiatric, developmental, medical, or neurological conditions that have directly affected their educational attainment. Similarly, racial/ethnic group adjustments are not appropriate for all members of a specific group. The background factors that impact the group as a whole may or may not be experienced by the individual being assessed. Demographic adjustment to norms are not appropriate for making decisions about an individual's ability to function in general society, or in vocational or educational settings, and the norms do not necessarily reflect their capacity to understand court proceedings, financial functioning, or to consent for treatment. The clinician is solely responsible for application of normative adjustments and must have a rationale for applying the adjustments to a specific patient.

KEY LEARNING

- Patient background characteristics impact expected level of performance on cognitive tests.
- Sex, education, and race/ethnicity have well documented effects on cognitive test performance.

- Adjusting cognitive tests for background characteristics of the patient is controversial but has been a part of clinical neuropsychological practice for decades.
- Demographic adjustments are available for Education, and Education/Sex/Ethnicity for the WAIS–IV and WMS–IV as an ACS report option.
- WAIS–IV and WMS–IV demographic norms are derived using inferential norming techniques and are presented as T-scores.
- Demographic adjustments have a large impact on patients at the extremes of the distribution (education level = 8 or 18 years) but only small changes occur for individuals in the middle (education level = 12 or 13–15 years) of the distribution.
- Demographic adjustments are larger for WAIS–IV than WMS–IV and the level of adjustment varies on measures within WAIS–IV (e.g., VCI > PSI). It is not possible to use a rule of thumb or clinical estimation to accurately adjust scores.
- Demographic adjustments lower the correlation between variables resulting in more and larger discrepancies in performance (use significance level and base rate data).
- Demographic adjustments are appropriate for estimating if an examinees performance is unexpectedly low or high signifying a change in cognitive functioning.
- Demographic adjustments assume that the variables are a reasonable estimation of an examinees pre-morbid functioning.
- Demographic adjustments are not appropriate for individuals with chronic psychiatric, medical, developmental, or neurological conditions, if those conditions had a significant impact on the patient's educational attainment.
- Demographic adjustments should not be used for determining eligibility for intellectual disability or learning disability.
- Demographic adjustments should not be used to determine functional capacity in the general population, job, or educational setting unless specific circumstances warrant such use. It is incumbent upon the examiner to provide a rationale in these situations.
- Demographic norms should not be used to determine competency or death penalty eligibility (e.g., culpability/intellectual disability) unless the purpose is to establish whether brain injury, loss of cognitive functioning, or dementia is affecting the patient.
- It is the responsibility of the clinician to use demographic adjustments responsibly and with clear understanding of how adjustments affect scores and the implications of making those adjustments on the patient.
- Adjusted norms are presented as T-scores (mean = 50, SD = 10). The T-scores are interpreted in ACS using the descriptors listed below.

A clinician, however, can choose to use look-up tables for T-score conversions to percentile ranks and apply the same classification descriptors as are used for age-adjusted normative data (e.g., superior, high average, and extremely low):

- \>55 "Above Average"
- 45—54 "Average"
- 40—44 "Low Average"
- 35—39 "Mild Impairment"
- 30—34 "Mild to Moderate Impairment"
- 25—29 "Moderate Impairment"
- 20—24 "Moderate to Severe Impairment"
- <20 "Severe Impairment".

References

Baker, D. P., Leon, J., Smith Greenaway, E., Collins, J., & Movit, M. (2011). The education effect on population health: a reassessment. *Population Development Review*, 37, 307—332. doi:10.1111/j.1728-4457.2011.00412.x.

Belzunces dos Santos, E., de Souza Silva Tudesco, I., Caboclo, L. O. S. F., & Yacubian, E. M. T. (2011). Low educational level effects on the performance of healthy adults on a neuropsychological protocol suggested by the commission on neuropsychology of the Liga Brasileira de Epilepsia. *Arquivos Neuropsychiatrica*, 65, 778—784.

Bernard, L. C. (1989). Halstead-Reitan neuropsychological test performance of black, hispanic, and white young adult males from poor academic backgrounds. *Archives of Clinical Neuropsychology*, 4, 267—274.

Boone, K. B., Victor, T. L., Wen, J., Ranzani, J., & Ponton, M. (2007). The association between neuropsychological scores and ethnicity, language, and acculturation variables in a large patient population. *Archives of Clinical Neuropsychology*, 22, 355—365.

Brickman, A. M., Cabo, R., & Manly, J. J. (2006). Ethical issues in cross-cultural neuropsychology. *Applied Neuropsychology*, 13, 91—100.

Byrd, D. A., Miller, S. W., Reilly, J., Weber, S., Wall, T. L., & Heaton, R. K. (2006). Early environmental factors, ethnicity, and adult cognitive test performance. *The Clinical Neuropsychologist*, 20, 243—260.

Camarata, S., & Woodcock, R. (2006). Sex differences in processing speed: developmental effects in males and females. *Intelligence*, 34, 231—252.

Dori, G. A., & Chelune, G. J. (2004). Education-stratified base-rate information on discrepancy scores within and between the Wechsler adult intelligence scale—third edition and the Wechsler memory scale—third edition. *Psychological Assessment*, 16, 146—154.

Golden, C. J., & van den Broek, A. (1998). Potential impact of age- and education-corrected scores on HRNB score patterns in participants with focal brain injury. *Archives of Clinical Neuropsychology*, 13, 683—694.

Gonzalez, H. M., Whitfield, K. E., West, B. T., Williams, D. R., Lichtenberg, P. A., & Jackson, J. S. (2007). Modified-symbol digit modalities test for African Americans, caribbean black americans, and non-latino whites: nationally representative normative data from the National Survey of American Life. *Archives of Clinical Neuropsychology*, 22, 605—613.

Gonzalez, R., Grant, I., Miller, S. W., Taylor, M. J., Schweinsburg, B. C., Carey, C. L., et al. (2006). Demographically adjusted normative standards for new indices of performance on the paced auditory serial addition task (PASAT). *The Clinical Neuropsychologist, 20,* 396–413.

Gorsuch, R. L. (2003, August). Update on continuous norming. Paper presented at the annual meeting of the american psychological association, Toronto, Canada. Heaton, R. K. & Grain, I. (1992). *Comprehensive norms for an expanded halstead-reitan battery: A supplement for the WAIS-R.* Odessa, FL: Psychological Assessment.

Gur, R. C., Richard, J., Calkins, M. E., Chiavacci, R., Hansen, J. A., Bilker, W. B., et al. (2012). Age group and sex differences in performance on a computerized neurocognitive battery in children age 8–21. *Neuropsychology, 26,* 251–265.

Heaton, R. K., Avitable, N., Grant, I., & Matthews, C. G. (1999). Further cross validation of regression-based neuropsychological norms with an update for the Boston Naming Test. *Journal of Clinical and Experimental Neuropsychology, 21,* 572–582.

Heaton, R. K., Grant, I., & Matthews, C. G. (1991). *Comprehensive norms for and expanded halstead-reitan battery: Demographic corrections, research findings, and clinical applications.* Odessa, FL: Psychological Assessment Resources.

Heaton, R. K., Taylor, M. J., & Manly, J. J. (2003). Demographic effects and the use of demographically corrected norms with the WAIS–III and WMS–III. In D. S. Tulsky, D. H. Saklofske, G. J. Chelune, R. K. Heaton, R. J. Ivnik, R. Bornstein, A. Prifitera, & M. F. Ledbetter (Eds.), Clinical interpretation of the WAIS–III and WMS–III. San Diego: Academic Press.

Herlitz, A., Airaksinen, E., & Nordstrom, E. (1999). Sex differences in episodic memory; the impact of verbal and visuospatial ability. *Neuropsychology, 13,* 590–597.

Jefferson, A. L., Gibbons, L. E., Rentz, D. M., Carvalho, J. O., Manly, J., Bennett, D. A., et al. (2011). A life course model of cognitive activities, socioeconomic status, education, reading ability, and cognition. *Journal of the American Geriatric Society, 59,* 1403–1411. doi:10.1111/j.1532-5415.2011.03499.x.

Karzmark, P., Heaton, R. K., Grant, I., & Matthews, C. G. (1984). Use of demographic variables to predict overall level of performance on the Halstead-Reitan Battery. *Journal of Consulting and Clinical Psychology, 52,* 663–665.

Kramer, J. H., Delis, D. C., Kaplan, E., O'Donnell, L., & Prifitera, A. (1997). Developmental differences in verbal learning. *Neuropsychology, 11,* 577–584.

Krueger, L. E., & Salthouse, T. A. (2010). Differences in acquisition, not retention, largely contribute to sex differences in multitrial word recall performance. *Personality and Individual Differences, 49,* 768–772.

Lejbak, L., Crossley, M., & Vrbancic, M. (2011). A male advantage for spatial and object but not verbal working memory using the n-back task. *Brain and Cognition, 76,* 191–196.

Lewin, C., Wolgers, G., & Herlitz, A. (2001). Sex differences favoring women in verbal but no visuospatial episodic memory. *Neuropsychology, 15,* 165–173.

Liu, Y., Julkunen, V., Paajanen, T., Westman, E., Wahlund, L. O., Aitken, A., et al. (2012). Education increases reserve against Alzheimer's disease-evidence from structural MRI analysis. *Neuroradiology, 54,* 929–938 [Epub ahead of print].

Longman, R. S., Saklofske, D. H., & Fung, T. S. (2007). WAIS–III percentile scores by education and sex for U.S. and Canadian populations. *Assessment, 14,* 426–432.

Lucas, J. A., Ivnik, R. J., Willis, F. B., Ferman, T. J., Smith, G. E., Parfitt, F. C., et al. (2005). Mayo's older African-Americans normative studies: Normative data for commonly used clinical neuropsychological measures. *The Clinical Neuropsychologist, 19,* 162–183.

Manly, J. J. (2005). Advantages and disadvantages of separate norms for African Americans. *The Clinical Neuropsychologist, 19,* 270–275.

Manly, J. J., & Echemendia, R. J. (2007). Race-specific norms: using the model of hypertension to understand issues of race, culture, and education in neuropsychology. *Archives of Clinical Neuropsychology, 22,* 319–325.

McBain, R., Norton, D., & Chen, Y. (2010). A female advantage in basic face recognition is absent in schizophrenia. *Psychiatry Research, 177,* 12–17.

McDaniel, M. A. (2006). Estimating state IQ: measurement challenges and preliminary correlates. *Intelligence, 34,* 607–619.

Moering, R. G., Schinka, J. A., Mortimer, J. A., & Graves, A. B. (2004). Normative data for elderly african americans for the stroop color and word test. *Archives of Clinical Neuropsychology, 19,* 61–71.

Morgan, E. E., Woods, S. P., Scott, J. C., Childers, M., Beck, J. M., Ellis, R. J., et al. HIV Neurobehavioral Research Center (HNRC) Group (2008). Predictive validity of demographically adjusted normative standards for the HIV Dementia Scale. *Journal of Clinical and Experimental Neuropsychology, 30,* 83–90.

Murray, A. D., Staff, R. T., McNeil, C. J., Salarirad, S., Ahearn, T. S., Mustafa, N., et al. (2011). The balance between cognitive reserve and brain imaging biomarkers of cerebrovascular and Alzheimer's diseases. *Brain, 134,* 3687–3696. [Epub 2011 Nov 18].

Norman, M. A., Evans, J. D., Miller, S. W., & Heaton, R. K. (2000). Demographically corrected norms for the california verbal learning test. *Journal of Clinical and Experimental Neuropsychology, 22,* 80–94.

Pearson (2009). *Advanced clinical solutions for the WAIS–IV/WMS–IV: Technical manual.* San Antonio, TX: NCS Pearson.

Ragland, J. D., Coleman, A. R., Gur, R. C., Glahn, D. C., & Gur, R. E. (2000). Sex differences in brain-behavior relationships between verbal episodic memory and resting regional cerebral blood flow. *Neuropsychologia, 38,* 451–461.

Randolph, C., Lansing, A. E., Ivnik, R. J., Cullum, C. M., & Hermann, B. P. (1999). Determinants of confrontation naming performance. *Archives of Clinical Neuropsychology, 14,* 489–496.

Reitan, R. M., & Wolfson, D. (1996). Differential relationships of age and education to WAIS subtest scores among brain-damaged and control groups. *Archives of Clinical Neuropsychology, 11,* 303–311.

Roid, G. H. (2003). *Stanford-Binet intelligence scales, fifth edition, technical manual.* Itasca, IL: Riverside.

Sharp, E. S., & Gatz, M. (2011). Relationship between education and dementia: an updated systematic review. *Alzheimer Disease and Associated Disorders, 24,* 289–304.

Taylor, M. J., & Heaton, R. K. (2001). Sensitivity and specificity of the WAIS–III/WMS–III demographically corrected factor scores in neuropsychological assessment. *Journal of the International Neuropsychological Society, 7,* 867–874.

Tombaugh, T. N. (2004). Trail making test A and B: normative data stratified by age and education. *Archives of Clinical Neuropsychology, 19,* 203–214.

Tombaugh, T. N., Kozak, J., & Rees, L. (1999). Normative data stratified by age and education for two measures of verbal fluency: FAS and animal naming. *Archives of Clinical Neuropsychology, 14,* 167–177.

Trahan, D. E., & Quintana, J. W. (1990). Analysis of gender effects upon verbal and visual memory performance in adults. *Archives of Clinical Neuropsychology, 5,* 325–334.

van der Sluis, S., Posthum, D., Dolan, C. V., de Geus, E. J. C., Colom, R., & Boomsma, D. I. (2006). Sex differences on the dutch WAIS-III. *Intelligence, 34,* 273–289.

Wechsler, D. (2007). *Wechsler memory scale (3rd ed.).* San Antonio, TX: The Psychological Corporation.

Weirich, S., Hoffmann, F., Meissner, L., Heinz, A., & Bengner, T. (2011). Sex influence on face recognition memory moderated by presentation duration and reencoding. *Neuropsychology, 25,* 806–813.

Weiss, L. G., Chen, H., Harris, J. G., Holdnack, J. A., & Saklofske, D. H. (2010). WAIS–IV use in societal context. In L. G. Weiss, D. H. Saklofske, D. L. Coalson, & S. E. Raiford

(Eds.), *WAIS–IV clinical use and interpretation: Scientist–practitioner perspectives*. San Diego: Academic Press.

Weiss, L. G., Harris, J. G., Prifitera, A., Courville, T., Rolfhus, E., Saklofske, D. H., et al. (2006). WISC–IV interpretation in societal context. In L. G. Weiss, D. H. Saklofske, A. Prifitera, & J. A. Holdnack (Eds.), WISC–IV advanced clinical interpretation. San Diego: Academic Press.

Wilkins, C., Rolfhus, E., Weiss, L. & Zhu, J. J. (2005). A new method for calibrating translated tests with small sample sizes. Paper presented at the 2005 annual meeting of the American Educational Research Association, Montreal, Canada.

Zahodne, L. B., Glymour, M. M., Sparks, C., Bontempo, D., Dixon, R. A., MacDonald, S. W., et al. (2011). Education does not slow cognitive decline with aging: 12-year evidence from the Victoria longitudinal study. *Journal of the International Neuropsychological Society, 17*, 1039–1046 [Epub 2011 Sep 19].

5

Predicting Premorbid Ability for WAIS–IV, WMS–IV and WASI–II

James A. Holdnack, Mike R. Schoenberg†,
Rael T. Lange‡ and Grant L. Iverson***

*Pearson Assessment, San Antonio, Texas, USA †University of South
Florida College of Medicine, Florida, USA ‡Defense and Veterans Brain
Injury Center, Walter Reed National Military Medical Center & University
of British Columbia, Washington, USA **Harvard Medical School, Boston,
Massachusetts, USA

INTRODUCTION

The accurate identification and quantification of decline in cognitive functioning is the *sine qua non* of neuropsychological assessment. Cognitive functioning after a neurological injury, illness, or condition can be adversely affected variably or globally, such that test scores will be lower in some domains but not others, or may even be grossly impaired. The obtained test scores are a measure of the patient's current level of functioning after a medical/neurological event. However, the obtained scores are also influenced by the patient's level of functioning prior to the injury or illness (i.e., premorbid ability). In neuropsychological assessment, the estimation of a premorbid intelligence is generally used as a comparison standard (i.e., comparison between current and expected premorbid levels of performance), although other comparison standards (e.g., serial assessment) are sometimes used (see Lezak, Howieson, & Loring, 2004; Schoenberg, Lange, Marsh, & Saklofske, 2010

© 2013 Elsevier Inc. All rights reserved.

for reviews). The clinician attempts to estimate the degree to which the current test scores reflect a change from premorbid ability as a result of a neurological injury, illness, or condition.

There are two common misconceptions associated with the prediction of premorbid cognitive functioning. First, some clinicians believe it is possible, given enough variables, to *precisely* estimate premorbid cognitive abilities, or to identify premorbid abilities within a small band of error and a high degree of confidence. Second, some believe premorbid ability can be *accurately* determined through clinical reasoning without applying statistical data. The belief of near perfect estimation of premorbid abilities assumes that: (a) measures of cognitive ability are perfectly reliable, (b) individual performance on measures of cognitive abilities are stable and there is only a small degree of variability between cognitive performances from one time to the next, which is not true (Salthouse, Nesselroade, & Berish, 2006), (c) different measures of cognitive ability almost always yield the same score, which is not true (see Chapter 6), and (d) predictors have a near perfect association with ability. These misconceptions are linked to another misconception that a person's performance on a battery of tests represents his or her "true ability," when in fact current performance is only an estimate of true ability (i.e., obtained scores = true scores + error). Measures of general cognitive ability include measurement error. A person's true cognitive ability can only be confidently identified as falling within a range of scores, rather than being represented by a single score (e.g., FSIQ = 100±4.4; VCI = 100±5.6; PRI = 100±6.9, for 95% C.I. based on SEM). In addition, test performance is variable over time, even when using the same measure of ability. Moreover, different versions of the same test do not yield the same specific score but a similar range of scores given imperfect correlation between measures (e.g., WAIS–III vs. WAIS–IV FSIQ, $r = 0.94$; WISC–IV vs. WAIS–IV FSIQ, $r = 0.91$). Common predictors of premorbid IQ, such as education and occupation, have only a moderate correlation with intelligence (e.g., $r = 0.54$ and $r = 0.49$, respectively). Beliefs that virtually all individuals who graduate from Harvard have an IQ of at least 140, or all individuals with a Ph.D. have an IQ of 120 or greater, are examples of misconceptions about the relationship between predictor and dependent variables. For all predictor variables, there is *always* a range of associated abilities and the best estimate for an individual for any specific predictor is the mean performance for that individual's specific comparison group, not the highest possible score for that group. In other words, just because some individuals with a Ph.D. have an IQ over 120 does not mean that all people with a Ph.D. have an IQ greater than 120. Therefore, assigning a premorbid IQ of 120 to a patient with a Ph.D. is erroneous.

The process of estimating an individual's premorbid cognitive functioning is complex; it requires evaluating multiple and overlapping sources of variance. In the absence of premorbid test data, psychologists have traditionally estimated premorbid cognitive ability from available historical data. These sources include: employment and education history, academic indicators such as grades and standardized test scores, family education and income level, and quality of educational experiences (Kareken & Williams, 1994). Although historical variables are known to correlate with level of intellectual functioning, it is difficult, without appropriate statistical data, to accurately determine: (a) if a particular psychosocial variable has a linear or non-linear relationship with ability, (b) if the variable is additive or incremental (e.g., education level and occupation have significant overlapping variance which can easily be double counted), and (c) the strength of the association between the psychosocial variable and ability level (e.g., high correlation of 0.7 vs. low of 0.3). The strength of the association between education and cognitive ability is often overestimated by clinicians, leading to an overestimation of a patient's premorbid ability (Kareken & Williams, 1994). Furthermore, clinicians who estimate premorbid functioning in the absence of statistical models do not have a means of evaluating the degree of error in their estimation, nor do they know if they are applying their own mental model consistently across patients. Because clinical estimation of premorbid abilities is subject to judgment errors, statistical models should be utilized to assist with obtaining an accurate, consistent, and reliable estimation of premorbid ability (Kareken, 1997).

Identifying loss of cognitive functioning in developmental or chronic neurological, psychiatric, and medical disorders is more challenging, particularly when the disorder began in childhood. The presence of neurological dysfunction in childhood impacts both cognitive development (e.g., intra- and inter-hemispheric reorganization of functional neuroanatomy and/or onset of alexia, agraphia, or acalculia) and the variables used to predict premorbid ability, such as educational and occupational attainment. Furthermore, a variety of environmental variables generally independent of the event/disease itself are also known to affect neurodevelopment (e.g., nutrition, sleep, education quality, quality of health care, and other family variables). Therefore, historical data is contaminated by the presence of neurological dysfunction present in childhood/adolescence. Another consideration in estimating premorbid ability is the influence of learning disorders that may affect educational and occupational attainment. Therefore, predicting premorbid ability in children and adolescents (or adults) years after the onset of known or suspected neurological condition is fraught with challenges. We now turn to reviewing some of the technical issues in predicting premorbid intellectual functioning.

METHODOLOGICAL, STATISTICAL, AND CLINICAL ISSUES

Affecting the Prediction of Premorbid Abilities

Estimating premorbid intellectual functioning has been the subject of clinical research for decades (e.g., Babcock, 1930; Wechsler, 1958; Wilson, Rosenbaum, Brown, Rourke, & Whitman, 1978; Yates, 1956; see also Schoenberg et al., 2010 for review). It is logistically and financially impractical to perform prospective, well-controlled, experimental paradigms to evaluate the best methods to predict premorbid cognitive ability, due to the impossibility (e.g., ethical and moral reasons) of inflicting neurological dysfunction on healthy individuals; or, alternatively, assessing a large sample of participants at baseline and then following them longitudinally, over decades, and re-assessing particular individuals after they sustain a known or suspected neurological disease or injury. Therefore, most studies rely on convenience samples of patients, population studies of unimpaired individuals, and estimation of premorbid functioning from current test data rather than historical test data. These research limitations yield imperfect models for predicting premorbid functioning. Despite the research limitations, these models are clearly superior to estimation without statistical data.

Based on decades of clinical research, multiple statistical models have been developed to predict premorbid cognitive ability (e.g., Lezak et al., 2004; Schoenberg et al., 2010 for reviews). Typically, multiple regression techniques are used to derive equations for the prediction of premorbid cognitive functioning using demographic data only, current performance data only, or a combination of demographic and current performance data (Crawford, 1992; Schretlen et al., 2009). A number of measures and types of data have been used for these approaches. There is no general consensus identifying the single best model for use in all cases; each model has strengths and weaknesses.

Demographic Data

Using demographic data to predict IQ scores has been studied at least since the 1970s (Crawford, 1992). Demographic variables (e.g., age, education, and occupation) have been shown to be correlated with measures of intelligence (e.g., Barona, Reynolds, & Chastain, 1984; Wilson et al., 1978). Demographic predictors can be thought of in two ways. First, there are demographic variables that are a reflection of an individual's choices, achievement orientation, work ethic, and innate abilities (e.g., education and occupation). The quantity and quality of obtained education also impacts intellectual development. Second, there are demographic variables related to group membership. Demographic groups can differ in either biological development (e.g., sex), serve as a proxy for a variety of socio-economic factors (i.e., ethnicity), or reflect differences in lifestyle (i.e., geographical region of residence). Individual factors (e.g., level of education) can be significantly affected by group membership such that level of success may be limited for many individuals within a specific demographic group (e.g., ethnic minority). Therefore, demographic variables represent individual achievement orientation and ability, as well as environmental variables. Similarly, occupational level can influence access to and quality of healthcare, nutrition, and other factors related to health and cognitive status. The use of group membership variables such as race/ethnicity and region of residence in prediction equations assumes that factors that impact minority groups (e.g., racism, lack of opportunity, low socioeconomic status, and linguistic and cultural differences), or people living in the same region (e.g., activity level, health status, education level), in general, accurately represent the experiences of the individual being assessed (see Chapter 4 for further discussion). Therefore, the clinician must consider whether the demographic variables to be used to predict premorbid functioning adequately generalize to a particular patient (i.e., does the demographic data accurately represents the patient's historical experiences).

There is considerable variability in the degree to which an individual's life experiences are well represented by the experiences within a specific demographic group. For example, many African-Americans experience economic disadvantage and a lack of opportunities for a high quality education. However, there are also many African-Americans raised in wealthy families with access to high quality educational experiences. Subsequently, there is considerable variability in the cognitive functioning of individuals within a group; such that within-group differences are frequently larger than between-group differences. For example, there are greater differences in cognitive ability among women in general than are observed between men and women. Therefore, knowing a patient's sex, ethnicity, occupation, or education level does not actually inform the clinician of his or her ability because the patient's ability could fall anywhere in the distribution of scores within that group. However, knowing this information provides a way for adjusting estimates of expected performance from the mean test score of a population sample (e.g., 100). That is, some variables are associated with increased likelihood of having estimated premorbid cognitive abilities greater than 100 and some variables are associated with increased probability of having estimated cognitive abilities below 100.

The specific demographic data used to predict premorbid ability varies among models. The most widely employed demographics model use age, education, occupation, sex, and/or race/ethnicity to predict WAIS (Wilson et al., 1978) and WAIS–R (Barona et al., 1984) IQ scores. Crawford and Allan (1997) used age, education, occupation, and sex for premorbid prediction of WAIS–R IQ scores in the UK. Additional data, such as family socioeconomic status (e.g., parent education), have been suggested to potentially improve estimates of premorbid ability (Reynolds, 1997). Studies using examinee interests and attitudes have yielded inconsistent results (Perez, Schlottmann, Holloway, & Ozolins, 1996; Schlottmann & Johnsen, 1991). In addition to using established demographic data, identifying personal variables that relate to the development or maintenance of cognitive abilities could potentially allow for more reliable or individualized estimations of premorbid cognitive functioning.

The concept of *cognitive reserve* is a promising area for future researchers to try to identify additional demographic or personal variables (e.g., daily activities such as health care, exercise, diet, and social activities) for improving prediction of premorbid functioning. Cognitive reserve is hypothesized to be the capacity to suffer brain injury and/or the physiological adverse effects of aging on the brain without demonstrating overt signs of cognitive impairment (Solé-Padullés et al., 2009). This model predicts that several historical factors impact the expression of cognitive disorders (e.g., a highly educated individual may perform well on cognitive tasks during the early stages of dementia). Factors such as education, occupation, and early socioeconomic environment are considered *passive* indicators of cognitive reserve, while active indicators of cognitive reserve include partaking in intellectually stimulating activities (e.g., reading), engaging in physical activity (e.g., sports, exercise), and being socially active (Solé-Padullés et al., 2009).

Cognitive reserve suggests that background variables are important in understanding individual differences in cognition, and personal choices and activity level (e.g., physical, social, and mental) also relate to maintaining cognitive functioning and could be helpful in predicting premorbid cognitive abilities. Salthouse (2006) reported that individuals who are mentally active lose cognitive functioning at a slower rate than those who are less mentally active. In healthy adults, exercise and mental activity relate to maintenance of brain function and cognition. Knowing the mental and physical activity level of an individual, particularly older adults, could be important in understanding their level of premorbid functioning.

The rationale for using demographic variables for predicting premorbid ability assumes that these variables are impervious to the impact of neurological disease/injury or dementia. That is, brain injury will not alter one's sex, ethnicity, parents' education level, socioeconomic status prior to injury, or education and occupation levels prior to the injury. This rationale is less true in children/adolescents, although assessment shortly after onset of known or suspected disease would retain these advantages. The fact that demographic, background, and personal factors are not influenced by the current disorder makes their use very compelling.

Another consideration in the use of demographic variables in predicting premorbid ability is the degree of variability in cognitive performance among members of specific demographic groups. Although individuals with a high degree of educational attainment have, in general, better performance results in cognitive tests, individuals within a specific group may have relatively higher or lower performance results. Table 5.1 presents the means, standard deviations, and score ranges for select WAIS–IV subsets by demographic variables.

People with more education or higher occupational levels, as a group, obtain higher intelligence scores. These data, however, illustrate the overlap of scores across groups (as indicated by the standard deviations and ranges of scores). As such, a substantial number of individuals will have higher or lower scores relative to other group members, or from those in other groups. Statistical models derived to estimate

TABLE 5.1 WAIS–IV Descriptive Data by Education, Sex, and Occupational Subgroups

Demographic Groups	WAIS–IV Verbal Comprehension Index			WAIS–IV Perceptual Reasoning Index		
	Mean	SD	Range	Mean	SD	Range
Education Level						
8 or fewer years	82.7	13.0	58–116	87.7	11.2	56–123
12 years	96.3	12.6	50–134	98.2	14.5	54–140
16 or more years	110.9	12.0	74–149	107.1	13.7	71–140
Sex						
Male	101.8	15.4	50–149	101.8	15.6	52–140
Female	98.4	14.5	56–138	98.3	14.2	54–140
Occupation Level						
General Laborer	85.2	14.2	56–130	88.9	15.1	58–127
Manager	103.0	12.7	70–138	104.0	13.7	73–138
Executive	111.8	11.6	80–138	109.3	13.9	79–140

Copyright © 2009 NCS Pearson, Inc. All rights reserved.

premorbid ability use the most probable score within a group; the mean. This may or may not be the best estimate for a particular patient, but will be the most probable for individuals belonging to that group. In some cases, the clinician may believe that the predicted ability level is inaccurate because a person with a certain education level *should* have a higher ability than the estimate indicates. This represents a tendency to overestimate the differences between education groups. In all fairness, there will be cases in which the estimated ability is less than the individual's actual ability (underestimate). However, in just as many cases, the estimated ability is likely higher than a person's actual ability (overestimate). Therefore, arbitrarily rejecting the results of a prediction in one instance, but finding a prediction acceptable in another instance, is an example of the potential application/consistency problems that can occur. Prediction equations are not intended to be a perfect prediction of a person's premorbid ability; rather, they reflect the most probabilistic ability level. The variability of scores from individuals within a group is reflected in large standard errors of estimate. These large standard errors of estimate are due to the lack of strong correlation between demographic variables and measures of cognitive functioning (see Schoenberg et al., 2010 for details).

Finally, a patient may provide inaccurate demographic data (e.g., years of education, occupational success) to the clinician, which would lead to additional error in predicting premorbid cognitive functioning. Individuals may inaccurately recall some aspects of their history (Johnson-Greene et al., 1997) or in some cases they may dissimulate for purposes of secondary gain. Not only can patients incorrectly recall important background information, they may also incorrectly recall symptoms and level of functioning prior to injury (Iverson, Lange, Brooks, & Rennison, 2010). Due to the drawbacks of using demographic data alone, alternative methods to predict premorbid cognitive ability have been developed using measures or indexes obtained at the time of the assessment. These current performance or "hold" models are discussed below.

Current Performance Data

Neuropsychological test scores represent a mix of current and premorbid cognitive ability (and, of course, measurement error). Therefore, the current performance "hold" model uses test results obtained from the current evaluation to estimate premorbid cognitive functioning. There are advantages to using test data obtained during the assessment compared to using demographic variables. Actual test results typically have a higher correlation with cognitive ability (e.g., better predictive accuracy) than do demographic variables (Pearson, 2001; Reynolds, 1997). The rationale for using current test performance lies in the assumption that some cognitive functions are *relatively resistant* to the effects of neurological insult and dementia (e.g., reading words, vocabulary). This is referred to as the "hold/don't hold" method for premorbid prediction (c.f., Franzen, Burgess, & Smith-Seemiller, 1997). However, tests purported as "hold" measures can be affected by brain injury or dementia (e.g., Larrabee, Largen, & Levin, 1985; Reynolds, 1997; Storandt, Stone, & LaBarge, 1995). Current performance data is typically captured through embedded test scores or stand alone tests.

Embedded Test Scores

The use of embedded test scores refers to using current scores, such as the Vocabulary subtest, to help predict premorbid intellectual functioning. They are considered as embedded measures because they are part of the battery of tests used to measure current intelligence; that is, no other tests are required to be administered to estimate premorbid ability. In this model, specific subtests within the measure of general ability are used in prediction equations to identify the expected "premorbid" level on the entire battery. A well-known embedded prediction model is the Oklahoma Premorbid Intelligence Estimate (OPIE) model (Krull, Scott, & Sherer, 1995; Schoenberg, Duff, Scott, & Adams, 2003; Schoenberg, Scott, Duff, & Adams, 2002; Scott, Krull, Iverson, Williamson, & Adams, 1997). The OPIE model was derived as a method to predict premorbid WAIS–R (and later WAIS–III) ability using a variety of estimation equations. These regression equations used subtests (Vocabulary, Matrix Reasoning, Information, and Picture Completion) that were relatively resistant to the effects of acute brain injury or deterioration due to dementia (e.g., Donders, Tulsky, & Zhu, 2001; Kaufman, 1990; Mittenberg et al., 2001; Wechsler, 1997). The OPIE model in its variations represents the "hold" model for predicting premorbid intellectual functioning.

Stand Alone (External) Test Scores

Stand-alone tests refer to any premorbid estimation model that uses tests that are not part of the general ability battery used in the evaluation. That is, the score on the test is used solely to predict premorbid functioning and is not also used to compute the patient's current intellectual functioning. This model uses "hold" functions typically not part of a neuropsychological assessment test battery (e.g., ability to read atypically pronounced words). These tests are given during the evaluation, and therefore represent a mix of current and premorbid abilities.

The most commonly used stand-alone measure to predict premorbid intellectual functioning is reading atypically pronounced words (e.g., "yacht"). Knowledge for pronouncing phonetically irregular words is generally resistant to neurological dysfunction and correlates well with intellectual functioning making it a good measure to predict premorbid functioning (Blair & Spreen, 1989; Crawford, 1992; Johnstone, Hogg, Schopp, Kapila, & Edwards, 2002; Schretlen et al., 2009). These tests are not a measure of current decoding ability; rather, these measures assess word knowledge (Crawford, 1992). Accurate pronunciation of phonetically irregular words does not necessarily equate to knowing the meaning of the word (this is not assessed). Rather, the individual need only pronounce the word, establishing prior experience/exposure to the word. Commonly used tests in the USA employing this method are the North American Adult Reading Test (NAART: Blair & Spreen, 1989), American National Adult Reading Test (AMNART: Grober & Sliwinski, 1991), Hopkins Adult Reading Test (HART: Schretlen et al., 2009), Wechsler Test of Adult Reading (WTAR: Pearson, 2001), and the Test of Premorbid Functioning (TOPF: Pearson, 2009). All of these tests estimate premorbid intelligence based on prediction equations using various editions of the Wechsler Adult Intelligence Scales. However, only the WTAR and TOPF were co-normed with these scales (i.e., WAIS–III and WAIS–IV, respectively). Co-norming of the tests yields more robust prediction equations and allows for sophisticated base rate analyses.

Standard reading decoding tests such as the Wide Range Achievement Test–Revised (WRAT–R: Jastak & Jastak, 1985) have also been used to predict premorbid intellectual ability (Kareken, Gur, & Saykin, 1995). These tests can serve the dual purpose of estimating current reading decoding ability as well as premorbid functioning. However, because these tests use standard grapheme-to-phoneme translation, individuals with good decoding skills may be able to identify words outside their usual reading/vocabulary range. Also, decoding skills reflect an active process that may be more affected by brain injury and subsequently may be more indicative of current rather than premorbid abilities.

Best Performance Method

The "Best Performance Method" (Lezak et al., 2004, p. 97) uses an individual's best performance on current testing, or evidence of premorbid achievements, as the best estimate of premorbid ability. In clinical practice, the method involves taking the person's one or two highest test scores and making the inferential leap that the person's "overall" premorbid ability was at that level. This approach, however, capitalizes on chance findings and systematically over-estimates past intellectual functioning in many people. More importantly, the approach does not take into account known variability in the cognitive test performance of healthy adults (see Chapter 3).

A comprehensive discussion of variability in test performance is provided in Chapter 3. Some of this information can be used to show problems with the Best Performance Method. Most healthy adults will have at least one subtest or index score well above the mean of their subtest scores. For example, the average highest obtained subtest score on the WAIS–IV for adults in the standardization sample is between 13 and 14. Thus, if applying the Best Performance Method to the standardization sample, the "average adult" would be estimated to have premorbid intellectual ability between the 84th and 91st percentile. When considering the WAIS–IV subtests, approximately 50% of the standardization sample has a highest score between 12 and 15. Moreover, 25% of healthy adults will have one or more subtest scores that are greater than the 95th percentile (i.e., scaled score of 16 or greater). Simply put, 25% of adults in the standardization sample would be estimated to have premorbid intellectual ability in the top 5% of the population using the Best Performance Method. Therefore, using the Best Performance Method on adults who do not have serious cognitive decline will likely result in serious over-estimation of their premorbid abilities.

Using this method in adults who clearly have cognitive decline, such as those with Alzheimer's disease or moderate-severe traumatic brain injury (TBI), will be more accurate and less prone to over-estimation; although some over-estimation is still possible. For example, on average, the highest WAIS–IV scaled score in patients with Alzheimer's disease (Chapter 9) or moderate-severe TBI (Chapter 10) is 11 (63rd percentile). Thus, using the Best Performance Method, we would estimate these groups of patients to have somewhat above average (63rd percentile vs. 50th percentile) premorbid intelligence. A more extreme example is illustrated by a sample of older adults diagnosed with Mild Cognitive Impairment (MCI: Chapter 9). This sample had a highest average WAIS–IV scaled score of 13, which would result in determining the average premorbid general cognitive ability of this sample at about the 84th percentile. In general, we do not recommend the Best Performance Method for estimating premorbid ability, and clearly overestimates premorbid ability.

Comparing Demographic and Current Performance Models

Each of the prediction models has advantages and disadvantages. One model will not be ideal for all situations and all patients; therefore, understanding the strengths and weaknesses of each model will enable the clinician to apply the most appropriate method for a specific patient. Evaluation of models (similar and dissimilar) needs to consider a number of factors such as statistical appropriateness, available data, prediction accuracy, prediction range, and the degree to which the estimate reflects premorbid rather than current ability.

The primary advantage of using a demographic model is the resistance of these variables to the impact of brain injury and dementia. The disadvantages of using demographic data include: low to moderate correlation with general intellectual ability (e.g., higher prediction error), results based on group membership not on individual's functioning within that group, and difficulty verifying some data all increasing likelihood of making a prediction error. The WTAR ($n > 1000$) and TOPF ($n > 1500$) were co-normed on a large sample of healthy adults with measures of intellectual functioning and demographic data (Pearson, 2001, 2009). These studies yield robust information regarding the relationship between demographic data and intellectual functioning. The results show education (FSIQ, $r = 0.54$; VCI, $r = 0.58$) and occupation level (FSIQ, $r = 0.49$; VCI, $r = 0.49$) are moderate predictors of intellectual functioning. Because education level and occupation are correlated ($r = 0.60$), the effect of using both measures to predict intellectual ability is incremental and not additive. In multiple regression equations, education (entered first into the equation) accounts for 31% of the variance in WAIS–IV FSIQ, while occupation (entered next in the equation) only adds an additional 4% of variance to predicted FSIQ. In the WAIS–IV standardization sample, region, sex, and ethnicity account for about an additional 10% of the variance in FSIQ, with ethnicity contributing the most of these three predictors.

For the TOPF demographic equations (e.g., excluding the reading test as a predictor), the variance accounted for by the simple demographic variables (education, occupation, region, sex, and ethnicity) ranged from 21% (PSI) to 46% (FSIQ). The largest prediction range for the TOPF simple demographics model was 67 to 121 for FSIQ, while the smallest was 79 to 112 for PSI. The variance in intellectual functioning accounted for in WTAR demographic regression equations (education, ethnicity, and sex) ranged from 22% to 37%. The largest prediction range for WTAR demographic equations was 78 to 118 for VCI and the most restricted range was 82 to 111 for PSI. The correlation between education and intellectual functioning was higher for the TOPF compared to the WTAR due to the expanded education range of less than 8 years to 21 years, which was accomplished through a greater sampling of higher education examinees. Also, the additional variables in the TOPF and the oversampling of Asian Americans improved the overall predictive accuracy of the equations and expanded the prediction range.

The TOPF demographic studies included additional research variables reflecting background and personal factors for individual examinees. These personal factors relate to the individual's personal choices and behaviors that might influence their test performance. The additional background factors were designed to better identify educational and family socioeconomic factors related to cognitive development and functioning. Personal factors that were significantly associated with intellectual performance included: (a) the amount of sleep prior to the evaluation, (b) current neighborhood wealth, (c) if job changes were related to getting a better position or not, and (d) frequency with which they lifted weights, did aerobic exercise, and engaged in social activities. The additional variables that significantly correlate with cognitive ability were mother and father's education and occupation level, neighborhood wealth as a child, and elementary school quality. The additional demographic and background information is subject to problems with verification; however, it can provide a more individualized estimate of premorbid functioning. The complex demographic models yield *slightly* better prediction equations accounting for 22% (PSI) to 48% (FSIQ) of the variance of WAIS−IV index scores (vs. 21% and 46% using basic demographic variables). Furthermore, the additional variables yield a larger prediction range with the maximum range being 63 to 134 for VCI while the most restricted was 74 to 119 for WMI (Working Memory Index). In addition, the inclusion of more diverse variables reduces the contribution of ethnicity to the equation by 1% on average.

In contrast to the demographic variables, WTAR reading scores correlated 0.46 (PSI) to 0.75 (VIQ) with WAIS−III Index scores, accounting for 22% to 56% of the variance. Similarly, the TOPF reading scores correlate 0.37 (PSI) to 0.75 (VCI) with WAIS−IV index scores, accounting for 14% to 56% of the variance in ability. The reading tests account for more of the variance in verbal and general intellectual skills compared to demographic data; however, demographic data perform similarly for processing speed. The rationale for using a reading test in predicting skills other than verbal and general intelligence levels is that reading and the dependent variables share an association with general intellectual functioning. The degree to which general ability relates to specific cognitive skills, such as processing speed and memory, influences the degree to which reading will also relate to those abilities, albeit to a lesser degree. The TOPF does not use regression to obtain estimated WAIS−IV/WMS−IV index scores; rather, equipercentile equating links the TOPF with the WAIS−IV/WMS−IV indexes. This method reduces the impact of regression to the mean effects at the extremes of the distribution yielding a larger prediction range. The TOPF range prediction range is 40−160 compared to the WTAR prediction range of 64−125 for FSIQ.

As an indicator of premorbid intellectual functioning, methods (measures) need to demonstrate accurate prediction of current ability in healthy participants (to assure no systematic over- or underestimation), and yield estimates of premorbid functions that are greater than actual abilities in individuals with known brain dysfunction (to assure ability to estimate premorbid functioning). Both the WTAR and the TOPF projects recruited patients with Alzheimer's disease and moderate to severe traumatic brain injury to complete reading and ability measures during the standardization of the tests. Patients with mild to moderate Alzheimer's disease performed less well than healthy controls on the WTAR reading test; however, only the difference for the moderate group was statistically significant (Pearson, 2001). Greater cognitive impairment, as measured by the Dementia Rating Scale (DRS: Mattis, 1988), was significantly associated with lower scores on the WTAR. In patients with moderate to severe traumatic brain injury, WTAR scores were also lower than matched controls but the differences were not significant. Mathias, Bowden, Bigler and Rosenfeld (2007) found patients with severe traumatic brain injury score lower on the WTAR than individuals with less severe injuries and healthy controls. Severe brain injury and moderate to severe levels of dementia appear to affect WTAR and TOPF performance.

Using WAIS–IV subtests (embedded prediction model) will produce similar advantages and disadvantages as the use of stand-alone measures. The ideal subtests for prediction will be those with the highest g-loading that are relatively resistant to the effects of brain injury. Historically, these subtests are Vocabulary, Information, and Matrix Reasoning. Vocabulary correlates from 0.41 (PSI) to 0.92 (VCI), Information correlates from 0.37 (PSI) to 0.89 (VCI), and Matrix Reasoning correlates from 0.46 (PSI) to 0.82 (PRI) with WAIS–IV indexes (Wechsler, 2008). Very high correlations are observed with the indexes in which the specific subtest contributes to the total score. Therefore, the relationship is inflated by the auto-correlation of the test with itself (e.g., correlating Information with Information embedded in the VCI). In patients suffering moderate to severe TBI and those diagnosed with Mild Cognitive Impairment, both Information and Matrix Reasoning were significantly lower than demographically matched controls, but Vocabulary was not. In patients diagnosed with probable dementia of the Alzheimer's type-mild severity, all of the subtests were significantly lower than matched controls (Wechsler, 2008). Clearly, performances on the "hold" WAIS–IV subtests can be negatively affected by brain injury and dementia.

The advantages of current performance measures are their superior correlation with general intellectual functioning, better ability to predict at the extremes of ability, more time efficient than "stand-alone" measures, and the more direct representation of an individual's ability. Alternatively, demographic models can be superior to "hold" based procedures in cases where the individual has known or suspected moderate to severe brain injury occurring in adulthood, as demographic variables are independent of brain injury. Using demographic and current performance data in combination to predict premorbid ability capitalizes on the advantages of each.

Combined Demographic and Current Performance

Demographic data and current performance on reading or embedded subtests can be combined to provide a more robust estimate of premorbid ability. Adding demographic variables to current performance data improves prediction iteratively rather than additively because current test performance is moderately correlated with demographic data. Education and occupation correlate at 0.55 and 0.45 with TOPF (TOPF/WAIS−IV standardization sample), respectively. Therefore, adding education to TOPF will incrementally improve prediction. The combined simple demographics with TOPF prediction equations account for 25% (PSI) to 67% (VCI) of the variance in WAIS−IV Indexes. This represents a 14% and 21% increase in variance accounted for above the TOPF only prediction model and a 4% to 22% increase compared to demographics only prediction model. Therefore, the combined demographics and current performance model is more accurate at estimating premorbid functioning. The prediction range for FSIQ is expanded compared to the demographics only prediction range; 67−121 compared to 53−141 for the combined method. This range is slightly truncated compared to the TOPF equated model; however, it is sufficient for all but very unusual cases of extremely high or low premorbid ability. The combined complex demographics with TOPF prediction model provide more accurate prediction than demographics or TOPF alone. Similar advantages were found for methods that combined embedded performance and demographics (e.g., OPIE, OPIE−III).

The OPIE−III prediction algorithms combined demographic variables with WAIS−III subtest raw scores to predict premorbid FSIQ, VCI, and PRI functioning (Schoenberg et al., 2002; 2004). We provide an update to the OPIE−III for the WAIS−IV termed the OPIE−IV. The OPIE−IV combines demographic variables with WAIS−IV subtests to predict premorbid intellectual functioning. There are significant differences in how demographic data can be combined with performance data, and the TOPF and OPIE−IV use different statistical modeling. This affects the calculation of the scores, and also what the scores represent and how they function across groups.

The WTAR, the predecessor of the TOPF, derived the combined prediction equations by entering the reading score first into the regression equation followed by education, ethnicity, and sex. This order represents the level of correlation between the predictor and dependent variables (e.g., highest correlation entered first and then in descending order). In this model, the common variance between education and reading was assigned to the reading score and the variance unique to education was only entered after common variance with reading had been removed. Therefore, reading performance has a greater impact on the predicted score compared to education because it is the stronger predictor and is entered first into the equation. This weights the equation more towards individual ability rather than group membership. As a result, this equation is more sensitive to effects of brain injury than a pure demographic based algorithm, but is less influenced by brain injury than a pure performance based method.

In order to reduce the impact of current cognitive impairment on the prediction of premorbid ability, the TOPF regression equations enter education and occupation *before* the reading scores are entered, followed by sex, region, and ethnicity. The resulting prediction equations assign the overlapping variance between education and occupation with reading to education and occupation. The resulting equation yields nearly equal weighting between educational attainment and reading. The advantage of this model is that the premorbid prediction is less affected by current injury or disease (if current injury or disease adversely affects the reading score). The disadvantage is that more weight was assigned to factors only indirectly related to the individual (e.g., group membership). This order of variable entry was selected because education and occupation represent aspects of the individual's achievement orientation and ability, while factors such as sex, region, and ethnicity are less directly associated with the individual's ability and choices. Therefore, this model significantly reduces the contribution of sex, region, and ethnicity in the prediction of premorbid ability. In the TOPF complex equations, years of education, occupation, and personal factors are entered before reading, while developmental factors are entered after reading.

The OPIE–III in both US and Canadian normative samples entered current performance data into the equation first followed by demographic factors (Lange, Schoenberg, Saklofske, Woodward, & Brickell, 2006; Schoenberg et al., 2002, 2003). The OPIE–III, presented later in the chapter, uses the same model which makes those prediction equations more representative of the individual's actual ability but is more susceptible to the impact of disease or injury. Additionally, OPIE–III for the Canadian WAIS–III (Lange et al., 2006), which is the most recent application of the OPIE model, and TOPF treat demographic and performance predictors slightly differently. For both equations, categorical variables such as ethnicity and region are dummy coded (i.e., 0 vs. 1 or 1 vs. 2) indicating the presence or absence of group membership. This yields multiple variables for those demographic indicators [e.g., northeast (yes, no), north central (yes, no), west (yes, no), and south (yes, no)]. In the past, ordinal level data (e.g., education and occupation) had been entered either as a continuous variable or dummy coded for each level of the variable. However, entering ordinal level data as a continuous variable can result in prediction errors because ordinal level data does not necessarily yield a linear change in performance across the groups. Using non-linear regression models manages the problem of non-linear changes in the dependent measure across the groups in the predictor variable. Dummy coding these variables is desirable because the measure is then not affected by non-linear changes in the predictor variable. The disadvantage is that it creates a large number of variables to be entered into the equation and computed to obtain the predicted scores. Also, dummy-coding demographic data can over-model the data yielding unexpected findings (e.g., post-bachelor's degree having lower ability than bachelor's degree). Finally, the TOPF uses age-adjusted reading scores in the prediction equation, eliminating the need to have age as a predictor in the equation. OPIE equations used raw scores rather than age-adjusted scaled scores. This creates a larger range of scores to correlate with the dependent variable because subtest scaled scores range 1–19. As a result, OPIE equations require age to be a predictor in the equation to account for the impact of age on test performance. The TOPF reading test standard scores have a range of 120 points, therefore, there is no concern about the TOPF having a sufficient score range as a predictor variable.

PREDICTING PREMORBID NEUROPSYCHOLOGICAL FUNCTIONING

The practice of premorbid prediction has primarily focused on predicting general intellectual ability, that is, Full-Scale IQ, Verbal Comprehension or Verbal IQ, and Perceptual Reasoning or Performance IQ. Prior to the publication of the WTAR, researchers began to explore whether other cognitive skills could be predicted, using similar models (e.g., Duff, 2010; Franzen et al., 1997; Gladsjo, Heaton, Palmer, Taylor, & Jeste, 1999; Hilsabeck & Sutker, 2009; Isella et al., 2005; Schretlen, Buffington, Meyer & Pearlson, 2005; Williams, 1997). The primary focus was memory, because memory impairment is associated with brain injury and dementia (Skeel, Sitzer, Fogal, Wells, & Johnstone, 2004). Typically, memory impairment was estimated by comparing current intellectual functioning with memory functioning to determine whether memory functioning was unexpectedly low given current intellectual functioning (e.g., IQ versus memory comparison; Wechsler, 2009). This method can be effective; however, if general cognitive functioning is mildly or moderately impaired, it can be difficult to identify concurrent memory impairment due to suppressed current intellectual functioning.

Some clinicians may question the use of a reading test to predict premorbid cognitive functions, such as memory or processing speed, when there is a relatively weak relationship between reading and these cognitive abilities. The concept of predicting memory functioning is based on the correlation between measures of general cognitive ability and other measures of cognitive functioning. Therefore, using tools that estimate premorbid general cognitive functioning (e.g., demographics and reading) can be used to estimate premorbid memory functioning. That is, reading performance used as an estimate of general cognitive ability can estimate expected memory functioning because general cognitive ability and memory functioning are correlated. These premorbid memory prediction equations are not as accurate as the equations predicting general cognitive ability because the correlation between general ability and memory is in the moderate range (e.g., $r = 0.4$ to 0.6; Wechsler, 2009). However, they do provide an estimate of expected memory functioning relatively resistant to brain injury or dementia. Similarly, premorbid working memory and processing speed also can be estimated.

The WTAR introduced the concept of predicting processing speed and working memory indexes from the WAIS–III. These predictions were provided as experimental measures. This procedure had some success in clinical populations with known deficits in these domains (Pearson, 2001). The WTAR also provided estimates of WMS–III memory indexes. Like the WTAR, the TOPF provides prediction equations for the WAIS–IV WMI and PSI, and the WMS–IV Immediate Memory Index (IMI), Delayed Memory Index (DMI), and Visual Working Memory Index (VWMI).

The correlation coefficients between the WTAR and the WAIS–III WMI and PSI were 0.62 and 0.47, respectively, and between WTAR and the WMS–III IMI and DMI was 0.47 and 0.49, respectively (i.e., WTAR scores accounted for 22% and 24% of variance in IMI and DMI scores, respectively). The TOPF correlated 0.61 and 0.37 with WAIS–IV WMI and PSI, respectively, and correlated 0.46, 0.41, and 0.47 with WMS–IV IMI, DMI, and VWMI, respectively. There have been arguments in the literature for the advantages of predicting premorbid indices of neuropsychological measures beyond general cognitive function (e.g., Duff, 2010; Franzen et al., 1997; Gladsjo et al., 1999; Hilsabeck & Sutker, 2009; Isella et al., 2005; Pearson, 2001, 2009; Schretlen et al., 2005; Williams,

1997). Although there are benefits to this approach, efforts to predict premorbid neuropsychological domains such as processing speed and memory have suffered from large standard errors of estimates due to the small to medium correlations between the "hold" measures/demographic variables used as predictors (because they are resistant to effects of brain dysfunction) and processing speed, working memory, and verbal memory scores. At this time, there is debate about the utility of separate premorbid prediction equations for PSI, WMI, or memory indexes.

For clinicians desiring to use premorbid prediction of additional WAIS–IV/WMS–IV indexes, the TOPF provides simple and complex demographic predictions (i.e., demographic variables only, not the reading test) for WAIS–IV WMI and PSI and WMS–IV VWMI: the R^2 values (i.e., percent variance accounted for) for these equations range from 0.19 (VWMI) to 0.34 (WMI). No demographic predictions are provided for WMS–IV IMI or DMI due to the low correlations of demographics with these measures. TOPF (using only the reading test) and demographics with the TOPF reading test combined prediction equations are available for WAIS–IV WMI and PSI and WMS–IV IMI, DMI, and VWMI: the R^2 values for the combined equations range from 0.20 (DMI) to 0.49 (WMI).

USING THE ACS TEST OF PREMORBID FUNCTIONING (TOPF)

The TOPF is part of the Advanced Clinical Solutions (ACS: Pearson, 2009) for the WAIS–IV/WMS–IV. The TOPF materials include a record form for recording responses and collecting demographic data, a word reading card for the examinee to read from, manual chapters for administration and interpretation information, and scoring software for calculation of WAIS–IV/WMS–IV predicted scores and supporting statistics. The TOPF takes approximately 5 to 10 minutes to administer and score. The examinee is given the word-reading card and asked to read up to 70 phonetically irregular words (i.e., there is a discontinue rule of five errors in a row) of increasing difficulty. The TOPF requires the use of the WAIS–IV and WMS–IV scoring software to obtain premorbid ability prediction and comparison data to current functioning. TOPF standard scores can be obtained by using the ACS Technical Manual.

Purpose for Using TOPF

The TOPF is used in cases where the clinician suspects the patient's current cognitive functioning has been compromised from a previous level. The TOPF quantifies the degree to which current cognitive performance is discrepant from estimated premorbid functioning. An observed discrepancy between current and estimated premorbid abilities *may indicate* the individual has experienced deterioration in cognitive functioning, or there may be other reasons why such a discrepancy is observed. The TOPF is not designed for evaluation of reading disorders; and individuals with a reading disorder will do poorly on the test. TOPF is not used for the evaluation of intellectual functioning for the purpose of identifying giftedness or intellectual disability, nor is it used as a replacement for assessing current intellectual functioning. The TOPF provides an estimate of premorbid intellectual and memory functions; and the results should not be considered as an absolute, perfect indicator of premorbid functioning.

Selecting a TOPF Model

The TOPF provides clinicians with three models for predicting premorbid functioning: (a) demographics only, (b) TOPF only, and (c) combined demographics and TOPF prediction equations. For each model using demographic data, a simple and complex prediction equation can be selected. In the simple model, only sex, race/ethnicity, and education, are used in predicting premorbid ability. In the complex model, developmental, personal, and more specific demographic data is incorporated into the equations. The clinician should select a model based on the patient's background and his or her current level of reading or language impairment. The background factors the clinician needs to consider include:

- History of childhood/adolescent medical condition, neurological illness, psychiatric illness, or learning disability affecting academic achievement.
- Representativeness of demographic variables.
  - Does the patient identify him or herself as an ethnic minority?
  - Does the patient's educational attainment seem consistent with his or her background?
  - Is the patient's occupational attainment consistent with his or her education level and is there any evidence that the patient may have been underemployed?
  - Is the patient very active and physically fit?
  - Does the patient report father and/or mother educational status being at either extreme of the distribution (e.g., very low or high)?
  - Is there any motive for the patient to provide incorrect information and can the background information provided be verified?

In most cases, using the TOPF, either alone or with simple demographic data, can likely provide a satisfactory estimation of premorbid abilities. Simple demographic data are easier to verify than the background information in the complex model and the level of prediction is generally the same as the complex model. The complex model may be selected in cases where elements of the simple model do not seem sufficient for capturing the nature of the patient's background. For example, ethnicity may not reflect issues of reduced access to education, healthcare, or other resources as well as those individual variables; or that an individual who is very active and fit, comes from a wealthy family, and whose parents have a high degree of education, may be better represented by the complex demographics. Moreover, the simple demographic model may not best represent an individual coming from very poor or disadvantaged backgrounds. The clinician must evaluate each patient to determine the most appropriate model for that individual.

The clinician may decide not to use demographic data when there is concern regarding the fidelity of that information, or when the clinician believes that the demographic data may not be representative of the patient's actual premorbid ability. The TOPF is a better indicator of the individual's actual ability level than demographic data; however, in some circumstances the TOPF may not be appropriate to use. Factors that may affect the clinician's decision to use the reading test to estimate premorbid ability are listed below.

- History of childhood/adolescent medical condition, neurological illness, psychiatric illness, or learning disability affecting the development of normal reading skills.
- Current impairment in reading functioning (e.g., alexia) due to aphasia, dementia, or severe brain injury due to any medical, traumatic, or neurological condition.
- Severe impairment in language functioning.
- Primary language other than English (particularly if English is learned as an adult), any cultural or linguistic difference that may have affected English reading development, English fluency, or very low educational attainment or illiteracy.

The clinician should obtain historical information about any possible learning disabilities, developmental disorder, or other medical or neurological condition that may have affected the patient's ability to learn to read. Similarly, the clinician must evaluate the patient's history for linguistic issues related to English acquisition or for very low educational attainment. The TOPF provides tools to help the clinician determine whether performance on the TOPF is unexpectedly low due to current reading impairment. The scoring assistant can alert the clinician when the TOPF reading score is significantly lower than expected given the examinees demographic data. If it is, the clinician should evaluate both statistical difference and base rate information. The TOPF may still be used in cases where the TOPF score is significantly below expectations based on demographic information, but the base rate of the difference occurs in more than 10%–15% of cases. The TOPF will lower the patient's score compared to demographics only, but not severely. The benefit of using the TOPF in this circumstance is a better prediction accuracy. The disadvantage is that the score could be an underestimate of the examinee's premorbid ability. In cases where the obtained TOPF score is significantly *worse* than predicted and the base rate is rare (<10%), the TOPF will underestimate premorbid functioning. If the result indicates significantly *better* TOPF performance than predicted, the examiner may wish to use the TOPF only score because the patient's actual performance is higher than expected for his or her background. This result can occur in individuals with high ability but reduced opportunity for educational or occupational success, or when the individual is at the upper-end of the ability level compared to their peers with similar education and occupation. Table 5.2 is a sample of the predicted TOPF standard scores found in a TOPF score report. The results show that the TOPF standard score of 106 is significantly lower than the predicted TOPF standard score of 118. The base rate of the difference is unusual, being observed in only 13.7% of the standardization sample.

In this particular case, the TOPF with simple demographic variables yielded a predicted premorbid FSIQ of 108, and the

TABLE 5.2   Sample of Predicted TOPF Score Report

Test of Premorbid Functioning Score Summary					
	Raw Score	Standard Score	Percentile Rank	SEM	Qualitative Description
Test of Premorbid Functioning	49	106	65.5	2.12	Average

Analysis							
Test of Premorbid Functioning Actual–Predicted Comparison							
	Actual Score	Predicted Score	Prediction Interval	Difference	Critical Value	Significant Difference	Base Rate
Actual–Predicted	106	118	89–147	−12	4.16	Y	13.7%

Actual–Predicted Comparsion based on Simple Demographics Predictive Model
Prediction Intervals reported at the 95% Level of Confidence.
Statistical significance (critical value) at the .05 level.

simple demographics only method estimated the FSIQ as 115. The TOPF with demographics equation suggested lower premorbid ability than the demographics only equation; however, compared to the examinee's actual FSIQ of 86, both equations indicated a significant and unusual difference between premorbid and current FSIQ. There will be situations in which using a significantly lowered TOPF score will result in a different interpretation of the premorbid versus current functioning compared to the demographic only equations. The clinician must decide if the low TOPF score is an accurate representation of low premorbid cognitive ability, and thus choose to use one of the TOPF models or if the TOPF has been compromised by the disorder itself and choose to use a demographics only model.

The decision to use demographics only, TOPF only, or combined demographics and TOPF predictions, can be made on a case-by-case basis. Alternatively, the clinician can choose to use a specific model for nearly all cases based on practical (e.g., consistency in clinical practice) and statistical reasons (e.g., simple demographics with the TOPF model have low error and simple demographics are easier to verify). However, when a single consistent model is selected, it is recommended that the clinician establish a rule by which he or she will not include the TOPF in the prediction equation or use the TOPF only (e.g., significant and base rate <10% or 15%). This is necessary to account for the effect of brain injury and dementia on current performance measures.

Interpreting TOPF Results

After the clinician has administered and scored the TOPF, these data are entered into the ACS software, which is part of the PsychCorp Center−II (PCC−II) test platform. The ACS software communicates with the WAIS−IV and WMS−IV scoring software within PCC−II. The TOPF software requests the clinician to select the desired demographics model, simple or complex, and to fill in that data. Before selecting the premorbid ability model, the software provides the clinician with the predicted TOPF data. This allows the examiner to determine if the TOPF has potentially been compromised by the neurological injury or process before selecting a prediction model. Finally, after the model is selected the software provides the premorbid estimate for each index (i.e., except for IMI and DMI when using the demographics only model).

See Table 5.3 for an example of a TOPF with simple a demographics report. The patient is a 71-year-old, white, woman, with a doctoral degree. She lives in the Midwest. Her self-reported highest

TABLE 5.3 Sample of TOPF with Simple Demographics Predicted WAIS-IV Score Report

WAIS–IV Actual–Predicted Comparison

Composite	Actual	Predicted	Prediction Interval	Difference	Critical Value	Significant Difference	Base Rate
PSIQ	86	108	84–132	−22	5.31	Y	1.3%
VCI	107	111	89–133	−4	6.14	N	34.1%
PRI	82	104	74–134	−22	7.06	Y	2.8%
WMI	89	105	77–133	−16	8.31	Y	6.8%
PSI	71	107	73–141	−36	9.06	Y	0.3%

WMS–IV Actual–Predicted Comparison

Index	Actual	Predicted	Prediction Interval	Difference	Critical Value	Significant Difference	Base Rate
IMI	58	108	75–141	−50	6.92	Y	0.2%
DMI	54	108	74–142	−54	9.02	Y	0.1%

Actual–Predicted Comparison based on Simple Demographics with Test of Premorbid Functioning Predictive Model
Prediction Intervals reported at the 95% Level of Confidence.
Statistical significance (critical value) at the 0.05 level.

employment level was management. She was referred for possible dementia. The TOPF results for this case are presented in Table 5.2. For each WAIS–IV and WMS–IV index (note: VWMI is not included in the WMS–IV older adult battery), the actual, predicted, prediction interval (e.g., in this example the 95% prediction interval is presented), actual minus predicted, critical value, significant difference, and base rate data are presented.

The actual score is the individual's current performance on the WAIS–IV/WMS–IV indexes which, in this case, range from 54 (DMI) to 107 (VCI). The predicted score is the expected premorbid score for each index based on the examinee's TOPF score of 106 and her demographic data. The predicted scores range from 104 (PRI) to 111 (VCI). The prediction interval is the range in which the predicted premorbid score could fall with a very high degree of confidence (e.g., 95%). The difference column represents the difference between predicted premorbid scores and current functioning (i.e., actual score). A negative value indicates a decline in abilities and a positive value indicates better than expected current functioning versus premorbid ability. In this case, difference scores range from −4 (VCI) to −54 (DMI). The critical value column presents the absolute value that the difference must exceed in order to be statistically reliable and not due to chance factors. The significant difference column indicates whether the difference has exceeded the critical value or not. The base rate column provides the percentages of cases in the standardization sample having the same or larger differences between estimated premorbid and actual abilities. The differences between actual and predicted of all the indexes except VCI are both statistically significant and occur infrequently in the normative sample (e.g., base rates <7%). These results indicate, particularly for processing speed and memory functions, a large decline in cognitive functioning across several domains. It is then up to the clinician to determine if the change is consistent with a neurological or medical condition, background and presenting symptoms, or if other factors may account for the discrepancy between predicted and obtained level of function.

Table 5.4 presents the WAIS–IV data when using the simple demographics model without the TOPF. Observe that WMS–IV data is not available when using demographics only equations, which can be important when evaluating individuals with possible dementia. The actual scores range from 71 (PSI) to 107 (VCI) and predicted scores range from 109 (PSI) to 115 (VCI, FSIQ). The difference between actual and predicted scores range from −8 (VCI) to −39 (PSI) and all of these are statistically significant. The demographics only and demographics with TOPF equations yield very similar results. The VCI score is statistically lower in the demographics only equation, but the cumulative

TABLE 5.4   Sample of WAIS–IV Actual Versus Premorbid Predicted Index Scores

Composite	Actual	Predicted	Prediction Interval	Difference	Critical Value	Significant Difference	Base Rate
PSIQ	86	115	87–143	−29	4.16	Y	0.3%
VCI	107	115	87–143	−8	5.09	Y	27%
PRI	82	109	77–141	−27	6.57	Y	1.3%
WMI	89	112	81–143	−23	7.2	Y	2.2%
PSI	71	110	76–144	−39	9.3	Y	0.6%

Actual–Predicted Comparison based on Simple Demographics with Test of Premorbid Functioning Predictive Model.
Prediction Intervals reported at the 95% Level of Confidence.
Statistical significance (critical value) at the 0.05 level.

percentage of the difference in scores was not rare (i.e., base rate = 27%). Therefore, the use of either model indicates global impairment with a relative sparing of verbal abilities. The advantage of using the TOPF in the prediction equation (i.e., Table 5.3) was the additional verification of severe memory impairment. In cases where the TOPF reading score is lower than expected, the two TOPF models may suggest different interpretations. The clinician needs to weigh the advantages and disadvantages of using the TOPF when it is lower than expected.

Using the TOPF with the WASI–II and WAIS–IV GAI and Cognitive Proficiency Index

There are many clinical situations in which the use of a full WAIS–IV is impractical due to administration length, client fatigue, or other clinical issues. The Wechsler Abbreviated Scale of Intelligence–Second Edition (WASI–II; Wechsler, 2009) may be given when the WAIS–IV cannot be administered. The WASI–II was equated with the WAIS–IV; therefore, regression models for predicting premorbid intellectual function can be derived using TOPF and WAIS–IV data. The WASI–II does not have WMI or PSI indexes or any memory indexes such as the WMS–IV. Predictions can be made for FSIQ/GAI, VCI, and PRI. The TOPF, as published in the ACS, did not provide prediction equations for GAI or the Cognitive Proficiency Index (CPI; see Chapter 1). The CPI summarizes performance on the working memory and processing speed indices of the WAIS–IV in a single score. These equations are included here for examiners who routinely use these measures.

Derivation of WASI−II prediction equations

A sample of 1764 cases with data across 13 levels of education and 9 levels of occupation from the WAIS−IV standardization sample was used to develop statistical data for premorbid estimation of WASI−II and WAIS−IV GAI and CPI indexes. The age range of the sample was restricted to 20−90 years, consistent with the adult age stratification used for the TOPF equations. The sample is differentiated by age this way because individuals under the age of 20 years are stratified in the US census by parent education and they have not had the opportunity to complete their formal education. Parent education is not as strong of a predictor of premorbid ability as self-education level so combining parent and self-education levels in the same prediction equation is inappropriate (Pearson, 2009). The sample demographics are presented in Table 5.5. The WAIS−IV subtests Vocabulary, Similarities, Block Design, and Matrix Reasoning were used to estimate WASI−II indexes, which use alternate forms of these subtests. Substitution studies demonstrate that WASI−II subtests can be used in WAIS−IV indexes with little observed difference in overall performance (Wechsler, 2010); therefore, it is expected that the WAIS−IV subtests can serve as substitutes for the actual WASI−II measures. The WAIS−IV subtest raw scores were converted to T-scores because the WASI−II subtests use T-scores not scaled scores. The T-scores are not those derived for WASI−II but are based on the WAIS−IV normative sample. The subtest T-scores were summed for each combination of indexes: 2-subtest FSIQ = Vocabulary + Block Design; 4-subtest FSIQ = Vocabulary + Block Design + Similarities + Matrix Reasoning; VCI = Vocabulary + Similarities; and PRI = Block Design + Matrix Reasoning. The sum of T-scores for each index was converted to index standard scores based on the WASI−II normative data. The GAI and CPI were calculated as described in the WAIS−IV Technical Manual for GAI (Wechsler, 2008) and Chapter 1 of this text for CPI.

Multiple Regression

Multiple hierarchical regression analysis was used to generate prediction equations for all of the calculated WASI−II and WAIS−IV indexes. The TOPF with simple demographics is the only model presented here and it applies only to individuals aged 20 to 90. For prediction models other than the TOPF with simple demographics or for premorbid predictions of patients aged 16 to 19, the ACS TOPF can be used. The independent variables were entered into the equation in the step-wise manner as follows: education, occupation, TOPF, sex, region, and ethnicity. Education and occupation include non-linear powers. Non-significant variables ($p<0.05$) were removed from the equation and the regression was re-run without these variables to

TABLE 5.5   Sample Characteristics for WASI–II and WAIS–IV Prediction Equations

Characteristic	Percentage/Mean (SD)
Age	49.6 (20.7)
Sex	
Male	52.8%
Female	47.2%
Education	
Kindergarten–7th Grade	2.7%
8th–10th Grade	8.4%
11th Grade	5.1%
GED/Skilled trade apprenticeship	5.8%
High school diploma	24.3%
Trade or vocational school	2.4%
1 year of college	6.9%
Associate's degree or 2 years of college	13.4%
3–5 years of college, no degree	5.3%
Bachelor's degree	12.0%
Post-bachelor's/master's degree	9.6%
Post master's, no doctorate	2.2%
Doctorate (e.g., PhD, MD, JD)	1.8%
Ethnicity	
White	72.7%
African-American	10.4%
Hispanic	12.5%
Asian	3.1%
Other	1.3%
Region	
Northeast	19.8%
North Central	25.2%
South	34.4%
West	20.6%

(*Continued*)

TABLE 5.5   (Continued)

Characteristic	Percentage/Mean (SD)
WAIS–IV	
FSIQ	101.5 (14.8)
GAI	101.4 (14.8)
VCI	101.3 (14.8)
PRI	101.1 (14.8)
WMI	101.3 (14.4)
PSI	101.1 (15.0)

Note: $n = 1764$; All variables are presented as percentages of the population with the exception of age and WAIS–IV variables which are presented as means (SDs).
Copyright 2008 NCS Pearson, Used with permission. All Rights Reserved.

obtain the final prediction equations. Tables 5.6 to 5.11 present the multiple hierarchical regression analysis summaries for the WASI–II and WAIS–IV indexes.

The results for the WASI–II indexes are generally consistent with the WAIS–IV TOPF with simple demographics equations. The R^2 values for the WASI–II indexes range from 0.33 (PRI) to 0.60 (VCI). Although lower than the prediction accuracy for the WAIS–IV indexes, these equations do account for a meaningful variance in the index scores. The equation has an R^2 of 0.59 for the WAIS–IV GAI and 0.39 for the WAIS–IV CPI. Table 5.12 presents descriptive statistics for predicted versus actual scores for the WASI–II and WAIS–IV indexes.

The premorbid estimation of WASI–II Full-Scale IQ estimates (using two and 4-subtests) have a prediction range of 84 points (range = $62-146$ and $59-143$, respectively). The range of prediction is applicable to most patients presenting with clinical problems. The 4-subtest index shows less variability (standard deviation of the difference = 9.58) in the predicted versus actual scores compared to the 2-subtest FSIQ (standard deviation of the difference = 12.04). The VCI and PRI predictions also have a large prediction range with VCI having more prediction accuracy than PRI (which is consistent with WAIS–IV). The WAIS–IV GAI and CPI indexes have large prediction ranges and prediction error rates similar to the standard WAIS–IV indexes.

Table 5.13 presents percentages of healthy adults whose actual performance and predicted premorbid performance differ by up to 15 points and within the same or different qualitative IQ category. For all of the prediction equations, at least 50% of the samples actual ability level was within ± 5 points of their predicted premorbid ability (50% to

TABLE 5.6 Multiple Hierarchical Regression Analysis Results: TOPF and Simple Demographics Predicted Estimated WASI–II 4-Subtest Full Scale IQ

Predictor	R	R^2	Adj R^2	SEE	R^2 Change	F Change	DF1	DF2	Sig F Change
Education	0.52	0.28	0.27	12.43	0.28	527.80	1	1390	0.000
Occupation	0.56	0.31	0.31	12.12	0.04	73.57	1	1389	0.000
TOPF	0.73	0.54	0.54	9.92	0.23	686.79	1	1388	0.000
Sex	0.74	0.55	0.54	9.86	0.01	18.08	1	1387	0.000
Region	0.74	0.55	0.55	9.83	0.00	5.26	2	1385	0.005
Ethnicity	0.75	0.57	0.57	9.61	0.02	64.87	1	1384	0.000

Note: Education = 13 education groups entered as a continuous variable. Occupation = 9 groups entered as a continuous variable. TOPF = Test of Premorbid Functioning, sex coded F = 1 and M = 2, Ethnicity coded 1 = belongs to group 0 = does not belong to group, Region coded 1 = lives in that region 0 = does not live in that region.
Copyright 2009 NCS Pearson. Used with permission. All rights reserved.

TABLE 5.7 Multiple Hierarchical Regression Analyses Results: TOPF and Simple Demographics Predicted Estimated WASI–II 2-Subtest Full Scale IQ

Predictor	R	R^2	Adj R^2	SEE	R^2 Change	F Change	DF1	DF2	Sig F Change
Education	0.49	0.24	0.24	12.82	0.24	432.14	1	1390	0.000
Occupation	0.52	0.27	0.27	12.52	0.04	67.67	1	1389	0.000
TOPF	0.71	0.51	0.51	10.28	0.24	672.49	1	1388	0.000
Sex	0.72	0.52	0.52	10.20	0.01	23.88	1	1387	0.000
Region	0.72	0.52	0.52	10.17	0.00	9.02	1	1386	0.003
Ethnicity	0.74	0.54	0.54	9.93	0.02	34.43	2	1384	0.000

Note: Education = 13 education groups entered as a continuous variable. Occupation = 9 groups entered as a continuous variable. TOPF = Test of Premorbid Functioning, sex coded F = 1 and M = 2, Ethnicity coded 1 = belongs to group 0 = does not belong to group, Region coded 1 = lives in that region 0 = does not live in that region.
Copyright 2009 NCS Pearson. Used with permission. All rights reserved.

65%), approximately 80% were within ±10 points (77% to 82%), and nearly all cases were within ±15 points. The proportion of cases in which predicted indexes and actual obtained indexes fell in the same classification category (e.g., Low average, Average, High Average) was greater than 50% for all WASI–II indexes and WAIS–IV GAI and CPI scores; and most individuals were within one category between predicted and actual performance.

TABLE 5.8   Multiple: Hierarchical Regression Analyses Results: TOPF and Simple Demographics Predicted Estimated WASI–II Verbal Comprehension Index

Predictor	R	R^2	Adj R^2	SEE	R^2 Change	F Change	DF1	DF2	Sig F Change
Education	0.54	0.29	0.29	12.31	0.29	576.18	1	1390	0.000
Occupation	0.57	0.32	0.32	12.04	0.03	64.82	1	1389	0.000
TOPF	0.77	0.59	0.59	9.41	0.26	886.33	1	1388	0.000
Sex	0.77	0.59	0.59	9.40	0.00	4.18	1	1387	0.041
Region	0.77	0.59	0.59	9.35	0.00	8.38	2	1385	0.000
Ethnicity	0.77	0.60	0.60	9.28	0.01	21.90	1	1384	0.000

Note: Education = 13 education groups entered as a continuous variable. Occupation = 9 groups entered as a continuous variable. TOPF = Test of Premorbid Functioning, sex coded F = 1 and M = 2, Ethnicity coded 1 = belongs to group 0 = does not belong to group, Region coded 1 = lives in that region 0 = does not live in that region

Copyright 2009 NCS Pearson. Used with permission. All rights reserved.

TABLE 5.9   Multiple Hierarchical Regression Analyses Results: TOPF and Simple Demographics Predicted Estimated WASI–II Perceptual Reasoning Index

Predictor	R	R^2	Adj R^2	SEE	R^2 Change	F Change	DF1	DF2	Sig F Change
Education	0.38	0.15	0.15	13.45	0.15	238.12	1	1390	0.000
Occupation	0.42	0.17	0.17	13.24	0.03	43.92	1	1389	0.000
TOPF	0.53	0.28	0.28	12.32	0.11	216.42	1	1388	0.000
Sex	0.54	0.29	0.29	12.24	0.01	19.66	1	1387	0.000
Region	0.54	0.30	0.29	12.23	0.00	2.63	1	1386	0.105
Ethnicity	0.58	0.33	0.33	11.92	0.04	37.62	2	1384	0.000

Note: Education = 13 education groups entered as a continuous variable. Occupation = 9 groups entered as a continuous variable. TOPF = Test of Premorbid Functioning, sex coded F = 1 and M = 2, Ethnicity coded 1 = belongs to group 0 = does not belong to group, Region coded 1 = lives in that region 0 = does not live in that region. Region had a significant beta weight in the prediction equation, $p<0.05$.

Copyright 2009 NCS Pearson. Used with permission. All rights reserved.

Using TOPF with Simple Demographic WASI–II/WAIS–IV Premorbid Predictions

All of the information required for using the TOPF prediction of WASI–II and WAIS–IV GAI and CPI are provided in Tables A5.1–A5.6 in the Appendix at the end of this chapter, except for the TOPF raw to standard score conversion which are found in the ACS

TABLE 5.10 Multiple Hierarchical Regression Analyses Results: TOPF and Simple Demographics Predicted WAIS–IV General Ability Index

Predictor	R	R^2	Adj R^2	SEE	R^2 Change	F Change	DF1	DF2	Sig F Change
Education	0.53	0.28	0.28	12.59	0.28	531.06	1	1390	0.000
Occupation	0.56	0.31	0.31	12.31	0.03	64.79	1	1389	0.000
TOPF	0.74	0.55	0.55	9.97	0.24	727.14	1	1388	0.000
Sex	0.75	0.57	0.56	9.77	0.02	59.99	1	1387	0.000
Region	0.75	0.57	0.57	9.75	0.00	6.80	1	1386	0.009
Ethnicity	0.77	0.59	0.59	9.50	0.02	75.20	1	1385	0.000

Note: Education = 13 education groups entered as a continuous variable. Occupation = 9 groups entered as a continuous variable. TOPF = Test of Premorbid Functioning, sex coded F = 1 and M = 2, Ethnicity coded 2 = belongs to group 1 = does not belong to group, Region coded 2 = lives in that region 1 = does not live in that region.
Copyright NCS 2009 Pearson. Used with permission. All rights reserved.

TABLE 5.11 Multiple Hierarchical Regression Analyses Results: TOPF and Simple Demographics Predicted WAIS–IV Cognitive Proficiency Index

Predictor	R	R^2	Adj R^2	SEE	R^2 Change	F Change	DF1	DF2	Sig F Change
Education	0.46	0.21	0.21	13.25	0.21	184.67	2	1389	0.000
Occupation	0.49	0.24	0.24	13.02	0.03	51.19	1	1388	0.000
TOPF	0.61	0.37	0.37	11.81	0.13	300.11	1	1387	0.000
Ethnicity	0.62	0.39	0.39	11.68	0.02	17.11	2	1385	0.000

Note: Education = 13 education groups entered as a continuous variable. Occupation = 9 groups entered as a continuous variable. TOPF = Test of Premorbid Functioning, sex coded F = 1 and M = 2, Ethnicity coded 2 = belongs to group 1 = does not belong to group, Region coded 2 = lives in that region 1 = does not live in that region.
Copyright 2009 NCS Pearson. Used with permission. All rights reserved.

Administration Manual (Pearson, 2009). The regression equations used for predicting WASI–II and WAIS–IV GAI and CPI are presented in Table A5.1. Each equation has somewhat different predictors and values associated with those predictors. For each equation, the clinician needs the highest reported education and occupation values, which are located in Table A5.2 and the TOPF equated scores for the specific score that is to be predicted (Table A5.3). Sex is coded as 1 for female and 2 for male. Region and ethnicity values are dummy coded (e.g., 0 = does not belong to the group while 1 = belongs to the group for WAIS equations; 2 = belongs to the group and 1 = does not belong to the group for

TABLE 5.12 Descriptive Statistics, Comparison Tests, and Prediction Ranges for Premorbid WASI–II and WAIS–IV Indexes for TOPF with Simple Demographics Equations

Dependent Variable	Independent Variables	Predicted Scores		Comparison Scores				Sample Prediction Range		Theoretical Prediction Range	
		Mean	SD	Mean Diff	Std Diff	Min	Max	Min	Max	Min	Max
WASI 4-Subtest FSIQ	Ed, Occ, TOPF, Sex, Region, Eth	101.43	11.02	0.11	9.58	−43	34	69	130	59	143
WASI 2-Subtest FSIQ	Ed, Occ, TOPF, Sex, Region, Eth	101.39	10.84	0.10	12.04	−62	51	68	129	62	146
WASI VCI	Ed, Occ, TOPF, Sex, Region, Eth	101.49	11.34	0.05	9.68	−41	34	65	132	59	146
WASI PRI	Ed, Occ, TOPF, Sex, Region, Eth	101.17	8.39	0.32	12.02	−60	51	74	121	69	130
WAIS–IV GAI	Ed, Occ, TOPF, Sex, Region, Eth	101.54	11.37	0.00	9.48	−43	35	62	130	54	142
WAIS–IV CPI	Ed, Occ, TOPF, Eth	101.48	9.29	0.00	11.67	−60	48	70	123	62	135

Note: Ed = Education level, Occ = Occupation level, TOPF = Test of Premorbid Functioning, Eth = Ethnicity.
Copyright 2009 Pearson, Inc. Reproduce with permission. All rights reserved.

TABLE 5.13 Predictive Accuracy of TOPF with Simple Demographics Equations for WASI–II and WAIS–IV GAI and CPI

| | Differences Between Predicted and Actual Scores | | | | |
| | Number of Points | | | Ability Classification | |
IQ or Index	±5	±10	±15	Same Category	One Category
WASI–II FSIQ 4	55.9	80.2	92.0	57.7	93.8
WASI–II FSIQ 2	60.1	78.8	89.1	55.2	92.9
WASI–II VCI	50.8	77.1	89.9	59.2	95.7
WASI–II PRI	59.5	79.2	89.4	47.9	89.2
WAIS–IV GAI	64.6	82.4	91.8	55.8	93.2
WAIS–IV CPI	62.5	81.4	91.0	40.2	84.9

Copyright 2009 Pearson, Inc. Reproduced with permission, All rights reserved.

WAIS–IV measures). These values, along with the equation constants, are used to obtain the predicted premorbid score for each of the indexes. Additional tables at the end of this chapter provide critical values for statistically significant differences between actual and predicted scores (Table A5.4) and base rates for the difference between actual and predicted scores (Tables A5.5 and 5.6).

Using the data from the previously presented case, premorbid predictions can be made for all the WASI–II scores and WAIS–IV indexes. For illustrative purposes, the WASI–II 4-subtest FSIQ and WAIS–IV CPI will be presented. The actual WASI–II 4-subtest FSIQ is 86. The first step is to identify the information needed to calculate the desired scores. According to Table A5.10, WASI–II 4-subtest FSIQ scores require education, occupation, TOPF WASI–II 4-subtest FSIQ equated score, sex, region, and ethnicity.

- Education level is doctorate = 13 (Table A5.2)
- Occupation level is manager = 7 (Table A5.2)
- TOPF = 106 and equates to a WASI–II 4-subtest FSIQ of 105 (Table A5.3)
- Sex = female = 1
- Region = Midwest, therefore Northeast = 0 and Midwest = 1 (uses 0 and 1)
- Ethnicity = white, therefore white = 1 (uses 0 and 1)
- Predicted FSIQ = 31.14939104 + (0.698346784 *Education) + (0.851680164 * 8 Occupation) + (0.533315988 *WASI–II equated score) + (2.310109011 * sex) + (−3.007567526 * Northeast) + (−1.485120726 * Midwest) + (4.983575051 * White)

- Predicted FSIQ = 31.14939104 + (0.698346784 *13) + (0.851680164 * 7) + (0.533315988 *105) + (2.310109011 * 1) + (−3.007567526 * 0) + (−1.485120726 * 1) + (4.983575051 * 1)
- Predicted FSIQ = 31.14939104 + 9.078508192 + 5.961761148 + 55.99817874 +2.310109011 + 0 + −1.485120726 + 4.983575051.
- Predicted WASI−II 4-subtests FSIQ = 108
- Actual−Predicted = 86−108 = −22
- Critical value p <0.01 = 7.43, difference is statistically significant (Table A5.4)
- Base Rate = 1.15% (Table A5.5)

The WAIS−IV actual CPI is 77. The predicted CPI requires the following data: education, occupation, TOPF_CPI equated, Asian, and White.

- Education level is doctorate = 13 (Table A5.2; Education^2 = 169)
- Occupation level is manager = 7 (Table A5.2)
- TOPF = 106 and equates to a WAIS−IV CPI of 105 (Table A5.3)
- Ethnicity = white therefore Asian = 1 and white = 2 (note WAIS−IV uses 1 and 2)
- Predicted FSIQ = 30.95822285 + (1.974000661*13) + (−0.095287171 * 169) + (0.844810128 * 7) + (0.416671256 *105) + (7.925180368 * 1) + (4.135941067 * 2)
- Predicted FSIQ = 30.95822285 + 25.66200859 − 16.1035319 + 5.913670896 + 43.75048188 + 7.925180368 + 8.271882134
- Predicted WAIS−IV CPI = 106
- Actual-Predicted = 77−106 = −29
- Critical value p <0.01 = 7.66, difference is statistically significant (Table A5.4)
- Base Rate = 0.86% (Table A5.6)

The predicted values for the WASI−II 4-subtest FSIQ and WAIS−IV CPI equations are similar to the values predicted for the standard WAIS−IV FSIQ and WMI/PSI. There is good convergence between the procedures for predicting premorbid ability. The large atypical difference between the predicted and actual scores indicates significantly lower current general ability and cognitive proficiency performance compared to premorbid levels.

Development and Use of OPIE−IV with WAIS−IV

Several methods are available to predict premorbid WAIS−III FSIQ scores. Schoenberg et al. (2002, 2003) developed a method to predict premorbid WAIS−III FSIQ scores termed the Oklahoma Premorbid

Intelligence Estimate-3 (OPIE–III). The OPIE–III was developed to estimate premorbid FSIQ scores in patients with brain injury by combining current performance on selected WAIS–III subtests with demographic variables (i.e., age, education, gender, region of the country, and ethnicity). The Vocabulary (VOC), Information (INFO), Matrix Reasoning (MR), and Picture Completion (PC) subtests were selected based on previous data indicating performances on these tasks were relatively unaffected by neurological dysfunction (e.g., Axelrod, Vanderploeg, & Schinka, 1999; Donders et al., 2001; Mittenberg et al., 2001; Ryan, Paolo, & Brungardt, 1990). Five OPIE–III algorithms were developed from the WAIS–III standardization sample (Wechsler, 1997) to predict FSIQ. Clinical validation using a mixed sample of patients with known brain injury found the OPIE–III algorithms employing single subtests combined with demographics performed well, particularly those using Vocabulary (OPIE–III V) and Matrix Reasoning (OPIE–III MR) subtests (Schoenberg et al., 2003). To date, similar algorithms have not yet been developed for the WAIS–IV.

In this section, algorithms for predicting WAIS–IV FSIQ by combining current performance on the WAIS–IV with demographic variables are presented. Estimating premorbid FSIQ with such an approach allows more flexibility of the WAIS–IV by providing an alternative method to predict premorbid FSIQ. The combined current performance and demographic approach may be particularly valuable for patients with known or suspected neurological disease that adversely affects reading and/or pronunciation.

There are some clinical situations in which the TOPF is not the best method to predict premorbid functioning. The TOPF should *not* be used on individuals with a history of developmental reading or language disorder, acquired reading or language deficits (agraphia and/or alexia), severe cognitive impairment, or chronic medical, neurological, or psychiatric conditions affecting educational attainment or reading development. The OPIE–IV model *may* be an effective alternative for predicting premorbid functioning in some of these cases. In cases of acquired language or reading impairment, developmental reading or language disorder, or in cases of chronic disorders that affect educational attainment, the OPIE–IV premorbid predictions model may be less impacted than the TOPF models; however, the OPIE–IV will also be affected by severe cognitive impairment.

The OPIE–IV equations were derived from hierarchical regression models using raw Vocabulary and Matrix Reasoning WAIS–IV subtest scores, age, education, sex, region, and ethnicity. Information and Picture Completion subtests were not used for the OPIE–IV, because these subtests did not "hold" well in patients with dementia (Wechsler, 2008). This finding of Information not holding well in dementia is not unique to WAIS–IV; similar findings were reported for the WAIS–R (Larrabee et al., 1985). Predictions are derived for FSIQ, GAI, VCI, and PRI. Because the OPIE–IV enters WAIS–IV subtest scores before demographic data are entered, these equations represent individual performance more than performance due to group membership. For this reason, the OPIE–IV premorbid predictions may be impacted by current performance impairments more than the TOPF predictions, unless a specific deficit in reading or language is present. The OPIE–IV prediction equations are provided here for clinicians wishing to use these equations.

Development of OPIE–IV WAIS–IV Prediction Equations

A sample of 2012 healthy adults aged 20 to 90 across 13 levels of education from the WAIS–IV standardization sample was randomly divided to development and validation samples. The development sample was used to develop statistical data for premorbid estimation of WAIS–IV FSIQ, GAI, VCI, and PRI indexes. The sample only includes subjects over the age of 19 because individuals under the age of 20 are stratified by parent education, which is not as strong a predictor of premorbid ability as self-education level (Pearson, 2009). The sample demographics are presented in Table 5.14. The development and validation samples were not significantly different on any demographic characteristic or WAIS–IV Index scores.

In addition to developing prediction equations for FSIQ, GAI, VCI, and PRI, equations were also derived for prorated and alternative FSIQ, GAI, VCI, and PRI. The equations for the standard form are influenced by the part-whole correlation of the Vocabulary and Matrix Reasoning subtests with the indexes to which they contribute. This results in an inflation of the R^2 value, which suggests greater accuracy in predicting premorbid abilities than is actually the case. These prediction equations should be restricted to the concept of predicting premorbid WAIS–IV ability not intellectual ability in a general sense. Using prorated or alternate index scores that do not include Vocabulary and/or Matrix Reasoning do not have the same issue with part-whole correlations, and do not have artificially reduced standard error of the estimate. Therefore, they can be interpreted as general estimates of premorbid functioning.

Multiple Regression

Multiple hierarchical regression analyses were used to create prediction equations for WAIS–IV FSIQ, GAI, VCI, and PRI standard,

TABLE 5.14   Demographic Characteristics of the OPIE–IV WAIS–IV Development and Validation Samples

	Development	Validation
Age	47.2 (22.2)	47.3 (22.2)
Sex		
Male	51.2%	52.7%
Female	48.2%	47.2%
Education		
Kindergarten–7th Grade	2.2%	2.9%
8th–10th Grade	9.7%	9.8%
11th Grade	8.2%	7.1%
GED/Skilled trade apprenticeship	4.9%	5.7%
High school diploma	27.5%	25.9%
Trade or vocational school	1.9%	2.6%
1 year of college	7.8%	8.7%
Associate's degree or 2 years of college	12.5%	12.1%
3–5 years of college, no degree	5.2%	3.8%
Bachelor's degree	8.9%	11.0%
Post-bachelor's/master's degree	8.2%	6.8%
Post master's, no doctorate	1.8%	1.6%
Doctorate (e.g., PhD, MD, JD)	1.1%	1.8%
Ethnicity		
White	72.3%	68.8%
African-American	11.7%	11.9%
Hispanic	11.4%	14.1%
Asian	3.3%	3.1%
Other	1.3%	2.1%
Region		
Northeast	20.2%	19.1%
North Central	24.3%	22.3%
South	34.2%	37.7%
West	21.3%	20.9%

(Continued)

TABLE 5.14   (Continued)

	Development	Validation
WAIS–IV		
FSIQ	100.4 (14.7)	99.8 (15.6)
VCI	100.3 (14.5)	99.7 (15.6)
PRI	100.4 (14.9)	99.7 (15.2)
WMI	100.1 (14.4)	99.9 (15.7)
PSI	100.4 (15.1)	99.9 (15.3)

Note: $n = 1018$ development group and $n = 1014$ for validation group. All variables are presented as the percentage of the population with the exception of age and WAIS–IV scores that are presented as mans (standard deviation).

prorated, and alternate forms. The OPIE–IV using basic demographic data is the only model presented here and it applies only to individuals age 20 to 90. For prediction models other than OPIE–IV with simple demographics or for premorbid predictions of patients aged 16 to 19, the ACS TOPF can be used. The independent variables are entered into the equation in the following steps: raw Vocabulary, raw Matrix Reasoning, age, education, sex, region, and ethnicity. The demographic variables in the OPIE–IV equations are: (a) non-linear age effects (entered as "age in years" and the "square of age in years"); (b) education level (coded 1 for "belongs to that level" or 0 for "does not belong to that level"); (c) sex (coded 1 for "males" and 0 for "females"); (d) region (coded 1 for "belongs to that region" and 0 for "does not belong to that region"); and (e) ethnicity (coded 1 for "belongs to that group" and 0 for "does not belong to that group"). Non-significant variables ($p<0.05$) are removed from the equation and the regression is re-run without these variables to obtain the final prediction equation. Tables 5.15 to 5.22 present the multiple regression summaries for the WASI–II and WAIS–IV indexes.

The predictive accuracy for the Vocabulary and Matrix Reasoning OPIE–IV equations vary considerably between the prediction of standard versus prorated and alternate WAIS–IV indexes. The R^2 values for the standard indexes range from 0.78 (FSIQ) to 0.84 (GAI); however, for prorated indexes the R^2 value was 0.67 (GAI, FSIQ). For the alternate indexes, the R^2 ranged from 0.69 (FSIQ) to 0.78 (GAI). The part-whole association in the standard index equations inflates the R^2 by 6% to 9%. The equations using only the Vocabulary subtest have R^2 values from 0.65 (FSIQ) to 0.84 (VCI) for standard index scores, values from 0.57 (FSIQ) to 0.67 (VCI) for prorated indexes, and values from 0.58 (FSIQ) to 0.70 (VCI) for alternate form indexes. Finally, the Matrix

TABLE 5.15 Hierarchical Multiple Regression Vocabulary, Matrix Reasoning, and Demographics Predicted Standard Full-Scale IQ Development Sample

Predictor	R	R²	Adj R²	SEE	R² Change	F Change	DF1	DF2	Sig F Change
Vocabulary and Matrix Reasoning									
Vocabulary	0.76	0.58	0.57	9.57	0.58	1375.78	1	1016	0.000
Matrix Reasoning	0.84	0.70	0.70	8.00	0.13	438.66	1	1015	0.000
Age	0.87	0.76	0.76	7.14	0.06	130.50	2	1013	0.000
Education	0.88	0.77	0.77	7.09	0.00	5.93	3	1010	0.001
Sex	0.88	0.77	0.77	7.05	0.00	12.05	1	1009	0.001
Region	0.88	0.77	0.77	7.04	0.00	3.70	1	1008	0.055
Ethnicity	0.89	0.78	0.78	6.86	0.01	56.17	1	1007	0.000
Vocabulary Only									
Vocabulary	0.76	0.58	0.57	9.57	0.58	1375.78	1	1016	0.000
Age	0.78	0.60	0.60	9.26	0.03	36.24	2	1014	0.000
Education	0.79	0.62	0.62	9.07	0.02	8.15	6	1008	0.000
Sex	0.79	0.63	0.63	8.98	0.01	20.15	1	1007	0.000
Ethnicity	0.81	0.65	0.65	8.68	0.03	73.58	1	1006	0.000
Matrix Reasoning Only									
Matrix Reasoning	0.63	0.40	0.40	11.36	0.40	683.61	1	1016	0.000
Age	0.74	0.54	0.54	9.94	0.14	311.99	1	1015	0.000
Education	0.78	0.61	0.61	9.22	0.07	19.12	9	1006	0.000
Sex	0.78	0.61	0.61	9.21	0.00	5.08	1	1005	0.024
Region	0.78	0.61	0.61	9.17	0.00	8.59	1	1004	0.003

Note: The demographic variables in the OPIE–IV equations are non-liner age effects (entered as age in years and the square of age in years); education level (coded 1 for belongs to that level or 0 does not belong to that level); sex (coded 1 for males and 0 for females); region (coded 1 belongs to that region and 0 does not belong to that region); and ethnicity (coded 1 belongs to that group and 0 does not belong to that group).

Reasoning only equations have R^2 values from 0.61 (FSIQ) to 0.67 (PRI) for standard index scores, values from 0.37 (PRI) to 0.52 (FSIQ) for pro-rated index scores, and values from 0.41 (PRI) to 0.60 (FSIQ) for alternate form index scores. The part-whole correlation for VCI results in a 14% inflation, and for PRI results in a 30% inflation, in variance accounted for in the standard index equations. The standard index equations should be not used given the statistical inflation of

TABLE 5.16 Hierarchical Multiple Regression Vocabulary, Matrix Reasoning, and Demographics Predicted Prorated Full-Scale IQ Development Sample

Predictor	R	R^2	Adj R^2	SEE	R^2 Change	F Change	DF1	DF2	Sig F Change
Vocabulary and Matrix Reasoning									
Vocabulary	0.70	0.49	0.49	10.45	0.49	976.54	1	1016	0.000
Matrix Reasoning	0.77	0.59	0.59	9.34	0.10	256.13	1	1015	0.000
Age	0.80	0.64	0.64	8.80	0.05	65.84	2	1013	0.000
Education	0.80	0.65	0.64	8.72	0.01	6.61	3	1010	0.000
Sex	0.81	0.65	0.65	8.68	0.00	12.29	1	1009	0.000
Ethnicity	0.82	0.67	0.67	8.44	0.02	57.58	1	1008	0.000
Vocabulary Only									
Vocabulary	0.70	0.49	0.49	10.52	0.49	960.62	1	1016	0.000
Age	0.71	0.51	0.51	10.27	0.02	25.77	2	1014	0.000
Education	0.73	0.53	0.53	10.05	0.02	8.41	6	1008	0.000
Sex	0.74	0.54	0.54	9.96	0.01	19.89	1	1007	0.000
Ethnicity	0.76	0.58	0.57	9.61	0.03	75.86	1	1006	0.000
Matrix Reasoning Only									
Matrix Reasoning	0.57	0.33	0.33	11.98	0.33	501.55	1	1016	0.000
Age	0.66	0.44	0.44	10.96	0.11	200.05	1	1015	0.000
Education	0.72	0.52	0.52	10.15	0.08	17.72	10	1005	0.000
Sex	0.73	0.53	0.52	10.13	0.00	4.98	1	1004	0.026
Region	0.73	0.53	0.52	10.10	0.00	8.37	1	1003	0.004

Note: The demographic variables in the OPIE–IV equations are non-liner age effects (entered as age in years and the square of age in years); education level (coded 1 for belongs to that level or 0 does not belong to that level); sex (coded 1 for males and 0 for females); region (coded 1 belongs to that region and 0 does not belong to that region); and ethnicity (coded 1 belongs to that group and 0 does not belong to that group).

association. Compared to the TOPF, using both Matrix Reasoning and Vocabulary yields higher R^2 values for GAI and FSIQ. In general, the TOPF equations are similar to Vocabulary only predictions and have somewhat higher R^2 values than the Matrix Reasoning equations.

Table 5.23 presents accuracy data for each OPIE–IV prediction equation. Approximately 75% of subjects have predicted scores within ±5 points and over 90% are within ±10 points of their actual index scores when the standard index scores are predicted from Vocabulary and Matrix Reasoning combined. When prorated indexes and alternate form

TABLE 5.17 Hierarchical Multiple Regression Vocabulary, Matrix Reasoning, and Demographics Predicted Alternate Form Full-Scale IQ Development Sample

Predictor	R	R^2	Adj R^2	SEE	R^2 Change	F Change	DF1	DF2	Sig F Change
Vocabulary and Matrix Reasoning									
Vocabulary	0.72	0.52	0.52	9.99	0.52	1103.91	1	1016	0.000
Matrix Reasoning	0.79	0.62	0.62	8.91	0.10	264.13	1	1015	0.000
Age	0.82	0.67	0.66	8.35	0.05	70.74	2	1013	0.000
Education	0.82	0.67	0.67	8.31	0.00	6.50	2	1011	0.002
Sex	0.82	0.67	0.67	8.26	0.00	13.62	1	1010	0.000
Ethnicity	0.83	0.69	0.69	8.05	0.02	54.01	1	1009	0.000
Vocabulary Only									
Vocabulary	0.73	0.53	0.53	9.98	0.53	1141.24	1	1016	0.000
Age	0.74	0.55	0.55	9.72	0.03	28.76	2	1014	0.000
Education	0.76	0.57	0.57	9.53	0.02	7.91	6	1008	0.000
Sex	0.76	0.58	0.58	9.46	0.01	16.35	1	1007	0.000
Matrix Reasoning Only									
Matrix Reasoning	0.63	0.40	0.40	11.33	0.40	667.68	1	1016	0.000
Age	0.73	0.53	0.53	9.96	0.14	299.64	1	1015	0.000
Education	0.77	0.60	0.59	9.28	0.06	18.11	9	1006	0.000
Region	0.78	0.60	0.60	9.26	0.00	5.91	1	1005	0.015

Note: The demographic variables in the OPIE–IV equations are non-liner age effects (entered as age in years and the square of age in years); education level (coded 1 for belongs to that level or 0 does not belong to that level); sex (coded 1 for males and 0 for females); region (coded 1 belongs to that region and 0 does not belong to that region); and ethnicity (coded 1 belongs to that group and 0 does not belong to that group).

indexes are used, a little more than 60% of the subjects have scores within ±5 points and more than 80% of subjects have scores within ±10 points of the actual obtained scores. For all equations, the examinees' ability level falls in the same classification level of their actual ability approximately 50 to 60% of the time, and the majority of the sample falls within one category of their actual ability (85% to 97%).

Table 5.24 presents results for the OPIE–IV validation sample. The mean predicted scores are very close to the overall mean of 100 for each index score. The difference between mean and actual scores in the validation sample is near zero. When applied to the validation sample, the OPIE–IV prediction equations show results consistent with the

TABLE 5.18   Hierarchical Multiple Regression Vocabulary, Matrix Reasoning, and Demographics Predicted Standard GAI Development Sample

Predictor	R	R^2	Adj R^2	SEE	R^2 Change	F Change	DF1	DF2	Sig F Change
Vocabulary and Matrix Reasoning									
Vocabulary	0.79	0.62	0.62	9.09	0.62	1672.52	1	1016	0.000
Matrix Reasoning	0.87	0.75	0.75	7.39	0.13	520.92	1	1015	0.000
Age	0.90	0.81	0.81	6.39	0.06	172.25	2	1013	0.000
Education	0.90	0.81	0.81	6.38	0.00	4.75	1	1012	0.030
Sex	0.91	0.83	0.83	6.18	0.01	67.47	1	1011	0.000
Ethnicity	0.91	0.84	0.83	6.02	0.01	54.86	1	1010	0.000
Vocabulary Only									
Vocabulary	0.79	0.62	0.62	9.09	0.62	1672.52	1	1016	0.000
Age	0.81	0.65	0.65	8.73	0.03	44.28	2	1014	0.000
Education	0.81	0.66	0.65	8.69	0.00	4.84	2	1012	0.008
Sex	0.82	0.68	0.67	8.44	0.02	63.36	1	1011	0.000
Ethnicity	0.83	0.70	0.69	8.17	0.02	67.74	1	1010	0.000
Matrix Reasoning Only									
Matrix Reasoning	0.65	0.42	0.42	11.28	0.42	729.36	1	1016	0.000
Age	0.75	0.57	0.57	9.74	0.15	348.45	1	1015	0.000
Education	0.79	0.62	0.62	9.11	0.06	17.01	9	1006	0.000
Sex	0.80	0.63	0.63	9.00	0.01	25.92	1	1005	0.000
Region	0.80	0.64	0.64	8.93	0.01	18.75	1	1004	0.000

Note: The demographic variables in the OPIE–IV equations are non-liner age effects (entered as age in years and the square of age in years); education level (coded 1 for belongs to that level or 0 does not belong to that level); sex (coded 1 for males and 0 for females); region (coded 1 belongs to that region and 0 does not belong to that region); and ethnicity (coded 1 belongs to that group and 0 does not belong to that group).

development sample, indicating good generalizability for the prediction equations in healthy adults. None of the equations produced significant differences between actual and predicted ability scores and the correlations are in the 0.70s to 0.90s range. The theoretical prediction range was largest for the Vocabulary and Matrix Reasoning prediction of standard GAI (44 to 150) and smallest for Vocabulary predicted prorated FSIQ (61–131) and Matrix Reasoning predicted alternate PRI (62–132). The theoretical prediction ranges are sufficient for most clinical cases.

TABLE 5.19 Hierarchical Multiple Regression Vocabulary, Matrix Reasoning, and Demographics Prorated GAI Development Sample

Predictor	R	R^2	Adj R^2	SEE	R^2 Change	F Change	DF1	DF2	Sig F Change
Vocabulary and Matrix Reasoning									
Vocabulary	0.70	0.49	0.49	10.82	0.49	1068.86	1	1098	0.000
Matrix Reasoning	0.77	0.59	0.59	9.74	0.10	258.52	1	1097	0.000
Age	0.79	0.63	0.63	9.25	0.04	60.30	2	1095	0.000
Sex	0.81	0.65	0.65	8.96	0.02	72.95	1	1094	0.000
Ethnicity	0.82	0.67	0.67	8.75	0.02	53.67	1	1093	0.000
Vocabulary Only									
Vocabulary	0.73	0.53	0.53	10.15	0.53	1162.59	1	1016	0.000
Age	0.75	0.56	0.56	9.86	0.03	31.75	2	1014	0.000
Education	0.76	0.58	0.57	9.72	0.01	5.90	6	1008	0.000
Sex	0.78	0.60	0.60	9.39	0.03	71.19	1	1007	0.000
Ethnicity	0.79	0.63	0.62	9.10	0.02	66.86	1	1006	0.000
Matrix Reasoning Only									
Matrix Reasoning	0.56	0.31	0.31	12.48	0.31	458.71	1	1016	0.000
Age	0.64	0.41	0.41	11.51	0.10	179.18	1	1015	0.000
Education	0.69	0.48	0.47	10.89	0.07	14.05	9	1006	0.000
Sex	0.70	0.49	0.49	10.75	0.01	28.98	1	1005	0.000
Region	0.71	0.50	0.50	10.66	0.01	16.98	1	1004	0.000

Note: The demographic variables in the OPIE–IV equations are non-liner age effects (entered as age in years and the square of age in years); education level (coded 1 for belongs to that level or 0 does not belong to that level); sex (coded 1 for males and 0 for females); region (coded 1 belongs to that region and 0 does not belong to that region); and ethnicity (coded 1 belongs to that group and 0 does not belong to that group).

OPIE–IV Prediction Equations

All of the information required for using the OPIE–IV WAIS–IV Indexes is provided in the Appendix as Tables A5.7–A5.13. The regression equations for predicting standard, prorated, or alternate WAIS–IV indexes appear in Tables A5.7, A5.10, and A5.12, respectively. Each equation has different predictors and values associated with those predictors. For each equation, the clinician will need to use the examinee's age, age to the third power, and/or age to the 6th power (e.g., because

TABLE 5.20 Hierarchical Multiple Regression Vocabulary, Matrix Reasoning, and Demographics Alternate GAI Development Sample

Predictor	R	R^2	Adj R^2	SEE	R^2 Change	F Change	DF1	DF2	Sig F Change
Vocabulary and Matrix Reasoning									
Vocabulary	0.73	0.53	0.53	10.15	0.53	1162.59	1	1016	0.000
Matrix Reasoning	0.82	0.68	0.68	8.43	0.15	459.36	1	1015	0.000
Age	0.86	0.75	0.75	7.47	0.07	138.42	2	1013	0.000
Sex	0.87	0.77	0.76	7.22	0.02	75.02	1	1012	0.000
Ethnicity	0.88	0.78	0.77	7.05	0.01	48.34	1	1011	0.000
Vocabulary Only									
Vocabulary	0.74	0.55	0.55	9.88	0.55	1245.91	1	1016	0.000
Age	0.76	0.58	0.58	9.60	0.03	31.29	2	1014	0.000
Education	0.77	0.59	0.59	9.47	0.01	6.64	5	1009	0.000
Sex	0.78	0.61	0.61	9.19	0.02	63.59	1	1008	0.000
Ethnicity	0.80	0.64	0.63	8.91	0.02	66.11	1	1007	0.000
Matrix Reasoning Only									
Matrix Reasoning	0.57	0.32	0.32	11.90	0.32	476.85	1	1016	0.000
Age	0.65	0.42	0.42	11.00	0.10	175.77	1	1015	0.000
Education	0.70	0.48	0.48	10.41	0.06	14.07	9	1006	0.000
Sex	0.70	0.50	0.49	10.31	0.01	20.96	1	1005	0.000
Region	0.71	0.50	0.50	10.25	0.01	12.60	1	1004	0.000
Ethnicity	0.73	0.53	0.53	9.93	0.03	65.51	1	1003	0.000

Note: The demographic variables in the OPIE−IV equations are non-liner age effects (entered as age in years and the square of age in years); education level (coded 1 for belongs to that level or 0 does not belong to that level); sex (coded 1 for males and 0 for females); region (coded 1 belongs to that region and 0 does not belong to that region); and ethnicity (coded 1 belongs to that group and 0 does not belong to that group).

the relationship is non-linear, age to specific power is calculated to create a curvilinear relationship). Education, region, and ethnicity are coded as "1" (belongs to that category) or "0" (does not belong to that category). Sex is coded as "0" for female and "1" for male. These values along with the equation constant are used to obtain the predicted premorbid score for each index. Additional tables at the end of this chapter provide critical values for statistically significant differences between actual and predicted scores (Table A5.8) and base rates

TABLE 5.21   Hierarchical Multiple Regression Vocabulary and Demographics Predicted Standard, Prorated, and Alternate VCI Development Sample

Predictor	R	R^2	Adj R^2	SEE	R^2 Change	F Change	DF1	DF2	Sig F Change
Standard VCI									
Vocabulary	0.88	0.78	0.78	6.77	0.78	3657.00	1	1016	0.000
Age	0.91	0.82	0.82	6.11	0.04	79.01	3	1013	0.000
Education	0.91	0.83	0.83	6.07	0.00	4.98	3	1010	0.002
Sex	0.91	0.84	0.83	5.91	0.01	55.99	1	1009	0.000
Ethnicity	0.92	0.84	0.84	5.87	0.00	8.75	2	1007	0.000
Prorated VCI									
Vocabulary	0.78	0.60	0.60	9.26	0.60	1547.90	1	1016	0.000
Age	0.80	0.64	0.64	8.86	0.03	32.60	3	1013	0.000
Education	0.80	0.65	0.64	8.78	0.01	5.30	4	1009	0.000
Sex	0.82	0.67	0.66	8.53	0.02	60.63	1	1008	0.000
Ethnicity	0.82	0.67	0.67	8.46	0.01	18.68	1	1007	0.000
Alternate VCI									
Vocabulary	0.80	0.65	0.65	8.58	0.65	1862.46	1	1016	0.000
Age	0.83	0.68	0.68	8.17	0.03	36.17	3	1013	0.000
Education	0.83	0.69	0.68	8.12	0.01	4.37	4	1009	0.002
Sex	0.84	0.70	0.70	7.92	0.02	51.25	1	1008	0.000
Ethnicity	0.84	0.71	0.70	7.86	0.01	17.48	1	1007	0.000

Note: The demographic variables in the OPIE–IV equations are non-liner age effects (entered as age in years and the square of age in years); education level (coded 1 for belongs to that level or 0 does not belong to that level); sex (coded 1 for males and 0 for females); region (coded 1 belongs to that region and 0 does not belong to that region); and ethnicity (coded 1 belongs to that group and 0 does not belong to that group).

for the difference between actual and predicted scores (Tables A5.9, A5.11, and A5.13).

Using the data from the previously presented case, premorbid predictions can be made for WAIS–IV FSIQ, GAI, VCI, and PRI indexes. For illustrative purposes, the WAIS–IV standard FSIQ and WAIS–IV standard PRI will be presented. The first step is to identify the information needed to calculate the desired scores. According to Table A5.28, WAIS–IV standard FSIQ scores from VC and MR require Vocabulary

TABLE 5.22 Hierarchical Multiple Regression Matrix Reasoning and Demographics Predicted Standard, Prorated, and Alternate PRI Development Sample

Predictor	R	R²	Adj R²	SEE	R² Change	F Change	DF1	DF2	Sig F Change
Standard PRCI									
Matrix Reasoning	0.69	0.48	0.48	10.80	0.48	921.44	1	1016	0.000
Age	0.81	0.66	0.66	8.74	0.18	536.60	1	1015	0.000
Education	0.81	0.66	0.66	8.69	0.00	11.48	1	1014	0.001
Sex	0.82	0.67	0.67	8.59	0.01	25.83	1	1013	0.000
Prorated PRI									
Matrix Reasoning	0.50	0.25	0.25	13.42	0.25	347.74	1	1016	0.000
Age	0.59	0.34	0.34	12.59	0.09	138.55	1	1015	0.000
Education	0.60	0.35	0.35	12.51	0.01	8.13	2	1013	0.000
Sex	0.61	0.37	0.37	12.34	0.02	28.45	1	1012	0.000
Alternate PRI									
Matrix Reasoning	0.53	0.28	0.28	12.00	0.28	388.88	1	1016	0.000
Age	0.60	0.36	0.36	11.26	0.09	138.32	1	1015	0.000
Education	0.61	0.37	0.37	11.21	0.01	10.93	1	1014	0.001
Sex	0.62	0.38	0.38	11.12	0.01	17.28	1	1013	0.000
Ethnicity	0.64	0.41	0.40	10.88	0.03	45.77	1	1012	0.000

Note: The demographic variables in the OPIE–IV equations are non-liner age effects (entered as age in years and the square of age in years); education level (coded 1 for belongs to that level or 0 does not belong to that level); sex (coded 1 for males and 0 for females); region (coded 1 belongs to that region and 0 does not belong to that region); and ethnicity (coded 1 belongs to that group and 0 does not belong to that group).

raw score, Matrix Reasoning raw score, age, age to the third power, education, sex, region, and ethnicity.

- Vocabulary raw score = 46
- Matrix Reasoning raw score = 10
- Age = 71 years, age to the third power = 357911 (i.e., $71 \times 71 \times 71$)
- Education level is doctorate, 0 for variables in this equation
- Sex is female = 0
- Region is Midwest = 1
- Ethnicity = white, 0 for variables in this equation
- Predicted FSIQ = 57.84718185 + (0.706570548 *Vocab Raw) + (1.38658557 * MR raw) + (−0.204106431*Age in years) + (0000415057 *

TABLE 5.23 Predictive Accuracy of OPIE Equations Validation Sample

Scores	Independent Variables		Differences Between Predicted and Actual Scores					
			Number of Points			Ability Classification		
			±5	±10	±15	Same Category	One Category
Full-Scale IQ	VC, MR, Age, Ed, Sex, Region, Eth	74.4	93.3	98.3	62.2	97.4	
Full-Scale IQ	VC, Age, Ed, Sex, Eth	68.0	86.9	95.2	53.7	94.0	
Full-Scale IQ	MR, Age, Ed, Sex, Region	45.0	75.1	90.3	53.7	92.8	
Full-Scale IQ Prorated	VC, MR, Age, Ed, Sex, Eth	66.6	87.5	96.3	55.3	94.8	
Full-Scale IQ Prorated	VC, Age, Ed, Sex, Eth	65.2	84.3	93.9	55.1	93.0	
Full-Scale IQ Prorated	MR, Age, Ed, Sex, Region	41.7	71.8	87.0	52.6	90.2	
Full Scale IQ Alternate	VC, MR, Age, Ed, Sex, Eth	66.8	89.0	97.0	57.5	95.7	
Full Scale IQ Alternate	VC, Age, Ed, Sex	45.2	72.7	91.4	55.4	93.1	
Full Scale IQ Alternate	MR, Age, Ed, Region	45.7	74.0	89.8	52.0	93.3	
General Ability Index	VC, MR, Age, Ed, Sex, Eth	75.6	94.0	99.3	62.9	99.5	
General Ability Index	VC, Age, Ed, Sex, Eth	69.3	88.0	95.3	55.6	95.1	
General Ability Index	MR, Age, Ed, Sex, Region	45.4	76.2	93.0	54.1	92.9	
General Ability Index Prorated	VC, MR, Age, Ed, Sex, Eth	64.4	84.9	94.1	51.7	95.3	
General Ability Index Prorated	VC, Age, Ed, Sex, Eth	66.1	84.7	93.8	51.3	93.2	

General Ability Index Prorated	MR, Age, Ed, Sex, Region	38.9	68.2	86.4	49.7	90.0
General Ability Index Alternate	VC, MR, Age, Ed, Sex, Eth	65.6	86.7	95.7	56.7	96.7
General Ability Index Alternate	VC, Age, Ed, Sex, Eth	66.8	84.8	93.8	53.5	93.7
General Ability Index Alternate	MR, Age, Ed, Sex, Region	56.5	81.2	93.3	50.4	90.6
Verbal Comprehension Index	VC, Age, Ed, Sex, Eth	76.4	95.1	99.1	64.8	99.0
Verbal Comprehension Index Prorated	VC, Age, Ed, Sex, Eth	61.6	86.0	95.0	52.8	94.9
Verbal Comprehension Index Alternate	VC, Age, Ed, Sex, Eth	64.5	88.3	96.6	58.8	96.4
Perceptual Reasoning Index	MR, Age, Ed, Sex	45.5	77.8	92.7	54.4	94.5
Perceptual Reasoning Index Prorated	MR, Age, Ed, Sex	32.7	62.1	80.2	43.4	85.0
Perceptual Reasoning Index Alternate	MR, Age, Ed, Sex, Eth	52.5	76.7	90.1	49.7	89.6

Copyright 2009 Pearson, Inc. Reproduced with Permission, All rights reserved.

TABLE 5.24 Descriptive Statistics, Comparison Tests, and Prediction Ranges for OPIE Prediction Equations Validation Sample

Dependent Variable	Independent Variables	Obtained Scores		Comparison Scores						Sample Prediction Range		Theoretical Prediction Range	
		Mean	SD	Mean Diff	Std Diff	Min	Max	p	r	Min	Max	Min	Max
Full-Scale IQ	VC, MR, Age, Ed, Sex, Region, Eth	99.57	13.88	0.21	7.17	−24	21	0.53	0.89	56	130	44	146
Full-Scale IQ	VC,Age,Ed,Sex,Eth	99.91	12.59	−0.14	9.11	−35	27	0.73	0.81	63	127	59	133
Full-Scale IQ	MR,Age,Ed,Sex,Region	99.67	11.90	0.10	9.49	−32	30	0.77	0.79	59	129	48	142
Full-Scale IQ Prorated	VC,MR,Age,Ed,Sex,Eth	99.50	12.83	0.23	8.84	−28	27	0.51	0.82	59	129	43	140
Full-Scale IQ Prorated	VC,Age,Ed,Sex,Eth	99.95	11.75	−0.16	10.11	−38	30	0.70	0.76	65	126	61	131
Full-Scale IQ Prorated	MR,Age,Ed,Sex,Region	99.73	11.04	0.10	10.46	−37	35	0.82	0.74	62	127	54	141
Full Scale IQ Alternate	VC,MR,Age,Ed,Sex,Eth	99.50	12.83	0.28	8.31	−28	24	0.46	0.84	59	128	46	142
Full Scale IQ Alternate	VC,Age,Ed,Sex	99.90	11.71	−0.16	9.49	−35	27	0.69	0.79	67	126	66	131
Full Scale IQ Alternate	MR,Age,Ed,Region	99.69	11.72	−0.01	9.61	−31	28	0.98	0.78	60	128	52	144
General Ability Index	VC,MR,Age,Ed,Sex,Eth	99.59	14.42	0.11	6.24	−15	20	0.68	0.92	54	133	44	150
General Ability Index	VC,Age,Ed,Sex,Eth	99.85	13.05	−0.15	8.41	−26	28	0.76	0.84	62	127	65	138
General Ability Index	MR,Age,Ed,Sex,Region	99.67	12.27	0.03	9.16	−27	25	0.94	0.81	59	131	47	144
General Ability Index Prorated	VC,MR,Age,Ed,Sex,Eth	100.17	13.26	0.12	9.06	−22	29	0.58	0.82	58	131	49	144
General Ability Index Prorated	VC,Age,Ed,Sex,Eth	100.18	12.53	−0.23	9.42	−30	31	0.58	0.80	64	129	59	135

General Ability Index Prorated	MR,Age,Ed,Sex,Region	99.98	11.03	0.08	11.01	−34	32	0.84	0.72	62	128	51	138
General Ability Index Alternate	VC,MR,Age,Ed,Sex,Eth	99.77	13.96	−0.11	8.53	−25	25	0.90	0.84	56	133	44	149
General Ability Index Alternate	VC,Age,Ed,Sex,Eth	99.85	12.52	−0.15	8.53	−29	28	0.54	0.80	63	128	59	135
General Ability Index Alternate	MR,Age,Ed,Sex,Region	99.50	11.07	0.20	9.22	−34	26	0.85	0.73	68	127	47	123
Verbal Comprehension Index	VC,Age,Ed,Sex,Eth	99.70	14.31	0.04	6.02	−17	24	0.90	0.92	62	130	58	133
Verbal Comprehension Index Prorated	VC,Age,Ed,Sex,Eth	100.15	13.01	−0.02	8.57	−25	35	0.97	0.84	64	128	56	129
Verbal Comprehension Index Alternate	VC,Age,Ed,Sex,Eth	99.62	13.12	0.17	7.82	−25	26	0.66	0.86	64	127	60	132
Perceptual Reasoning Index	MR, Age, Ed, Sex	99.56	12.63	0.11	8.81	−23	26	0.77	0.82	58	131	48	149
Perceptual Reasoning Index Prorated	MR, Age, Ed, Sex	100.20	9.76	0.24	12.69	−38	39	0.66	0.60	66	125	58	138
Perceptual Reasoning Index Alternate	MR, Age, Ed, Sex, Eth	99.50	9.39	0.21	11.46	−34	41	0.68	0.61	70	121	62	132

Copyright 2009 Pearson, Inc. Reproduced with Permission, All rights reserved.

Age^3) + (−4.213630131 * Kinder) + (−1.880854304 * 8–10th grade) + (1.765273315* Bachelor's degree) + (1.568961576 * sex) + (1.061002858 * Midwest) + (−5.143182795 * African-American)

- Predicted FSIQ = 57.84718185 + (0. 706570548 *46) + (1.38658557 * 10) + (−0.204106431 * 71) + (.0000415057 * 357911) + (− 4.213630131 * 0) + (−1.880854304 * 0) + (1.765273315 * 0) + (1.568961576 * 0) + (1.061002858 * 1) + (−5.143182795 * 0)
- Predicted
  FSIQ = 57.84718185 + 32.50224521 + 13.8658557 − 14.4915566 + 14.85534659 + 0 + 0 + 0 + 0 + 1.061002858 + 0
- Predicted standard FSIQ = 106
- Actual-Predicted = 86−106 = − 20
- Critical value p <0.01 = 9.01, difference is statistically significant (Table A5.8)
- Base Rate = 0.20% (Table A5.9).

The WAIS–IV actual PRI is 82. The predicted PRI requires the following data: Matrix Reasoning raw score, age to the third power, education, and sex.

- Matrix Reasoning raw score = 10
- Age = 71 years, age to the third power = 357911
- Education level is doctorate, 0 for variables in this equation
- Sex is female = 0
- Predicted PRI = 48.98035805 + (2.560129553 * MR raw) + (0000386971 * Age^3) + (−3.365709173 * 8–10th grade) + (2.759698382 * sex)
- Predicted PRI = 48.98035805 + (2.560129553 * 10) + (0000386971 * 357911) + (−3.365709173 * 0) + (2.759698382 * 0)
- Predicted FSIQ = 48.98035805 + 25.60129553 + 13.85011776 + 0 + 0
- Predicted WAIS–IV PRI = 88
- Actual-Predicted = 82−88 = −6
- Critical value p > 0.05 = 7.96, difference is not statistically significant (Table A5.8)
- Base Rate = 28.25% (Table A5.9)

The OPIE–IV and TOPF with simple demographics yield similar predictions and interpretations. In both cases, actual FSIQ is significantly below estimates of premorbid ability, indicative of cognitive decline. The PRI premorbid prediction was 88 for the OPIE–IV equation and 104 for the TOPF with simple demographics. The OPIE–IV equation indicated no significant difference between actual and premorbid abilities; however, the TOPF scores indicated a large, significant, discrepancy between actual and predicted PRI. These results show that different results may be obtained depending upon which model is used.

CASE STUDIES

Two case studies are presented in this chapter to illustrate the application of the TOPF and OPIE–IV models. These procedures are used to estimate premorbid functioning in adults with known or suspected neurological dysfunction, and OPIE–IV and TOPF are not to be used in lieu of formal intellectual assessment or as a replacement for a comprehensive evaluation of intellectual abilities. Each model has strengths and weaknesses. The clinician must determine the most appropriate model for a specific individual based on presenting problems and background information.

CASE STUDY 1

Mr. J. is a 25-year-old Hispanic man, referred for neuropsychological evaluation after sustaining a moderate traumatic brain injury. Mr. J. was injured in a motorcycle accident in which he struck a brick and lost control of his vehicle. He crashed into the rear end of a parked car and was ejected from his motorcycle head first into the car. He lost consciousness for approximately 55 minutes. He had a GCS score of 11 and post-traumatic amnesia for approximately 36 hours. A day-of-injury CT scan performed in the ER indicated a large right temporal/parietal subdural hematoma. He was released from the hospital after 2 days.

After a 6-week recovery period, Mr. J. returned to his position as lead HVAC installation technician for a small heating and air conditioning company. He struggled to complete his work on time and made multiple mistakes that were inconsistent with his work history. He reported disrupted sleep but otherwise denied any physical difficulties. Cognitively, he reported mild problems with attention and concentration. Neurological evaluation showed no signs of significant impairment and his EEG was normal. He was referred by his treating neurologist for a neuropsychological evaluation to assess his cognitive symptoms.

Mr. J.'s family emigrated from Mexico when he was an infant. He was raised in California where his father worked as a mechanic and his mother worked at a local grocery store. Mr. J. learned English from an early age, even though his family primarily spoke Spanish at home. He attended day care and local public schools. He was an average to above average student. He graduated from high school and completed 1 year of college. Mr. J. left school and obtained employment as a mechanic. He is married and has one child. He still lives in California close to his parent's home.

The WAIS–IV, WMS–IV, and TOPF were administered as part of the evaluation. His TOPF standard score was 98, which was not significantly different from the predicted TOPF score of 94. Therefore, his TOPF score did not appear to be affected by the injury. Table 5.25 provides Mr. J.'s TOPF with simple demographics predicted and actual scores for WAIS–IV and WMS–IV indexes. Based on the TOPF with simple demographics, his predicted FSIQ is 99 and his actual FSIQ is 92. This is significantly different at the p <0.01 level but has a base rate of 24.1% indicating the difference is not unusual in the standardization sample. VCI, PRI, WMI, and GAI predicted premorbid scores are not significantly different from his obtained scores. Therefore, there is no obvious decline in verbal abilities, perceptual reasoning, or auditory working memory abilities relative to estimated premorbid functioning. However, PSI and CPI show significant discrepancies between premorbid and actual scores and occurred infrequently (e.g., 0.4% and 1.08%, respectively). It is not necessary, however, for the clinician to interpret the CPI discrepancy because it is being driven by the very large PSI discrepancy (CPI = WMI + PSI). Actual WMS–IV Immediate, Delayed, and Visual Working Memory Index scores were all statistically lower than predicted memory scores; although, only immediate and delayed memory discrepancies were uncommon in the standardization sample. The TOPF equations indicate generally preserved intellectual functioning with declines in processing speed and immediate and delayed memory functioning.

OPIE–IV based estimates are provided below. The OPIE–IV is less reliant on demographic variables and generally reflects the individual's

TABLE 5.25 TOPF with Simple Demographics WAIS–IV/WMS–IV Actual–Predicted Comparison for Mr. J.

Composite	Actual	Predicted	Difference	Critical Value	Significant Difference	Base Rate (%)
FSIQ	92	99	−7	5.8	Y	24.10
GAI	102	103	−1	7.52	N	48.90
VCI	107	100	7	7.23	N	20.10
PRI	98	100	−2	6.67	N	46.50
WMI	95	97	−2	7.48	N	46.00
PSI	65	98	−33	9.64	Y	0.40
CPI	77	98	−21	7.66	Y	1.08
IMI	84	101	−17	6.45	Y	10.40
DMI	80	100	−20	6.33	Y	7.00
VWMI	91	102	−11	7.72	Y	22.80

ability more than the TOPF. The results of OPIE–IV equations for Mr. J. are presented in Table 5.26. FSIQ is significantly lower than predicted and the degree of difference is rare in the general population. No other comparison is statistically significant. The results suggest a general decline in intellectual functioning but not specifically associated with loss of verbal or perceptual reasoning abilities.

Both the TOPF and the OPIE–IV identified a decline in cognitive functioning. The TOPF identified impairments in processing speed, and immediate and delayed memory functioning. The OPIE–IV identified a decline in general cognitive functioning that was not specifically related to verbal or perceptual functioning. The FSIQ is lower than the PRI and VCI indexes due to very low PSI scores, which may be the reason there is a significant discrepancy on that index.

CASE STUDY 2

Mr. Q. is a 60-year-old married African-American man. Mr. Q. retired 6 months ago. His wife noticed a decline in his cognitive functioning over the past year. She was concerned that since his retirement, he has appeared depressed and his cognitive symptoms have intensified. She noted that his recent memory is quite poor though his memory for past events is quite good. Mr. Q. reports that he has felt down since his retirement but he would not say he was depressed. He is also concerned about his declining memory functioning. Mr. Q. was referred for a neuropsychological assessment to evaluate memory problems and possible depression.

Mr. Q. has a bachelor's degree in accounting. He worked for many years as an accountant for a small manufacturing business. Later, he returned to school and obtained a M.B.A. He then worked 20 years as an operations manager at a large distribution company in Atlanta. Prior to his retirement, he was experiencing difficulties keeping up with his monthly reports and at times appeared confused and forgetful. Given his on-going problems, he was offered an early retirement package, which he accepted.

TABLE 5.26 OPIE–IV WAIS–IV Actual–Predicted Comparison for Mr. J.

Composite	Actual	Predicted	Difference	Critical Value	Significant Difference	Base Rate (%)
FSIQ	92	105	−13	9.08	Y	3.54
GAI	102	105	−3	7.68	N	33.60
VCI	107	114	−7	8.83	N	12.77
PRI	98	91	7	10.46	N	22.99

TABLE 5.27   OPIE–IV WAIS–IV Actual–Predicted Comparison for Mr. Q.

Composite	Actual	Predicted	Difference	Critical Value	Significant Difference	Base Rate (%)
FSIQ	98	104	−6	9.08	N	20.92
GAI	98	103	−5	7.68	N	22.20
VCI	95	97	−2	8.83	N	40.67
PRI	102	106	−4	10.46	N	37.13

The WAIS–IV, WMS–IV, and TOPF were administered as part of the neuropsychological evaluation. Mr. Q's TOPF score of 88 was significantly lower than predicted given his education and occupation. Instead of using the TOPF for estimating premorbid intellectual functioning, the examiner decided the OPIE–IV would be more appropriate due to the unexpectedly low TOPF scores. Table 5.27 presents the OPIE–IV predicted and actual WAIS–IV FSIQ, GAI, VCI, and PRI indexes for Mr. Q. The results indicated no difference between predicted and actual general cognitive functioning.

Mr. Q.'s performance on the WMS–IV was in the deficient to average range. His Immediate Memory Index of 78 was in the borderline range and his Delayed Memory Index was extremely low (61). Mr. Q. performed in the average range on visual (VWMI = 97) and auditory (WMI = 105) working memory measures and processing speed (PSI = 92). Overall, the results indicated generally average cognitive functioning with significant impairments in immediate and delayed memory. Based on the presenting symptoms, history, and test results, the clinician diagnosed Mr. Q. with Mild Cognitive Impairment.

SUMMARY

The estimation of premorbid cognitive functioning is an important component of most neuropsychological evaluations with adults. However, it is not possible to precisely calculate or determine an individual's exact level of premorbid ability. Cognitive functioning, in general, is quite variable in its measurement due to natural fluctuations in human performance. Statistical models are needed to evaluate *probable* levels of premorbid functioning.

Several models have been used to evaluate premorbid functioning. These include demographic models, current performance models, and combined demographic and performance models. Each model has strengths and weaknesses. The advantage of demographic models is that they are independent of the impact of current neurological dysfunction. However, demographic data have lower correlation with ability and large standard errors of estimate. In addition, demographic based methods suffer from referencing the individual to the average of a population and the information can be difficult to verify. Performance based prediction models use either subtests embedded in the cognitive battery or stand-alone reading tests. The advantage of current performance models is their higher correlation with cognitive ability, easily verifiable information, and better representation of the individual's ability. However, current performance models are susceptible to the effects of the current illness or injury making premorbid estimations less accurate. Combined models use both demographics and current performance data, taking advantage of the strengths and minimizing the disadvantages of each model.

The TOPF and the OPIE−IV were developed as statistical techniques to estimate premorbid functioning based on the WAIS−IV battery. The TOPF provides estimation of WAIS−IV and WMS−IV indexes using demographics only, TOPF only, or combined TOPF and demographic data. Prediction of WASI−II performance is available in this chapter. The OPIE−IV algorithms predict WAIS−IV indexes using Vocabulary and Matrix Reasoning subtests and demographic data. Each model has strengths and weaknesses to be considered when determining which approach to use for a particular patient.

KEY LEARNING

- It is impossible to predict premorbid ability with 100% accuracy. Intellectual assessments provide a range of abilities for an individual and intellectual functioning fluctuates over time. The goal of predicting premorbid functioning is to provide a *reasonable estimate* of an individual's previous level of functioning.
- The purpose of estimating premorbid cognitive functioning is to establish a comparison standard in order to determine if there has been a decline in ability due to injury or illness.
- Demographic data, particularly education, occupation, sex, and ethnicity, have low to moderate correlations with cognitive functioning, and can be used to estimate premorbid abilities. The advantage of demographic data is that it is resistant to the impact of injury or illness. The disadvantage of using demographic data is that it can be difficult to verify, estimation error is higher due to moderate correlation with ability, and there is a high degree of variability within demographic groups.

- Test scores from within the cognitive ability battery, or *embedded measures*, can be used to estimate premorbid ability. Subtests such as Vocabulary and Matrix Reasoning are *relatively* resistant to the effects of brain injury, dementia, or illness and can be used to estimate premorbid abilities. The advantages of using these measures are that they represent the individual's actual ability, scores are easy to verify, and they have a high correlation with overall ability. The drawback of using embedded measures is that they tend to inflate the accuracy of premorbid predictions and are susceptible to effects of injury and illness.
- Reading tests, particularly those with atypical phoneme-grapheme associations (such as the TOPF and HART), have been used effectively as measures of premorbid ability. The advantages of using reading tests are that they represent the patient's actual ability, are easy to verify, have a high correlation with intellectual functioning, and are relatively resistant to the effects of injury and illness. The disadvantage of using reading tests is that they cannot be used in individuals with a history of reading disability or current impairment in reading ability.
- The best model for estimating premorbid functioning can be combining demographic and performance variables, either reading tests or embedded measures. The combination of performance and demographic data maximizes the advantages of both models and minimizes the impact of the disadvantages.
- Commonly used reading tests for the prediction of premorbid abilities include the Hopkins Adult Reading Test (HART; Schretlen et al., 2009), WTAR and its revised edition the Test of Premorbid Functioning (TOPF). The WTAR and TOPF were co-normed with the WAIS–III and WAIS–IV, respectively. The TOPF is part of the Advanced Clinical Solutions for the WAIS–IV/WMS–IV. The HART was developed using the WAIS-R and WAIS–III.
- The TOPF provides premorbid estimation for WAIS–IV VCI, PRI, WMI, FSIQ, GAI, and CPI, as well as the WMS–IV IMI, DMI, and VWMI. Equations using the TOPF only, the TOPF with simple demographics, the TOPF with complex demographics, and demographics only models are available. The TOPF can also be used to predict WASI–II scores. The equations for predicting CPI and WASI–II scores are provided in this chapter.
- OPIE–IV provides premorbid estimation of WAIS–IV FSIQ, GAI, VCI, and PRI. The OPIE–IV combines current raw WAIS–IV subtest scores with demographic variables. Equations are available to predict standard, prorated, and alternate versions of WAIS–IV indexes.
- Education and reading skills are likely more generalized correlates of premorbid cognition functioning than the results of individual WAIS

subtests, such as Vocabulary and Matrix Reasoning. Therefore, theoretically, if the clinician wishes to generalize the findings to overall pre-morbid functioning rather than performance related to a specific ability battery (e.g., WAIS–IV), then education and reading skills are usually preferred in a premorbid prediction model over using current performance on a specific subtests.

- The TOPF reading test should not be used in cases where there is a history of reading disability or in cases where reading is significantly affected by the presenting injury or illness. The TOPF provides estimation of expected TOPF performance based on demographic data. Data suggest the TOPF can be used even when the predicted TOPF is significantly higher than the actual TOPF unless the base rate of the discrepancy exceeds 10% of the standardization sample. The TOPF demographic models can be used when the TOPF reading score is unexpectedly low.
- The OPIE–IV may be used when TOPF is unexpectedly low and in cases of severe language impairment or a history of speech-language impairment. In these cases, the models using Matrix Reasoning may be preferable.
- When selecting a model for predicting premorbid ability, the clinician must consider the strengths and weaknesses of each method, and use the model that is most appropriate for the individual being assessed.
- The use of premorbid prediction equations for determining decline in cognitive functioning is enhanced when statistical significance data and base rate of discrepancies are also applied. These data are available for both the TOPF and OPIE–IV.

The Appendix containing tables for Chapter 5 can be found online at: http://booksite.elsevier.com/9780123869340

References

Axelrod, B. N., Vanderploeg, R. D., & Schinka, J. A. (1999). Comparing methods for estimating premorbid intellectual functioning. *Archives of Clinical Neuropsychology, 14*(4), 341–346.

Babcock, H. (1930). An experiment in the measurement of mental deterioration. *Archives of Psychology, 18*(117), 5–105.

Barona, A., Reynolds, C., & Chastain, R. (1984). A demographically based index of premorbid intelligence for the WAIS-R. *Journal of Consulting and Clinical Psychology, 52*(5), 885–887.

Blair, J., & Spreen, O. (1989). Predicting premorbid IQ: A revision of the national adult reading test. *The Clinical Neuropsychologist, 3*(2), 129–136.

Crawford, J. R. (1992). Current and premorbid intelligence measures in neuropsychological assessment. In J. R. Crawford, D. M. Parker, & W. W. McKinlay (Eds.), *A handbook of neuropsychological assessment* (pp. 21–50). Hove, UK: Erlbaum.

Crawford, J. R., & Allan, K. M. (1997). Estimating premorbid WAIS-R IQ with demographic variables: Regression equations derived from a UK sample. *The Clinical Neuropsychologist*, *11*(2), 192–197.

Donders, J., Tulsky, D. S., & Zhu, J. (2001). Criterion validity of new WAIS–III subtest scores after traumatic brain injury. *Journal of the International Neuropsychological Society*, *7*(7), 892–898.

Duff, K. (2010). Predicting premorbid memory functioning in older adults. *Applied Neuropsychology*, *17*(4), 278–282.

Franzen, M. D., Burgess, E. J., & Smith-Seemiller, L. (1997). Method of estimating premorbid functioning. *Archives of Clinical Neuropsychology*, *12*(8), 711–738.

Gladsjo, J. A., Heaton, R. K., Palmer, B. W., Taylor, M. J., & Jeste, D. V. (1999). Use of oral reading to estimate premorbid intellectual and neuropsychological functioning. *Journal of the International Neuropsychological Society*, *5*(3), 247–254.

Grober, E., & Sliwinski, M. (1991). Development and validation of a model for estimating premorbid verbal intelligence in the elderly. *Journal of Clinical and Experimental Neuropsychology*, *13*(6), 933–949.

Hilsabeck, R. C., & Sutker, P. B. (2009). Using an implicit memory task to estimate premorbid memory. *Archives of Clinical Neuropsychology*, *24*(2), 179–191.

Isella, V., Villa, M. L., Forapani, E., Piamarta, F., Russo, A., & Appollonio, I. M. (2005). Ineffectiveness of an Italian NART-equivalent for the estimation of verbal learning ability in normal elderly. *Journal of Clinical & Experimental Neuropsychology*, *27*(5), 618–623.

Iverson, G. L., Lange, R. T., Brooks, B. L., & Rennison, V. L. A. (2010). "Good old days" bias following mild traumatic brain injury. *The Clinical Neuropsychologist*, *24*(1), 17–37.

Jastak, J. F., & Jastak, S. (1985). *The wide range achievement test–revised*. Wilmington, DE: Jastak Associates.

Johnson-Greene, D., Dehring, M., Adams, K. M., Miller, T., Arora, S., & Beylin, A., et al. (1997). Accuracy of self-reported educational attainment among diverse patient populations: A preliminary investigation. *Archives of Clinical Neuropsychology*, *12*(7), 635–643.

Johnstone, B., Hogg, J. R., Schopp, L. H., Kapila, C., & Edwards, S. (2002). Neuropsychological deficit profiles in senile dementia of the Alzheimer's type. *Archives of Clinical Neuropsychology*, *17*(3), 273–281.

Kareken, D. (1997). Judgment pitfalls in estimating premorbid intellectual function. *Archives of Clinical Neuropsychology*, *12*(8), 701–709.

Kareken, G., Gur, R., & Saykin, A. (1995). Reading on the wide range achievement test–revised and parental education as predictors of IQ: Comparison with the Barona formula. *Archives of Clinical Neuropsychology*, *10*(2), 147–157.

Kareken, D., & Williams, M. (1994). Human judgment and estimation of premorbid intellectual functioning. *Psychological Assessment*, *6*(2), 83–91.

Kaufman, A. S. (1990). *Assessing adolescent and adult intelligence*. Boston: Allyn and Bacon.

Krull, K. R., Scott, J., & Sherer, M. (1995). Estimation of premorbid intelligence from combined performance and demographic variables. *The Clinical Neuropsychologist*, *9*(1), 83–88.

Lange, R. T., Schoenberg, M. R., Saklofske, D. H., Woodward, T. S., & Brickell, T. A. (2006). Expanding the WAIS–III estimate of premorbid ability for Canadians (EPAC). *Journal of Clinical and Experimental Neuropsychology*, *28*(5), 773–789.

Larrabee, G. J., Largen, J. W., & Levin, H. S. (1985). Sensitivity of age-decline resistant ("Hold") WAIS subtests to Alzheimer's disease. *Clinical and Experimental Neuropsychology*, *7*(5), 497–504.

Mathias, J. L., Bowden, S. C., Bigler, E. D., & Rosenfeld, J. V. (2007). Is performance on the Wechsler test of adult reading affected by traumatic brain injury? *British Journal of Clinical Psychology*, *46*(4), 457–466.

Mattis, S. (1988). *Dementia rating scale*. Odessa, FL: Psychological Assessment Resources.

Mittenberg, W., Theroux, S., Aguila-Puentes, G., Bianchini, K., Greve, K., & Tayls, K. (2001). Identification of Malingered head injury on the Wechsler adult intelligence scale–third edition. *The Clinical Neuropsychologist, 15*(4), 440–445.

Perez, S. A., Schlottmann, R. S., Holloway, J. A., & Ozolins, M. S. (1996). Measurement of premorbid intellectual ability following brain injury. *Archives of Clinical Neuropsychology, 11*(6), 491–501.

Pearson (2001). *Manual for the Wechsler test of adult reading.* San Antonio, TX: Pearson Education.

Pearson (2009). *Test of premorbid functioning: Advanced clinical solutions for use with WAIS–IV and WMS–IV.* San Antonio: Pearson Education.

Reynolds, C. R. (1997). Postscripts on premorbid ability estimation: Conceptual addenda and a few words on alternative and conditional approaches. *Archives of Clinical Neuropsychology, 12*(8), 769–778.

Ryan, J. J., Paolo, A. M., & Brungardt, T. M. (1990). Standardization of the WAIS-R for persons 75 years and older. *Psychological Assessment, 2*(4), 404–411.

Salthouse, T. A. (2006). Mental exercise and mental aging: Evaluating the validity of the "use it or lose it" hypothesis. *Perspectives on Psychological Science, 1*(1), 68–87.

Salthouse, T. A., Nesselroade, J. R., & Berish, D. E. (2006). Short-term variability in cognitive performance and the calibration of longitudinal change. *Journal of Gerontology: Psychological Sciences, 61*(3), 144–151.

Schoenberg, M. R., Duff, K., Scott, J. G., & Adams, R. L. (2003). An evaluation of the clinical utility of the OPIE-3 as an estimate of premorbid WAIS-III FSIQ. *The Clinical Neuropsychologist, 17*(3), 308–321.

Schoenberg, M. R., Lange, R. T., Marsh, P., & Saklofske, D. H. (2010). Premorbid intelligence. In J. S. Kreutzer, J. DeLuca, & B. Caplan (Eds.), *Encyclopedia of clinical neuropsychology.* New York: Springer.

Schoenberg, M. R., Scott, J. G., Duff, K., & Adams, R. L. (2002). Estimation of WAIS–III intelligence from combined performance and demographic variables: Development of the OPIE-3. *The Clinical Neuropsychologist, 16*(4), 426–438.

Schretlen, D. J., Buffington, A. L., Meyer, S. M., & Pearlson, G. D. (2005). The use of word-reading to estimate "premorbid" ability in cognitive domains other than intelligence. *Journal of the International Neuropsychological Society, 11*(6), 784–787.

Schretlen, D. J., Winicki, J. M., Meyer, S. M., Testa, S. M., Pearlson, G. D., & Gordon, B. (2009). Development of psychometric properties, and validity of the Hopkins adult reading test (HART). *The Clinical Neuropsychologist, 23*(6), 926–943.

Scott, J. G., Krull, K. R., Iverson, G. L., Williamson, D. J. G., & Adams, R. L. (1997). Oklahoma premorbid intelligence estimation (OPIE): Validation on clinical samples. *The Clinical Neuropsychologist, 11*(2), 146–154.

Skeel, R. L., Sitzer, D., Fogal, T., Wells, J., & Johnstone, B. (2004). Comparison of predicted-difference, simple-difference, and premorbid-estimation methodologies for evaluating IQ and memory score discrepancies. *Archives of Clinical Neuropsychology, 19*(3), 363–374.

Solé-Padullés, C., Bartrés-Faz, D., Junqué, C., Vendrell, P., Rami, L., & Clemente, I. C., et al. (2009). Brain structure and function related to cognitive reserve variables in normal aging, mild cognitive impairment and Alzheimer's disease. *Neurobiology of Aging, 30*(7), 1114–1124.

Storandt, M., Stone, K., & LaBarge, E. (1995). Deficits in reading performance in very mild dementia of the Alzheimer type. *Neuropsychology, 9*(2), 174–176.

Wechsler, D. (1958). *The measurement and appraisal of adult intelligence* (4th ed.). Baltimore, MD: Williams & Wilkins.

Wechsler, D. (1997). *Wechsler adult intelligence scale–third edition (WAIS–III).* San Antonio, TX: Pearson.

Wechsler, D. (2008). *Wechsler adult intelligence scale–fourth edition (WAIS–IV)*. San Antonio, TX: Pearson.

Wechsler, D. (2009). *Wechsler abbreviated scale of intelligence–second edition (WAIS–III)*. San Antonio, TX: Pearson.

Williams, M. (1997). The prediction of premorbid memory ability. *Archives of Clinical Neuropsychology, 12*(8), 745–756.

Wilson, R., Rosenbaum, G., Brown, G., Rourke, D., & Whitman, D. (1978). An index of premorbid intelligence. *Journal of Consulting and Clinical Psychology, 46*(6), 1554–1555.

Yates, A. (1956). The use of vocabulary in the measurement of intelligence deterioration: A review. *Journal of Mental Science, 102*, 409–440.

Serial Assessment with WAIS–IV and WMS–IV

James A. Holdnack[*], *Lisa Whipple Drozdick*[*],
Grant L. Iverson[†] *and Gordon J. Chelune*[‡]

[*]Pearson Assessment, San Antonio, Texas, USA [†]Harvard Medical School,
Boston, Massachusetts, USA [‡]University of Utah, Salt Lake City,
Utah, USA

INTRODUCTION

Clinicians frequently re-evaluate patients in clinical and research contexts to identify changes in cognitive functioning. In most cases, the clinical question at re-evaluation involves determining if an individual's cognitive status has changed since the initial assessment. In other words, has there been a clinically significant decline or improvement in the person's cognitive functioning, or has it remained stable over the retest interval? In addition, in some legal contexts, multiple clinicians conduct assessments on the same individual within a short period of time using the same or related cognitive instruments. In this context, no significant change in cognitive performance would be expected between evaluations. However, to make this judgment, the clinician must evaluate and compare test scores within the context of multiple evaluations to ensure the accuracy of the results and subsequent interpretation (Heilbronner et al., 2010). Applying the same conceptual models for evaluating variability within an assessment (e.g., difference of ± 1 standard deviation), would result in an incorrect evaluation of a significant change in performance in Serial Assessments. Regardless of the context, statistical data are required to reject or support a hypothesis of either

 © 2013 Elsevier Inc. All rights reserved.

stable cognitive performance or significant change in cognitive performance.

Research hypotheses concerning test–retest change are most often bidirectional or two-tailed and take the form: *"Has the client's performance changed (for the better or for the worse)?"* In clinical settings, hypotheses are almost always directional or one-tailed, seeking to determine if the client has changed in a specific direction (Tulsky, Rolfhus, & Zhu, 2000). The clinical question of interest in a reassessment may involve a concern about decline in specific cognitive functions, such as: *"Is the patient's memory getting worse over time"*; *"Did the examinee experience a loss of visual-perceptual functions after surgical repair of a cerebral aneurysm"*; or *"Is the patient's medication impairing performance on processing speed measures?"* In other instances, the purpose of the re-evaluation is to identify general improvement in cognitive functioning or improvement in specific abilities; for example: *"To what extent has the person with a severe brain injury improved from three months to one year following injury"*; *"Does a new medication improve memory functioning in older adults"*; *"Does the patient have improved working memory skills following treatment with CogMed"* (Klingberg, et al., 2005); or *"Is cognitive rehabilitation improving the patient's language skills?"* To answer these questions, the clinician must know the degree of change expected on re-administration of cognitive tests in normally developing and aging individuals in whom no cognitive changes are expected, and the base rates of change for scores that deviate from those expected. As we will describe, changes in cognitive performance between test administrations are related to a number of statistical and test factors (e.g., susceptibility to practice effects, measurement error, test–retest interval between administrations, and regression to the mean). In addition, several client-specific factors can also influence scores across test sessions (e.g., initial level of performance, motivation, and effort). The degree to which all of these factors influence changes in test performance is not consistent across tests or across specific cognitive abilities. For example, memory tests may be more susceptible to practice effects than tests of verbal abilities, and motivation can change within or across test sessions. Interpreting clinically meaningful cognitive change requires the clinician to isolate changes in performance due to the variable of interest (e.g., disease process, treatment effect, or intervention) from those due to other sources. These factors are discussed in detail later in this chapter. As will be seen, there are relatively simple and useful statistical approaches for evaluating change in test performance that can aid the clinician in controlling for these extraneous sources of variance.

Interpretation of test–retest changes is further complicated when different editions or alternate forms of the same test are used; for example, Wechsler Adult Intelligence Scale–Third Edition (WAIS–III: Wechsler,

1997a) followed later by Wechsler Adult Intelligence Scale–Fourth Edition (WAIS–IV: Wechsler, 2008). Common factors that influence changes in test performance across editions of a test include the Flynn Effect (Flynn, 1984), changes in the composition of the normative sample, and changes to index and subtest content. Therefore, clinicians need to determine not only if an examinee's test score has significantly changed between evaluations, but whether the change is simply due to differences between the editions or forms of the tests used.

Interpretation of test results from serial assessments is complex, yet can provide critical information concerning a client's cognitive status, trajectory and prognosis. In this chapter, information is provided on using the Wechsler Adult Intelligence Scale–Fourth Edition (WAIS–IV: Wechsler, 2008) and Wechsler Memory Scale–Fourth Edition (WMS–IV: Wechsler, 2009) in serial assessments that will assist clinicians in identifying statistically significant and clinically meaningful change in cognition, both across time and across test editions.

FACTORS INFLUENCING CHANGE IN PERFORMANCE ACROSS EVALUATIONS

Historically, clinicians were faced with the need to interpret test performance in the absence of comprehensive statistical data. As noted in Chapters 2 and 3, the observance that a high degree of intra-individual variability in test scores, and frequent occurrence of low scores, are consistent with the performance of healthy controls, requires adequate statistical data to comprehend and apply in clinical practice. In cases where statistical data are absent, clinicians frequently develop heuristics based on clinical and psychometric reasoning to facilitate interpretation of complex data points. Where serial assessment is concerned, the clinician may use a rule of thumb that a change in performance of one standard deviation (e.g., consistent within an assessment score comparison model) between two administrations is clinically and statistically significant. In this case, both are likely to be true; however, this estimate is very conservative (e.g., $\frac{1}{2}$ standard deviation is statistically significant in some cases) in comparison to actual statistical and base rate data. This rule significantly reduces the sensitivity to identifying change in performance in serial assessments.

Using a specific value (e.g., one standard deviation or 15 points), does not account for the myriad of factors that influence how scores change from one assessment to another. In some cases, a reduction in performance of only 3–4 points may be statistically significant but an improvement of 7–8 points would be required to be significant.

For examinees with high ability, a very small drop in performance could be atypical, while larger differences may be required for low ability examinees. Other factors, such as the examinees age, sex, and education level influences the degree of change that is typical between test sessions. While applying a conservative rule of thumb in the absence of statistical data is clinically useful, it will result in inaccurate assessment of cognitive change over time. Multiple independent and inter-related factors can influence how scores change in serial assessments. Initial level of performance, reliability, measurement error, regression to the mean, and practice affects all impact test results on reassessments. Although these factors can be controlled statistically, their impact should still be considered when interpreting change in performance. In addition to statistical and test-related factors, client-specific attributes such as motivation and effort, education level, age, and sex, can differentially impact test–retest changes in performance. Finally, the use of alternate forms or different editions of a test between assessments introduces additional extraneous sources of variance between test–retest comparisons.

Regression to the Mean, Measurement Error, and Initial Level of Performance

Regression to the mean is a non-cognitive statistical phenomenon whereby scores at the end of a frequency distribution move toward the mean on retesting. For example, an examinee having a very superior scaled score on initial testing will likely obtain lower scaled score on retesting. This change has nothing to do with a loss in ability; rather, the second score is lower due to statistical probability. Similarly, a borderline initial score will likely be higher on retest. Score changes, particularly at the very extremes of the distribution, can appear to be substantial (e.g., a score of 19 dropping to 16 or a score of 1 rising to 5); however, such large changes often do not indicate real change in cognitive abilities. Although scores at the extremes of the distribution have a higher probability of regression to the mean and are associated with large changes in scores, above average or low average scores are also susceptible to regression to the mean effects. Regression to the mean occurs when two variables are not perfectly correlated and is considered a consequence of measurement error. However, even a test with perfect or near perfect internal consistency can show regression to the mean due to an imperfect correlation with other cognitive variables, or with itself over time. This is due to normal variability in cognitive functioning within (Binder, Iverson, & Brooks, 2009) and across test sessions (Salthouse, 2007).

Measurement error is all of the variance in test performance that is not directly attributable to the construct that a test purports to measure. Some sources of error variance are systematic and relate to how the test is constructed (although they have more or less impact, depending on examinee characteristics). For example, tests of processing speed often require intact fine-motor functioning. In the presence of fine-motor impairments, the test loses some specificity for measuring processing speed. Additional sources of error include poor motivation, disruptive non-compliant behavior during testing, or physical difficulties such as poor vision, hearing, or motor functions. These will likely have a negative impact on multiple measures throughout the assessment process reducing the degree to which the construct in question is accurately measured. A significant change in a non-construct source of variance can result in large changes in performance over time. The resolution of an orthopedic injury, correction of a visual/hearing issue, or improved behavior control related to changes in medication may result in better scores across domains initially affected by the sensory, motor, or behavioral issues.

Random sources of measurement error consist of *unpredictable* person and situational factors. Interruptions during the testing—ambient noise, lapses in attention, fatigue, poor comprehension or misinterpretation of instructions by the examinee, and acute onset of medical issues (e.g., headache, absence seizures)—during the assessment are all random sources of error. These types of factors cannot be controlled for statistically and are closely related to test reliability.

Reliability is associated with score consistency over time (i.e., test–retest stability) or the consistency with which the test items in a measure assess the same construct. According to classical test theory, reliability is the relation between "true" scores and obtained scores (Crocker & Algina, 1986). Obtained scores contain an error component, which influences both the consistency and stability of a particular score. Thus, reliability may be viewed as the strength of a test to measure an individual's ability taking into account random error. It is important to recognize, particularly when considering change in performance over time, that internal consistency measures are usually higher than test–retest coefficients. Moreover, test–retest reliability is affected by the internal consistency of the test, additional sources of error related to time and situational variables (Franzen, 1989, 2000), and normal variability in human cognition. Therefore, even in highly reliable tests, there is greater error in measuring change in the construct of interest over time than in measuring the construct at a specific point in time. A test with low test–retest reliability will have larger changes in scores between assessments than a test with high test–retest reliability.

In addition to variables related to test construction, the construct being assessed influences changes in test scores across assessments. Constructs with high variability (e.g., state anxiety) are expected to show greater variability over time, due to the nature of the construct being measured. In addition, some cognitive skills may be subject to more situational variability (e.g., attention) than other cognitive skills (e.g., language). Therefore, greater score discrepancies occur normally in some measures more than others. Applying a simple rule to assess change across all measures (e.g., interpreting any index change of 15 points as meaningful) could either overestimate or underestimate atypicality. Although non-construct related variability can be caused by systematic sources of error, most often variability is introduced by temporal, situational, or clinical factors. Consequently, stability estimates will be attenuated in measures of more variable constructs (e.g., attention, memory, processing speed).

One concept related to regression to the mean and measurement error is the effect of the examinee's *initial level of performance*. For example, on a test with a scaled score range of 1 to 19, an examinee with a scaled score of 15 on initial testing can show a decline of up to 14 scaled score points on reassessment, while an examinee with an initial scaled score of 5 can only show a decline of four scaled score points. Similarly, an improvement of only 4 points can be achieved when the initial value is 15; while up to 14 scaled score points of improvement can be observed for an initial score of 5. The initial level of performance sets finite limitations on the amount of improvement or decline that can be observed between test sessions. Initial levels of performance also affect change in scores due to test scaling issues. For some tests, a change in one raw score point at the upper end (younger age groups) or lower end of the distribution (older age groups) can yield a two-scaled score increase while in the middle of the distribution a one- or even two-point raw score improvement yields only one-scaled score improvement. Greater raw score improvement or decline is often required to change scores in the middle of the distribution compared to the extremes of the distribution. Depending on the nature of the distribution, these effects can be even more dramatic.

In cases where initial performance is extreme, it may appear to be futile—due to ceiling or floor effects—to attempt to determine if a specific change in performance has occurred. For example, if the assessment is conducted to determine if there is a decline from an initial performance of a scaled score of 1, then a lower score cannot be observed on retest and a decline cannot be detected, even if a raw score decline was observed. Similarly, improvement cannot be observed if the initial performance results in a scaled score of 19. When a simple difference model is used, this is the case. However, when regression-based methods are applied, it is possible to determine if scores on retest are unexpectedly low or high even at the extremes of the distribution. Initial performance levels are related to other factors that influence change in test performance (e.g., practice effects and regression to the mean) and to client-specific factors (e.g., education level, general ability level, and level of effort and motivation). For some measures, these client-specific factors can influence how much change is observed in test performance.

For example, baseline test scores that are very low are more susceptible to large changes due to greater change from combined practice effects and regression to the mean (a statistical occurrence whereby a score in one tail of a distribution is more likely to move toward the mean on retesting). Baseline test scores in the high average and superior classification ranges, in contrast, are susceptible to regression, and therefore somewhat less likely to show large practice effects. In part, this is because situational factors are more likely to artificially lower, rather than artificially inflate, a test score. Psychometric and situational factors alone predict that very low scores are more likely to improve on retesting than above average scores. In some clinical situations, combined psychometric and situational factors might lead the clinician to over-estimate the degree to which a person has improved or recovered following a neurological injury.

Initial level of performance, regression to the mean, and measurement error produce independent and inter-related effects on score change between test sessions. When initial performance is in the tails of the distribution and test internal consistency and temporal stability are low, regression to the mean effects are greater; however, for highly consistent measures the impact of these factors is less. For stable constructs, scores near the middle of the distribution tend to have less score-change over time, but for highly unstable constructs, changes can be quite large. In general, measurement error, regression to the mean, initial level of performance, and practice effects, singly or in combination, can influence change in test performance across test sessions. Therefore, it is not possible to accurately apply a rule of thumb, such as a one standard deviation change on retesting, as the criteria for interpreting change.

Practice Effects

When discussing the relationship between learning and memory, Squire (1987, p. 3) noted that *the experiences an animal has can modify its nervous system,* and because of this capacity *it will later behave differently as a result.* It is therefore not surprising that prior exposure to test materials can impact future performance on those test materials. In the absence of other discernible reasons, when test scores increase on re-administration of an instrument simply due to prior exposure or experi-ence with the measure, this is conceptualized as a *practice effect*. Practice effects are a systematic source of construct (e.g., people with better memory remember more on re-assessment) and non-construct related (e.g., familiarity with the test procedures improves performance) var-iances that affect retest performance and must be considered when eval-uating whether a client's retest performance is significantly changed from baseline (Lineweaver & Chelune, 2003; McCabe, Langer, Borod, & Bender, 2011). Tests vary considerably in their susceptibility to practice effects and these differences can be directly related to the construct being assessed (McCaffrey, Ortega, & Haase, 1993). Tests tapping highly crys-tallized intellectual functions such as Vocabulary on WAIS–IV tend to show very little change in performance across assessments. In contrast, measures of fluid reasoning and episodic memory, which rely on testing a person's response to novel tasks, are more susceptible to practice effects (i.e., prior exposure reduces the degree of novelty). Due to this variability in practice effects across tests, it is not possible to use a single rule-of-thumb (e.g., three scaled score points higher or lower) to interpret a change in performance as being indicative of significant loss or gain in functioning. Memory and processing speed tests show greater practice effects than simple auditory discrimination tasks (McCaffrey et al., 1993) and tests of verbal intelligence (Wechsler, 2008).

In the WAIS–IV and WMS–IV, the smallest practice effects, as indi-cated by the effect size of the mean differences between time one and time two evaluations, are observed on the Verbal Comprehension Index (VCI) ($d = 0.17$; Wechsler, 2008). The largest effects are observed on the WMS–IV Adult Battery Delayed Memory Index ($d = 0.95$; Wechlser, 2009). Typically, the largest practice effects are observed between the first and second assessments, with minimal to no additional increases in scores observed on subsequent administrations (Ivnik et al., 1999). Despite the plateauing of performance, practice effects can be observed as long as 7 years past the initial assessment (Salthouse, Schroeder, & Ferrer, 2004). Average practice effects for the WAIS–IV and WMS–IV Index scores are presented in Table 6.1.

Not only do constructs/tests vary in susceptibility to practice effects, there are also a number of specific client factors that can exacerbate or attenuate the degree to which practice effects occur (Lineweaver & Chelune, 2003). These personal factors can be identified and controlled for statistically. The demographic characteristics known to influence practice effects include age (Lineweaver & Chelune, 2003), education level and gender (Duff et al., 2005). Relative change in performance between test sessions has also been associated with initial level of

TABLE 6.1 Average practice effects on the WAIS–IV and the WMS–IV Index scores

WAIS–IV IQ & Indexes	Average Practice Effect	WAIS–IV IQ & Indexes	Average Practice Effect
Age: 16–29 years		Age: 55–69 years	
Full Scale IQ	4.4	Full Scale IQ	4.9
Verbal Comprehension Index	2.2	Verbal Comprehension Index	3.3
Perceptual Reasoning Index	4.6	Perceptual Reasoning Index	3.6
Working Memory Index	2.7	Working Memory Index	4.3
Processing Speed Index	4.8	Processing Speed Index	5.0
Age: 30–54 years		Age: 70–90 years	
Full Scale IQ	4.4	Full Scale IQ	3.5
Verbal Comprehension Index	2.7	Verbal Comprehension Index	2.1
Perceptual Reasoning Index	4.5	Perceptual Reasoning Index	3.2
Working Memory Index	1.9	Working Memory Index	3.2
Processing Speed Index	5.3	Processing Speed Index	2.7
WMS–IV Indexes			
Age: 16–69 years (Adult Battery)		Age: 65–90 years (Older Adult Battery)	
Auditory Memory Index	11.5	Auditory Memory Index	10.6
Visual Memory Index	12.1	Visual Memory Index	11.0
Visual Working Memory Index	4.3	Immediate Memory Index	12.4
Immediate Memory Index	12.4	Delayed Memory Index	11.0
Delayed Memory Index	13.7		

Notes: WAIS–IV: $n = 228$, Mean test interval was 22 days (range = 8–82 days). WMS–IV: Adult battery, $N = 144–173$; Older adult battery, $n = 69–71$. Average practice effects are calculated by subtracting the age-adjusted mean score at time two − mean score at time one.
Copyright © 2009 NCS Pearson, Inc. All rights reserved.

functioning (Ferrer et al., 2005); the interval between test sessions (Duff et al., 2005); and intellectual ability at first assessment (Lineweaver & Chelune, 2003). However, other research has not found interval effects for memory or intellectual functioning measures (Basso, Carona, Lowery & Axelrod, 2002), and some cognitive skills may not show differential practice effects as a function of intellectual ability (Basso, Bornstein, & Lang, 1999). Because cognitive skills vary in the degree to which practice effects are observed, each test may have a different set of factors that impact practice effects. These factors need to be identified for each test and uniquely applied to tests when indicated.

Practice effects also interact with the initial level of performance and a test's susceptibility to regression to the mean: that is, the impact of practice effects is greater or lesser depending on initial level of performance and subsequent regression to the mean. Superior scores on baseline testing cannot show large practice effects because of the limits imposed by ceiling effects described earlier. However, examinees with high initial ability on a construct may learn more from experience/exposure to the test and experience practice effects that are less apparent. At the upper end of the distribution, practice effects may not yield substantially higher post-test scores but might attenuate the influence of regression to the mean. Thus, small improvements at the upper end of the distribution may be as meaningful as larger ones in the middle of the distribution. Conversely, low initial scores can theoretically show exaggerated improvements on retest due to the combination of potential practice effects and regression to the mean. However, in reality, low ability on the construct may inhibit learning effects due to test exposure/experience and attenuate regression to the mean effects. Thus, the interaction between initial level of performance, regression to the mean, and practice effects can be difficult to understand for individual cases without the appropriate statistical tools to account for the complexities of this interaction.

The fidelity of the relationship among ability level, regression to the mean, and practice effects cannot be perfect, because situational factors introduce additional sources of variance. For example, a patient may obtain an unusually low score at time one on Symbol Search due to a lapse of attention, other distractions, or variable effort. On retesting, the patient may have a substantially higher score, not due to improvement in processing speed but due to better attention and effort. Although it is virtually impossible for a clinician to determine precisely the impact that such factors may have on a specific comparison, these factors nonetheless have obvious relevance for interpreting results obtained in serial testing.

It should be obvious to the reader that relying solely on the examination of the simple difference in a person's performance from time 1 to time 2 can lead to erroneous clinical decisions as to whether the person has actually shown a meaningful change from baseline. Without appropriate statistical controls that account for the differential effects of practice, measurement error, regression to the mean, and other sources of systematic variance on a specific test measure, a clinician might easily over-interpret a large test–retest difference as meaningful when they are common, or conversely dismiss small changes when they are quite rare and clinically important. When evaluating change in performance, the test–retest coefficient and internal consistency coefficient are insufficient for interpreting change in individual cases. The test–retest coefficient provides information regarding the stability of score distributions, but it does not describe dispersion, regression, or practice effects. Additional information, such as change in mean scores and the standard deviation of the difference scores, provides the clinician useful information, but is still inadequate for determining if a particular change in performance is significant and atypical. Our interpretation of change scores from serial assessments must be done within the context of appropriate psychometric information. In subsequent sections of this chapter we will discuss the application of regression-based methods for interpreting change that attempts to control for the differential effects of practice, measurement error, regression to the mean, and other sources of systematic influence on test change.

Motivational Factors

All tests are influenced by motivational factors and level of effort. Just as these factors need to be considered when interpreting results obtained within a test session, level of motivation needs to be considered when interpreting results obtained across test sessions. Suboptimal effort can have a significant impact on performance within one or both test sessions, and have a marked impact on change scores between sessions. Chapter 7 discusses, in detail, the use of the Advanced Clinical Solutions for WAIS–IV and WMS–IV (ACS: Pearson, 2009) for assessing suboptimal effort. The accuracy of neuropsychological test results is largely dependent upon an appropriate amount of effort on the part of the examinee. It is important to note that effort is a state, not a trait. Although certain personality factors, such as achievement orientation and conscientiousness, can influence the likelihood that adequate or inadequate effort occurs, even among highly motivated examinees, effort can be variable, not constant. Moreover, effort can be variable within an evaluation and can be the cause of significant discrepancies between scores or of isolated low test scores within and between assessments. Other than applying specific tools designed to identify suboptimal effort, there is no particular methodology related to serial assessment that can specifically identify effort as the cause of unexpected changes in performance over time. The possibility of variable effort should be considered, particularly when there are external incentives associated with having cognitive impairments.

Use of Revised Test Editions in Serial Assessment

In some clinical cases, a patient that presents for re-evaluation was administered a different version or edition of the specified test. This occurs most frequently when a new edition is published (e.g., WAIS–III versus WAIS–IV) or when the examinee has transitioned from the child edition to the adult edition of a test (e.g., WISC–IV to WAIS–IV). The need to compare performance across editions poses a unique challenge. The clinical questions and hypotheses associated with the assessment of cognitive change are essentially the same, but the factors affecting change scores are somewhat different. In these circumstances, statistical models developed for within-edition comparisons do not apply. Even if the test structure and subtest configuration are similar, the differences between the normative samples and test content can impact the level of practice effects. Therefore, the expected change in performance will be different than within-version comparisons. Even subtests designed to measure the same construct will have fewer or perhaps no overlapping items (e.g., Vocabulary in WAIS–III versus WAIS–IV has some but not all identical items). Modifications to subtest items, subtest configurations for index scores, and other content changes all impact the interpretation of changes in performance. The degree of similarity between editions impacts the correlation between the tests. Additionally, normative data collected at different times yields lower scores on a new edition compared to a previous edition of the test, a phenomenon known as the Flynn effect. These cross-instrument factors need to be considered and controlled for by creating specific equations that compare re-testing using the different editions.

Reliable Change Methods

A wide variety of methods for evaluating reliable change have been developed and applied in neuropsychological research (Hinton-Bayre, 2010). Each method has specific strengths and weaknesses affecting the obtained results. Although these procedures differ widely in terms of how they deal with practice effects, measurement error, regression to the mean, and other sources of variance, when simplified, they all are based on a ratio of a measure of difference between two scores divided by a measure of the dispersion of the difference scores (Chelune & Duff, 2013). In the simplest form, the simple difference between Time 1 and Time 2 is divided by the observed standard deviation of the difference scores [(T2 − T1)/SD]. Because researchers often did not have direct access to the SD of the difference scores, Jacobson and Truax (1991) developed a procedure for estimating the standard error of the differences based on the standard error of the measurement of a scale and its test–retest reliability, coining the method the *Reliable Change Index*. Chelune, Naugle, Lüders, Sedlak, & Awad (1993) introduced a modification of this approach that attempted to account for expected practice effects, and others have made additional refinements (e.g., Iverson, 2001). The ratio of the simple difference between scores divided by these observed or estimated measures of dispersion of score results in a z-score that can be directly linked to the area under the normal curve. A z-score of ±1.04 identifies an area under the curve where the base rate of difference scores would be 70%, with the base rate of those showing larger or smaller differences would be 15% (assuming normally distributed difference scores). A 90% Reliable Change Index (z-scores ± 1.64) identifies a base rate of difference scores where only 5% of cases would be above or below the mean of the differences. The *base rate* of a specific change in scores from Time 1 to Time 2 in non-clinical populations provides information about the relative atypicality of the difference. When the frequency of a change score that is relatively rare in a non-clinical population is found to be much more common in a clinical population, then the clinician can assert that such difference scores are clinically meaningful (Lineweaver & Chelune, 2003). A lookup table for reliable change differences scores for the WAIS–IV and WMS–IV has been published (Brooks, Strauss, Sherman, Iverson, & Slick, 2009).

The standard application of the simple difference method for calculating reliable change scores (Jacobson & Truax, 1991) control for the effects of measurement error; however, it did not control for practice effects or regression to the mean (Lineweaver & Chelune, 2003). Although researchers have modified this approach to account for practice effects (Chelune et al., 1993; Iverson, 2001), it only controls for practice effects treated as a constant (Lineweaver & Chelune, 2003). A more sophisticated reliable change method is based on the predicted difference model in which linear regression is used to develop an equation to predict Time 2 scores from Time 1 scores (McSweeny, Naugle, Chelune, & Luders, 1993). The difference between the *observed* Time 2 score and the *predicted* Time 2 score is the measure of change, and the measure of dispersion is the Standard Error of the Estimate (SEE) of the regression equation. In its simplest form, the predicted difference model based on the standard regression approach takes the observed Time 2 score minus the predicted Time 2 score and divides this difference by the SEE [(Observed T2 − Predicted T2)/SEE] to obtain a z-score. These z-scores can then be related to the normal curve to determine the base rates associated with them. The predicted difference method based on the standard regression approach provides statistical controls for both measurement error and regression to the mean, while modeling practice as a function of baseline performance. When expanded to a multivariate model, the standard regression based approach can also consider other factors that influence practice effects, such as ability level, demographic variables (e.g., education level), and retest interval (Lineweaver & Chelune, 2003).

Levine et al. (2007) applied both a standard regression based model and a simple difference model of reliable change with a correction for practice effects in multiple samples of patients with HIV + / AIDS. The standard regression based model was more sensitive to cognitive decline but less sensitive to cognitive improvement than the reliable change method (Levine et al., 2007). Heaton et al. (2001) used reliable change scores to identify improved cognitive functioning in patients recovering from brain injury and to identify declines in cognitive performance in patients who suffered additional brain injury. Complex and simple regression models yielded similar results in identifying cognitive change, and both models were sensitive to identifying improvement and decline in cognitive functioning (Heaton et al., 2001). The best model, from a statistical standpoint, is the standard regression-based change model to produce predicted difference scores. Research suggests both simple and complex models are able to identify changes in cognitive functioning. In the ACS: Serial Assessment, the standard regression-based change score model was used to derive prediction equations for evaluating the differences between observed and predicted Time 2 scores.

WAIS–IV SERIAL ASSESSMENT

ACS: Serial Assessment for WAIS–IV Indexes and Subtests

Multiple hierarchical regression was used with data from the WAIS–IV test–retest sample to derive prediction equations for all WAIS–IV indexes and subtests. For each prediction equation, cut-off scores were computed to identify statistically significant differences between predicted and actual Time 2 WAIS–IV scores. Base rates of the difference scores were also derived. The retest sample included 298 healthy controls aged 16–90, who completed the WAIS–IV on two separate test sessions, with a mean interval of 22 days, ranging from 8 to 82 days. The sample was 44.6% male and 55.4% female; 72.2% White, 12.1% Hispanic, 10.7% African-American, 3.0% Asian, and 2.0% Other; and 9.1% completed 8 years of education or fewer, 12.7% completed between 9 and 11 years of education, 31.5% completed 12 years of education, 23.5% completed 13–15 years of education, and 23.2% completed 16 years of education or more. The sample demographic characteristics roughly reflect the demographics of the general population.

Hierarchical regression equations were derived in the following steps. In each equation, the dependent variable was the Time 2 WAIS–IV Index or subtest score. The independent variables were entered hierarchically into the equations. In the first step, the Time 1 index or subtest score was entered into the equation. In the second step, a Time 1 measure of intellectual ability was entered, controlling for ability on practice effects. In most cases, the ability measure was GAI; however, for VCI and PRI predictions, GAI was not used to avoid part-whole correlation effects. For VCI, PRI was entered into the equation; for PRI, VCI was entered into the equation. In the third step, length of retest interval was entered. In the fourth step, demographic variables including age, education level, and sex were entered. All non-significant predictors (e.g., $p > 0.05$) were dropped from the equation. In some instances, the only significant predictor was the Time 1 score of interest, while for other scores multiple predictors were significant.

The simple or multiple regression equations used to predict WAIS–IV reliable change are part of the ACS software. The ACS software applies the prediction rules from the derived equations and compares the examinee's actual Time 2 scores to his or her predicted Time 2 scores. The level of statistical significance of the difference (e.g., $p < 0.05$) and the base rate of the discrepancy in the test–retest sample are provided in the ACS clinical reports. Interval data are applied only for retest intervals of eight to 82 days, the interval collected in the test–retest sample on which the equations were based; information about longer or shorter intervals was not available. *If the test interval is outside this range, the equation applies a minimum value of eight for intervals less than eight days and a maximum value of 82 for intervals greater than 82 days.* Table 6.2 summarizes the significant predictors for the WAIS–IV composites and subtests.

WAIS–IV index R^2 values range from 0.74 (PSI) to 0.91 (FSIQ), showing a high degree of association between the predictor(s) and dependent variables and accuracy of the predicted value. The accuracy of the prediction is evident in the size of the Standard Error of the Estimate (SEE); the smaller the value of the standard error of the estimate, the more accurate the predicted values. Longer intervals produced smaller practice effects on the Working Memory Index (WMI). Demographic predictors of PSI indicate older examinees and men did not demonstrate as large a practice effect as did younger examinees and women.

WAIS–IV subtest R^2 values range from 0.53 (VP) to 0.85 (IN). The subtest correlations are generally lower than those observed in the index equations, except for verbal subtests. Therefore, subtest predictions are generally less accurate than index predictions. Smaller practice effects occur for longer retest intervals on Digit Span, older examinees show smaller practice effects on Block Design and Symbol Search, and women have greater practice effects on Coding and Symbol Search than do men.

TABLE 6.2   ACS WAIS–IV Index and Subtest Prediction Equations

			Independent Variables			
Dependent Variable	R^2	SEE	Time 1 Measure	Ability Measure	Test Interval	Demographics
Full Scale IQ (FSIQ)	0.91	4.58	FSIQ	–	–	–
Verbal Comprehension Index (VCI)	0.90	4.82	VCI	–	–	–
Perceptual Reasoning Index (PRI)	0.75	7.17	PRI	VCI	–	–
Working Memory Index (WMI)	0.77	7.11	WMI	GAI	Interval in days	–
Processing Speed Index (PSI)	0.74	7.68	PSI	GAI	–	Age, Sex
Vocabulary (VC)	0.83	1.24	VC	GAI	–	–
Similarities (SI)	0.72	1.53	SI	GAI	–	–
Information (IN)	0.85	1.23	IN	GAI	–	–
Block Design (BD)	0.66	1.66	BD	GAI	–	Age
Matrix Reasoning (MR)	0.61	1.95	MR	GAI	–	–
Visual Puzzles (VP)	0.53	2.06	VP	GAI	–	–
Digit Span (DS)	0.69	1.66	DS	GAI	Interval in days	–
Arithmetic (AR)	0.70	1.58	AR	GAI	–	–
Coding (CD)	0.72	1.52	CD	GAI	–	Sex
Symbol Search (SS)	0.68	1.82	SS	GAI	–	Age, Sex

Note: Significant predictors, such as the Time 1 score, ability level, time interval, age, and sex, are presented.
Copyright © 2009 NCS Pearson, Inc. All rights reserved.

Additional Serial Assessment Equations for WAIS–IV Indexes and Subtests

Many of the standard ACS prediction equations require complete ability measures to compute the equation (e.g., GAI, VCI, or PRI); however, in certain clinical situations, a full battery cannot be completed. In these situations, the ACS software will not calculate serial assessment scores. Additional equations are provided in this chapter to enable clinicians to identify significant change in performance in the absence of comprehensive ability measures. Education level replaces GAI, VCI, or

PRI, in these equations. When interpreting these equations, the clinician must keep in mind that the equations used within the ACS software reflect the examinees actual intellectual functioning, thus better representing his or her ability to profit from practice. Education level (used in the equations below) estimates pre-morbid ability, which can overestimate the examinee's ability to profit from past exposure to the test, particularly when there is a rather significant impairment in intellectual functioning related to the patient's condition. However, education has a relatively small contribution to the overall equation so any overestimation of practice effects would be small. The use of education level improves the predictive power of the equation and reduces prediction errors for most subjects. Table 6.3 provides regression data and beta weights for all WAIS–IV indexes and subtests using education instead of ability level in the prediction equations. FSIQ and VCI are not included because neither education nor ability were included in their prediction equations.

WAIS–IV index R^2 values range from 0.71 (PSI) to 0.74 (PRI, WMI) indicating a high degree of correlation between the predictor(s) and dependent variables. WAIS–IV subtest correlations range from 0.49 (VP) to 0.84 (IN). These WAIS–IV retest equations based on education instead of ability are consistently lower than those reported in the ACS indicating less predictive accuracy. It is recommended that clinicians use the equations from the ACS when possible. However, in circumstances where a full battery cannot be administered, these equations provide an adequate estimate of significant change in WAIS–IV performance over time. For all equations where education is a significant predictor, higher levels of education are associated with greater practice effects. Age is negatively associated with practice effects on Symbol Search and women gain more on retest on PSI, Coding, and Symbol Search. In order to calculate the predicted Time 2 score, the examiner must calculate the predicted score from the equation values provided in the table. For example, a woman examinee (code = 2), with 15 years of education (code = 4), and a Time 1 PSI index score of 85 would have the prediction equation below for her Time 2 PSI score.

Step 1: Time 2 PSI = 9.091 + (0.887 × Time 1 PSI) + (0.873 × education level) + (2.305 × sex)
Step 2: Time 2 PSI = 9.091 + (0.887 × 85) + (0.873 × 4) + (2.305 × 2)
Step 3: Time 2 PSI = 9.091 + (74.545) + (3.492) + (4.61)
Result: Time 2 PSI = 91.737 or 92

At the subtest level, if the same examinee is 75 years old and has a Symbol Search subtest score of eight at Time 1, the equation below provides the expected Time 2 Symbol Search score.

TABLE 6.3   WAIS–IV Index and Subtest Scores Alternate Retest Prediction Equations

WAIS–IV Index/Subtest Time 2	R^2	SEE	Constant	WAIS–IV Index/Subtest Time 1	Education Level	Age	Sex
PRI	0.74	7.34	15.838	0.826	1.625	–	–
WMI	0.74	7.44	12.546	0.870	1.003	–	–
PSI	0.71	8.01	9.091	0.887	0.873	–	2.305
Vocabulary	0.82	1.28	0.719	0.848	0.271	–	–
Similarities	0.69	1.58	1.940	0.858	–	–	–
Information	0.84	1.27	0.833	0.873	0.332	–	–
Block Design	0.64	1.72	2.480	0.739	0.290	–	–
Matrix Reasoning	0.58	2.03	2.061	0.710	0.368	–	–
Visual Puzzles	0.49	2.15	2.636	0.685	0.413	–	–
Digit Span	0.67	1.72	1.733	0.814	0.218	–	–
Arithmetic	0.64	1.73	1.733	0.787	0.259	–	–
Coding	0.70	1.55	1.145	0.824	0.162	–	0.449
Symbol Search	0.66	1.92	2.119	0.868	–	– 0.015	0.568

Note: WAIS–IV Time 1 Index/Subtest is the same as the WAIS–IV Time 2 Index/Subtest (e.g., PRI Time 1 predicts PRI Time 2). Education Level Coded: 1 = 8 or less years, 2 = 9–11 years, 3 = 12 years, 4 = 13–15 years, and 5 = 16 or more years. Age = age in years. Sex Coded: male = 1, female = 2. All index equations use age adjusted standard scores for Time 1 and Time 2. All WAIS–IV subtest scores are age-adjusted scaled scores.

Copyright 2008 by Pearson, Inc. Reproduced with permission. All rights reserved.

Step 1: Time 2 SS = 2.119 + (0.868 × Time 1 SS) + (− 0.015 × age) + (0.568 × sex)
Step 2: Time 2 SS = 2.119 + (0.868 × 8) + (− 0.015 × 75) + (0.568 × 2)
Step 3: Time 2 SS = 2.119 + (6.944) − (1.125) + (1.136)
Result: Time 2 SS = 9.074 or 9

The difference between the actual Time 2 score and the predicted Time 2 score is used to determine if a decline or improvement in cognitive functioning has occurred. Tables A6.1 and A6.2 in the Appendix (available at: http://booksite.elsevier.com/9780123869340), provide cut-off scores to identify whether a difference between actual and predicted Time 2 WAIS–IV scores is statistically significant. In this example, the actual PSI is 78 and the difference (e.g., actual − predicted) equals −13.26. According to Table A6.1, a cut-off score of 11.86 or greater is significant at the $p < 0.05$ level; therefore, the difference is significant at the $p < 0.05$ level. If the Symbol Search actual Time 2 score is 6, then the subtest difference is -3.07. The cut-off score in Table A6.2 for Symbol Search is 3.22; therefore, the difference in Symbol Search scores is not statistically different. Tables A6.3 and A6.4 provide base rate data for WAIS–IV index and subtest retest discrepancies. Base rate data informs the clinician if the difference is atypical or potentially clinically meaningful in the retest sample. A difference of 13 points where actual PSI is less than predicted PSI occurs in only 4.73% of the sample. The Symbol Search difference of three points occurs in only 7.53% of the sample. The PSI index score is both statistically different and unusual; however, the Symbol Search difference is not statistically significant even though the degree of difference is unusual in the retest sample.

WAIS–IV Index and Subtest Serial Assessment Interpretation

As discussed previously, the ACS uses regression methodology to identify significant change in performance over time. When the predicted difference regression method is used, the actual Time 1 and Time 2 scores are never directly compared. Rather, the Time 1 values are used to predict Time 2 values. Subsequently, the predicted score can be lower or higher than the actual Time 1 scores. This occurs because the equation accounts for regression to the mean effects and the impact of practice effects. Subsequently, the clinician may observe that the actual difference between the Time 1 and Time 2 scores is much smaller than the predicted versus actual Time 2 score.

The regression equations occasionally yield counter-intuitive results. A very small change between Time 1 and Time 2 scores will sometimes be interpreted as a significant decline in performance because the predicted Time 2 score was influenced by anticipated regression to the mean and practice effects. Thus, the absence of improvement or even a slight improvement might actually represent a "decline" in certain cases. This effect only occurs when initial performance is very low.

The clinician evaluates whether or not a difference is statistically reliable and atypical. Results may be statistically significant yet still occur at a relatively high rate in the retest sample. There is no specific cut-off for identifying an uncommon or rare base rate; however, the base rate serves as an indicator of the false positive rate of stating that a difference is clinically significant when in actuality it is observed in a healthy sample. Using a 10% base rate indicates that a conclusion that the difference is indicative of a clinically significant cognitive decline or improvement would be inaccurate only 10% of the time (relative to the healthy test–retest sample). This is the false positive rate for misidentifying a normally occurring change in performance as atypical. Therefore, using a higher base rate (e.g., 25%) will result in identifying more cases of atypical cognitive change (that is, it will increase sensitivity to real change in performance); however, it also increases the false positive rate.

The primary level of analysis for evaluating differences is the index level because these scores are more stable and reliable. Subtest level analysis can be used when a whole battery has not been administered or to identify specific cognitive changes. It is recommended that the clinician uses the ACS software to evaluate cognitive change with ability measures to estimate practice effects due to the greater accuracy of the equations. When a whole battery has not been used, the equations provided in this chapter may be helpful.

An effective strategy for evaluating cognitive change is to start with the primary WAIS–IV index scores. If the predicted Perceptual Reasoning is both significantly lower and occurs at a low base rate, the results can be interpreted as *"Ms. X shows a decline in her perceptual reasoning abilities on re-evaluation, as demonstrated by her significantly lower obtained PRI in comparison to her predicted PRI (p <0.05, BR = 4.5%)."* Evaluation of the Perceptual Reasoning subtests will inform the clinician if the decline in functioning is general, or if the change in the PRI is due to a change on a specific subtest. For example, if there is very little difference between two of the Perceptual Reasoning subtests (e.g., Visual Puzzles, Matrix Reasoning) from Time 1 to Time 2, but a very large difference in one of the subtest (e.g., Block Design), then that particular subtest is producing the change in the PRI score. In this scenario, the clinician will want to modify the general statement about decline in perceptual reasoning abilities to state a specific decline on the Block Design subtest. The clinician will need to evaluate the examinee's performance to understand why such a change has occurred. Also, consider whether the change is indicative of a real change in ability, or due to fluctuations in effort, situational factors, or other transient difficulties in performing that task. A similar approach can be employed when evaluating significant gains in a cognitive domain.

It is important to appreciate that test–retest changes can reflect real change in a person's cognitive functioning, due to injury, illness, or disease, or these changes can be due to situational or motivational factors. Real change and situational change can both be present during the same evaluation too. It is also important to note that when a battery of tests is re-administered, it is common to have at least one large change in performance. We do not know, however, how often this occurs. Furthermore, changes in index scores can occur due to a large change in a single subtest. In such cases, the clinician needs to consider if the change is due to a real specific loss in ability or if some other factors influenced performance on the specific subtest.

WAIS–IV Serial Assessment Using Revised Editions

In some cases, examinees present for re-evaluation having completed an edition of a test that is different from the one that the examiner currently uses. This occurs when a new edition has been published between evaluations (e.g., WAIS–III to WAIS–IV) or when a patient was initially tested with a children's edition (for example, Wechsler, 2003) and then outgrown that edition (e.g., WISC–IV to WAIS–IV). Determining if there has been a significant change in performance across test editions adds another level of complexity given that the editions are typically not strictly parallel. Fortunately, the Wechsler family of tests has similar structure across age editions and revisions. There are usually small differences in the number of tests contributing to an index, or the specific tests contributing to an index—but the overall structure is nearly identical, making the batteries comparable. While differences in test content provide an alternative hypothesis for change in performance, the content between editions is frequently similar enough for this to be a minor issue.

Comparing tests normed on different populations at different times affects the obtained results. Due to Flynn effects, a recently revised and re-normed test will yield lower scores than the predecessor edition. This has an impact on observed practice effects depending on the order of administration. If the newer version was administered second, then practice effects can be masked by the lowering of scores on the new version. In the more unusual case where the older version is administered after the new version, the practice effects will be magnified. Therefore, test order has a significant impact on the observed differences between the tests. Equations for statistically comparing change in performance between different test editions are provided below.

WAIS–III versus WAIS–IV

Multiple regression was used to derive predicted WAIS–IV index and subtest scores from WAIS–III index and subtest scores. Statistical cut-offs and base-rates were computed for each equation. The WAIS–III/WAIS–IV validity sample from the WAIS–IV standardization was used to create the equations. A sample of 240 healthy controls (62.1% female, 37.9% male), ages 16–88, completed the WAIS–IV and WAIS–III on two separate test sessions, using a counter-balanced design. The interval between test sessions ranged from six to 163 days, with an average of 36 days. The racial/ethnic distribution was 66.6% White, 8.8% Hispanic, 17.9% African American, 3.8% Asian and 2.9% Other. The sample education level distribution was 5.8% completed eight years of education or fewer, 9.6% completed between nine and 11 years of education, 32.1% completed 12 years of education, 27.9% completed 13–15 years of education, and 24.6% completed 16 years of education or more.

Hierarchical regression equations were computed in several steps. In each equation, the dependent variable was the WAIS–IV index or subtest, regardless of administration order. Subtests not included in both WAIS–IV and WAIS–III (e.g., Visual Puzzles) are not included. The independent variables were entered into the equations in steps. In the first step, the WAIS–III index or subtest score was entered into the equation. In the second step, test order (e.g., WAIS–IV or WAIS–III administered first) was entered. In the third step, education level (parent education level was used for ages 16–19) was entered. In the fourth step, demographic variables, including age at Time 1 and sex, were entered. All non-significant predictor variables (e.g., $p > 0.05$) were dropped from the equation.

Table 6.4 contains the R^2, SEE, and beta weights for the WAIS–III/ WAIS–IV index and subtest prediction equations. In the Appendix, Tables A6.1, A6.2, A6.5, and A6.6 provide cut-offs for statistical significance and frequencies of specific differences between actual and predicted WAIS–IV scores in the normal control sample.

WAIS–III predicted WAIS–IV index R^2 values range from 0.65 (PRI) to 0.84 (FSIQ) which are lower than WAIS–IV retest equations but still show a moderate to high degree of predictive accuracy. WAIS–III predicted WAIS–IV subtest R^2 values range from 0.44 (SS) to 0.78 (IN). The subtest equations are generally in the moderate range with the exception of the Vocabulary and Information subtests, which show a high degree of association between editions.

Test order is a significant predictor for most equations. The positive predictor value indicates that WAIS–IV predicted scores are much higher when WAIS–III was administered first, rather than when WAIS–IV was administered first. This is consistent with expected lower scores on the WAIS–IV due to Flynn effects and confirms that WAIS–III content and format overlap still produces practice effects. Higher levels of education are associated with greater practice effects. Age has mixed effects when comparing performance across tests. Age is negatively associated with Information across editions and positively associated with changes in PRI and Block Design. When using these equations, the WAIS–IV score is always the dependent variable even when it has been administered first. In most clinical settings, the new edition will be administered in the second test session; however, there

TABLE 6.4 WAIS–III Prediction Equations for WAIS–IV Index and Subtest Scores

WAIS–IV Index/Subtest	R^2	SEE	Constant	WAIS–III Index/ Subtest	Test Order	Education Level	Time 1 Age
FSIQ	0.84	5.96	0.667	0.854	5.057	0.747	–
VCI	0.82	6.24	7.427	0.786	2.725	1.599	–
PRI	0.65	8.93	9.316	0.718	5.438	1.182	0.048
WMI	0.72	7.33	16.01	0.749	2.554	1.133	–
PSI	0.69	8.20	22.197	0.715	3.914	–	–
Vocabulary	0.75	1.46	0.362	0.737	0.371	0.264	–
Similarities	0.55	2.01	1.503	0.598	–	0.558	–
Information	0.78	1.38	– 0.453	0.85	0.726	0.24	– 0.011
Block Design	0.65	1.93	– 1.121	0.833	0.882	–	0.02
Matrix Reasoning	0.51	2.15	1.315	0.639	–	0.513	–
Digit Span	0.60	1.78	0.65	0.698	0.761	0.296	–
Arithmetic	0.59	1.78	1.95	0.685	–	0.285	–
Coding	0.70	1.58	2.614	0.724	–	–	–
Symbol Search	0.44	2.33	3.967	0.604	–	–	–

Note: WAIS–III Index/Subtest is the same as the WAIS–IV (e.g., FSIQ WAIS–III predicts FSIQ WAIS–IV).
Test Order coded: 1 = WAIS–IV administered first, 2 = WAIS–III administered first.
Education Level Coded: 1 = 8 or less years, 2 = 9–11 years, 3 = 12 years, 4 = 13–15 years, and 5 = 16 or more years.
Age = age in years.
All index equations use age adjusted standard scores for both WAIS–IV and WAIS–III. All WAIS–IV and WAIS–III subtest scores are age-adjusted scaled scores.
Copyright 1997, 2008 by Pearson, Inc. Reproduced with permission. All rights reserved.

are instances when an examiner will use an older edition to avoid using the same edition on retest.

In this example of applying the regression equations, a 70-year-old-man with 16 years of education (code = 5) was administered the WAIS–III as part of a dementia evaluation. Six months later he was administered the WAIS–IV (order code = 2) as part of a follow-up evaluation to assess for cognitive decline because his family noticed a pronounced change in his functioning. On the first assessment, he obtained a WAIS–III WMI score of 90, and on reassessment his WAIS–IV WMI was 74. Using the equations in Table 6.4, the following predicted versus actual scores are obtained:

> Step 1: WAIS–IV WMI = 16.01 + (0.749 × WAIS–III WMI) + (2.554 × test order) + (1.133 × Education Level)
> Step 2: WAIS–IV WMI = 16.01 + (0.749 × 90) + (2.554 × 2) + (1.133 × 5)
> Step 3: WAIS–IV WMI = 16.01 + (67.41) + (5.108) + (5.665)
> Result: WAIS–IV WMI = 94.19 or 94

The difference between the actual and predicted WAIS–IV scores is −20.19 (e.g., 74 − 94.19). This difference is statistically significant at the p <0.01 and has a base rate <2% (see Table A6.5 in the chapter Appendix). These results indicate a significant decline in WMI scores. If the same parameters are used, but the WAIS–IV administered first and the WAIS–III second, the results would be as follows:

> Step 1: WAIS–IV WMI = 16.01 + (0.749 × WAIS–III WMI) + (2.554 × test order) + (1.133 × Education Level)
> Step 2: WAIS–IV WMI = 16.01 + (0.749 × 90) + (2.554 × 1) + (1.133 × 5)
> Step 3: WAIS–IV WMI = 16.01 + (67.41) + (2.554) + (5.665)
> Result: WAIS–IV WMI = 91.639 or 92

The difference between the actual and predicted WAIS–IV scores is −17.64 (e.g., 74 − 91.64). This difference is statistically significant at the p <0.01 and occurs at a base rate <3% (see Table A6.5). These results also indicate a significant decline in working memory ability. Because the WAIS–IV score is the dependent variable, the interpretation is different from when the WAIS–IV is given first; the Time 1 WAIS–IV scores are compared to the Time 2 WAIS–IV predicted scores. The WAIS–III scores are considered to be much lower than expected because the predicted WAIS–IV scores were much lower than the actual WAIS–IV scores. These results indicate a significant decline in WMI from Time 1 to Time 2. The same concepts apply to the WAIS–III/WAIS–IV subtest prediction equations.

WAIS–IV versus WISC–IV

Another clinical scenario involving a comparison between test editions occurs when an adolescent is administered a children's edition of a test and subsequently re-evaluated using the adult edition. In a more unusual scenario, a 16-year-old examinee may have completed the WAIS–IV and then subsequently been re-evaluated with the WISC–IV on re-evaluation. The same methodology used for the WAIS–III is applied when comparing the WAIS–IV and WISC–IV. The multiple regression equations for WAIS–IV predicted from WISC–IV is derived from the WISC–IV/WAIS–IV validation sample.

A sample of 157 healthy, 16-year-old controls (45.9% female, 54.1% male) completed the WAIS–IV and WISC–IV on two separate test sessions, using a counter-balanced design. The interval between test sessions ranged from 7 to 73 days, with an average of 17 days. The racial/ethnic distribution was 75.0% White, 18.5% Hispanic, 5.1% African-American, 1.9% Asian, and 3.2% Other. The sample parent education level distribution was 3.2% completed 8 years of education or fewer, 5.7% completed between nine and 11 years of education, 24.8% completed 12 years of education, 31.9% completed 13–15 years of education, and 34.4% completed 16 years of education or more.

Hierarchical regression models were derived for all common index and subtest scores. In each equation, the dependent variable was the WAIS–IV index or subtest, regardless of administration order. The independent variables were entered into the equations in steps. In the first step, the WISC–IV index or subtest score was entered into the equation. In the second step, test order (e.g., WAIS–IV or WISC–IV administered first) was entered. In the third step, parent education level was entered. In the fourth step, sex was entered. All non-significant predictor variables (e.g., $p > 0.05$) were dropped from the equation.

Table 6.5 contains the R^2, SEE, and beta weights for the WISC–IV/WAIS–IV index and subtest prediction equations. In the Apppendix, Tables A6.1, A6.2, A6.7, and A6.8 provide cut-offs for statistical significance and frequencies of specific differences between actual and predicted WAIS–IV scores.

WISC–IV predicted WAIS–IV index R^2 values range from 0.48 (PSI) to 0.75 (FSIQ) which are lower than WAIS–IV retest and WAIS–III/WAIS–IV prediction equations. The child and adult versions have less content overlap relative to the adult versions. The WISC–IV/WAIS–IV equations have a moderate to high degree of predictive accuracy. WISC–IV predicted WAIS–IV subtest R^2 values range from 0.32 (MR) to 0.62 (VC). These equations are lower than other models but can still be used to estimate change in performance between editions.

Similar to the WAIS–III equations, test order is a significant, positive predictor of WAIS–IV scores in the WISC–IV equations. The effect is similar to the WAIS–III results described previously. Parent education level is also a significant predictor of some WAIS–IV indexes and subtests with higher parent education related to increased practice effects. Few demographic variables are significant predictors of WAIS–IV scores after controlling for WISC–IV scores. The WAIS–IV predicted scores should be approached in the same manner as the WAIS–III predictions, which were detailed in the previous example.

TABLE 6.5   WISC–IV Prediction Equations for WAIS–IV Index and Subtest Scores

WAIS–IV Index/Subtest	R^2	SEE	Constant	WISC–IV Index/ Subtest	Test Order	Parent Education Level	Sex
FSIQ	0.75	6.21	6.862	0.834	6.154	–	–
VCI	0.69	7.38	8.657	0.841	–	1.542	–
PRI	0.50	8.92	27.049	0.655	5.241	–	–
WMI	0.58	8.84	22.781	0.665	3.247	1.524	–
PSI	0.48	8.66	26.843	0.585	5.948	1.692	–
Vocabulary	0.62	1.71	0.113	0.839	–	–	0.584
Similarities	0.38	2.18	3.5	0.65	–	–	–
Information	0.53	1.98	1.603	0.692	–	0.355	–
Block Design	0.50	1.97	1.471	0.694	1.349	–	–
Matrix Reasoning	0.32	2.35	3.656	0.587	–	–	–
Digit Span	0.57	1.70	1.811	0.581	0.601	0.317	–
Arithmetic	0.51	2.02	2.687	0.703	–	–	–
Coding	0.41	1.89	3.416	0.537	0.877	–	–
Symbol Search	0.33	2.21	1.493	0.557	1.057	0.409	–

Note: WISC–IV Index/Subtest is the same as the WAIS–IV (e.g., FSIQ WISC–IV predicts FSIQ WAIS–IV).
Test Order coded: 1 = WAIS–IV administered first, 2 = WISC–IV Administered first. Parent Education Level Coded: 1 = 8 or less years, 2 = 9–11 years, 3 = 12 years, 4 = 13–15 years, and 5 = 16 or more years. Sex coded: male = 1, female = 2.
All index equations use age adjusted standard scores for both WAIS–IV and WISC–IV.
All WAIS–IV and WISC–IV subtest scores are age-adjusted scaled scores.
Copyright 2003, 2008 by Pearson, Inc. Reproduced with permission. All rights reserved.

Additional WAIS–IV Interpretative Considerations and Using Alternate Editions

There are a few notable trends across all of the prediction equations that need to be considered when evaluating a change in performance over time. First, in every model, index scores show the greatest stability and most predictive accuracy between Time 1 and Time 2 assessments. Second, FSIQ and VCI provide the most consistent performance while the other indexes are more variable, with PRI being substantially more variable when using alternate versions. Therefore, expect larger changes in performance on PRI, WMI, and PSI, than on VCI and FSIQ (e.g., use statistical significance and base rates to identify atypicality of the differences). Third, subtests have less stability than indexes and the predictive strength varies substantially from one subtest to another. In the verbal domain Similarities consistently has the lowest stability over time, an effect that is magnified when alternate forms are used. Perceptual Reasoning subtests Block Design and Matrix Reasoning have greater stability than Visual Puzzles on WAIS–IV retest. Both Block Design and Matrix Reasoning show consistent stability on WAIS–IV retest and WAIS–IV versus WAIS–III retest; however, Matrix Reasoning in the WAIS–IV versus WISC–IV comparison is more variable. Working Memory subtests have the most stability with WAIS–IV retest but there is little difference when comparing WAIS–III or WISC–IV Digit Span and Arithmetic to WAIS–IV. Finally, Coding shows a high degree of stability between WAIS–IV retest and with WAIS–III but the stability is considerably lower when compared to the WISC–IV. Symbol Search has less stability when either the WAIS–III or WISC–IV is used.

The differences in stability across indexes, subtests, and editions will yield variable profiles in change scores depending on the measures and editions used. Large differences in some subtests or indexes relative to other measures could easily be mistaken for a meaningful profile of cognitive change when no real change has occurred. It is important to consider the non-random effects of changes in test–retest stability across testing conditions. The observed differences in stability across editions reflect real changes to the test content and structure (e.g., fewer subtests in VCI and PRI in the WAIS–IV versus WAIS–III, structural change of Digit Span, Visual Puzzles replacing Picture Completion, Symbol Search changing format). In addition, statistical artifacts such as a relatively homogenous age used for the WISC–IV versus WAIS–IV comparison may have attenuated correlations in this comparison, while the interval between test editions varies to a slight degree.

Overall, there will be greater stability and predictive accuracy when using the same edition of a test. Because practice effects can be accounted for in the ACS prediction equations when using the same edition, avoiding practice effects by using an alternate version should not be a primary consideration. Rather, whenever possible, the clinician should try to use the same edition of the test. If the patient has previous testing with a different edition, the prediction equations presented here will work well as long as the clinician carefully evaluates whether changes in cognition are occurring primarily in domains or on subtests where the content or structure is quite different between editions. Using statistical data mitigates some of these effects; however, patterns of what appear to be significant changes in cognition may reflect a change in the test structure across editions more than impaired cognition. Further evaluation of the test results and/or observational data can be useful in deciphering if something about the test parameters has influenced a change in performance (e.g., change in time limits, reduced motor demands).

Interpretation of change scores when using alternate editions should follow the same general principals outlined for interpreting WAIS–IV retest data. That is, the initial focus is to evaluate generality of change within a cognitive ability (e.g., PRI) and then to look at the subtest data to determine if a specific rather than general change occurred. When multiple specific changes occur at the subtest level but no index changes emerge, the clinician may want to evaluate FSIQ to determine if a more general decline in abilities is present. Very disparate findings within an index (e.g., no change or minimal change in two of three scores and one very large change), may signal difficulties with the task for reasons other than cognitive decline such as fluctuations in attention, mood, fatigue, or some specific misunderstanding about the task. This is not to say that a large change in a single score can never indicate cognitive decline; rather, additional information would be required to corroborate such a finding.

WMS–IV SERIAL ASSESSMENT

ACS: Serial Assessment for WMS–IV Indexes and Subtests

The same procedure used to derive prediction equations across Time 1 and Time 2 WAIS–IV evaluations was applied to the WMS–IV subtest and index scores. For each equation, cut-off scores identifying statistically significant differences between predicted and actual Time 2 WMS–IV scores were computed and base rates of the difference scores were derived. The test–retest sample of the WMS–IV was used to create the prediction equations. A sample of 244 healthy controls, ages 16–90, completed the WMS–IV on two separate test sessions. The interval between test sessions ranged from 14 to 84 days, with an average of 23 days. Of the 244 cases, 173 examinees completed the Adult battery, and 71 completed the Older Adult battery. The Adult sample was 49% male and 51% female; 68.7% White, 13.3% Hispanic, 11.6% African-American, 3.5% Asian, and 2.9% Other; and 5.8% completed eight years of education or fewer, 8.1% completed 9–11 years of education, 32.9% completed 12 years of education, 28.3% completed 13–15 years of education, and 24.9% completed 16 years of education or more. The Older Adult sample was 41% male and 59% female; 84.5% White, 8.5% Hispanic, 5.6% African American, and 1.4% Asian; 9.9% completed eight years of education or fewer, 14.1% completed

9–11 years of education, 35.2% completed 12 years of education, 22.5% completed 13–15 years of education, and 18.3% completed 16 years of education or more. The demographic characteristics of the retest samples are similar to the general population demographics.

Hierarchical regression models were derived in several steps. In each equation, the dependent variable was the Time 2 WMS–IV index or subtest score. The independent variables were entered into the equations in steps. In the first step, the Time 1 index or subtest score was entered into the equation. In the second step, Time 1 WAIS–IV GAI was entered to control for ability effects on practice. In the third step, length of retest interval was entered into the equation. In the fourth step, demographic variables including age, education level, and sex were entered. All non-significant predictor variables (e.g., $p > 0.05$) were dropped from the equation. In some instances, the only significant predictor was the Time 1 score of interest while for other scores multiple predictors were significant.

The multiple regression equations used to predict WMS–IV reliable change are part of the ACS software. The ACS software applies the prediction rules from the derived equations and compares the examinee's actual Time 2 scores to his or her predicted Time 2 scores. The level of statistical significance of the difference (e.g., $p < 0.05$) and the base rate of the discrepancy in the test–retest sample are also provided. In the ACS Software, interval data are only applied for testing intervals from 14 to 84 days, the range obtained in the retest sample. In cases where the test interval is outside this range, the equation applies a minimum value of 14 if the interval is less than 14 days and a maximum value of 84 if the interval is greater than 84 days. Table 6.6 summarizes the significant predictors for the WMS–IV index and subtest scores.

WMS–IV index correlations R^2 values range 0.69 (VMI, VWMI) to 0.73 (IMI) showing a high degree of association between the predictor (s) and dependent variables. The WMS–IV prediction equations have more error than the WAIS–IV equations; therefore, larger score differences are expected for the WMS–IV compared to the WAIS–IV. Examinees with higher GAI scores benefit from practice more than those with lower GAI scores do. Interval data indicate that the more days between test sessions, the less practice effects are observed on Visual, Immediate, and Delayed Memory Indexes. Women show greater practice effects on memory tests than men.

WMS–IV subtest R^2 values range from 0.44 (VR II) to 0.66 (VPA I). Therefore, subtest predictions tend to be less accurate than index predictions. Smaller practice effects occur at longer retest intervals for Visual Reproduction I and II and Designs II. Higher ability examinees benefit more from practice than do lower ability examinees. Older

TABLE 6.6　ACS WMS–IV Index and Subtest Prediction Equations

| Dependent Variable | R^2 | SEE | Independent Variables | | | |
			Time 1 Measure	Ability Measure	Test Interval	Demographics
Auditory Memory Index (AMI)	0.71	7.88	AMI	GAI	–	Sex
Visual Memory Index (VMI)	0.69	9.46	VMI	GAI	Interval in days	Sex
Visual Working Memory Index (VWMI)	0.69	8.76	VWMI	GAI	–	–
Immediate Memory Index (IMI)	0.73	8.11	IMI	GAI	Interval in days	Sex
Delayed Memory Index (DMI)	0.70	8.34	DMI	GAI	Interval in days	Sex
Logical Memory I (LM I)	0.60	1.77	LM I	GAI	–	Sex
Logical Memory II (LM II)	0.54	1.96	LM II	GAI	–	Sex
Verbal Paired Associates I (VPA I)	0.66	1.92	VPA I	GAI	–	Age
Verbal Paired Associates II (VPA II)	0.61	1.72	VPA II	GAI	–	Sex
Visual Reproduction I (VR I)	0.50	2.03	VR I	GAI	Interval in days	–
Visual Reproduction II (VR II)	0.44	2.26	VR II	GAI	Interval in days	–
Designs I (DE I)	0.60	2.14	DE I	GAI	–	Sex
Designs II (DE II)	0.60	2.05	DE II	GAI	Interval in days	Sex
Spatial Addition (SA)	0.60	1.93	SA	GAI	–	–
Symbol Span (SYS)	0.54	2.11	SYS	GAI	–	–

Copyright 2009 by Pearson, Inc. Reproduced with permission. All rights reserved.

WAIS-IV, WMS-IV, AND ACS

examinees show smaller practice effects on Verbal Paired Associates I than younger examinees, and women improve more following exposure than men on WMS–IV subtests (except for Verbal Paired Associates I).

Additional Serial Assessment Equations for WMS–IV Indexes and Subtests

Like the WAIS–IV, complete ability measures are required by the ACS software to obtain a serial assessment report. In some cases, a WMS–IV may be administered without a full WAIS–IV or with a different ability measure (e.g., WASI–II). In these situations, it is not possible to obtain ACS serial assessment scores for WMS–IV. Additional equations are provided here to enable clinicians to identify significant change in WMS–IV performance without using WAIS–IV. Rather than using GAI, VCI, or PRI as a predictor variable, education level is used. As stated for the WAIS–IV, when interpreting these alternate equations, the clinician must keep in mind that the ACS equations reflect the examinee's current intellectual functioning and better represent his or her ability to profit from practice. Education level is an estimate of premorbid ability and may potentially overestimate the examinees ability to profit from practice effects. For most individuals, the use of education level will improve the predictive power of the equation when ability scores are not available and reduce prediction error. Table 6.7 provides regression data and beta weights for all WMS–IV indexes and subtests.

WMS–IV index R^2 values range from 0.67 (VMI, VWMI, DMI) to 0.71 (IMI) showing a high degree of association between the predictor (s) and dependent variables, and indicating moderate to high levels of predictive accuracy. Examinees with higher education levels benefit from practice more than those with lower education levels. Interval data indicate that the more days between test sessions, the less practice effects are observed on Auditory, Visual, Immediate, and Delayed Memory Indexes. Women show greater practice effects on memory tests than men, with the exception of visual working memory subtests on which no sex effects are observed.

WMS–IV subtest R^2 values range from 0.40 (VR II) to 0.62 (VPA I). The subtest prediction equations are generally lower than the index equations. Therefore, subtests will show more variability between Time 1 and Time 2 assessments. Examinees with higher levels of education benefit more from practice than examinees with lower education levels. Reduced practice effects are observed at longer retest intervals on Visual Reproduction I. Older examinees show smaller practice effects on Verbal Paired Associates I. Women have greater practice effects on Logical Memory I, Verbal Paired Associates II, and Designs I and II.

TABLE 6.7   WMS–IV Index and Subtest Scores Alternate Retest Prediction Equations

WMS–IV Index/Subtest Time 2	R^2	SEE	Constant	WMS–IV Time 1 Index/ Subtest	Interval	Education Level	Time 1 Age	Sex
AMI	0.68	8.26	22.009	0.817	− 0.094	1.569	−	2.743
VMI	0.67	9.64	17.424	0.878	− 0.191	1.911	−	3.01
VWMI	0.67	8.99	15.615	0.886	−	−	−	−
IMI	0.71	8.29	23.932	0.824	− 0.159	1.597	−	2.755
DMI	0.67	8.59	21.231	0.798	− 0.13	2.593	−	3.861
Logical Memory I	0.55	1.89	4.003	0.709	−	−	−	0.557
Logical Memory II	0.46	2.11	5.305	0.698	−	−	−	−
Verbal Paired Associates I	0.62	2.02	3.275	0.801	−	0.476	− 0.016	−
Verbal Paired Associates II	0.61	1.72	2.02	0.7	−	0.376	−	0.453
Visual Reproduction I	0.48	2.11	5.122	0.652	− 0.03	0.263	−	−
Visual Reproduction II	0.40	2.33	4.442	0.602	−	0.607	−	−
Designs I	0.55	2.26	1.258	0.817	−	−	−	1.103
Designs II	0.58	2.07	− 0.145	0.806	−	0.469	−	1.416
Spatial Addition	0.55	2.07	2.808	0.793	−	−	−	−
Symbol Span	0.52	2.14	2.283	0.709	−	0.356	−	−

Note: WMS–IV Time 1 Index/Subtest is the same as the Time 2 Index/Subtest (e.g., Auditory Index Time 1 predicts Auditory Index Time 2). Interval difference between Time 1 and Time 2 assessment in days. Education Level Coded: 1 = 8 or less years, 2 = 9–11 years, 3 = 12 years, 4 = 13–15 years, and 5 = 16 or more years. Sex coded: male = 1, female = 2. All index equations use age adjusted standard scores for both WMS–IV.

Copyright 2009 by Pearson, Inc. Reproduced with permission. All rights reserved.

In the same manner as was illustrated for the WAIS–IV, the examiner calculates the predicted WMS–IV Time 2 score from the equations in the table. For example, a 55-year-old man with secondary progressive multiple sclerosis (code = 1) with eight years of education (code = 1), was re-evaluated 180 days (interval = 84) after his initial evaluation. If his Time 1 AMI score is 75, he would have the following prediction equation for his Time 2 AMI score.

Step 1: Time 2 AMI = 22.009 + (0.817 × Time 1 AMI)
+ (− 0.094 × interval) + (1.569 × education) + (2.743 × sex)
Step 2: Time 2 AMI = 22.009 + (0.817 × 75) + (− 0.094 × 84)
+ (1.569 × 1) + (2.743 × 1)
Step 3: Time 2 AMI = 22.009 + (61.275) − (7.896) + (1.569) + (2.743)
Result: Time 2 AMI = 79.70 or 80

At the subtest level, if the same examinee had a Logical Memory I subtest score of seven at Time 1, the following equation provides the expected Time 2 Logical Memory I score.

Step 1: Time 2 LM I = 4.003 + (0.709 × Time 1 LM I) + (0.557 × sex)
Step 2: Time 2 LM I = 4.003 + (0.709 × 7) + (0.557 × 1)
Step 3: Time 2 LM I = 4.003 + (4.963) + (0.557)
Result: Time 2 LM I = 9.52 or 10

The difference between the actual Time 2 score and the predicted Time 2 score is used to determine if there is an unexpected decline or improvement in memory functioning. Tables A6.9 and A6.10 in the Appendix provide cut-off scores to determine if a difference between actual and predicted Time 2 WMS–IV index, and subtest scores, is statistically significant. In this example, if the actual Time 2 AMI is 62 then the difference (e.g., actual − predicted) equals −17.7. According to Table A6.9, that difference is significant at the p <0.01 level (cut-off = 14.18). If the Logical Memory I actual Time 2 score is 5, then the subtest actual versus predicted difference is −4.52 which is statistically significant at the p <0.01 level (cut-off = 4.08). Base rate data for WMS–IV actual versus predicted differences is found in Tables A6.11 and A6.12 in the Appendix. An AMI actual versus predicted difference of 17 points where the actual score is less than the predicted score occurs in 2.11% of the retest sample and the Logical Memory I difference of −4.52 occurs in 3.72% of the retest sample. In both cases, the difference is statistically significant and atypical.

WMS–IV Index and Subtest Serial Assessment Interpretation

Evaluating change in performance on the WAIS–IV allowed identification of general intellectual decline or decline in a specific intellectual process (i.e., verbal comprehension, perceptual reasoning, working memory, or processing speed). On the WMS–IV, the focus of evaluating change is a little narrower. The WMS–IV is primarily a measure of memory functioning; therefore, the rationale for comparing Time 1 and

Time 2 scores is to identify memory decline or improvement. Again, Time 1 and Time 2 scores are never directly compared and occasionally what seems to be a relatively small Time 1 versus Time 2 difference is statistically significant when the predicted difference method is used. This was illustrated in the example above of the man with multiple sclerosis whose AMI score declined from 75 to 62. An actual Time 1 versus Time 2 score difference of 13 points became over 17 points when the *predicted difference method* is applied. This effect is magnified on the WMS–IV due to the large practice effects observed on memory measures. In the example presented above, the predicted scores would have been even larger if the examinee was a highly educated woman.

The statistical significance level informs the examiner if the difference is statistically reliable. The base rate identifies the rarity of the difference. Scores that are both statistically significant and rare may indicate clinically meaningful improvement or decline in memory functioning. However, obtaining a single measure that is unusual does not necessarily indicate a real decline in functioning. Consider that multivariate base rate rules still apply here (see Chapter 2) and that one low score is usually not atypical within an entire battery of tests. Other cognitive and situational factors contribute to changes in performance across time and may have an even greater impact on memory functioning. Inattention, fatigue, poor effort, and presence of distractions may adversely impact memory test performance and need to be considered when significant changes in memory scores are observed.

As was suggested for the WAIS–IV, the clinician will want to evaluate differences at the index level as the primary level of analysis because these are more stable and reliable. Subtest-level analysis can be used when a whole battery has not been administered or to identify specific cognitive changes. It is strongly recommended that the clinician use the ACS model to evaluate memory change with current ability measures to estimate dynamic practice effects. When WAIS–IV data is not available, the equations provided in this chapter can be useful for identifying change in memory functioning.

On the WMS–IV, the examiner will want to start with the indexes that best answer the clinical question. Generic referral questions focused on identifying a general loss in memory functioning would be best answered by evaluating the Immediate and Delayed Memory Indexes, initially. If the predicted Immediate Memory Index, is both significantly lower and occurs at a low base rate, the results can be interpreted as *"Ms. X shows a decline in her immediate memory functioning compared to previous testing, as demonstrated by her significantly lower obtained IMI relative to her predicted IMI (p <0.05, BR = 4.48%)."* Next, the examiner evaluates change in DMI performance. If both IMI and DMI are significantly lower, the clinician can confidently state that general memory functioning is significantly lower on re-evaluation. The examiner then reviews the subtest changes to determine if the change is general or specific to large changes in a few subtests. In the latter case, if there is a consistency in findings (e.g., verbal or visual subtests) then the examiner may wish to evaluate the AMI and VMI to determine if modality specific memory loss is causing the IMI and DMI to be lower. The examiner should use the same approach outlined for the WAIS–IV when determining if a result is specific to a single subtest or not. If all of the subtests in the index are not significantly different, but one subtest is very different, then it is unlikely that a general decline in memory is present. Carefully reviewing performance on the significantly different subtest and behavioral observations associated with that subtest can provide additional information to understand the change better.

When the referral question relates to modality specific changes in memory functioning (e.g., post left-hippocampectomy), the examiner will start with the AMI and VMI indexes rather than IMI and DMI and follow the same process described in the previous paragraph. If the modality specific aspects of the referral question include working memory as well (e.g., improvement in visual versus auditory working memory after CogMed (Klingberg et al., 2005) training), then the examiner would also evaluate changes in WMI from the WAIS–IV and VWMI from the WMS–IV. If differences are found in the indexes, a thorough evaluation of subtests is completed. Again, if only a few very large changes in specific subtests appear to be creating the lowered scores in AMI, VMI, WMI, or VWMI then non-cognitive factors need to be considered. Alternately, if the changes in AMI and VMI are selective to immediate and delayed memory measures, then the IMI and DMI indexes should also be evaluated. As stressed throughout this book, the clinician is evaluating the examinee's performance for consistency and trying to identify cognitive factors that could be caused by the clinical disorders under consideration (e.g., memory impairment following traumatic brain injury, improved memory after treatment for depression).

WMS–IV Serial Assessment Using Alternate Editions

As with the WAIS–IV, there are occasions when patients will present for re-evaluation having data from a previous test edition. For the Wechsler Memory Scale, this occurs when a new edition is published (e.g., WMS–III to WMS–IV). As discussed in Chapter 1, substantial changes were made to the structure and content of the test between

WMS–III (Wechsler 1997b) and WMS–IV. The index structure has been reduced to five core measures from eight and the visual memory tests contributing to the Visual Memory Indexes have completely new content. To facilitate evaluation of a change in scores between editions, the ACS WMS–IV additional index structure, which replicates the WMS–III index structure, should be used. This ACS index structure replicates the division of the Auditory and Visual Indexes into immediate and delayed subsets. The WMS–III has three subtests that have sufficient content overlap with the new edition to make them comparable. Discrepancies occurring between the WMS–III and WMS–IV in the visual and working memory domains will need to be carefully evaluated due to the substantial revision of the content in these domains. The verbal subtests are very similar across editions, making content effects a very minor issue.

The WMS–IV and WMS–III were normed at different times and on different populations. This affects the amount of practice effects that are observed when comparing scores across editions. If WMS–IV was administered second, then practice effects can be masked by the lowering of scores on WMS–IV due to the Flynn effect. In the more unusual case, where WMS–III is administered after WMS–IV, practice effects will appear to be magnified. Therefore, test order has a significant impact on the observed differences between the tests.

Equations to assess reliable change between the WMS–III and WMS–IV have not been previously published. The equations were derived using the methodology described above. Statistical cut-offs and base-rates were computed for each equation. The WMS–III/WMS–IV validity sample from the WMS–IV standardization was used to create the equations. A sample of 224 healthy controls (50.4% female, 49.6% male), ages 17–69, completed the WMS–IV and WMS–III on two separate test sessions, using a counter-balanced design. The interval between test sessions ranged from 13 to 89 days, with an average of 22 days. The racial/ethnic distribution was 70.5% White, 13.9% Hispanic, 11.6% African-American, 3.1% Asian, and 0.9% Other. The sample education level distribution was 7.6% completed 8 years of education or fewer, 7.6% completed between 9 and 11 years of education, 29.5% completed 12 years of education, 29.5% completed 13–15 years of education, and 25.8% completed 16 years of education or more.

Hierarchical regression models were derived in several steps. In each equation, the dependent variable was the WMS–IV index or subtest, regardless of administration order. The independent variables were entered into the equations in steps. In the first step, the WMS–III index or subtest score was entered into the equation. In the second step, test order (e.g., WMS–IV or WMS–III administered first) was entered. In the third step, interval in days was entered. In the fourth and final step, education level (parent education level for ages 16–19), age at Time 1, and sex were entered. All non-significant predictor variables (e.g., $p > 0.05$) were dropped from the equation.

Table 6.8 contains the R^2, SEE, and beta weights for the WMS–III/WMS–IV index and subtest prediction equations. At the end of this chapter, Tables A6.9, A6.10, A6.13 in conjunction with A6.14, and A6.15 in the Appendix provide cut-offs for statistical significance and frequencies of specific differences between actual and predicted WMS–IV scores.

The WMS–III predicted WMS–IV index R^2 values range from 0.34 (Visual Immediate) to 0.69 (Auditory Immediate). The level of predictive accuracy varies significantly among the indexes. As expected, the Visual Indexes have a moderate association and a higher standard error of estimate than other comparisons. The Working Memory Indexes have a moderate degree of association despite having no overlapping content. The test sequence has a large impact on the predicted scores, particularly when WMS–III is administered first. Examinees with higher education levels benefit from practice more than those with lower education levels. Older examinees have lower observed practice effects on Auditory Immediate, Immediate, and Delayed Memory Indexes. Women show greater practice effects on the Auditory Delayed Index than men.

WMS–IV subtest R^2 values range from 0.48 (VPA II, VR I) to 0.64 (LM I & II). The subtest equations predictive accuracy is generally lower than the index equations, except for VR scores that are more stable than the visual memory indexes. Logical Memory and Visual Reproduction comparisons with WMS–III are similar to those reported for the WAIS–IV retest sample. This is expected because the content is very similar across the editions. VPA I and II scores are lower when comparing across editions rather than within editions and is likely due to changes in content. Test sequence has a large impact on predicted WMS–IV subtest scores. Education, age, and sex effects occur intermittently across subtests.

In the same manner as was illustrated for the WAIS–IV alternate equations, the examiner must calculate the predicted WMS–IV Time 2 score from the equations in the table. For example, a 40- year-old man (code = 2) with 12 years of education (code = 3), was re-evaluated 60 days (interval = 60) after his initial evaluation. If his Time 1 WMS–III Auditory Immediate index score is 95, he would have the following prediction equation for his WMS–IV Time 2 Auditory Immediate Index score.

Step 1: Time 2 AII = 5.788 + (0.756 × Time 1 AII) + (12.717 × test order) + (1.369 × education) + (− 0.118 × age)

TABLE 6.8   WMS–III Prediction Equations for WMS–IV Index and Subtest Scores

WMS–IV Index/Subtest	R^2	SEE	Constant	WMS–III Index/ Subtest	Test Order	Education Level	Time 1 Age	Sex
Auditory Immediate	0.69	9.09	5.788	0.756	12.717	1.369	−0.118	−
Auditory Delayed	0.66	9.27	−0.932	0.773	13.521	−	−	2.609
Visual Immediate	0.34	11.92	40.787	0.376	7.082	3.317	−	−
Visual Delayed	0.40	13.13	37.723	0.407	11.417	3.878	−	−
Immediate Memory	0.65	9.46	14.179	0.642	11.069	2.513	−0.086	−
Delayed Memory	0.61	10.72	9.87	0.684	15.005	1.736	−0.098	−
Visual Working Memory	0.54	10.98	29.674	0.561	3.583	−	−	−
Logical Memory I	0.64	1.96	−2.156	0.781	3.784	−	−0.026	−
Logical Memory II	0.64	1.99	−4.117	0.775	4.324	−	−	−
Verbal Paired Associates I	0.54	2.10	1.262	0.648	0.637	0.34	−	−
Verbal Paired Associates II	0.48	2.14	1.879	0.689	−	−	−	0.868
Visual Reproduction I	0.48	2.25	0.949	0.524	2.808	−	−	−
Visual Reproduction II	0.56	2.49	−3.012	0.693	4.51	−	−0.026	−

Note: WMS–III Index/Subtest is the same as the WMS–IV Index/Subtest (e.g., Auditory Immediate WMS–III predicts Auditory Immediate WMS–IV, exceptions WMS–III GMI predicts WMS–IV Delayed and WMS–III WMI predicts WMS–IV Visual Working Memory Index).
Test Order coded: 1 = WMS–IV administered first, 2 = WMS–III administered first. Education Level Coded: 1 = 8 or less years, 2 = 9–11 years, 3 = 12 years, 4 = 13–15 years, and 5 = 16 or more years. Age = age in years. Sex coded: male = 1, female = 2. All index equations use age-adjusted standard scores for both WMS–IV and WMS–III. All WMS–IV and WMS–III subtest scores are age-adjusted scaled scores.

Copyright 2009 by Pearson, Inc. Reproduced with permission. All rights reserved.

Step 2: Time 2 AII = 5.788 + (0.756 × 95) + (12.717 × 2) + (1.369 × 3) + (− 0.118 × 40)
Step 3: Time 2 AII = 5.788 + (71.82) + (25.434) + (4.107) − (4.72)
Result: Time 2 AII = 102.429 or 102

At the subtest level, if the same examinee has a WMS–III Logical Memory I subtest score of eight at Time 1, the following equation provides the expected Time 2 Logical Memory I score.

Step 1: Time 2 LM I = − 2.156 + (0.781 × Time 1 LM I) + (3.784 × test order) + (− 0.026 × age)
Step 2: Time 2 LM I = − 2.156 + (0.781 × 8) + (3.784 × 2) − (0.026 × 40)
Step 3: Time 2 LM I = − 2.156 + (6.248) + (7.568)−(1.04)
Result: Time 2 LM I = 10.62 or 11

The difference between the actual Time 2 score and the predicted Time 2 score is used to determine if there is an unexpected decline or improvement in memory functioning. Use Tables A6.13 to A6.15 to determine the statistical significance and base rate for actual versus predicted WMS–IV differences. In this case, if the actual Time 2 AII is 89, a difference of 13.43 is significant at the p <0.05 level and occurs in 5.36% of the retest sample. For a Logical Memory I actual Time 2 score of 8, the *predicted difference* of 2.62 is not statistically significant and has a base rate of 11.16%. The index score is statistically significant and has a low base rate; however, the LM I subtest is not reliably different across editions (despite being relatively uncommon).

Additional WMS–IV Interpretative Considerations and Using Alternate Editions

There are a few notable trends across all of the prediction equations that need to be taken into consideration when evaluating a change in WMS–IV performance over time. First, index scores show the greatest stability and most predictive accuracy between Time 1 and Time 2 assessments. Among WMS–IV indexes, the Immediate Memory Index has the best predictive accuracy. The WMS–IV retest indexes are all quite similar, so big variations in cross-assessment performance are not expected. However, when using the WMS–III, the Visual indexes have substantially lower predictive accuracy so larger serial assessment differences may be observed without being statistically significant or rare. This can result in large differences on re-evaluation on these subtests, which could appear as a modality specific change but may be related to differences in the content of the test.

In most cases, subtests are less stable than indexes. Therefore, more variability will occur at the subtest level. In the verbal domain, Verbal

Paired Associates has greater predictive accuracy than Logical Memory on retest but the opposite occurs when WMS–III is used. Some variability in change between these subtests can occur. Likewise, prediction of Visual Reproduction is less accurate than for Designs. Variations in change scores (e.g., when the size of simple differences are considered) across subtests can appear to represent a specific profile; however, due to variations in statistical accuracy these may occur by chance. Using statistical significance and base rates enables determination of true versus chance differences.

The differences in stability across indexes, subtests, and editions will yield variable profiles in change scores depending on the measure and edition used. Large differences in some subtests or indexes relative to other measures could easily be mistaken for a meaningful profile of cognitive change. It is important to consider the non-random effects of changes in test–retest stability across testing conditions. The observed differences in stability across editions reflect real changes to the test content and structure (e.g., different visual memory tests, changes in VPA content). As noted previously with the WAIS–IV, there is greater stability and predictive accuracy when using the same edition of a test. Therefore, in most situations using the same edition for re-evaluation will yield the best results. For patients with previous testing, often an alternate version was used. In these cases, the prediction equations presented here will work well as long as the clinician carefully evaluates whether changes in cognition are occurring in domains or on subtests where the content or structure is quite different between editions. Using statistical data mitigates some of these effects; however, patterns of what appear to be significant changes in cognition may really reflect a change in the test content or structure that has impacted the patient's performance, and not a significant change in memory ability.

Interpretation of change scores when using alternate editions should follow the same general principals outlined for interpreting WMS–IV retest data. That is, indexes that directly answer the clinical question associated with change in memory functioning should be evaluated first (e.g., modality related deficits or general memory changes). Subsequently, the subtests within those indexes are reviewed. The purpose is to evaluate generality of change within a memory function (e.g., Auditory Memory) and then to use subtest data to identify specific rather than general deficits. Very disparate findings within an index (e.g., no change or minimal change in two of three scores and one very large change) may signal difficulties with the task for reasons other than cognitive decline, such as fluctuations in attention, mood, fatigue, or a specific misunderstanding of the task.

CASE STUDIES

CASE STUDY 1

Mr. D. is a 63-year-old, married, African-American man, with a Master's degree in business administration. He was referred for re-evaluation by his primary care physician following continuing complaints of attention and memory problems.

Mr. D. was born and raised in Boston, Massachusetts. He did well in school and graduated college with a degree in Accounting. He enlisted in the Air Force as a commissioned officer and completed 12 years of service. He met and married his wife during this time. After leaving the Air Force he returned to school and completed his Master's degree. Upon completion of his degree, he worked as a manager for a hardware store chain where he has remained for 20 years. He has received regular promotions and is currently the regional manager for 12 stores.

Several years ago, Mr. D reports noticing more stress at work, frequent headaches, fatigue, and difficulty completing tasks he had previously completed easily. He reports that the company began using new computer systems at this time and stated that he just was not good with computers. Mr. D. has a long history of hypertension, which has not been well controlled by medication. He suffered a significant myocardial infarction at the age of 60. He required resuscitation by paramedics responding to the emergency. Subsequently, he underwent successful quadruple by-pass surgery. After the surgery, he experienced a bout of depression that was successfully treated with medication but he still complained that he did not feel himself. An MRI performed 12 months after the surgery showed white matter ischemia. He completed an initial evaluation 6 months prior at the request of his company following concerns about his memory and increasing difficulty keeping up with tasks.

He reported a high degree of anxiety over his difficulties. His scores during this initial evaluation reflected average to low average performance on most index and subtest scores of the WAIS−IV. His overall FSIQ was 96 with a GAI of 97. His performance on processing speed tasks was notably lower than on the other indexes with performance in the borderline range. On the WMS−IV, his scores were in the low average to borderline range with particularly low scores on delayed recall. Given his relatively poor performance in comparison to his attained education and employment history, his doctor recommended that he be re-evaluated in 12−18 months. His employer made accommodations for him, including providing him with an assistant to help with his job duties. However, he continued to struggle with his job and is currently on disability leave. Despite medication, Mr. D.'s high blood pressure was not well-controlled and he experienced two to three episodes of confusion and disorientation. The most recent episode resulted in his hospitalization for 4 days secondary to a mild cerebrovascular accident. The current assessment was completed 12 months after the initial evaluation.

Mr. D. was on time for his second evaluation and accompanied by his wife. He was well dressed and groomed. During the interview, he frequently deferred to his wife to answer questions and appeared anxious and withdrawn. His speech was fluent and he was well spoken although he had difficulty with word finding. He observed that he just did not feel like himself anymore but attributed that to getting older. He indicated that he was nervous during the first assessment and he did not do as well as he would have liked. He did not feel that the results reflected his abilities and expressed concern that the current evaluation would produce the same results. Throughout testing, he denied difficulty with the questions and tasks and explained difficulties by stating that this was not anything like the real world. Despite this, he appeared to give good effort and was motivated to do well. He performed well on the Word Choice (Pearson, 2009) test and the embedded effort indices for the WAIS–IV and WMS–IV (see Chapter 7 for additional information).

Mr. D. completed the WAIS–IV and WMS–IV as part of his evaluation. On the WAIS–IV, he obtained an FSIQ of 87. His scores on the WAIS–IV were in the low average to borderline range and his WMS–IV scores were in the borderline and extremely low range. All his index and subtest scores were lower than those obtained on the initial evaluation. The ACS software was used to compare his performances across the two assessments to determine if the change in performance was statistically and clinically meaningful. The results of the serial assessment analyses are provided in Tables 6.9 and 6.10.

On the WAIS–IV, Mr. D.'s index scores were significantly different between Time 1 and Time 2, with the greatest difference observed on WMI and PSI. Notice that the actual minus predicted differences for the WMI and PSI are greater than the absolute Time 1 − Time 2 differences in part because the prediction model assumes some degree of practice effects would be present. These scores indicate that Mr. D. has experienced a decline in his abilities over the past eight months. At the subtest level, while all scores have decreased, only Block Design, Visual Puzzles, and Arithmetic were significant at the $p < 0.01$ level. Similar declines were observed in 10% or less of the normative sample.

On WMS–IV, Mr. D.'s performance appeared to decline from his initial assessment. His scores were in the borderline to extremely low range on all index and subtest scores. Moreover, every score was lower

TABLE 6.9 Mr. D.'s ACS WAIS–IV Index and Subtest Time 1 versus Time 2 Comparisons

Index/ Subtest	Time 1 Index/ Subtest	Time 2 Index/ Subtest	Time 2 Predicted	Actual Minus Predicted	Statistical Significance	Base Rate (%)
VCI	96	85	100.1	−15.1	<0.01	<1
PRI	98	84	100.6	−16.6	<0.01	<1
WMI	83	71	91.0	−20.0	<0.01	<1
PSI	76	71	93.7	−22.7	<0.01	<1
FSIQ	87	75	91.2	−16.2	<0.01	<2
VC	11	9	10.8	−1.8	>0.05	<25
SI	8	6	9.0	−3.0	<0.05	<10
IN	9	7	9.7	−2.7	<0.05	<5
BD	12	8	11.8	−3.8	<0.01	<5
MR	10	8	10.2	−2.2	>0.05	<15
VP	7	6	9.3	−3.3	<0.01	<10
DS	6	5	6.2	−1.2	>0.05	>25
AR	8	5	9.0	−4.0	<0.01	<2
CD	6	5	7.1	−2.1	>0.05	<15
SS	5	4	6.5	−2.5	>0.05	<15

than those obtained at the initial assessment. He is clearly demonstrating significant problems with his memory at this time. The ACS comparison analysis indicates that his decline in performance was significant and atypical at the index level. Every actual score was lower than the predicted score, indicating a significant decline in performance. At the subtest level, with the exception of Designs and Symbol Span, Mr. D.'s decline was statistically significant at the $p < 0.01$ level and occurred in 10% or less of the normative sample.

The results of the second assessment confirm the difficulties observed at the initial evaluation. In addition, the decline in performance over the 8-month interval between assessments suggests a progressive decline in abilities. It was recommended that Mr. D. be referred to a memory clinic where he and his wife can obtain support services and ongoing medical and psychological services. It is unlikely that Mr. D. will be able to return to work at his former position.

TABLE 6.10   Mr. D.'s ACS WMS–IV Index and Subtest Time 1 versus Time 2 Comparisons

Index/ Subtest	Time 1 Index/ Subtest	Time 2 Index/ Subtest	Time 2 Predicted	Actual Minus Predicted	Statistical Significance	Base Rate (%)
IMM	84	70	88.3	−18.3	<0.01	<2
DEL	72	60	80.7	−20.7	<0.01	<1
AMI	80	64	93.3	−29.3	<0.01	<1
VMI	84	73	84.2	−11.2	<0.05	<10
VWMI	83	77	90.5	−13.5	<0.01	<10
LM I	8	6	10.3	−4.3	<0.01	<2
LM II	5	3	8.6	−5.6	<0.01	<1
VPA I	7	5	9.3	−4.3	<0.01	<2
VPA II	6	2	7.9	−5.9	<0.01	<1
VR I	9	6	9.1	−3.1	<0.01	<10
VR II	6	5	8.7	−3.7	<0.01	<10
DE I	7	5	8.1	−3.1	<0.05	<10
DE II	7	6	6.7	−0.7	>0.05	>25
SA	8	6	9.2	−3.2	<0.01	<10
SyS	6	6	7.9	−1.9	>0.05	>25

CASE STUDY 2

Mrs. W. is a 42-year-old, married Hispanic woman, with 12 years of education. She was referred for re-evaluation following continuing difficulties following a recent flare up of multiple sclerosis symptoms.

Mrs. W. was born and raised in San Diego, California. She was an average student and completed high school. She reported no difficulty in school but found it boring and was more interested in being with her friends than school. She worked in retail settings for many years after high school and enjoyed spending time with family and friends. She married her husband 15 years ago and had two children; she was not employed while her children were young. She is currently employed as an administrative assistant at a medical office.

Eight years ago, Mrs. W. was diagnosed with multiple sclerosis— presenting initially as optic neuritis. Initially her symptoms were mild—primarily related to weakness, fatigue, and pain in her extremities, particularly her ankles and feet. She has continued to work despite occasional flare ups of her symptoms. Within the past year, she experienced a more progressive course of decline with increased motor and cognitive symptoms. She complains of fatigue, memory problems, and reduced attention. She was referred by her neurologist for a neuro-psychological evaluation to assess memory functioning.

As part of the neuropsychological evaluation, she was administered the WAIS–III and WMS–III. Overall, her performance was average on both the WAIS–III and the WMS–III. Her WAIS–III FSIQ was 98, in the average range. Her index scores were variable with a noticeable strength in verbal comprehension abilities (VCI = 115). Her processing speed was low average. These strengths and weaknesses were reflected in the subtest scores with her highest scores on Similarities and Vocabulary and her lowest score on Coding. Her WMS–III scores were also in the average range, although her performance was less varied than observed on the WAIS–III. All her WMS–III subtest scores were in the average range. Following the initial evaluation, Mrs. W. reported continuing problems and went on medical disability. She has not been able to return to work due to her weakness, fatigue, and attention pro-blems. She was referred for a second evaluation to determine if she qualified for long-term disability. The WAIS–IV and WMS–IV were administered as part of that evaluation. The current evaluation was completed 75 days after the initial evaluation.

Mrs. W. was driven to the appointment by her mother. She was slightly disheveled and appeared distracted during the interview, requiring several questions to be repeated. Her speech was slow but fluid and she responded appropriately to questions. She reported feel-ing tired but refused to reschedule saying that she has not had much energy lately and could not predict when she might feel better. She did not recall the results of the previous assessment, stating that they were sent to her work but she was not concerned about the results or about the request for re-evaluation. She reported that she would like to return to work because disability did not pay as much but she felt over-whelmed by the idea of returning immediately. She appeared to give good effort throughout testing but she required frequent breaks.

Mrs. W. completed the WAIS–IV and WMS–IV as part of her evalu-ation. On WAIS–IV, she obtained an FSIQ of 97, consistent with her previous evaluation. Her index scores were also relatively consistent with her previous performance with a similar pattern of scores. Her scores were all in the average to low average range at both the index and subtest level. Her WMS–IV scores were typically lower than those observed on the initial evaluation although there was some variability. The results of the serial assessment analyses are provided in Tables 6.11 and 6.12.

TABLE 6.11   Mrs. W.'s WAIS–III/WAIS–IV Index and Subtest Time 1 versus Time 2 Comparisons

Index/ Subtest	Time 1 Index/ Subtest	Time 2 Index/ Subtest	Time 2 Predicted	Actual Minus Predicted	Statistical Significance	Base Rate (%)
VCI	115	110	108.1	1.9	>0.05	<25
PRI	95	102	94.0	8.0	>0.05	>25
WMI	94	89	94.9	− 5.9	>0.05	>25
PSI	86	81	91.5	− 10.5	>0.05	>25
FSIQ	98	97	96.7	0.3	>0.05	<25
VC	12	14	10.7	3.3	<0.01	>5
SI	14	10	11.5	− 1.5	>0.05	<25
IN	11	12	10.6	1.4	>0.05	<25
BD	8	9	8.1	0.9	>0.05	<25
MR	10	12	9.2	2.8	<0.05	>25
DS	9	7	9.3	− 2.3	<0.05	>25
AR	8	9	8.3	0.7	>0.05	<25
CD	6	6	7.0	− 1.0	>0.05	<25
SS	9	7	9.4	− 2.4	>0.05	<25

On WAIS–IV, Mrs. W.'s index scores were not significantly different across assessments, indicating no significant change in her cognitive abilities. Given the relatively consistent performance, this is not surprising. A significant change was observed at the subtest level with her performance on Vocabulary increasing two scaled score points. Fewer than 5% of the normative sample had a similar increase. This indicates an unexpectedly higher score on this subtest. Given that this improvement was not reflected in other verbal subtests, it is unlikely this reflects a general improvement in verbal comprehension ability and may be related to the changes in content from WAIS–III to WAIS–IV and/or situational factors slightly lowering her score during the first evaluation.

On WMS–IV, Mrs. W.'s performance appeared to decline from her initial assessment. Her scores were in the average to low average range on both index and subtest scores. Her performances on the Auditory Immediate, Visual Delayed, Immediate, and General Memory Indexes were significantly lower on retest. This was also unusual with fewer

TABLE 6.12   Mrs. W.'s WMS–III/WMS–IV Index and Subtest Time 1 versus Time 2 Comparisons

Index/Subtest	Time 1 Index/ Subtest	Time 2 Index/ Subtest	Time 2 Predicted	Actual Minus Predicted	Statistical Significance	Base Rate (%)
Auditory Immediate	105	86	109.8	− 23.8	<0.01	<1
Auditory Delayed	102	103	110.2	− 7.2	>0.05	>25
Visual Immediate	97	97	101.4	− 4.4	>0.05	>25
Visual Delayed	106	92	115.3	− 23.3	<0.01	<5
Immediate	103	89	113.6	− 24.6	<0.01	<2
Delayed	98	86	116.2	− 30.2	<0.01	<1
Visual Working Memory	93	85	89.0	− 4.0	>0.05	>25
LM I	10	8	14.3	− 6.3	<0.01	<2
LM II	11	9	13.1	− 4.1	<0.05	<5
VPA I	12	7	11.3	− 4.3	<0.01	<10
VPA II	10	6	10.5	− 4.5	<0.01	<10
VR I	9	9	11.3	− 2.3	<0.05	<25
VR II	11	8	14.7	− 6.7	<0.01	<5

than 5% of the sample having similar declines in performance. All the common subtest scores were significantly lower at retest (i.e., LM, VPA, and VR).

The results of the second assessment indicate a decline in memory abilities for Mrs. W. Some of her difficulties on these tests appeared to be related to difficulties in maintaining attention and fatigue. Memory functioning is susceptible to disruption from poor attention and varying ability to sustain effort. Mrs. W. appears to be suffering from significant fatigue, weakness, and poor attention, making it difficult to determine if there truly is a memory deficit or her poor memory is a function of her low energy and ability to sustain effort. Mrs. W. performed within normal limits on measures of effort suggesting no obvious attempts at feigning memory difficulty. It is evident that Mrs. W. will have difficulty returning to work. It is recommended that Mrs. W. receive outpatient rehabilitation services to improve physical strength and to identify factors that exacerbate feelings of fatigue.

SUMMARY

Psychologists frequently conduct evaluations to determine if a person's cognitive functioning has improved, remained stable, or declined. It is essential to appreciate that some variability in performance from test to retest is common in healthy adults. That is, changes in scores do not necessarily reflect a change in a clinical condition. Cognitive functioning can improve in tandem with clinical improvement in a neurological or psychiatric condition or as the result of cognitive-enhancing or condition-modifying medications (e.g., selective serotonin reuptake inhibitors or methylphenidate). It can also improve as a result of regression to the mean, practice effects, and situational factors. Cognitive functioning can decline due to a progressive neurodegenerative condition, worsening psychiatric condition, regression to the mean, motivational factors, and/or other situational factors.

The regression and reliable change methodologies allow the clinician to reduce the adverse impact of measurement error, regression to the mean, and practice effects on test interpretation. To represent clinically significant improvement or decline, ideally the change score should be statistically reliable. However, the converse is not true; a statistically reliable change does not necessarily guarantee a clinically meaningful change. Simply put, these methods for assessing change are used to determine if there has been improvement or deterioration in functioning that exceeds the probable range of measurement error. Thus, regression and reliable change methodologies are used to supplement, not replace, clinical judgment.

KEY LEARNING

- Changes on WAIS–IV and WMS–IV index and subtest scores, from test to retest, can occur for multiple reasons.
- Initial levels of performance are associated with, or can influence, practice effects, regression to the mean, and relations among individual test scores (e.g., discrepancy scores). Baseline test scores that are very low are more susceptible to greater change from combined practice effects and regression to the mean. Baseline test scores in the high average and superior classification ranges, in contrast, are susceptible to regression, but are somewhat less likely to show large practice effects.
- Regression to the mean is a non-cognitive statistical phenomenon whereby scores at either end of a frequency distribution move toward the mean on retesting.

- Measurement error is all the variance in test performance that is not directly attributable to the construct a test purports to measure.
- Reliability is associated with score consistency over time (i.e., test—retest stability) or the consistency with which the test items in a measure assess the same construct.
- Practice effects describe the phenomenon where test scores increase on re-administration of an instrument due to prior exposure or experience with the measure. Practice effects are a systematic source of extraneous variance when evaluating change in cognitive functioning over time.
- Using a rule of thumb to determine a significant change in performance between evaluations will result in reduced sensitivity or specificity. Due to the complexity of factors that influence change scores, setting one cut-off based on the simple difference between test sessions will result in inaccurate assessment of change in cognitive functioning.
- All tests are influenced by motivational factors and level of effort. Just as these factors need to be considered when interpreting results obtained within a test session, they also need to be considered when interpreting results obtained across test sessions.
- Multiple regression is an effective statistical model for evaluating serial change given the ability to control for initial performance, regression to the mean, and practice effects.
- Index level scores generally provide the most stable estimate of change in cognitive functioning between evaluations.
- When calculating regression equations, do not enter interval values greater than the maximum interval listed in the retest sample (e.g., 84 days for WMS—IV). Using the maximum value returns the practice effects to zero (i.e., at 84 days, it is thought that the examinee had never taken the test before because there is no gain from the previous exposure). Using a greater value would result in a negative practice effect. For example, because the predictor value is negative, once the zero effect of practice at 84 days is reached, any additional days will reduce this to a lower score than if the examinee had never taken the test before creating a negative practice effect, that is, exposure to test results in worse performance.
- Assessing changes in cognitive functioning across different test editions (e.g., WAIS—III versus WAIS—IV) presents unique challenges due to normative changes (e.g., Flynn effect) and changes to test content and structure.
- A significant change in one test should not be considered a strong indicator of cognitive decline. Rather, the examiner should evaluate change in performance for consistency across similar skills, consistency with the disorder in question, motivational factors, and

applying the concept of multivariate base rates (e.g., one low score or one change may not be atypical in an entire battery of tests).

The Appendix containing tables for Chapter 6 can be found online at: http://booksite.elsevier.com/9780123869340

References

Basso, M. R., Bornstein, R. A., & Lang, J. M. (1999). Practice effects on commonly used measures of executive function across twelve months. *The Clinical Neuropsychologist*, 13(3), 283−292.

Basso, M. R., Carona, F. D., Lowery, N., & Axelrod, B. N. (2002). Practice effects on the WAIS–III across 3- and 6-month intervals. *The Clinical Neuropsychologist*, 16(1), 57−63.

Binder, L. M., Iverson, G. L., & Brooks, B. L. (2009). To err is human: "abnormal" neuropsychological scores and variability are common in healthy adults. *Archives of Clinical Neuropsychology*, 24(1), 31−46.

Brooks, B. L., Strauss, E., Sherman, E. M. S., Iverson, G. L., & Slick, D. J. (2009). Developments in neuropsychological assessment: refining psychometric and clinical interpretivemethods. *Canadian Psychology*, 50(3), 196−209.

Chelune, G. J., & Duff, K. (2013). The assessment of change: serial assessments in dementia evaluations. In L. D. Ravdin, & H. I. Katzen (Eds.), *Handbook on the neuropsychology of aging and dementia* (pp. 43−57). New York: Springer Science.

Chelune, G. J., Naugle, R. I., Lüders, H., Sedlak, J., & Awad, I. A. (1993). Individual change after epilepsy surgery: Practice effects and base-rate information. *Neuropsychology*, 7(1), 41−52.

Crocker, L., & Algina, J. (1986). *Introduction to classical and modern test theory*. Fort Worth, TX: Harcourt Brace Jovanovich College.

Duff, K., Schoenberg, M. R., Patton, D., Paulsen, J. S., Bayless, J. D., Mold, J., et al. (2005). Regression based formulas for predicting change in RBANS subtests with older adults. *Archives of Clinical Neuropsychology*, 20(3), 281−290.

Ferrer, E., Salthouse, T. A., McArdle, J. J., Stewart, W. F., & Schwartz, B. S. (2005). Multivariate modeling of age and retest in longitudinal studies of cognitive abilities. *Psychology of Aging*, 20(3), 412−422.

Flynn, J. R. (1984). The mean IQ of Americans: Massive gains 1932 to 1978. *Psychological Bulletin*, 95(1), 29−51.

Franzen, M. D. (1989). *Reliability and validity in neuropsychological assessment*. New York, NY: Plenum Press.

Franzen, M. D. (2000). *Reliability and validity in neurological assessment* (2nd ed.). New York, NY: Kluwer Academic/Plenum Press.

Heaton, R. K., Temkin, N., Dikmen, S., Avitable, N., Taylor, M. J., Marcotte, T. D., et al. (2001). Detecting change: a comparison of three neuropsychological methods, using normal and clinical samples. *Archives of Clinical Neuropsychology*, 16(1), 75−91.

Heilbronner, R. L., Sweet, J. J., Attix, D. K., Krull, K. R., Henry, G. K., & Hart, R. P. (2010). Official position of the american academy of clinical neuropsychology on serial neuropsychological assessments: the utility and challenges of repeat test administrations in clinical and forensic contexts. *The Clinical Neuropsychologist*, 24(8), 1267−1278.

Hinton-Bayre, A. D. (2010). Deriving reliable change statistics from test−retest normative data: comparison of models and mathematical expressions. *Archives of Clinical Neuropsychology*, 25(3), 244−256.

Iverson, G. L. (2001). Interpreting change on the WAIS–III/WMS–III in clinical samples. *Archives of Clinical Neuropsychology*, 16(2), 183−191.

Ivnik, R. J., Smith, G. E., Lucas, J. A., Petersen, R. C., Boeve, B. F., Kokmen, E., et al. (1999). Testing normal older people three or four times at 1- to 2-year intervals: Defining normal variance. *Neuropsychology, 13*(1), 121−127.

Jacobson, N. S., & Truax, P. (1991). Clinical significance: A statistical approach to defining meaningful change in psychotherapy research. *Journal of Consulting and Clinical Psychology, 59*(1), 12−19.

Klingberg, T., Fernell, E., Oleson, P., Johnson, M., Gustafsson, P., Dahlstrom, K., et al. (2005). Computerized training of working memory in children with ADHD-A randomized, controlled trial. *Journal of the American Academy of Child and Adolescent Psychiatry, 44*(2), 177−186.

Levine, A. J., Hinkin, C. H., Miller, E. N., Becker, J. T., Selnes, O. A., & Cohen, B. A. (2007). The generalizability of neurocognitive test/retest data derived from a nonclinical sample for detecting change among two HIV+ cohorts. *Journal of Clinical and Experimental Neuropsychology, 29*(6), 669−678.

Lineweaver, T. T., & Chelune, G. J. (2003). Use of the WAIS−III and WMS−III in the context of serial assessments: Interpreting reliable and meaningful change. In D. S. Tulsky, D. H. Saklofske, G. J. Chelune, R. K. Heaton, R. J. Ivnik, & R. Bornstein, et al. *Clinical interpretation of the WAIS−III and WMS−III* (pp. 303−337). Burlington, MA: Academic Press.

McCabe, D., Langer, K. G., Borod, J. C., & Bender, A. (2011). Practice effects. In J. S. Kreutzer, J. DeLuca, & B. Caplan (Eds.), *Encyclopedia of clinical neuropsychology* (pp. 1998−1999). New York: Springer Science.

McCaffrey, R. J., Ortega, A., & Haase, R. F. (1993). Effects of repeated neuropsychological assessments. *Archives of Clinical Neuropsychology, 8*(6), 519−524.

McSweeny, A. J., Naugle, R. I., Chelune, G. J., & Luders, H. (1993). "T-scores for change:" An illustration of a regression approach to depicting change in clinical neuropsychology. *The Clinical Neuropsychologist, 7*(3), 300−312.

Pearson (2009). *Advanced clinical solutions for the WAIS−IV/WMS−IV: technical manual.* San Antonio, TX: Pearson.

Salthouse, T. A. (2007). Implications of within-person variability in cognitive and neuropsychological functioning for the interpretation of change. *Neuropsychology, 21*(4), 401−411.

Salthouse, T. A., Schroeder, D. H., & Ferrer, E. (2004). Estimating retest effects in longitudinal assessments of cognitive functioning in adults between 18 and 60 years of age. *Developmental Psychology, 40*(5), 813−822.

Squire, L. R. (1987). *Memory and Brain.* New York: Oxford University Press.

Tulsky, D. S., Rolfhus, E. L., & Zhu, J. (2000). Two-tailed versus one-tailed base rates of discrepancy scores in the WAIS−III. *The Clinical Neuropsychologist, 14*(4), 451−460.

Wechsler, D. (1997a). Wechsler adult intelligence scale−third edition. San Antonio, TX: The Psychological Corporation.

Wechsler, D. (1997b). Wechsler memory scale, third edition. San Antonio, TX: The Psychological Corporation.

Wechsler, D. (2003). Wechsler intelligence scale for children−fourth edition. San Antonio, TX: Pearson.

Wechsler, D. (2008). Wechsler adult intelligence scale−fourth edition. San Antonio, TX: Pearson.

Wechsler, D. (2009). Wechsler memory scale−fourth edition. San Antonio, TX: Pearson.

Assessing Performance Validity with the ACS

James A. Holdnack*, Scott Millis[†], Glenn J. Larrabee[‡] and Grant L. Iverson**

*Pearson Assessment, San Antonio, Texas, USA [†]Wayne State University School of Medicine, Detroit, Michigan, USA [‡]Sarasota, Florida, USA **Harvard Medical School, Boston, Massachusetts, USA

INTRODUCTION

The evaluation of response bias is an important aspect of all types of psychological assessment. Various tools have been developed for evaluating the validity of personality measures, rating scales, and cognitive tests. *Response bias* occurs when an individual approaches a test, questionnaire, rating scale, or survey attempting to create a specific impression that could be either overly positive or negative. In other words, the examinee is not completing the test to give an accurate perception of his or her abilities; instead, he or she is biasing his or her responses to portray that he or she has more or less symptoms/problems than is actually the case. Response bias can be intentional or it can be a subconscious process that reflects other psychological processes (e.g., need for sick role). Neuropsychological evaluations frequently occur in settings wherein there can be substantial external incentives, such as monetary gain in personal injury litigation, disability payments, avoidance of criminal prosecution, and/or mitigation of criminal charges. Hence, assessment for negative response bias is important.

Negative response bias occurs in one of two ways in a neuropsychological evaluation: (a) exaggeration or fabrication of symptoms, or (b) intentional portrayal of deficit on measures of neuropsychological

WAIS-IV, WMS-IV, and ACS.
DOI: http://dx.doi.org/10.1016/B978-0-12-386934-0.00007-9
© 2013 Elsevier Inc. All rights reserved.

abilities such as motor function, attention, memory, processing speed, intellectual ability, or problem solving skills (Boone, 2007; Iverson, 2003; Larrabee, 2007). Larrabee (2012) espoused the use of separate terms to distinguish between exaggerated symptoms and biased performance on cognitive testing. He encouraged the use of the term Symptom Validity Tests (SVTs) for tests that measure exaggerated symptoms, and Performance Validity Tests (PVTs) for tests that measure biased performance on cognitive assessment. Embedded SVTs exist for measures such as the MMPI-2-RF, including F-r, Fp-r, Fs, FBS-r, and RBS scales (Ben-Porath, 2012). PVTs can either be free-standing, such as the Test of Memory Malingering, or derived from atypical patterns of performance on standard tests of ability such as the Wechsler Adult Intelligence Scale and Wechsler Memory Scale. In the current chapter we use the PVT terminology to refer to procedures which were previously referred to as measures of "suboptimal effort" in the ACS Manual.

The assessment of performance validity requires the identification of scores that are atypical in pattern or degree for *bona fide* neurological, psychiatric, or developmental disorders. Historically, these patterns include impaired attention in the context of normal memory (Mittenberg, Azrin, Millsaps, & Heilbronner, 1993), extremely poor recognition memory following minor injury and at a level inconsistent with that seen in severe traumatic brain injury (Langeluddecke & Lucas, 2003), and impaired immediate memory in the context of preserved verbal intellectual functions (Mittenberg, Theroux-Fichera, Zielinski, & Heilbronner, 1995). Although invalid performance can be present in any type of psychological or neuropsychological evaluation, it is particularly important in high stakes assessments (e.g., forensic, medical-legal) where having a specific diagnosis, high levels of symptoms, or demonstrated impairment is advantageous.

The use of performance validity indicators is common in neuropsychological practice, and it is strongly recommended by professional organizations (Bush et al., 2005; Heilbronner, Sweet, Morgan, Larrabee, & Millis, 2009). A survey of neuropsychologists identified as experts in forensic assessments (i.e., medical-legal evaluations) found that 79% of them include at least one performance validity measure in assessments for litigation cases (Slick, Tan, Strauss, & Hultsch, 2004). Similarly, a survey of practicing clinical neuropsychologists reported that 57% of these practitioners regularly use PVTs as part of neuropsychological evaluations (Sharland & Gfeller, 2007). Because the use of PVTs has become an important and frequent component of neuropsychological practice, such measures were included in the standardization of the Wechsler Adult Intelligence Scale–Fourth Edition (WAIS–IV: Wechsler, 2008) and Wechsler Memory Scale–Fourth Edition (WMS–IV: Wechsler, 2009) and are published as part of the ACS.

MEASURING PERFORMANCE VALIDITY

External/Stand-Alone Validity Checks

External or stand-alone PVTs are developed solely to measure invalid performance, that is, they are not used to measure any other construct. These tests are designed to be easily performed by patients with significant cognitive impairment. In past surveys, the most common stand alone performance validity measures used by experts include: the Test of Memory Malingering, Rey 15-Item, and Recognition Memory Test (Slick et al., 2004) and clinical neuropsychologists most commonly use the Test of Memory Malingering and Rey 15-Item (Sharland & Gfeller, 2007). Other PVTs shown to be sensitive in differentiating invalid from valid performance include: Word Memory Test, Medical Symptom Validity Test, Victoria Symptom Validity Test, Portland Digit Recognition, Dot Counting Test, Digit Memory Test and 21-Item Test (Iverson, 2010; Mossman, Wygant, & Gervais, 2012; Strauss et al., 2002; Vickery, Berry, Inman, Harris, & Orey, 2001). Many external PVTs use a forced choice memory paradigm. The examinee is given multiple stimuli to remember, in some cases the number of items to be remembered appears to be quite large, or the nature of the stimuli appears complex and difficult to memorize. In some models, immediately after the examinee sees one of the stimuli, he or she is asked to identify the item to be recalled from a foil. In other tasks, the examinee is presented with all of the stimuli and then asked to identify the target stimuli from a foil. In all cases, the foil is different enough from the original stimuli to be easily identifiable as incorrect. The sensitivity of identifying potential invalid performance in forced choice memory tasks differs with different stimuli, with word stimuli superior to digits and pictures (Gervais, Rohling, Green, & Ford, 2004). Even though these types of forced choice memory tasks appear challenging to the examinee, they are in actuality quite easy—yielding a high level of performance in clinical samples.

Embedded Performance Validity Checks

Embedded validity checks are subtests or trials/conditions/measures within a subtest that have been identified as sensitive to invalid performance. These tests were developed to measure a specific construct (e.g., memory, attention, working memory) but have characteristics that make them useful for detecting feigned impairment. In addition to external validity tests, experts use embedded PVTs from a variety of commonly used tests, such as the Digit Span subtest from the Wechsler Adult Intelligence Scale—Third Edition (WAIS—III: Wechsler, 1997), and verbal learning measures, particularly atypical performance on recognition memory measures (Slick et al., 2004). Using embedded performance validity measures within standard neuropsychological tests is an effective model for simultaneously assessing the validity of test performance and providing assessment of important cognitive constructs in examinees displaying valid performance (Meyers & Volbrecht, 2003). Embedded performance validity checks also provide a means of tracking validity of performance throughout the course of the assessment, not at just at a single point in time (Boone, 2009).

Identifying Invalid Performance

Invalid test performance is identified by comparing an examinee's performance to the performances of a large mixed clinical population (Boone et al., 2002), and clinical populations of interest, such as traumatic brain injury (Boone et al., 2002; Greve et al., 2007), as well as to the performance of uninjured persons known to be feigning impairment (simulation design) or identified by the presence of multiple PVTs in the context of external incentive as probable malingerers (Slick, Sherman, & Iverson, 1999). If the examinee's performance falls below the performance of a majority of clinical patients, and resembles the performance more commonly seen in persons feigning impairment or engaging in probable malingering, it is identified as being an invalid performance. This is very different from standard normative procedures in which the examinee's performance is ranked relative to healthy controls. In other words, patterns of performance that typically occur in non-injured persons feigning impairment (simulation research design), or in persons identified as probable malingerers ("known groups" or criterion groups research design), but which rarely occur in patients with actual psychological or neuropsychological impairment secondary to *bona fide* neurologic, psychiatric, or developmental disorders are identified as invalid performance patterns.

Invalid performance can be evaluated using different cut scores across clinical samples and simulators. For each indicator, cut scores can be derived for each measure identifying atypical performance (e.g., base rates of 10%, 5%, and 2%) relative to a large clinical sample. Using multiple validity indicators and requiring at least two scores to be identified as atypical (e.g., at or below the specified clinical cut-off) maximizes sensitivity and specificity for identifying response bias (Larrabee, 2003; Victor, Boone, Serpa, Buehler, & Ziegler, 2009) and improving diagnostic accuracy (Larrabee, 2008; Victor et al., 2009). Certainly, a single score in the atypical range does not necessarily indicate invalid performance. However, if the examinee's performance is grossly atypical (e.g., demonstrating multiple positive invalid performance indicators, or performance that is significantly worse than chance on a two-alternative forced choice test), would indicate that the level of cognitive impairment being expressed is significantly different from the degree of cognitive impairment observed in the vast majority of patients.

It is essential to appreciate that most members of clinical populations perform adequately on performance validity measures. For example, patients with memory impairment due to substance abuse (Arnett & Franzen, 1997), low functioning psychiatric patients (Gierok, Dickson, & Cole, 2005), and patients suffering from depression and anxiety (Ashendorf, Constantinou, & McCaffrey, 2004) do not show atypical performance on PVTs. Similarly, patients with severe brain injury perform adequately on some performance validity measures (Macciocchi, Seel, Alderson, & Godsall, 2006). Patients with dementia or intellectual disability, particularly those requiring a supervised living setting, will often score below cut-offs for suspecting invalid performance. Obviously, caution must be used when interpreting atypically low scores in these populations because they may be "false positive" scores that are not indicative of invalid performance (Milanovich, Axelrod, & Millis, 1996).

As evaluation of invalid test performance occurs within the context of high stakes assessments, it is important to minimize false positives (i.e., identifying invalid performance when it is not present). In forensic assessment with substantial external incentive, multiple PVT failure might lead to a diagnosis of malingering. Consequently, the impact of an incorrect conclusion of malingering, when in fact performance is reflecting actual impaired ability, is obvious. PVTs associated with low false positive rates are desirable.

It is possible that embedded PVTs could be influenced by low intellectual ability or low education level. For example, studies using Reliable Digit Span (RDS) identify a cut-off of less than or equal to seven points as sensitive to response bias in toxic exposure cases (Greve et al., 2007), traumatic brain injury (Mathias, Greve, Bianchini, Houston, & Crouch, 2002), and pain-related disorders (Etherton, Bianchini, Greve, & Heinly, 2005b). A cut-off of RDS less than or equal to seven also has a relatively high false positive rate (Babikian, Boone, Lu, & Arnold, 2006), particularly in individuals with low educational attainment and among ethnic minorities (Echemendia & Holdnack, 2007). These findings highlight the need to compare an examinee's performance on validity measures to those of individual's with similar backgrounds.

Two-alternative forced-choice tests are commonly used as measures of performance validity. For these tests, it is possible to compute a theoretical guess rate (i.e., the probable range of random responding) and to document the performance of a "no stimulus" sample. A no stimulus sample is a group of examinees that responds to the test items without hearing or seeing the test stimuli (e.g., not hearing stories to be recalled or seeing designs to copy: Flowers, Bolton, & Brindle, 2008). Flowers et al. (2008) found that individuals simulating cognitive impairment performed more poorly than examinees in the no stimulus condition. Although a single atypical result is not necessarily indicative of a globally invalid test performance, having multiple scores that are consistent with guessing, or with the performance of individuals who never saw or heard the test stimuli, has a high probability of being associated with an invalid response to psychological or neuropsychological assessment.

DEVELOPMENT OF ACS EXTERNAL AND EMBEDDED PERFORMANCE VALIDITY INDICATORS

The ACS Suboptimal Effort measures (hereafter referred to as performance validity measures) were developed based on methods previously validated in clinical research. Additionally, the ACS performance validity measures were designed to take advantage of the co-norming of the WAIS–IV/WMS–IV and ACS. Throughout the development of the WAIS–IV/WMS–IV and ACS, different types of external validity measures were developed and tested. In each research phase, pilot, tryout, and standardization, a sample of individuals simulating impairment completed each battery of tests. These studies were completed to identify the best external and embedded validity measures. Early versions of the external validity measure used either visual stimuli or numbers and letters. These versions were not effective in identifying simulated brain injury and response bias. Finally, a forced choice word memory test was shown to be effective at identifying simulators from patients suffering moderate to severe traumatic brain injury (TBI). The ACS offers five performance validity measures for examinees aged 16–69; one external and four embedded.

External Performance Validity Measure: Word Choice

The Word Choice test is the external validity measure developed specifically to assess performance validity, not memory. On this test, the examinee is shown and read 50 words in succession. To focus the examinee's attention on the words during the presentation of the Learning Items, the examinee is asked to identify each word as either synthetic or occurring in nature. During the Test Items, the examinee is shown a card with 50 pairs of words and asked to select the word that was previously presented from each pair.

The average theoretical guess rate for the Word Choice test is 50%. A no stimulus group was collected as part of the ACS Suboptimal Effort standardization and validation. This group was presented with the card with 50 word pairs, and they were asked to identify the stimulus word that they had never seen. This group simulated random responding or pure guessing. The no stimulus group scores ranged from 42% to 68% accuracy (i.e., raw scores ranging from 21−34/50) with the middle 50% of scores being between 48% and 56%. Even guessing can yield scores above the average theoretical guess rate of 50%. The probable range of random responding on this 50-item test is 20−30 (representing the 90% confidence interval of random responding according to the binomial distribution).

Embedded Performance Validity Indicators

The embedded performance validity measures in the ACS are derived from the WAIS−IV and WMS−IV subtests. The tests were designed to measure specific cognitive skills: working memory and recognition memory. The WAIS−IV measure is Reliable Digit Span (RDS) and the three WMS−IV measures are Logical Memory II Recognition (LMR), Verbal Paired Associates II Recognition (VPAR), and Visual Reproduction II Recognition (VRR). Cognitively impaired individuals perform poorly on these measures when compared to the normative sample. However, they are able to achieve some points on these measures. In addition, there is sufficient range in performance among patients to identify atypical performance. The measures from the WMS−IV have known guess rates and are relatively easy to perform. The WAIS−IV Reliable Digit Span was selected because it has a long-history of use as a measure of response bias and there is significant research support for this application (Babikian et al., 2006; Etherton, Bianchini, Ciota, & Greve, 2005a; Etherton et al., 2005b; Greiffenstein, Baker, & Gola, 1994; Greve et al., 2007; Mathias et al., 2002; Meyers & Volbrecht, 1998; Shum, O'Gorman, & Alpar, 2004).

The theoretical average guess rate for LMR, VPAR, and VRR is 50%, 50%, and 17%, respectively. The no stimulus group completed each of the measures as part of the ACS Suboptimal Effort validation. The no stimulus group accuracy on LMR ranged from 33% to 70% with the middle 50% of subjects scoring from 47% to 57% correct. The accuracy scores ranged from 35% to 65% correct for VPAR and 0% to 43% for VRR. The middle 50% had accuracy scores of 43% to 50% on VPAR and 0−17% on VRR. Scores in this range are consistent with random responding.

Identifying Cut-offs for Atypical Performance

The no stimulus group and theoretical random responding guess rates provide some information about atypical performance. However, most instances of invalid performance will not yield scores that are random. In order to improve the sensitivity of the response bias measures, cut-off scores based on the performance of individuals with varying degrees of cognitive impairment were derived. The cut-off scores were derived utilizing the large mixed clinical sample (i.e., overall clinical sample) that was collected as part of the WAIS–IV/WMS–IV/ACS standardization and validation. The overall clinical sample ($n = 371$) was composed of individuals identified with the following neurological, psychiatric, or developmental disorders: moderate to severe TBI, right and left temporal lobectomy, schizophrenia, major depressive disorder, anxiety disorder, intellectual disability-mild severity (ID-Mild), autistic disorder, Asperger's disorder, reading disorder, mathematics disorder, and attention-deficit/hyperactivity disorder. The frequency distribution of scores in the overall clinical sample was evaluated for each of the validity measures. The raw score associated with the 25%, 15%, 10%, 5%, and 2% base rates were identified for each measure. These raw scores are used as cut-offs for identifying atypical performance. For a single measure the base rate is equivalent to the presumed false positive rate in the overall clinical sample. In other words, when using a cut-off of 25% of the clinical sample, 25% of patients will be considered to have an atypical performance that could indicate response bias. However, none of the patients in this sample were litigating or had any obvious benefit from doing poorly on the tests. Therefore, in other words, these 25% would be probable false positives.

One of the primary benefits of the ACS performance validity measures is that there is more than one response bias indicator and the clinician can use up to five while only administering one additional test, the Word Choice Test (i.e., assuming the full WMS–IV and core WAIS–IV are administered). As discussed in Chapter 2, when multiple tests are given the probability of achieving at least one low score is increased. When multivariate base rates are applied, it is possible to identify atypical performance. That is, we can identify how many low scores in a cognitive profile occur before that is considered unusual. One low score, when multiple measures are applied, will have a false positive rate that is greater than the base rate when only that single test is used (e.g., at the 10% base rate more than 10% of examinees will have a low score when multiple tests are used). Therefore, the multivariate base rate for using all five measures was determined in order to accurately assess the false positive rate, and to define an atypical performance pattern when multiple measures are used.

Applying Multivariate Base Rates

The multivariate base rates for the validity indicators are important for assessing the validity of WAIS–IV/WMS–IV test performance. The base rates of low scores at various cut-offs were derived for the overall clinical sample and for individual clinical groups of interest. Deriving base rates for specific clinical conditions (e.g., moderate to severe TBI) can give the clinician an estimate of the presumed false positive rate for a group that is comparable to the patient they are evaluating. Additionally, the individual clinical groups and other groups of interest (e.g., simulators) evaluate how well the cut-off scores identify atypical responding rather than actual cognitive impairment. The actual cut-off scores are presented in the ACS technical manual, for reasons of test security they are not presented here. Tables 7.1–7.5 present base rates of scores below five different cut-off scores for various clinical groups and for the WMS–IV normative sample.

As seen in Table 7.1, if the clinician selects the 15% cut-off then the base rates of certain samples having low scores can be looked up. For example, 22% of the total clinical sample, 36% of the TBI sample, and 11% of the normative sample will have one or more scores in this range. However, only 7% of the total clinical sample, 9% of the TBI sample, and 1% of the normative sample will have two or more scores in this range. In fact, having two scores below the 15% cut-off is uncommon in all clinical groups with the exception of those with mild intellectual disability. The no stimulus group had most scores at or below the 15% base rate. For the no stimulus group, random responding frequently yields four scores at or below the 15% cut-off. Over 1/3rd of the individuals simulating cognitive impairment had two or more scores at or below the 15% cut-off, four times as many as the TBI group.

Table 7.2 presents the same results using a more restrictive cut-off of 10% of the overall clinical sample. For example, 19% of the total clinical sample, 30% of the TBI sample, and 7% of the normative sample will have one or more scores in this range. However, only 5% of the total clinical sample, 6% of the TBI sample, and 1% of the normative sample will have two or more scores in this range. In fact, having two scores below the 10% cut-off is uncommon in all clinical groups with the exception of those with mild intellectual disability.

Some clinicians might feel uncomfortable using the 25% cut-off because they believe it is too liberal and it might be prone to higher rates of false positives (see Table 7.3). This concern represents a misunderstanding of multivariate base rates. Without question, it is common to have one score below this cut-off. Having three scores, however, below the 25% cut-off is very uncommon in clinical samples and in the normative sample. This pattern occurs in a small number of people

TABLE 7.1   Percentages of Cases in Groups of Interest Having Various Numbers of Scores At or Below the 25% Cut-off

Group of Interest	Number of Scores at or below the 25% Base Rate				
	1	2	3	4	5
No Stimulus	100	100	100	92	–
Simulators	76	58	38	24	16
Overall Clinical Sample	38	19	6	3	1
Traumatic Brain Injury	48	18	3	0	0
Temporal Lobectomy	29	25	4	0	0
Schizophrenia	71	31	7	2	0
Major Depressive Disorder	34	12	2	0	0
Anxiety Disorder	8	3	0	0	–
Intellectual Disability-Mild	91	88	47	31	13
Autistic Disorder	55	14	9	0	0
Asperger's Syndrome	20	6	0	0	0
Reading Disorder	27	0	0	0	0
Math Disorder	36	5	0	0	0
ADHD	12	9	0	0	0
WMS–IV Normative Sample	23	7	2	0	0
≤8 Years Education	63	27	7	0	0
9–11 Years Education	42	13	5	1	0
12 Years Education	27	9	3	0	0
13–15 Years Education	19	5	2	0	0
≥16 Years Education	9	2	0	0	0
General Ability Index: 69 or Less	81	38	13	0	0
General Ability Index: 70–84	52	25	10	2	0
General Ability Index: 85–99	28	8	2	0	0
General Ability Index: 100–114	13	1	0	0	0
General Ability Index: 115 or Greater	4	0	0	0	0

Copyright 2009 by Pearson, Inc. Reproduced with permission. All rights reserved.

TABLE 7.2   Percentages of Cases in Groups of Interest Having Various Numbers of Scores At or Below the 15% Cut-off

Group of Interest	Number of Scores at or below the 15% Base Rate				
	1	2	3	4	5
No Stimulus	100	100	96	72	–
Simulators	70	36	22	12	8
Overall Clinical Sample	22	7	2	0	0
Traumatic Brain Injury	36	9	0	0	0
Temporal Lobectomy	21	4	0	0	0
Schizophrenia	35	9	2	0	0
Major Depressive Disorder	16	2	0	0	0
Intellectual Disability-Mild	72	41	22	9	0
Autistic Disorder	27	9	5	0	0
Asperger's Syndrome	11	6	0	0	0
Reading Disorder	7	0	0	0	0
Math Disorder	18	0	0	0	0
ADHD	9	3	0	0	0
WMS–IV Normative Sample	11	1	0	0	0
≤8 Years Education	34	2	0	0	0
9–11 Years Education	23	5	1	1	0
12 Years Education	13	1	0	0	0
13–15 Years Education	8	1	0	0	0
≥16 Years Education	5	0	0	0	0
General Ability Index: 69 or Less	44	13	0	0	0
General Ability Index: 70–84	29	4	1	1	0
General Ability Index: 85–99	12	1	0	0	0
General Ability Index: 100–114	7	1	0	0	0
General Ability Index: 115 or Greater	0	0	0	0	0

Copyright 2009 by Pearson, Inc. Reproduced with permission. All rights reserved.

TABLE 7.3 Percentages of Cases in Groups of Interest Having Various Numbers of Scores At or Below the 10% Cut-off

	Number of Scores at or below the 10% Base Rate				
Group of Interest	1	2	3	4	5
No Stimulus	100	100	96	60	—
Simulators	64	36	20	10	8
Overall Clinical Sample	19	5	1	0	0
Traumatic Brain Injury	30	6	0	0	0
Temporal Lobectomy	17	0	0	0	0
Schizophrenia	35	7	0	0	0
Major Depressive Disorder	12	2	0	0	0
Intellectual Disability-Mild	63	31	16	6	0
Autistic Disorder	27	9	0	0	0
Asperger's Syndrome	9	3	0	0	0
Reading Disorder	7	0	0	0	0
Math Disorder	14	0	0	0	0
ADHD	9	3	0	0	0
WMS–IV Normative Sample	7	1	0	0	0
≤8 Years Education	27	2	0	0	0
9–11 Years Education	17	4	1	1	0
12 Years Education	5	0	0	0	0
13–15 Years Education	5	1	0	0	0
≥16 Years Education	4	0	0	0	0
General Ability Index: 69 or Less	38	6	0	0	0
General Ability Index: 70–84	19	2	1	1	0
General Ability Index: 85–99	7	1	0	0	0
General Ability Index: 100–114	4	0	0	0	0
General Ability Index: 115 or Greater	0	0	0	0	0

Copyright 2009 by Pearson, Inc. Reproduced with permission. All rights reserved.

TABLE 7.4 Percentages of Cases in Groups of Interest Having Various Numbers of Scores At or Below the 5% Cut-off

Group of Interest	Number of Scores at or below the 5% Base Rate				
	1	2	3	4	5
No Stimulus	100	100	88	38	—
Simulators	40	24	14	10	2
Overall Clinical Sample	9	2	0	0	0
Traumatic Brain Injury	9	3	0	0	0
Temporal Lobectomy	8	0	0	0	0
Schizophrenia	15	2	0	0	0
Major Depressive Disorder	4	0	0	0	0
Intellectual Disability-Mild	38	13	3	3	0
Autistic Disorder	23	5	0	0	0
Asperger's Syndrome	3	0	0	0	0
Reading Disorder	0	0	0	0	0
Math Disorder	14	0	0	0	0
ADHD	6	3	0	0	0
WMS–IV Normative Sample	2	0	0	0	0
≤8 Years Education	15	2	0	0	0
9–11 Years Education	9	1	0	0	0
12 Years Education	2	0	0	0	0
13–15 Years Education	1	0	0	0	0
≥16 Years Education	1	0	0	0	0
General Ability Index: 69 or Less	19	6	0	0	0
General Ability Index: 70–84	7	1	0	0	0
General Ability Index: 85–99	2	0	0	0	0
General Ability Index: 100–114	1	0	0	0	0
General Ability Index: 115 or Greater	0	0	0	0	0

Copyright 2009 by Pearson, Inc. Reproduced with permission. All rights reserved.

TABLE 7.5   Percentages of Cases in Groups of Interest Having Various Numbers of Scores At or Below the 2% Cut-off

Group of Interest	Number of Scores at or below the 2% Base Rate				
	1	2	3	4	5
No Stimulus	100	92	50	8	–
Simulators	22	18	8	4	0
Overall Clinical Sample	4	0	0	0	0
Traumatic Brain Injury	6	0	0	0	0
Temporal Lobectomy	0	0	0	0	0
Schizophrenia	4	0	0	0	0
Major Depressive Disorder	1	0	0	0	0
Intellectual Disability-Mild	31	3	3	0	0
Autistic Disorder	14	0	0	0	0
Asperger's Syndrome	0	0	0	0	0
Reading Disorder	0	0	0	0	0
Math Disorder	0	0	0	0	0
ADHD	0	0	0	0	0
WMS–IV Normative Sample	1	0	0	0	0
≤8 Years Education	7	0	0	0	0
9–11 Years Education	4	0	0	0	0
12 Years Education	1	0	0	0	0
13–15 Years Education	0	0	0	0	0
≥16 Years Education	0	0	0	0	0
General Ability Index: 69 or Less	19	0	0	0	0
General Ability Index: 70–84	2	0	0	0	0
General Ability Index: 85–99	1	0	0	0	0
General Ability Index: 100–114	0	0	0	0	0
General Ability Index: 115 or Greater	0	0	0	0	0

Copyright 2009 by Pearson, Inc. Reproduced with permission. All rights reserved.

with low intellectual functioning (e.g., 10% of adults with General Ability Index scores between 70 and 84), and a substantial number of people with mild intellectual disability. However, the vast majority of clinical patients should not show this pattern.

The tables reproduced here are available as part of the ACS technical manual. These tables identify the cut-offs that are considered atypical for most clinical patients. Clearly, having two or more scores at the 15% or 10% cut-off, or three or more scores at the 25% cut-off, is an unusual finding for most clinical groups with the exception of intellectually disabled individuals.

Tables 7.1 through 7.5 can be used with an *a priori* criterion for interpreting a performance pattern as possibly or probably invalid. That is, a clinician might say that if my university educated client who sustained a very mild TBI 2 years ago obtains a single score at or below the 15th percentile, then it is *possible* this reflects invalid performance (base rates = 11% in the WMS−IV normative sample, 5% in healthy adults with university degrees, 0% in healthy adults with above average intelligence, 22% in the overall clinical sample, and 36% in the moderate-severe TBI sample). If this client obtains two scores at or below the 10% cut-off, then it is *probable* that this reflects invalid performance (base rates = 1% in the WMS−IV normative sample, 0% in healthy adults with university degrees, 0% in healthy adults with above average intelligence, 5% in the overall clinical sample, and 6% in the moderate-severe TBI sample).

In the ACS Technical Manual, Tables 3.7 through 3.11 (see Tables 7.1−7.5 in this chapter as examples) provide data on how the five ACS PVTs perform based on the various subject groups, and the number of test scores exceeding various cut-offs for performance of the combined clinical group, ranging from 2% to 25%. A widely used cut-off for individual PVTs and SVTs in the literature is one defining a 10% false positive rate (Boone, 2007; Larrabee, 2007). The results for the 10% false positive rate are depicted in Table 7.1. Note that as the number of scores exceeding the cut-off increases, there is a corresponding decrease in the percentage of clinical subjects that are identified. Thus, for one PVT exceeding the 10% cut-off, 19% of clinical cases are (mis-) identified (false positives), whereas for two PVTs exceeding this cut-off, this value drops to 5%. At three PVTs exceeding the 10% cut-off, the false positive rate drops to 1%, and at four tests, the rate drops to zero. The decrease in false positive rate associated with increased number of failed PVTs is a reliable finding in the malingering research literature (Larrabee, 2008; Victor et al., 2009), and supports recommendations for relying upon multiple PVT and SVT failure in the diagnosis of malingering (Slick et al., 1999).

INTERPRETATION

There are multiple techniques that can be applied to the performance validity measures. All the approaches used to detect possible invalid performance are based on probabilities. There is no procedure that can identify invalid performance absolutely, with the possible exception of significantly worse than chance performance on forced choice testing, which has been characterized as the "smoking gun of intent" by Pankratz (1988). The purpose of performance validity measures is to provide an estimation, or likelihood, that a particular assessment has atypical findings that might be attributed to invalid performance. Conceptually, low scores on cognitive tests are expected in cases of specific psychiatric, developmental, neurological, or acquired conditions. However, in many of these disorders, the degree of impairment relative to the normative standard is not exceptionally large. For many measures, the average difference in performance between individuals who are cognitively compromised and healthy controls is approximately one standard deviation ($\pm 0.5\,\text{SD}$) unless the disorder is associated with dementia or intellectual disability. Therefore, scores that are more than three standard deviations below the mean are the exception among clinical populations rather than the rule. The difficulty for the clinician is to know what level of performance represents the actual level of cognitive impairment versus an exaggeration of cognitive impairment.

Standard Interpretation of ACS Invalid Performance Scores

The ACS Clinical and Interpretative Manual and suboptimal effort software report provide the clinician with base rate data that is used to help interpret whether invalid performance may be present. The base rates are designed to be used when all five measures are administered. To maximize objectivity, it is recommended that the examiner select specific criteria (e.g., three scores at or below 15% or two scores at or below 10%) for identifying invalid performance prior to the evaluation. Setting the criteria *a priori* reduces the likelihood of obtaining a false negative or false positive finding. One author reviewed a recent case in which the psychologist evaluated a client with a remote mild TBI and noted three scores at or below the 10% cut-off but no scores at the 2% cut-off, so he chose to interpret the 2% cut-off and state that there was no clear concern about response validity. This, clearly, is an inappropriate use of the base rates.

Setting Performance Validity Criteria

The criterion used should be based on two factors: the sensitivity to identifying invalid performance and the false positive rate. Tables 3.7–3.11

in the ACS Clinical and Interpretative Manual provide data for identifying sensitivity and specificity. For example, Table 3.10 in the ACS Clinical and Interpretative Manual or Table 7.2 in this chapter provides data for estimating the sensitivity and specificity at the 15% clinical base rate. The sensitivity is established by the percentage of simulators scoring at or below the 15% criterion for 1−5 validity measures (i.e., 70, 36, 22, 12, and 8, respectively). One positive indicator at the 15% base rate will identify 70% of individuals simulating cognitive impairment. Two indicators will identify 36% of the simulators and three indicators will identify only 22% of the simulators. Therefore, it is important to appreciate that the performance validity indicators do not have high sensitivity for detecting biased responding in the simulating sample collected as part of the ACS validation. More research is needed to study the sensitivity of the ACS validity indicators in other samples.

The presumed false positive rate is established by evaluating the overall clinical sample at the 15% base rate for 1−5 positive indicators (i.e., 22, 7, 2, 0, and 0, respectively). The false positive rate for one validity indicator at the 15% base rate is 22%. Ideally, the false positive rate should be low, such as 10% or less, because the emotional and financial cost of misattributing real cognitive impairment as exaggerated cognitive impairment can be quite high for a patient and their family, and for the importance of a low false positive rate to overall diagnostic accuracy, on a statistical basis.

Examiners may choose to select a specific criterion such as two scores at the 10% base rate, or they can establish multiple criteria. Selecting *a priori* criteria can help reduce *post hoc* biases when interpreting the data. For example, the examiner could set an *a priori* criterion that either two scores at the 10% base rate or three scores at the 15% base rate suggest

TABLE 7.6 Example of ACS Suboptimal Effort Score Report, Valid Performance

Effort Score Summary

Score	Overall Clinical Sample Base Rates					
	≤2%	≤5%	≤10%	≤15%	≤25%	>25%
Word Choice	−	−	−	−	−	X
LM II Recognition	−	−	−	X	X	−
VPA II Recognition	−	−	−	X	X	−
VR II Recognition	−	−	−	−	−	X
Reliable Digit Span	−	−	−	−	−	X
Totals	0	0	0	2	2	−

that the evaluation may have been influenced by response bias. Invalid performance is interpreted as being present when the examinee's performance on suboptimal effort measures equals or exceeds the criteria set by the examiner.

Table 7.6 presents information provided by the ACS Suboptimal Effort score report for an examinee. The first portion of the table shows the examinee's performance on the five validity indicators. The Word Choice, Visual Reproduction II Recognition, and Reliable Digit Span were all within the expected range for the clinical sample (e.g., the 6th column of base rates indicates scores that occur in greater than 25% of the clinical sample). On two of the measures, LM II Recognition and VPA II Recognition, the examinee had scores that were at or below certain cut-offs. Both were identified as unusual at the 15 and 25% base rate. For this case, if the examiner had adopted the *a priori* criterion stated above, then the examiner might choose to interpret the performance validity tests as suspicious, but not invalid, because the scores did not meet *a priori* criterion (i.e., three scores at the 15% cut-off or two scores at the 10% cut-off). Depending on the overall evaluation results, however, two scores at the 15% cut-off might be evidence of invalid responding because this pattern has a low false positive rate in healthy adults and in clinical samples (see Table 7.2).

Table 7.7 illustrates a case that shows the criteria met for two scores at the 10% base rate and three scores at the 15% base rate. Portions of Table 7.1 are also printed in the ACS Suboptimal Effort (invalid performance) Report. Table 7.8 displays the base rates for various groups of interest related to this example presented in Table 7.7. The table shows that only 5% of the overall clinical sample and 6% of moderate to severe

TABLE 7.7   Example of ACS Suboptimal Effort Score Report, Possible Invalid Performance

Effort Score Summary

Score	Overall Clinical Sample Base Rates					
	≤2%	≤5%	≤10%	≤15%	≤25%	>25%
Word Choice	–	–	X	X	X	–
LM II Recognition	–	–	–	X	X	–
VPA II Recognition	–	–	–	–	X	–
VR II Recognition	–	–	–	–	–	X
Reliable Digit Span	–	–	X	X	X	–
Totals	0	0	2	3	4	–

TABLE 7.8 Example of ACS Suboptimal Effort Score Report, Clinical and Background Comparisons

Effort Score Analysis

Group of Interest	Percentages With Matching Number of Scores at Cut-off				
	Number of Scores at 10% Cut-off				
	1	2	3	4	5
No Stimulus	100	100	96	60	—
Simulators	64	36	20	10	8
Overall Clinical Sample	19	5	1	0	0
Traumatic Brain Injury	30	6	0	0	0
Major Depressive Disorder	12	2	0	0	0
Normative Sample: Education Level	6	0	0	0	0
Normative Sample: Race/Ethnicity	4	1	0	0	0
Normative Sample: GAI	19	2	1	1	0

Copyright 2009 by Pearson, Inc. Reproduced with permission. All rights reserved.

TBI cases have two scores at the 10% base rate criterion. The false positive rate is very low for individuals in those groups making it unlikely the examinee's performance is a false positive for invalid performance. Similarly, individuals diagnosed with Major Depressive Disorder and individuals of similar background and intellectual ability also rarely meet this criterion. Therefore, co-morbid psychiatric symptoms, level of intelligence, education, and ethnicity are not contributing factors to this profile.

Advanced Interpretation Using Likelihood Ratios and Logistic Regression

Likelihood Ratios

Every diagnostic test has a sensitivity (the conditional probability of a positive test, given the presence of the disorder) and a specificity (the conditional probability of a negative test, given the absence of the disorder of interest). However, the question that clinicians encounter is the inverse *"Given a positive test result, what is the probability that the patient has the disorder?"* This conditional probability is not equivalent to the conditional probability posed by the test's sensitivity. In order to understand the meaning of a positive test result without knowing the patient's actual disorder status, one first starts with the test's likelihood ratio (LR), which is a single summary statistic based on a test's sensitivity and specificity (Straus, Richardson, Glasziou, & Haynes, 2005):

$$LR = Sensitivity/(1 - Specificity)$$

The LR tells us how many times more (or less) likely individuals with the disorder are to have a positive test result than individuals without the disorder. A likelihood ratio greater than one indicates that the test result is associated with the presence of the disorder of interest. The likelihood ratio is then multiplied by the pre-test odds (i.e., base rate odds) to obtain the post-test odds and converted algebraically back to a probability that answers the question *"Given a positive test result or score, what is the probability that the patient has the disorder?"*

- As an example, let's say that a clinician, in reviewing previous medical records and interviewing a hypothetical patient, makes an assessment that the patient has a probability of 30% of having Disorder X. There is still considerable uncertainty about the patient's disorder status. Accordingly, the clinician will conduct additional testing, but first, converts this estimated base rate probability of 30% to pre-test odds:

  $$Odds = probability/(1 - probability) = 0.30/(1 - 0.30) = 0.43$$

- Let's say that the clinician will then give a test that has a likelihood ratio of 8. We then multiply the pre-test odds with the LR to obtain the post-test odds:

  $$Post\text{-}test\ Odds = (0.43) \times (8) = 3.44$$

- We convert the post-test odds to a post-test probability:

  $$Probability = Odds/(1 + odds) = 3.44/(1 + 3.44) = 0.77,\ or\ 77\%$$

Hence, we estimate that, given this positive test score, this hypothetical patient has a probability of 77% of having Disorder X. The positive test result "moved" our initial base rate estimate of 30% to 77%. The diagnostic uncertainty has been substantially reduced following the use of our hypothetical test. Nonetheless, this is an extremely simplistic example. Many tests may not have LRs this large (i.e., sensitivity = 0.80 and specificity = 0.90). In addition, it is rare that a clinician will use a single test in diagnostic decision-making. It is more realistic that several tests will be used. We now turn our attention to methods of combining several diagnostic tests or indices.

Naïve Bayes

Perhaps the simplest way to combine test results is to use the first test's posterior probability (i.e., the probability obtained in three above) for the next test's prior probability (updated base rate used in one above). Next, use that in combination with the second test's likelihood ratio to obtain its posterior probability, and so on. This method of combined multiple test results has been called Naïve Bayes estimation (Steyerberg, 2009). Although this method's simplicity is appealing, it is problematic that Naïve Bayes estimation does not take the test inter-correlations into consideration. Consequently, the effects of the tests' predictions are overestimated, which produce predictions that are too high or too low (Steyerberg, 2009). Yet, other investigators have found good performance with Naïve Bayes estimation for group discrimination (Spiegelhalter, 1986), particularly if the variables utilized are weakly correlated (Larrabee, 2008).

Tables 3.2 to 3.11 in the ACS Technical Manual provide information on the ACS performance validity tests that can be utilized in Naïve Bayes estimation. These tables show the percentages of various subject groups, including simulators, a "no stimulus group", and various clinical patient groups, achieving various scores on the five tests comprising the ACS Performance Validity Tests (PVTs). One can compute LRs by comparing the percent of the simulating group achieving a particular score (i.e., the sensitivity of the PVT at that score) by the percent of the clinical groups achieving the same score (i.e., the false positive rate at that score, referred to earlier as one minus specificity). For example, in Table 3.2, a score of 43 on ACS Word Choice occurs in 54% (interpolated) of simulators, but only 10% of the Overall Clinical Sample. This yields a LR of 5.4 which, multiplied by the base rate odds of 0.43 from our previous example, yields a post-test odds of 2.322 or a post-test probability of biased responding of 0.70. Moreover, these post-test odds could be chained in combination with the likelihood ratio of a PVT or SVT independent of the ACS PVTs, such as the MMPI-2-RF Response Bias Scale (RBS). Assume the person producing a score of 43 on Word Choice also produces an RBS of 100. This RBS score is associated with a sensitivity of 0.24 and specificity of 0.98 (Wygant et al., 2010), resulting in a likelihood ratio of 0.24/0.02 or 12.0. The value of 12.0 can be multiplied by the post-test odds for the ACS Word Choice test determined above to be 2.322 to yield new post-test odds of 27.864, converting to a post-test probability of 0.965.

Although scores from the five different ACS PVT measures can also be chained using Naïve Bayes estimation, logistic regression equations exist that both take into account test score inter-correlations, as well as optimally weight the various test scores for saliency in relation to the criterion. These are described further below.

Discriminant Function Analysis

Discriminant Function Analysis (DFA) has been used extensively in the past to derive optimal combinations of variables to differentiate groups because of its computational simplicity. However, DFA assumes that the predictors (i.e., tests included in the model) are each normally distributed and the set of predictors has a multivariate normal distribution along with homogeneous variance-covariance matrices (Harrell, 2001). These are strong statistical assumptions that are rarely met in clinical research and with performance validity measures in particular. In addition, there is no consensus regarding whether one should use the discriminant weights (standardized coefficients) or discriminant loadings (structure correlations) when interpreting the DFA model. Finally, DFA has no inferential tests for the individual predictors to determine which are statistically reliable in differentiating the groups.

Logistic Regression

Logistic regression is another approach to derive multivariable composites to differentiate two or more groups. It does not have the restrictive statistical assumptions of DFA. Logistic regression offers many advantages over other statistical methods in this context. Interpretation of the relative importance of individual predictors is straightforward in logistic regression. The logistic regression function can also be used to calculate the probability that an individual belongs to one of the groups in the following manner. Analogous to ordinary least squares (OLS) multiple regression for continuous dependent variables, coefficients are derived for each predictor variable (or covariate) in logistic regression. Rather than using OLS to fit the model and derive the coefficients, logistic regression uses the method of maximum likelihood to iteratively fit the model. Once a model is derived, a linear composite known as the logit (also known as the logged odds or linear predictor) is calculated by multiplying each predictor variable's raw score by its respective coefficient (e.g., $b1 \times 1 + b2 \times 2$) and a constant is added. The logit is exponentiated in the following manner to yield the probability that an individual belongs to one of two groups, based on the raw scores entered into this formula, where e is the mathematical constant e and is the base of the natural logarithm. Its value to the sixth decimal digit is $e = 2.718281$:

$$probability = \frac{e^{\alpha + \beta 1x1 + \beta 2x2}}{1 + e^{\alpha + \beta 1x1 + \beta 2x2}}$$

Given the advantages of logistic regression over other methods, we now turn our attention to its application to the ACS performance validity subtests. Miller et al. (2011) evaluated the capacity of the ACS subtests to distinguish poor performance due to intentional response bias among simulators from poor performance due to actual traumatic brain injury. Participants were 45 survivors of moderate to severe TBI and 39 healthy adults coached to simulate TBI. Two logistic regression models were fitted: a five-subtest model containing Visual Reproduction II Recognition, Logical Memory II Recognition, Verbal Paired Associates II Recognition, Word Choice Test (WCT), and Reliable Digit Span; and a single subtest model containing only WCT. Both models were statistically reliable and had excellent discrimination in differentiating the TBI group from the simulator group: the Area Under the Curve (AUC) was 0.95 for the five-variable model and 0.84 for the WCT model.

However, these logistic regression formulas need external validation. In other words, to determine the extent to which the predicted values from these formulas accurately predict responses, research with participants not used to develop the original formulas is needed. To that end, we applied the two logistic regression formulas from Miller et al. (2011) to two subgroups from the WMS–IV standardization sample: a moderate-severe traumatic brain injury group (TBI: $n = 28$) and a simulator group ($n = 49$). For each participant, a linear predicted score was calculated using the coefficients from the original study. For example, for the five-subtest model:

$$\text{Linear predicted score} = [10.61 - (0.65 \times \text{RDS}) - (0.23 \times \text{WCT})$$
$$- (0.007 \times \text{LMR}) + (0.24 \times \text{VPAR}) - (0.95 \times (\text{VRR})].$$

This was also done with the WCT model for each participant. Next, the linear predicted scores were exponentiated for each participant, as shown in Formula 1, to produce the probability of group membership; in this case, the probability of invalid performance or poor effort.

ROC curve analysis was then performed on the new predicted probability scores to determine how well the original logistic regression formulas fared in this external validation. As expected, we observed some shrinkage in our estimates of discrimination. AUC for the WCT formula still acceptable (AUC = 0.73) (Hosmer & Lemeshow, 2000) and excellent for the five-subtest model (AUC = 0.87). Based on the Bayesian Information criterion (BIC) and Akaike Information criterion (AIC), there was very strong evidence of support for the five-subtest model over the WCT model (Hardin & Hilbe, 2012), with BIC and AIC discrepancies of more than 20 in favor of the multivariable model.

This pattern of findings provides additional support for the ACS performance validity subtests, particularly for the five-subtest model. Its performance in this external validation study is notable, given the small and unbalanced cross validation sample. Further, as we discussed above, logistic regression offers the advantage over Naïve Bayes estimation, in that variable inter-correlation is accounted for, as well as providing differential weighting of predictors as to their salience. In this regard, note how LMR has a very small B weight, 0.007, in comparison to VRR, at 0.95. In the Miller et al. (2011) paper, this is understood as a function of a very small effect size in association with LMR, $d = 0.21$ in contrast with $d = 1.81$ for VRR, in the comparison of feigned versus *bona fide* test performance.

Applying Response Bias Results

The ACS PVT procedures can be used for evaluation of invalid test performance. Invalid performance can be present for a variety of reasons including unintentional psychological reasons and intentional malingering. The ACS Suboptimal Effort (performance validity) measures can be used as evidence to support the results of the assessment *"were invalid, inconsistent with the injury, or indicative of exaggeration"* (Slick et al., 2004). Slick, Sherman and Iverson (1999) proposed specific criteria for identification of suspected malingerers. They propose three levels of diagnostic certainty for identifying malingering: definite, probable, and possible. The three criteria proposed for definite malingering of neurocognitive deficit are:

Criterion 1:   Presence of a substantial external incentive
Criterion 2:   Definite negative response bias, and
Criterion 3:   The response bias is not accounted for by psychiatric, neurological, or developmental factors.

The first criterion is established by the context of the evaluation (e.g., high stakes disability, medical-legal, or forensic evaluations). Criterion two can be established by significantly worse than chance performance on the ACS Word Choice Test. Alternatively, both Boone (2007) and Larrabee et al. (2007) have argued that failure of three PVTs at a false positive rate of 10% per test is associated with essentially zero false positives and can support a diagnosis of definite non-credible performance/malingering. The third criterion is identified by comparing the examinee's level of performance to individuals with various psychiatric, developmental, and neurological conditions. The ACS Suboptimal Effort score report automatically provides information about the performance of other clinical groups on these measures. Therefore, the criteria for probable malingering posited by Slick et al. that two or more PVTs are failed, in the context of external incentive with no evidence to support that failure was due to actual neurologic, psychiatric, or developmental problems, can be examined using the ACS score report.

The *a priori* cut-off established by the clinician provides an indication that invalid performance is present. Further investigation of the obtained scores is necessary to identify probable malingering. The ACS samples include individuals with intellectual disability, malingering simulators, and a no-stimulus group. These special groups provide the examiner with comparison groups which represent the extremes of performance. After the examiner establishes that a response bias is present (i.e., using an *a priori* criterion), he or she can further explore if the number of measures at other cut-offs are unusual for examinees with intellectual disability and consistent with simulators or random responding (i.e., no stimulus condition). Table 7.9 presents an example of ACS data strongly indicative of invalid test performance. In this example, the examinee clearly meets criterion of two or more scores at the 10% cut-off and also meets criteria for two scores at the 2% base rate. Table 7.10 presents base rate data for intellectual disability, simulators, and no-stimulus groups. The examinee's five scores at the 10% cut-off are obtained by less than 1% of individuals with intellectual disability or TBI and only 8% of simulators. The three scores at the 5% base rate and two scores at the 2% base rate are unusual for all clinical samples (see Tables 7.4 and 7.5) and are most consistent with random responding. As seen in Table 7.10, 0% of the TBI sample obtained so many low validity scores and only 2−3% of those with mild intellectual disability showed this pattern.

Case Studies

CASE STUDY 1

Mr. J. is a 43-year-old, married white man, with 13 years of education. He was injured at work when he fell 10 feet off a ladder onto the concrete floor. Mr. J. was repairing electrical wiring when he was accidently shocked which caused the accident. He struck his head and suffered a mild uncomplicated TBI. He also experienced a fractured forearm. Mr. J. has been out of work for the past six months and is

TABLE 7.9 Example of ACS Suboptimal Effort Score Report Showing Negative Response Bias

			Effort Score Summary			
			Overall Clinical Sample Base Rates			
Score	≤2%	≤5%	≤10%	≤15%	≤25%	>25%
Word Choice	−	X	X	X	X	−
LM II Recognition	X	X	X	X	X	−
VPA II Recognition	−	−	X	X	X	−
VR II Recognition	−	−	X	X	X	−
Reliable Digit Span	X	X	X	X	X	−
Totals	2	3	5	5	5	−

TABLE 7.10 Example of ACS Suboptimal Effort Score Report Clinical Base Rates

	Effort Score Analysis				
	Percentages With Matching Number of Cut Scores at Cut-off				
Number of Scores at 2% Cut-off					
Group of Interest	1	2	3	4	5
No Stimulus	100	92	50	8	–
Simulators	22	18	8	4	0
Intellectual Disability	31	3	3	0	0
Traumatic Brain Injury	6	0	0	0	0
Number of Scores at 5% Cut-off					
No Stimulus	100	100	88	38	–
Simulators	40	24	14	10	2
Intellectual Disability	38	13	3	3	0
Traumatic Brain Injury	9	3	0	0	0
Number of Scores at 10% Cut-off					
No Stimulus	100	100	96	60	–
Simulators	64	36	20	10	8
Intellectual Disability	63	31	16	6	0
Traumatic Brain Injury	30	6	0	0	0

Copyright 2009 by Pearson, Inc. Reproduced with permission. All rights reserved.

applying for long-term disability. He reports headaches, dizziness, memory loss, and difficulty concentrating. Mr. J. also reports chronic pain in his back, and pain in his elbow and shoulder. As part of the disability evaluation, the WAIS–IV/WMS–IV and ACS performance validity measures were administered.

The WAIS–IV/WMS–IV results for Mr. J. are presented in Table 7.11. On the WAIS–IV, he obtained three primary index scores below the 10th percentile (PRI, WMI, and PSI). On the WMS–IV, four primary index scores were at or below the 5th percentile (Auditory Memory, Visual Memory, Immediate Memory, and Delayed Memory).

The examiner administered the ACS Suboptimal Effort (performance validity) measures as part of the evaluation. The *a priori* criteria of two scores at the 10% base rate or three scores at the 15% base rate were applied. The results of the ACS Suboptimal Effort measures are presented in Table 7.12. Mr. J. performed at the 10% base rate on the Word Choice

TABLE 7.11 Mr. J.'s WAIS–IV/WMS–IV Results

WAIS–IV Scores			WMS–IV Scores		
WAIS–IV Index	Index/Scaled Score	%ile	WMS–IV Index	Index/Scaled Score	%ile
Verbal Comprehension	99	45	Auditory Memory	75	5
Perceptual Reasoning	79	8	Visual Memory	74	4
Working Memory Index	80	9	Visual Working Memory	83	13
Processing Speed	68	2	Immediate Memory	70	2
Full-Scale IQ	79	8	Delayed Memory	72	3
WAIS–IV Subtests			**WMS–IV Subtest**		
Similarities	10	50	Logical Memory I	6	9
Vocabulary	9	37	Logical Memory II	6	9
Information	10	50	Verbal Paired Associates I	6	9
Block Design	5	5	Verbal Paired Associates II	5	5
Matrix Reasoning	8	25	Designs I	5	5
Visual Puzzles	6	9	Designs II	7	16
Digit Span	9	37	Visual Reproduction I	5	5
Arithmetic	4	2	Visual Reproduction II	6	9
Symbol Search	4	2	Spatial Addition	7	16
Coding	4	2	Symbol Span	7	16

and VPA II Recognition measures. The examiner compared these results to individuals with TBI and similar backgrounds (see Table 7.13). Only 6% of individual's suffering moderate to severe TBI had two scores at the 10% base rate. Individuals of similar education and intellectual ability (GAI) rarely achieve two scores at the 10% base rate (i.e., 1% of cases).

Based on the overall results, the examiner concluded that Mr. J.'s evaluation was affected by invalid test performance. Applying the logistic regression equation for these scores (Miller et al., 2011) yields a 0.17 probability for the full five subtest model and 0.54 for the Word Choice only model. The likelihood that Mr. J. belongs to the simulator sample is quite low for the full model and about 50% for the single variable. The degree of memory, perceptual reasoning, and processing speed deficits appears inconsistent with the severity of the injury. Consequently,

TABLE 7.12   Mr. J.'s ACS Suboptimal Effort Summary

Effort Score Summary

Overall Clinical Sample Base Rates

Score	≤2%	≤5%	≤10%	≤15%	≤25%	>25%
Word Choice	–	–	X	X	X	–
LM II Recognition	–	–	–	–	–	X
VPA II Recognition	–	–	X	X	X	–
VR II Recognition	–	–	–	–	–	X
Reliable Digit Span	–	–	–	–	–	X
Totals	0	0	2	2	2	–

TABLE 7.13   Base Rate of Low Scores in Groups of Interest

Effort Score Analysis

	Percentages With Matching Number of Cut Scores at Cut-off				
	Number of Scores at 10% Cut-off				
Group of Interest	1	2	3	4	5
No Stimulus	100	100	96	60	–
Simulators	64	36	20	10	8
Overall Clinical Sample	19	5	1	0	0
Traumatic Brain Injury	30	6	0	0	0
WMS–IV Normative Sample	7	1	0	0	0
Education Level	5	1	0	0	0
Race/Ethnicity	4	1	0	0	0
GAI	7	1	0	0	0

poor performances are more likely the result of invalid test performance than they are of actual impaired abilities. Moreover, normal range scores are themselves likely underestimates of the actual level of ability.

CASE STUDY 2

Ms. T. is a 24-year-old, white woman, who completed 16 years of education. She was employed as a district wide sales representative for a large manufacturing company. Ms. T. was involved in a motor vehicle accident while on company business. According to medical records, she sustained a mild concussion and there were no signs of significant injury on her CAT scan. She was released from the hospital on the same day as the accident. Following her accident, Ms. T. began to experience anxiety about driving and reported symptoms of headache, neck pain, and poor concentration to her family physician. She reported having difficulty working due to pain and cognitive symptoms. She used all of her sick and vacation time. Ms. T. requested to be placed on disability until her symptoms subsided.

A neuropsychological evaluation was completed as part of her application for disability. Table 7.14 presents the results of Ms. T.'s WAIS–IV/WMS–IV. Her overall intellectual functioning (FSIQ) was in the low average range. She had average verbal and processing speed

TABLE 7.14 Ms. T.'s WAIS–IV/WMS–IV Results

	WAIS–IV Scores			WMS–IV Scores	
WAIS–IV Index	Index/Scaled Score	%ile	WMS–IV Index	Index/ Scaled Score	%ile
Verbal Comprehension	91	27	Auditory Memory	88	21
Perceptual Reasoning	84	14	Visual Memory	73	4
Working Memory Index	80	9	Visual Working Memory	70	2
Processing Speed	94	34	Immediate Memory	83	13
Full-Scale IQ	84	14	Delayed Memory	72	3
WAIS–IV Subtests			**WMS–IV Subtest**		
Similarities	5	5	Logical Memory I	7	16
Vocabulary	10	50	Logical Memory II	6	9
Information	10	50	Verbal Paired Associates I	10	50
Block Design	7	16	Verbal Paired Associates II	9	37
Matrix Reasoning	8	25	Designs I	5	5
Visual Puzzles	7	16	Designs II	5	5
Digit Span	4	2	Visual Reproduction I	8	25
Arithmetic	9	37	Visual Reproduction II	4	2
Symbol Search	7	16	Spatial Addition	5	5
Coding	11	63	Symbol Span	5	5

TABLE 7.15 Ms. T.'s ACS Suboptimal Effort Scores

| | Effort Score Summary | | | | | |
| | Overall Clinical Sample Base Rates | | | | | |
Score	≤2%	≤5%	≤10%	≤15%	≤25%	>25%
Word Choice	–	X	X	X	X	–
LM II Recognition	–	–	–	X	X	–
VPA II Recognition	–	–	X	X	X	–
VR II Recognition	–	X	X	X	X	–
Reliable Digit Span	–	–	–	–	X	–
Totals	0	2	3	4	5	–

scores and low average perceptual reasoning and working memory. WAIS–IV subtest performance ranged from borderline (Digit Span: SS = 4) to average (Coding: SS = 11). The WMS–IV results indicated unusually low delayed memory, visual memory, and visual working memory indexes.

The ACS performance validity measures were administered as part of this evaluation. The results of these tests are displayed in Table 7.15. She met *a priori* criteria for two scores at 10% and three scores at 15%. Further review of her scores indicated that four scores at the 15% base rate are very unusual for all clinical groups, including those with intellectual disability (see Table 7.16). Application of the Miller et al. (2011) logistic regression equations indicated a 0.99 probability of belonging to the simulator group based on the full five test model and 0.95 probability for the Word Choice model.

The level of performance on the WAIS–IV/WMS–IV appeared inconsistent with the severity of the sustained injury, particularly for an individual with 16 years of education. The ACS Suboptimal Effort (performance validity) scores strongly indicated that Ms. T.'s test performance was invalid. Based on interviewing and these test results, the clinician suspected malingering of neurocognitive deficits.

SUMMARY

Evaluating the validity of a test performance is an important aspect of psychological and neuropsychological assessments. Invalid test performance can create a mismatch between the severity of an examinee's injury or illness and the level of cognitive impairment observed on neuropsychological tests. A variety of methods have been developed

TABLE 7.16 Base Rates for Groups of Interest for Ms. T.'s Suboptimal Effort Performance

	Effort Score Analysis				
	Percentages With Matching Number of Cut Scores at Cut-off				
	Number of Scores at 15% Cut-off				
Group of Interest	1	2	3	4	5
No Stimulus	100	100	96	92	–
Simulators	70	36	22	12	8
Overall Clinical Sample	22	7	2	0	0
Traumatic Brain Injury	36	9	0	0	0
Intellectual Disability – Mild Severity	72	41	22	6	0

for identifying invalid performance on neuropsychological tests. These methods include: inconsistency in performance between or within measures, unexpectedly low performance on very simple tasks, and performance on tests that is well below typical performance of cognitively impaired patients.

The ACS Suboptimal Effort (performance validity) measures use an external test (Word Choice) and multiple embedded scores (e.g., from tests within the WAIS–IV/WMS–IV) to identify unexpectedly low performance. Cut-off scores are derived for each measure based on the performance of a large clinical sample that includes cases with significant cognitive impairment. Performing well below the overall clinical sample (e.g., worse that 90% of all clinical cases) suggests that the examinee's performance is atypical. Multiple atypical scores strongly suggest that the evaluation has been affected by invalid performance. In other words, the examinee is trying to appear more cognitively impaired than they actually are. A high number of atypical scores may indicate intentional feigning of cognitive symptoms or malingering neurocognitive deficits, if these results occur in the context of a significant external incentive (e.g., personal injury litigation or criminal prosecution).

KEY LEARNING

- *Response bias* occurs when an individual approaches a test, questionnaire, rating-scale, or survey attempting to create a specific impression that could be overly positive or negative.

- Response bias in neuropsychological testing has been referred to as suboptimal effort because the examinee did not put forth adequate effort to accurately assess his or her current cognitive functioning. More recently, the terms invalid performance, performance validity, and performance validity test (PVT) have been suggested as more descriptive of negative response bias than the term effort (Larrabee, 2012).
- Invalid test performance can be intentional, as in malingering neurocognitive deficits, or unintentional as in a person needing to appear sick or impaired for psychological reasons.
- The ACS Suboptimal Effort (performance validity) assessment used one external and four embedded measures to identify atypical performance. These measures include the Word Choice test, the WAIS−IV Reliable Digit Span score, and the Verbal Paired Associates Delayed Recognition, Logical Memory Delayed Recognition, and Visual Reproduction Delayed Recognition tests from the WMS−IV.
- Identification of atypical performance on the ACS Suboptimal Effort measures is based on a large clinical sample that includes individuals with significant cognitive impairment. Cut-off scores were derived for each measure identifying the 25%, 15%, 10%, 5%, and 2% clinical base rate (i.e., false positive rate).
- Multivariate base rate analysis indicates that having three or more scores at the 15% clinical base rate or two or more scores at the 10% clinical base rate yields a false positive rate well below 10%. That is, having this level of performance is more typical of individuals simulating cognitive impairment than individuals with actual cognitive impairment.
- Sophisticated techniques such as calculating likelihood ratios and using logistic regression equations can improve the identification of invalid test performance.
- The ACS performance validity tests cannot be used to draw the inference that a person gave his or her "best" or "optimal" effort. They were not designed to measure effort or motivation in that sense. Rather, they were designed to detect unusually low and atypical scores suggestive of invalid performance.
- The ACS Suboptimal Effort (performance validity) measures include comparison to important clinical groups and other groups of special interest. These groups enable the clinician the ability to rule out atypical performance due to background factors such as low education level, or atypical performance due to low intellectual ability, psychiatric problems, or a developmental disorder.

- The ACS Suboptimal Effort (performance validity) measures can be used to provide evidence for identification of malingered neurocognitive deficits.

References

Arnett, P. A., & Franzen, M. D. (1997). Performance of substance abusers with memory deficits on measures of malingering. *Archives of Clinical Neuropsychology, 12*(5), 513−518.

Ashendorf, L., Constantinou, M., & McCaffrey, R. J. (2004). The effect of depression and anxiety on the TOMM in community-dwelling older adults. *Archives of Clinical Neuropsychology, 19*(1), 125−130.

Babikian, T., Boone, K. B., Lu, P., & Arnold, G. (2006). Sensitivity and specificity of various digit span scores in the detection of suspect effort. *The Clinical Neuropsychologist, 20*(1), 145−159.

Ben-Porath, Y. S. (2012). Addressing challenges to MMPI-2-RF-based testimony: Questions and answers. *Archives of Clinical Neuropsychology, 27*(7), 691−705.

Boone, K. B. (Ed.), (2007). *Assessment of feigned cognitive impairment: A neuropsychological perspective.* New York: The Guilford Press.

Boone, K. B. (2009). The need for continuous and comprehensive sampling of effort/response bias during neuropsychological examinations. *The Clinical Neuropsychologist, 23*(4), 729−741.

Boone, K. B., Lu, P., Back, C., King, C., Lee, A., Philpott, L., et al. (2002). Sensitivity and specificity of the Rey Dot Counting Test in patients with suspect effort and various clinical samples. *Archives of Clinical Neuropsychology, 17*(7), 625−642.

Bush, S. S., Ruff, R. M., Troster, A. I., Barth, J. T., Koffler, S. P., Pliskin, N. H., et al. (2005). Symptom validity assessment: Practice issues and medical necessity NAN policy & planning committee. *Archives of Clinical Neuropsychology, 20*(4), 419−426.

Echemendia, R. J., & Holdnack, J. A. (2007). *The use of reliable digit span cut scores with ethnic minorities.* Paper presented at the thirty-fifth annual meeting of the international neuro-psychological society (February), Portland, OR.

Etherton, J. L., Bianchini, K. J., Ciota, M. A., & Greve, K. W. (2005a). Reliable digit span is unaffected by laboratory-induced pain: Implications for clinical use. *Assessment, 12*(1), 101−106.

Etherton, J. L., Bianchini, K. J., Greve, K. W., & Heinly, M. T. (2005b). Sensitivity and specificity of reliable digit span in malingered pain-related disability. *Assessment, 12*(2), 130−136.

Flowers, K. A., Bolton, C., & Brindle, N. (2008). Chance guessing in a forced-choice recognition task and the detection of malingering. *Neuropsychology, 22*(2), 273−277.

Gervais, R. O., Rohling, M. L., Green, P., & Ford, W. (2004). A comparison of WMT, CARB, and TOMM failure rates in non-head injury disability claimants. *Archives of Clinical Neuropsychology, 19*(4), 475−487.

Gierok, S. D., Dickson, A. L., & Cole, J. A. (2005). Performance of forensic and non-forensic adult psychiatric inpatients on the Test of Memory Malingering. *Archives of Clinical Neuropsychology, 20*(6), 755−760.

Greiffenstein, M. F., Baker, W. J., & Gola, T. (1994). Validation of malingered amnesia measures with a large clinical sample. *Psychological Assessment, 6*(3), 218−224.

Greve, K. W., Springer, S., Bianchini, K. J., Black, F. W., Heinly, M. T., Love, J. M., et al. (2007). Malingering in toxic exposure: Classification accuracy of reliable digit span and WAIS−III Digit Span scaled scores. *Assessment, 14*(1), 12−21.

Hardin, J. W., & Hilbe, J. M. (2012). *Generalized linear models and extensions* (3rd ed.). College Station, TX: StataCorp LP.

Harrell, F. E., Jr. (2001). *Regression modeling strategies: With applications to linear models, logistic regression, and survival analysis.* New York: Springer-Verlag.

Heilbronner, R. L., Sweet, J. J., Morgan, J. E., Larrabee, G. J., & Millis, S. R. (2009). American Academy of Clinical Neuropsychology consensus conference statement on the neuropsychological assessment of effort, response bias, and malingering. *The Clinical Neuropsychologist, 23*(7), 1093–1129.

Hosmer, D. W., & Lemeshow, S. (2000). *Applied logistic regression* (2nd ed.). New York: Wiley Interscience.

Iverson, G. L. (2003). Detecting malingering in civil forensic evaluations. In A. M. Horton, L. C. Hartlage (Eds.), *Handbook of forensic neuropsychology* (pp. 137–177). New York: Springer.

Iverson, G. L. (2010). Detecting exaggeration, poor effort, and malingering in neuropsychology. In A. M. Horton, Jr., & L. C. Hartlage (Eds.), *Handbook of forensic neuropsychology* (2nd ed., pp. 91–135). New York: Springer.

Langeluddecke, P. M., & Lucas, S. K. (2003). Quantitative measures of memory malingering on the Wechsler Memory Scale–Third edition in mild head injury litigants. *Archives of Clinical Neuropsychology, 18*(2), 181–197.

Larrabee, G. J. (2003). Detection of malingering using atypical performance patterns on standard neuropsychological tests. *The Clinical Neuropsychologist, 17*(3), 410–425.

Larrabee, G. J. (2008). Aggregation across multiple indicators improves the detection of malingering: Relationship to likelihood ratios. *The Clinical Neuropsychologist, 22*(4), 666–679.

Larrabee, G. J. (2012). Performance validity and symptom validity in neuropsychological assessment. *Journal of the International Neuropsychological Society, 18*(4), 625–630.

Larrabee, G. J. (Ed.), (2007). *Assessment of malingered neuropsychological deficits* New York: Oxford University Press.

Macciocchi, S. N., Seel, R. T., Alderson, A., & Godsall, R. (2006). Victoria Symptom Validity Test performance in acute severe traumatic brain injury: Implications for test interpretation. *Archives of Clinical Neuropsychology, 21*(5), 395–404.

Mathias, C. W., Greve, K. W., Bianchini, K. J., Houston, R. J., & Crouch, J. A. (2002). Detecting malingered neurocognitive dysfunction using the reliable digit span in traumatic brain injury. *Assessment, 9*(3), 301–308.

Meyers, J. E., & Volbrecht, M. (1998). Validation of reliable digits for detection of malingering. *Assessment, 5*(3), 303–307.

Meyers, J. E., & Volbrecht, M. E. (2003). A validation of multiple malingering detection methods in a large clinical sample. *Archives of Clinical Neuropsychology, 18*(3), 261–276.

Milanovich, J. R., Axelrod, B. N., & Millis, S. R. (1996). Validation of the simulation index— Revised with a mixed clinical population. *Archives of Clinical Neuropsychology, 11*(1), 53–59.

Miller, J. B., Millis, S. R., Rapport, L. J., Bashem, J. R., Hanks, R. A., & Axelrod, B. N. (2011). Detection of insufficient effort using the advanced clinical solutions for the Wechsler Memory Scale, 4th ed. *The Clinical Neuropsychologist, 25*(1), 160–172.

Mittenberg, W., Azrin, R. L., Millsaps, C., & Heilbronner, R. L. (1993). Identification of malingered head injury on the Wechsler Memory Scale-Revised. *Psychological Assessment, 5*(1), 34–40.

Mittenberg, W., Theroux-Fichera, S. T., Zielinski, R. E., & Heilbronner, R. L. (1995). Identification of malingered head injury on the Wechsler Adult Intelligence Scale-Revised. *Professional Psychology: Research and Practice, 26*(5), 491–498.

Mossman, D., Wygant, D. B., & Gervais, R. O. (2012). Estimating the accuracy of neurocognitive effort measures in the absence of a "gold standard". *Psychological Assessment, 24*(4), 815–822.

Pankratz, L. (1988). Malingering on intellectual and neuropsychologic measures. In R. Rogers (Ed.), *Clinical assessment of malingering and deception* (pp. 169–192). New York: Guilford.

Sharland, M. J., & Gfeller, J. D. (2007). A survey of neuropsychologists' beliefs and practices with respect to the assessment of effort. *Archives of Clinical Neuropsychology, 22*(2), 213–223.

Shum, D. H., O'Gorman, J. G., & Alpar, A. (2004). Effects of incentive and preparation time on performance and classification accuracy of standard and malingering-specific memory tests. *Archives of Clinical Neuropsychology, 19*(6), 817–823.

Slick, D., Sherman, E. M., & Iverson, G. L. (1999). Diagnostic criteria for malingered neurocognitive dysfunction: Proposed standards for clinical practice and research. *The Clinical Neuropsychologist, 13*(4), 545–561.

Slick, D., Tan, J. E., Strauss, E. H., & Hultsch, D. F. (2004). Detecting malingering: A survey of experts' practices. *Archives of Clinical Neuropsychology, 19*(4), 465–473.

Spiegelhalter, D. J. (1986). Probabilistic prediction in patient management and clinical trials. *Statistics in Medicine, 5*(5), 421–433.

Steyerberg, E. W. (2009). *Clinical prediction models: A practical approach to development, validation, and updating.* New York: Springer.

Straus, S., Richardson, W. S., Glasziou, P., & Haynes, R. B. (2005). Diagnosis and screening. In S. Straus, W. S. Richardson, P. Glasziou, & R. B. Haynes (Eds.), *Evidence-based medicine: How to practice and teach EBM* (3rd ed.). London: Elsevier.

Strauss, E., Slick, D. J., Levy-Bencheton, J., Hunter, M., MacDonald, S. W., & Hultsch, D. F. (2002). Intraindividual variability as an indicator of malingering in head injury. *Archives of Clinical Neuropsychology, 17*(5), 423–444.

Vickery, C. D., Berry, D. T., Inman, T. H., Harris, M. J., & Orey, S. A. (2001). Detection of inadequate effort on neuropsychological testing: A meta-analytic review of selected procedures. *Archives of Clinical Neuropsychology, 16*(1), 45–73.

Victor, T. L., Boone, K. B., Serpa, J. G., Buehler, J., & Ziegler, E. A. (2009). Interpreting the meaning of multiple symptom validity test failure. *The Clinical Neuropsychologist, 23*(2), 297–313.

Wechsler, D. (1997). Wechsler adult intelligence scale–third edition. San Antonio, TX: Psychological Corporation.

Wechsler, D. (2008). Wechsler adult intelligence scale–fourth edition. San Antonio, TX: Pearson.

Wechsler, D. (2009). *Wechsler memory scale–fourth edition.* San Antonio, TX: The Psychological Corporation.

Wygant, D. B., Sellbom, M., Gervais, R. O., Ben-Porath, Y. S., Stafford, K. P., & Freeman, D. B., et al. (2010). Further validation of the MMPI-2 and MMPI-2-RF Response Bias Scale: Findings from disability and criminal forensic settings. *Psychological Assessment, 22*(4), 745–756.

Assessing Social Cognition Using the ACS for WAIS–IV and WMS–IV

Yana Suchy [*] *and James A Holdnack* [†]

[*]University of Utah, Salt Lake City, Utah, USA [†]Pearson Assessment, San Antonio, Texas, USA

INTRODUCTION

Social Cognition (SC) is an umbrella term for cognitive and emotional processes and abilities involved in effective interaction with other members of one's social group. Although SC was originally studied primarily by social and cognitive psychologists, over the last few decades various aspects of SC have become central topics of research in cognitive and affective neurosciences. This research yielded a growing understanding of the neuroanatomic underpinnings of the components of SC, as well as a growing understanding of the prevalence of SC deficits among a variety of neurologic and neuropsychiatric populations. In some individuals, these deficits are sometimes masked by more prominent deficits in cognition, while in others they may mimic, or present as, cognitive dysfunction. Consequently, there is growing recognition that neuropsychological evaluations need to include assessments of SC.

Among the many processes that fall under the umbrella of SC are verbal and nonverbal communication, emotional memory and learning, emotion and affect regulation, incentive sensitivity, comprehension of other's and one's own emotions, and moral and ethical judgment. As can be gleaned from this list of SC components, there is some considerable overlap between SC and emotional processing (which, too, has

WAIS-IV, WMS-IV, and ACS.
DOI: http://dx.doi.org/10.1016/B978-0-12-386934-0.00008-0

© 2013 Elsevier Inc. All rights reserved.

gained increased visibility in clinical neuropsychology). However, it is important to note that this overlap is not perfect. In fact, many aspects of emotional processing are not necessarily "social" in nature. For example, individuals with autism exhibit deficits in processing of emotional stimuli, but at least some research suggests that these deficits are evident only for stimuli that have social relevance (South et al., 2008). Conversely, many aspects of SC are not necessarily "emotional." For example, "cognitive empathy" requires that one *cognitively understand*, but not necessarily *feel*, the predicaments of others. Needless to say, a thorough review of all the processes that fall under the SC umbrella is beyond the scope of this text. This chapter will focus on nonverbal communication, a subset of SC processes that are particularly relevant for a practicing neuropsychologist.

DOMAINS OF NONVERBAL COMMUNICATION

Nonverbal communication spans two primary domains: Paralinguistic and Situational. The *Paralinguistic* domain of nonverbal communication has both receptive and expressive modalities. It refers to nonverbal signals that have the capacity to communicate without the use of language, or that add information above and beyond what is explicitly stated verbally. This can occur via a variety of channels (e.g., prosody, gestures, posture, and facial expressions) (Borod, Bloom, Brickman, Nakhutina, & Curko, 2002). Paralinguistic communication can convey an emotional tone (e.g., sadness, happiness, disappointment), meaning (e.g., sarcasm communicates that the *opposite* of what is being explicitly stated is actually true), or grammatical concepts, which are sometimes referred to as "linguistic intonation" or "propositional prosody" (e.g., questions vs. statements).

Importantly, while some basic aspects of paralinguistic communication are learned, others appear to be innate. The learned forms of paralinguistic communication include the ability to understand or produce nonverbal signals that are specific to a particular culture or even a particular person, the ability to convey and comprehend grammatical concepts, and the ability to assign labels or meanings to various nonverbal expressions. The inherent aspects of paralinguistic communication refer to hardwired basic emotional expressions that are processed rapidly, sometimes even pre-consciously, and involve a variety of species-specific visual and auditory signals that are important to one's survival. Additionally, in response to such signals, all normal individuals automatically and without any conscious effort produce nonverbal vocal, postural, and facial expressions that can be helpful for the survival of other members of one's social group. For example, in response to a threatening stimulus, one automatically generates a fearful facial expression. This expression, in turn, is rapidly and automatically detected by other members of the group, serving as a warning of an approaching danger.

The *Situational* domain of nonverbal communication has only a receptive mode. It refers to one's ability to comprehend complex social situations that may involve an interaction among several people, between people and their environment, or between people and their social contexts. As such, Situational communication relies on a good grasp of social norms, the ability to detect discrepancies between expectations and reality, the ability to engage in perspective taking, and the ability to integrate multiple pieces of information. Additionally, comprehension of situations often requires good receptive paralinguistic skills, although these skills are not always necessary. For example, seeing a lethal car accident, hearing about a friend's terminal illness, or reading about a devastating earthquake, should evoke an empathic understanding of the emotional reactions likely experienced by the victims of these events, without necessarily requiring the ability to comprehend other people's facial expressions.

Understanding of complex situations can also be conceptualized as a person's capacity for either Emotional or Cognitive empathy. *Emotional* empathy refers to the capacity to intuitively *feel* what others are feeling. In contrast, *Cognitive* empathy refers to the ability to cognitively *understand* how others might be feeling. Dissociation between Emotional and Cognitive empathy occurs in both clinical (Dziobek et al., 2008; Rankin, Kramer, & Miller, 2005; Shamay-Tsoory, Aharon-Peretz, & Perry, 2009; Shamay-Tsoory, Tomer, Yaniv, & Aharon-Peretz, 2002) and healthy populations (Davis, Hull, Young, & Warren, 1987). Emotional empathy is thought to rely on one's implicit or unconscious mimicking of the affective displays of others (whether these displays are real or imagined), and as such is thought to rely at least in part on the Mirror Neuron System (MNS). In contrast, Cognitive empathy is thought to rely on the capacity for perspective taking also known as the "Theory of Mind" (ToM) (Premack & Woodruff, 1978).

NEUROANATOMIC UNDERPINNINGS

Paralinguistic Communication

Subcortical and Brainstem Networks

A substantial body of research supports the notion that rapid *detection* of affective displays of others (vocal, facial, and postural) is subserved by the amygdala (Adolphs, Damasio, & Tranel, 2002; Derntl et al., 2009; Hadjikhani & de Gelder, 2003). Although older research suggested that the amygdala plays a role in the detection of only *negatively* valenced expressions (Adolphs, Russell, & Tranel, 1999; Adolphs, Tranel, et al., 1999), newer studies have demonstrated that the amygdala plays a role in the detection of emotional expressions that are *positive* as well (Burgdorf & Panksepp, 2006; Hamann & Mao, 2002; Lee et al., 2004; Liberzon, Phan, Decker, & Taylor, 2003). In line with the notion that rapid detection of nonverbal signals from other members of one's social group is important for survival, research demonstrates that the amygdala becomes activated in response to emotional stimuli even when they are presented subliminally, without the person's conscious awareness (Diaz & McCarthy, 2007; Naccache et al., 2005; Ohman, 2002, 2005). For a more thorough review of this topic, see Suchy (2011, pp. 45–69).

In addition to the ability to automatically detect important social cues, we also have the ability to rapidly generate behavioral responses. Such automatic responses consist of facial, postural, and vocal signals and are clearly designed for rapid communication. As such, they are not a product of the relatively slow volitional motor system controlled by the frontal-basal ganglia circuitry, but rather emanate from various brainstem nuclei located in the mesencephalon, lower brainstem and the cerebellum. For a more thorough review of this topic, see Suchy (2011, pp. 70–93).

Cortical Networks

Beyond the rapid subcortical and brainstem processing, slower and more conscious processing takes place in cortical (or cortico-striatal) networks involving primarily the right hemisphere. In particular, damage to the right cerebral hemisphere is associated with deficits in both expression (Blonder et al., 2005; Wertz, Henschel, Auther, Ashford, & Kirshner, 1998) and comprehension (Ross, Thompson, & Yenkosky, 1997; Shapiro & Danly, 1985; Tompkins & Flowers, 1985) of prosody, as well as recognition (Bowers, Bauer, Coslett, & Heilman, 1985) and expression (Blonder et al., 2005; Montreys & Borod, 1998) of facial affect. Importantly, research suggests that such deficits are *not* secondary to other cognitive or perceptual impairments, because they appear to persist even after other relevant aspects of cognition, such as perceptual, attentional, and conceptual abilities, have been accounted for (Blonder et al., 1993; Blonder et al., 2005; Borod et al., 1998; Bowers, Coslett, Bauer, & Speedie, 1987; Orbelo, Grim, Talbott, & Ross, 2005).

Despite the clear dominance of the right hemisphere for paralinguistic processing in general, it is important to note that some components of prosody appear to rely on left-hemisphere resources. In particular, while the right hemisphere is dominant for the processing of pitch (Lattner, Meyer, & Friederici, 2005; Murayama, Kashiwagi,

Kashiwagi, & Mimura, 2004), other prosodic cues, such as emphasis (Pell, 1998) and tempo (Platel et al., 1997), are processed primarily by the left hemisphere. Additionally, it appears that the grammatical aspects of paralinguistic communication (i.e., propositional prosody), while overlapping with the networks for affective prosody (Barrett, Pike, & Paus, 2004), show a greater tendency toward bilateral involvement (Heilman, Bowers, Speedie, & Coslett, 1984). Consistent with these notions, several studies found *no* differences between patients with left and right hemisphere damage with respect to prosody production (Baum & Pell, 1999; Bradvik, Dravins, Holtas, & Rosen, 1991; Cancelliere & Kertesz, 1990; Ross, Thompson, & Yenkosky, 1997) or prosody comprehension (Van Lancker & Sidtis, 1992). Thus, while the patients with right hemisphere damage may make prosody errors due to poor processing of pitch, the patients with left hemisphere damage may make prosody errors due to poor understanding of timing (Van Lancker & Sidtis, 1992). Alternatively, it has been suggested that prosody production difficulties among patients with left hemisphere damage may be caused by a disconnection between the two hemispheres, which would preclude normal integration of the linguistic and paralinguistic components of speech (Ross & Monnot, 2008).

With respect to localization *within* the hemispheres, older conceptualizations proposed that *paralinguistic* processing is localized within the right hemisphere in an analogous fashion to the localization of *linguistic* processing within the left hemisphere (Ross, 1981, 1984; Ross, & Mesulam, 2000). In other words, while the expressive paralinguistic processing was presumed to be localized in the inferior lateral frontal cortex, the receptive processing was presumed to be localized within the posterior temporal lobe. However, newer research has challenged this conceptualization. In particular, although research has generally supported the notion of *expressive* paralinguistic communication being localized anteriorly, an overwhelming body of research has refuted the notion of *comprehension* being localized posteriorly. These literatures are briefly reviewed.

With respect to *expressive* abilities, lesions in the right basal ganglia and the right medial frontal lobe are associated with deficits in comprehending prosody (Cancelliere & Kertesz, 1990; Heilman, Leon, & Rosenbek, 2004; Karow, Marquardt, & Marshall, 2001). In addition, imitation of emotional expressions leads to activation in the right inferior frontal gyrus (Lee, Josephs, Dolan, & Critchley, 2006). With respect to *receptive* abilities, studies have localized facial and prosodic affect *recognition* to the orbitofrontal/frontal opercular and/or anterior cingulate cortex, primarily on the right (Blood, Zatorre, Bermudez, & Evans, 1999; Buchanan et al., 2000; Frey, Kostopoulos, & Petrides, 2000; Hornak et al., 2003), as well as the basal ganglia and/or the thalamus

(Breitenstein, Daum, & Ackermann, 1998; Cancelliere & Kertesz, 1990; Ross & Monnot, 2008; Weddell, 1994). Further, at least one study has shown that basal ganglia lesions are *necessary and sufficient* for a receptive impairment in paralinguistic processing (Karow et al., 2001). Although some studies of receptive paralinguistic communication have also implicated regions outside of the right frontal lobe, including the temporoparietal cortex, bilateral frontal poles, right frontoparietal operculum, right temporal operculum, and left frontal operculum (Adolphs et al., 2002; Ross & Monnot, 2008; Starkstein, Federoff, Price, & Leiguarda, 1994), such findings are less common. Lastly, it is important to note that some investigations have identified discrete networks for recognition of *specific* emotions, although this line of research is marked by many inconsistencies across studies and is beyond the scope of this chapter.

Situational Communication

As mentioned earlier, situational communication can be conceptualized as empathy. Empathy consists of at least two distinct and neuroanatomically dissociable (Shamay-Tsoory et al., 2009) components, emotional empathy and cognitive empathy.

Emotional Empathy

Emotional empathy refers to the capacity to feel what others feel. Interestingly, exposure to affective displays of others appears to trigger covert or overt mimicry, and it is presumably the neural feedback from this mimicry that helps us understand and relate to what others feel. Thus, it should not be surprising that simple exposure to affective displays of others is often sufficient for automatic generation of subjective empathic feelings (Wild, Erb, & Bartels, 2001).

Mimicry, which is thought to play a role in Emotional empathy (Varcin, Bailey, & Henry, 2010), has been shown to be subserved by a distributed network of supramodal neurons known as MNS (Pineda, Moore, Elfenbeinand, & Cox, 2009). This system becomes activated both by observation of actions of others and by performance of actions by self (Heyes, 2011). Additionally, the MNS is also involved in abstract intentions, social interactions, and shared emotional states (Borroni, Gorini, Riva, Bouchard, & Cerri, 2011; Liew, Han, & Aziz-Zadeh, 2011). Not surprisingly then, the MNS becomes activated not only by observation of another person's emotions, but also by simply just hearing or reading about scenarios involving others. In humans, the MNS network includes the inferior frontal gyrus and the somatosensory cortex. Importantly, the strength of activation in this network correlates with self-reported empathy (Carr, Iacoboni, Dubeau, Mazziotta, & Lenzi, 2003; Schulte-Ruether, Markowitsch, Fink, & Piefke, 2007), and the capacity for Emotional empathy appears to be abolished by lesions in the inferior frontal gyrus (Shamay-Tsoory et al., 2009).

Cognitive Empathy

In contrast to Emotional empathy, *Cognitive* empathy does not require that one feel how the other person feels. Rather, Cognitive empathy is a cognitive *understanding* of how another person might feel. The ability to arrive at such an understanding is thought to rely on the network that subserves the ToM. This network includes the medial prefrontal and medial orbitofrontal cortex, and, to a lesser degree, the anterior paracingulate cortex, superior temporal lobe, and temporal-parietal juncture (Carrington & Bailey, 2009; Gallagher & Frith, 2003). Although functional imaging research has shown activation in various components of this network in response to different empathy paradigms (Hooker, Verosky, Germine, Knight, & D'Esposito, 2010; Preston et al., 2007; Schulte-Ruether et al., 2007), the specific patterns of activation vary. However, at least one lesion study has shown that the medial orbitofrontal cortex is *necessary* for cognitive empathy to take place (Shamay-Tsoory et al., 2009).

COGNITIVE CORRELATES OF NONVERBAL COMMUNICATION

Given that ToM is related to both cognitive flexibility (Milders, Ietswaart, Crawford, & Currie, 2008) and empathy, it should not be surprising that empathy and cognitive flexibility are also correlated with each other (Shamay-Tsoory, Harari, Szepsenwol, & Levkovitz, 2009; Shamay-Tsoory, Tomer, Goldsher, Berger, & Aharon-Peretz, 2004). Additionally, it is well recognized that deficits in nonverbal communication are sometimes associated with weaknesses in visual–spatial (i.e., right-hemisphere) functions. For example, individuals with nonverbal learning disability are typically characterized both by affect recognition deficits (Dimitrovsky, Spector, & Levy-Shiff, 2000; Dimitrovsky, Spector, Levy-Shiff, & Vakil, 1998) and by visual–spatial deficits (Forrest, 2004; Worling, Humphries, & Tannock, 1999).

However, in at least some populations, deficits in nonverbal communication are associated with a much broader array of cognitive problems. For example, among patients with schizophrenia, poor affect recognition correlates not only with poor visual–spatial abilities, but also with poor performance on measures of executive functioning, vocabulary, and learning (Bozikas, Kosmidis, Anezoulaki, Giannakou, & Karavatos, 2004;

Sachs, Steger-Wuchse, Kryspin-Exner, Gur, & Katschnig, 2004; Whittaker, Deakin, & Tomenson, 2001). Such deficits are difficult to explain as reflecting a right-hemisphere dysfunction and have sometimes been explained as stemming from a low general intelligence (Bozikas et al., 2004; Whittaker et al., 2001). However, this interpretation has been questioned, as the association between affect recognition deficits and poor test performance on verbal measures has been observed even after intelligence and educational background have been accounted for (Suchy, Rau, Whittaker, Eastvold, & Strassberg, 2009).

One possible explanation for the apparent association between nonverbal communication and performance on some verbal measures is that some verbal tests employ visual stimuli. For example, reading comprehension tests sometimes require that patients select a scene that corresponds to a given statement. However, correct interpretation of such scenes assumes normal SC. In fact, at least one study found that nonverbal communication was related to performances on cognitive measures that contained emotionally significant content, but *not* to measures that were emotionally neutral (Suchy, Rau, et al., 2009). Alternately, facial features of emotion can be verbally labeled (e.g., corners of the mouth are up, eyes are open wide) and verbal strategies can be used to decipher expressions if sufficient time is allotted.

RATIONALE FOR ASSESSING SOCIAL COGNITION

There are a number of reasons why neuropsychological evaluations should include assessment of SC in general and nonverbal communication in particular. First, deficits in nonverbal communication are prone to cause misunderstandings, affecting patients' daily functioning across a variety of domains. Importantly, because nonverbal communication involves not only the ability to convey or receive information, but also the ability to experience and express empathy for others, it is critical for healthy interpersonal functioning at all levels, from successful interactions with teachers, colleagues, or supervisors to successful development and maintenance of intimate relationships.

Second, deficits in nonverbal communication may sometimes masquerade as problems in several different cognitive domains, most notably executive functioning, judgment, attention, or memory. Patients who do not appropriately notice nonverbal cues in their daily interactions with others are likely to misunderstand the contents of conversations or the thrust of situations around them. Consequently, they may fail to react appropriately (thus appearing to suffer from lapses in judgment or executive functioning) or may fail to encode relevant aspects of conversations (thus appearing to suffer from lapses in memory and attention). Additionally, as mentioned earlier, deficits in SC may inadvertently impact performance on cognitive measures that contain socially relevant visual stimuli (e.g., some tests of reading comprehension).

Third, research is beginning to suggest that some aspects of SC may be specifically impaired in certain populations. For example, there is growing evidence that patients with Huntington's chorea tend to be impaired specifically on processing disgust, but not other discrete emotions (Hayes, Stevenson, & Coltheart, 2007). This is thought to stem from the fact that processing disgust appears to rely more heavily on the basal ganglia than does processing of other emotions (Adolphs, 2002). In contrast, patients with Alzheimer's disease, whose basal ganglia structures are relatively spared, show relatively normal recognition of facial disgust, while exhibiting deficits in processing of other emotional expressions (Henry et al., 2008). Teasing apart, such relevant SC components and employment of assessment methods that would allow dissociation of these components might aid in differential diagnosis of various neurodegenerative and neurodevelopmental disorders.

Lastly, perhaps due to its reliance on complex neuroanatomic networks, SC in general, and nonverbal communication in particular, represent areas of impairment that are extremely common among many neurologic and neuropsychiatric populations typically seen by clinical neuropsychologists. These impairments can have many different etiologies: they can be present congenitally, may develop in the course of a neurodegenerative disorder, or may result from a brain injury. This section will review the most representative clinical populations that are characterized by such deficits.

CLINICAL POPULATIONS

Neurodevelopmental Disorders

Autism Spectrum Disorders (ASD) are often seen as the prototypical example of SC deficits. This is well warranted, given that ASD is characterized by deficits across an array of SC domains. Most relevant for this chapter, however, are the deficits in recognition of both facial and prosodic affect, as well as deficits in empathy (Hubbard & Trauner, 2007; Humphreys, Minshew, Leonard, & Behrmanna, 2007). These deficits begin to emerge by the age of 3 years, and cannot be explained by limitations in general intellectual functioning or perceptual deficits (Dawson, Webb, & McPartland, 2005). Interestingly, emotional empathy appears to be relatively spared as compared to cognitive empathy

(Dziobek et al., 2008). Research suggests that the various SC deficits in this population likely involve both abnormalities in the amygdala, and abnormalities in more distributed cortical networks that subsume the ToM network and the MNS (Bernier & Dawson, 2009; Pinkham, Hopfinger, Pelphrey, Piven, & Penn, 2008; Sugranyes, Kyriakopoulos, Corrigall, Taylor, & Frangou, 2011).

However, ASD is not the only neurodevelopmental disorder characterized by deficits in nonverbal communication. Deficits in recognition of facial or prosodic affect have also been identified among both children and adults with Down syndrome (Kasari, Freeman, & Hughes, 2001; Wishart, Cebula, Willis, & Pitcairn, 2007), individuals with fetal alcohol syndrome (Monnot, Lovallo, Nixon, & Ross, 2002), women and girls with Turner syndrome (Mazzola et al., 2006; Skuse, Morris & Dolan, 2005), and individuals with Attention Deficit/Hyperactivity Disorder (Boakes, Chapman, Houghton, & West, 2008; Da Fonseca, Seguier, Santos, Poinso, & Deruelle, 2009).

Neurodegenerative Disorders

From among various neurodegenerative disorders, Frontotemporal Lobar Degeneration (FTD) represents the best-known example of impaired SC. With respect to nonverbal communication, FTD individuals exhibit impairment in both facial and prosodic affect recognition, as well as in cognitive empathy (Fernandez-Duque & Black, 2005; Lough et al., 2006; Snowden et al., 2008). Although the frontal variant exhibits a greater severity of deficits, the temporal variant is also affected, with cognitive and emotional empathy being particularly problematic among patients with semantic dementia (Rankin Kramer & Miller, 2005).

In addition to FTD, other dementias, including Amyotrophic Lateral Sclerosis, and Alzheimer's, Huntington's, Parkinson's, and vascular dementias (Dujardin et al., 2004; Lavenu & Pasquier, 2004; Rankin, Baldwin, Pace-Savitsky, Kramer, & Miller, 2005; Snowden et al., 2008; Zimmerman, Eslinger, Simmons, & Barrett, 2007), are all characterized by varying degrees of receptive nonverbal communication deficits. Importantly, nonverbal communication deficits can begin to emerge early in some diseases, long predating the onset of dementia. This is the case primarily in Parkinson's disease (with deficits unrelated to the severity of motor symptoms) (Dujardin et al., 2004) and in Amyotrophic Lateral Sclerosis (particularly the bulbar variant) (Zimmerman et al., 2007). Lastly, as noted previously, some specificity with respect to individual emotions has been described, such that dementias involving the basal ganglia structures (i.e., Parkinson's and Huntington's) tend to have greater deficits in disgust (Snowden et al., 2008), whereas disgust tends to be relatively spared in individuals with Alzheimer's disease (Henry et al., 2008).

Acquired Brain Injury

As previously discussed, aside from amygdala lesions, lesions in the right hemisphere and in the right (and sometimes left) frontal lobe, including the basal ganglia, can lead to deficits in nonverbal communication. Such lesions are most commonly a result of cerebral-vascular accidents, traumatic brain injuries, tumors, or epilepsy surgeries. Additionally, lesions in the ventral frontal areas, which are commonly associated with traumatic brain injury, have also been associated with an array of deficits in SC, including poor facial affect recognition (Radice-Neumann, Zupan, Babbage, & Willer, 2007), and poor cognitive and emotional empathy (Shamay-Tsoory et al., 2004).

Seizure Disorder

Seizure disorder represents the most common cause of acquired amygdala damage, typically due to prolonged febrile seizures in childhood, that have been linked to amygdala gliosis (Gloor & Aggleton, 1992) and volume reduction by 10% to 30% (Cendes et al., 1993a,b). Additionally, individuals with intractable epilepsy may elect to undergo surgical intervention, which in some cases involves the removal of the amygdala. Consequently, some individuals with seizure disorder have deficits in nonverbal communication. Because the amygdala damage in seizure disorders is virtually always unilateral, these deficits are typically relatively mild.

Neuropsychiatric Disorders

Deficits in various aspects of SC are by definition present in a variety of neuropsychiatric disorders. For example, schizophrenia is characterized by deficits in both receptive and expressive paralinguistic communication, as well as deficits in empathy (Addington & Addington, 1998; Shamay-Tsoory, Shur, Harari, & Levkovitz, 2007). Similarly, mood disorders are often characterized by readily obvious deficits in affective expression, as well as less obvious deficits in facial affect recognition (Bozikas, Tonia, Fokas, Karavatos, & Kosmidis, 2006; Weniger, Lange, Rather, & Irle, 2004).

In addition to axis I disorders, personality disorders, are also characterized by weaknesses in SC. For example, it has been hypothesized that violent criminals are capable of committing heinous crimes in part due to impairment in empathy (Kirsch & Becker, 2007), as well as well-documented deficits in recognizing facial affect (Carr et al., 2003; Dolan & Fullam, 2006; Hastings, Tangney, & Stuewig, 2008; Kosson, Suchy, Mayer, & Libby, 2002; McCown, Johnson, & Austin, 1986, 1988; Suchy, Whittaker, Strassberg, & Eastvold, 2008). Interestingly, while many criminal offenders tend to have difficulty recognizing emotions that they are likely to encounter among their victims, in particular *fear* (Dolan & Fullam, 2006), they also appear to erroneously interpret other emotions, such as *anger* (Cadesky, Mota, & Schachar, 2000; Kosson et al., 2002; Matheson & Jahoda, 2005; Suchy, Whittaker, Strassberg, & Eastvold, 2009). This may explain their sometimes apparently unprovoked acts of violence.

Lastly, there is a considerable overlap between substance abuse, aggression, and antisocial personality disorder and/or psychopathy. Thus, it should not be surprising that individuals who abuse substances exhibit deficits in nonverbal communication that are similar to those seen in criminal populations (Foisy et al., 2005; Kornreich et al., 2001; Monnot et al., 2002; Monnot, Nixon, Lovallo, & Ross, 2001; Philippot et al., 1999; Uekermann, Daum, Schlebusch, & Trenckmann, 2005).

ACS MEASURES OF SOCIAL COGNITION

Overview

The Advanced Clinical Solutions for the WAIS–IV and WMS–IV (ACS) provides the examiner with a variety of tools for evaluating components of SC. The tests that comprise SC in the ACS are Social Perception, Faces, and Names.

The Social Perception test loosely draws upon prior advances in methods developed for the assessment of affective communication. These include the Florida Affect Battery (Bowers, Blonder, & Heilman, 1991), role playing assessments and interventions (Bellack, Brown, & Thomas-Lohrman, 2006), facial emotion tasks developed for neuroimaging research (Gur et al., 2002; Gur, Skolnick, & Gur, 1994), and social cognition screening measures within a larger battery of neuropsychological tests (Korkman, Kirk, & Kemp, 2007), to name a few. The Social Perception test was designed to be a screening tool. As such, it assesses multiple aspects of SC simultaneously in order to maximize sensitivity to any type of SC deficit, rather than aiming to be specific to discrete SC problems. In other words, the tasks within the Social Perception test are designed to assess integrated, rather than singular, functions. The Social

Perception test is the core measure of SC; the Faces and Names subtests are supplementary tests that provide additional information about face processing.

The Faces subtest was developed primarily as a memory test; however, face recognition was found to be sensitive to Asperger's Syndrome and Autism in a previous battery (Korkman et al., 2007) which is the reason for its inclusion in the broad umbrella of SC. Similarly, the Names subtest is designed as an associative learning task but it also requires face learning, incidental recall of emotional expressions, and the ability to link a name with a specific face. These are important aspects of social functioning not typically assessed in other emotion batteries.

The ACS tools are not designed as a comprehensive evaluation of all components of SC; rather, they are designed to screen for assessment of deficits in nonverbal comprehension and face processing. Specifically, the Social Perception test measures facial affect recognition, prosody recognition, and interactions between pairs of people. The Face Memory subtest assesses the examinee's facial discrimination and recognition abilities. The Memory for Names test, evaluates face memory, face–name associative memory, and face–semantic memory. Importantly, as a screening tool, the ACS tests were designed to maximize sensitivity to any deficits in nonverbal comprehension and face processing. As such, they assess multiple aspects of nonverbal communication and face processing simultaneously, rather than identifying very discrete problems with SC.

PRIMARY MEASURES OF SOCIAL COGNITION

Social Perception

As stated previously, the Social Perception test measures multiple aspects of SC. The test is divided into three conditions: affect naming, prosody–face expression matching, and prosody–pairs emotion matching. Professional models were used for most of the photographs in the Social Perception test. Multiple photographs were obtained for each expression for all of the models. Pearson staff reviewed all of the photographs initially in order to identify the best expressions for each of the models. All of the selected photographs were then rated for emotions expressed, intensity of expression, and believability of the expressed emotion. Approximately 30 raters were used in this initial evaluation of the potential test stimuli. Photographs with the highest degree of agreement among raters for expressed emotion and believability were selected for the pilot edition of the Social Perception test. Emotions of varying intensity were selected to increase the difficulty range of the test.

The prosody stimuli were obtained in a similar fashion. Professional voice actors were used to create the verbal emotional stimuli. More prosody items were obtained than were actually used in the pilot through final editions of the test. A professional recording studio was engaged to capture the stimuli. Pearson staff reviewed all items and the items that best represented the intended emotion were selected for the pilot edition.

The Social Perception test was evaluated in three development phases: pilot, tryout, and standardization. The pilot phase evaluated the functioning of items in a healthy sample. Initial reliability and item functioning estimates were used to refine the test. The tryout phase evaluated the Social Perception test in a large, nationally stratified sample. Additionally, clinical samples were collected to determine if the test was adequately sensitive in patients with expected deficits in SC, for example, Traumatic Brain Injury (TBI) or epilepsy. The standardization phase provided information for final item selection, normative data, clinical sensitivity, and concurrent validity. The Social Perception test was co-normed with the WAIS–IV, allowing the development of comparison scores between the WAIS–IV and the Social Perception test.

The Social Perception test yields four primary scores (a total score and one score for each of the three conditions), as well as three contrast scores. The primary scores include the Social Perception Total Scaled Score, Affect Naming Scaled Score, Prosody Scaled Score, and the Pairs Total Scaled Score. The contrast scores are WAIS–IV General Ability Index (GAI) versus Social Perception Total Contrast Scaled Score, WAIS–IV Verbal Comprehension Index (VCI) versus Social Perception Total Contrast Scaled Score, and WAIS–IV Perceptual Reasoning Index (PRI) versus Social Perception Total Contrast Scaled Score. These scores enable the clinician to identify general and specific deficits in social perception, and to rule out low cognitive ability as the source of low social perception scores.

Affect Naming

The Affect Naming condition of the Social Perception test measures basic recognition and naming of facial expression of emotions. Deficits on this measure could indicate problems with recognition of emotional expressions or with the ability to accurately name emotional expressions. A more general naming deficit (i.e., anomia or dysnomia) can produce low scores on this test, but can easily be ruled out by assessment of confrontation naming skills. Similarly, a severe deficit in face perception (i.e., anosognosia) can produce poor performance on this measure, but can be ruled out by assessment of face discrimination and face memory functions. Low scores on Affect Naming, in the absence of other significant cognitive impairments, signal problems in identification and labeling basic facial emotional expressions.

The Affect Naming task utilizes basic emotional expressions described by (Ekman, Friesen, and Tomkins,1971). These emotions are believed to be inherently present in all cultures throughout the world and include happy, sad, angry, fearful, disgusted, surprised, and neutral expressions. The patient is shown a page with six photographs of people expressing one of the seven emotions and a card with the names of the seven emotions listed. The patient then names (or points to the emotion name) the expression on each face.

There are 24 items in the Affect Naming section. The raw score is the total number of correct responses and is converted to a scaled score. Most of the items in the Affect Naming subtest were correctly identified by subjects in the normative sample; subsequently, the range of scores is somewhat constrained, and internal consistency reliabilities range from low to good (0.54–0.87) and range from moderate very high in clinical samples (0.71–0.97). The Affect Naming condition has a low correlation with WAIS–IV (0.19–0.26) and WMS–IV indexes (0.20–0.26), as well as with measures of Reading (0.30) and Oral Language (0.36) from the Wechsler Individual Achievement Test–Second Edition (WIAT–II: Pearson, 2001). These results indicate that performance on Affect Naming is not strongly influenced by other cognitive abilities.

Prosody

The Prosody condition of the Social Perception test assesses the examinee's ability to match auditory emotional statements with facial expressions of emotion. As noted for the Affect Naming condition, other cognitive or affective abilities can influence the Prosody score. For example, examinees who are unable to name basic emotions may be less likely to accurately match auditory emotional expressions with facial emotional expressions, especially if their Affect Naming deficit reflects difficulty discriminating among the various facial expressions (rather than difficulty attaching verbal labels to such expressions). Similarly, examinees with difficulties discriminating rhythm or pitch may have difficulties with prosody perception. In contrast, impaired language functioning may not necessarily result in impaired scores on the prosody section, as long as auditory and visual discrimination abilities are intact. Low scores on Prosody suggest deficits in the ability to match auditory expression of emotions with facial expressions of emotions. In the absence of any clear deficit in discrimination of facial expression of emotions, a more specific deficit in prosody identification can be inferred.

The Prosody score of the Social Perception test is comprised of items from the Prosody and Pairs sections. All items related to matching a photographic expression with an auditory expression of emotion are included in the Prosody score. In the Prosody section, the patient is shown a page of six people with facial expressions. The expressions include the seven emotions found in the Affect Naming section and two additional expressions, sarcasm and confusion. The auditory prosody emotions are happy, sad, angry, surprised, fearful, disgusted, neutral, and sarcastic. The facial expressions are the same as the auditory emotions, with the exception of confused, which is added as a distracter for sarcasm. The patient listens to a statement spoken in a tone of voice that expresses one of the eight emotions and selects a facial expression that best matches the prosody of what was said. The emotion can be congruent or incongruent to the meaning of the words and the sex of the speaker may or may not match the sex of the person with the matching facial expression. This forces the patient to focus on the emotions rather than linguistic content or features of the person.

As noted before, the Pairs condition also contributes to the total Prosody score. Across the Prosody and Pairs conditions, there are 24 items that require the patient to match prosody to a photograph showing an emotional expression. The total raw score ranges from 0 to 24 and is converted to an age adjusted scaled score. The internal consistencies range from low to moderate (0.64–0.79). In the clinical samples, the reliability is very good (0.81–0.94). The Prosody Scaled Score has low to moderate correlations with the WAIS–IV indexes (0.29–0.42). The moderate correlations are with GAI and FSIQ. Similarly, the Prosody scale score has low to moderate correlations with WMS–IV indexes (0.34–0.40), with Immediate Memory yielding the moderate correlation. Prosody correlates in the low to moderate range with WIAT–III academic achievement indexes (0.15–0.50), with the highest correlation being with the Listening Comprehension component of Oral Language (0.58). These results indicate that Prosody is relatively unrelated to most cognitive skills, with the possible exception of general cognitive ability, immediate memory, and aural comprehension. The meaning of these associations is not fully understood at this time. While it is possible that general cognition, immediate memory, and aural comprehension all contribute to performance on the Prosody test, it is equally possible that adequate prosody abilities are important for comprehension of spoken language, thereby contributing to how well one encodes information in short term memory, and how well one develops a solid fund of knowledge.

Pairs

The Pairs condition of the ACS Social Perception test assesses multiple aspects of social perception. This condition requires the examinee to identify the emotional relationship between two people. For example, the emotional tone can be anger and conflict where both parties are angry, or anger and fear where one person is attacking the other. Similarly, sadness can be met with either empathy or neutrality. The emotional exchange, as well as other social cues such as distance, gestures, and touching, provides additional information about the nature of the interaction. The patient must understand the prosody of the speaker, its relationship to the linguistic content of what was said, and what that information represents about the interaction between the two people. For example, if the spoken content is, "you're a jerk," but the tone of voice is happy and the recipient of the comment is expressing a positive emotion, then it can be inferred that the people are friendly with each other and the comment was made in jest. On the other hand, if the tone of voice is angry and the recipient also has an angry expression, then the interaction would be considered more aggressive and confrontational. Therefore, the Pairs section requires the patient to integrate and consider multiple sources of information, and the interpretive and integrative demands are greater than those in previous sections (i.e., Affect Naming and Prosody). Additionally, the patient must be able to verbally identify the emotion expressed by the prosody and determine if the emotional expression is congruent or incongruent with the linguistic content of the statement. Low scores on this test can occur due to deficits in prosody identification, difficulties identifying interpersonal social cues and facial expressions, and, to some degree, cognitive and emotional empathy (i.e., feeling and/or knowing that the person being yelled at would be afraid if threatened). As such, the Pairs section of the test may, to some extent, tap into the ToM and Mirror Motor Neuron functions. The Pairs condition requires more verbal responding; therefore deficits in language expression may impact performance.

In the Pairs condition, the patient is shown a page with four photographs showing two people interacting. Each person has one of the eight emotional expressions (or confusion as a distractor) that are the same as those in the prosody section. The patient has to carefully examine the expression of both people in the picture and interpret other social cues (e.g., distance, gestures, etc.) in order to understand the emotional context of the interaction. Although a specific emotional expression may be present in multiple scenes, no two scenes are the same with respect to *all* the available cues. In other words, the second person in the scenes will have different expressions across the photos, and other information in the scenes will provide different clues about the emotional tone of the interaction. The patient hears a statement spoken in a tone of voice that expresses one of the eight emotions from the prosody condition, and must select one of the four pictures that best represents the emotional tone of what was said.

The Pairs section consists of 12 items, which are used to derive the Pairs total raw score. The total raw score ranges from 0 to 42 and is converted into an age-adjusted scaled score. For each item, a point is awarded for choosing the correct photograph, for correctly naming the prosody, and for correctly identifying if the prosody is congruent or incongruent with the linguistic content of the statement. For incongruent items (six of these), an additional point can be obtained if the patient can correctly state how the prosody changed the meaning of what was said. Points can be obtained on any item, even if the wrong photograph was selected. The clinician will need to evaluate where points were gained or lost on this test to identify why a low score was observed.

The internal consistency for the Pairs section is moderate to good across all ages in the normative sample (0.78–0.85) and is very good in the clinical samples (0.86–0.98). The Pairs scaled score correlates in the low to moderate range with WAIS–IV indexes (0.31–0.46), with VCI (0.46) and FSIQ (0.46) having the highest index correlations and Vocabulary (0.46) the highest subtest correlation. The correlations with the WMS–IV are also low to moderate (0.32–0.40), with Immediate Memory being the most strongly correlated WMS–IV index. The Pairs scaled score correlations with WIAT–II are low to moderate (0.14–0.49), with Oral Language Composite having the highest index correlation and Oral Expression the highest subtest correlation (0.47). These results indicate that the Pairs subtest is modestly related to oral verbal skills and, to a lesser degree, immediate memory.

Social Perception Total Score

The Social Perception Total Raw Score is derived from summing the item level scores across the three conditions of the test: Affect Naming, Prosody, and Pairs. Not all components of the Pairs item scores are included in the Social Perception Total Raw Score. Rather, only the scores indicating the correct selection of a photograph are part of the total score. The Social Perception Total Score ranges from 0 to 42. The raw score is converted to an age-adjusted scaled score.

The Social Perception Total Scaled Score is an index of the patient's ability to integrate verbal, auditory, and visual aspects of emotional expression. Specifically, each section requires the ability to discriminate among facial expressions of emotions. Additionally, some items require that examinees identify emotions from auditory cues and match them to corresponding facial expressions. Lastly, all the sections require some integration of auditory or verbal (i.e., naming) emotional components with a visual expression of emotion. Consequently, deficits in several different abilities contribute to a low total score, including deficits in facial affect discrimination, deficits in prosody identification, and deficits in integrating auditory/verbal information with visual information. For some examinees, component scores such as Affect Naming, Prosody, or Pairs may be lower or higher than the Social Perception Total Scaled Score. This indicates a profile of relative strengths and weaknesses in social perception skills.

The Social Perception Total Score has good internal consistency (0.70–0.84) across age groups and very good reliability in clinical samples (0.80–0.98). The Social Perception Total Score has low to moderate correlations with WAIS–IV Indexes (0.29–0.42) and low correlations with WMS–IV Indexes (0.32–0.39). WIAT–III Index correlations are in the low to moderate range (0.25–0.44), with the highest index association with Oral Language and the highest subtest association with Listening Comprehension (0.51). These results indicate only modest association of general cognitive, memory, and academic skills with the Social Perception Total Scaled Score. Listening comprehension abilities have the strongest association with the total score, although the meaning of this association is not understood at this time. While it is possible that listening comprehension abilities are important for good performance on tests of Social Perception (or, perhaps, on any test, due to the need to comprehend test instructions), it is equally possible that good Social Perception abilities play an important role in one's ability to comprehend spoken language. Similarly, individuals with low general intellectual ability may exhibit lower scores on Social Perception, with the directionality of the association not yet well understood. Importantly, because the correlations are only modest, the effects of low ability in other cognitive domains would not solely account for impairment on this measure.

Social Perception Contrast Scores

The co-norming of the Social Perception test with the WAIS–IV enables a direct statistical comparison between cognitive measures from the WAIS–IV and the Social Perception test. The comparison allows the examiner to evaluate if general cognitive deficits or more specific cognitive deficits may be contributing to low scores on Social Perception. As reported previously, the correlation between the WAIS–IV and the Social Perception Tests was generally low to moderate. Therefore, the adjustments made to Social Perception scores are small to moderate depending upon cognitive ability level.

Contrast scores use a regression-based model to adjust the distribution of scores in one variable controlling for another variable. In this case, the dependent variable is the Social Perception total scaled-score and the control variable is one of the following WAIS–IV Indexes: GAI, VCI, or PRI. *The clinician uses the index that answers a specific hypothesis about the patient's social perception functioning.*

The GAI versus Social Perception Contrast Scaled Score evaluates if low scores on Social Perception are similar to overall intellectual deficits. This contrast score is used when the clinician evaluates a patient who has global deficits in intellectual functioning. The contrast scaled score is interpreted the same as age-adjusted scaled scores, with the exception that the comparison group is comprised of individuals of similar age and intellectual ability. Therefore, a contrast scaled score of six indicates that the examinee is at the ninth percentile on Social Perception compared to individuals of similar age and GAI ability level. This interpretation does not change in relation to their GAI score. In other words, if GAI is 120 and the contrast score is six, the patient's Social Perception ability is at the ninth percentile compared to age- and general ability-matched peers. Similarly, if the GAI is 75 and the contrast score is six, the patient's Social Perception ability is at the ninth percentile compared to individuals of similar age and ability.

The VCI versus Social Perception Contrast Scaled Score compares performance on the Verbal Comprehension Index to the Social Perception Total Score. As stated previously, language skills have a small effect on the Social Perception Total Score. Therefore, low verbal abilities will have only a modest impact on the test performance. In cases where the examinee has apparent language or verbal intellectual difficulties, the contrast score informs the examiner whether the Social Perception Total Score is deficient or within normal limits after controlling these cognitive difficulties.

The PRI versus Social Perception Contrast Scaled Score compares performance on the Perceptual Reasoning Index to the Social Perception Total Score. Perceptual Reasoning skills have a small correlation with the Social Perception Total Score. Therefore, low perceptual reasoning abilities will have only a modest impact on test performance. In cases where the examinee has apparent perceptual reasoning difficulties, the contrast score informs the examiner whether the Social Perception Total Score is deficient or within normal limits after controlling for low perceptual reasoning abilities.

Clinical Studies

The majority of clinical studies using the Social Perception test will be presented in the chapters associated with specific clinical groups (e.g., the psychiatric chapter will present data for patients with Schizophrenia; the developmental disorders chapter will present data for Autism). Additional clinical case studies are presented here not as exemplars, but rather to provide information about how the Social Perception test can be used in various clinical samples. In addition to clinical samples, a group of examinees identified as gifted were also evaluated to illustrate the impact of high general ability on the Social Perception test score.

Table 8.1 presents descriptive data for a small sample of patients who underwent left ($n = 4$) or right ($n = 9$) temporal lobectomy surgery for intractable seizures secondary to chronic epilepsy. Comparison of the combined left and right temporal lobectomy groups versus matched controls are reported elsewhere (Pearson, 2009). Because combining the right and left groups masks the group differences in performance on tests of SC, they are presented separately here. The samples are small, and are intended only to illustrate possible patterns of findings. Thus, they should not be viewed as being representative of all patients who have undergone temporal lobectomy surgery.

As seen in Table 8.1, the patients with left temporal lobotomies performed in the borderline to low average range on all measures of social perception. The left temporal lobectomy group also performed in the borderline to low average range on measures of intellectual functioning.

TABLE 8.1   ACS Social Perception Descriptive Statistics for Left and Right Temporal Lobectomy Patients

Score	Left Temporal Lobectomy		Right Temporal Lobectomy	
	Mean	SD	Mean	SD
Social Perception Total	5.2	3.4	7.8	2.6
Affect Naming	5	3.4	7.8	2.3
Prosody	6	3.5	8.4	2.8
Pairs	5.4	2.1	7.7	2.9
General Ability Index	80	17	91.2	14.4
Verbal Comprehension Index	77.4	11.6	90	13.2
Perceptual Reasoning Index	86.2	19.5	94.1	11
GAI versus Social Perception Contrast Scaled Score	7	1.9	8.7	1.8
VCI versus Social Perception Contrast Scaled Score	7	2.7	8.5	2.3
PRI versus Social Perception Contrast Scaled Score	6.6	2.1	8.9	1.9

Note: $n = 4$ for left and 9 for right temporal lobectomy patients.
Copyright 2009 by Pearson, Inc. Reproduced with permission. All rights reserved.

One potential explanation for this finding is that low intellectual performance, particularly low verbal ability, is the cause of low social perception scores. The contrast scores indicate that after controlling for low intellectual functioning, social perception scores improved somewhat, falling into the low average range. Thus, low intellectual functioning may have impacted the severity of the social perception deficits in this group, although it did not fully explain the weakness in social perception: patients still show low ability on social perception even after controlling for other cognitive limitations.

Table 8.1 shows that the right temporal lobectomy group performed in the low average-to-average range on social perception measures. The right temporal lobectomy scores were better than those obtained by the left temporal lobectomy group, but still indicate a weakness in this domain. Intellectual functioning is in the average range and would likely have only a small impact on Social Perception test scores. As was the case with the left temporal lobectomy, controlling intellectual functioning somewhat improves the Social Perception Total score: For right temporal lobectomy, this score now falls in the average range, suggesting that social perception difficulties can in part be explained by intellectual weaknesses. These results indicate that the Social Perception test is a useful tool when evaluating lobectomy patients.

In addition to its utility with temporal lobectomy patients, the Social Perception test also yielded expected clinical findings for specific neurodevelopmental (e.g., Autism, Asperger's Syndrome) and psychiatric disorders (e.g., schizophrenia), and traumatic brain injury. Table 8.2 provides a summary of Social Perception data for various neurological, developmental, and psychiatric conditions collected as part of the ACS standardization. More detailed clinical results are presented in other chapters in this book. Lastly, in addition to clinical samples, a group of 16 adults identified as gifted also completed the Social Perception test. The average GAI for the group is 129.4 ($\pm$8.6). The social perception scores for the group range from 11.4 (Affect Naming) to 12.2 (Prosody), demonstrating that individuals with superior intelligence do not show any obvious deficits in social perception. By the same token, having superior intellectual abilities does not necessarily translate into superior performance on the Social Perception test.

SUPPLEMENTARY ACS MEASURES OF SOCIAL COGNITION

Faces

The Faces test measures face discrimination, face recognition, spatial identification, and spatial memory. Although the Faces test was initially

TABLE 8.2 Social Perception Descriptive Data for Various Clinical Populations

	N	Social Perception		Affect Naming		Prosody		Pairs	
		M	SD	M	SD	M	SD	M	SD
Intellectual Disability-Mild	36	3.6	2.8	4.9	3.5	4.2	2.8	3.9	2.3
Intellectual Disability-Moderate	16	1.6	1.5	1.9	1.2	2.1	1.5	2.1	1.1
Autistic Disorder	15–16	4.4	2.7	6.4	4.1	4.9	3.6	4.9	3.4
Asperger's Disorder	26–27	8.2	3.0	7.9	2.6	9.0	3.2	8.3	3.2
Schizophrenia	45–46	6.3	2.3	7.4	2.8	6.5	2.5	5.6	2.2
Depression	114–115	8.2	3.3	8.9	3.3	8.3	3.3	8.0	3.2
Traumatic Brain Injury	23–24	5.0	2.9	5.5	3.1	6.0	2.9	5.8	3.4
Temporal Lobectomy	14	6.9	3.1	6.8	2.9	7.6	3.2	6.9	2.8
Mild Cognitive Impairment	41–42	9.8	3.2	10.0	3.1	10.0	3.2	9.9	3.0
Probable Alzheimer's Disease	26	8.1	4.4	8.7	4.4	8.0	3.6	7.7	3.7

Copyright 2009 by Pearson, Inc. Reproduced with permission. All rights reserved.

developed as a memory measure, it can provide important supplementary information when interpreting the results of the Social Perception test. Additionally, since the ability to discriminate among and remember people's faces can have an impact on social interactions, the Faces test can, in its own right, help explicate a patient's social difficulties.

In the Faces subtest, the patient is shown a 4×4 grid containing 10 pictures of faces. After seeing the stimuli for a period of 10 seconds, the patient is given 20 cards with pictures of faces (10 targets and 10 distracters) and asked to select the previously seen faces and place them in the correct locations in the 4×4 grid. There are four learning trials and a delayed trial. Each trial is scored for content, spatial locations, and bonus points. The content score is the number of correctly identified faces, and ranges from 0 to10 for each trial. The spatial score is the number of correctly identified locations on the grid and ranges from 0 to10 for each trial. An additional bonus point is awarded when the correct face is placed in the correct location. A total trial score is calculated from the sum of the content, spatial, and bonus points across the four trials. Each trial total score ranges from 0 to 30 and the immediate total score (Faces I) ranges from 0 to 120. The immediate content score is the sum of the individual trial content scores across the four immediate learning trials (0–40). The immediate spatial score is calculated in the same way. The delayed trial is administered 10 to 15 minutes after the last immediate trial and is scored in the same manner as the individual immediate trials. Faces II is the total for the delayed task and ranges from 0 to 30. Faces I and II combine all aspects of the memory test including face recognition, spatial memory, and the correct placement of the correct face.

The Faces test measures cognitive abilities beyond just SC. Of the scores obtained on the Faces test, the content total score measures important aspects of face processing. This score assesses the ability to discriminate between similar faces, face learning, and long-term face memory/recognition. This score is the primary focus of social perception interpretation. The Faces I and II and spatial memory total scores are used when memory functioning is the basis for evaluation.

Internal consistencies for the Faces content total score range from 0.76 to 0.94 in the normative sample, and 0.84 to 0.97 in clinical samples. Clinical studies using the Faces test found that patients with moderate to severe TBI performed in the low average range on the Faces content score, significantly below matched controls (Pearson, 2009). Similarly, patients diagnosed with probable Alzheimer's disease scored significantly lower than matched controls on the Faces content score. The findings in the TBI and Alzheimer's disease groups are consistent with the expected memory impairment in these populations, and memory deficits may account for the findings rather than deficits in face processing. Further research is needed in patients with psychiatric and developmental disorders that are known to exhibit impairments in face recognition/discrimination (e.g., schizophrenia, autism).

Names

Like Faces, Names was initially developed as a memory measure, but also assesses components of face processing, including face recognition, discrimination, and affect recognition. In addition to face processing, Names measures the patient's ability to learn people's names and other information about them. The ability to remember people's names can have an impact on social interactions.

The Names test consists of presenting examinees with 10 photographs of children's faces, one at a time. Each face will have a happy, sad, angry, or fearful expression. Each photograph presentation is comprised of three learning trials, which yield an immediate recall score, and a delayed recall trial. The patient is told the child's first and last name, and an activity the child likes to do. For example, an examinee is shown a picture of a girl, and told that the girl's name is Mary Smith and that she likes to play golf. Although the examinee is told to remember the child's name and the preferred activity, he or she is warned that they would also need to remember the child's facial expression. For two of the faces, the patient is asked to make up a name and activity for the child to facilitate their recall. After all the 10 photos are presented, the patient is shown the 10 photos again and asked to recall the name and activity that go with each face. For the delayed condition, the examinee is also asked to recall the facial expression of each child.

The Names I score is the sum of all the first and last names and activities correctly recalled across the three learning trials for a total of up to 90 points. The Delayed recall trial is the sum of last and first names, activities, and emotional expressions correctly recalled for a sum of up to 40 points. The Names Proper Names total score is the sum of all correctly recalled first and last names on the immediate learning and delayed recall trials, up to 80 points. The Names Activity total score is the sum of all correctly recalled activities on the immediate learning and delayed recall trials for a sum of up to 40 points. The Names Emotion total score is the sum of the correctly recalled emotions on the delayed recall trial for a sum of up to 10 points. Each score, except the Names Emotion score, is converted to an age-adjusted scaled score. The Names Emotion normative scores are presented as percentile groups. Normative data are available on this test for ages 16–69.

The Names test has very good reliability both in the normative sample (0.87–0.95) and in clinical samples (0.83–0.94). Patients suffering moderate to severe traumatic brain injury perform in the low average-to-average range, which is significantly below matched controls (Pearson, 2009). In contrast, patients with right or left temporal lobe epilepsy perform in the average range. The level of performance in the TBI group was similar to their performance on other memory measures. The results are not surprising given that SC deficits in these groups are typically not due to basic impairments in facial discrimination and recognition.

The Names test is primarily a visual–verbal association memory test. Memory functions include immediate learning and delayed recall for proper names, faces, and other associated information, and incidental recall for facial expression of emotions. Performance on the Names test can also be influenced by difficulties in face discrimination, expressive and receptive language skills, and auditory acuity and discrimination. The various scores provided on the Names test can help with the interpretation of low performance on this test.

The Names I total score combines all aspects of the immediate associative learning component of the test, except incidental recall of emotional expressions. Therefore, a low score on Names I could indicate impairments in immediate face memory, verbal memory, visual–verbal association memory, memory for proper names, and/or memory for semantic information.

Similarly, the Names II score measures all aspects of delayed associative recall, except for incidental recall of emotional expressions. Low scores on Names II could indicate difficulties with long-term recall for faces, verbal information, visual–verbal associations, proper names, and/or semantic information.

The Proper Names score measures the examinees ability to learn and retain name–face associations. The Activity score measures the examinees ability to relate visual and semantic information. When the Proper Names score is higher than the Activity score, the examinee may struggle with semantic memory or semantic–face associations. When the opposite finding occurs, recall of the association between Proper Names and Faces is deficient but semantic recall is intact. In either case, if one of the Activity or Proper Names scores is average while the other is significantly lower, face memory would not be considered impaired and a general deficit in verbal memory can be ruled out. This finding suggests a more specific deficit in verbal–visual associative memory functioning.

The Emotion total score specifically evaluates the patient's ability to identify facial expressions of emotion and delayed incidental learning of emotional information. When Names II is average but the Emotion total score is low, it indicates difficulties with either affect recognition or incidental recall. When scores are low on Names II and Emotion total score, more general problems with face memory may also be present.

INTEGRATING SOCIAL COGNITION ASSESSMENT AND WAIS–IV/WMS–IV

The SC tests reviewed in this chapter measure multiple cognitive skills, making it difficult to identify the exact nature of examinees' cognitive difficulties if administered in isolation. Clinicians can test hypotheses about why low scores were obtained on SC measures by comparing performance to other SC scores and to scores on specific WAIS–IV and WMS–IV subtests. Previously, normative data for specific contrast scores were described for identifying whether general cognitive, verbal, or perceptual deficits were affecting performance on the Social Perception Total Score. This section describes specific test comparisons for which normative statistical comparisons are unfortunately not available. Therefore, when interpreting performance differences across individual measures, using restrictive criteria to identify specific strengths and weaknesses is recommended. Also, individual test score comparisons are not intended to be diagnostic of a specific condition, but rather are used to clarify, to the degree possible, underlying cognitive difficulties.

WMS–IV Designs versus Faces

The WMS–IV Designs subtest parallels the Faces test in modality of information presentation, structure, and scoring rubrics. Both tests present information visually, and both have content and spatial scores, enabling the differentiation of memory into object versus location. There are two primary differences between these two tests; the content of what is to be recalled (i.e., abstract designs versus faces) and the number of trials to learn the information (i.e., single trial learning versus four learning trials).

In the context of evaluating social perception, the primary comparison is between Designs Content and Faces Content scores. When Designs Content scores are significantly higher than Faces Content, this result indicates that visual object memory is better for abstract designs than for faces. If the Design Content score is within normal limits and the Faces Content score is significantly lower, then visual object memory is likely to be intact while there may be a specific weakness or impairment in memory for faces. If low scores are observed on all or most visual memory scores, including Faces Spatial and Designs Spatial, then a more general deficit in visual memory functioning is likely to be present.

In the context of a possible memory encoding or attentional impairment, the differences in the number of presentation trials between the Designs and the Faces tests needs to be carefully considered. Specifically, because Designs is a single trial learning test, whereas Faces is a multi-trial learning test, disparities in performance between the two tests can also occur due to poor single trial learning (e.g., Designs < Faces) or due to difficulty benefitting from practice (e.g., Designs > Faces). Comparing performance on other single- and multi-trial learning measures such as WMS–IV Logical Memory and WMS–IV Paired Associates can help clarify if the number of learning trials impacts performance more generally.

WMS–IV Verbal Paired Associates versus Names

The WMS–IV Verbal Paired Associates (VPA) subtest measures verbal associative learning and recall. Comparing VPA to Names enables the clinician to identify whether the examinee has a general deficit in associative learning, or if a deficit is material specific. When patients have low Names scores, while VPA scores are within normal limits, this suggests a specific deficit in visual–verbal associations, possibly specific to face–name associations. This could indicate deficits in face discrimination or recognition. However, if both Names and VPA are low, this could suggest a more general deficit in associative learning and recall.

Faces versus Names

The Faces and Names subtests both require face memory and recognition. When determining if low scores on Names may be due to problems with face recognition and discrimination, the Faces Content score can be used to help clarify the nature of the cognitive difficulties. For example, if the patient has low scores both on Names I and/or II and on Faces Content, then deficits in Face Memory may be present. This would be further confirmed if WMS–IV VPA scores were within normal limits. In contrast, when Names I and/or II are low, but the Faces Content score is within normal limits, the results suggest that Face Memory may be intact but visual–verbal association memory may be deficient. Lastly, in some cases, Faces I and/or II are low and Names is within normal limits. This suggests that verbal labels help the patient remember faces, but in the absence of verbal cues, face memory is weak.

Social Perception versus Faces

The Social Perception and Faces subtests both require processing facial information. When patients have low scores on Social Perception and Faces, they may have a general deficit in face processing that may be affecting their performance on the Social Perception test. In contrast, patients whose Social Perception scores are low and whose Faces scores are within normal limits are likely to have intact face processing, suggesting a specific deficit in emotion recognition or processing of emotional content. Lastly, low scores on Faces with Social Perception scores within normal limits suggest difficulties with face memory, but not necessarily with other aspects of face discrimination.

Social Perception versus Names

The Social Perception and Names tests measure face processing, facial affect recognition, and associating auditory/verbal information with faces. A low Affect Naming score can be compared to the Emotion recall score from Names. If both scores are low, this verifies difficulties identifying and labeling facial expressions of emotion. If Affect Naming is low in the context of normal performance on Names Emotion recall, this result is likely related to the limited number of emotions needed to be identified on the Names Emotion Recall. This result suggests a more discrete deficit in affect naming/recognition of certain emotions may be present. In contrast, if the Names Emotion Recall score is low while the Affect Naming is within normal limits, difficulties with delayed incidental recall are the most fitting interpretation.

WAIS–IV Comprehension versus Social Perception

The WAIS–IV Comprehension subtest is not a direct measure of SC or ToM; however, this test requires significant verbal expression, cognitive flexibility, reasoning, and some knowledge of social conventions.

The Social Perception Pairs subtest also requires significant verbal expression, social reasoning, and some degree of cognitive flexibility (e.g., understanding difference between literal meaning and intended meaning). Low scores on the Pairs test, with relatively good scores on other Social Perception measures could signal verbal expression, reasoning, or cognitive flexibility problems. Comparing the Pairs score to Comprehension clarifies whether the deficit is specific to ToM or represents a more general problem with verbal expression, reasoning, and/or flexibility. Low scores on Pairs with Comprehension scores within normal limits may indicate difficulties with ToM. Low Pairs and Comprehension scores suggest more general difficulties with verbal expression, reasoning, or flexibility.

CASE STUDY

Mr. S. is a 33-year-old Caucasian man currently living alone. His history is remarkable for few friendships throughout his life and poor interpersonal relationships in general. He holds a Bachelor's degree in computer science and a Masters in Business Administration, and for the past 8 years has been employed as a computer specialist in a large business firm. Despite receiving very positive work reviews, Mr. S. has been passed up for promotion on several occasions. He has also been reprimanded twice for making inappropriate comments to his supervisor. The Human Resources department suggested that Mr. S. seek psychological counseling to help him develop more appropriate social skills to facilitate interactions with his boss and peers.

During therapy, Mr. S.'s psychologist noted that Mr. S. appeared to have difficulty listening to what was being said to him, and did not appear to fully process therapeutic suggestions. He also noted that Mr. S. had problems discussing topics other than his interests in computers and computer games. After 3 months of therapy, Mr. S.'s psychologist decided to perform a thorough psychological assessment to help him better understand Mr. S.'s personality and cognitive strengths and weaknesses. On the basis of this evaluation, the psychologist diagnosed Mr. S. with Asperger's Syndrome and a Personality Disorder with Schizotypal features.

As part of the psychological evaluation, the psychologist administered the WAIS–IV, and the Names, Faces, and Social Perception subtests from the ACS. The psychologist noted that Mr. S. had difficulty staying on task during the assessment, but was easily redirected. Additionally, Mr. S. frequently asked tangential questions (e.g., *"Why aren't these tests computerized?"*), or made derogatory remarks about the faces in the different tests (e.g., *"Hey that chick's fat"* or *"That guy looks like an idiot"*). The results of the WAIS–IV and the ACS are presented in Table 8.3.

TABLE 8.3   Case Study WAIS−IV and Social Perception Scores

WAIS−IV Index	Standard Score	Percentile
Verbal Comprehension	127	96
Perceptual Reasoning	105	63
Working Memory	120	91
Processing Speed	88	21
WAIS−IV Subtest	**Scale Score**	**Percentile**
Similarities	15	95
Vocabulary	17	99
Information	16	98
Block Design	9	37
Matrix Reasoning	13	84
Visual Puzzles	10	50
Digit Span	15	95
Arithmetic	14	91
Coding	6	9
Symbol Search	8	25
Social Perception Score	**Scale Score**	**Percentile**
Social Perception Total	5	5
Affect Naming	5	5
Prosody	7	16
Pairs	8	25
Verbal Comprehension Vs. Social Perception	3	1
Perceptual Reasoning Vs. Social Perception	5	5
Faces Score	**Scale Score**	**Percentile**
Faces I	6	9
Faces II	7	16
Faces Content	5	5
Faces Spatial	8	25
Names Score	**Scale Score**	**Percentile**
Names I	9	37
Names II	6	9
Names Proper Names	6	9
Names Activity	11	63

The results of the cognitive assessment indicated superior verbal abilities and working memory. Mr. S.'s visual perceptual skills were in the average range and were significantly below his verbal intellectual functioning. Among perceptual measures, Mr. S. had most difficulty with tasks requiring the ability to construct designs from a model, while his visual reasoning skills were strong. Mr. S. also showed a significant weakness in his processing speed. He appeared poorly coordinated and had rather weak graphomotor skills (e.g., sloppy drawing of symbols on the coding task). Additionally, Mr. S. had low average immediate memory and delayed recognition of faces and their locations, and average immediate recall and low average delayed recall of names and activities associated with faces. He was better at recalling the activities associated with each face rather than being able to recall names. Mr. S.'s lowest scores across the whole assessment were on the Social Perception Total Score and Affect Naming. He exhibited significant difficulties identifying and labeling facial expressions of emotion. He also showed low average ability to associate prosody with facial expressions of emotion. His best performance on this subtest was on the Pairs section. This indicates that when there is more information and greater verbalization of responses, his performance improves. In other words, he is better able to describe the interaction between people, rather than identify individual expressions of basic emotion.

To sum up, the profile of strengths and weaknesses suggests highly developed verbal abilities in the context of weaknesses in face processing and affect recognition. Mr. S. is able to use his verbal skills to describe interactions between people, but his ability to effectively read the emotional states of others is a weakness. Therapeutically, the treating psychologist used this information to better understand the apparent gap between Mr. S.'s detailed verbal description of interpersonal events and the seemingly unexpected outcomes resulting from those interactions.

SUMMARY

Social cognition is a broad term that describes a group of abilities needed for effective interpersonal functioning. Increasingly, neuroscientists are researching the brain—behavior associations underlying these cognitive functions. One set of important abilities involves paralinguistic communication. Receptive and expressive nonverbal communication facilitates normal day-to-day social functioning. Similarly, empathy and ToM skills enable an understanding of other's thoughts, emotions, and needs impacting a variety of social behaviors.

The skills often studied as exemplifying nonverbal communication abilities are facial affect and prosody recognition, and face processing (i.e., discrimination and recognition). The amygdala and the right frontal regions, among other cortical and subcorticol systems, are the neuroanatomical regions associated with these abilities. Additionally, ToM and empathy play a key role in understanding situations, and are subserved primarily by the mirror neuron system networks (primarily inferior frontal gyrus and somatosensory cortex), as well as medial frontal and temporoparietal cortices. Many clinical populations including patients diagnosed with neurological, psychiatric, and developmental disorders, as well as patients suffering traumatic brain injury, have impairments in components of SC. The ACS for WAIS–IV and WMS–IV provides multiple measures of receptive paralinguistic communication that can be used as part of a larger neuropsychological assessment.

KEY LEARNING

- Social Cognition is a global term used to describe cognitive and emotional abilities that facilitate interpersonal relationships.
- Paralinguistic communication can convey an emotional tone (e.g., sadness, happiness, disappointment), meaning (e.g., sarcasm communicates that the *opposite* of what is being explicitly stated is actually true), or grammatical concepts, which are sometimes referred to as "linguistic intonation" or "propositional prosody" (e.g., questions vs. statements). Paralinguistic communication and can be expressed through multiple channels (e.g., facial expression, gestures, posture, and prosody).
- *Emotional empathy* refers to the capacity to intuitively *feel* what others are feeling while *cognitive empathy* refers to the ability to cognitively understand how others might be feeling. The latter skill is associated with *theory of mind* or the ability to understand the thoughts, feelings, and perspective of others.
- Rapid *detection* of affective displays of others (vocal, facial, and postural) is subserved by the amygdala, while slower and more conscious processing takes place in cortical networks.
- *Expressive* prosody deficits have been associated with lesions in the right basal ganglia, and right medial frontal lobe. Imitation of emotional expressions is believed to be related to the right inferior frontal gyrus. *Receptive* abilities, including facial and prosodic affect *recognition*, are associated with the orbitofrontal/frontal opercular and/or anterior cingulate cortex, primarily in the right hemisphere, as well as the basal ganglia and/or the thalamus.
- Social cognition skills can be associated with other cognitive abilities such as cognitive flexibility, language abilities, and

visual—perceptual abilities. General cognitive deficits can mask underlying deficits in SC.
- Developmental disorders commonly associated with deficits in SC include ASD, Down syndrome, and Turner syndrome.
- Neurological conditions associated with deficits in SC include: seizure disorder, traumatic brain injury, Huntington's disease, Parkinson's disease, Alzheimer's disease, FLD, and amyotrophic lateral sclerosis.
- Psychiatric conditions associated with deficits in SC include schizophrenia, mood disorders, substance abuse disorders, and personality disorders.
- The ACS for the WAIS—IV and WMS—IV provides reliable, normed tools, for measuring components of receptive paralinguistic skills and face processing.
- The Social Perception test measures facial affect naming, prosody—facial affect recognition, and the ability to understand an interaction between people (i.e., emotion, gesture, and posture). Initial clinical studies indicate that the Social Perception test is sensitive to patients with epilepsy, traumatic brain injury, schizophrenia, and ASD.
- The Faces subtest measures face discrimination and memory. The Names subtest measures name—face association, face recognition, verbal learning and memory, and affect recognition and incidental recall.
- Comparisons of the Social Perception, Names, and Faces subtest scores to WAIS—IV and WMS—IV scores can help identify SC deficits.

References

Addington, J., & Addington, D. (1998). Facial affect recognition and information processing in schizophrenia and bipolar disorder. *Schizophrenia Research, 32*(3), 171—181.

Adolphs, R. (2002). Neural systems for recognizing emotion. *Current Opinion in Neurobiology, 12*(2), 169—177.

Adolphs, R., Damasio, H., & Tranel, D. (2002). Neural systems for recognition of emotional prosody: A 3-D lesion study. *Emotion, 2*(1), 23—51.

Adolphs, R., Russell, J. A., & Tranel, D. (1999). A role for the human amygdala in recognizing emotional arousal from unpleasant stimuli. *Psychological Science, 10*(2), 167—171.

Adolphs, R., Tranel, D., Hamann, S., Young, A. W., Calder, A. J., Phelps, E. A., et al. (1999). Recognition of facial emotion in nine individuals with bilateral amygdala damage. *Neuropsychologia, 37*(10), 1111—1117.

Barrett, J., Pike, G. B., & Paus, T. Å. (2004). The role of the anterior cingulate cortex in pitch variation during sad affect. *European Journal of Neuroscience, 19*(2), 458—464.

Baum, S. R., & Pell, M. D. (1999). The neural bases of prosody: insights from lesion studies and neuroimaging. *Aphasiology, 13*(8), 581—608.

Bellack, A. S., Brown, C. H., & Thomas-Lohrman, S. (2006). Psychometric characteristics of role-play assessments of social skill in schizophrenia. *Behavior Therapy*, 37(4), 339–352.

Bernier, R., & Dawson, G. (2009). The role of mirror neuron dysfunction in autism. In J. A. Pineda (Ed.), *Mirror neuron systems: The role of mirroring processes in social cognition* (pp. 261–286). Totowa, NJ US: Humana Press.

Blonder, L. X., Burns, A. F., Bowers, D., Moore, R. W., & Heilman, K. M. (1993). Right hemisphere facial expressivity during natural conversation. *Brain and Cognition*, 21(1), 44–56.

Blonder, L. X., Heilman, K. M., Ketterson, T., Rosenbek, J., Raymer, A., Crosson, B., et al. (2005). Affective facial and lexical expression in aprosodic versus aphasic stroke patients. *Journal of the International Neuropsychological Society*, 11(6), 677–685.

Blood, A. J., Zatorre, R. J., Bermudez, P., & Evans, A. C. (1999). Emotional responses to pleasant and unpleasant music correlate with activity in paralimbic brain regions. *Nature Neuroscience*, 2(4), 382–387.

Boakes, J., Chapman, E., Houghton, S., & West, J. (2008). Facial affect interpretation in boys with attention deficit/hyperactivity disorder. *Child Neuropsychology*, 14(1), 82–96.

Borod, J. C., Bloom, R. L., Brickman, A. M., Nakhutina, L., & Curko, E. A. (2002). Emotional processing deficits in individuals with unilateral brain damage. *Applied Neuropsychology*, 9(1), 23–36.

Borod, J. C., Cicero, B. A., Obler, L. K., Welkowitz, J., Erhan, H. M., Santschi, C., et al. (1998). Right hemisphere emotional perception: Evidence across multiple channels. *Neuropsychology*, 12(3), 446–458.

Borroni, P., Gorini, A., Riva, G., Bouchard, S., & Cerri, G. (2011). Mirroring avatars: Dissociation of action and intention in human motor resonance. *European journal of neuroscience*, 34(4), 662–669.

Bowers, D., Bauer, R. M., Coslett, H. B., & Heilman, K. M. (1985). Processing of faces by patients with unilateral hemisphere lesions. I. Dissociation between judgments of facial affect and facial identity. *Brain and Cognition*, 4(3), 258–272.

Bowers, D., Blonder, L., & Heilman, K. (1991). *Florida affect battery: Test manual*. Gainesville, FL: University of Florida.

Bowers, D., Coslett, H. B., Bauer, R. M., & Speedie, L. J. (1987). Comprehension of emotional prosody following unilateral hemispheric lesions: Processing defect versus distraction defect. *Neuropsychologia*, 25(2), 317–328.

Bozikas, V. P., Kosmidis, M. H., Anezoulaki, D., Giannakou, M., & Karavatos, A. (2004). Relationship of affect recognition with psychopathology and cognitive performance in schizophrenia. *Journal of the International Neuropsychological Society*, 10(4), 549–558.

Bozikas, V. P., Tonia, T., Fokas, K., Karavatos, A., & Kosmidis, M. H. (2006). Impaired emotion processing in remitted patients with bipolar disorder. *Journal of Affective Disorders*, 91(1), 53–56.

Bradvik, B., Dravins, C., Holtas, S., & Rosen, I. (1991). Disturbances of speech prosody following right hemisphere infarcts. *Acta Neurologica Scandinavica*, 84(2), 114–126.

Breitenstein, C., Daum, I., & Ackermann, H. (1998). Emotional processing following cortical and subcortical brain damage: Contribution of the fronto-striatal circuitry. *Behavioural Neurology*, 11(1), 29–42.

Buchanan, T. W., Lutz, K., Mirzazade, S., Specht, K., Shah, N. J., Zilles, K., et al. (2000). Recognition of emotional prosody and verbal components of spoken language: An fMRI study. *Cognitive Brain Research*, 9(3), 227–238.

Burgdorf, J., & Panksepp, J. (2006). The neurobiology of positive emotions. *Neuroscience & Biobehavioral Reviews*, 30(2), 173–187.

Cadesky, E. B., Mota, V. L., & Schachar, R. J. (2000). Beyond words: How do problem children with ADHD and/or conduct problems process nonverbal information about affect? *Journal of the American Academy of Child & Adolescent Psychiatry*, *39*(9), 1160−1167.

Cancelliere, A. E., & Kertesz, A. (1990). Lesion localization in acquired deficits of emotional expression and comprehension. *Brain and Cognition*, *13*(2), 133−147.

Carr, L., Iacoboni, M., Dubeau, M. C., Mazziotta, J. C., & Lenzi, G. L. (2003). Neural mechanisms of empathy in humans: A relay froom neural systems for imitations to limbic areas. *Proceedings of the National Academy of Sciences*, *100*, 5497−5502.

Carrington, S. J., & Bailey, A. J. (2009). Are there theory of mind regions in the brain? A review of the neuroimaging literature. *Human Brain Mapping*, *30*(8), 2313−2335.

Cendes, F., Andermann, F., Dubeau, F., Gloor, P., Evans, A., Jones-Gotman, M., et al. (1993a). Early childhood prolonged febrile convulsions, atrophy and sclerosis of mesial structrues, and temporal lobe epilepsy: An MRI volumentric study. *Neurology*, *43*(6), 1083−1087.

Cendes, F., Andermann, F., Gloor, P., Evans, A., Jones-Gotman, M., Watson, C., et al. (1993b). MRI volumentric measurement of amygdala and hippocampus in temporal lobe epilepsy. *Neurology*, *43*(4), 719−725.

Da Fonseca, D., Seguier, V. R., Santos, A., Poinso, F. O., & Deruelle, C. (2009). Emotion understanding in children with ADHD. *Child Psychiatry & Human Development*, *40*(1), 111−121.

Davis, M. H., Hull, J. G., Young, R. D., & Warren, G. G. (1987). Emotional reactions to dramatic film stimuli: The influence of cognitive and emotional empathy. *Journal of Personality and Social Psychology*, *52*(1), 126−133.

Dawson, G., Webb, S. J., & McPartland, J. (2005). Understanding the nature of face processing impairment in autism: Insights from behavioral and electrophysiological studies. *Developmental Neuropsychology*, *27*(3), 403−424.

Derntl, B., Habel, U., Windischberger, C., Robinson, S., Kryspin-Exner, I., Gur, R. C., et al. (2009). General and specific responsiveness of the amygdala during explicit emotion recognition in females and males. *BMC Neuroscience*, *10*, 91. doi:10.1186/1471-2202-10-91.

Diaz, M. T., & McCarthy, G. (2007). Unconscious word processing engages a distributed network of brain regions. *Journal of Cognitive Neuroscience*, *19*(11), 1768−1775.

Dimitrovsky, L., Spector, H., & Levy-Shiff, R. (2000). Stimulus gender and emotional difficulty level: Their effect on recognition of facial expressions of affect in children with and without LD. *Journal of Learning Disabilities*, *33*(5), 410−416.

Dimitrovsky, L., Spector, H., Levy-Shiff, R., & Vakil, E. (1998). Interpretation of facial expressions of affect in children with learning disabilities with verbal or nonverbal deficits. *Journal of Learning Disabilities*, *31*(3), 286−292.

Dolan, M., & Fullam, R. (2006). Face affect recognition deficits in personality-disordered offenders: Association with psychopathy. *Psychological Medicine*, *36*(11), 1563−1569.

Dujardin, K., Blairy, S., Defebvre, L., Duhem, S., Noël, Y., Hess, U., & Destée, A. (2004). Deficits in decoding emotional facial expressions in Parkinson's disease. *Neuropsychologia*, *42*(2), 239−250.

Dziobek, I., Rogers, K., Fleck, S., Bahnemann, M., Heekeren, H. R., Wolf, O. T., et al. (2008). Dissociation of cognitive and emotional empathy in adults with asperger syndrome using the multifaceted empathy test (MET). *Journal of Autism and Developmental Disorders*, *38*(3), 464−473.

Ekman, P., Friesen, W. V., & Tomkins, S. S. (1971). Facial affect scoring technique: a first validity study. *Semiotica*, *3*(1), 37−58.

Fernandez-Duque, D., & Black, S. E. (2005). Impaired recognition of negative facial emotions in patients with frontotemporal dementia. *Neuropsychologia*, *43*(11), 1673−1687.

Foisy, M. -L., Philippot, P., Verbanck, P., Pelc, I., Van Der Straten, G., & Kornreich, C. (2005). Emotional facial expression decoding impairment in persons dependent on multiple substances: impact of a history of alcohol dependence. *Journal of Studies on Alcohol*, *66*(5), 673–681.

Forrest, B. J. (2004). The utility of math difficulties, internalized psychopathology, and visual–spatial deficits to identify children with the nonverbal learning disability syndrome: Evidence for a visualspatial disability. *Child Neuropsychology*, *10*(2), 129–146.

Frey, S., Kostopoulos, P., & Petrides, M. (2000). Orbitofrontal involvement in the processing of unpleasant auditory information. *European Journal of Neuroscience*, *12*(10), 3709–3712.

Gallagher, H. L., & Frith, C. D. (2003). Functional imaging of 'theory of mind. *Trends in Cognitive Sciences*, *7*(2), 77–83.

Gloor, P., & Aggleton, J. P. (1992). Role of the amygdala in temporal lobe epilepsy. *The amygdala: Neurobiological aspects of emotion, memory, and mental dysfunction* (pp. 505–538). New York, NY US: Wiley-Liss.

Gur, R. C., Sara, R., Hagendoorn, M., Marom, O., Hughett, P., Macy, L., et al. (2002). A method for obtaining 3-dimensional facial expressions and its standardization for use in neurocognitive studies. *Journal of Neuroscience Methods*, *115*(2), 137–143.

Gur, R. C., Skolnick, B. E., & Gur, R. E. (1994). Effects of emotional discrimination tasks on cerebral blood flow: regional activation and its relation to performance. *Brain and Cognition*, *25*(2), 171–286.

Hadjikhani, N., & de Gelder, B. (2003). Seeing fearful body expressions activates the fusiform cortex and amygdala. *Current Biology*, *13*(24), 2201–2205.

Hamann, S., & Mao, H. (2002). Positive and negative emotional verbal stimuli elicit activity in the left amygdala. *Neuroreport: For Rapid Communication of Neuroscience Research*, *13*(1), 15–19.

Hastings, M. E., Tangney, J. P., & Stuewig, J. (2008). Psychopathy and identification of facial expressions of emotion. *Personality and Individual Differences*, *44*(7), 1474–1483.

Hayes, C. J., Stevenson, R. J., & Coltheart, M. (2007). Disgust and huntington's disease. *Neuropsychologia*, *45*(6), 1135–1151.

Heilman, K. M., Bowers, D., Speedie, L., & Coslett, H. B. (1984). Comprehension of affective and nonaffective prosody. *Neurology*, *34*(7), 917–921.

Heilman, K. M., Leon, S. A., & Rosenbek, J. C. (2004). Affective aprosodia from a medial frontal stroke. *Brain and Language*, *89*(3), 411–416.

Henry, J. D., Ruffman, T., McDonald, S., O'Leary, M. -A. P., Phillips, L. H., Brodaty, H., et al. (2008). Recognition of disgust is selectively preserved in Alzheimer's disease. *Neuropsychologia*, *46*(5), 1363–1370.

Heyes, C. (2011). Automatic imitation. *Psychological Bulletin*, *137*(3), 463–483.

Hooker, C. I., Verosky, S. C., Germine, L. T., Knight, R. T., & D'Esposito, M. (2010). Neural activity during social signal perception correlates with self-reported empathy. *Brain Research*, *1308*, 100–113.

Hornak, J., Bramham, J., Rolls, E. T., Morris, R. G., O'Doherty, J., Bullock, P. R., et al. (2003). Changes in emotion after circumscribed surgical lesions of the orbitofrontal and cingulate cortices. *Brain: A Journal of Neurology*, *126*(7), 1691–1712.

Hubbard, K., & Trauner, D. A. (2007). Intonation and emotion in autistic spectrum disorders. *Journal of Psycholinguistic Research*, *36*(2), 159–173.

Humphreys, K., Minshew, N., Leonard, G. L., & Behrmanna, M. (2007). A fine-grained analysis of facial expression processing in high-functioning adults with autism. *Neuropsychologia*, *45*(4), 685–695.

Karow, C. M., Marquardt, T. P., & Marshall, R. C. (2001). Affective processing in left and right hemisphere brain-damaged subjects with and without subcortical involvement. *Aphasiology*, *15*(8), 715–729.

Kasari, C., Freeman, S. F. N., & Hughes, M. A. (2001). Emotion recognition by children with Down syndrome. *American Journal on Mental Retardation*, *106*(1), 59–72.

Kirsch, L. G., & Becker, J. V. (2007). Emotional deficits in psychopathy and sexual sadism: Implications for violent and sadistic behavior. *Clinical Psychology Review*, 27(8), 904–922.

Korkman, M., Kirk, U., & Kemp, S. (2007). *NEPSY-II: Clinical and Interpretive Manual*. San Antonio, TX: NCS Pearson.

Kornreich, C., Blairy, S., Philippot, P., Dan, B., Foisy, M. -L., Hess, U., et al. (2001). Impaired emotional facial expression recognition in alcoholism compared with obsessive-compulsive disorder and normal controls. *Psychiatry Research*, 102(3), 235–248.

Kosson, D. S., Suchy, Y., Mayer, A. R., & Libby, J. (2002). Facial affect recognition in criminal psychopaths. *Emotion*, 2(4), 398–411.

Lattner, S., Meyer, M. E., & Friederici, A. D. (2005). Voice perception: Sex, pitch, and the right hemisphere. *Human Brain Mapping*, 24(1), 11–20.

Lavenu, I., & Pasquier, F. (2004). Perception of emotion on faces in frontotemporal dementia and Alzheimer's disease: a longitudinal study. *Dementia and Geriatric Cognitive Disorders*, 19(1), 37–41.

Lee, G. P., Meador, K. J., Loring, D. W., Allison, J. D., Brown, W. S., Paul, L. K., et al. (2004). Neural substrates of emotion as revealed by functional magnetic resonance imaging. *Cognitive and Behavioral Neurology*, 17(1), 9–17.

Lee, T. -W., Josephs, O., Dolan, R. J., & Critchley, H. D. (2006). Imitating expressions: Emotion-specific neural substrates in facial mimicry. *Social Cognitive and Affective Neuroscience*, 1(2), 122–135.

Liberzon, I., Phan, K. L., Decker, L. R., & Taylor, S. F. (2003). Extended amygdala and emotional salience: a PET activation study of positive and negative affect. *Neuropsychopharmacology*, 28(4), 726–733.

Liew, S. L., Han, S., & Aziz-Zadeh, L. (2011). Familiarity modulates mirror neuron and mentalizing regions during intention understanding. *Human Brain Mapping*, 32(11), 1986–1997.

Lough, S., Kipps, C. M., Treise, C., Watson, P., Blair, J. R., & Hodges, J. R. (2006). Social reasoning, emotion and empathy in frontotemporal dementia. *Neuropsychologia*, 44(6), 950–958.

Matheson, E., & Jahoda, A. (2005). Emotional understanding in aggressive and nonaggressive individuals with mild or moderate mental retardation. *American Journal on Mental Retardation*, 110(1), 57–67.

Mazzola, F., Seigal, A., MacAskill, A., Corden, B., Lawrence, K., & Skuse, D. H. (2006). Eye tracking and fear recognition deficits in Turner syndrome. *Social Neuroscience*, 1(3), 259–269.

McCown, W. G., Johnson, J., & Austin, S. (1986). Inability of delinquents to recognize facial affects. *Journal of Social Behavior & Personality*, 1(4), 489–496.

McCown, W. G., Johnson, J. L., & Austin, S. H. (1988). Patterns of facial affect recognition errors in delinquent adolescent males. *Journal of Social Behavior & Personality*, 3(3), 215–224.

Milders, M., Ietswaart, M., Crawford, J. R., & Currie, D. (2008). Social behavior following traumatic brain injury and its association with emotion recognition, understanding of intentions, and cognitive flexibility. *Journal of the International Neuropsychological Society*, 14(2), 318–326.

Monnot, M., Lovallo, W. R., Nixon, S. J., & Ross, E. (2002). Neurological basis of deficits in affective prosody comprehension among alcoholics and fetal alcohol-exposed adults. *Journal of Neuropsychiatry and Clinical Neuroscience*, 14(3), 321–328.

Monnot, M., Nixon, S., Lovallo, W., & Ross, E. (2001). Altered emotional perception in alcoholics: Deficits in affective prosody comprehension. *Alcoholism: Clinical and Experimental Research*, 25(3), 362–369.

Montreys, C. R., & Borod, J. C. (1998). A preliminary evaluation of emotional experience and expression following unilateral braiin damage. *International Journal of Neuroscience, 96*(3), 269–283.

Murayama, J., Kashiwagi, T., Kashiwagi, A., & Mimura, M. (2004). Impaired pitch production and preserved rhythm production in a right brain-damaged patient with amusia. *Brain and Cognition, 56*(1), 36–42.

Naccache, L., Gaillard, R. l., Adam, C., Hasboun, D., Clémenceau, S. P., Baulac, M., et al. (2005). A direct intracranial record of emotions evoked by subliminal words. *PNAS Proceedings of the National Academy of Sciences of the United States of America, 102*(21), 7713–7717.

Ohman, A. (2002). Automaticity and the amygdala: Nonconscious responses to emotional faces. *Current Directions in Psychological Science, 11*(2), 62–66.

Ohman, A. (2005). The role of the amygdala in human fear: automatic detection of threat. *Psychoneuroendocrinology, 30*(10), 953–958.

Orbelo, D. M., Grim, M. A., Talbott, R. E., & Ross, E. D. (2005). Impaired comprehension of affective prosody in elderly subjects is not predicted by age-related hearing loss or age-related cognitive decline. *Journal of Geriatric Psychiatry and Neurology, 18*(1), 25–32.

Pearson (2001). *Manual for the wechsler test of adult reading (WTAR).* San Antonio, TX: Pearson Education.

Pearson (2009). *Advanced clinical solutions for the WAIS–IV/WMS–IV.* San Antonio, TX: Pearson Education.

Pell, M. D. (1998). Recognition of prosody following unilateral brain lesion: influence of functional and structural attributes of prosodic contours. *Neuropsychologia, 36*(8), 701–715.

Philippot, P., Kornreich, C., Blairy, S., Den Dulk, A., Le Bon, O., Streel, E., et al. (1999). Alcoholics' deficits in the decoding of emotional facial expression. *Alcoholism: Clinical and experimental research, 23*(6), 1031–1038.

Pineda, J. A., Moore, A. R., Elfenbeinand, H., & Cox, R. (2009). Hierarchically organized mirroring processes in social cognition: The functional neuroanatomy of empathy. In J. A. Pineda (Ed.), *Mirror neuron systems: The role of mirroring processes in social cognition* (pp. 135–160). Totowa, NJ US: Humana Press.

Pinkham, A. E., Hopfinger, J. B., Pelphrey, K. A., Piven, J., & Penn, D. L. (2008). Neural bases for impaired social cognition in schizophrenia and autism spectrum disorders. *Schizophrenia Research, 99*(1–3), 164–175.

Platel, H., Price, C., Baron, J.-C., Wise, R., Lambert, J., Frackowiak, R. S. J., et al. (1997). The structural components of music perception: A functional anatomical study. *Brain: A Journal of Neurology, 120*(2), 229–243.

Premack, D., & Woodruff, G. (1978). Does the chimpanzee have a theory of mind? *Behavioral and Brain Sciences, 1*(4), 515–526.

Preston, S. D., Bechara, A., Damasio, H., Grabowski, T. J., Stansfield, R. B., Mehta, S., et al. (2007). The neural substrates of cognitive empathy. *Social Neuroscience, 2*(3), 254–275.

Radice-Neumann, D., Zupan, B., Babbage, D. R., & Willer, B. (2007). Overview of impaired facial affect recognition in persons with traumatic brain injury. *Brain Injury, 21*(8), 807–816.

Rankin, K. P., Baldwin, E., Pace-Savitsky, C., Kramer, J. H., & Miller, B. L. (2005). Self awareness and personality change in dementia. *Journal of Neurology, Neurosurgery & Psychiatry, 76*(5), 632–639.

Rankin, K. P., Kramer, J. H., & Miller, B. L. (2005). Patterns of cognitive and emotional empathy in frontotemporal lobar degeneration. *Cognitive and Behavioral Neurology, 18* (1), 28–36.

Ross, E. D. (1981). The aprosodias: Functional-anatomic organization of the affective components of language in the right hemisphere. *Archives of Neurology, 38*(9), 561–569.

Ross, E. D. (1984). Right hemisphere's role in language, affective behavior and emotion. *Trends in Neurosciences, 7*(9), 342–346.

Ross, E. D., & Mesulam, M. M. (2000). *Affective prosody and the aprosodias principles of behavioral and cognitive neurology* (2nd ed., pp. 316–331).). New York, NY US: Oxford University Press.

Ross, E. D., & Monnot, M. (2008). Neurology of affective prosody and its functional-anatomic organization in right hemisphere. *Brain and Language, 104*(1), 51–74.

Ross, E. D., Thompson, R. D., & Yenkosky, J. (1997). Lateralization of affective prosody in brain and the callosal integration of hemispheric language functions. *Brain and Language, 56*(1), 27–54.

Sachs, G., Steger-Wuchse, D., Kryspin-Exner, I., Gur, R. C., & Katschnig, H. (2004). Facial affect recognition deficits and cognition in schizophrenia. *Schizophrenia Research, 68*(1), 27–35.

Schulte-Ruether, M., Markowitsch, H. J., Fink, G. R., & Piefke, M. (2007). Mirror neuron and theory of mind mechanisms involved in face-to-face interactions: a functional magnetic resonance imaging approach to empathy. *Journal of Cognitive Neuroscience, 19*(8), 1354–1372.

Shamay-Tsoory, S. G., Aharon-Peretz, J., & Perry, D. (2009). Two systems for empathy: a double dissociation between emotional and cognitive empathy in inferior frontal gyrus versus ventromedial prefrontal lesions. *Brain: A Journal of Neurology, 132*(3), 617–627.

Shamay-Tsoory, S. G., Harari, H., Szepsenwol, O., & Levkovitz, Y. (2009). Neuropsychological evidence of impaired cognitive empathy in euthymic bipolar disorder. *The Journal of Neuropsychiatry and Clinical Neurosciences, 21*(1), 59–67.

Shamay-Tsoory, S. G., Shur, S., Harari, H., & Levkovitz, Y. (2007). Neurocognitive basis of impaired empathy in schizophrenia. *Neuropsychology, 21*(4), 431–438.

Shamay-Tsoory, S. G., Tomer, R., Goldsher, D., Berger, B. D., & Aharon-Peretz, J. (2004). Impairment in cognitive and affective empathy in patients with brain lesions: Anatomical and cognitive correlates. *Journal of Clinical and Experimental Neuropsychology, 26*(8), 1113–1127.

Shamay-Tsoory, S. G., Tomer, R., Yaniv, S., & Aharon-Peretz, J. (2002). Empathy deficits in asperger syndrome: A cognitive profile. *Neurocase, 8*(3), 245–252.

Shapiro, B. E., & Danly, M. (1985). The role of the right hemisphere in the control of speech prosody in propositional and affective contexts. *Brain and Language, 25*(1), 19–36.

Skuse, D. H., Morris, J. S., & Dolan, R. J. (2005). Functional dissociation of amygdala-modulated arousal and cognitive appraisal, in Turner syndrome. *Brain: A Journal of Neurology, 128*(9), 2084–2096.

Snowden, J. S., Austin, N. A., Sembi, S., Thompson, J. C., Craufurd, D., & Neary, D. (2008). Emotion recognition in Huntington's disease and frontotemporal dementia. *Neuropsychologia, 46*(11), 2638–2649.

South, M. D., Ozonoff, S., Suchy, Y., Kesner, R. P., McMahon, W. M., & Lainhart, J. E. (2008). Intact emotion facilitation for non-social stimuli in autism: is amygdala impairment in autism specific for social information? *Journal of International Neuropsychological Society, 14*(1), 42–54.

Starkstein, S. E., Federoff, J. P., Price, T. R., & Leiguarda, R. C. (1994). Neuropsychological and neuroradiologic correlates of emotional prosody comprehension. *Neurology, 44*(3), 515–522.

Suchy, Y. (2011). *Clinical neuropsychology of emotion.* New York: Guilford Press.

Suchy, Y., Rau, H., Whittaker, W. J., Eastvold, A., & Strassberg, D. S. (2009). Facial affect recognition as a predictor of performance on a reading comprehension test among criminal sex offenders. *Applied Psychology in Criminal Justice, 5*(1), 73–89.

Suchy, Y., Whittaker, W. J., Strassberg, D., & Eastvold, A. (2009). Facial and prosodic affect recognition among pedophilic and non-pedophilic criminal child molesters. *Sexual Abuse: A journal of Research and Treatment, 21*(1), 93–110.

Sugranyes, G., Kyriakopoulos, M., Corrigall, R., Taylor, E., & Frangou, S. (2011). Autism spectrum disorders and schizophrenia: meta-analysis of the neural correlates of social cognition. *PLoS ONE, 6*(10), e26322.

Tompkins, C. A., & Flowers, C. R. (1985). Perception of emotional intonation by brain-damaged adults: The influence of task processing levels. *Journal of Speech & Hearing Research, 28*(4), 527–538.

Uekermann, J., Daum, I., Schlebusch, P., & Trenckmann, U. (2005). Processing of affective stimuli in alcoholism. *Cortex, 41*(2), 189–194.

Van Lancker, D., & Sidtis, J. J. (1992). The identification of affective-prosodic stimuli by left- and right-hemisphere-damaged subjects: all errors are not created equal. *Journal of Speech & Hearing Research, 35*(5), 963–970.

Varcin, K. J., Bailey, P. E., & Henry, J. D. (2010). Empathic deficits in schizophrenia: The potential role of rapid facial mimicry. *Journal of the International Neuropsychological Society, 16*(4), 621–629.

Weddell, R. A. (1994). Effects of subcortical lesion site on human emotional behavior. *Brain and Cognition, 25*(2), 161–193.

Weniger, G., Lange, C., Rather, E., & Irle, E. (2004). Differential impairments of facial affect recognition in schizophrenia subtypes and major depression. *Psychiatry Research, 128* (2), 135–146.

Wertz, R. T., Henschel, C. R., Auther, L. L., Ashford, J. R., & Kirshner, H. S. (1998). Affective prosodic disturbance subsequent to right hemisphere stroke: A clinical application. *Journal of Neurolinguistics, 11*(1), 89–102.

Whittaker, J. F., Deakin, J. F. W., & Tomenson, B. (2001). Face processing in schizophrenia: Defining the deficit. *Psychological Medicine, 31*(3), 499–507.

Wild, B., Erb, M., & Bartels, M. (2001). Are emotions contagious? Evoked emotions while viewing emotionally expressive faces: quality, quantity, time course and gender differences. *Psychiatry Research, 102*(2), 109–124.

Wishart, J. G., Cebula, K. R., Willis, D. S., & Pitcairn, T. K. (2007). Understanding of facial expressions of emotion by children with intellectual disabilities of differing aetiology. *Journal of Intellectual Disability Research, 51*(7), 551–563.

Worling, D. E., Humphries, T., & Tannock, R. (1999). Spatial and emotional aspects of language inferencing in nonverbal learning disabilities. *Brain and Language, 70*(2), 220–239.

Zimmerman, E. K., Eslinger, P. J., Simmons, Z., & Barrett, A. M. (2007). Emotional perception deficits in amyotrophic lateral sclerosis. *Cognitive and Behavioral Neurology, 20*(2), 79–82.

Assessing Cognition in Older Adults with the WAIS–IV, WMS–IV, and ACS

Lisa Whipple Drozdick*, James A. Holdnack*, Timothy Salthouse† and C. Munro Cullum‡

*Pearson Assessment, San Antonio, Texas, USA †University of Virginia, Charlottesville, Virginia, USA ‡UT Southwestern Medical Center, Dallas, Texas, USA

INTRODUCTION

The population of older adults is one of the fastest growing demographic groups in the United States (Vincent & Velkoff, 2010). Clinicians are increasingly assessing this diverse group and facing unique challenges. Psychological evaluation of older adults requires knowledge and consideration of many issues to appropriately assess with and interpret results obtained on cognitive instruments such as the Wechsler Adult Intelligence Scale–Fourth Edition (WAIS–IV: Wechsler, 2008) and the Wechsler Memory Scale–Fourth Edition (WMS–IV: Wechsler, 2009). Although many older adults do not experience significant physical or cognitive impairment, the likelihood of experiencing physical and/or sensory impairment increases with age. Chronic health conditions affecting cognitive functioning are frequently experienced in older adults, as are physical and sensory limitations that affect cognitive performance. Several chronic health conditions increase in prevalence with age, including arthritis, cancer, cardiovascular, and pulmonary disease, and diabetes. These conditions can impact cognitive

    © 2013 Elsevier Inc. All rights reserved.

abilities or produce or exacerbate physical/sensory impairment. In addition, these conditions may co-occur with neurological conditions known to impact cognitive ability, such as Alzheimer's (ALZ) disease, making it difficult to determine the effects of the conditions independently. Many activities, such as shopping and driving, can be significantly compromised by sensory impairment.

In addition to health conditions and sensory impairments, medications can impact performance and should be considered when examining scores and score profiles. Medication use, both in isolation and in combination, is common in older adults. In a survey of 1100 community-dwelling older adults, 43.4% were taking more than one medication with 51.1% of these taking more than five medications (Heuberger & Caudell, 2011). The use of multiple medications increases the risk of drug interactions and poor health outcomes in older adults, such as cognitive impairment and acute confusional state (Hanlon et al., 2006; Starr et al., 2004; Wright et al., 2009). The effects of medication are particularly problematic if cognitive impairment, financial considerations, or other medical or sensory conditions impair the individual's ability to take medication as prescribed. The overuse, underuse, or improper use of medication among older adults can frequently be attributed to the complexity of the medication regimen (including multiple prescriptions or multiple prescribers), sensory impairment, cognitive and memory deficits, concerns about medication effects or side effects, and cost (Hajjar et al., 2005; MacLaughlin et al., 2005; O'Carroll et al., 2011). When evaluating an older adult, a clinician should assess the number and type of medications the client is taking as well as the examinee's use of those medications.

Cognitive assessment is essential for detecting declines in ability, a requirement for evaluating and diagnosing Mild Cognitive Impairment (MCI) and dementia (AGS Clinical Practice Committee, 2003; Knopman et al., 2001; Petersen et al., 2001). Early detection of cognitive change is imperative for applying pharmacological and other interventions as early as possible in a dementing process. Neuropsychological measures, particularly memory measures such as the WMS–IV and California Verbal Learning test–Second Edition (CVLT–II; Delis, Kaplan, Kramer, & Ober, 2000) demonstrate predictive powers in identifying the likelihood of cognitive decline in healthy older adults and those with MCI (Albert, Moss, Blacker, Tanzi, & McArdle, 2007; Derrer et al., 2001; Guarch, Marcos, Salamero, Gastó, & Blesa, 2008; Jungwirth et al., 2009; Masur, Fuld, Blau, Crystal, & Aronson, 1990; Tierney, Moineddin, & McDowell, 2010). Finally, the use of cognitive testing reduces the likelihood of misdiagnosing dementia (Brooks, Iverson, Feldman, & Holdnack, 2009). Mansdorf, Harrington, Lund and Wohl (2008) assessed individuals residing in a skilled nursing facility with cognitive measures and found that 84.2% of those individuals with a diagnosis of "suspected" dementia did not meet the criteria for dementia. Moreover, only 25% of the misdiagnosed individuals met the criteria for MCI, while the vast majority met criteria for other disorders, most commonly depression.

In addition to assessing cognitive decline, clinicians are frequently called on to evaluate the capacity of an older adult to perform complex behaviors such as driving or making medical or financial decisions. Measures of executive functioning, memory, and visuospatial processing may assist in predicting these complex behaviors and everyday functioning (Baird, Podell, Lovell, & McGinty, 2001; Bell-McGinty, Podell, Franzen, Baird, & Williams, 2002; Bieliauskas, 2005; Brand & Markowitsch, 2010; Farias et al., 2009; Whelihana, DiCarloa, & Paula, 2005). The assessment of adaptive functioning, particularly Activities of Daily Living (ADL) and Instrumental Activities of Daily Living (IADL) status, is an important aspect of the evaluation of older adults and is addressed later in this chapter.

Numerous books and chapters have been devoted to the assessment of older adults and are good sources for clinicians new to the field (e.g., Carstensen, Edelstein, & Dornbrand, 1996; Lezak, Howieson, & Loring, 2004; Lichtenberg, 2011; Storandt, 1994). Moreover, the American Psychological Association (APA) has published guidelines for psychologists working with older adults (APA, 2004). This chapter focuses on the use of the WAIS–IV, WMS–IV, Advanced Clinical Solutions for the WAIS–IV and WMS–IV (ACS: Pearson, 2009), WMS–IV Flexible Approach (Pearson, 2010), and Texas Functional Living Scale (TFLS: Cullum, Saine, & Weiner, 2009) in the assessment of older adults, particularly in the evaluation of cognitive decline. Other chapters in this book provide detailed information on the methodological processes described in this chapter while the focus of this chapter is on the use of these methods in older adults.

RELATIONSHIP OF AGE TO COGNITIVE FUNCTIONING

Most research examining the relations between age and measures of cognitive functioning has been based on cross-sectional rather than longitudinal samples. This distinction between cognitive differences based on cross-sectional comparisons and individual changes in cognition based on longitudinal comparisons is important because age trends can differ across the two types of comparisons. In both paradigms, non-age related factors may impact the results of the study. For example, people of different ages could differ in a variety of characteristics (e.g., education level) related to cognitive performance, which could distort cross-sectional comparisons, or people might benefit from prior test experience associated with the first longitudinal measurement (e.g., practice effects) which influence longitudinal comparisons. Research on the relation of age to cognitive functioning needs to be evaluated in light of the study design utilized. At the current time, cross-sectional research on the relations between age and cognitive functioning is much more extensive than longitudinal research; therefore, only cross-sectional comparisons will be discussed in this section.

For almost 100 years, a consistent pattern of age effects on cognition has been reported in cross-sectional comparisons. What has come to be known as the classic pattern of aging consists of *higher* scores on tests of knowledge such as vocabulary and information (at least until about age 70 or so), but nearly linear age-related *declines* on tests of reasoning, such as block design and matrix reasoning, and more precipitous declines on tests of processing speed, such as digit symbol substitution and symbol search. These patterns are portrayed in Figure 9.1 with data from the WAIS–IV standardization sample. In order to facilitate comparisons across tests, all scores have been converted to T-scores, with means of 50 and standard deviations of 10. It can be seen that on reasoning and speed tests the average 50-year-old performs about 0.5 standard deviations lower than the average 20-year-old, but performs about 1 standard deviation higher than the average 70-year-old. However, performance on vocabulary and information among adults in their 50 s is about 0.3 standard deviations above that of both adults in their 20 s and adults in their 70 s.

Although the patterns illustrated in Figure 9.1 are robust and have been well documented for almost 100 years with a variety of clinical and experimental tests, the reasons for the age-related associations with

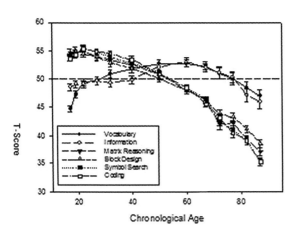

FIGURE 9.1 WAIS–IV Subtest Performance across Normative Age Bands.

cognition are still not well understood. It seems likely that much of the age-related increase in knowledge reflects greater cumulative exposure to information, coupled with relative preservation of the capacity to access previously acquired information. However, the negative relationship between age and other cognitive abilities remains a puzzle.

In addition to patterns observed directly with age, a number of strong correlates of age differences in cognitive functioning have been identified, and some have been found to be effective statistical mediators of the relations between age and cognitive functioning. For example, Salthouse (1996) reported that statistical control of various measures of processing speed reduced the cross-sectional relations between age and measures of reasoning, memory, and spatial ability. Although these findings have been quite consistent, the correlational nature of the data precludes strong causal inferences. That is, the moderate relations between measures of speed and measures of other types of cognition could reflect a causal sequence in which increased age is associated with decreased speed, which in turn contributes to lower levels of performance in other cognitive measures. However, it is also possible that the speed measures may be influenced by aspects of cognition such as working memory or efficient allocation of attention, or that the relations reflect the operation of a third variable, such as cardiovascular and cerebrovascular health status, that affects both types of variables. Because it is impossible to experimentally manipulate the critical variable of age, it is very difficult to identify the causes, as opposed to correlates, of age-related differences in cognitive functioning.

One of the earliest speculations suggested that the negative age relations were attributable to lower amounts of education in older ages. In other words, the current older adult population attained lower levels of formal education than younger adult cohorts due to societal influences on the importance of education, access to advanced education, and major historical disruptions to completing formal education (e.g., military draft). Although intuitively plausible, this interpretation of the age-cognition relations has a number of weaknesses. For example, education influences would be expected to be greatest with knowledge measures and yet these exhibit little age-related decline, and numerous analyses have found similar age trends when amount of education is controlled (see Salthouse, 2010a, for a review).

In recent years another category of explanation based on unspecified changes in the physical and social environment has become popular. Increases over time in the average score on various cognitive tests among people of the same age has been well documented (i.e., the Flynn Effect), and some authors propose that generational improvements in performance may be responsible for the cross-sectional relations between age and cognitive functioning (Ronnlund, Nyberg,

Backman, & Nilsson, 2005; Schaie, 2005). For example, if the average 20-year-old in 2010 performs one standard deviation higher than the average 20-year-old in 1980, and if there were little or no actual change in cognitive ability after the individual reached maturity, generational improvements might account for the nearly one standard deviation difference between 20- and 50-year-olds in cross-sectional data in 2010. However, it is important to recognize that this argument is based on the assumption that there is little historical or time-related increase in cognitive performance after about age 20, which might not be the case. In fact, Salthouse (2010a) suggested that if the time lag effects were similar at all ages, the Flynn phenomenon could be analogous to the effect of inflation on salaries, in which a contrast at two different points in time would reveal historical "improvements," without affecting the relative differences between adults of different ages. An implication of this inflationary interpretation is that regardless of the absolute level of performance, the relative age differences in cognitive performance might be expected to be similar across different historical periods. Comparisons of the age trends on the same tests in different versions of the Wechsler tests are consistent with this implication. Salthouse (2010a) reported that the relative age trends in Vocabulary, Similarities, Block Design, and Digit Symbol tests have been very similar from the 1955 to 2008 standardizations of the test battery. Results such as these suggest that although there has been a shift over time in the absolute level of performance, the relation of older adult performance to younger adult performance has remained fairly similar.

Another possible interpretation of the negative age relations in some measures of cognitive functioning is that they reflect qualitative differences in how the tests are perceived and performed by different age groups rather than a quantitative shift in ability. That is, increased age could be associated with a reduction in motivation, or a difference in how the tests relate to one's life goals. Unfortunately, few objective methods are available to assess the meaning of tests in particular individuals. One potentially informative method involves examining the pattern of correlations among different cognitive tests because age-related shifts in the strengths of the interrelations among measures might reflect an age difference in what the tests are representing. However, most of the available research has revealed relatively small age differences in factor structure patterns.

It is likely that some of the relations of age to certain types of cognitive functioning are associated with age-related neurobiological changes. Many age differences in measures of brain structure and brain function are well documented, and some have been related to performance on cognitive tests (See review in Salthouse, 2011). However, a major challenge has been to establish a causal linkage between age differences and changes in brain measures, and age difference and changes in measures of cognitive functioning (Salthouse, 2011).

WAIS–IV, WMS–IV, AND ACS MEASURES FOR ASSESSING COGNITIVE CHANGE

During the development of the WAIS–IV and WMS–IV, numerous adjustments were made to the instruments to accommodate the changes in sensory and psychomotor abilities frequently experienced by older adults. In addition to modifications to the core instruments, several subtests and procedures were developed to address specific clinical questions and concerns that often arise while working with older adults, such as quickly assessing cognitive status, estimating premorbid ability, or applying demographically adjusted norms or serial change scores. Some of these measures are included or can be derived from the standard WAIS–IV or WMS–IV while others require the Advanced Clinical Solutions for WAIS–IV and WMS–IV (ACS) or the WMS–IV Flexible Approach. This section describes the modifications made to the WAIS–IV and WMS–IV to improve the assessment of older adults, as well as the new measures included in the WMS–IV, ACS, and WMS–IV Flexible Approach.

Modifications to WAIS–IV for Older Adults

The WAIS–IV was modified to reduce the influence of known aging changes on scores, including processing speed, visual and auditory acuity, motor skills, and fatigue. The specific modifications from the WAIS–III to the WAIS–IV include:

- Age range extended to 90.
- Time-bonus points minimized on the perceptual reasoning subtests. No time-bonus points are included within Arithmetic and fewer items include time bonus points on Block Design.
- The occurrence of phonologically similar letters and numbers within a trial on Digit Span and Letter–Number Sequencing (LNS) was reduced. In addition, LNS is not used in individuals over the age of 70.
- Overall level of vocabulary and sentence structure used in verbal instructions was reduced to decrease complexity.
- All visual stimuli were enlarged.
- Cancellation was developed to provide an alternative processing speed measure with reduced fine motor demands compared to Coding, available up to age 70.

- Visual Puzzles replaced Picture Arrangement and Object Assembly as a core subtest. This reduced the motor demands of subtests in the perceptual reasoning domain.
- On teaching items, all examinees received the same instruction, practice opportunities, and feedback regardless of performance, thus reducing differential teaching and ensuring low scores are not due to an examinee's misunderstanding of the task.
- The number of core subtests was reduced to 10, resulting in a reduced administration time of 67 minutes, an average savings of approximately 13 minutes over the WAIS–III.
- Clinical validity groups relevant to older adults were collected (e.g., ALZ, MCI).

Coalson, Raiford, Saklofske and Weiss (2010); Sattler and Ryan (2010); Wechsler (2008); and Woodard (2011) provide a detailed description of the WAIS–IV and modifications made to accommodate older adult assessment.

Modifications to WMS–IV for Older Adults

The WMS–IV is frequently used to assess memory in older adults. Some of the design features incorporated into the WMS–IV to make the test more amenable for use with older adults include having fewer and shorter subtests, reducing fatigue effects, and modification of content to improve floor effects, and increase sensitivity across the older age groups. For example, the older adult battery does not require manipulatives, increasing the portability of the kit for clinicians testing in non-traditional settings, such as hospitals or long-term care facilities. To improve the assessment of older adults, the WMS–IV introduces a cognitive screening tool designed to identify significant cognitive difficulties that may indicate dementia or other cognitive impairment. Additional modifications from WMS–III to WMS–IV include:

- Age range extended to 90.
- The optional Brief Cognitive Status Exam (BCSE) was developed to assess gross cognitive functioning and provides an age- and education-adjusted classification level of general cognitive status.
- Overall level of vocabulary used in verbal instructions was reduced to decrease complexity.
- A new story was developed for Logical Memory with reduced syntactic complexity and vocabulary level and content more relevant to older adults.
- The total number of words in Verbal Paired Associates was increased from eight (WMS–III) to 14; however, for the older adult battery

there are only 10 items and four of the items are semantically similar (i.e., easy items) to improve the floor (e.g., the ability to differentiate amongst the lowest ability individuals) in the older age groups.
- Designs provides an alternative visual memory assessment with reduced fine motor demands compared to Visual Reproduction, available up to age 69 in the adult battery.
- Symbol Span reduces the auditory acuity and motor demands in the working memory domain. It replaces Digit Span and Spatial Span, which are no longer included in the WMS–IV.
- The number of core subtests was reduced to four, resulting in a reduced administration time for older adults.
- The normative sample was screened for significant medical and psychiatric difficulties, cognitive impairment, and effort. This reduced the influence of MCI on scores in older adults where such disorders increase in frequency with increased age (Luck et al., 2007; Petersen, 2011).
- WAIS–IV scores were co-collected and used to establish a mean GAI of 100 for each age group, ensuring that ability and memory were equally scaled.
- Clinical validity groups relevant to older adult were collected (e.g., ALZ, dementia, MCI).

Drozdick, Holdnack and Hilsabeck (2011); Holdnack and Drozdick (2010); and Wechsler (2009) provide thorough descriptions of the WMS–IV and more detailed descriptions of the modifications made to accommodate older adults.

Brief Cognitive Status Exam

The BCSE is designed to quickly assess general cognitive functioning. It provides a broad classification level of current cognitive status (i.e., average, low average, borderline, low, and very low) adjusted for age and education level. Items assess orientation to time, mental control/processing speed, incidental memory, planning and visual–perceptual processing, inhibition of over-learned responses, and verbal production. Item raw scores are converted to weighted raw scores. The weighting of each item raw score reflects the percent of individuals in the normative sample that achieved a specific score. The highest values, which range from 4 to 8 across scores, are based on the clinical significance of the score and typically represent at least 25% of the normative sample and indicate little to no impairment on the item; the lowest score represents the score attained by less than 2% of the normative sample and indicates impairment on that item. The weighted raw item scores are summed to obtain the total raw score.

Total raw scores range from 0 to 58, with scores reflecting different levels of overall cognitive functioning. The total score is weighted toward measures of processing speed and mental control to increase the sensitivity of the BCSE to dementia or other cognitive impairment. The total score is converted to a classification level. The classification levels—Average, Low Average, Borderline, Low, and Very Low—represent 25% through 100%, 10% through 24%, 5% through 9%, 2% through 4%, and <2% of the normative sample, respectively. The BCSE Classification Level describes the general cognitive ability level of the individual being assessed.

WMS–IV Flexible Approach

The WMS–IV Flexible Approach manual is included in the WMS–IV kit and provides alternate measures and index scores for the WMS–IV. These alternate indexes were designed to create shorter or alternate memory assessments utilizing the WMS–IV subtests alone or in conjunction with the new supplemental subtests included in the WMS–IV Flexible Approach: Logos and Faces. Chapter 1 of this book provides an overview of the new subtests and indexes available in the WMS–IV Flexible Approach. The availability of alternate indexes and subtests maximizes the flexibility of the WMS–IV for clinicians serving vastly different populations. However, it should be noted that the WMS–IV Flexible Approach alternate batteries do not provide comparisons to WAIS–IV scores.

Advanced Clinical Solutions for WAIS–IV and WMS–IV (ACS)

The ACS provides face memory and memory for names measures not found in the standard WMS–IV. These additional memory measures are particularly helpful when working with clients suspected of having social perception deficits in addition to memory problems, such as those observed in frontotemporal dementia (Kipps, Mioshi, & Hodges, 2009; Snowden et al., 2003). The WMS–IV does not accommodate substitution of any of these subtests into any of the WMS–IV indexes; the ACS expands the assessment of memory beyond the constructs found in the WMS–IV. The ACS includes additional indexes described in Chapter 1, the Test of Premorbid Functioning (TOPF), demographically adjusted norms (DAN), and serial assessment scores.

Test of Premorbid Functioning

Estimating premorbid cognitive functioning provides valuable information for clinicians assessing older adults, particularly when evaluating cognitive functioning following a stroke or establishing a decline in functioning for diagnosing MCI or dementia. Chapter 5 in this book provides a detailed review of estimating premorbid functioning. The TOPF is a performance measure for the prediction of premorbid cognitive ability. It utilizes words with atypical grapheme to phoneme translation; thus, the test is not a measure of decoding ability but a test of word knowledge (Crawford, 1992). Reading skills are less susceptible to brain injury or decline than other performance measures and have been shown to effectively predict intellectual functioning (Crawford, 1992; Johnstone, Hogg, Schopp, Kapila, & Edwards, 2002). Unlike many cognitive abilities, reading recognition is *relatively* stable in the presence of cognitive decline associated with normal aging or brain insult, although it is not impervious to the effects of significant intellectual impairments (see Crawford 1992; Putnam, Ricker, Ross, & Kurtz, 1999; and Spreen & Strauss, 1998 for reviews).

The TOPF was co-developed for use with the WAIS–IV and WMS–IV and provides premorbid prediction based on demographic data only, current performance data only, or a combination of demographic data and current performance data. The co-norming with WAIS–IV and WMS–IV improves prediction estimates of intelligence and memory ability through direct comparison data between predicted and actual ability in a large, representative sample and a variety of clinical groups. The current performance models use test results from the TOPF to predict the examinee's premorbid ability. Although prediction accuracy of TOPF is lower for memory measures, using predicted premorbid memory scores significantly improves diagnostic accuracy in cases of dementia (Pearson, 2001).

Demographic Norms in ACS

Demographically adjusted norms are frequently used to identify a change in cognitive functioning by evaluating whether a test score is consistent with the patient's background characteristics. Standard norms, such as those provided in the WAIS–IV and WMS–IV, adjust test scores by age, a variable with well-known effects on cognitive performance. Demographically adjusted norms adjust normative scores by other background characteristics associated with performance on general cognitive ability, memory, and neuropsychological measures, such as education, gender, and ethnicity. Demographically adjusted norms allow an examiner to evaluate an obtained score in comparison to specific comparison groups, such as individuals with similar educational backgrounds. Demographically adjusted norms answer the question *"Are the examinee's current scores consistent with what is expected given his or her age and education and/or other background characteristics?"* For a comprehensive discourse on the appropriate use and application of demographic adjustments, see Chapter 4 of this book, Heaton, Ryan and Grant (2009), or Heaton, Taylor and Manly (2003).

Demographically adjusted norms were developed for the WAIS–IV and WMS–IV utilizing the normative sample and additional samples of examinees with low and high education levels and from minority ethnic groups. See the ACS Technical Manual (Pearson, 2009) for detailed information on the methods used to develop the demographically adjusted norms. Two sets of demographically adjusted norms are available: age and education only adjusted norms and full demographic adjusted norms. The full demographic adjustments account for age, education, gender, ethnicity, and region.

Serial Change Scores in ACS

The ability to compare scores across assessments provides insight into and documentation of changes in cognitive functioning over time, a key requirement for diagnosing MCI or dementia. Although changes in scores across evaluations may represent important clinical information, changes in test performance may occur for reasons other than actual changes in cognitive functioning, including normal fluctuations in cognitive skills (Salthouse, 2007; Sliwinski, Hofer, Hall, Bushke, & Lipton, 2003). Variability in cognitive functioning over time is normal; however, a consistent decline in cognitive skills may signal a significant clinical issue.

In addition to normal variability in performance, change in scores over time can be influenced by *practice effects*; that is, improved performance due to exposure and learning (McCaffrey, Ortega, & Haase, 1993). Measures of memory and processing speed are particularly susceptible to practice effects (McCaffrey et al., 1993; Wechsler, 2008, 2009). In the WAIS–IV and WMS–IV retest studies, the largest composite score changes were observed on the WMS–IV Delayed Memory Index ($d = 0.95$; Wechsler, 2009). Practice effects are not transient, with reports of effects lasting up to 7 years on measures of associative learning, memory, and inductive reasoning (Salthouse, Schroeder, & Ferrer, 2004). Although they can be long-lasting, practice effects are not equal across tests or examinees. Demographic or cognitive characteristics of an examinee—such as age, education, gender, and level of functioning at the initial assessment—may predispose that examinee to benefit more or less from exposure and learning than other examinees (Duff et al., 2005; Ferrer, Salthouse, McArdle, Stewart, & Schwartz, 2005; Lineweaver & Chelune, 2003; Salthouse, 2010b). See Chapter 6 of this book for a review of serial assessment and the development of the hierarchical equations derived in the ACS to assess changes in scores over time.

Evaluation of the Measures Used in Older Adults

The validity of the WAIS–IV, WMS–IV, ACS measures, and WMS–IV Flexible Approach are described in detail in their respective technical manuals (Wechsler, 2008, 2009, 2010; Pearson, 2009, 2010). To evaluate the utility of the measures described above and others proposed in relation to the WAIS–IV and WMS–IV, a series of additional comparison studies were conducted. For each study, data was obtained from subsamples of the WAIS–IV and WMS–IV standardization, demographic oversample and clinical samples. The studies include evaluation of prediction equations based on the Oklahoma Premorbid Intelligence Estimate (OPIE; Krull, Scott, & Sherer, 1995) or TOPF simple demographics methods, comparisons of measures of variability in performance across scores, multivariate base rates of low scores in older adults, and descriptions of performance on the standard and new index and subtest scores. In addition to comparison of performance to matched control groups, the ALZ and MCI groups are compared to randomly selected low and high education groups. This provides a comparison of results to populations in which predicted scores are frequently used, the extremes of the population. The demographic characteristics of the clinical, matched control, and high and low education groups are provided in Table 9.1.

WAIS–IV AND WMS–IV PERFORMANCE IN ALZHEIMER AND MILD COGNITIVE IMPAIRMENT GROUPS

Prior to presenting the prediction equation data, it is important to understand the actual performance differences observed between the clinical, matched controls, and low and high education groups. Tables 9.2–9.17 list the obtained scores on the WAIS–IV and WMS–IV for the ALZ and MCI and the related comparison groups. Scores are provided for the standard indexes as well as the new indexes described in Chapter 1 (i.e., Cognitive Proficiency Index, CPI; General Memory Index, GMI; Retention Index; Retrieval Index; Working Memory Index). Comparisons using the demographically adjusted norms for the standard indexes and subtests are reported as well.

For each study, actual means and standard deviations are provided followed by base rates for various cut-off points. The base rates describe

TABLE 9.1 Demographic Characteristics of the Clinical and Comparison Groups

Demographic Characteristic	Alzheimer Study Groups				MCI Study Groups			
	Alzheimer	Matched Controls	Low Education	High Education	MCI	Matched Controls	Low Education	High Education
N	51	51	50	50	75	75	50	50
Age Mean (SD)	77.2 (7.7)	77.3 (7.8)	77.2 (7.3)	77.1 (7.5)	72.5 (9.5)	72.5 (9.5)	77.2 (7.4)	77.3 (7.5)
Sex								
Male	27.5%	25.5%	44.0%	70.0%	50.7%	49.3%	42.0%	58.0%
Female	72.5%	74.5%	56.0%	30.0%	49.3%	50.7%	58.0%	42.0%
Education								
8 years or less	3.9%	3.9%	48.0%	0.0%	6.7%	6.7%	52.0%	0.0%
9–11 years	2.0%	2.0%	52.0%	0.0%	4.0%	4.0%	48.0%	0.0%
12 years	27.4%	27.4%	0.0%	0.0%	32.0%	32.0%	0.0%	0.0%
13–15 years	27.4%	27.4%	0.0%	0.0%	21.3%	25.3%	0.0%	0.0%
16 or more years	39.3%	39.3%	0.0%	100.0%	36.0%	32.0%	0.0%	100.0%

Ethnicity

White	90.2%	90.2%	70.0%	80.0%	93.3%	93.3%	74.0%	80.0%
African-American	9.8%	9.8%	18.0%	10.0%	4.0%	4.0%	10.0%	10.0%
Hispanic	0.0%	0.0%	10.0%	4.0%	2.7%	2.7%	14.0%	4.0%
Asian	0.0%	0.0%	2.0%	6.0%	0.0%	0.0%	2.0%	6.0%
Region								
Northeast	3.9%	21.6%	22.0%	14.0%	33.3%	21.3%	18.0%	18.0%
North Central	13.7%	33.3%	16.0%	38.0%	14.7%	24.0%	22.0%	34.0%
South	54.9%	29.4%	42.0%	38.0%	44.0%	36.0%	44.0%	36.0%
West	27.5%	15.7%	20.0%	10.0%	8.0%	18.7%	16.0%	12.0%

Copyright 2009 by Pearson, Inc. Reproduced with permission. All rights reserved.

TABLE 9.2 WAIS–IV Standard and New Index Scores and Subtest Scores in Alzheimer Disease and Matched Control Samples

Score	Alzheimer					Matched Control					Between-Group Differences	
	Mean	SD	25th %ile	16th %ile	9th %ile	Mean	SD	25th %ile	16th %ile	9th %ile	p	Effect Size
VCI	86.0	16.5	65	60	43	103.8	13.9	16	10	6	<0.001	−1.07
PRI	87.4	17.6	64	46	34	103.7	14.2	16	6	2	<0.001	−0.93
WMI	81.0	17.2	67	45	41	101.5	13.4	14	8	6	<0.001	−1.19
PSI	76.4	15.2	76	68	58	102.6	12.2	14	4	4	<0.001	−1.72
GAI	85.4	17.2	64	56	53	104.1	13.6	16	8	6	<0.001	−1.08
CPI	77.5	16.2	81	72	64	102.1	13.5	12	8	6	<0.001	−1.53
FSIQ	81.0	17.2	74	63	54	103.7	13.7	12	9	6	<0.001	−1.32
Vocabulary	8.2	2.9	65	43	24	10.9	2.7	22	12	4	<0.001	−0.90
Similarities	7.9	3.9	60	51	38	10.8	2.9	22	8	6	<0.001	−0.73
Information	6.5	2.8	70	70	65	10.5	3.1	24	20	18	<0.001	−1.41
Block Design	8.0	4.0	57	41	32	10.8	2.9	24	8	8	<0.001	−0.71
Matrix Reasoning	7.8	3.6	67	53	42	11.0	3.1	20	10	2	<0.001	−0.89

Visual Puzzles	7.8	2.5	76	62	35	10.2	2.7	31	12	2	<0.001	−0.97
Digit Span	7.5	3.3	68	46	43	10.3	2.7	22	8	8	<0.001	−0.88
Digit Span Forward	8.8	2.7	57	26	17	9.8	2.9	35	12	8	>0.05	−0.39
Digit Span Backward	8.0	3.0	60	43	31	9.9	2.7	31	22	16	<0.01	−0.63
Digit Span Sequencing	6.9	3.7	74	57	43	10.8	3.0	14	14	8	<0.001	−1.07
Arithmetic	7.1	2.4	76	65	38	10.3	2.7	18	14	6	<0.001	−1.35
Coding	6.0	3.5	75	67	56	10.5	2.5	14	6	6	<0.001	−1.31
Symbol Search	5.3	2.7	87	73	70	10.5	2.5	16	10	8	<0.001	−1.94

Note: Listwise deletion of cases, Alzheimer $n = 35$.
VCI = Verbal Comprehension Index; PRI = Perceptual Reasoning Index; WMI = Working Memory Index; PSI = Processing Speed Index; GAI = General Ability Index; CPI = Cognitive Proficiency Index; FSIQ = Full Scale IQ.

Copyright 2009 by Pearson, Inc. Reproduced with permission. All rights reserved.

TABLE 9.3 WAIS–IV Standard Index Scores in Alzheimer Disease and Low and High Education Samples

	Alzheimer					Low Education					Between Group Differences	
Score	Mean	SD	25th %ile	16th %ile	9th %ile	Mean	SD	25th %ile	16th %ile	9th %ile	p	ES
VCI	86.0	16.5	65	60	43	88.6	16.1	48	44	34	>0.05	−0.16
PRI	87.4	17.6	64	46	34	90.1	12.6	66	32	18	>0.05	−0.15
WMI	81.0	17.2	67	45	41	90.4	14.1	48	38	28	>0.05	−0.55
PSI	76.4	15.2	76	68	58	90.7	17.8	48	38	24	<0.001	−0.94
GAI	85.4	17.2	64	56	53	88.2	14.6	58	46	30	>0.05	−0.16
FSIQ	81.0	17.2	74	63	54	87.8	15.9	64	50	32	>0.05	−0.39

	Alzheimer					High Education					Between Group Differences	
Score	Mean	SD	25th %ile	16th %ile	9th %ile	Mean	SD	25th %ile	16th %ile	9th %ile	p	ES
VCI	86.0	16.5	65	60	44	114.4	11.3	4	0	0	<0.001	−1.71
PRI	87.4	17.6	64	46	34	109.2	15.0	14	4	0	<0.001	−1.24
WMI	81.0	17.2	67	45	41	109.8	14.1	12	2	0	<0.001	−1.68
PSI	76.4	15.2	76	68	58	104.7	11.4	12	2	0	<0.001	−1.86
GAI	85.4	17.2	64	56	53	113.4	12.6	4	0	0	<0.001	−1.63
FSIQ	81.0	17.2	74	63	54	112.3	12.1	6	4	0	<0.001	−1.82

Note: Listwise deletion of cases, Alzheimer n = 35.
%ile
VCI = Verbal Comprehension Index; PRI = Perceptual Reasoning Index; WMI = Working Memory Index; PSI = Processing Speed Index; GAI = General Ability Index; FSIQ = Full Scale IQ.
Copyright 2009 by Pearson, Inc. Reproduced with permission. All rights reserved.

the percentage of individuals in the sample that obtained a score for that variable at or below the 25th, 16th, and 9th percentiles, respectively. Finally, comparison data are provided, including statistical significance and effect size information.

Table 9.2 describes the performance on the WAIS–IV index and subtest scores by the ALZ and matched control samples. *Significant differences are observed on all index scores with the greatest differences on the Processing Speed Index (PSI) and CPI.* All subtest scores are significantly different between groups with the exception of Digit Span Forward. The greatest difference was observed on Symbol Search. Interestingly, Information, frequently described as a hold task (e.g., relatively impervious to effects of cognitive

TABLE 9.4 WAIS–IV Full Demographically Adjusted Standard Index and Subtest Scores in Alzheimer Disease and Matched Control Samples

Score	Alzheimer					Matched Control					Between Group Differences	
	Mean	SD	25th %ile	16th %ile	9th %ile	Mean	SD	25th %ile	16th %ile	9th %ile	p	ES
VCI	34.0	11.7	77	71	66	50.1	8.2	27	8	2	<0.001	−1.38
PRI	38.0	12.2	74	60	57	51.2	9.7	20	16	8	<0.001	−1.08
WMI	34.5	10.6	83	71	63	48.8	8.4	22	10	8	<0.001	−1.34
PSI	29.4	12.2	83	83	77	49.2	7.1	14	6	2	<0.001	−1.62
FSIQ	30.2	12.5	83	80	74	49.8	8.4	18	14	4	<0.001	−1.57
Vocabulary	38.2	10.3	71	54	46	50.2	9.2	24	8	6	<0.001	−1.17
Similarities	38.3	14.2	63	57	49	50.6	10.1	26	16	8	<0.001	−0.87
Information	31.8	11.4	83	77	66	50.1	8.3	18	14	12	<0.001	−1.61
Block Design	40.0	14.5	63	49	40	51.8	9.6	24	12	8	<0.001	−0.81
Matrix Reasoning	39.0	11.7	71	63	57	51.1	10.5	22	14	8	<0.001	−1.04
Visual Puzzles	39.9	10.0	71	57	46	50.2	8.7	29	12	12	<0.001	−1.03
Digit Span	37.3	11.8	77	71	40	49.1	9.3	28	22	10	<0.001	−1.00
Arithmetic	34.6	9.4	83	71	57	48.9	8.2	24	14	6	<0.001	−1.52
Coding	30.3	14.8	86	77	69	49.0	8.1	26	10	8	<0.001	−1.26
Symbol Search	30.3	10.2	91	86	74	49.6	7.6	18	8	6	<0.001	−1.89

Note: Listwise deletion of cases, Alzheimer $n = 35$.
VCI = Verbal Comprehension Index; PRI = Perceptual Reasoning Index; WMI = Working Memory Index; PSI = Processing Speed Index; FSIQ = Full Scale IQ.

Copyright 2009 by Pearson, Inc. Reproduced with permission. All rights reserved.

TABLE 9.5 WAIS–IV Full Demographically Adjusted Standard Index Scores in Alzheimer Disease and Low and High Education Samples

											Between Group Differences	
	Alzheimer					Low Education						
Score	Mean	SD	25th %ile	16th %ile	9th %ile	Mean	SD	25th %ile	16th %ile	9th %ile	p	ES
VCI	34.0	11.7	77	71	66	52.7	10.3	16	12	8	<0.001	−1.60
PRI	38.0	12.2	74	60	57	51.1	8.5	36	14	12	<0.001	−1.07
WMI	34.5	10.6	83	71	63	52.0	10.0	28	18	14	<0.001	−1.65
PSI	29.4	12.2	83	83	77	50.2	10.3	28	18	8	<0.001	−1.70
FSIQ	30.2	12.5	83	80	74	52.1	10.6	32	14	6	<0.001	−1.75

											Between Group Differences	
	Alzheimer					High Education						
Score	Mean	SD	25th %ile	16th %ile	9th %ile	Mean	SD	25th %ile	16th %ile	9th %ile	p	ES
VCI	34.0	11.7	77	71	66	51.3	8.9	24	16	6	<0.001	−1.48
PRI	38.0	12.2	74	60	57	50.4	10.4	14	6	6	<0.001	−1.01
WMI	34.5	10.6	83	71	63	49.4	10.5	20	16	8	<0.001	−1.40
PSI	29.4	12.2	83	83	77	49.0	8.0	24	20	10	<0.001	−1.60
FSIQ	30.2	12.5	83	80	74	50.2	8.8	18	14	10	<0.001	−1.60

Note: Listwise deletion of cases, Alzheimer $n = 35$.
VCI = Verbal Comprehension Index; PRI = Perceptual Reasoning Index; WMI = Working Memory Index; PSI = Processing Speed Index; FSIQ = Full Scale IQ.
Copyright 2009 by Pearson, Inc. Reproduced with permission. All rights reserved.

decline), produced the second highest effect size. For all significant differences, the ALZ group obtained lower scores, producing large effect sizes. Base rates of low scores were much higher in the ALZ group; for example, 65% of the ALZ sample obtained a VCI score at or below the 25th percentile compared to 16% of the matched control sample. The low and high education sample comparisons are shown in Table 9.3. In comparison to the low education group, the ALZ group obtained a significantly lower score on PSI. All other index scores were similar between the two groups. In contrast, all index scores were significantly lower in the ALZ group in comparison to the high education group. *For clinicians working with individuals with low education levels, it may be difficult to accurately differentiate dementia from low pre-morbid ability.*

Table 9.4 presents statistical comparisons for the demographic adjusted WAIS–IV index and subtest scores between ALZ and matched

TABLE 9.6 WAIS–IV Standard and New Index and Subtest Scores in Mild Cognitive Impairment and Matched Control Samples

Score	MCI					Matched Control					Between Group Differences	
	Mean	SD	25th %ile	16th %ile	9th %ile	Mean	SD	25th %ile	16th %ile	9th %ile	p	ES
VCI	98.1	14.0	27	22	13	102.2	13.0	19	13	4	>0.05	−0.29
PRI	92.9	13.6	41	27	18	101.9	13.9	24	9	3	<0.001	−0.66
WMI	95.3	17.4	43	20	20	102.2	12.0	19	7	3	>0.05	−0.40
PSI	94.5	15.9	41	26	18	101.4	15.2	21	15	11	>0.05	−0.44
GAI	94.9	13.7	41	25	14	102.3	13.3	20	9	4	<0.01	−0.54
CPI	94.1	16.3	39	31	20	102.0	13.7	16	15	9	<0.01	−0.49
FSIQ	94.2	15.0	46	32	15	102.4	13.3	19	13	5	<0.01	−0.55
Vocabulary	9.7	2.7	32	28	13	10.5	2.7	23	16	8	>0.05	−0.32
Similarities	9.7	2.8	35	22	17	10.6	2.7	21	11	4	>0.05	−0.31
Information	9.7	3.1	30	25	20	10.3	2.8	25	20	11	>0.05	−0.18
Block Design	8.9	2.8	41	27	22	10.5	3.1	32	15	11	<0.01	−0.58
Matrix Reasoning	9.1	2.8	47	30	22	10.7	3.1	24	19	4	<0.01	−0.57
Visual Puzzles	8.5	2.8	60	43	18	9.9	3.0	37	21	5	<0.01	−0.50

(*Continued*)

TABLE 9.6 (Continued)

Score	MCI						Matched Control						Between Group Differences	
	Mean	SD	25th %ile	16th %ile	9th %ile		Mean	SD	25th %ile	16th %ile	9th %ile		p	ES
Digit Span	9.2	3.5	40	28	25		10.6	2.4	20	8	4		<0.01	−0.41
Digit Span Forward	9.8	3.0	35	18	12		10.3	2.8	24	11	7		>0.05	−0.15
Digit Span Backward	9.4	3.1	35	18	13		10.3	2.3	24	12	5		>0.05	−0.29
Digit Span Sequencing	8.7	3.7	38	32	23		10.8	2.7	12	11	11		<0.001	−0.57
Arithmetic	9.2	3.3	45	35	18		10.2	2.6	29	15	7		>0.05	−0.30
Coding	8.9	2.8	42	30	22		10.5	3.0	20	15	12		<0.01	−0.56
Symbol Search	9.0	3.5	43	37	23		10.0	3.1	28	19	15		>0.05	−0.30

Note: Listwise deletion of cases, MCI $n = 59$.

VCI = Verbal Comprehension Index; PRI = Perceptual Reasoning Index; WMI = Working Memory Index; PSI = Processing Speed Index; GAI = General Ability Index; CPI = Cognitive Proficiency Index; FSIQ = Full Scale IQ.

Copyright 2009 by Pearson, Inc. Reproduced with permission. All rights reserved.

control groups. All index and subtest scores are significantly lower in the ALZ group with large effect sizes. The largest effect sizes are observed on Symbol Search and PSI. The base rates of low scores in the ALZ sample are higher when using demographic adjustments than those observed using the standard scores. Otherwise, the results are very similar across groups because the samples are matched on demographics, so each is adjusted in the same manner (i.e., by a constant). Table 9.5 shows the demographically adjusted norm comparisons between the ALZ and low and high education samples. In comparison to both groups, the ALZ group obtained significantly lower scores on all index scores. *The significant differences for all indexes in the low*

TABLE 9.7 WAIS–IV Standard Index Scores in Mild Cognitive Impairment and Low and High Education Samples

	Mild Cognitive Impairment					Low Education					Between Group Differences	
Score	Mean	SD	25th %ile	16th %ile	9th %ile	Mean	SD	25th %ile	16th %ile	9th %ile	p	ES
VCI	98.1	14.0	27	22	13	89.2	16.5	48	38	32	<0.01	0.64
PRI	92.9	13.6	41	27	18	91.1	12.3	60	26	14	>0.05	0.13
WMI	95.3	17.4	43	20	20	89.3	15.5	48	40	26	>0.05	0.34
PSI	94.5	15.9	41	26	18	90.7	16.9	52	36	24	>0.05	0.24
GAI	94.9	13.7	41	25	14	89.3	14.3	44	38	24	>0.05	0.41
FSIQ	94.2	15.0	46	32	15	88.1	15.7	54	46	32	>0.05	0.41

	Mild Cognitive Impairment					High Education					Between Group Differences	
Score	Mean	SD	25th %ile	16th %ile	9th %ile	Mean	SD	25th %ile	16th %ile	9th %ile	p	ES
VCI	98.1	14.0	27	22	13	114.9	11.5	2	2	0	<0.001	−1.20
PRI	92.9	13.6	41	27	18	109.5	14.5	14	2	0	<0.001	−1.21
WMI	95.3	17.4	43	20	20	107.7	15.6	14	6	2	<0.001	−0.71
PSI	94.5	15.9	41	26	18	104.5	12.4	16	6	2	<0.001	−0.63
GAI	94.9	13.7	41	25	14	113.8	12.6	4	2	0	<0.001	−1.38
FSIQ	94.2	15.0	46	32	15	112.0	12.6	6	0	0	<0.001	−1.18

Note: Listwise deletion of cases, MCI $n = 59$.
VCI = Verbal Comprehension Index; PRI = Perceptual Reasoning Index; WMI = Working Memory Index; PSI = Processing Speed Index; GAI = General Ability Index; FSIQ = Full Scale IQ.
Copyright 2009 by Pearson, Inc. Reproduced with permission. All rights reserved.

TABLE 9.8 WAIS–IV Full Demographically Adjusted Standard Index and Subtest Scores in Mild Cognitive Impairment and Matched Control Samples

Score	Mild Cognitive Impairment					Matched Control					Between Group Differences	
	Mean	SD	25th %ile	16th %ile	9th %ile	Mean	SD	25th %ile	16th %ile	9th %ile	p	ES
VCI	44.3	10.4	48	36	22	49.0	8.8	28	17	13	<0.01	−0.45
PRI	41.6	9.7	59	49	39	49.2	9.4	29	24	12	<0.001	−0.78
WMI	42.7	13.0	54	49	31	49.2	7.9	25	15	12	<0.01	−0.50
PSI	43.5	12.5	49	41	34	49.2	9.9	27	17	9	<0.01	−0.45
FSIQ	41.0	11.5	58	42	37	48.8	8.7	28	17	9	<0.001	−0.68
Vocabulary	44.7	11.4	44	32	27	49.6	9.5	27	17	13	<0.01	−0.42
Similarities	45.5	10.7	46	34	24	49.8	9.6	27	17	7	<0.05	−0.40
Information	45.5	10.5	46	29	20	48.6	9.3	29	17	12	>0.05	−0.29
Block Design	40.0	14.5	52	32	24	49.4	10.6	32	20	19	<0.001	−0.64
Matrix Reasoning	43.9	10.5	49	44	34	50.5	10.5	24	20	13	<0.001	−0.63
Visual Puzzles	42.2	10.8	63	48	32	48.2	9.3	33	17	9	<0.01	−0.56
Digit Span	43.7	13.6	51	39	27	50.0	8.7	20	15	9	<0.01	−0.47
Arithmetic	43.4	12.8	49	42	30	48.8	8.6	31	20	11	<0.01	−0.42
Coding	43.5	11.9	49	32	27	50.1	10.2	24	12	11	<0.01	−0.55
Symbol Search	44.2	12.7	46	41	32	48.3	9.9	32	19	12	<0.05	−0.32

Note: Listwise deletion of cases, MCI n = 59.

VCI = Verbal Comprehension Index; PRI = Perceptual Reasoning Index; WMI = Working Memory Index; PSI = Processing Speed Index; FSIQ = Full Scale IQ.

Copyright 2009 by Pearson, Inc. Reproduced with permission. All rights reserved.

TABLE 9.9 WAIS–IV Full Demographically Adjusted Standard Index Scores in Mild Cognitive Impairment and Low and High Education Samples

											Between Group Differences	
	Mild Cognitive Impairment					Low Education						
Score	Mean	SD	25th %ile	16th %ile	9th %ile	Mean	SD	25th %ile	16th %ile	9th %ile	p	ES
VCI	44.3	10.4	48	36	22	52.9	11.6	16	8	4	<0.001	−0.82
PRI	41.6	9.7	59	49	39	51.4	8.7	26	14	10	<0.001	−1.01
WMI	42.7	13.0	54	49	31	50.8	11.0	32	18	16	<0.01	−0.62
PSI	43.5	12.5	49	41	34	49.5	10.3	30	24	10	<0.01	−0.47
FSIQ	41.0	11.5	58	42	37	51.8	11.4	28	16	8	<0.001	−0.94

											Between Group Differences	
	Mild Cognitive Impairment					Low Education						
Score	Mean	SD	25th %ile	16th %ile	9th %ile	Mean	SD	25th %ile	16th %ile	9th %ile	p	ES
VCI	44.3	10.4	48	36	22	51.6	8.6	26	22	8	<0.001	−0.70
PRI	41.6	9.7	59	49	39	50.9	9.6	18	8	8	<0.001	−0.96
WMI	42.7	13.0	54	49	31	48.3	11.2	26	20	16	<0.01	−0.43
PSI	43.5	12.5	49	41	34	48.4	8.3	28	24	12	<0.01	−0.39
FSIQ	41.0	11.5	58	42	37	50.0	8.6	24	18	14	<0.001	−0.78

Note: Listwise deletion of cases, MCI $n = 59$.
VCI = Verbal Comprehension Index; PRI = Perceptual Reasoning Index; WMI = Working Memory Index; PSI = Processing Speed Index; FSIQ = Full Scale IQ.
Copyright 2009 by Pearson, Inc. Reproduced with permission. All rights reserved.

education group demonstrate greatly improved sensitivity and specificity to dementia and the importance of using demographically adjusted norms in this group. In contrast, the large differences observed in the high education group are similar to the differences observed without demographic adjustments. Therefore, using demographically adjusted norms results in relatively stable sensitivity and specificity across different patient populations.

As observed in Table 9.6, the MCI group scored significantly lower on the Perceptual Reasoning Index (PRI), General Ability Index (GAI), Cognitive Proficiency Index (CPI), and Full Scale Intelligence Quotient (FSIQ) indexes. At the subtest level, the greatest effect sizes were observed on the PRI subtests and Coding. Most effect sizes were small to moderate. Table 9.7 describes the comparisons to the low and high education groups. In comparison to the low education group, the MCI group did not differ

TABLE 9.10 WMS–IV Standard and New Index and Subtest Scores in Alzheimer Disease and Matched Control Samples

Score	Alzheimer					Matched Control					Between Group Differences	
	Mean	SD	25th %ile	16th %ile	9th %ile	Mean	SD	25th %ile	16th %ile	9th %ile	p	ES
GMI	67.2	17.9	90	90	81	105.5	10.8	9	9	2	<0.001	−2.13
IMI	69.2	19.4	85	88	85	104.0	12.0	14	9	2	<0.001	−1.80
DMI	64.3	19.7	90	88	85	103.6	11.6	14	14	2	<0.001	−1.99
IMI vs. DMI	4.9	4.3	78	68	63	9.8	2.5	30	21	9	<0.001	−1.14
AMI	67.7	19.9	88	85	81	104.1	12.1	16	9	5	<0.001	−1.83
AII	70.1	20.5	90	78	73	104.1	12.0	16	5	5	<0.001	−1.66
ADI	64.6	20.8	90	83	78	103.7	12.3	16	9	2	<0.001	−1.88
ARI	70.7	18.1	88	80	68	105.0	11.2	7	7	2	<0.001	−1.90
VMI	68.1	20.1	85	85	73	103.4	12.7	21	9	5	<0.001	−1.76
Retention Index	77.4	18.3	76	73	63	101.8	12.1	16	5	5	<0.001	−1.34
Retrieval Index	71.6	16.6	88	83	78	103.0	11.0	9	7	2	<0.001	−1.89
WMI	82.4	17.6	76	68	49	103.9	12.2	11	5	2	<0.001	−1.23
LM I	5.3	3.6	81	78	68	10.9	2.6	18	7	7	<0.001	−1.53
LM II	3.8	3.4	83	78	73	11.0	2.8	14	14	7	<0.001	−2.11
LM I vs. II	5.8	4.2	73	68	66	10.5	3.2	23	21	9	<0.001	−1.14

LM II vs. Rec	5.0	3.6	81	76	68	10.7	2.7	18	18	7	<0.001	−1.61
VPA I	4.9	3.1	88	88	83	10.3	2.3	9	7	2	<0.001	−1.76
VPA II	4.9	3.3	90	83	76	10.2	2.7	16	11	9	<0.001	−1.64
VPA I vs. II	8.4	3.7	46	42	34	9.3	2.9	48	18	18	>0.05	−0.25
VPA II vs. Rec	7.4	3.1	70	48	45	9.5	2.4	39	18	7	<0.001	−0.67
VPA II Free Recall	4.3	3.1	90	83	76	10.7	2.7	18	11	7	<0.001	−2.04
VPA Trial A	6.6	3.0	78	66	66	10.7	3.1	23	23	9	<0.001	−1.39
VPA Trial B	4.9	3.4	85	85	66	10.3	2.3	23	9	5	<0.001	−1.61
VPA A vs. D	5.9	2.2	73	66	49	9.7	2.4	27	21	5	<0.001	−1.70
VPA Total Intrusions	6.6	4.4	66	56	44	10.5	2.5	16	7	7	<0.001	−0.88
VPA Easy Items	5.0	3.2	85	81	73	11.2	3.1	16	9	9	<0.001	−1.95
VPA Hard Items	5.2	3.1	85	83	81	10.3	2.8	27	18	7	<0.001	−1.64
VR I	4.9	3.6	85	78	68	10.6	2.5	18	14	5	<0.001	−1.60
VR II	4.2	3.3	85	85	85	10.6	3.0	23	9	9	<0.001	−1.96
VR I vs. II	6.4	2.9	81	78	66	10.4	3.0	23	16	9	<0.001	−1.36
VR II vs. Rec	5.9	3.0	85	73	63	10.5	3.0	21	16	11	<0.001	−1.53

Note: Listwise deletion of cases, Alzheimer $n = 42$.

GMI = General Memory Index; IMI = Immediate Memory Index; DMI = Delayed Memory Index; AMI = Auditory Memory Index; AII = Auditory Immediate Index; ADI = Auditory Delayed Index; ARI = Auditory recognition Index; VMI = Visual Memory Index; WMI = Working Memory Index; LM = Logical memory; VPA = Verbal Paired Associates; VR = Visual Reproduction.

Copyright 2009 by Pearson, Inc. Reproduced with permission. All rights reserved.

TABLE 9.11 WMS–IV Standard Index Scores in Alzheimer Disease and Low and High Education Samples

											Between Group Differences	
	Alzheimer					Low Education Sample						
Score	Mean	SD	25th %ile	16th %ile	9th %ile	Mean	SD	25th %ile	16th %ile	9th %ile	p	ES
IMI	69.2	19.4	85	88	85	91.8	17.3	43	33	18	<0.001	−1.17
DMI	64.3	19.7	90	88	85	92.2	18.4	50	40	23	<0.001	−1.41
AMI	67.7	19.9	88	85	81	92.4	17.2	45	38	28	<0.001	−1.24
VMI	68.1	20.1	85	85	73	92.7	17.7	43	33	15	<0.001	−1.23

											Between Group Differences	
	Alzheimer					High Education Sample						
Score	Mean	SD	25th %ile	16th %ile	9th %ile	Mean	SD	25th %ile	16th %ile	9th %ile	p	ES
IMI	69.2	19.4	85	88	85	103.4	12.1	13	10	3	<0.001	−1.77
DMI	64.3	19.7	90	88	85	103.0	14.8	16	16	10	<0.001	−1.96
AMI	67.7	19.9	88	85	81	101.7	14.0	16	13	13	<0.001	−1.71
VMI	68.1	20.1	85	85	73	105.3	13.3	10	7	3	<0.001	−1.85

Note: Listwise deletion of cases, Alzheimer $n = 40$.
IMI = Immediate Memory Index; DMI = Delayed Memory Index; AMI = Auditory Memory Index; VMI = Visual Memory Index.
Copyright 2009 by Pearson, Inc. Reproduced with permission. All rights reserved.

on any index except VCI, which was significantly higher in the MCI group than in the low education group. In contrast, all index scores are significantly lower in the MCI group in comparison to the high education group. *In this case, clinicians serving individuals with high levels of education may overestimate the level of impairment, reducing the specificity of the tests.*

Table 9.8 describes the demographically adjusted norm comparison for the WAIS–IV in the MCI sample and matched controls. At the index level, all scores are significantly lower in the MCI sample although effect sizes are relatively moderate. All subtests, with the exception of Information, are significantly lower in the MCI group. The MCI group also shows a greater percentage of low scores than observed in the standard age-adjusted score comparisons highlighting the importance of demographic norm comparisons. Table 9.9 provides the comparisons to the low and high education groups. All index scores are significantly lower in the MCI group in comparison to either the low or high education group. These results are similar to those observed in the

TABLE 9.12 WMS–IV Full Demographic Adjusted Standard Index and Subtest Scores in Alzheimer Disease and Matched Control Samples

	Alzheimer					Matched Control					Between Group Differences	
Score	Mean	SD	25th %ile	16th %ile	9th %ile	Mean	SD	25th %ile	16th %ile	9th %ile	ES	p
IMI	24.1	12.9	93	91	83	50.1	7.8	21	14	9	−2.02	<.001
DMI	22.4	12.5	93	93	90	50.4	7.3	14	11	9	−2.24	<.001
AMI	24.4	12.5	93	93	88	50.1	8.1	23	11	7	−2.06	<.001
VMI	27.5	11.7	91	83	83	50.9	8.3	21	14	5	−2.00	<.001
LM I	30.1	12.7	84	84	80	50.2	8.9	23	18	5	−1.59	<.001
LM II	25.9	11.0	91	91	84	50.8	9.1	23	11	11	−2.25	<.001
VPA I	29.3	11.4	89	86	75	50.2	7.9	23	9	7	−1.82	<.001
VPA II	31.5	9.9	91	86	74	49.1	7.6	16	11	9	−1.77	<.001
VR I	30.7	11.3	86	82	75	50.6	7.6	16	11	5	−1.76	<.001
VR II	29.7	10.6	89	84	82	51.5	9.8	21	11	7	−2.06	<.001

Note: Listwise deletion of cases, Alzheimer n = 42.
IMI = Immediate Memory Index; DMI = Delayed Memory Index; AMI = Auditory Memory Index; VMI = Visual Memory Index; LM = Logical memory; VPA = Verbal Paired Associates; VR = Visual Reproduction.
Copyright 2009 by Pearson, Inc. Reproduced with permission. All rights reserved.

ALZ sample, where demographic adjustments show greater sensitivity and specificity particularly when compared to specific samples (e.g., low or high education).

Table 9.10 describes performance on the WMS–IV index and subtest scores by the ALZ and matched control samples. Significant differences are observed on all index scores with the greatest differences on the GMI and DMI. All subtest scores are significantly different between groups with the exception of the VPA I versus II contrast scaled score. The greatest difference was observed on Logical Memory II. For all significant differences, the ALZ group obtained lower scores, producing large effect sizes. Base rates of low scores were much higher in the ALZ group; for example, 90% of the ALZ sample obtained a GMI score at or below the 25th percentile compared to 9% of the matched control sample. Base rates of low scores were also higher for WMS–IV scores than for WAIS–IV scores. The low and high education sample comparisons are shown in Table 9.11. In comparison to both groups, the ALZ group obtained significantly lower scores on all measures. The effect sizes are smaller when comparing ALZ to a low

TABLE 9.13 WMS–IV Full Demographically Adjusted Standard Index Scores in Alzheimer Disease and Low and High Education Sample

	Alzheimer					Low Education					Between Group Differences	
Score	Mean	SD	25th %ile	16th %ile	9th %ile	Mean	SD	25th %ile	16th %ile	9th %ile	p	ES
IMI	24.1	12.9	93	91	83	50.3	11.4	21	15	15	<.001	−2.04
DMI	22.4	12.5	93	93	90	49.2	11.1	31	21	8	<.001	−2.15
AMI	24.4	12.5	93	93	88	49.6	10.5	28	21	18	<.001	−2.02
VMI	27.5	11.7	91	83	83	49.8	10.1	23	10	8	<.001	−1.91

	Alzheimer					Low Education					Between Group Differences	
Score	Mean	SD	25th %ile	16th %ile	9th %ile	Mean	SD	25th %ile	16th %ile	9th %ile	p	ES
IMI	24.1	12.9	93	91	83	47.7	9.8	40	30	13	<.001	−1.83
DMI	22.4	12.5	93	93	90	48.3	10.7	30	17	13	<.001	−2.08
AMI	24.4	12.5	93	93	88	47.4	10.1	30	17	17	<.001	−1.84
VMI	27.5	11.7	91	83	83	49.9	10.1	27	20	10	<.001	−1.91

Note: Listwise deletion of cases, ALZ n = 42.
IMI = Immediate Memory Index; DMI = Delayed Memory Index; AMI = Auditory Memory Index; VMI = Visual Memory Index.
Copyright 2009 by Pearson, Inc. Reproduced with permission. All rights reserved.

education sample, although still highly significant and large. Compared to intellectual functioning, memory impairment in ALZ is evident across all group comparisons, even when compared to individuals with lower education levels. This result occurs because education has a smaller effect on memory ability in comparison to its effect on general intellectual functioning.

Table 9.12 describes the comparison of the ALZ and matched control groups utilizing the ACS demographically adjusted norms. All index and subtest scores are significantly lower in the ALZ group with large effect sizes. *The largest effect sizes are observed on DMI and Logical Memory II. The base rates in the ALZ sample are higher when using demographic adjustments than those observed using the standard scores.* Table 9.13 shows the demographically adjusted norm comparisons between the ALZ and low and high education samples. In comparison to both groups, the ALZ group obtained significantly lower scores on all index scores. The effect sizes are greater in the comparisons using the demographic norms than those

TABLE 9.14 WMS–IV Standard and New Index and Subtest Scores in Mild Cognitive Impairment and Matched Control Samples

Score	Mild Cognitive Impairment					Matched Control					Between Group Differences	
	Mean	SD	25th %ile	16th %ile	9th %ile	Mean	SD	25th %ile	16th %ile	9th %ile	p	ES
GMI	88.2	15.5	48	40	29	101.6	12.2	12	10	4	<0.001	−0.86
IMI	90.6	13.8	50	36	28	102.1	13.0	14	10	8	<0.001	−0.83
DMI	87.5	17.2	50	42	29	101.6	11.8	12	10	4	<0.001	−0.82
IMI vs. DMI	8.1	4.1	46	40	33	9.8	3.2	35	22	14	<0.01	−0.41
AMI	90.0	15.1	43	33	27	103.1	11.3	18	6	4	<0.001	−0.87
AII	91.9	13.9	40	28	24	102.2	10.9	16	6	4	<0.001	−0.75
ADI	88.5	17.2	43	31	29	103.5	11.6	18	8	6	<0.001	−0.87
ADR	91.6	17.6	39	37	31	104.7	13.0	14	14	10	<0.001	−0.74
VMI	89.6	14.8	53	47	31	100.4	12.7	27	18	8	<0.01	−0.73
Retention Index	90.2	15.2	46	35	31	100.0	14.7	29	14	8	<0.01	−0.64
Retrieval Index	89.3	17.9	52	35	23	98.9	14.8	18	6	2	<0.01	−0.54
WMI	95.1	17.7	45	29	12	102.7	11.4	16	8	2	<0.01	−0.43
LM I	8.4	2.7	52	40	30	10.8	2.7	20	12	8	<0.001	−0.91
LM I	7.3	3.3	59	41	33	11.0	2.6	18	12	6	<0.001	−1.09
LM I vs. II	7.6	3.9	45	43	37	10.5	2.8	16	16	6	<0.001	−0.76
LM II vs. Rec	7.8	3.5	55	45	35	10.5	2.7	20	14	8	<0.001	−0.78
VPA I	8.9	2.9	36	32	28	10.0	2.4	26	12	6	<0.05	−0.38

(Continued)

TABLE 9.14 (Continued)

Score	Mild Cognitive Impairment					Matched Control					Between Group Differences	
	Mean	SD	25th %ile	16th %ile	9th %ile	Mean	SD	25th %ile	16th %ile	9th %ile	p	ES
VPA II	8.8	2.9	38	28	24	10.1	2.7	22	14	6	<0.05	−0.46
VPA I vs. II	9.5	2.4	30	16	12	9.9	2.9	34	16	16	>0.05	−0.16
VPA II vs. Rec	9.3	2.9	44	18	12	9.8	2.7	34	16	6	>0.05	−0.17
VPA II Free Recall	8.2	2.8	44	40	26	10.3	2.9	26	16	8	<0.001	−0.77
VPA Trial A	9.1	2.4	36	28	8	10.1	2.5	24	20	6	>0.05	−0.40
VPA Trial D	8.8	3.5	46	34	28	9.7	2.8	32	16	6	>0.05	−0.26
VPA A vs. D	9.3	4.0	46	42	30	9.5	2.9	32	22	14	>0.05	−0.05
VPA Total Intrusions	9.7	2.9	28	16	12	10.8	1.9	4	4	4	<0.05	−0.35
VPA Easy Items	9.1	3.3	38	32	24	10.3	2.9	24	18	12	>0.05	−0.36
VPA Hard Items	8.9	2.9	42	30	18	9.9	2.8	20	12	10	>0.05	−0.35
VR I	8.6	3.1	42	30	22	10.3	3.4	30	18	12	<0.05	−0.54
VR II	8.0	4.0	57	51	39	9.7	3.0	38	20	18	<0.05	−0.43
VR I vs. II	8.8	4.0	51	49	33	9.5	2.8	34	24	12	>0.05	−0.17
VR II vs. Rec	9.0	3.8	85	73	63	9.5	2.8	36	30	16	>0.05	−0.15

Note: Listwise deletion of cases MCI n = 48.

GMI = General Memory Index; IMI = Immediate Memory Index; DMI = Delayed Memory Index; AMI = Auditory Memory Index; AII = Auditory Immediate Index; ADI = Auditory Delayed Index; ARI = Auditory recognition Index; VMI = Visual Memory Index; WMI = Working Memory Index; LM = Logical memory; VPA = Verbal Paired Associates; VR = Visual Reproduction.

Copyright 2009 by Pearson, Inc. Reproduced with permission. All rights reserved.

TABLE 9.15 WMS–IV Standard Index Scores in Mild Cognitive Impairment and Low and High Education Samples

	Mild Cognitive Impairment					Low Education Sample					Between Group Differences	
Score	Mean	SD	25th %ile	16th %ile	9th %ile	Mean	SD	25th %ile	16th %ile	9th %ile	p	ES
IMI	90.6	13.8	50	36	28	93.5	19.1	46	39	18	>0.05	−0.21
DMI	87.5	17.2	50	42	29	94.7	20.6	54	36	21	>0.05	−0.42
AMI	90.0	15.1	43	33	27	94.2	19.2	49	39	21	>0.05	−0.28
VMI	89.6	14.8	53	47	31	95.5	21.4	39	28	21	>0.05	−0.39

	Mild Cognitive Impairment					Low Education Sample					Between Group Differences	
Score	Mean	SD	25th %ile	16th %ile	9th %ile	Mean	SD	25th %ile	16th %ile	9th %ile	p	ES
IMI	90.6	13.8	50	36	28	105.7	14.2	13	9	6	<0.001	−1.08
DMI	87.5	17.2	50	42	29	104.3	15.6	16	13	9	<0.001	−0.98
AMI	90.0	15.1	43	33	27	104.4	16.3	19	16	13	<0.001	−0.96
VMI	89.6	14.8	53	47	31	104.6	12.5	16	6	6	<0.001	−1.01

Note: Listwise deletion of cases, MCI $n = 42$.
IMI = Immediate Memory Index; DMI = Delayed Memory Index; AMI = Auditory Memory Index; VMI = Visual Memory Index.
Copyright 2009 by Pearson, Inc. Reproduced with permission. All rights reserved.

observed in the standard score comparisons. In addition, there are fewer low scores in the low education sample when demographic adjustments are applied indicating better specificity for the tests.

As observed in Table 9.14, the MCI group scored significantly lower on all WMS–IV new and standard indexes. Effect sizes for index scores were moderate to large. *At the subtest level, the greatest effect size was observed on Logical Memory II.* In both the ALZ and MCI groups, Logical Memory II was the most sensitive measure. Most subtest effect sizes were moderate. Table 9.15 describes the comparisons to the low and high education groups. The MCI group performed at the same level as the low education group. Clinicians working with individuals with low education levels may have difficulty identifying MCI when applying standard age adjusted scores. Compared to the high education sample, all scores were significantly lower in the MCI group with large effect sizes.

Table 9.16 describes the demographically adjusted norm comparison for the WMS–IV in the MCI and matched control samples. At the index

TABLE 9.16 WMS–IV Full Demographically Adjusted Index and Subtest Scores in Mild Cognitive Impairment and Matched Control Samples

	Mild Cognitive Impairment					Matched Control					Between Group Differences	
Score	Mean	SD	25th %ile	16th %ile	9th %ile	Mean	SD	25th %ile	16th %ile	9th %ile	p	ES
IMI	40.8	10.2	58	52	36	49.8	8.7	26	14	8	<0.001	−0.88
DMI	39.5	12.3	54	46	42	49.6	7.4	17	12	6	<0.001	−0.82
AMI	41.2	10.6	51	43	33	50.5	7.3	16	10	4	<0.001	−0.88
VMI	41.3	11.1	59	43	39	48.9	9.6	29	21	15	<0.001	−0.69
LM I	42.2	9.2	56	44	30	51.2	9.5	18	10	4	<0.001	−0.98
LM II	39.0	11.4	61	53	37	51.8	8.9	18	10	8	<0.001	−1.12
VPA I	45.3	10.0	38	30	28	49.0	8.0	24	10	8	<0.05	−0.38
VPA II	45.2	9.5	38	30	24	49.6	8.4	22	10	6	<0.05	−0.47
VR I	43.9	10.4	44	28	22	49.8	11.2	31	20	10	<0.01	−0.57
VR II	42.6	13.4	59	51	45	48.2	9.6	39	20	14	<0.05	−0.42

Note: Listwise deletion of cases, MCI $n = 42$.
IMI = Immediate Memory Index; DMI = Delayed Memory Index; AMI = Auditory Memory Index; VMI = Visual Memory Index; LM = Logical memory; VPA = Verbal Paired Associates; VR = Visual Reproduction.
Copyright 2009 by Pearson, Inc. Reproduced with permission. All rights reserved.

level, all scores are significantly lower in the MCI sample and effect sizes are moderate to large. All subtests are significantly lower in the MCI sample; Logical Memory II has the largest effect size. Demographic adjustments do not have a large impact when compared to matched controls given that each group is adjusted by a similar amount. Table 9.17 provides the comparisons to the low and high education groups. All index scores are significantly lower in the MCI group in comparison to either the low or high education group. These results show improved sensitivity for the memory tests when compared to a low pre-morbid ability group. The application of demographic norms improves sensitivity and specificity in this sample.

OPIE AND WAIS–IV

Krull and colleagues (1995) developed the Oklahoma Premorbid Intelligence Estimate (OPIE) to predict premorbid IQ for the WAIS–R. The OPIE utilized measures of current performance from the WAIS–R

TABLE 9.17   WMS–IV Full Demographically Adjusted Standard Index Scores in Mild Cognitive Impairment and Low and High Education Samples

	MCI				Low Education					Between Group Differences	
Score	Mean	SD	25th %ile	16th %ile	9th %ile	Mean	SD	25th %ile	16th %ile	9th %ile	p	ES
IMI	40.8	10.2	58	52	36	49.4	10.1	34	22	12	<0.001	−0.84
DMI	39.5	12.3	54	46	42	49.4	10.9	28	16	16	<0.001	−0.80
AMI	41.2	10.6	51	43	33	49.1	11.3	31	19	19	<0.01	−0.74
VMI	41.3	11.1	59	43	39	50.3	9.2	25	19	9	<0.001	−0.82

	MCI				Low Education					Between Group Differences	
Score	Mean	SD	25th %ile	16th %ile	9th %ile	Mean	SD	25th %ile	16th %ile	9th %ile	p	ES
IMI	40.8	10.2	58	52	36	51.3	12.3	24	16	11	<0.001	−1.03
DMI	39.5	12.3	54	46	42	50.8	12.3	30	16	5	<0.001	−0.92
AMI	41.2	10.6	51	43	33	51.0	12.1	30	11	11	<0.001	−0.93
VMI	41.3	11.1	59	43	39	50.5	10.8	19	14	11	<0.001	−0.84

Note: Listwise deletion of cases, MCI $n = 42$.
IMI = Immediate Memory Index; DMI = Delayed Memory Index; AMI = Auditory Memory Index; VMI = Visual Memory Index.
Copyright 2009 by Pearson, Inc. Reproduced with permission. All rights reserved.

(i.e., Vocabulary, Picture Completion) and demographic measures (i.e., age, education, race, and occupation) to derive regression equations to predict premorbid IQ. Vocabulary and Picture Completion were selected because performance on these tasks was *relatively* resistant to brain damage (Donders, Tulsky, & Zhu, 2001) and would thus be least affected by cognitive decline. The OPIE – III reflected updates to the OPIE to accommodate the release of the WAIS–III (Schoenberg, Scott, Duff, & Adams, 2002). OPIE – III performance measures included Vocabulary, Matrix Reasoning, Picture Completion, and Information. In addition, prediction equations were derived that included subsets of the performance scores.

OPIE–IV equations (i.e., using within-test performance measures and demographic prediction variables) were derived for the WAIS–IV. Performance measures included Vocabulary and Matrix Reasoning, and demographic variables included age, sex, education, ethnicity, and region. Tables 9.18–9.21 provide data on the OPIE–IV equations predicted

TABLE 9.18 OPIE–IV Predicted Versus Actual WAIS–IV Standard, Prorated, and Alternate Index Scores in Alzheimer and Matched Controls

Score	Predictors	Alzheimer										Matched Control										Between Group Differences				
		Actual Mean	Actual SD	Pred. Mean	Pred. SD	Diff. Mean	Diff. SD	25% Cut	15% Cut	10% Cut	p	Actual Mean	Actual SD	Pred. Mean	Pred. SD	Diff. Mean	Diff. SD	25% Cut	15% Cut	10% Cut	p	Actual ES	p	Pred ES	p	Diff ES
FSIQ	VC, MR, A, Ed, S, R, Et	81.0	17.2	90.2	15.7	-9.1	7.9	71	69	57	<0.001	103.7	13.7	104.1	12.5	-0.4	6.3	24	12	10	<0.001	-1.32	<0.001	-0.89	<0.001	-1.12
FSIQ	VC, A, Ed, S, Et	81.0	17.2	94.5	13.1	-13.5	11.2	74	71	69	<0.001	103.7	13.7	104.2	11.6	-0.5	8.5	18	8	8	<0.001	-1.32	<0.01	-0.74	<0.001	-1.16
FSIQ	MR, A, Ed, S, R	81.0	17.2	94.9	12.5	-13.8	9.7	86	63	57	<0.001	103.7	13.7	104.7	11.5	-1.0	7.6	16	12	10	<0.001	-1.32	<0.001	-0.79	<0.001	-1.33
Prorated FSIQ	VC, MR, A, Ed, S, Et	79.8	17.1	91.7	14.4	-11.9	9.6	74	69	66	<0.001	103.1	13.6	103.7	11.5	-0.6	7.7	25	12	10	<0.001	-1.36	<0.001	-0.83	<0.001	-1.18
Prorated FSIQ	VC, A, Ed, S, Et	80.4	17.7	95.5	12.4	-15.1	12.3	77	69	69	<0.001	103.5	13.9	104.0	10.8	-0.5	9.4	20	10	8	<0.001	-1.31	<0.01	-0.69	<0.001	-1.18
Prorated FSIQ	MR, A, Ed, S, R	80.6	16.8	94.9	12.5	-13.8	9.7	86	66	60	<0.001	103.4	13.5	104.7	11.5	-1.0	7.6	14	12	8	<0.001	-1.36	<0.001	-0.79	<0.001	-1.33
Alternate FSIQ	VC, MR, A, Ed, S, Et	79.7	17.8	91.5	15.0	-11.8	9.1	81	69	62	<0.001	103.1	14.1	103.5	11.6	-0.4	7.6	29	14	12	<0.001	-1.31	<0.001	-0.80	<0.001	-1.26
Alternate FSIQ	VC, A, Ed, S	79.7	19.0	95.9	12.3	-16.2	13.5	81	73	65	<0.001	103.7	14.7	104.2	10.4	-0.5	9.9	18	14	12	<0.001	-1.27	<0.01	-0.67	<0.001	-1.17
Alternate FSIQ	MR, A, Ed, R	80.1	18.0	94.4	13.2	-14.3	9.2	85	67	59	<0.001	104.1	13.6	104.9	11.3	-1.1	8.5	28	16	12	<0.001	-1.33	<0.001	-0.79	<0.001	-1.44
GAI	VC, MR, A, Ed, S, Et	84.7	17.5	92.1	14.0	-7.4	10.2	58	42	28	<0.001	103.7	14.5	103.3	11.5	0.8	8.6	22	14	8	<0.001	-1.09	<0.001	-0.80	<0.001	-0.80
GAI	VC, A, Ed, S, Et	84.7	17.5	92.1	14.0	-7.4	10.2	61	56	44	<0.001	104.1	13.6	103.3	11.5	0.8	8.6	22	14	8	<0.001	-1.11	<0.01	-0.80	<0.001	-0.80
GAI	MR, A, Ed, S, R	84.7	17.5	94.5	14.3	-9.8	7.8	64	50	47	<0.001	104.1	13.6	104.3	11.9	-0.2	7.2	14	10	8	<0.001	-1.11	<0.01	-0.68	<0.001	-1.24
Prorated GAI	VC, MR, A, Ed, S, Et	84.0	18.0	89.8	15.7	-5.8	10.3	56	44	25	<0.001	103.9	13.9	103.5	12.2	0.5	8.4	22	9	6	<0.001	-1.11	<0.001	-0.87	<0.01	-0.61

Prorated GAI	VC, A, Ed, S, Et	83.8	18.5	94.3	13.7	−10.2	12.1	67	64	53	104.0	14.1	103.8	11.3	0.0	8.6	20	12	10	<0.001	−1.09	<0.01	−0.69	<0.01	−0.84
Prorated GAI	MR, A, Ed, S, R	85.0	17.0	96.2	12.9	−11.2	9.3	61	47	42	104.0	13.4	104.1	10.5	−0.1	8.7	12	4	4	<0.001	−1.12	<0.01	−0.61	<0.01	−1.19
Alternate GAI	VC, MR, A, Ed, S, Et	82.5	18.1	89.4	17.4	−6.9	8.6	63	56	48	103.2	14.3	103.5	12.9	−0.4	7.9	33	22	14	<0.001	−1.14	<0.01	−0.82	<0.01	−0.75
Alternate GAI	VC, A, Ed, S, Et	83.3	18.9	93.6	13.9	−8.7	10.1	69	66	60	103.8	13.9	104.3	12.3	−0.9	8.0	20	14	10	<0.001	−1.09	<0.01	−0.77	<0.01	−0.77
Alternate GAI	MR, A, Ed, S, R	82.9	16.8	95.1	13.8	−12.3	8.1	79	61	54	103.4	14.0	103.6	10.1	−0.2	8.2	20	12	10	<0.001	−1.22	<0.01	−0.61	<0.001	−1.50
VCI	VC, A, Ed, S, Et	87.2	18.3	92.6	15.4	−5.4	7.8	51	46	43	103.8	13.9	104.1	12.7	−0.4	6.3	24	16	12	<0.001	−0.91	<0.001	−0.75	<0.01	−0.65
Prorated VCI	VC, A, Ed, S, Et	98.3	14.6	100.3	13.0	−2.1	9.6	32	25	15	102.4	13.6	103.7	12.4	−1.3	8.8	25	17	9	>0.05	−0.28	>0.05	−0.26	>0.05	−0.08
Alternate VCI	VC, A, Ed, S, Et	97.1	14.6	100.2	13.2	−3.2	9.6	39	26	19	102.7	13.2	103.5	12.5	−0.9	7.9	25	15	11	>0.05	−0.38	>0.05	−0.25	>0.05	−0.24
PRI	MR, A, Ed, S	93.7	13.6	96.5	12.6	−2.8	6.8	26	22	14	101.9	13.9	102.2	12.8	−0.3	8.8	25	15	11	<0.001	−0.60	<0.01	−0.45	>0.05	−0.37
Prorated PRI	MR, A, Ed, S	93.5	13.5	98.3	9.9	−4.8	9.8	30	22	18	101.6	14.8	102.3	9.8	−0.7	12.5	24	19	13	<0.01	−0.60	<0.05	−0.40	<0.05	−0.41
Alternate PRI	MR, A, Ed, S, Et	92.1	12.2	98.0	8.5	−5.9	8.7	43	28	15	101.4	14.2	101.9	8.8	−0.5	11.4	27	20	15	<0.001	−0.77	<0.01	−0.25	<0.01	−0.62

FSIQ = Full Scale IQ; GAI = General Ability Score; VCI = Verbal Comprehension Index; PRI = Perceptual Reasoning Index; VC = Vocabulary; MR = Matrix Reasoning; A = Age; Ed = Education; S = Sex; R = Region; Et = Ethnicity.

Copyright 2009 by Pearson, Inc. Reproduced with permission. All rights reserved.

TABLE 9.19 OPIE–IV Predicted Versus Actual WAIS–IV Standard Index Scores in Alzheimer and Random Low and High Education Samples

Score	Predictors	Alzheimer										Low Education Sample										Between Group Differences				
		Actual Mean	Actual SD	Pred Mean	Pred SD	Diff. Mean	Diff. SD	25% Cut	15% Cut	10% Cut	p	Actual Mean	Actual SD	Pred Mean	Pred SD	Diff. Mean	Diff. SD	25% Cut	15% Cut	10% Cut	p	Actual ES	p	Pred. ES	p	Diff ES
FSIQ	VC, MR, A, Ed, S, R, Et	81.0	17.2	90.2	15.7	−9.1	7.9	71	69	57		87.8	15.9	87.5	13.6	0.3	7.4	24	12	4	>0.05	−0.39	>0.05	0.17	<0.001	−1.20
FSIQ	VC, A, Ed, S, Et	81.0	17.2	94.5	13.1	−13.5	11.2	74	71	69		87.8	15.9	88.2	12.7	−0.5	9.0	24	12	8	>0.05	−0.39	<0.05	0.48	<0.001	−1.16
FSIQ	MR, A, Ed, S, R	81.0	17.2	94.9	12.5	−13.8	9.7	86	63	57		87.8	15.9	86.7	9.0	1.1	9.8	24	20	10	>0.05	−0.39	<0.01	0.65	<0.001	−1.54
GAI	VC, MR, A, Ed, S, Et	84.7	17.5	92.1	14.0	−7.4	10.2	58	42	28		88.2	14.6	88.4	13.7	−0.1	5.6	20	10	8	>0.05	−0.20	>0.05	0.27	<0.01	−0.71
GAI	VC, A, Ed, S, Et	84.7	17.5	92.1	14.0	−7.4	10.2	61	56	44		88.2	14.6	89.6	13.5	−1.4	7.4	22	22	8	>0.05	−0.20	>0.05	0.18	<0.01	−0.59
GAI	MR, A, Ed, S, R	84.7	17.5	94.5	14.3	−9.8	7.8	64	50	47		88.2	14.6	87.9	9.7	0.3	8.2	26	10	6	>0.05	−0.20	>0.05	0.46	<0.001	−1.31
VCI	VC, A, Ed, S, Et	87.2	18.3	92.6	15.4	−5.4	7.8	51	46	43		88.6	16.1	88.2	12.7	−0.5	9.0	30	20	14	>0.05	−0.08	<0.05	0.29	<0.001	−0.63
PRI	MR, A, Ed, S	86.6	17.6	90.8	13.7	−4.2	9.2	34	22	16		90.1	12.6	90.5	9.7	−0.5	7.0	20	12	6	>0.05	−0.20	>0.05	0.02	<0.05	−0.41

Score	Predictors	Alzheimer									High Education Sample										Between Group Differences				
		Actual Mean	Actual SD	Pred Mean	Pred SD	Diff. Mean	Diff. SD	25% Cut	15% Cut	10% Cut	Actual Mean	Actual SD	Pred Mean	Pred SD	Diff. Mean	Diff. SD	25% Cut	15% Cut	10% Cut	p	Actual ES	p	Pred. ES	p	Diff ES
FSIQ	VC, MR, A, Ed, S, R, Et	81.0	17.2	90.2	15.7	−9.1	7.9	71	69	57	112.3	12.1	111.6	10.7	0.7	7.5	22	12	12	<0.001	−1.82	<0.001	−1.37	<0.001	−1.24
FSIQ	VC, A, Ed, S, Et	81.0	17.2	94.5	13.1	−13.5	11.2	74	71	69	112.3	15.9	112.7	8.6	−0.4	10.5	32	20	16	<0.001	−1.82	<0.001	−1.38	<0.001	−1.17
FSIQ	MR, A, Ed, S, R	81.0	17.2	94.9	12.5	−13.8	9.7	86	63	57	112.3	15.9	111.0	9.9	1.3	8.9	22	14	8	<0.001	−1.82	<0.001	−1.29	<0.001	−1.57
GAI	VC, MR, A, Ed, S, Et	84.7	17.5	92.1	14.0	−7.4	10.2	58	42	28	113.4	12.6	112.4	11.5	1.0	7.2	22	16	12	<0.001	−1.64	<0.001	−1.45	<0.01	−0.82
GAI	VC, A, Ed, S, Et	84.7	17.5	92.1	14.0	−7.4	10.2	61	56	44	113.4	12.6	111.6	9.9	1.8	9.8	24	16	12	<0.001	−1.64	<0.001	−1.39	<0.001	−0.90
GAI	MR, A, Ed, S, R	84.7	17.5	94.5	14.3	−9.8	7.8	64	50	47	113.4	12.6	112.0	10.7	1.3	8.6	18	12	6	<0.001	−1.64	<0.001	−1.22	<0.001	−1.44
VCI	VC, A, Ed, S, Et	87.2	18.3	92.6	15.4	−5.4	7.8	51	46	43	114.4	11.3	113.4	10.0	0.9	6.6	10	6	4	<0.001	−1.49	<0.05	−1.35	<0.001	−0.81
PRI	MR, A, Ed, S	92.1	12.2	98.0	8.5	−5.9	8.7	43	28	15	109.5	14.5	107.9	12.4	1.5	8.9	22	8	4	<0.001	−1.42	<0.001	−0.25	<0.01	−0.85

FSIQ = Full Scale IQ; GAI = General Ability Score; VCI = Verbal Comprehension Index; PRI = Perceptual Reasoning Index; VC = Vocabulary; MR = Matrix Reasoning; A = Age; Ed = Education; S = Sex; R = Region; Et = Ethnicity.

Copyright 2009 by Pearson, Inc. Reproduced with permission. All rights reserved.

TABLE 9.20 OPIE–IV Predicted Versus Actual WAIS–IV Standard, Pro-Rated, and Alternate Index Scores in Mild Cognitive Impairment and Matched Controls

Score	Predictors	Mild Cognitive Impairment									Matched Control										Between Group Differences				
		Actual Mean	Actual SD	Pred. Mean	Pred. SD	Diff. Mean	Diff. SD	25% Cut	15% Cut	10% Cut	Actual Mean	Actual SD	Pred. Mean	Pred. SD	Diff. Mean	Diff. SD	25% Cut	15% Cut	10% Cut	p	Actual ES	p	Pred ES	p	Diff ES
FSIQ	VC, MR, A, Ed, S, R, Et	94.2	15.0	97.1	13.0	−2.9	7.3	36	25	17	102.4	13.3	102.9	12.6	−0.5	7.1	24	11	8	<0.01	−0.55	<0.05	−0.45	>0.05	−0.33
FSIQ	VC, A, Ed, S, Et	94.2	15.0	100.3	12.5	−6.1	9.5	49	31	24	102.4	13.3	103.1	11.7	−0.7	8.9	25	15	11	<0.01	−0.55	>0.05	−0.23	<0.01	−0.57
FSIQ	MR, A, Ed, S, R	94.2	15.0	98.2	11.3	−4.0	10.5	44	24	20	102.4	13.3	102.9	11.7	−0.4	8.6	20	12	8	<0.01	−0.55	<0.05	−0.41	<0.05	−0.34
Prorated FSIQ	VC, MR, A, Ed, S, Et	93.9	15.4	98.0	11.8	−4.1	8.9	46	27	25	102.0	13.4	102.8	11.4	−0.8	8.7	31	13	11	<0.01	−0.53	<0.05	−0.41	<0.05	−0.36
Prorated FSIQ	VC, A, Ed, S, Et	93.7	15.2	100.7	11.6	−6.9	10.4	51	36	29	102.3	13.4	103.1	10.9	−0.9	9.7	27	19	11	<0.01	−0.57	>0.05	−0.21	<0.01	−0.58
Prorated FSIQ	MR, A, Ed, S, R	94.3	15.2	98.8	10.4	−4.6	11.4	37	20	20	102.1	13.2	102.7	10.7	−0.5	9.4	17	12	8	<0.01	−0.52	<0.05	−0.36	<0.05	−0.36
Alternate FSIQ	VC, MR, A, Ed, S, Et	93.6	15.0	97.7	12.0	−4.1	8.3	39	25	18	102.3	13.7	102.6	11.4	−0.3	8.6	29	12	12	<0.01	−0.58	<0.05	−0.41	<0.05	−0.46
Alternate FSIQ	VC, A, Ed, S	93.9	15.0	100.3	11.7	−6.4	10.0	45	34	23	102.9	14.0	102.7	11.0	0.2	10.1	23	17	8	<0.01	−0.60	>0.05	−0.21	<0.001	−0.66
Alternate FSIQ	MR, A, Ed, R	94.2	14.7	98.1	10.9	−3.9	10.6	42	27	20	102.8	13.8	102.7	11.5	0.0	9.3	27	13	9	<0.05	−0.58	<0.01	−0.43	<0.01	−0.37

GAI	VC, MR, A, Ed, S, Et	94.9	13.7	97.1	13.8	-2.2	5.5	32	22	20	102.3	13.3	103.1	13.1	-0.8	6.4	32	20	13	<0.01	-0.54	<0.05	-0.43	>0.05	-0.26
GAI	VC, A, Ed, S, Et	94.9	13.7	99.3	13.2	-4.4	7.6	46	29	19	102.3	13.3	102.9	11.7	-0.6	8.5	28	17	12	<0.01	-0.54	>0.05	-0.27	<0.01	-0.51
GAI	MR, A, Ed, S, R	94.9	13.7	98.1	12.0	-3.2	9.0	39	29	20	102.3	13.3	102.8	12.0	-0.5	8.6	20	12	8	<0.01	-0.54	<0.05	-0.39	>0.05	-0.30
Prorated GAI	VC, MR, A, Ed, S, Et	95.1	14.1	97.8	12.9	-2.7	8.0	34	24	10	102.3	13.9	103.3	12.1	-1.0	9.4	31	19	9	<0.01	-0.51	<0.05	-0.42	>0.05	-0.21
Prorated GAI	VC, A, Ed, S, Et	95.3	13.9	100.7	12.7	-5.4	8.7	44	31	20	102.4	13.6	103.5	11.8	-1.1	9.3	28	16	13	<0.01	-0.52	>0.05	-0.22	<0.01	-0.50
Prorated GAI	MR, A, Ed, S, R	94.7	13.9	98.9	10.9	-4.2	10.3	36	24	20	102.1	13.6	102.7	10.6	-0.6	10.1	21	12	8	<0.01	-0.53	<0.05	-0.35	<0.05	-0.34
Alternate GAI	VC, MR, A, Ed, S, Et	94.0	13.7	97.3	13.6	-3.3	8.2	41	34	29	102.3	13.9	103.2	12.8	-0.9	8.9	39	29	24	<0.01	-0.61	<0.05	-0.43	>0.05	-0.30
Alternate GAI	VC, A, Ed, S, Et	94.7	14.1	100.5	12.7	-5.8	8.9	50	34	30	102.5	13.6	103.3	11.6	-0.8	9.2	28	17	13	<0.01	-0.56	>0.05	-0.22	<0.01	-0.57
Alternate GAI	VC, A, Ed, S, Et	94.2	13.3	99.4	14.2	-5.2	10.0	51	37	25	102.0	13.9	102.8	10.0	-0.8	10.1	27	16	12	<0.01	-0.58	>0.05	-0.34	<0.05	-0.43
VCI	MR, A, Ed, S, R	97.9	14.0	99.2	13.0	-1.4	6.6	33	23	15	102.2	13.0	103.2	13.2	-1.0	6.1	25	13	13	<0.01	-0.31	>0.05	-0.28	>0.05	-0.06
Prorated VCI	VC, A, Ed, S, Et	98.3	14.6	100.3	13.2	-2.1	9.6	32	25	15	102.4	13.6	103.7	12.4	-1.3	8.8	25	17	9	>0.05	-0.28	>0.05	-0.26	>0.05	-0.08
Alternate VCI	VC, A, Ed, S, Et	97.1	14.6	100.2	13.2	-3.2	9.6	39	26	19	102.7	13.2	103.5	12.5	-0.9	7.9	25	15	11	<0.05	-0.38	>0.05	-0.25	>0.05	-0.24
PRI	MR, A, Ed, S	93.7	13.6	96.5	12.6	-2.8	6.8	26	22	14	101.9	13.9	102.2	12.8	-0.3	8.8	25	15	11	<0.001	-0.60	<0.01	-0.45	>0.05	-0.37

(Continued)

TABLE 9.20 (Continued)

Score	Predictors	Mild Cognitive Impairment									Matched Control										Between Group Differences				
		Actual Mean	Actual SD	Pred. Mean	Pred. SD	Diff. Mean	Diff. SD	25% Cut	15% Cut	10% Cut	Actual Mean	Actual SD	Pred. Mean	Pred. SD	Diff. Mean	Diff. Mean	25% Cut	15% Cut	10% Cut	p	Actual ES	p	Pred ES	p	Diff ES
Prorated PRI	MR, A, Ed, S	93.5	13.5	98.3	9.9	−4.8	9.8	30	22	18	101.6	14.8	102.3	9.8	−0.7	12.5	24	19	13	<0.01	−0.60	<0.05	−0.40	<0.05	−0.41
Alternate PRI	MR, A, Ed, S, Et	92.1	12.2	98.0	8.5	−5.9	8.7	43	28	15	101.4	14.2	101.9	8.8	−0.5	11.4	27	20	15	<0.001	−0.77	<0.01	−0.25	<0.01	−0.62

FSIQ = Full Scale IQ; GAI = General Ability Score; VCI = Verbal Comprehension Index; PRI = Perceptual Reasoning Index; VC = Vocabulary; MR = Matrix Reasoning; A = Age; Ed = Education; S = Sex; R = Region; Et = Ethnicity.

Copyright 2009 by Pearson, Inc. Reproduced with permission. All rights reserved.

TABLE 9.21 OPIE–IV Predicted Versus Actual WAIS–IV Standard Index Scores in Mild Cognitive Impairment and Random Low and High Education Samples

Score	Predictors	Mild Cognitive Impairment									Low Education Sample										Between Group Differences				
		Actual Mean	Actual SD	Pred Mean	Pred SD	Diff. Mean	Diff. SD	25% Cut	15% Cut	10% Cut	Actual Mean	Actual SD	Pred Mean	Pred SD	Diff. Mean	Diff. SD	25% Cut	15% Cut	10% Cut	p	Actual ES	p	Pred ES	p	Diff ES
FSIQ	VC, MR, A, Ed, S, R, Et	94.2	15.0	97.1	13.0	-2.9	7.3	36	25	17	88.1	15.7	88.7	13.2	-0.6	7.5	28	14	8	<0.05	0.41	<0.01	0.65	>0.05	-0.31
FSIQ	VC, A, Ed, S, Et	94.2	15.0	100.3	12.5	-6.1	9.5	49	31	24	88.1	15.7	89.4	12.6	-1.3	8.5	28	16	12	<0.05	0.41	<0.001	0.87	<0.01	-0.50
FSIQ	MR, A, Ed, S, R	94.2	15.0	98.2	11.3	-4.0	10.5	44	24	20	88.1	15.7	86.6	8.8	1.5	10.6	24	20	12	<0.05	0.41	<0.001	1.03	<0.01	-0.53
GAI	VC, MR, A, Ed, S, Et	94.9	13.7	97.1	13.8	-2.2	5.5	32	22	20	89.3	14.3	89.7	13.6	-0.5	5.5	26	14	10	<0.05	0.41	<0.01	0.53	>0.05	-0.31
GAI	VC, A, Ed, S, Et	94.9	13.7	99.3	13.2	-4.4	7.6	46	29	19	89.3	14.3	91.2	13.4	-1.9	6.3	26	22	12	<0.05	0.41	<0.01	0.62	>0.05	-0.33
GAI	MR, A, Ed, S, R	94.9	13.7	98.1	12.0	-3.2	9.0	39	29	20	89.3	14.3	87.7	9.7	1.6	9.3	26	16	10	<0.05	0.41	<0.001	0.86	<0.01	-0.53
VCI	VC, A, Ed, S, Et	97.9	14.0	99.2	14.2	-1.4	6.6	33	23	15	89.2	16.5	90.5	15.8	-1.3	6.2	32	18	14	<0.01	0.62	<0.01	0.61	>0.05	-0.01
PRI	MR, A, Ed, S, Et	92.1	12.2	98.0	8.5	-5.9	8.7	43	28	15	91.1	12.3	91.0	9.6	0.1	7.7	22	14	10	>0.05	0.08	<0.01	-0.25	>0.05	-0.69

		Mild Cognitive Impairment									High Education Sample									Between Group Differences				
Score	Predictors	Actual Mean	Actual SD	Pred Mean	Pred SD	Diff. Mean	Diff. SD	25% Cut	15% Cut	10% Cut		Actual Mean	Actual SD	Pred Mean	Pred SD	Diff. Mean	Diff. SD	25% Cut	15% Cut	10% Cut	Actual ES	p	Pred ES	p	Diff ES
FSIQ	VC, MR, A, Ed, S, R, Et	94.2	15.0	97.1	13.0	-2.9	7.3	36	25	17		112.0	12.6	111.3	11.4	0.7	7.5	22	16	16	-1.18	<0.001	-1.10	<0.05	-0.49
FSIQ	VC, A, Ed, S, Et	94.2	15.0	100.3	12.5	-6.1	9.5	49	31	24		112.0	12.6	112.0	9.1	0.0	10.0	24	16	12	-1.18	<0.001	-0.94	<0.01	-0.64
FSIQ	MR, A, Ed, S, R	94.2	15.0	98.2	11.3	-4.0	10.5	44	24	20		112.0	12.6	111.3	11.4	0.7	7.5	20	10	4	-1.18	<0.001	-1.15	<0.05	-0.45
GAI	VC, MR, A, Ed, S, Et	94.9	13.7	97.1	13.8	-2.2	5.5	32	22	20		113.8	12.6	111.9	12.3	1.9	6.4	16	10	10	-1.38	<0.001	-1.07	<0.05	-0.75
GAI	VC, A, Ed, S, Et	94.9	13.7	99.3	13.2	-4.4	7.6	46	29	19		113.8	12.6	111.1	10.4	2.8	8.9	18	12	8	-1.38	<0.001	-0.89	<0.001	-0.94
GAI	MR, A, Ed, S, R	94.9	13.7	98.1	12.0	-3.2	9.0	39	29	20		113.8	12.6	111.8	10.4	2.0	7.0	12	6	2	-1.38	<0.001	-1.15	<0.01	-0.57
VCI	VC, A, Ed, S, Et	97.9	14.0	99.2	14.2	-1.4	6.6	33	23	15		114.9	11.5	112.9	10.7	2.0	6.3	16	8	6	-1.22	<0.001	-0.96	<0.01	-0.51
PRI	MR, A, Ed, S, Et	92.1	12.2	98.0	8.5	-5.9	8.7	43	28	15		109.5	14.5	107.9	12.4	1.5	8.9	22	8	4	-1.42	<0.001	-0.25	<0.01	-0.85

Copyright 2009 by Pearson, Inc. Reproduced with permission. All rights reserved.

WAIS–IV FSIQ and index scores in the ALZ and MCI groups. Different equations were developed to accommodate different groupings of performance and demographics predictors. The tables also provide comparison data on the prediction equations in low and high education groups. Base rates reflect the percentage of individuals in the sample who obtained a score lower than 25%, 15%, and 10% of the normative sample.

Table 9.18 compares OPIE–IV WAIS–IV FSIQ, GAI, VCI, and PRI predicted and obtained scores in the ALZ group and matched controls. For each composite score, comparison data is provided for the standard index score, a prorated score obtained without the score used for prediction (e.g., PRI without Matrix Reasoning), and an alternate score using a supplemental subtest score in place of the predictor score to obtain the composite score. The presentation of the prorated and alternate scores allows evaluation of the OPIE approach without inflating scores by using the same variable as a predictor and dependent measure. The variables used in each prediction equation are listed in the predictors column.

The OPIE predicted WAIS–IV index scores were significantly lower in the ALZ group compared to matched controls, except for the Vocabulary predicated alternate and prorated VCI scores. Because the groups are matched on measures related to pre-morbid ability, it was expected that the predicted scores would not be significantly different. *This result indicates that the OPIE equations generally underpredict premorbid ability in patients with ALZ.* The effect sizes for the predicted score differences are smaller than for the actual score differences; therefore, some aspects of pre-morbid functioning are being assessed. The predicted minus actual index differences were all significant and large but did not improve sensitivity (e.g., similar effect sizes) compared to the actual score differences.

The base rate data presented in Table 9.18 (i.e., 25%, 15%, and 10%) represent the cut-off in the normative sample where the predicted score is greater than the actual score. In other words, the difference score obtained by 25%, 15%, and 10% of the normative sample, respectively. In the ALZ sample, 71% had a difference between predicted and actual FSIQ that equaled or exceeded the 25% cut-off in the normative sample when all predictor variables are included in predictions. Nearly three times as many ALZ patients as normal controls achieved such a large discrepancy. Clearly, the base rates of the difference scores indicate that patients with ALZ are more likely to have large differences between predicted and actual WAIS–IV scores than matched controls. However, the under-prediction of pre-morbid scores in the OPIE method described above makes it less likely to identify a true cognitive decline relative to the predicted pre-morbid state—which limits the utility of the OPIE method.

Table 9.19 compares the WAIS–IV actual and OPIE–IV predicted composite scores obtained in the ALZ group to those obtained in randomly selected low education and high education groups. These comparisons allow examination of predictions in groups at the educational extremes where predictions are frequently needed. In comparison to the low education group, the ALZ group produced significantly different actual and predicted score differences across all scores; however, actual scores and predicted scores were not different between groups. In other words, the patient sample did not show worse performance on their current test scores than the low education group. This could be mistaken as either no impairment in the clinical sample or impairment in the low education sample. However, the large discrepancy between the predicted scores and actual scores in the patient but not the low education sample reveals impairment versus low premorbid ability. This highlights the importance of examining difference scores in this demographic group. This profile enables clinicians to identify a low ability examinee from a patient with ALZ.

The ALZ group obtained significantly lower actual and predicted scores, and significantly greater score differences than the high education group. Given the large effect sizes of differences in actual scores, premorbid prediction from actual score differences may not be as helpful in the high education groups. However, given that large differences between predicted and actual scores occur mostly in the clinical sample and not in the low or high education samples, the presence of a large discrepancy between premorbid and current functioning can help a clinician identify cognitive impairment associated with clinical populations. Finally, the base rates of large predicted versus actual discrepancies were much higher in the ALZ than the low education and high education groups.

Table 9.20 compares OPIE–IV, WAIS–IV, FSIQ, GAI, VCI, and PRI predicted and obtained scores in the MCI group and matched controls. The same methods were used as previously described. Actual scores significantly differ between groups on most measures, except VCI. The predicted scores were very similar across groups. The groups were significantly different when Matrix Reasoning was entered into the equation but not for equations where Vocabulary was the only included performance measure. Using Vocabulary provides a good estimate of pre-morbid ability in individuals with MCI. *The discrepancy between predicted and actual ability did not yield larger effect sizes than observed in the actual between group differences in the matched control samples.* All effect sizes were smaller than those seen in the ALZ sample. Base rates of large discrepancies were slightly higher in the ALZ sample in comparison to matched controls and the normative sample.

Table 9.21 compares the WAIS–IV actual and OPIE–IV predicted composite scores obtained in the MCI group to those obtained in randomly selected low education and high education groups. These comparisons allow examination of predictions in comparison to groups at the educational extremes where predictions are frequently used. In comparison to the low education group, the MCI group produced significantly higher actual and predicted WAIS–IV index scores (except for actual PRI). Several difference scores were significantly different but the effect sizes were small. By comparison, the MCI group had slightly higher ability but tended to show greater predicted versus actual score differences than the low education sample. Larger differences are observed in the comparisons to the high education group. In all actual and predicted score comparisons the MCI group obtained lower actual and predicted scores, and greater score differences were observed on most scores. As was reported in the ALZ sample, the lower scores in the clinical sample are accompanied by lower actual than predicted score differences, unlike the pattern observed in the low education sample, in which low scores contrast with relatively equal predicted and actual scores. All effect sizes were lower than those observed in the ALZ group comparisons.

TOPF AND WAIS–IV AND WMS–IV

TOPF prediction equations were applied to samples similar to those described for the OPIE studies (some cases were missing TOPF scores). See Table 9.1 for demographic information on the TOPF samples. In addition to WAIS–IV predictions, TOPF predictions for WMS–IV are also provided. TOPF simple demographics prediction equations were used to derive predicted index scores for the ALZ and MCI groups. In addition, TOPF equations were derived for a new index in the WAIS–IV, the Cognitive Proficiency Index (CPI). Tables 9.22 and 9.23 compare the actual and TOPF-predicted difference scores obtained by the ALZ and MCI group, respectively, and the matched control, low education, and high education groups.

Table 9.22 provides the comparison data between actual and TOPF simple demographics predicted scores on WAIS–IV and WMS–IV for the ALZ group and matched control, low education, and high education groups. *The most important finding is that the ALZ group predicted scores were not statistically different from the matched controls. This indicates that the TOPF with simple demographics model provides a good estimation of pre-morbid functioning in this clinical population.* The ALZ group obtained lower actual scores, and greater differences between actual and predicted scores than the matched controls. The effect sizes for the predicted versus actual difference scores within the ALZ group were similar to the effect sizes observed when comparing actual scores of the ALZ and matched control groups. This suggests a similar degree of sensitivity to differences with the matched control sample. In addition, the

TABLE 9.22 TOPF Simple Demographics Predicted Versus Actual WAIS–IV/WMS–IV Index Scores in Alzheimer and Matched Control, High and Low Education Samples

Score	Alzheimer										Matched Control Group										Between Group Differences				
	Actual Mean	Actual SD	Pred. Mean	Pred. SD	Diff. Mean	Diff. SD	25% Cut	15% Cut	10% Cut	p	Actual Mean	Actual SD	Pred. Mean	Pred. SD	Diff. Mean	Diff. SD	25% Cut	15% Cut	10% Cut	p	Actual ES	p	Pred. ES	p	Diff. ES
VCI	87.4	18.9	99.8	15.7	−12.4	10.9	71	62	59	<0.001	103.3	15.0	104.5	11.2	−1.2	8.6	28	15	8	<0.001	−0.84	>0.05	−0.30	<0.001	−1.03
PRI	86.0	17.6	99.9	9.6	−13.9	14.9	70	52	50	<0.001	102.2	14.4	103.0	8.3	−0.8	12.5	25	23	8	<0.001	−0.92	>0.05	−0.32	<0.001	−0.88
WMI	85.3	17.2	99.3	11.1	−14.0	12.6	66	64	49	<0.001	100.5	13.7	103.6	9.0	−3.1	10.9	25	15	10	<0.001	−0.89	>0.05	−0.39	<0.001	−0.86
PSI	77.8	17.1	101.8	6.8	−23.9	15.7	80	77	74	<0.001	101.8	13.0	104.0	6.3	−2.2	10.4	15	5	3	<0.001	−1.40	>0.05	−0.33	<0.001	−1.39
GAI	84.5	17.8	99.1	14.6	−14.6	11.5	79	67	64	<0.001	103.1	14.9	103.9	10.9	−0.8	9.9	30	15	5	<0.001	−1.04	>0.05	−0.32	<0.001	−1.20
CPI	79.1	18.4	101.1	9.8	−22.0	14.7	83	83	80	<0.001	101.3	14.4	104.7	8.0	−3.5	11.2	23	8	8	<0.001	−1.20	>0.05	−0.37	<0.001	−1.26
FSIQ	80.8	17.5	100.1	13.5	−19.3	12.4	88	78	72	<0.001	102.7	15.0	104.5	10.6	−1.8	10.2	33	15	8	<0.001	−1.25	>0.05	−0.32	<0.001	−1.42
IMI	70.2	19.7	102.1	7.2	−31.8	18.1	90	87	82	<0.001	102.6	13.7	103.9	6.7	−1.2	12.4	32	16	11	<0.001	−1.65	>0.05	−0.25	<0.001	−1.69
DMI	64.0	19.6	102.3	6.3	−38.3	18.9	90	88	85	<0.001	103.5	13.5	104.0	5.9	−0.5	12.3	26	15	9	<0.001	−2.02	>0.05	−0.25	<0.001	−2.00

	Alzheimer									Low Education Group										Between Group Differences				
Score	Actual Mean	Actual SD	Pred. Mean	Pred. SD	Diff. Mean	Diff. SD	25% Cut	15% Cut	10% Cut	Actual Mean	Actual SD	Pred. Mean	Pred. SD	Diff. Mean	Diff. SD	25% Cut	15% Cut	10% Cut	p	Actual ES	p	Pred. ES	p	Diff. ES
VCI	87.4	18.9	99.8	15.7	−12.4	10.9	71	62	59	89.3	15.8	89.9	10.9	−0.6	9.2	25	19	16	>0.05	−0.10	<0.01	0.63	<0.001	−1.08
PRI	86.0	17.6	99.9	9.6	−13.9	14.9	70	52	50	90.5	13.8	93.4	7.7	−2.9	10.8	28	13	9	>0.05	−0.25	<0.01	0.68	<0.01	−0.74
WMI	85.3	17.2	99.3	11.1	−14.0	12.6	66	64	49	91.1	13.7	92.6	9.4	−1.5	9.7	25	9	6	>0.05	−0.34	<0.01	0.60	<0.001	−0.99
PSI	77.8	17.1	101.8	6.8	−23.9	15.7	80	77	74	91.3	18.4	92.9	6.7	−1.6	15.1	28	22	19	<0.001	−0.79	<0.01	1.32	<0.001	−1.42
GAI	84.5	17.8	99.1	14.6	−14.6	11.5	79	67	64	88.8	15.1	90.2	10.5	−1.3	9.5	34	19	6	>0.05	−0.24	<0.01	0.61	<0.001	−1.16
CPI	79.1	18.4	101.1	9.8	−22.0	14.7	83	83	80	90.0	17.1	90.9	8.8	−1.0	12.5	34	25	13	<0.05	−0.59	<0.001	1.04	<0.001	−1.43
FSIQ	80.8	17.5	100.1	13.5	−19.3	12.4	88	78	72	88.5	16.4	90.4	10.4	−1.9	10.5	31	25	19	>0.05	−0.44	<0.001	0.72	<0.001	−1.41
IMI	70.2	19.7	102.1	7.2	−31.8	18.1	90	87	82	92.5	17.1	92.9	7.3	−0.4	13.2	21	13	4	<0.001	−1.13	<0.001	1.28	<0.001	−1.74
DMI	64.0	19.6	102.3	6.3	−38.3	18.9	90	88	85	92.9	17.9	93.9	6.0	−1.0	15.9	31	11	3	<0.001	−1.48	<0.001	−0.25	<0.001	−1.97

	Alzheimer									High Education Group										Between Group Differences				
Score	Actual Mean	Actual SD	Pred. Mean	Pred. SD	Diff. Mean	Diff. SD	25% Cut	15% Cut	10% Cut	Actual Mean	Actual SD	Pred. Mean	Pred. SD	Diff. Mean	Diff. SD	25% Cut	15% Cut	10% Cut	p	Actual ES	p	Pred. ES	p	Diff. ES
VCI	87.4	18.9	99.8	15.7	−12.4	10.9	71	62	59	116.7	9.3	116.2	7.0	0.6	8.6	21	11	0	<0.001	−1.55	<0.001	−1.05	<0.001	−1.19
PRI	86.0	17.6	99.9	9.6	−13.9	14.9	70	52	50	112.2	13.1	110.8	4.8	1.4	12.3	24	10	8	<0.001	−1.49	<0.001	−1.13	<0.001	−1.03
WMI	85.3	17.2	99.3	11.1	−14.0	12.6	66	64	49	112.6	13.1	112.2	6.0	0.3	12.2	24	18	13	<0.001	−1.59	<0.001	−1.17	<0.001	−1.14
PSI	77.8	17.1	101.8	6.8	−23.9	15.7	80	77	74	105.8	11.0	107.4	3.8	−1.6	11.6	18	13	11	<0.001	−1.63	<0.001	−0.84	<0.001	−1.42
GAI	84.5	17.8	99.1	14.6	−14.6	11.5	79	67	64	116.5	10.6	115.1	6.5	1.4	9.2	19	13	5	<0.001	−1.79	<0.001	−1.09	<0.001	−1.39
CPI	79.1	18.4	101.1	9.8	−22.0	14.7	83	83	80	110.5	10.6	111.7	4.6	−1.2	10.9	29	21	13	<0.001	−1.70	<0.001	−1.08	<0.001	−1.41
FSIQ	80.8	17.5	100.1	13.5	−19.3	12.4	88	78	72	115.2	10.1	114.7	5.8	0.6	9.4	21	18	8	<0.001	−1.97	<0.001	−1.08	<0.001	−1.60
IMI	70.2	19.7	102.1	7.2	−31.8	18.1	90	87	82	106.7	11.4	107.7	4.2	−1.0	11.0	28	16	8	<0.001	−1.86	<0.001	−0.79	<0.01	−1.71
DMI	64.0	19.6	102.3	6.3	−38.3	18.9	90	88	85	103.4	14.9	106.5	12.3	−3.1	14.5	28	16	13	<0.001	−2.02	<0.001	−0.67	<0.01	−1.86

Copyright 2009 by Pearson, Inc. Reproduced with permission. All rights reserved.

TABLE 9.23 TOPF Simple Demographics Predicted Versus Actual WAIS–IV/WMS–IV Index Scores in Mild Cognitive Impairment and Matched Controls, High and Low Education Groups

	Mild Cognitive Impairment									Matched Control Group										Between Group Differences				
Score	Actual Mean	Actual SD	Pred. Mean	Pred. SD	Diff. Mean	Diff. SD	25% Cut	15% Cut	10% Cut	Actual Mean	Actual SD	Pred. Mean	Pred. SD	Diff. Mean	Diff. SD	25% Cut	15% Cut	10% Cut	p	Actual ES	p	Pred. ES	p	Diff. ES
VCI	97.1	14.2	102.6	10.0	−5.4	9.6	44	19	4	103.5	13.1	103.3	9.7	0.2	8.1	22	10	5	<0.05	−0.44	>0.05	−0.07	<0.01	−0.59
PRI	94.2	13.4	103.0	6.5	−8.8	12.5	47	43	28	102.6	13.3	103.2	6.9	−0.6	11.2	22	15	10	<0.05	−0.62	>0.05	−0.03	<0.01	−0.65
WMI	96.0	15.6	102.6	7.7	−6.6	13.0	44	41	8	102.2	12.1	103.1	7.6	−0.9	10.1	25	17	7	<0.05	−0.39	>0.05	−0.06	<0.01	−0.44
PSI	93.2	15.6	102.2	5.6	−9.1	15.4	45	43	41	101.6	14.0	102.4	6.2	−0.9	11.6	20	12	9	<0.01	−0.54	>0.05	−0.04	<0.01	−0.53
GAI	94.6	13.4	103.0	9.5	−8.4	10.3	53	43	34	103.5	13.4	103.5	9.4	0.0	9.4	25	17	9	<0.01	−0.66	>0.05	−0.05	<0.001	−0.82
CPI	93.2	15.0	102.9	7.3	−9.7	13.4	51	37	35	102.0	13.1	103.4	7.5	−1.4	10.2	23	8	8	<0.01	−0.59	>0.05	−0.07	<0.001	−0.62
FSIQ	93.6	14.4	103.7	9.1	−10.1	11.2	60	49	45	103.1	13.3	103.9	9.0	−0.7	9.0	25	14	9	<0.001	−0.66	>0.05	−0.02	<0.001	−0.84
IMI	90.5	14.2	101.0	4.5	−10.5	14.1	58	41	30	102.4	13.0	101.5	6.7	0.8	11.7	17	8	4	<0.001	−0.84	>0.05	−0.13	<0.001	−0.80
DMI	87.5	17.2	99.1	10.4	−13.3	16.9	54	42	33	101.1	12.2	101.4	13.4	−0.3	11.7	21	14	4	<0.001	−0.79	>0.05	−0.25	<0.001	−0.77

| | Mild Cognitive Impairment | | | | | | | | | Low Education Group | | | | | | | | | | Between Group Differences | | | | |
Score	Actual Mean	Actual SD	Pred. Mean	Pred. SD	Diff. Mean	Diff. SD	25% Cut	15% Cut	10% Cut	Actual Mean	Actual SD	Pred. Mean	Pred. SD	Diff. Mean	Diff. SD	25% Cut	15% Cut	10% Cut	p	Actual ES	p	Pred. ES	p	Diff. ES
VCI	97.1	14.2	102.6	10.0	−5.4	9.6	44	19	4	88.3	16.3	90.5	11.5	−2.2	8.9	30	21	15	<0.05	0.62	<0.001	1.21	<0.05	−0.33
PRI	94.2	13.4	103.0	6.5	−8.8	12.5	47	43	28	90.9	13.5	94.2	7.7	−3.3	10.3	33	18	12	>0.05	0.24	<0.001	1.34	<0.05	−0.44
WMI	96.0	15.6	102.6	7.7	−6.6	13.0	44	41	8	89.3	15.6	92.8	10.3	−3.5	10.9	33	12	9	<0.05	0.43	<0.001	1.27	>0.05	−0.23
PSI	93.2	15.6	102.2	5.6	−9.1	15.4	45	43	41	91.6	18.0	93.2	6.4	−1.5	15.8	30	18	18	>0.05	0.10	<0.001	1.63	<0.05	−0.49
GAI	94.6	13.4	103.0	9.5	−8.4	10.3	53	43	34	88.6	14.8	91.0	10.6	−2.4	8.1	33	21	9	>0.05	0.45	<0.001	1.27	<0.01	−0.58
CPI	93.2	15.0	102.9	7.3	−9.7	13.4	51	37	35	89.3	17.6	91.0	9.4	−1.7	13.0	33	24	15	>0.05	0.25	<0.001	1.63	<0.01	−0.60
FSIQ	93.6	14.4	103.7	9.1	−10.1	11.2	60	49	45	88.0	16.4	90.9	10.8	−2.9	9.9	33	27	21	>0.05	0.39	<0.001	1.41	<0.01	−0.64
IMI	90.5	14.2	101.0	4.5	−10.5	14.1	58	41	30	93.9	18.3	93.5	7.2	0.4	15.7	21	8	8	>0.05	−0.24	<0.001	1.67	<0.01	−0.77
DMI	87.5	17.2	99.1	10.4	−13.3	16.9	54	42	33	95.2	16.5	94.7	5.3	0.6	15.2	24	14	3	<0.05	−0.45	<0.001	−0.25	<0.001	−0.82

| | Mild Cognitive Impairment | | | | | | | | | High Education Group | | | | | | | | | | Between Group Differences | | | | |
Score	Actual Mean	Actual SD	Pred. Mean	Pred. SD	Diff. Mean	Diff. SD	25% Cut	15% Cut	10% Cut	Actual Mean	Actual SD	Pred. Mean	Pred. SD	Diff. Mean	Diff. SD	25% Cut	15% Cut	10% Cut	p	Actual ES	p	Pred. ES	p	Diff. ES
VCI	97.1	14.2	102.6	10.0	-5.4	9.6	44	19	4	117.1	11.2	115.9	8.2	1.2	9.0	17	14	11	<0.001	-1.41	<0.001	-1.33	<0.01	-0.69
PRI	94.2	13.4	103.0	6.5	-8.8	12.5	47	43	28	112.7	12.9	110.2	5.7	2.4	11.8	20	8	6	<0.001	-1.38	<0.001	-1.12	<0.001	-0.90
WMI	96.0	15.6	102.6	7.7	-6.6	13.0	44	41	8	110.9	15.4	111.9	6.9	-1.0	13.3	31	19	11	<0.001	-0.95	<0.001	-1.21	<0.05	-0.43
PSI	93.2	15.6	102.2	5.6	-9.1	15.4	45	43	41	105.9	12.8	107.6	4.5	-1.7	12.8	22	17	14	<0.001	-0.82	<0.001	-0.97	<0.05	-0.48
GAI	94.6	13.4	103.0	9.5	-8.4	10.3	53	43	34	116.9	11.7	114.5	7.5	2.4	9.3	17	8	0	<0.001	-1.66	<0.001	-1.21	<0.001	-1.05
CPI	93.2	15.0	102.9	7.3	-9.7	13.4	51	37	35	109.6	12.3	111.6	5.2	-1.9	11.9	36	25	17	<0.001	-1.09	<0.001	-1.19	<0.01	-0.58
FSIQ	93.6	14.4	103.7	9.1	-10.1	11.2	60	49	45	115.2	11.6	114.3	6.9	0.9	9.8	22	17	6	<0.001	-1.51	<0.001	-1.17	<0.001	-0.98
IMI	90.5	14.2	101.0	4.5	-10.5	14.1	58	41	30	108.2	10.4	108.6	5.5	-0.3	10.9	23	18	9	<0.001	-1.25	<0.001	-1.71	<0.01	-0.72
DMI	87.5	17.2	99.1	10.4	-13.3	16.9	54	42	33	105.0	15.1	107.2	4.6	-2.3	15.1	31	16	13	<0.001	-1.02	<0.001	-0.25	<0.01	-0.65

Copyright 2009 by Pearson, Inc. Reproduced with permission. All rights reserved.

ALZ group had a high number of cases showing unusually large differences where predicted scores were higher than actual tests scores (e.g., 90% were at or greater than the 25% population based cut-off).

In comparison to the low education group, the ALZ group obtained lower actual scores on PSI, CPI, Immediate Memory Index (IMI), and Delayed Memory Index (DMI), higher predicted scores on all measures, and greater difference scores across all scores. *ALZ patients can be differentiated from low ability subjects based on higher pre-morbid prediction scores and large discrepancies between actual and predicted scores.* The effect sizes for the discrepancy are 1.5 to 9 times larger than the actual score differences. Given this pattern of similar actual scores, the use of predictions was particularly useful in this group. In comparison to the high education group, the ALZ group obtained lower actual and predicted scores, and greater difference scores on all measures. When compared to a high education sample, the ALZ group is significantly lower on all variables. The TOPF predicted ability model is helpful because it enables the clinician to rule out low pre-morbid ability as the reason for obtained low scores.

Table 9.23 provides the comparison data between actual and TOPF simple demographics predicted scores on WAIS–IV and WMS–IV for the MCI group and the matched control, low education, and high education groups. There is no difference between the predicted scores in the MCI and matched control groups. This indicates that the TOPF with simple demographics is a good measure of pre-morbid functioning in this group.

In comparison to the matched controls, the MCI group obtained lower actual WAIS–IV and WMS–IV index scores, and greater differences between actual and predicted scores on all measures than the matched controls. In the matched control sample, the effect sizes are similar for the actual score differences and the predicted versus actual score differences. In comparison to the low education group, the MCI group obtained similar actual scores, higher predicted scores, and greater difference scores on GAI, CPI, FSIQ, IMI, and DMI. In comparison to the high education group, the MCI group obtained lower actual and predicted scores on all measures. The TOPF pre-morbid model relies on the discrepancy between the predicted versus actual test scores to enable the clinician to determine if the examinee has low ability or if the scores suggest a change in cognitive functioning from a previous level.

SCATTER IN OLDER ADULT CLINICAL POPULATIONS

Variability in performance across subtests within a battery is sometimes considered an indicator of cognitive impairment. However, variability in performance occurs in normally developing and aging individuals as well as those with clinical diagnoses (Binder, Iverson, & Brooks, 2009; Brooks, Iverson, Holdnack, & Feldman, 2008). In order to utilize variability measures as indicators of impairment, the base rates for scores in these measures need to be established in non-clinical populations. Chapter 3 of this book describes the derivation and interpretation of the variability measures and provides a review of variability in performance on the WAIS–IV and WMS–IV. This section is restricted to variability measures in older adult populations.

Table 9.24 provides data on a variety of measures of score variability for the WAIS–IV and WMS–IV in ALZ and matched control groups. The presented scores are scaled scores with lower scores representing greater variability. Scores were placed on the scaled score metric to allow similar interpretation of results, low scaled scores indicate lower performance, or in this case greater variability. The WAIS–IV variability measures indicate the highest obtained subtest scaled score is significantly lower in the ALZ group compared to controls. The ALZ sample also obtained a lower lowest score than the control group. The level of performance suggests that both the highest and lowest subtest scores for the ALZ group are in the low average range. The variability measure comparing the highest versus lowest subtest scaled scores does not differ between the ALZ and control sample. The standard deviation of the subtest scaled scores also does not differ from controls. The same results are observed for the WAIS–IV index scores. On the WAIS–IV, the ALZ group shows a suppressed but not unusually variable cognitive profile.

The WMS–IV results indicate borderline performance on the highest and lowest subtest scores and deficient highest and lowest WMS–IV index scores. These are significantly lower than controls and have very large effect sizes. The WMS–IV variability measures reveal no difference between the ALZ and control sample for subtest and index scores. When the WAIS–IV/WMS–IV batteries are considered together, the ALZ group has significantly more variability on the subtest standard deviation and the index highest versus lowest and standard deviation measures. *These results indicate that the ALZ subjects have significant variability when considering intellectual and memory functions together but not within those constructs.*

Variability measures are affected by the highest score obtained. In the ALZ sample, the highest score is very low and suppresses variability; therefore, it is difficult to identify whether true profile variability occurs. Table 9.25 provides data on variability measures obtained in the ALZ group controlling for the highest score. *When controlling for the highest score, the ALZ group showed significantly more variability than controls on WAIS–IV subtests and indexes and WMS–IV indexes.* The degree

TABLE 9.24 WAIS–IV/WMS–IV Variability Measures in Alzheimer Disease and Matched Controls

Score	Alzheimer		Matched Control		Between Group Differences	
	Mean	SD	Mean	SD	p	ES
WAIS–IV Subtest High vs. Low	10.3	3.1	10.7	2.7	>0.05	−0.12
WAIS–IV Subtest Standard Deviation	10.3	3.5	11.1	2.9	>0.05	−0.23
WAIS–IV Subtest Highest Score	6.8	3.2	10.3	2.8	<0.001	−1.08
WAIS–IV Subtest Lowest Score	6.5	3.5	11.2	2.9	<0.001	−1.32
WAIS–IV Index High vs. Low	11.2	3.5	11.5	3.4	>0.05	−0.09
WAIS–IV Index Standard Deviation	10.8	3.7	11.6	3.3	>0.05	−0.23
WAIS–IV Index Highest Score	6.9	3.6	11.3	2.8	<0.001	−1.21
WAIS–IV Index Lowest Score	6.7	3.2	10.2	2.8	<0.001	−1.08
WMS–IV Subtest High vs. Low	10.5	3.7	10.1	2.8	>0.05	0.10
WMS–IV Subtest Standard Deviation	10.5	3.5	10.5	2.9	>0.05	0.00
WMS–IV Subtest Highest Score	4.5	3.8	10.8	2.5	<0.001	−1.65
WMS–IV Subtest Lowest Score	4.3	3.4	10.8	2.4	<0.001	−1.92
WMS–IV Index High vs. Low	9.6	3.6	10.3	2.8	>0.05	−0.21
WMS–IV Index Standard Deviation	9.8	3.6	10.4	3.0	>0.05	−0.17
WMS–IV Index Highest Score	3.6	3.6	10.7	2.3	<0.001	−1.98
WMS–IV Index Lowest Score	3.6	3.5	10.8	2.5	<0.001	−2.08
WAIS–IV/WMS–IV Subtest High vs. Low	9.1	4.1	10.5	3.1	>0.05	−0.35
WAIS–IV/WMS–IV Subtest Standard Deviation	8.4	4.0	10.8	3.2	<0.01	−0.59
WAIS–IV/WMS–IV Subtest Highest Score	6.4	3.9	10.6	2.9	<0.001	−1.06
WAIS–IV/WMS–IV Subtest Lowest Score	5.1	3.4	10.8	2.9	<0.001	−1.69
WAIS–IV/WMS–IV Index High vs. Low	7.9	3.8	11.1	3.2	<0.001	−0.85
WAIS–IV/WMS–IV Index Standard Deviation	6.8	3.9	11.2	3.6	<0.001	−1.14
WAIS–IV/WMS–IV Index Highest Score	6.3	3.9	10.7	3.1	<0.001	−1.13
WAIS–IV/WMS–IV Index Lowest Score	4.2	4.0	11.5	2.9	<0.001	−1.82

Note: See Chapter 3 for description of variability measures.
Copyright 2009 by Pearson, Inc. Reproduced with permission. All rights reserved.

TABLE 9.25 WAIS–IV/WMS–IV Variability Measures Controlling for Highest
Subtest or Index Score in Alzheimer Disease and Matched Controls

Score	Alzheimer		Matched Control		Between Group Differences	
	Mean	SD	Mean	SD	*p*	ES
WAIS–IV Subtest High vs. Low	7.9	3.7	11.1	2.7	<0.001	−0.85
WAIS–IV Subtest Standard Deviation	7.9	4.1	11.5	3.1	<0.001	−0.88
WAIS–IV Index High vs. Low	10.1	4.2	11.8	2.9	<0.01	−0.40
WAIS–IV Index Standard Deviation	9.6	4.3	11.9	3.1	<0.05	−0.53
WMS–IV Subtest High vs. Low	8.2	3.5	10.4	2.5	>0.05	−0.62
WMS–IV Subtest Standard Deviation	9.4	3.8	10.5	2.9	>0.05	−0.30
WMS–IV Index High vs. Low	8.9	3.9	10.2	2.8	<0.001	−0.35
WMS–IV Index Standard Deviation	9.1	3.7	10.8	3.1	<0.001	−0.46
WAIS–IV/WMS–IV Subtest High vs. Low	6.9	3.7	10.8	2.8	<0.001	−1.05
WAIS–IV/WMS–IV Subtest Standard Deviation	6.8	4.1	11.2	3.1	<0.001	−1.06
WAIS–IV/WMS–IV Index High vs. Low	5.3	4.4	10.9	3.0	<0.001	−1.30
WAIS–IV/WMS–IV Index Standard Deviation	4.6	4.3	11.4	3.0	<0.001	−1.57

Note: See Chapter 3 for description of variability measures.
Copyright 2009 by Pearson, Inc. Reproduced with permission. All rights reserved.

of variability is much greater when the WAIS–IV and WMS–IV are
considered together. These differences yield large effect sizes. These
variability indicators may be additional sources of diagnostic information in patients with ALZ.

Table 9.26 provides data on a variety of measures of score variability
for the WAIS–IV and WMS–IV in MCI and matched control groups.
The WAIS–IV results indicate that the MCI group has significantly
lower highest obtained subtest scores and significantly lower lowest
obtained subtest scaled scores. These scores were not as low as those
observed in the ALZ sample. The variability measures for the
WAIS–IV subtests were not significantly different from controls. The
WAIS–IV Index scores had the same pattern as the subtests, significantly lower highest and lowest scores but no differences in variability
from controls. Similarly, the WMS–IV subtest and index scores were

TABLE 9.26 WAIS–IV/WMS–IV Variability Measures in Mild Cognitive Impairment and Matched Controls

Score	Mild Cognitive Impairment		Matched Control		Between Group Differences	
	Mean	SD	Mean	SD	p	ES
WAIS–IV Subtest High vs. Low	10.4	2.9	9.9	2.8	>0.05	0.17
WAIS–IV Subtest Standard Deviation	10.2	2.9	10.2	2.9	>0.05	0.00
WAIS–IV Subtest Highest Score	9.1	3.1	10.6	2.9	<0.01	−0.47
WAIS–IV Subtest Lowest Score	9.3	3.4	10.6	3.0	<0.05	−0.40
WAIS–IV Index High vs. Low	10.5	3.3	10.3	3.0	>0.05	0.06
WAIS–IV Index Standard Deviation	10.0	3.1	10.5	3.0	>0.05	−0.14
WAIS–IV Index Highest Score	8.9	3.0	10.3	2.6	<0.01	−0.44
WAIS–IV Index Lowest Score	9.1	3.3	10.7	2.8	<0.01	−0.49
WMS–IV Subtest High vs. Low	9.2	3.4	9.6	3.4	>0.05	−0.12
WMS–IV Subtest Standard Deviation	9.6	3.3	9.9	3.3	>0.05	−0.10
WMS–IV Subtest Highest Score	8.4	2.9	10.4	2.7	<0.01	−0.69
WMS–IV Subtest Lowest Score	7.8	3.2	10.0	2.7	<0.001	−0.69

WMS–IV Index High vs. Low	9.5	3.5	9.8	2.8	>0.05	−0.10
WMS–IV Index Standard Deviation	9.4	3.4	9.8	2.7	>0.05	−0.12
WMS–IV Index Highest Score	7.9	2.9	10.3	2.4	<0.001	−0.82
WMS–IV Index Lowest Score	7.7	3.1	10.5	2.4	<0.001	−0.89
WAIS–IV/WMS–IV Subtest High vs. Low	9.3	4.0	9.8	3.2	>0.05	−0.12
WAIS–IV/WMS–IV Subtest Standard Deviation	9.5	4.0	10.8	2.5	>0.05	−0.32
WAIS–IV/WMS–IV Subtest Highest Score	9.2	3.0	10.8	2.9	<0.01	−0.55
WAIS–IV/WMS–IV Subtest Lowest Score	8.0	3.4	10.4	3.0	<0.001	−0.71
WAIS–IV/WMS–IV Index High vs. Low	9.9	4.1	10.3	3.0	>0.05	−0.11
WAIS–IV/WMS–IV Index Standard Deviation	9.8	4.3	10.5	3.2	>0.05	−0.15
WAIS–IV/WMS–IV Index Highest Score	8.7	2.9	10.6	2.3	<0.001	−0.65
WAIS–IV/WMS–IV Index Lowest Score	8.3	3.0	11.0	2.8	<0.001	−0.91

Note: See Chapter 3 for description of variability measures.
Copyright 2009 by Pearson, Inc. Reproduced with permission. All rights reserved.

significantly lower in the MCI group for highest and lowest scores but not on any variability measures. Compared to the WAIS–IV, the lowest and highest scores were lower for the WMS–IV in the MCI group. The pattern of results did not change when both the WAIS–IV and WMS–IV were considered together. The profile is somewhat suppressed; although the highest scores were not as severely limited as in the ALZ sample.

Just as in the ALZ group, the variability measures may be affected by the highest score obtained. Table 9.27 provides data on variability measures obtained in the MCI samples controlling for the highest score. Unlike that observed in the ALZ group, only the WAIS–IV index standard deviation and the combined WAIS–IV/WMS–IV measures were significantly lower in the MCI group than in the matched controls, and these differences produced small effect sizes. *In general, the MCI group does not display a high degree of variability in intellectual or memory functioning. There is a small increase in variability when memory and intellectual functioning are considered together.*

MULTIVARIATE BASE RATES

Another way to examine performance is to evaluate the base rates of low performance across multiple measures in various groups. A single low score within a battery of tests is not uncommon in healthy older adults (see Chapter 2 for detailed information on the use of multivariate base rates) and over-interpretation of a single low score may lead to misdiagnosis of impairment. As additional low scores are obtained, more confidence can be placed in poor performance being due to poor ability and not random error. It is important to note that sometimes a single low finding or a cluster of low findings may be meaningful depending upon the specific clinical hypotheses and presentations. For example, a low PSI score in an individual with a TBI is not likely due to random error. Multivariate base rates are particularly helpful when there are no specific clinical hypotheses about cognitive deficits. Depending on the pre-morbid ability of the examinee, many low scores may be required to establish cognitive impairment. Tables 9.28 and 9.29 provide the descriptive statistics and base rates of low scores obtained in the ALZ and MCI groups and their matched control groups, respectively. Low scores are defined as a score at or below 1 standard deviation below the mean, and at or below the fifth percentile. The first group of scores presented describes the actual number of obtained scores at the cut-offs on WAIS–IV, WMS–IV, or on both WAIS–IV and WMS–IV; the second group of scores describes the number of ACS demographically adjusted T-scores at the cut-offs.

TABLE 9.27 WAIS–IV/WMS–IV Variability Measures Controlling for Highest subtest or Index Score in Mild Cognitive Impairment and Matched Controls

Score	Mild Cognitive Impairment		Matched Control		Between Group Differences	
	Mean	SD	Mean	SD	p	ES
WAIS–IV Subtest High vs. Low	9.7	3.5	10.2	2.8	>0.05	−0.12
WAIS–IV Subtest Standard Deviation	9.5	3.5	10.4	3.2	>0.05	−0.26
WAIS–IV Index High vs. Low	10.4	3.6	11.0	2.9	>0.05	−0.16
WAIS–IV Index Standard Deviation	9.7	3.3	10.7	2.8	<0.05	−0.31
WMS–IV Subtest High vs. Low	8.4	3.6	9.6	3.4	>0.05	−0.32
WMS–IV Subtest Standard Deviation	8.8	3.7	10.0	3.5	>0.05	−0.32
WMS–IV Index High vs. Low	8.9	3.7	9.9	2.6	>0.05	−0.27
WMS–IV Index Standard Deviation	9.1	3.6	10.2	2.7	>0.05	−0.30
WAIS–IV/WMS–IV Subtest High vs. Low	8.6	4.2	10.0	3.3	<0.001	−0.35
WAIS–IV/WMS–IV Subtest Standard Deviation	9.0	4.2	10.4	3.0	<0.001	−0.34
WAIS–IV/WMS–IV Index High vs. Low	8.9	4.1	10.4	2.9	<0.001	−0.35
WAIS–IV/WMS–IV Index Standard Deviation	8.9	4.2	10.7	2.9	<0.001	−0.43

Note: See Chapter 3 for description of variability measures.
Copyright 2009 by Pearson, Inc. Reproduced with permission. All rights reserved.

TABLE 9.28 Descriptive Statistics and Base Rates of Low Scores in Alzheimer Disease and Matched Controls

Score	Alzheimer At or below 1 SD		Alzheimer At or below 5%		Matched Control At or below 1 SD		Matched Control At or below 5%		Between Group Differences At or below 1 SD		Between Group Differences At or below 5%	
	Mean	SD	Mean	SD	Mean	SD	Mean	SD	p	ES	p	ES
WAIS–IV Index Low Scores	2.3	1.9	1.5	1.7	0.4	1.1	0.2	0.8	<0.001	1.7	<0.001	1.7
WAIS–IV Subtest Low Scores	5.2	3.4	2.9	3.0	1.1	2.0	0.4	1.3	<0.001	2.0	<0.001	1.9
WMS–IV Index Low Scores	3.4	1.2	3.1	1.4	0.4	1.0	0.1	0.3	<0.001	3.0	<0.001	9.0
WMS–IV Subtest Low Scores	5.0	1.9	4.0	2.1	0.7	1.2	0.3	0.7	<0.001	3.6	<0.001	5.5
WAIS–IV/WMS–IV Index Low Scores	5.5	2.8	4.5	2.7	0.7	1.6	0.2	0.8	<0.001	3.0	<0.001	5.2
WAIS–IV/WMS–IV Subtest Low Scores	10.5	5.0	6.9	4.4	1.6	2.7	0.6	1.6	<0.001	3.4	<0.001	4.0
WAIS–IV Index Low Scores DAN	2.9	1.8	2.2	2.0	0.5	1.1	0.2	0.6	<0.001	2.2	<0.001	3.4
WAIS–IV Subtest Low Scores by DAN	5.9	3.2	4.1	3.2	1.3	1.6	0.3	0.9	<0.001	2.9	<0.001	4.2
WMS–IV Index Low Scores by DAN	3.5	1.2	3.2	1.4	0.5	1.1	0.1	0.5	<0.001	2.7	<0.001	6.2
WMS–IV Subtest Low Scores by DAN	5.2	1.8	4.3	2.1	0.8	1.2	0.2	0.5	<0.001	3.8	<0.001	7.9
WAIS–IV/WMS–IV Index Low Scores by DAN	6.5	2.6	5.4	2.9	1.1	1.7	0.3	0.9	<0.001	3.1	<0.001	5.9
WAIS–IV/WMS–IV Subtest Low Scores by DAN	11.9	4.8	8.9	5.0	2.2	2.5	0.6	1.2	<0.001	3.9	<0.001	6.8

Note: DAN = demographically adjusted norms. Visual Working Memory Index not included in the WMS–IV or combined WAIS–IV/WMS–IV analysis.

Copyright 2009 by Pearson, Inc. Reproduced with permission. All rights reserved.

TABLE 9.29 Descriptive Statistics and Base Rates of Low Scores in Mild Cognitive Impairment and Matched Controls

| Score | Mild Cognitive Impairment | | | | Matched Control | | | | Between Group Differences | | | |
| | At or below 1 sd | | At or below 5 % | | At or below 1 sd | | At or below 5 % | | At or below 1 sd | | At or below 5 % | |
	Mean	SD	Mean	SD	Mean	SD	Mean	SD	p	ES	p	ES
WAIS–IV Index Low Scores	1.1	1.5	0.5	0.9	0.6	1.2	0.2	0.6	<0.05	0.4	<0.05	0.46
WAIS–IV Subtest Low Scores	2.7	2.8	0.9	1.7	1.6	2.3	0.4	1.1	<0.01	0.5	<0.05	0.49
WMS–IV Index Low Scores	1.6	1.7	0.9	1.4	0.4	1.0	0.1	0.5	<0.001	1.2	<0.001	1.64
WMS–IV Subtest Low Scores	3.1	3.1	1.8	2.4	1.3	1.8	0.4	0.9	<0.01	1.0	<0.001	1.64
WAIS–IV/WMS–IV Index Low Scores	2.5	2.6	1.2	1.6	0.9	1.6	0.2	0.7	<0.001	1.0	<0.001	1.46
WAIS–IV/WMS–IV Subtest Low Scores	6.1	4.2	2.5	2.7	2.4	3.1	0.6	1.3	<0.001	1.2	<0.001	1.55
WAIS–IV Index Low Scores DAN	1.8	1.8	0.9	1.4	0.8	1.2	0.3	0.7	<0.01	0.8	<0.001	0.86
WAIS–IV Subtest Low Scores by DAN	3.3	2.7	1.8	2.2	1.7	1.8	0.6	1.1	<0.001	0.9	<0.001	1.09
WMS–IV Index Low Scores by DAN	2.0	1.8	1.1	1.6	0.6	1.1	0.2	0.5	<0.001	1.2	<0.001	1.74
WMS–IV Subtest Low Scores by DAN	2.6	2.3	1.5	1.8	0.9	1.2	0.2	0.7	<0.001	1.4	<0.001	1.86
WAIS–IV/WMS–IV Index Low Scores by DAN	3.7	3.1	2.0	2.3	1.3	1.8	0.4	0.9	<0.001	1.3	<0.001	1.75
WAIS–IV/WMS–IV Subtest Low Scores by DAN	6.2	4.4	3.4	3.0	2.6	2.5	0.8	1.3	<0.001	1.5	<0.001	1.89

Note: Visual Working Memory Index not included in the WMS–IV or combined WAIS–IV/WMS–IV analysis.
Copyright 2009 by Pearson, Inc. Reproduced with permission. All rights reserved.

The ALZ sample obtained more low scores, for all subtest and index combinations, for age and demographically adjusted scores. The effect sizes for these base rates were large. That is, ALZ patients are likely to have more low scores than seen in matched controls. In the matched control sample, it is common for examinees to have one or two scores at or below one standard deviation below the mean, but for individuals with ALZ the average number of low scores was 10 to 11 when considering the combined WAIS–IV and WMS–IV. Those in the MCI sample also had a greater number of low scores than matched controls. They had fewer low scores, however, than the ALZ sample.

TEXAS FUNCTIONAL LIVING SCALE

The TFLS was included as part of the standardization of the WAIS–IV, WMS–IV, and ACS. The TFLS (Cullum et al., 2001, 2009), also referred to as the Texas Evaluation of Functional Abilities (TEFA: Weiner, Gehrmann, Hynan, Saine, & Cullum, 2006), is a brief, perfor- mance- based measure of IADL originally designed for use in indivi- duals with known or suspected dementia. A performance-based IADL tool was selected for inclusion with the ACS in order to avoid potential rater bias of IADL rating scales. The tasks selected for inclusion on the TFLS were designed to focus on areas of functional ability that met the following criteria: (a) represent common everyday tasks, (b) require minimal equipment, (c) can be administered in a brief amount of time, and (d) place clear demands on cognitive operations while avoiding floor and ceiling effects in older individuals.

The TFLS consists of 24 items that represent various common IADL tasks that require various cognitive skills and can be completed in 15–20 minutes. A total score is rendered which reflects the summation of four component subscales. TFLS subscales and representative tasks are listed in Table 9.30.

Total scores (highest total raw score = 50) and normative T-scores are provided in the TFLS manual, with a mean of 50, SD of 10. The range of T-scores is 20–63, with scores of ≤20 (severe impairment) to ≥61 (high average). Cumulative percentages, rather than T-scores, are pro- vided for TFLS subscales in the test manual, because subscale scores were skewed in the normal population due to the relative ease of com- pletion and restricted scores. Along these lines, it should be kept in mind that *most healthy individuals can complete most or all TFLS items without difficulty*, because it was designed to assess impaired older sub- jects with known or suspected dementia.

The correlation between TFLS total score and the total score on the Independent Living Scales (ILS; Loeb, 1996) was 0.45 in a small group

TABLE 9.30 TFLS Subscales Component Tasks

Subscale	Representative Task
Time	Ability to read and use clocks and calendars
Money and Calculation	Performing calculations using time and money
Communication	Bill-paying, phonebook use, emergency calling, and meal preparation
Memory	Prospective memory task, recall of bill paying task details

of healthy controls (Weiner et al., 2006), lower than what would be expected in clinical populations because of the restricted range of scores in controls where most individuals obtain high scores on IADL measures. As indicated in the TFLS manual (Cullum et al., 2009), the TFLS was co-normed with the WAIS–IV and WMS–IV in a sample of 1210 normally aging individuals from ages 16 to 90, providing an opportunity to explore its relationship with other neuropsychological measures. Among normally developing and aging adults, correlations with WMS–IV scores are small, in the 0.3 to 0.4 range. Slightly lower correlations are observed with WAIS–IV subtests (i.e., 0.25 to 0.30) and the Test of Premorbid Function ($r = 0.26$). The correlations with GAI and FSIQ scores were 0.37 and 0.41, respectively. Similar correlations are observed between the TFLS and RBANS (e.g., $r = 0.44$ with total RBANS score), suggesting a modest relationship between TFLS and overall cognitive functioning in healthy developing/aging populations. In clinical groups, however, supporting the cognitive-orientation of the measures, the TFLS has shown generally strong correlations with the MMSE, typically at or above 0.80. Correlations with the WAIS–IV range from 0.63 on Visual Puzzles to 0.80 on Letter-Number Sequencing, and 0.77 with GAI and 0.79 with FSIQ. Relationships with VCI, PRI, WMI, and PSI scores ranged from 0.71 to 0.74. Correlations with WMS–IV subscale and Index scores in clinical groups are similar, typically in the 0.7 to 0.8 range.

Overall, the TFLS has shown highest correlations with measures of global cognitive ability and working memory, perhaps suggesting the importance of these dimensions of neuropsychological functioning in relationship to IADLs. Contrast scores have also been developed for comparing the TFLS more directly with WAIS–IV and WMS–IV results (Drozdick & Cullum, 2011). These scores provide useful additional interpretive assistance for the TFLS insofar as higher functioning individuals (i.e., those with higher GAI scores) are expected to obtain higher scores on the TFLS. Hence, when a discrepancy score reveals a TFLS that is below expectation *given that subject's overall cognitive ability*, then a problem with that individual's functioning is suggested.

The TFLS has also been used in individuals who require greater levels of assistance in their living environment (Weiner et al., 2007). Specifically, a sample of 77 older individuals with evidence of cognitive impairment (mean age = 86) were recruited from three settings: (1) independent living (receiving some assistance, $n = 26$), (2) assisted living ($n = 25$), and (3) a special care unit for patients with dementia ($n = 26$). Results of this study showed that the TFLS total score distinguished the groups at a high level ($p < 0.00001$), with very little overlap between groups. Furthermore, a caregiver-based rating of TFLS performance domains showed that caregivers tended to modestly but significantly overestimate patients' abilities, although both forms of the TFLS were highly correlated [rho(72) = 0.86, $p < 0.00001$]. As such, the TFLS has shown promise in assisted living and nursing home settings as a tool that can help determine functional placement needs. In addition, the TFLS has shown sensitivity to the effects of medication, specifically donepezil (Saine et al., 2002).

In summary, the TFLS provides an integrated means of assessing and documenting IADL functioning in older individuals. It utilizes standard performance-based tasks that depict several everyday-type of behaviors required by adults (e.g., use of calendar, clocks, making change, paying bills, and following directions, in addition to items requiring prospective and episodic memory). It was co-normed with the WAIS–IV and WMS–IV, thereby allowing for direct comparison of standard scores across measures, use of contrast scores for functional interpretation, and an improved understanding of the relationship between aspects of IADL and cognitive test performance.

CASE STUDIES

Many of the methods and techniques discussed in the other chapters of this book are used with older adults. More detailed case studies for a particular method or approach can be found in the relevant chapter.

CASE STUDY 1

Mrs. P. is a 70-year-old white female, with 11 years of education. She dropped out of high school following her junior year to marry her high school sweetheart who graduated prior to her. She remained at home raising her three children and never worked outside of the home. Her husband of 52 years passed away 14 months ago following a long battle with cancer. Mrs. P. was his caregiver throughout the illness and reports that she *"misses him every day and prefers to stay at home rather than do things without him."* She has hypothyroidism and hypertension, both of which are well-controlled with medication. She was referred for an evaluation by her daughter due to concerns with increasing forgetfulness, difficulties managing her daily activities, and loss of interest in activities.

As part of her evaluation, Mrs. P. was administered the WAIS–IV, WMS–IV Older Adult battery, TOPF, TFLS, and Geriatric Depression Scale (Yesavage et al., 1982–1983). She was on time for her appointment, was well dressed and groomed, and was accompanied by her daughter. She reported being tired but willing to complete the evaluation *"for her daughter."* She denied having significant problems with her memory but did endorse symptoms of depression. Her score on the GDS was 14, indicating a mild to moderate degree of depression. She appeared to give forth good effort throughout the test session, although she had difficulty concentrating and required frequent prompting. Multiple breaks were given throughout the assessment to allow her to rest.

Mrs. P.'s WAIS–IV and WMS–IV scores and demographically adjusted scores are displayed in Table 9.31. In addition to the scores listed in the table, Mrs. P. obtained an average rating on the BCSE and a T-score of 44 on the TFLS. All Mrs. P.'s WAIS–IV index scores were in the borderline to low average range, with her lowest score on the Verbal Comprehension Index. Her WMS–IV index scores were all in the average range, and contrast scores indicated that her memory scores were within the expected range given her cognitive ability. When her scores were demographically adjusted, only VCI fell in the mild impairment range; all other index scores were average to low average.

Multivariate base rates for the combined WAIS–IV and WMS–IV were reviewed for Mrs. P's standard index scores. She obtained six index scores below 25th percentile (base rate = 18.5%), four below the 16th percentile (base rate = 17.9%), three below the 9th percentile (base rate = 14.0%), two at or below the 5th percentile (base rate = 11.3%), and zero below the 2nd percentile (base rate = 89.8%). Base rates are for the standardization sample. For demographically adjusted index scores, again combining WAIS–IV and WMS–IV, she obtained four index scores below the 25th percentile (base rate = 31.1%), four below the 16th percentile (base rate = 19.1), and zero below the 9th percentile (base rate = 65.2%).

Mrs. P.'s scores are generally consistent with her age and demographic background. Her working memory, processing speed, and memory scores were all in the average range, suggesting that

TABLE 9.31 WAIS–IV and WMS–IV Composite and Subtest Scores for Mrs. P.

Score Name	Actual Score	Percentile	Demographically Adjusted Score	Percentile
VCI	74	4	37	9.7
PRI	82	12	40	15.9
WMI	86	18	46	34.5
PSI	89	23	45	30.9
FSIQ	78	7	39	13.6
GAI	76	5	37	9.7
Similarities	5	5	37	9.7
Vocabulary	5	5	37	9.7
Information	6	9	43	24.2
Block Design	9	37	51	54.0
Matrix Reasoning	6	9	39	13.6
Visual Puzzles	6	9	37	9.7
Digit Span	8	25	47	38.2
Arithmetic	9	16	46	34.5
Symbol Search	7	16	41	18.4
Coding	9	37	50	50
AMI	91	27	46	34.5
VMI	95	37	48	42.1
IMI	90	25	44	27.4
DMI	93	32	48	42.1
Logical Memory I	5	5	35	6.7
Logical Memory II	7	16	40	15.9
VPA I	11	63	56	72.6
VPA II	11	63	56	72.6
Visual Repro. I	9	37	48	42.1
Visual Repro. II	9	37	50	50

depressive symptoms did not impact her performance. To assess the possibility of a decline from a previous level, she was administered the TOPF and results were compared to her current score. Her TOPF predicted score comparisons to actual performance are listed in Table 9.32.

The TOPF-Predicted score comparisons indicate that Mrs. P. may be experiencing some decline in her verbal and perceptual reasoning abilities. However, she does not appear to be experiencing any gross decline in her working memory, processing speed, or memory abilities. It was recommended that she be re-evaluated in 6–12 months to determine if her performance represents a progressive decline.

CASE STUDY 2

Mr. O. is an 81-year-old African-American male, with 20 years of education (J.D.). He joined the army at 18 and served in Korea. He used his GI benefits to complete college and law school. He worked as a lawyer in the army until he retired from service at 60. He continued to provide legal services until the age of 75 when he began having difficulty remembering appointments and making mistakes on documents. Mr. O. has hypertension and diabetes, both well controlled medically. Over the past 6 years, he has experienced increasing memory problems and

TABLE 9.32 Mrs. P's TOPF Predicted Score Comparisons

Composite	Actual Score	Predicted Score	Prediction Interval	Difference	Critical Value	Significant Difference	Base Rate
TOPF Actual–Predicted[a]	95	92	63 – 121	3	5.47	N	42.9%
FSIQ[b]	78	93	69 – 117	−15	6.99	Y	6.4%
VCI[b]	74	94	72 – 116	−20	8.08	Y	1%
PRI[b]	82	94	64 – 124	−12	9.29	Y	15.7%
WMI[b]	86	95	67 – 123	−9	10.93	N	20.5%
PSI[b]	89	98	64 – 132	−9	11.93	N	24.1%
IMI[b]	90	96	63 – 129	−6	9.11	N	32%
DMI[b]	93	99	65 – 133	−6	11.88	N	35.5%

[a]Actual–Predicted Comparison based on Simple Demographics Predictive Model.
[b]Actual–Predicted Comparison based on Simple Demographics with Test of Premorbid Functioning Predictive Model.
Prediction Intervals reported at the 95% Level of Confidence.
Statistical significance (critical value) at the 0.01 level.

was referred for evaluation after failing to recognize several family members at a family reunion.

As part of his evaluation, Mr. O. was administered the WAIS–IV, WMS–IV Older Adult battery, and TFLS. He was on time for his appointment, was slightly disheveled but groomed, and was accompanied by his wife. He reported concern for his problems which he felt were preventing him from enjoying time with his family. He appeared to give forth good effort throughout the test session, although he had difficulty concentrating and lost focus frequently. He worked steadily, refusing to take breaks, and completed all testing within a single session.

Mr. O.'s WAIS–IV and WMS–IV scores and demographically adjusted scores are displayed in Table 9.33. In addition to the scores listed in the table, Mr. O. obtained a very low rating on the BCSE and a T-score of 32 on the TFLS, suggesting cognitive impairment. All of Mr. O.'s WAIS–IV index scores were in the borderline to low average range, with his lowest score on the Processing Speed Index. His WMS–IV index scores were in the extremely low to borderline range, and contrast scores indicate that all of his memory scores were well below the expected range given his cognitive ability. Demographically adjusted WAIS–IV scores indicated mild to moderate impairment on all indexes, with the exception of the PRI, which was in the low average range. Demographically adjusted WMS–IV scores were in the moderately to severely impaired range.

Multivariate base rates for combined WAIS–IV and WMS–IV performance were reviewed for Mr. O's standard index scores. He obtained 10 index scores at or below the 25th percentile (base rate = 3.4%), eight were at or below the 16th percentile (base rate = 4.8%), five were below the 9th percentile (base rate = 6.9%), five were at or below the 5th percentile (base rate = 3.9%), and four were below the 2nd percentile (base rate = 2.6%). All four that were below the 2nd percentile were WMS–IV index scores. For demographically adjusted index scores, 10 WAIS–IV index scores were below the 25th percentile (base rate = 1.1%), nine were below the 16th and 9th percentile (base rates = 1.5% and 0.3%, respectively), seven below the 5th percentile (base rate = 0.9%), and five below the 2nd percentile (base rate = 0.4%); all four WMS–IV index scores were below the 2nd percentile.

Mr. O.'s scores were very low given his education and demographic background, clearly indicating that he was experiencing significant cognitive and memory impairments consistent with dementia. Given his performance, it was recommended that he and his wife receive education on dementia and available community support, treatment options, and ongoing counseling and support.

TABLE 9.33 WAIS—IV and WMS—IV Composite and Subtest Scores for Mr. O.

Score Name	Actual Score	Percentile	Demographically Adjusted Score	Percentile
VCI	85	16	28	1.4
PRI	90	25	42	21.2
WMI	86	18	34	5.5
PSI	76	5	36	8.1
FSIQ	81	10	31	2.9
GAI	86	18	33	4.5
Similarities	7	16	30	2.3
Vocabulary	9	37	36	8.1
Information	6	9	27	1.1
Block Design	11	63	56	72.6
Matrix Reasoning	7	16	34	5.5
Visual Puzzles	7	16	41	18.4
Digit Span	8	25	38	11.5
Arithmetic	7	16	33	4.5
Symbol Search	4	2	32	3.6
Coding	7	16	41	18.4
AMI	64	1	25	0.6
VMI	69	2	24	0.5
IMI	75	5	28	1.4
DMI	51	0.1	16	< 0.1
Logical Memory I	7	16	38	11.5
Logical Memory II	2	0.4	23	0.3
Verbal Paired Associates I	5	5	33	4.5
Verbal Paired Associates II	2	0.4	26	0.8
Visual Reproduction I	6	9	31	2.9
Visual Reproduction II	3	1	24	0.5

SUMMARY

Normal aging is associated with declines in cognitive skills, particularly related to processing speed and memory functioning. It is possible, however, to differentiate pathological changes in cognitive functioning from normal aging. Multiple tools and analyses are included in the WAIS–IV, WMS–IV, ACS, and TFLS that may be used in the neurocognitive assessment of older adults. Performance on the WAIS–IV and WMS–IV index and subtest scores differentiates ALZ and MCI groups from normally aging controls, as does performance on the TFLS. Base rates of low scores on the WAIS–IV and WMS–IV are also higher in ALZ and MCI groups than in the normally aging controls. Similar results are observed with demographically adjusted WAIS–IV and WMS–IV norms.

OPIE–IV and TOPF prediction equations were calculated for the WAIS–IV and WMS–IV in older adults. The TOPF better predicted pre-morbid ability in ALZ but both models differentiated predicted pre-morbid ability from actual performance. These models are useful for differentiating low ability from loss in cognitive functioning. The application of pre-morbid models improves specificity in clinical practice. Similarly, the application of multivariate base rates enables clinicians to differentiate meaningful low score performance from low ability. Taken together, it appears that many of the measures and standard scores from the WAIS–IV, WMS–IV and ACS provide useful information in the characterization and detailed assessment of the older individual with known or suspected cognitive impairment.

KEY LEARNING

- Normal aging is associated with declines in many domains of cognitive functioning, particularly processing speed and memory.
- Older adults often have multiple medical issues that need to be considered as part of the psychological evaluation.
- Older adults are frequently prescribed multiple medications that can affect cognition. In addition, cognitive impairment can lead to improper use of medications.
- Older adults are frequently referred for evaluation for symptoms related to depression or cognitive decline. It is important to differentiate the effects of mood disorder from loss in cognitive ability.
- Older adults are frequently referred for questions about capacity to perform IADL's particularly the ability to drive, manage finances,

and live independently. Specific tools should be used to answer these questions.

- The WAIS–IV and WMS–IV are sensitive to ALZ disease and Mild Cognitive Impairment, particularly when the batteries are used in conjunction.
- Logical Memory II was one of the most sensitive measures in both ALZ and MCI.
- Additional tools found in the ACS, such as demographic adjustment to norms and pre-morbid prediction, improves the specificity of the WAIS–IV and WMS–IV, particularly for individuals of low pre-morbid functioning. Moreover, demographic norms and pre-morbid predictions improve sensitivity and specificity in routine clinical evaluations because these models are a means of comparing the subject to similar individuals.
- The TOPF prediction model provides better estimation of pre-morbid functioning than OPIE equations, particularly in patients with ALZ disease. For OPIE, OPIE equations using Matrix Reasoning were best in individuals with ALZ disease but OPIE equations using Vocabulary were better in MCI.
- The ALZ and MCI groups did not show significant profile variability; rather both groups had suppressed profiles due to low highest scores. When controlling for low highest scores, the ALZ but not the MCI group showed significant variability, particularly for combined WAIS–IV and WMS–IV subtest and index scores.
- The ALZ and MCI groups obtain more low index and subtest scores than matched controls. Although it is common for healthy older adults to have a few low scores, it is unusual for healthy adults to have a large number of low scores. Using demographic adjusted normative data for multivariate base rates improved test specificity.
- The Texas Functional Living Scales was designed to help clinicians objectively identify deficits in cognitively related IADLs that limit an older adult's capacity to live independently.

References

Albert, M., Moss, M. B., Blacker, D., Tanzi, R., & McArdle, J. J. (2007). Longitudinal change in cognitive performance among individuals with mild cognitive impairment. *Neuropsychology*, *21*(2), 158–169.

AGS Clinical Practice (2003). Guidelines abstracted from the American Academy of Neurology's dementia guidelines for early detection, diagnosis and management of dementia. *Journal of the American Geriatrics Society*, *51*(6), 869–873.

APA (2004). Guidelines for psychological practice with older adults. *American Psychologist*, *59*(4), 236–260.

Baird, A., Podell, K., Lovell, M., & McGinty, S. B. (2001). Complex real-world functioning and neuropsychological test performance in older adults. *Clinical Neuropsychologist*, *15*(3), 369–379.

Bell-McGinty, S., Podell, K., Franzen, M., Baird, A. D., & Williams, M. J. (2002). Standard measures of executive function in predicting instrumental activities of daily living in older adults. *International Journal of Geriatric Psychiatry, 17*(9), 828–834.

Bieliauskas, L. A. (2005). Neuropsychological assessment of geriatric driving competence. *Brain Injury, 19*(3), 221–226.

Binder, L. M., Iverson, G. L., & Brooks, B. L. (2009). To err is human: "Abnormal" neuropsychological scores and variability are common in healthy adults. *Archives of Clinical Neuropsychology, 24*(1), 31–46.

Brand, M., & Markowitsch, H. J. (2010). Aging and decision-making: A neurocognitive perspective. *Gerontology, 56*(3), 319–324.

Brooks, B. L., Iverson, G. L., Feldman, H. H., & Holdnack, J. A. (2009). Minimizing misdiagnosis: Psychometric criteria for possible or probable memory impairment. *Dementia and Geriatric Cognitive Disorders, 27*(5), 439–450.

Brooks, B. L., Iverson, G. L., Holdnack, J. A., & Feldman, H. H. (2008). The potential for misclassification of mild cognitive impairment: A study of memory scores on the Wechsler Memory Scale–III in healthy older adults. *Journal of the International Neuropsychological Society, 14*(3), 463–478.

Carstensen, L. L., Edelstein, B. A., & Dornbrand, L. (1996). *The practical handbook of clinical gerontology.* Thousand Oaks, California: Sage Publications.

Coalson, D. L., Raiford, S. E., Saklofske, D. H., & Weiss, L. G. (2010). WAIS–IV: Advances in the assessment of intelligence. In L. G. Weiss, D. H. Saklofske, D. Coalson, & S. E. Raiford (Eds.), *WAIS–IV clinical use and interpretation: Scientist practitioner perspectives* (pp. 1–24). London, UK: Academic Press.

Crawford, J. R. (1992). Current and premorbid intelligence measures in neuropsychological assessment. In J. R. Crawford, D. M. Parker, & W. W. McKinlay (Eds.), *A handbook of neuropsychological assessment* (pp. 21–50). Hove, UK: Erlbaum.

Cullum, C. M., Saine, K., Chan, L. D., Martin-Cook, K., Gray, K., & Weiner, M. F. (2001). A performance-based instrument to assess functional capacity in dementia: the Texas functional living scale. *Neuropsychiatry, Neuropsychology, and Behavioral Neurology, 14*(2), 103–108.

Cullum, C. M., Saine, K., & Weiner, M. F. (2009). *Texas functional living scales.* San Antonio, TX: Pearson.

Delis, D. C., Kaplan, E., Kramer, J. H., & Ober, B. A. (2000). *California verbal learning test–second edition.* San Antonio, TX: Pearson.

Derrer, D. S., Howieson, D. B., Mueller, E. A., Sexton, G., Camicioli, R. M., & Kaye, J. A. (2001). Memory testing in dementia: how much is enough? *Journal of Geriatric Psychiatry & Neurology, 14*(1), 1–6.

Donders, J., Tulsky, D. S., & Zhu, J. (2001). Criterion validity of new WAIS–III subtest scores after traumatic brain injury. *Journal of International Neuropsychological Society, 7*(7), 892–898.

Drozdick, L. W., & Cullum, C. M. (2011). Expanding the ecological validity of WAIS–IV and WMS–IV with the texas functional living scale. *Assessment, 18*(2), 141–155.

Drozdick, L. W., Holdnack, J. A., & Hilsabeck, R. C. (2011). *Essentials of WMS–IV assessment.* Hoboken, New Jersey: John Wiley & Sons.

Duff, K., Schoenberg, M. R., Patton, D., Paulsen, J. S., Bayless, J. D., Mold, J., et al. (2005). Regression based formulas for predicting change in RBANS subtests with older adults. *Archives of Clinical Neuropsychology, 20*(3), 281–290.

Farias, S. T., Cahn-Weiner, D. A., Harvey, D. J., Reed, B. R., Mungas, D., Kramer, J. H., et al. (2009). Longitudinal changes in memory and executive functioning are associated with longitudinal change in instrumental activities of daily living in older adults. *The Clinical Neuropsychologist, 23*(3), 446–461.

Ferrer, E., Salthouse, T. A., McArdle, J. J., Stewart, W. F., & Schwartz, B. S. (2005). Multivariate modeling of age and retest in longitudinal studies of cognitive abilities. *Psychology and Aging, 20*(3), 412–422.

Guarch, J., Marcos, T., Salamero, M., Gastó, C., & Blesa, R. (2008). Mild cognitive impairment: A risk indicator of later dementia, or a preclinical phase of the disease? *International Journal of Geriatric Psychiatry, 23*(3), 257–265.

Hajjar, E. R., Hanlon, J. T., Sloane, R. J., Lindblad, C. I., Pieper, C. F., Ruby, C. M., et al. (2005). Unnecessary drug use in frail older people at hospital discharge. *Journal of the American Geriatrics Society, 53*(9), 1518–1523.

Hanlon, J. T., Pieper, C. F., Hajjar, E. R., Sloan, R. J., Lindblad, C. I., Ruby, C. M., et al. (2006). Incidence and predictor of all preventable adverse drug reactions in frail elderly persons after hospital stay. *Journals of Gerontology Series A: Biological Sciences & Medical Sciences, 61A*(5), 511–515.

Heaton, R. K., Ryan, L., & Grant, I. (2009). Demographic influences and use of demographically corrected norms in neuropsychological assessment. In I. Grant, & K. M. Adams (Eds.), *Neuropsychological assessment of neuropsychiatric & neuromedical disorders* (3rd ed., pp. 127–155). New York: Oxford University Press.

Heaton, R. K., Taylor, M. J., & Manly, J. (2003). Demographic effects and the use of demographically corrected norms with the WAIS–III and WMS–III. In D. S. Tulsky, D. H. Saklofske, G. J. Chelune, R. K. Heaton, R. J. Ivnik, R. Bornstein, et al. *Clinical interpretation of the WAIS–III and WMS–III* (pp. 181–210). San Diego: Academic Press.

Heuberger, R. A., & Caudell, K. (2011). Polypharmacy and nutritional status in older adults. *Drugs & Aging, 28*(4), 315–323.

Holdnack, J. A., & Drozdick, L. W. (2010). Using WAIS–IV with WMS–IV. In L. G. Weiss, D. H. Saklofske, D. Coalson, & S. E. Raiford (Eds.), *WAIS–IV clinical use and interpretation: Scientist practitioner perspectives* (pp. 237–291). London, UK: Academic Press.

Johnstone, B., Hogg, J. R., Schopp, L. H., Kapila, C., & Edwards, S. (2002). Neuropsychological deficit profiles in senile dementia of the Alzheimer's type. *Archives of Clinical Neuropsychology, 17*(3), 273–281.

Jungwirth, S., Zehetmayer, S., Bauer, P., Weissgram, S., Tragl, K. H., & Fischer, P. (2009). Screening for Alzheimer's dementia at age 78 with short psychometric instruments. *International Psychogeriatrics, 21*(3), 548–559.

Kipps, C. M., Mioshi, E., & Hodges, J. R. (2009). Emotion, social functioning and activities of daily living in frontotemporal dementia. *Neurocase, 15*(3), 182–189.

Knopman, D. S., DeKosky, S. T., Cummings, J. L., Chui, H., Corey-Bloom, J., Relkin, N., et al. (2001). Practice parameter: Diagnosis of dementia (an evidence-based review). Report of the quality standards subcommittee of the american academy of neurology. *Neurology, 56*(9), 1143–1153.

Krull, K. R., Scott, J. G., & Sherer, M. (1995). Estimation of premorbid intelligence from combined performance and demographic variables. *The Clinical Neuropsychologist, 9*(1), 83–88.

Lezak, M. D., Howieson, D. B., Loring, D. W., Hannay, H. J., & Fischer, J. S. (2004). *Neuropsychological assessment* (4th ed.). New York: Oxford University Press.

Lichtenberg, P. A. (2011). *Handbook of assessment in clinical gerontology*. London, UK: Academic Press.

Lineweaver, T. T., & Chelune, G. J. (2003). Use of the WAIS–III and WMS–III in the context of serial assessments: Interpreting reliable and meaningful change. In D. S. Tulsky, D. H. Saklofske, G. J. Chelune, R. K. Heaton, R. J. Ivnik, R. Bornstein, et al. *Clinical interpretation of the WAIS–III and WMS–III* (pp. 303–337). Burlington, MA: Academic Press.

Loeb, P. A. (1996). *Independent living scales*. San Antonio, Texas: Pearson.

Luck, T., Riedel-Heller, S. G., Kaduszkiewicz, H., Bickel, H., Jessen, F., Pentzek, M., et al. (2007). Mild Cognitive Impairment in general practice: Age-specific prevalence and correlate. Results from the German study on ageing, cognition and dementia in primary care patients (AgeCoDe). *Dementia & Geriatric Cognitive Disorders, 24*(4), 307–316.

MacLaughlin, E. J., Raehl, C. L., Treadway, A. K., Sterling, T. L., Zoller, D. P., & Bond, C. A. (2005). Assessing medication adherence in the elderly: Which tools to use in clinical practice? *Drugs and Aging, 22*(3), 231–255.

Mansdorf, I. J., Harrington, M., Lund, J., & Wohl, N. (2008). Neuropsychological testing in skilled nursing facilities: The failure to confirm diagnoses of dementia. *Journal of the American Medical Directors Association, 9*(4), 271–274.

Masur, D. M., Fuld, P. A., Blau, A. D., Crystal, H., & Aronson, M. K. (1990). Predicting development of dementia in the elderly with the Selective Reminding Test. *Journal of Clinical and Experimental Neuropsychology, 12*(4), 529–538.

McCaffrey, R. J., Ortega, A., & Haase, R. F. (1993). Effects of repeated neuropsychological assessments. *Archives of Clinical Neuropsychology, 8*(6), 519–524.

O'Carroll, R., Whittaker, J., Hamilton, B., Johnston, M., Sudlow, C., & Dennis, M. (2011). Predictors of adherence to secondary preventive medication in strike patients. *Annals of Behavioral Medicine, 41*(3), 383–390.

Pearson (2010). *WMS-IV flexible approach*. San Antonio, TX: Author.

Pearson (2009). Advanced clinical solutions for WAIS–IV and WMS–IV. San Antonio, TX: Author.

Pearson (2001). *Wechsler test of adult reading*. San Antonio, TX: Author.

Petersen, R. C. (2011). Mild cognitive impairment. *New England Journal of Medicine, 364*(23), 2227–2234.

Petersen, R. C., Stevens, J. C., Ganguli, M., Tangalos, E. G., Cummings, J. L., & DeKosky, S. T. (2001). Practice parameter. Early detection of dementia: Mild cognitive impairment (an evidence-based review). Report of the quality standards subcommittee of the american academy of neurology. *Neurology, 56*(9), 1133–1142.

Putnam, S. H., Ricker, J. H., Ross, S. R., & Kurtz, J. E. (1999). Considering premorbid functioning: Beyond cognition to a conceptualization of personality in postinjury functioning. In J. J. Sweet (Ed.), *Forensic neuropsychology: Fundamentals and practice* (pp. 39–81). Lisse, The Netherlands: Swets & Zeitlinger.

Ronnlund, M., Nyberg, L., Backman, L., & Nilsson, L.-G. (2005). Stability, growth, and decline in adult life span development of declarative memory: Cross-sectional and longitudinal data from a population-based study. *Psychology and aging, 20*(1), 3–18.

Saine, K., Cullum, C. M., Martin-Cook, K., Hynan, L., Svetlik, D. A., & Weiner, M. F. (2002). Comparison of functional and cognitive donepezil effects in Alzheimer's disease. *International Psychogeriatrics, 14*(2), 181–185.

Salthouse, T. A. (2011). Neuroanatomical substrates of age-related cognitive decline. *Psychological Bulletin, 137*(5), 753–784.

Salthouse, T. A. (2010a). *Major issues in cognitive aging*. New York: Oxford University Press.

Salthouse, T. A. (2010b). Influence of age on practice effects in longitudinal neurocognitive change. *Neuropsychology, 24*(5), 563–572.

Salthouse, T. A. (2007). Implications of within-person variability in cognitive and neuropsychological functioning for the interpretation of change. *Neuropsychology, 21*(4), 401–411.

Salthouse, T. A. (1996). The processing speed theory of adult age differences in cognition. *Psychological Review, 103*(3), 403–428.

Salthouse, T. A., Schroeder, D. H., & Ferrer, E. (2004). Estimating retest effects in longitudinal assessments of cognitive functioning in adults between 18 and 60 years of age. *Developmental Psychology, 40*(5), 813–822.

Sattler, J. M., & Ryan, J. J. (2010). Assessment with the WAIS–IV. San Diego, CA: Jerome M. Sattler, Publisher, Inc.

Schaie, K. W. (2005). *Developmental influences on adult intelligence: The seattle longitudinal study*. New York, NY: Oxford University Press.

Schoenberg, M. R., Scott, J. G., Duff, K., & Adams, R. L. (2002). Estimation of WAIS–III intelligence from combined performance and demographic variables: Development of the OPIE–3. *Clinical Neuropsychology, 16*(4), 426–437.

Sliwinski, M. J., Hofer, S. M., Hall, C., Bushke, H., & Lipton, R. B. (2003). Modeling memory decline in older adults: The importance of preclinical dementia, attrition, and chronological age. *Psychology and Aging, 18*(4), 658–671.

Snowden, J. S., Gibbons, Z. C., Blackshaw, A., Doubleday, E., Thompson, J., Craufurd, D., et al. (2003). Social cognition in frontotemporal dementia and Huntington's disease. *Neuropsychologia, 41*(6), 688–702.

Spreen, O., & Strauss, E. (1998). *A compendium of neuropsychological tests: Administration, norms, and commentary* (2nd ed.). New York: Oxford University Press.

Starr, J. M., McGurn, B., Whiteman, M., Pattie, A., Whalley, L. J., & Deary, I. J. (2004). Life long changes in cognitive ability are associated with prescribed medications in old age. *International Journal of Geriatric Psychiatry, 19*(4), 327–332.

Storandt, M. (1994). *Neuropsychological assessment of dementia and depression in older adults*. New York, NY: American Psychological Association.

Tierney, M. C., Moineddin, R., & McDowell, I. (2010). Prediction of all-cause dementia using neuropsychological tests within 10 and 5 years of diagnosis in a community-based sample. *Journal of Alzheimer's Disease, 22*(4), 1231–1240.

Vincent, G. K., & Velkoff, V. A. (2010). *The next four decades, the older population in the United States: 2010 to 2050* (P25–1138). *Current population reports*. Washington, DC: US Census Bureau.

Wechsler, D. (2010). *WMS-IV flexible approach*. San Antonio, TX: Pearson.

Wechsler, D. (2009). Wechsler memory scale–fourth edition. San Antonio, TX: Pearson.

Wechsler, D. (2008). *Wechsler adult intelligence scale–fourth edition*. San Antonio, TX: Pearson.

Weiner, M. F., Davis, B., Martin-Cook, K., Hynan, L. S., Saine, K. C., & Cullum, C. M. (2007). A direct functional measure to help ascertain optimal level of residential care. *American Journal of Alzheimers Disease and Other Dementias, 22*(5), 355–359.

Weiner, M. F., Gehrmann, H. R., Hynan, L. S., Saine, K. C., & Cullum, C. M. (2006). Comparison of the test of everyday functional abilities with a direct measure of daily function. *Dementia and Geriatric Cognitive Disorders, 22*(1), 83–86.

Whelihana, W. M., DiCarloa, M. A., & Paula, R. H. (2005). The relationship of neuropsychological functioning to driving competence in older persons with early cognitive decline. *Archives of Clinical Neuropsychology, 20*, 217–228.

Woodard, J. L. (2011). Geriatric neuropsychological assessment. In P. A. Lichtenberg (Ed.), *Handbook of assessment in clinical gerontology* (pp. 461–503). London, UK: Academic Press.

Wright, R. M., Roumani, Y. F., Boudreau, R., Newman, A. B., Ruby, C. M., Studenski, S. A., et al. (2009). Effect of central nervous system medication use on decline in cognition in community-dwelling older adults: Findings of the health, aging and body composition study. *Journal of the American Geriatrics Society, 57*(2), 243–250.

Yesavage, J. A., Brink, T. L., Rose, T. L., Lum, O., Huang, V., Adey, M., et al. (1982–1983). Development and validation of a geriatric depression screening scale: A preliminary report. *Journal of Psychiatric Research, 17*(1), 37–49.

Using the WAIS–IV/WMS–IV/ ACS Following Moderate-Severe Traumatic Brain Injury

Grant L. Iverson[*], James A. Holdnack[†] and
Rael T. Lange[‡]

[*]Harvard Medical School, Boston, Massachusetts, USA [†]Pearson
Assessment, San Antonio, Texas, USA [‡]Defense and Veterans Brain Injury
Center, Walter Reed National Military Medical Center & University of
British Columbia, Washington DC, USA

INTRODUCTION

Traumatic brain injuries (TBI) are common in daily life and in military service. These injuries occur on a broad continuum of severity, from very mild transient injuries to catastrophic injuries resulting in death or severe disability. In the initial hours and days following injury, TBI is associated with both primary (e.g., axonal injury, contusions, edema, vascular injury, and hemorrhage) and secondary systemic pathophysiologies (e.g., hypotension or hypoxia). In addition, endogenous secondary pathophysiologies include: (a) ischemia, excitotoxicity, energy failure, and cell death cascades (e.g., necrosis and apoptosis), (b) edema, (c) traumatic axonal injury, and (d) inflammation (Kochanek, Clark, & Jenkins, 2007). Over time, ventricular dilation can occur following severe TBI. Cortical atrophy and ventricular dilation have been identified in patients with TBIs imaged 6 weeks to 1 year post injury (Anderson & Bigler, 1995; Bigler, Kurth, Blatter, & Abildskov, 1992).

WAIS-IV, WMS-IV, and ACS.
DOI: http://dx.doi.org/10.1016/B978-0-12-386934-0.00010-9

© 2013 Elsevier Inc. All rights reserved.

In general, as injury severity increases, the magnitude of physical and cognitive impairment increases. Moderate and severe TBIs can result in time-limited or permanent neurological or neuropsychiatric problems. Diverse motor, sensory, language, cognitive, emotional, and interpersonal problems can occur following injury. Some of these problems are listed below (summarized from Iverson and Lange, 2011, 2012).

- *Motor Impairments and Movement Disorders.* Weakness (paresis) or paralysis (plegia), spasticity (increased muscle tone and exaggerated reflexes), ataxia (loss of muscle coordination), or post-traumatic movement disorders (hypokinesia or hyperkinesia).
- *Balance and Dizziness.* Imbalance and dizziness can be related to damage to the vestibular system, visual system, somatosensory system, proprioceptive system, brainstem, or cerebellum. Peripheral damage to the vestibular system is fairly common following head trauma.
- *Visual Impairments.* Blurred vision, binocular vision problems [e.g., double vision (diplopia), changes in depth perception, or difficulty localizing objects in space], nystagmus, difficulty with visual tracking (i.e., deficit of smooth pursuit), or difficulty reading or rapidly localizing objects in space (i.e., deficit of saccadic movement) (Kapoor & Ciuffreda, 2005; Padula et al., 2007).
- *Cranial Nerve Impairments.* These nerves can be damaged due to skull fractures, shearing forces, intracranial hemorrhages or hematomas, or uncal herniation, and result in problems with olfaction, vision, hearing, balance, eye movements, facial sensation, facial movement, swallowing, tongue movements, and neck strength.
- *Headaches.* Common types of headaches are: (a) musculoskeletal headaches (cap-like discomfort), (b) cervicogenic headaches (unilateral sub-occipital head pain with secondary oculo-frontotemporal discomfort), (c) neuritic and neuralgic head pain (sharp and shooting pain in the occipital or parietal region of the scalp), (d) post-traumatic migraine (throbbing with associated nausea and sometimes vomiting), and (e) post-traumatic tension headache (bilateral vice-like pain in the temporal regions) (Zasler, Horn, Martelli, & Nicolson, 2007).
- *Fatigue and Sleep Disturbance.* Fatigue is a commonly reported persistent symptom following TBI (Bushnik, Englander, & Wright, 2008; Hillier, Sharpe, & Metzer, 1997; Olver, Ponsford & Curran, 1996). Sleep disturbances (Thaxton & Patel, 2007) can relate to insomnia, hypersomnia, or disturbed sleep-wake (circadian) cycles. These problems can be caused or exacerbated by lifestyle factors and mental health problems.

- *Mental Health Problems.* Depression is common following TBI (e.g., Ashman et al., 2004; Dikmen, Bombardier, Machamer, Fann, & Temkin, 2004; Jorge et al., 2004; Jorge, Robinson, Starkstein, & Arndt, 1993; Silver, Kramer, Greenwald, & Weissman, 2001; Varney, Martzke, & Roberts, 1987). It is not clear whether depression arises as a biological consequence of the TBI, as a psychological reaction to deficits and psychosocial problems associated with having a brain injury, or both. Anxiety disorders are also common in people who have sustained brain injuries (Warden & Labbate, 2005).
- *Personality Changes, Apathy, and Motivation.* Personality changes are fairly common and they can result from structural damage to specific regions of the brain, from secondary reactions to impairment or loss, or both (Lezak, Howieson, & Loring, 2004; O'Shanick & O'Shanick, 2005). Damage to the frontal lobes can result in impulsivity, emotional lability, socially inappropriate behaviors, apathy, decreased spontaneity, lack of interest, and emotional blunting.
- *Lack of Awareness.* A substantial percentage of people with TBIs experience reduced awareness of medical, physical, and/or cognitive deficits (Flashman & McAllister, 2002). In general, patients tend to underestimate the severity of their cognitive and behavioral impairments, or changes in personality or behavior, when compared to ratings of family members.

According to meta-analyses, TBIs have a large adverse effect on cognition. The overall effect of moderate to severe TBI on cognition, after two or more years of recovery, was $d = -0.74$ (Schretlen & Shapiro, 2003). Cognitive impairments are relatively common in attention, concentration, working memory, speed of processing, and memory domains (Dikmen, Machamer, & Temkin, 2001; Dikmen, Machamer, Powell, & Temkin, 2003; Dikmen, Machamer, Winn, & Temkin, 1995; Dikmen, McLean, Temkin, & Wyler, 1986; Iverson, 2005; Lezak et al., 2004; Mearns & Lees-Haley, 1993; Spikman, Timmerman, Zomeren van, & Deelman, 1999; Whyte, Schuster, Polansky, Adams, & Coslett, 2000). As injury severity increases, there is a greater likelihood of global cognitive deficits including motor skills, verbal and visual-spatial ability, and executive functioning (Dikmen et al., 1995).

The cognitive effects of a TBI are highly individualized and difficult to predict. Careful assessment is needed to identify the nature and extent of these cognitive deficits during different time periods following injury (e.g., the first few months versus more than two years post injury). Iverson and colleagues provided a framework for conceptualizing cognitive impairment on a continuum (Iverson & Brooks, 2010; Iverson, Brooks, & Ashton, 2008; Iverson, Brooks, & Holdnack, 2008, 2012). This framework proposed a number of categories that reflect five levels of cognitive impairment in a face valid manner—the specific criteria for each level have not been codified or agreed upon. These categories can be helpful for conceptualizing cognitive problems following moderate or severe TBI.

- *Mild cognitive diminishment.* This is not cognitive "impairment." Instead, this represents a mild diminishment in cognitive functioning. This cognitive diminishment may or may not be identifiable using neuropsychological tests. This diminishment can, but does not always, have a mild adverse impact on a person's social and/or occupational functioning. This diminishment may or may not be noticeable by others.
- *Mild cognitive impairment.* This level of cognitive impairment should be identifiable using neuropsychological tests. This impairment has a mild (sometimes moderate) adverse impact on a person's social and/or occupational functioning. This category corresponds to the DSM–IV diagnosis of Cognitive Disorder Not Otherwise Specified (NOS).
- *Moderate cognitive impairment.* This level of cognitive impairment would have a substantial impact on everyday functioning. This impairment would be noticeable to others in regards to the person's social and/or occupational functioning. This category is in between the DSM–IV Cognitive Disorder NOS and Dementia diagnoses. Either diagnosis might apply, depending upon the severity of the person's problems.
- *Severe cognitive impairment/dementia.* The cognitive impairment would have a substantial adverse impact on everyday functioning. This level of impairment would render the individual incapable of competitive employment. The person should not be driving a motor vehicle, and might have difficulty with activities of daily living. This category is consistent with the DSM–IV diagnosis of Dementia.
- *Profound cognitive impairment/severe dementia.* The cognitive impairment would render the person incapable of living outside of a nursing home or an institution. If the person lived at home, he or she likely would require 24-hour supervision.

It is important to consider that cognitive outcomes following TBI are quite variable. Some patients may show significant changes in functioning; while others will show only modest changes on cognitive testing. The variability in outcomes are likely due to a number of factors such as premorbid abilities, pre-injury health status, severity of injury, and a variety of biopsychosocial post-injury individual differences. A person with a TBI can have any of the five general cognitive outcomes listed above. Individuals who sustain MTBIs are likely to have good cognitive recovery, but a subset might have mild diminishment or mild impairment for many weeks post injury. Patients with moderate or severe TBIs are, of course, at risk for worse cognitive outcomes. The majority of those patients have cognitive outcomes within the first three categories listed above.

WAIS–IV, WMS–IV, AND THE ADVANCED CLINICAL SOLUTIONS FOR ADULTS WITH TRAUMATIC BRAIN INJURIES

The Wechsler Adult Intelligence Scale–Fourth Edition (WAIS–IV: Wechsler, 2008), the Wechsler Memory Scale–Fourth Edition (WMS–IV: Wechsler, 2009), and the Advanced Clinical Solutions for the WAIS–IV/WMS–IV (ACS: Pearson Assessment, 2009) can be used as part of a comprehensive battery for assessing cognition following TBI. The purpose of this chapter is to illustrate a range of interpretive strategies for use with the WAIS–IV, WMS–IV, and ACS in adults following TBI. A group of 37 patients diagnosed with moderate to severe TBI was collected as part of the WAIS–IV/WMS–IV clinical standardization sample. Demographic data for the TBI sample and three control groups used throughout this chapter are presented in Table 10.1.

For decades, past and present editions of the WAIS and WMS have been used in numerous studies to examine cognitive functioning following TBI. Selected studies in which all (or nearly all) of the subtests and/or indexes from the Wechsler Adult Intelligence Scale–Third Edition (WAIS–III: Wechsler, 1997a) or Wechsler Memory Scale–Third Edition (WMS–III: Wechsler, 1997b) have been administered, are presented in Tables 10.2 and 10.3. These studies illustrate the level of performance of various TBI groups. As seen in Table 10.2, the Processing Speed Index is most affected by TBI. The Digit Symbol Coding subtest is most sensitive to the effects of TBI. Contrary to longstanding clinical lore, the Working Memory Index is only slightly lower relative to the Verbal Comprehension and Perceptual Organization Indexes. As seen in Table 10.3, the visual memory indexes tend to be more sensitive to the effects of TBI than the auditory indexes. In general, comparing Tables 10.2 and 10.3, the memory indexes tend to be lower than the WAIS–III Verbal Comprehension Index (VCI), Perceptual Reasoning Index (PRI), and Working Memory Index (WMI).

In the final column of Tables 10.2 and 10.3, we present clinical meta-norms for people with moderate to severe TBIs. They were calculated based weighting each M and SD in the table by the sample size and then calculating the average of these weighted values. These meta-norms are useful for clinicians in that the majority of patients are expected to have scores within one standard deviation of the mean.

TABLE 10.1   Demographic Characteristics of TBI and Control Groups

	Moderate to Severe TBI	Matched Controls	Random Low Education Sample	Random High Education Sample
N	37	37	37	37
Age	29.4 (7.1)	30.3 (7.9)	31.6 (10.4)	31.9 (9.8)
Sex				
Female	24.3%	35.1%	45.9%	62.2%
Male	75.7%	64.9%	54.1%	37.8%
Education				
8 years or less	0.0%	0.0%	70.3%	0.0%
9–11 years	16.2%	18.9%	29.3%	0.0%
12 years	37.8%	35.1%	0.0%	0.0%
13–15 years	32.4%	29.7%	0.0%	0.0%
16 or more years	13.5%	16.2%	0.0%	100.0%
Ethnicity				
White	48.6%	54.1%	35.1%	86.5%
African-American	8.1%	8.1%	8.2%	5.4%
Hispanic	32.5%	29.7%	51.3%	5.4%
Asian	2.7%	2.7%	2.7%	2.7%
Other	8.1%	5.4%	2.7%	0.0%
Region				
Northeast	10.8%	8.1%	8.1%	10.8%
North Central	8.1%	21.7%	10.8%	37.8%
South	48.6%	40.5%	54.1%	45.9%
West	32.4%	29.7%	27.0%	5.5%

This helps the clinician determine if a specific patient is functioning comparably, better, or worse than the average patient who has a moderate to severe TBI.

WAIS–IV

Descriptive statistics for the WAIS–IV index and subtest scores in the moderate to severe TBI group and matched controls are presented

TABLE 10.2 WAIS–III Scores in those with Moderate-Severe TBIs

	1	2	3	4	5	6	7	8	9	10	Meta Norms
	M (SD)	M (SD)	M (SD)	M (SD)	M (SD)	M (SD)	M (SD)	M (SD)	M (SD)	M (SD)	M (SD)
IQ & Index Scores											
Full Scale IQ	105.4 (15.7)	97.2 (12.6)	101.7 (14.4)	92.7 (14.3)	87.3 (14.3)	92.6 (18.9)	88.4 (19.8)	86.5 (10.9)	88.5 (11.7)	86.5 (10.9)	92.7 (13.9)
Verbal IQ	106.6 (14.6)	99.2 (13.2)	102.1 (14.7)	94.5 (14.6)	89.7 (15.1)	95.8 (18.8)	92.6 (19.7)	89.6 (12.4)	91.5 (10.0)	89.6 (12.4)	94.9 (14.2)
Performance IQ	103.0 (15.8)	95.1 (13.3)	100.9 (14.4)	91.7 (13.6)	86.4 (12.5)	90.1 (20.3)	83.2 (20.3)	84.5 (13.8)	86.6 (14.1)	84.5 (13.8)	91.1 (14.3)
Verbal Comprehension	104.5 (12.9)	99.4 (13.0)	103.0 (15.5)	95.2 (15.0)	90.5 (14.5)	97.2 (17.5)	94.8 (18.4)	89.6 (12.7)	91.1 (9.6)	89.6 (12.7)	95.2 (14.1)
Perceptual Organization	103.1 (15.9)	98.3 (13.0)	104.7 (15.4)	95.6 (14.4)	91.2 (12.7)	96.5 (20.2)	89.4 (20.2)	92.1 (15.0)	92.2 (14.1)	92.1 (15.0)	95.7 (14.8)
Working Memory	101.1 (15.9)	96.2 (13.0)	101.9 (14.4)	94.4 (14.1)	90.1 (16.9)	92.2 (19.5)	90.0 (20.4)	89.8 (13.1)	94.1 (13.0)	89.8 (13.1)	94.3 (14.8)
Processing Speed	94.7 (16.1)	86.5 (10.9)	93.1 (12.6)	88.1 (12.9)	80.1 (13.0)	82.8 (17.7)	76.6 (17.7)	73.4 (10.7)	79.8 (12.6)	73.4 (10.7)	84.2 (13.0)
Subtest Scores											
Vocabulary	11.5 (3.1)	10.0 (2.3)	11.1 (3.1)	9.6 (3.1)	8.8 (3.3)	9.2 (3.5)	9.3 (3.7)	—	—	—	9.9 (3.1)
Similarities	11.0 (3.6)	10.0 (3.1)	9.9 (3.2)	8.2 (2.7)	7.1 (2.3)	10.4 (3.2)	8.6 (3.4)	—	—	—	8.8 (2.9)
Information	10.1 (1.8)	9.7 (2.9)	10.8 (2.7)	9.7 (3.1)	8.9 (3.2)	9.1 (3.2)	9.4 (3.4)	—	—	—	9.7 (2.9)
Comprehension	12.3 (2.9)	10.9 (3.0)	10.4 (3.0)	8.8 (3.4)	7.7 (3.2)	—	—	—	—	—	9.4 (3.2)
Arithmetic	9.8 (2.8)	9.5 (2.7)	10.4 (3.5)	9.4 (3.3)	8.2 (3.6)	8.5 (3.4)	8.5 (3.6)	—	—	—	9.3 (3.3)

(Continued)

TABLE 10.2 (Continued)

	1	2	3	4	5	6	7	8	9	10	Meta Norms
	M (SD)	M (SD)	M (SD)	M (SD)	M (SD)	M (SD)	M (SD)	M (SD)	M (SD)	M (SD)	M (SD)
Digit Span	11.4 (3.9)	9.5 (2.9)	9.9 (2.4)	9.1 (2.5)	9.2 (2.7)	9.5 (3.6)	8.7 (3.8)	–	–	–	9.5 (2.8)
Letter Number Sequencing	9.5 (2.7)	9.3 (2.7)	10.9 (3.1)	8.8 (2.7)	8.0 (3.1)	8.2 (3.6)	7.9 (3.8)	–	–	–	9.0 (3.0)
Picture Completion	10.0 (3.6)	9.6 (3.2)	10.3 (3.0)	9.2 (3.2)	7.5 (2.6)	8.6 (4.2)	7.0 (4.1)	–	–	–	9.0 (3.2)
Block Design	11.0 (3.1)	10.1 (2.3)	11.4 (3.1)	9.6 (3.0)	9.5 (2.7)	10.3 (3.5)	8.3 (3.5)	–	–	–	10.0 (3.0)
Matrix Reasoning	10.8 (2.8)	10.0 (2.8)	10.7 (2.4)	9.1 (2.5)	9.0 (2.7)	9.3 (3.7)	9.7 (3.7)	–	–	–	9.6 (2.7)
Picture Arrangement	11.4 (3.1)	9.8 (2.4)	10.2 (3.0)	8.3 (2.4)	8.0 (2.4)	–	–	–	–	–	9.1 (2.6)
Digit Symbol Coding	8.4 (3.2)	7.1 (2.1)	8.4 (2.4)	7.5 (2.9)	5.9 (2.6)	5.6 (3.3)	4.6 (3.3)	–	–	–	7.1 (2.8)
Symbol Search	9.8 (3.3)	7.9 (2.6)	9.1 (2.8)	8.0 (2.6)	6.5 (3.0)	7.4 (4.6)	7.5 (4.6)	–	–	–	8.0 (2.8)

1st Author	Group	N	TBI severity	Time Post Injury
Clement (2003)	1	20	Moderate	1–204 months after injury
Clement (2003)	2	19	Severe	1–204 months after injury
Langeluddecke (2003)	3	35	Moderate	$M = 32.1$ months (19.7)
Langeluddecke (2003)	4	74	Severe-very severe	$M = 34.1$ months (24.6)
Langeluddecke (2003)	5	41	Extremely severe	$M = 33.9$ months (23.1)
High (2010)	6[a]	12	Moderate-severe	$M = 11.0$ years (9.2)
High (2010)	7[a]	11	Moderate-severe	$M = 5.1$ years (3.6)
Fisher (2000)	8	22	Moderate-severe	6–18 months
Curtis (2009)	9	26	Moderate-severe	$M = 18.2$ months (32.3)
The Psych. Corp. (1997)	10	22	Moderate-severe	6–18 months

[a]*Calculated SD for WAIS/WMS scores from reported SEE.*

TABLE 10.3 WMS–III Index Scores in those with Moderate-Severe TBIs

	1	2	3	4	5	6	7	8	9	Meta Norms
	M (SD)	M (SD)	M (SD)	M (SD)	M (SD)	M (SD)	M (SD)	M (SD)	M (SD)	M (SD)
Auditory Immediate	94.9 (15.6)	92.1 (16.7)	85.1 (17.0)	94.2 (19.2)	86.6 (16.1)	97.4 (14.3)	89.3 (19.3)	87.5 (14.4)	89.3 (19.3)	90.3 (16.7)
Auditory Delayed	95.8 (13.5)	92.2 (16.6)	83.5 (18.1)	93.2 (20.8)	88.1 (17.8)	96.4 (17.9)	89.6 (21.8)	86.0 (18.8)	89.6 (21.8)	90.3 (17.9)
Auditory Recognition Delayed	98.6 (16.9)	94.8 (15.8)	90.1 (17.3)	95.1 (18.2)	91.8 (18.5)	99.5 (18.1)	93.6 (16.6)	94.6 (17.3)	93.6 (16.6)	94.3 (17.2)
Visual Immediate	88.8 (14.0)	85.3 (15.1)	74.9 (13.1)	89.8 (20.4)	84.0 (14.9)	86.1 (17.6)	74.9 (13.9)	85.2 (15.9)	74.9 (13.9)	83.5 (15.3)
Visual Delayed	88.1 (13.3)	86.3 (15.0)	75.9 (11.6)	90.4 (21.9)	84.7 (17.0)	85.6 (19.4)	74.3 (13.9)	86.4 (19.2)	74.3 (13.9)	84.0 (16.0)
Immediate Memory	90.3 (15.4)	86.6 (17.7)	76.2 (16.6)	90.3 (22.4)	82.4 (17.4)	90.8 (17.9)	78.9 (17.7)	83.5 (16.0)	78.9 (17.7)	84.5 (17.6)
General Memory	92.2 (14.1)	88.8 (17.0)	79.1 (15.9)	91.1 (23.2)	85.9 (17.9)	92.0 (19.6)	81.9 (16.5)	86.0 (19.2)	81.9 (16.5)	86.9 (17.7)
Working Memory	104.2 (14.7)	96.0 (12.0)	91.8 (14.9)	93.1 (14.8)	—	101.0 (15.9)	91.9 (11.9)	95.7 (11.2)	91.9 (11.9)	95.9 (13.4)

1st Author	Group	N	TBI severity	Time Post Injury
Langeluddecke (2005)	1	44	Complicated Mild or Moderate	M = 35.6 months (24.8)
Langeluddecke (2005)	2	86	Severe-Very Severe	M = 29.9 months (17.4)
Langeluddecke (2005)	3	50	Extremely Severe	M = 34.1 months (22.4)
West (2011)	4	40	Complicated Mild, Moderate, Severe	M = 37.0 months (18.5)
Johnstone (2003)	5[a]	78	Not stated (Moderate-Severe)	M = 9.2 years (9.6)
Ord (2008)	6	28	Moderate-Severe	M = 16 months
Fisher (2000)	7	22	Moderate-Severe	6–18 months
Axelrod (2001)	8	38	Complicated Mild or Moderate	M = 4.9 months (5.8)
The Psychological Corporation (1997)	9	22	Moderate-Severe	6–18 months

[a]Sample sizes ranged from 68–71 across the indexes

in Table 10.4. All WAIS–IV Indexes are significantly lower in the TBI group compared to the matched controls. The effect sizes range from medium (Cohen's $d = -0.65$; VCI) to very large ($d = -1.53$; PSI). The level of performance in the TBI group falls within the unusually low (i.e., borderline) to average ranges. This table also provides the percentage of cases obtaining scores below specific cut-offs (e.g., 25th, 16th, and 9th percentiles). In the TBI group: (a) 78% had scores at or below the 25th percentile compared to 27% of the matched controls (i.e., three times as many patients have low scores compared to controls), and (b) 60% had scores at or below the 9th percentile versus 8% of the matched controls. These results show that PSI, seven times as many patients have scores below the 9th percentile; however, 40% of the TBI group has scores greater than the 9th percentile.

For the WAIS–IV subtests, there were significant differences between the TBI group and matched controls on all measures, with the exception of the Information subtest. The level of performance ranged from the borderline to average range. The largest effect sizes were observed for Symbol Search ($d = -1.36$, very large), Coding ($d = -1.29$, very large), Digit Span Sequencing ($d = -1.28$, very large), and Visual Puzzles ($d = -0.96$, large). When comparing Digit Span measures, the moderate to severe TBI group performed worse on Digit Span Sequencing (-1.28) followed by Digit Span Forward ($d = -0.63$) and Backward ($d = -0.44$). On Symbol Search, 84% of the TBI group had a scaled score of eight or less and 70% had a scaled score of six or less; compared to 35% and 16% of controls, respectively. Similar to the index scores, the TBI group clearly show deficits in processing speed; however, not all TBI patients show large decrements in processing speed.

At a group level, the TBI group has relatively low processing speed (PSI) scores compared to verbal abilities (VCI). The average difference is approximately 12 standard score points between PSI and VCI. However, it is important to note that these are group averages and they likely mask intra-individual variability. This issue will be discussed in more detail later in the chapter.

By comparing the TBI group with demographically matched controls, areas of cognitive difficulties can be identified while controlling for background factors that can affect test performance (e.g., education level, sex, and ethnicity). However, such comparisons control for premorbid level of functioning at a group level, but not an individual level. Often clinicians evaluate patients that have low or high levels of education. In cases where education is low, it may be difficult to identify if a low level of cognitive ability represents an acquired impairment or is simply consistent with low premorbid ability. Similarly, it may be difficult for clinicians working with high education patients to know what level of performance would be expected from them. Table 10.5

TABLE 10.4 WAIS–IV Standard and New Index Scores and Subtests in Moderate to Severe TBI and Matched Controls

Index Scores	Moderate to Severe TBI					Matched Control					Between Group Differences	
	Mean	SD	25th %ile At or below	16th %ile At or below	9th %ile At or below	Mean	SD	25th %ile At or below	16th %ile At or below	9th %ile At or below	ES	p
Verbal Comprehension	91.1	16.1	46	39	33	99.1	12.3	24	19	3	−0.65	<0.05
Perceptual Reasoning	86.6	15.9	62	51	43	101.1	16.3	22	21	11	−0.89	<0.01
Working Memory	86.3	15.3	67	44	36	100.4	14.3	24	14	11	−0.98	<0.001
Processing Speed	79	17.6	78	65	60	100.2	13.9	27	22	8	−1.53	<0.001
General Ability	87.6	16.4	64	58	30	100	14.1	27	19	5	−0.87	<0.01
Cognitive Proficiency	80.4	16.6	69	69	56	100.1	13.7	22	14	11	−1.44	<0.001
Full Scale IQ	84	17.3	69	62	47	100.2	13.8	24	16	8	−1.17	<0.001
Subtest Scores												
Vocabulary	8.5	3.1	53	42	36	9.8	2.2	24	14	5	−0.60	<0.05
Similarities	8	3.3	45	40	34	9.9	2.6	27	19	8	−0.74	<0.01
Information	8.6	3.1	53	39	36	9.9	2.6	38	22	8	−0.48	>0.05
Block Design	8	3.1	62	54	43	10.6	3.2	24	22	14	−0.82	<0.001
Matrix Reasoning	7.5	3	62	48	43	9.8	3.5	43	27	19	−0.66	<0.01
Visual Puzzles	7.6	3.3	70	62	62	10.2	2.7	35	22	7	−0.96	<0.001

Digit Span	7.7	3.1	54	68	46	10.2	3	24	22	8	−0.83	<0.001
Digit Span Forward	8.3	3.3	51	43	35	10.2	3.1	27	16	8	−0.63	<0.01
Digit Span Backward	9	2.5	46	30	30	10.6	3.6	24	14	3	−0.44	<0.05
Digit Span Sequencing	6.9	2.4	73	62	38	10.7	2.9	27	22	14	−1.28	<0.001
Arithmetic	7.4	2.6	72	56	44	9.9	2.6	24	16	14	−0.95	<0.001
Coding	6.2	3.8	73	60	57	10.2	3.1	32	24	16	−1.29	<0.001
Symbol Search	6	3.3	84	73	70	9.9	2.8	35	27	16	−1.36	<0.001

Note: $n = 37$ in each group.

Copyright © 2008. NCS Pearson, Inc. All rights reserved.

TABLE 10.5 WAIS–IV Standard Index Scores in Moderate to Severe TBI versus Low and High Education Sample

Score	Moderate to Severe TBI		Low Education		Between Group Differences		High Education		Between Group Differences	
	Mean	SD	Mean	SD	ES	p	Mean	SD	ES	p
Verbal Comprehension	91.1	16.1	84.4	13.4	0.50	>.05	109.1	12.1	−1.49	<.001
Perceptual Reasoning	86.6	15.9	90.1	12.1	−0.29	>.05	106.5	13.4	−1.48	<.001
Working Memory	86.3	15.3	85.9	12.5	0.03	>.05	105.5	12.7	−1.51	<.001
Processing Speed	79.0	17.6	90.6	15.0	−0.78	<.01	105.4	12.5	−2.11	<.001
General Ability Index	87.6	16.4	85.8	12.2	0.15	>.05	108.8	12.2	−1.74	<.001
Full Scale IQ	84.0	17.3	85.0	12.2	−0.08	>.05	108.3	10.3	−2.36	<.001

Copyright © 2008 NCS Pearson, Inc. All rights reserved.

compares data from the moderate to severe TBI group to two randomly selected groups of individuals with low and high education levels from the WAIS–IV/WMS–IV standardization sample. Compared to the low education group, the PSI is the only score that is significantly lower in the TBI group. Compared to high education group, the TBI group shows very large differences on all WAIS–IV measures. Therefore, when clinicians interpret age adjusted scores, it may be difficult to differentiate low premorbid ability from the effects of TBI on WAIS–IV scores.

WMS–IV

Descriptive statistics for the WMS–IV index and subtest scores in the moderate to severe TBI group and matched controls are presented in Table 10.6. On the WMS–IV indexes, the TBI group performed in the borderline to low average range. The largest effect size was found for the Auditory Delayed Memory Index ($d = -1.70$, very large). However, all of the Auditory Indexes had large to very large effect sizes. Lower effect sizes were found on the visual memory indexes when compared to the auditory memory indexes, though effect sizes were still large ($d = -0.84$ to $d = -1.05$). Combined auditory and visual memory measures including General, Immediate, and Delayed Memory Indexes have large effects that fall between auditory and visual memory measures. Retention measures (i.e., Immediate versus Delayed Memory Index and the Retention Index) were not significantly different from controls indicating that the rate of forgetting in the TBI group is not different from controls. Although recognition memory indexes were generally higher than delayed recall, the retrieval index was significantly lower in the TBI group compared to controls indicating that delayed free recall is lower than expected compared to the recognition measures. Large effect sizes were observed on measures of visual working memory, consistent with the WAIS–IV working memory results. In terms of level of performance, the lowest achieved score in the TBI group was on the Delayed Memory Index (76.8), with 71% having scores at or below the 9th percentile compared to only 8% of controls.

In the TBI group, performance on the WMS–IV subtest scores ranged from the borderline to average range. The largest effect sizes were found for the Verbal Paired Associates (VPA) subtest; specifically Verbal Paired Associates Trial D ($d = -2.06$, very large), Verbal Paired Associates I Easy Items ($d = -1.94$, very large), Verbal Paired Associates I ($d = -1.87$, very large), and Verbal Paired Associates I Hard Items ($d = -1.73$, very large). The only VPA measures not significantly different between the TBI group and matched controls were VPA I Intrusions

TABLE 10.6 WMS–IV Standard and New Index Scores and Subtest Scores in Moderate to Severe TBI and Matched Controls

Score	Moderate to Severe TBI					Matched Control					Between Group Differences	
	Mean	SD	At or Below 25th %ile	At or Below 16th %ile	At or Below 9th %ile	Mean	SD	At or Below 25th %ile	At or Below 16th %ile	At or Below 9th %ile	ES	p
General Memory	78.8	21.1	67	67	62	98.2	16.1	31	23	8	−1.21	<0.01
Immediate Memory	80.2	20.4	65	58	58	98.9	15.5	29	21	7	−1.21	<0.001
Delayed Memory	76.8	24.0	76	71	71	97.0	14.4	35	19	8	−1.40	<0.01
Immediate vs. Delayed	7.1	4.8	62	57	57	9.2	2.2	42	31	8	−0.93	<0.01
Auditory Memory	80.0	20.4	68	61	57	99.6	11.9	21	11	4	−1.65	<0.001
Auditory Immediate	81.1	19.7	68	57	54	100.9	12.2	14	7	4	−1.63	<0.001
Auditory Delayed	78.8	22.6	68	57	50	98.6	11.6	18	11	11	−1.70	<0.001
Auditory Delayed Recognition	86.4	18.2	54	50	46	99.0	14.0	14	14	7	−0.91	<0.01
Visual Memory	80.9	20.9	67	57	52	96.9	17.4	42	23	15	−0.92	<0.01
Visual Immediate	83.5	19.4	54	54	46	97.4	16.7	32	21	18	−0.84	<0.01
Visual Delayed	79.4	23.3	67	67	57	96.7	16.5	35	31	19	−1.05	<0.01
Visual Delayed Recognition	86.7	17.9	67	57	48	98.0	13.1	40	20	16	−0.86	<0.05
Designs Content Index	79.5	19.0	81	57	52	100.9	15.4	29	21	8	−1.38	<0.001

Designs Spatial Index	82.9	17.0	62	52	48	99.1	16.2	25	21	8	−1.00	<0.01
Retention Index	84.6	24.0	62	52	48	94.7	13.1	38	31	15	−0.78	>0.05
Retrieval Index	78.6	23.0	71	67	57	98.5	15.2	28	12	12	−1.31	<0.01
Visual Working Memory Index	85.2	18.0	61	57	36	101.3	17.7	21	21	21	−0.91	<0.01
Working Memory	87.6	16.0	59	48	44	101.3	15.9	29	21	7	−0.86	<0.01
Quantitative Reasoning Index	89.0	15.5	52	48	44	105.1	17.5	29	11	0	−0.92	<0.01
Logical Memory I	7.9	4.1	57	50	39	10.0	3.1	25	18	14	−0.68	<0.05
Logical Memory I	7.2	4.5	54	54	46	9.5	3.2	32	21	11	−0.69	<0.05
Logical Memory I *vs.* II	8.1	3.8	50	46	25	9.2	3.4	39	36	14	−0.34	>0.05
Logical Memory II *vs.* Rec	7.1	4.6	64	50	46	9.6	4.1	36	14	14	−0.62	<0.05
Verbal Paired Associates I	5.9	3.3	75	75	61	10.3	2.3	21	14	4	−1.87	<0.001
Verbal Paired Associates II	5.9	3.7	82	68	46	10.0	2.6	25	11	11	−1.56	<0.001
Verbal Paired Associates I *vs.* II	8.5	4.2	50	42	36	9.3	2.6	36	18	18	−0.30	>0.05
Verbal Paired Associates II *vs.* Recognition	7.1	2.7	68	54	46	9.8	2.1	25	7	4	−1.26	<0.001
Verbal Paired Associates II Free Recall	5.1	3.6	75	68	61	10.0	2.9	32	25	14	−1.68	<0.001

(Continued)

TABLE 10.6 (Continued)

Score	Moderate to Severe TBI					Matched Control					Between Group Differences	
	Mean	SD	At or Below 25th %ile	At or Below 16th %ile	At or Below 9th %ile	Mean	SD	At or Below 25th %ile	At or Below 16th %ile	At or Below 9th %ile	ES	p
Verbal Paired I Associates Trial A	7.1	2.8	79	57	32	10.5	2.5	21	11	4	−1.37	<0.001
Verbal Paired I Associates Trial D	6.0	3.7	71	61	57	10.5	2.2	14	14	7	−2.06	<0.001
Verbal Paired I Associates A vs. D	7.1	3.3	61	54	46	10.1	2.0	18	14	4	−1.46	<0.001
Verbal Paired I Associates Total Intrusions	8.9	4.2	32	32	29	9.9	2.4	29	18	4	−0.42	>0.05
Verbal Paired I Associates Easy Items	6.3	3.6	75	64	50	10.6	2.2	18	7	4	−1.94	<0.001
Verbal Paired I Associates Hard Items	5.9	3.5	75	71	57	10.3	2.5	18	14	7	−1.73	<0.001
Visual Reproduction I	7.9	3.8	50	50	39	9.1	3.6	54	39	39	−0.34	>0.05
Visual Reproduction II	7.0	4.0	61	54	50	9.0	3.2	50	32	21	−0.62	<0.05
Visual Reproduction I vs. II	7.8	3.1	64	46	36	9.5	2.8	25	18	14	−0.62	<0.05
Visual Reproduction II vs. Recognition	7.7	4.1	68	54	46	9.1	3.0	25	7	4	−0.48	>0.05

Designs I	6.7	3.4	54	42	42	10.0	3.2	32	29	14	−1.04	<0.01
Designs I Content	6.8	3.8	69	65	46	9.7	2.8	30	22	18	−1.04	<0.01
Designs I Spatial	6.8	2.7	77	50	35	9.7	3.1	30	18	18	−0.92	<0.01
Designs II	6.3	4.1	67	62	57	10.0	3.2	31	19	8	−1.13	<0.01
Designs II Content	6.0	3.9	76	62	52	10.2	3.3	24	16	8	−1.31	<0.001
Designs II Spatial	7.3	3.9	57	52	38	10.0	3.2	28	16	12	−0.84	<0.05
Designs I vs. II	8.3	3.9	62	52	33	9.8	2.9	23	15	15	−0.53	>0.05
Designs II vs. Recognition	7.4	4.6	48	48	48	10.6	3.4	24	12	8	−0.95	<0.05

Note: $n = 28$.

Controls Copyright © 2009 NCS Pearson, Inc. All rights reserved.

and VPA I/VPA II contrast score. In the visual memory domain, the Designs subtest had larger effect sizes compared to Visual Reproduction, particularly the Designs II Content score ($d = -1.31$, very large). The lowest mean subtest score in the TBI group was 5.1 (SD = 3.6) on Verbal Paired Associates Delayed Free Recall. On average, 70% of the TBI group had a scaled score of eight or lower on many of the VPA measures.

A comparison of WMS–IV performance between the moderate to severe TBI group and both the low and high education control groups is presented in Table 10.7. The only WMS–IV index that was significantly different between the low education control group and the TBI group was the Delayed Memory Index ($d = -0.70$). In contrast, all five WMS–IV indexes were significantly different when comparing the high education control group and the TBI group, with very large effect sizes greater than $d = -2.0$ for the majority of comparisons.

MULTIVARIATE BASE RATES

Chapter 2 presented data on the frequency of low scores on the WAIS–IV/WMS–IV in healthy adults when multiple subtests or indexes are considered simultaneously (i.e., multivariate base rate analysis). In the previous section of this chapter, we demonstrated that moderate to severe TBI is associated with low scores on some WAIS–IV/WMS–IV measures. However, what is not clear from these data is whether or not the TBI group has multiple low scores at a rate that is unexpected (e.g., greater than occurs in healthy controls). Previously, Brooks, Holdnack, and Iverson (2011) reported that over 70% of patients with moderate to severe TBI have greater than expected number of low WAIS–IV/WMS–IV index and subtest scores compared to the general population. The sample from Brooks et al. (2011), a clinical group used as part of the WAIS–IV/WMS–IV standardization, was also used in this chapter.

The number of low scores in the moderate to severe TBI sample versus matched controls for the WAIS–IV, WMS–IV, and combined WAIS–IV/WMS–IV are presented in Table 10.8. The prevalence of low scores is represented using two cut-off score criteria: (a) ≤1 SD, and (b) ≤5th percentile. The moderate to severe TBI group had a significantly greater number of low scores compared to matched controls. The effect sizes are largest when using the 5th percentile cut-off criterion, with effect sizes ranging from $d = -2.4$ to $d = -2.9$ for the WAIS–IV, WMS–IV, and combined WAIS–IV/WMS–IV indexes. These data show that applying multivariate base rates can effectively differentiate normal from atypical cognitive profiles. However, having multiple low scores is not diagnostic of a specific condition or disorder because many factors

TABLE 10.7 WMS–IV Standard Index Scores in Moderate to Severe TBI and Low Education Sample

Score	Moderate to Severe TBI		Low Education Sample		Between Group Difference		High Education Sample		Between Group Differences	
	Mean	SD	Mean	SD	ES	p	Mean	SD	ES	p
Immediate Memory	80.2	20.4	86.7	17.0	−0.38	>0.05	110.2	12.5	−2.41	<0.001
Delayed Memory	76.8	24.0	90.0	18.9	−0.70	<0.05	109.7	14.6	−2.25	<0.001
Auditory Memory	80.0	20.4	90.8	20.7	−0.52	>0.05	106.3	12.1	−2.17	<0.001
Visual Memory	80.9	20.9	88.3	14.4	−0.52	>0.05	111.6	14.9	−2.06	<0.001
Visual Working Memory	85.2	18.0	86.8	15.9	−0.10	>0.05	109.4	14.8	−1.64	<0.001

Copyright © 2009 NCS Pearson, Inc. All rights reserved.

can influence the rate of observed low scores. Interpretation of the reason for the large number of low scores must take into account the overall clinical picture and data collected from multiple sources.

INTRAINDIVIDUAL VARIABILITY

Variability in cognitive functioning is sometimes thought to indicate the presence of cognitive impairment, brain injury, or abnormal brain functioning. Chapter 3 describes methods for identifying intra-individual variability including: (a) highest and lowest obtained scores, (b) difference between highest and lowest index and subtest scores, and (c) the standard deviation of indexes and subtests. The data presented in Chapter 3 demonstrate that cognitive variability is common in healthy adolescents and adults, such that large differences in ability are the norm rather than the exception.

WAIS–IV, WMS–IV, and WAIS–IV/WMS–IV index and subtest variability measures for the moderate to severe TBI sample and matched controls are presented in Table 10.9. The WAIS–IV index and subtest variability measures were *not* statistically different between the TBI and matched control groups. The mean variability scaled scores were in the average range for both the moderate to severe TBI and control groups. The highest and lowest obtained index and subtest scores were significantly lower in the TBI sample compared to controls. The level of performance was in the low average range (highest and lowest obtained scores) which is consistent with a suppressed rather than variable cognitive profile.

Similarly, the WMS–IV index and subtest variability measures were in the average range for both the TBI and matched control groups. The highest and lowest obtained WMS–IV index and subtest scores were significantly lower in the TBI group compared to controls. The level of performance in the TBI group was in the low average range (highest and lowest obtained scores) which is again consistent with a suppressed rather than variable memory profile. In the combined WAIS–IV/WMS–IV batteries, there is significant general variability among the index scores (i.e., WAIS–IV/WMS–IV Index standard deviation). Similar to the individual batteries, the TBI group has lower than expected "highest" and "lowest" obtained scores, indicating a general suppression of the cognitive profile. However, there is some variability when memory and intellectual functioning are considered simultaneously.

Because the moderate to severe TBI sample has a suppressed cognitive profile, it is necessary to adjust the variability measures by the highest achieved score (see Chapter 3 for details). WAIS–IV/WMS–IV variability measures, controlling for the highest achieved score in the

TABLE 10.8 Descriptive Statistics and Base Rates of Low Scores in Moderate to Severe TBI and Matched Controls.

| Score | Moderate to Severe TBI | | | | Matched Control | | | | Between Group Differences | | | |
| | At or below 1 SD | | At or below 5th %ile | | At or below 1 SD | | At or below 5th %ile | | At or below 1 SD | | At or below 5th %ile | |
	Mean	SD	Mean	SD	Mean	SD	Mean	SD	ES	p	ES	p
WAIS–IV Index Low Scores	2.5	1.9	1.7	1.7	0.9	1.4	0.2	0.6	1.1	<0.001	2.4	<0.001
WAIS–IV Subtest Low Scores	5.1	3.4	2.9	2.9	2.1	2.4	0.5	0.9	1.3	<0.001	2.6	<0.001
WMS–IV Index Low Scores	2.7	2.1	2.1	2.0	0.9	1.4	0.3	0.6	1.3	<0.001	2.9	<0.001
WMS–IV Subtest Low Scores	5.6	3.6	4.0	3.3	2.3	2.4	0.9	1.3	1.4	<0.001	2.4	<0.001
WAIS–IV/WMS–IV Index Low Scores	4.7	3.3	3.3	3.0	1.8	2.7	0.5	1.0	1.1	<0.001	2.9	<0.001
WAIS–IV/WMS–IV Subtest Low Scores	9.7	6.3	5.6	4.8	4.0	4.2	1.2	1.8	1.4	<0.001	2.5	<0.001

Note: ES = Effect size.

Copyright © 2009 NCS Pearson, Inc. All rights reserved.

TABLE 10.9   WAIS–IV/WMS–IV Variability Measures in Moderate to Severe TBI and Matched Controls

Score	Moderate to Severe TBI		Matched Control		Between Group Differences	
	Mean	SD	Mean	SD	ES	p
WAIS–IV Subtest High Versus Low	10.1	2.9	10.5	3.3	−0.10	>0.05
WAIS–IV Subtest Standard Deviation	10.2	3.2	10.2	3.6	−0.01	>0.05
WAIS–IV Subtest Highest Score	7.2	3.0	9.6	3.0	−0.79	<0.01
WAIS–IV Subtest Lowest Score	6.7	3.1	9.9	3.1	−1.04	<0.001
WAIS–IV Index High Versus Low	10.3	3.7	9.9	3.0	0.13	>0.05
WAIS–IV Index Standard Deviation	10.1	3.8	9.9	3.0	0.08	>0.05
WAIS–IV Index Highest Score	6.8	2.9	10.1	2.8	−1.21	<0.001
WAIS–IV Index Lowest Score	6.5	3.3	10.0	2.9	−1.22	<0.001
WMS–IV Subtest High Versus Low	9.3	3.4	9.6	2.4	−0.15	>0.05
WMS–IV Subtest Standard Deviation	9.3	3.2	9.3	3.6	−0.02	>0.05
WMS–IV Subtest Highest Score	7.3	4.0	10.3	2.8	−1.07	<0.05
WMS–IV Subtest Lowest Score	6.3	3.5	10.4	3.0	−1.40	<0.01
WMS–IV Index High Versus Low	10.0	3.9	10.2	2.8	−0.08	>0.05
WMS–IV Index Standard Deviation	9.3	3.7	9.7	2.6	−0.15	>0.05
WMS–IV Index Highest Score	6.3	3.9	9.8	3.0	−1.16	<0.001
WMS–IV Index Lowest Score	5.9	4.1	9.9	3.6	−1.12	<0.001
WAIS–IV/WMS–IV Subtest High Versus Low	9.5	2.8	10.4	3.4	−0.27	>0.05
WAIS–IV/WMS–IV Subtest Standard Deviation	8.8	3.2	10.1	3.6	−0.39	>0.05
WAIS–IV/WMS–IV Subtest Highest Score	7.4	3.0	9.4	2.7	−0.74	<0.001
WAIS–IV/WMS–IV Subtest Lowest Score	6.3	3.7	9.6	3.6	−0.92	<0.001
WAIS–IV/WMS–IV Index High Versus Low	8.9	3.8	10.2	3.6	−0.27	>0.05
WAIS–IV/WMS–IV Index Standard Deviation	8.3	3.8	10.2	3.4	−0.39	<0.05
WAIS–IV/WMS–IV Index Highest Score	7.1	3.2	9.9	3.1	−0.74	<0.01
WAIS–IV/WMS–IV Index Lowest Score	5.9	4.4	9.9	3.3	−0.92	<0.001

Note: Scores are in scaled score units; low scores indicate more variability for highest versus lowest and highest obtained scores.
Copyright © 2009 NCS Pearson, Inc. All rights reserved.

TBI and matched control groups, are presented in Table 10.10 (see Chapter 3 for a discussion of the methodology for variability analyses). Controlling for the low "highest" index score, there was no significant variability on the WAIS–IV or WMS–IV indexes in the moderate to severe TBI group. However, there was significant subtest variability for WAIS–IV extremes of performance (i.e., highest versus lowest subtest scores) and WAIS–IV and WMS–IV general variability (i.e., standard deviation of subtest scaled scores). The TBI group shows significant variability on the combined WAIS–IV/WMS–IV batteries at the index and subtest level for both general profile variability and extremes of performance. The level of variability is in the low average range (e.g., scaled score <8). The overall intellectual and memory profile indicates that there was a suppressed cognitive profile in the TBI group which limits the degree to which cognitive variability can be identified compared to the general population. When you control for the profile suppression, the TBI group shows a mild degree of cognitive variability particularly when combining intellectual and memory functions.

In conclusion, patients who sustained a moderate to severe TBI *did not* show greater cognitive variability than healthy controls. The impact of brain injury is a suppression of cognitive functioning that is evidenced by few scores above the mean and several low scores in the borderline and extremely low range.

DEMOGRAPHICALLY-ADJUSTED NORMS

Chapter 4 described the derivation and application of demographically-adjusted norms (DANs). The primary purpose of these normative adjustments is to identify unexpectedly low levels of performance compared to individuals with similar background characteristics. The use of DANs can be very helpful in many assessments of patients with TBIs because these norms control for the effects of education, gender, and ethnicity (in addition to age).

Previously, we presented WAIS–IV and WMS–IV data in a moderate to severe TBI group, a matched control group, and two low and high education control groups. There were large effect sizes for most WAIS–IV/WMS–IV measures when comparing the TBI group to the matched control and high education control groups, but not when comparing the TBI group to the low education control group. WAIS–IV DAN scores (i.e., age, education, sex, and ethnicity adjusted) for the moderate to severe TBI group and matched controls are presented in Table 10.11. The effect sizes for DAN scores should be very similar to the standard age-only adjusted scores because both the clinical and control sample are matched on these factors. All WAIS–IV index scores are

TABLE 10.10   WAIS–IV/WMS–IV Variability Measures Controlling for Highest subtest or Index Score in Moderate to Severe TBI and Matched Controls

Score	Moderate to Severe TBI		Matched Control		Between Group Differences	
	Mean	SD	Mean	SD	ES	p
WAIS–IV Subtest High vs. Low	8.0	3.5	10.3	3.4	−0.68	<0.01
WAIS–IV Subtest Standard Deviation	8.0	3.5	10.2	3.7	−0.60	<0.05
WAIS–IV Index High vs. Low	9.8	4.4	9.9	3.1	−0.06	>0.05
WAIS–IV Index Standard Deviation	9.0	4.0	9.9	2.9	−0.33	>0.05
WMS–IV Subtest High vs. Low	8.0	3.3	9.7	3.9	−0.43	>0.05
WMS–IV Subtest Standard Deviation	7.6	3.1	9.8	3.7	−0.58	<0.05
WMS–IV Index High vs. Low	8.0	4.2	9.9	3.2	−0.60	>0.05
WMS–IV Index Standard Deviation	7.9	4.1	9.8	3.0	−0.63	>0.05
WAIS–IV/WMS–IV Subtest High vs. Low	7.6	3.1	10.0	3.5	−0.68	<0.05
WAIS–IV/WMS–IV Subtest Standard Deviation	7.1	3.4	10.1	3.4	−0.87	<0.01
WAIS–IV/WMS–IV Index High vs. Low	6.6	4.9	10.0	3.7	−0.91	<0.01
WAIS–IV/WMS–IV Index Standard Deviation	6.3	4.8	10.3	3.2	−1.25	<0.01

Note: Scores are in scaled score units; low scores indicate more variability for highest versus lowest and highest obtained scores.

Copyright © 2009 NCS Pearson, Inc. All rights reserved.

significantly different between the TBI and control group. The effect sizes are slightly larger when using DANs (range: $d = 0.65$ to $d = 1.56$) compared to the age-only adjusted norms (range: $d = 0.44$ to $d = 1.53$). The sensitivity is not substantially higher because a similar number of cases fall below specific cut-scores; although, specificity may be slightly higher because fewer controls are scoring below cut-offs. All the WAIS–IV subtests are significantly different except Vocabulary. The largest effects are observed on Coding and Symbol Search. The overall results are consistent with those reported for age-only adjusted scores. Small observed differences may be due to missing data and a smaller sample in the DAN analysis.

WAIS–IV DAN index scores for the TBI group, and the low and high education control groups, are presented in Table 10.12. The TBI group performed significantly lower than both the low and high education groups on all WAIS–IV indexes. The effect sizes are consistent with those reported for the matched control group. These results illustrate the usefulness of the DANs approach. Simply put, when using

TABLE 16.11 WAIS–IV Full Demographically Adjusted Standard Index Scores and Subtests in Moderate to Severe TBI and Matched Controls

Score	Moderate to Severe TBI				Matched Control				Between Group Differences	
	Mean SD	At or below 25th %ile	At or below 16th %ile	At or below 9th %ile	Mean SD	At or below 25th %ile	At or Below 16th %ile	At or below 9th %ile	ES	p
Verbal Comprehension	43.2 12.0	48	39	32	50.8 8.8	18	15	0	−0.86	<0.01
Perceptual Reasoning	40.0 10.9	64	58	42	51.5 10.8	24	12	9	−1.06	<0.001
Working Memory	40.2 9.7	62	53	44	51.9 8.8	12	9	3	−1.34	<0.001
Processing Speed	36.9 13.1	73	64	47	52.1 9.5	15	15	9	−1.61	<0.001
Full Scale IQ	37.5 12.3	60	49	47	51.8 9.2	21	9	6	−1.56	<0.001
Vocabulary	46.3 11.2	41	38	25	51.1 7.4	15	6	0	−0.65	>0.05
Similarities	41.7 11.8	56	50	31	50.9 9.4	24	15	3	−0.98	<0.01
Information	44.8 11.1	45	30	27	50.5 8.1	24	12	0	−0.70	<0.05
Block Design	41.9 10.7	58	52	33	51.9 11.3	21	12	12	−0.89	<0.01
Matrix Reasoning	42.2 10.2	58	52	33	50.6 11.0	30	21	6	−0.76	<0.01
Visual Puzzles	40.2 12.2	64	48	42	50.8 9.7	27	15	3	−1.09	<0.001
Digit Span	42.8 10.7	58	48	27	53.3 9.5	18	6	3	−1.11	<0.001
Arithmetic	39.5 8.7	66	59	31	50.4 8.9	12	12	6	−1.23	<0.001
Coding	37.7 15.4	70	52	42	53.2 10.7	12	12	12	−1.44	<0.001
Symbol Search	37.5 12.0	73	67	54	50.4 10.0	30	24	12	−1.29	<0.001

Note: $n = 32$.
Copyright © 2009 NCS Pearson, Inc. All rights reserved.

TABLE 10.12 WAIS–IV Full Demographically Adjusted Standard Index Scores in Moderate to Severe TBI and Low and High Education Groups

Score	Moderate to Severe TBI		Low Education		Between Group Differences		High Education		Between Group Differences	
	Mean	SD	Mean	SD	ES	p	Mean	SD	Actual ES	p
Verbal Comprehension Index	43.2	12.0	51.5	10.6	−0.78	<0.01	46.5	10.5	−0.31	<0.01
Perceptual Reasoning Index	40.0	10.9	50.9	9.8	−1.12	<0.001	48.0	9.2	−0.87	<0.001
Working Memory Index	40.2	9.7	51.5	10.5	−1.09	<0.001	46.5	10.4	−0.61	<0.001
Processing Speed Index	36.9	13.1	50.1	9.8	−1.34	<0.001	48.0	9.5	−1.18	<0.001
Full Scale IQ	37.5	12.3	51.4	10.6	−1.31	<0.001	46.4	8.4	−1.06	<0.001

Note: $n = 32$.

Copyright © 2009 NCS Pearson, Inc. All rights reserved.

age-adjusted norms it is difficult to differentiate TBI from the effects of low education. However, this is not a problem when using DANs. Using DANs enables the clinician to identify cognitive deficits that are not due to low education level or other background factors. Consistent application of DANs will improve test sensitivity and specificity.

DANs scores for the WMS–IV index and subtests for the moderate to severe TBI group and matched controls are presented in Table 10.13. The results are consistent with those reported when using age-adjusted normative data. The DANs effect sizes are very similar to the age-adjusted effect sizes when comparing the results to matched controls. At a subtest level, the largest effect sizes were again found on the Verbal Paired Associates and Design Memory subtests. WMS–IV DANs scores for the TBI group and the low and high education control groups are presented in Table 10.14. WMS–IV DANs index scores are significantly lower in the TBI group compared to low and high education groups. The effect sizes are similar to those reported for the matched control sample demonstrating the usefulness of the DANs approach.

The use of DANs improves the clinician's ability to identify cognitive deficits in patients regardless of their background. When patients have low educational attainment, it can be difficult to determine if cognitive deficits are present or if achieved scores are consistent with low premorbid functioning. Similarly, patients with a high education level (and high premorbid ability) may show average scores on age-adjusted indexes and subtests following TBI. It may be difficult to determine if these scores represent an actual decline in ability or not. DANs provide information about the examinee's relative standing compared to examinees of similar background making it easier to identify cognitive deficits in highly educated patients.

It should be noted that the matched control group data presented in this chapter does not change significantly when DANs are applied because the scores are adjusted for factors that the examinees are matched on, so scores in both groups are adjusted by the same constant. In clinical practice, clinicians do not have matched controls to compare a patient's performance against unless DANs scores are used. Clinicians tend to use age-adjusted normative scores that means that the patient is being compared to a general sample, not a demographically similar sample. DANs data essentially provides the clinician a matched control sample by which to compare individual patients. Overall, sensitivity and specificity is improved when using DANs scores enabling clinicians to more accurately identify cognitive impairment when education level is high or low.

TABLE 10.13 WMS–IV Full Demographically Adjusted Standard Index and Subtest Scores in Moderate to Severe TBI and Matched Controls

Score	Moderate to Severe TBI					Matched Control					Between Group Differences	
	Mean	SD	At or below 25th %ile	At or below 16th %ile	At or below 9th %ile	Mean	SD	At or below 25th %ile	At or below 16th %ile	At or below 9th %ile	ES	p
Immediate Memory	36.2	15.7	65	65	53	50.6	11.8	26	13	4	−1.22	<0.01
Delayed Memory	34.9	16.9	71	59	59	49.1	9.5	16	13	0	−1.49	<0.01
Auditory Memory	38.1	15.3	65	65	65	50.4	9.3	17	13	4	−1.33	<0.01
Visual Memory	36.2	14.1	71	59	59	49.0	11.3	35	26	4	−1.13	<0.01
Visual Working Memory	40.2	13.6	65	65	65	52.2	11.7	17	17	17	−1.02	<0.01
Logical Memory I	42.3	15.9	59	47	47	50.6	10.2	17	9	9	−0.81	>0.05
Logical Memory II	41.3	17.1	59	59	53	49.2	11.5	22	17	9	−0.69	>0.05
Verbal Paired Associates I	38.2	12.1	65	65	41	51.6	9.3	22	9	0	−1.44	<0.001
Verbal Paired Associates II	40.1	11.3	65	53	41	50.2	9.1	17	9	9	−1.10	<0.01
Designs I	38.4	12.6	71	53	41	51.1	10.6	30	17	4	−1.21	<0.01
Designs II	37.2	12.8	71	64	59	51.7	9.6	26	9	0	−1.52	<0.001

Visual Reproduction I	41.8	13.2	59	47	35	47.8	11.5	40	30	26	−0.53	> 0.05
Visual Reproduction II	39.9	14.1	59	53	53	46.4	10.9	48	26	22	−0.59	> 0.05
Spatial Addition	42.1	10.7	65	47	35	52.7	11.1	22	22	9	−0.96	< 0.01
Symbol Span	41.8	13.4	71	53	41	50.8	9.9	26	17	13	−0.91	< 0.05

Note: $n = 32$.

Copyright © 2009 NCS Pearson, Inc. All rights reserved.

TABLE 10.14 WMS–IV Full Demographically Adjusted Index Scores in Moderate to Severe TBI and Low Education Sample

Score	Moderate to Severe TBI		Low Education		Between Group Differences		High Education		Between Group Differences	
	Mean	SD	Mean	SD	ES	p	Mean	SD	ES	p
Immediate Memory	36.2	15.7	49.7	13.1	-1.03	<0.01	50.8	8.8	-1.66	<0.001
Delayed Memory	34.9	16.9	49.2	13.4	-1.07	<0.01	50.8	10.1	-1.57	<0.01
Auditory Memory	38.1	15.3	49.2	13.4	-0.83	<0.05	48.7	8.5	-1.25	<0.01
Visual Memory	36.2	14.1	49.6	10.9	-1.23	<0.01	53.0	11.0	-1.53	<0.001
Visual Working Memory	40.2	13.6	49.2	11.6	-0.77	<0.05	50.9	11.9	-0.90	<0.01

Copyright 2009 Pearson, Inc. Reproduced with Permission. All rights reserved.

PREMORBID FUNCTIONING

Chapter 5 of this book is devoted to predicting premorbid cognitive functioning. The purpose of estimating premorbid functioning is to determine if current cognitive functioning represents a loss or decline in ability due to injury, disease, or dementia, or if current functioning is within expected performance given the patient's background characteristics. The Test of Premorbid Functioning (TOPF) and the Oklahoma Premorbid Intelligence Estimate—IV have been developed to aid the clinician in identifying a significant discrepancy between current cognitive functioning and expected levels of performance. The presence of a discrepancy is not diagnostic of a specific disorder or condition but is evidence that current levels of performance are different from what is expected.

Test of Premorbid Functioning

The TOPF premorbid prediction model was described in detail in Chapter 5. For the purposes of this chapter, the TOPF with simple demographic data were calculated for the moderate to severe TBI group and the three control groups (e.g., matched, low education, and high education controls). The TOPF provides information about the predicted scores, significant difference between actual and predicted scores, base rates of differences, and other relevant information. The information presented here focuses on the: (a) actual, (b) predicted, and (c) difference between actual and predicted scores for each group.

TOPF scores using the simple demographic prediction data for the TBI and matched control groups are presented in Table 10.15. The "actual" data indicates the person's obtained WAIS–IV/WMS–IV index scores. The "predicted" data is the value predicted by the TOPF using the simple demographics equation. The "difference" data refers to the difference between actual and predicted scores. The "base rate" data refers to the percentages of cases that exceed specific cut-off differences (e.g., specifically where actual is lower than predicted, a potential loss in functioning) established by the normative sample.

Group comparisons revealed that the TBI group had significantly lower "actual" WAIS–IV and WMS–IV scores compared to the matched controls, with effect sizes ranging from $d = -0.65$ (VCI) to $d = -1.41$ (PSI). There were significant differences between the TBI group and matched controls on "predicted" premorbid VCI, WMI, and Full Scale Intelligence Quotient (FSIQ) scores. As such, it appears as if the TOPF reading score could be modestly affected by moderate to severe TBI. Consequently, premorbid cognitive abilities are likely to be

TABLE 10.15 TOPF with Simple Demographics Predicted WAIS–IV/WMS–IV Indexes in TBI and Matched Controls

Score	Moderate-Severe TBI									Matched Controls									Between Group Differences					
	Actual Mean	Actual SD	Pred Mean	Pred SD	Diff	SD of Diff	Actual < Predicted 25% Cut-off	Actual < Predicted 15% Cut-off	Actual < Predicted 10% Cut-off	Actual Mean	Actual SD	Pred Mean	Pred SD	Diff	SD of Diff	Actual > Predicted 25% Cut-off	Actual > Predicted 15% Cut-off	Actual > Predicted 10% Cut-off	Actual ES d	p	Pred ES d	p	Diff ES d	p
Verbal Comprehension	89.7	16.7	95.2	11.9	−5.5	8.7	31	32	24	100.5	12.5	101.3	8.9	−0.7	8.7	26	19	10	−0.65	<0.01	−0.68	<0.05	−0.55	<0.05
Perceptual Reasoning	87.4	16.1	98.6	7.7	−11.2	11.7	52	44	40	103.9	15.8	101.8	6.4	2.1	13.5	19	13	10	−1.03	<0.001	−0.50	>0.05	−0.98	<0.001
Working Memory	87.2	15.6	95.8	10.4	−8.6	10.0	52	46	44	102.2	14.6	101.2	7.7	1.0	10.7	16	13	10	−0.96	<0.01	−0.69	<0.05	−0.90	<0.01
Processing Speed	77.0	17.1	97.6	7.1	−20.6	15.3	68	68	64	101.2	13.3	100.3	5.2	0.8	13.1	19	19	10	−1.41	<0.001	−0.53	>0.05	−1.64	<0.001
General Ability	87.0	17.0	97.6	10.6	−10.6	10.2	40	32	20	102.4	13.7	102.3	8.5	0.2	9.5	38	23	3	−0.90	<0.001	−0.55	>0.05	−1.13	<0.001
Cognitive Proficiency	79.5	16.4	96.1	10.5	−16.6	12.1	80	60	48	101.6	13.2	100.6	7.1	1.0	10.7	38	19	6	−1.35	<0.001	−0.64	>0.05	−1.64	<0.001
Full-Scale IQ	83.0	17.4	96.0	11.6	−13.0	10.5	76	48	44	102.4	13.3	101.5	8.3	0.9	9.4	13	13	8	−1.11	<0.001	−0.67	<0.001	−1.47	<0.001
Immediate Memory	78.6	20.8	98.7	6.8	−20.1	18.3	70	56	56	100.5	15.6	101.3	4.5	−0.8	15.4	36	8	4	−1.05	<0.001	−0.57	>0.05	−1.25	<0.001
Delayed Memory	75.3	23.6	98.5	6.5	−23.2	21.2	75	70	70	97.6	14.2	100.3	5.0	−2.7	13.5	36	8	4	−0.95	<0.001	−0.38	>0.05	−1.51	<0.001

Note: $n = 30$ in each group.

Copyright © 2009 NCS Pearson, Inc. All rights reserved.

somewhat underestimated in the TBI group. The "difference" columns indicate that for every index, the predicted versus actual score is significantly different in the TBI versus matched control sample. The TBI group has much lower actual scores compared to predicted scores (i.e., decline in cognitive functioning) with effect sizes ranging from $d = -0.55$ (VCI) to $d = -1.64$ (PSI, Cognitive Proficiency Index: CPI).

TOPF scores using the simple demographic prediction data for the TBI group and low education control group is presented in Table 10.16. These analyses illustrate the usefulness of premorbid predictions for differentiating: (a) loss of cognitive functioning, from (b) low premorbid ability associated with low education. As reported previously, actual score differences between the TBI group and the low education control group are observed for PSI, CPI, Immediate Memory Index (IMI), and Delayed Memory Index (DMI) with moderate to large effect sizes. The predicted scores show very large and significant differences between the groups. The TBI group has significantly higher predicted scores compared to the low education control group. However, the most important finding is the large significant difference between the TBI and low education control group on the actual versus predicted score. The TBI group shows large discrepancies between actual and predicted scores, but the low education control group does not show a discrepancy between actual and predicted scores. Therefore, the clinician can differentiate low premorbid ability from possible loss in functioning by examining the discrepancy between actual and predicted scores. The premorbid prediction model reduces the impact of background variables on the test performance yielding a better estimate of the impact of brain injury on cognitive performance.

Table 10.17 provides data comparing the TBI group with the high education control sample on the TOPF using simple demographic predicted scores. The TBI group shows large and significant differences between all actual, predicted, and actual versus predicted scores. Similar to the DANs, the application of premorbid adjustments reduces the differences between the TBI and high education control group. The adjustment of background factors that influence test performance yields effect sizes closer to those observed in the matched control sample that may be a better estimate of the impact of brain injury on cognitive functioning.

The TOPF with simple demographics prediction equations are an efficient and effective model for identifying potential impairments in cognitive functioning following brain injury. In general, the predicted scores represent a reasonable estimate of premorbid ability. The TOPF reading scores are mildly affected by moderate to severe brain injury and this needs to be considered when reporting premorbid abilities. Significant differences were observed for all actual versus TOPF predicted WAIS–IV and WMS–IV indexes; however, the largest effect

TABLE 10.16 Simple Demographics with Test of Premorbid Functioning Predicted Versus Actual WAIS–IV/WMS–IV Index Scores in Moderate to Severe TBI and Random Low Education Sample

Score	Moderate-Severe TBI									Low Education Sample									Between Group Differences					
	Actual Mean	Actual SD	Pred Mean	Pred SD	Diff	SD of Diff	Actual < Predicted 25% Cut-off	Actual < Predicted 15% Cut-off	Actual < Predicted 10% Cut-off	Actual Mean	Actual SD	Pred Mean	Pred SD	Diff	SD of Diff	Actual > Predicted 25% Cut-off	Actual > Predicted 15% Cut-off	Actual > Predicted 10% Cut-off	Actual ES d	p	Pred ES d	p	Diff ES d	p
Verbal Comprehension	89.7	16.7	95.2	11.9	−5.5	8.8	31	32	24	86.3	13.0	85.2	9.0	1.1	9.9	18	7	7	0.27	>0.05	1.11	<0.01	−0.66	<0.05
Perceptual Reasoning	87.4	16.1	98.6	7.7	−11.2	12.0	52	44	40	90.0	11.7	91.2	5.1	−1.2	10.3	25	18	5	−0.23	>0.05	1.45	<0.001	−0.97	<0.01
Working Memory	87.2	15.6	95.8	10.4	−8.6	10.1	52	46	44	85.9	11.3	88.1	6.7	−2.2	9.5	39	18	7	0.12	>0.05	1.16	<0.01	−0.68	<0.01
Processing Speed	77.0	17.1	97.6	7.1	−20.6	14.7	68	68	64	91.6	13.5	91.3	4.9	0.3	13.3	25	14	7	−1.08	<0.01	1.28	<0.01	−1.57	<0.001
General Ability	87.0	17.0	97.6	10.6	−10.6	10.2	40	32	20	86.7	11.8	87.9	7.3	−1.2	9.7	29	14	7	0.03	>0.05	1.34	<0.001	−0.98	<0.01
Cognitive Proficiency	79.5	16.4	96.1	10.5	−16.6	11.6	80	60	48	87.2	11.0	87.5	6.0	−0.3	10.4	29	21	11	−0.70	<0.05	1.43	<0.01	−1.57	<0.001
Full-Scale IQ	83.0	17.4	96.0	11.6	−13.0	10.6	76	48	44	85.7	10.6	87.4	7.6	−1.7	8.2	25	21	7	−0.26	>0.05	1.13	<0.05	−1.37	<0.001
Immediate Memory	78.6	20.8	98.7	6.8	−20.1	18.3	70	56	56	90.3	15.2	90.0	4.4	0.3	14.8	15	12	4	−0.77	<0.05	1.28	<0.001	−1.12	<0.001
Delayed Memory	75.3	23.6	98.5	6.5	−23.2	21.2	75	70	70	90.0	17.6	91.8	4.4	−0.8	17.4	26	18	12	−0.83	<0.01	1.05	<0.001	−1.05	<0.001

Note: $n = 30$ in each group.

Copyright © 2009 NCS Pearson, Inc. All rights reserved.

TABLE 10.17 Simple Demographics with Test of Premorbid Functioning Predicted Versus Actual WAIS–IV/WMS–IV Index Scores in Moderate to Severe TBI and Random High Education Sample

Score	Moderate-Severe TBI									High Education Sample									Between Group Differences						
	Actual Mean	Actual SD	Pred Mean	Pred SD	Diff	SD of Diff	Actual > Predicted 25th% Cut-off	Actual > Predicted 15th% Cut-off	Actual > Predicted 10th% Cut-off	Actual Mean	Actual SD	Pred Mean	Pred SD	Diff	SD of Diff	Actual > Predicted 25th% Cut-off	Actual > Predicted 15th% Cut-off	Actual > Predicted 10th% Cut-off	Actual ES d	p	Pred ES d	p	Diff ES d	p
Verbal Comprehension	89.7	16.7	95.2	11.9	−5.5	8.8	31	32	24	107.8	11.0	109.1	7.5	−1.4	7.7	29	14	11	−1.65	<0.001	−1.86	<0.001	−0.53	>0.05
Perceptual Reasoning	87.4	16.1	98.6	7.7	−11.2	12.0	52	44	40	105.9	13.6	106.5	5.6	−0.5	12.9	34	17	11	−1.37	<0.001	−1.41	<0.001	−0.83	<0.01
Working Memory	87.2	15.6	95.8	10.4	−8.6	10.1	52	46	44	105.0	12.9	106.9	6.4	−1.9	11.8	34	17	11	−1.38	<0.001	−1.73	<0.001	−0.57	<0.05
Processing Speed	77.0	17.1	97.6	7.1	−20.6	14.7	68	68	64	106.2	12.5	106.3	5.1	−0.1	12.0	23	11	6	−2.34	<0.001	−1.71	<0.001	−1.70	<0.001
General Ability	87.0	17.0	97.6	10.6	−10.6	10.2	40	32	20	107.8	11.7	108.4	7.6	−0.6	10.5	43	31	6	−1.77	<0.001	−1.42	<0.001	−0.95	<0.01
Cognitive Proficiency	79.5	16.4	96.1	10.5	−16.6	11.6	80	60	48	106.3	11.3	107.5	5.8	−1.1	10.8	49	20	8	−2.38	<0.001	−1.96	<0.001	−1.44	<0.001
Full-Scale IQ	83.0	17.4	96.0	11.6	−13.0	10.6	76	48	44	107.7	10.3	108.9	6.9	−1.1	8.8	31	14	6	−2.40	<0.001	−1.87	<0.001	−1.34	<0.001
Immediate Memory	78.6	20.8	98.7	6.8	−20.1	18.3	70	56	56	109.5	12.3	105.6	5.4	3.9	9.9	5	3	3	−2.52	<0.001	−1.01	<0.001	−1.31	<0.001
Delayed Memory	75.3	23.6	98.5	6.5	−23.2	21.2	75	70	70	109.8	14.4	105.9	5.3	3.9	12.5	18	9	6	−2.39	<0.001	−1.14	<0.01	−1.28	<0.001

Note: $n = 30$ in each group.

Copyright © 2009 NCS Pearson, Inc. All rights reserved.

sizes were observed for the Processing Speed, Cognitive Proficiency Index, Immediate Memory Index, and Delayed Memory Index. Applying the premorbid prediction model controls for the impact of background variables on test performance enabling more accurate identification of loss of functioning.

Oklahoma Premorbid Intelligence Estimate–IV (OPIE–IV)

Multiple OPIE–IV prediction equations were calculated for the moderate to severe TBI and control groups based on the equations presented in Chapter 5. The OPIE–IV provides information about the predicted score, significant difference between actual and predicted scores, base rates of differences, and a variety of other pieces of data. The information presented here focuses on the actual, predicted, and difference between actual and predicted scores for each group. OPIE–IV prediction data for the TBI and matched control groups are presented in Table 10.18.

The actual scores in the moderate to severe TBI group are significantly lower than the matched control group for VCI ($d = -0.42$, medium), PRI ($d = -0.75$, large), General Ability Index (GAI) ($d = -0.91$, large), and FSIQ ($d = -1.24$, very large). The predicted scores in the TBI group were consistently lower than the matched controls. All equations using Matrix Reasoning or a combination of Vocabulary and Matrix Reasoning were significantly lower in the TBI group versus matched controls indicating that Matrix Reasoning is affected by TBI. The equations using Vocabulary only were not significantly different from controls. This suggests that Vocabulary may be a good option for predicting premorbid functioning for this clinical group. The predicted scores are generally lower in the OPIE–IV model compared to the TOPF with the exception of some of the predictions using Vocabulary. The biggest difference is observed in the prediction of the PRI with the TOPF prediction of 98.6 and the OPIE–IV of 90.9.

The predicted versus actual difference was significantly different in the TBI versus matched control groups for all WAIS–IV indexes. These results suggest deficits in general cognitive functioning, including Verbal Comprehension and Perceptual Reasoning. The equations using Matrix Reasoning yielded lower effect sizes than the Vocabulary only equations. The OPIE–IV equations identify diminished cognitive functioning due to brain injury; although, not in specific cognitive domains such as memory.

OPIE–IV predicted WAIS–IV indexes in the moderate to severe TBI group and the low education group are presented in Table 10.19. The actual WAIS–IV index scores do not significantly differ between the

TABLE 10.18 Demographics with OPIE Predicted Versus Actual WAIS–IV Standard Index Scores in Moderate to Severe TBI and Matched Controls

Score	Predictor	Moderate-Severe TBI									Matched Control											Between Group Differences			
		Actual Mean	Actual SD	Pred Mean	Pred SD	Diff	SD of Diff	Actual > Predicted 25th% Cut-off	Actual > Predicted 15th% Cut-off	Actual > Predicted 10th% Cut-off	Actual Mean	Actual SD	Pred Mean	Pred SD	Diff	SD of Diff	Actual > Predicted 25th% Cut-off	Actual > Predicted 15th% Cut-off	Actual > Predicted 10th% Cut-off	Actual ES	p	Pred ES	p	Diff ES	p
Full Scale IQ	VC,MR,Age,Ed, Sex,Region, Eth	84.0	17.3	92.9	13.9	−8.9	7.7	62	59	53	100.8	13.5	100.3	11.6	0.4	6.7	17	11	6	−1.24	<0.05	−0.64	<0.05	−1.40	<0.001
Full Scale IQ	VC,Age,Ed, Sex,Eth	84.0	17.3	97.0	12.3	−13.0	9.5	75	59	47	100.8	13.5	100.8	10.2	−0.1	8.3	28	11	8	−1.24	<0.05	−0.38	>0.05	−1.56	<0.001
Full Scale IQ	MR,Age,Ed,Sex, Region	84.0	17.3	93.8	12.1	−9.8	10.3	66	56	53	100.8	13.5	100.1	11.4	0.7	9.3	25	14	8	−1.24	<0.05	−0.54	<0.05	−1.13	<0.001
General Ability Index	VC,MR,Age,Ed, Sex,Eth	87.6	16.4	92.8	14.6	−5.2	6.1	61	36	24	100.4	14.1	100.4	12.3	0.0	6.4	25	11	11	−0.91	<0.01	−0.62	<0.01	−0.81	<0.01
General Ability Index	VC,Age,Ed, Sex,Eth	87.6	16.4	96.9	12.6	−9.3	8.4	67	58	52	100.4	14.1	100.9	10.8	−0.5	8.9	33	19	14	−0.91	<0.01	−0.37	>0.05	−0.99	<0.001
General Ability Index	MR,Age,Ed,Sex, Region	87.6	16.4	93.6	12.7	−6.0	9.3	42	36	33	100.4	14.1	100.3	12.0	0.2	9.1	25	19	11	−0.91	<0.01	−0.55	<0.01	−0.68	<0.01
Verbal Comprehension Index	VC,Age,Ed, Sex,Eth	91.1	16.1	95.1	14.2	−4.1	5.4	54	46	36	99.2	12.4	99.9	11.4	−0.7	5.5	19	11	6	−0.66	<0.05	−0.42	>0.05	−0.62	<0.05
Perceptual Reasoning Index	MR, Age, Ed, Sex	86.6	15.9	90.9	13.6	−4.3	9.5	57	30	24	101.7	16.1	100.1	12.2	1.6	9.8	19	11	8	−0.94	<0.001	−0.75	<0.01	−0.60	<0.01

Note: $n = 33$.

Copyright © 2009 NCS Pearson, Inc. All rights reserved.

TABLE 10.19 Demographics with OPIE Predicted Versus Actual WAIS–IV Standard Index Scores in Moderate to Severe TBI and Random Low Education Group

Score	Predictor	Moderate-Severe TBI									Low Education Control									Between Group Differences					
		Actual Mean	Actual D	Pred Mean	Pred SD	Diff	SD of Diff	Actual > Predicted 25th% Cut-off	Actual > Predicted 15th% Cut-off	Actual > Predicted 10th% Cut-off	Actual Mean	Actual SD	Pred Mean	Pred SD	Diff	SD of Diff	Actual > Predicted 25th% Cut-off	Actual > Predicted 15th% Cut-off	Actual > Predicted 10th% Cut-off	Actual ES	p	Pred ES	p	Diff ES	p
Full Scale IQ	VC,MR,Age,Ed,Sex,Region, Eth	84.0	17.3	92.9	13.9	−8.9	7.7	62	59	53	84.4	11.7	85.8	12.0	−1.4	6.1	25	17	11	−0.03	>0.05	0.59	<0.05	−1.22	<0.001
Full Scale IQ	VC,Age,Ed,Sex,Eth	84.0	17.3	97.0	12.3	−13.0	9.5	75	59	47	84.4	11.7	86.7	9.2	−2.3	6.7	25	17	11	−0.03	>0.05	1.12	<0.05	−1.59	<0.001
Full Scale IQ	MR,Age,Ed,Sex,Region	84.0	17.3	93.8	12.1	−9.8	10.3	86	66	56	84.4	11.7	86.4	10.8	−2.0	8.6	36	19	11	−0.03	>0.05	0.69	<0.001	−0.91	<0.01
General Ability Index	VC,MR,Age,Ed, Sex,Eth	87.6	16.4	92.8	14.6	−5.2	6.1	61	36	24	85.4	12.1	86.4	12.3	−1.0	5.3	28	11	11	0.19	>0.05	0.52	<0.01	−0.78	<0.01
General Ability Index	VC,Age,Ed,Sex,Eth	87.6	16.4	96.9	12.6	−9.3	8.4	67	58	52	85.4	12.1	87.4	10.2	−2.1	6.4	39	19	11	0.19	>0.05	0.93	<0.01	−1.13	<0.001
General Ability Index	MR,Age,Ed,Sex,Region	87.6	16.4	93.6	12.7	−6.0	9.3	42	36	33	85.4	12.1	87.1	11.2	−1.8	8.3	33	19	14	0.19	>0.05	0.58	<0.05	−0.51	>0.05
Verbal Comprehension Index	VC,Age,Ed,Sex,Eth	91.1	16.1	95.1	14.2	−4.1	5.4	54	46	36	84.1	13.5	85.5	12.2	−1.4	6.3	33	22	14	0.52	>0.05	0.79	<0.01	−0.43	>0.05
Perceptual Reasoning Index	MR, Age, Ed, Sex	86.6	15.9	90.9	13.6	−4.3	9.5	57	30	24	89.6	11.7	89.8	12.1	−0.2	7.2	19	6	6	−0.25	>0.05	0.09	>0.05	−0.57	<0.05

Note: $n = 33$.

Copyright © 2009 NCS Pearson, Inc. All rights reserved.

TBI and low education control groups. All OPIE–IV predicted scores were significantly higher in the TBI group compared to the low education control group, except the PRI. The discrepancy between premorbid estimates and actual performance were significantly different in the TBI versus low education control groups for all equations except VCI and Matrix Reasoning predicted GAI. These results show that general cognitive difficulties associated with moderate to severe TBI can be differentiated from low ability using the OPIE–IV equations. The effect sizes are similar to those observed in the matched control group except for the non-significant findings.

OPIE–IV predicted WAIS–IV indexes in the TBI and high education control groups are presented in Table 10.20. The actual scores for the moderate to severe TBI group are well below those when compared to the high education control group. Similarly, predicted scores were substantially higher for the high education control group compared to the TBI group. Finally, the actual versus predicted score discrepancy was significantly different for all the OPIE–IV equations showing loss of functioning in the TBI group and not in the matched controls. The effect sizes are similar to those reported for the TBI versus matched control groups.

Like the TOPF, the OPIE–IV model is an effective method for identifying acquired cognitive deficits (i.e., lower actual scores compared to premorbid estimations). The premorbid model enables clinicians to differentiate low premorbid ability from acquired cognitive impairment. Additionally, the level of impairment is not overstated (i.e., compared to age adjusted actual scores) in high education populations. In the TBI group, equations using Vocabulary were most accurate in estimating premorbid ability.

SUBOPTIMAL EFFORT

It is standard practice to assess for suboptimal effort in patients undergoing evaluations following TBI. See Chapter 7 for a detailed description of the effort indices for WAIS–IV/WMS–IV/ACS. The ACS suboptimal effort indicators include embedded WAIS–IV (e.g., Reliable Digit Span) and WMS–IV measures (Logical Memory Delayed Recognition, Visual Reproduction Recognition, and Verbal Paired Associates Delayed Recognition) and a standalone measure of response bias (i.e., Word Choice). Healthy adults perform perfectly, near perfectly, or with a high level of accuracy on these measures. Not only do healthy adults complete these tests quite easily, patients with various degrees of cognitive impairment also perform well on these measures. Low scores can indicate cognitive problems; however, very

TABLE 10.20 Demographics with OPIE Predicted Versus Actual WAIS–IV Standard Index Scores in Moderate to Severe TBI and Random High Education Group

Score	Predictor	MS-TBI Actual Mean	Actual SD	Pred Mean	Pred SD	Diff	SD of Diff	Actual > Predicted 25th% Cut-off	Actual > Predicted 15th% Cut-off	Actual > Predicted 10th% Cut-off	HEC Actual Mean	Actual SD	Pred Mean	Pred SD	Diff	SD of Diff	Actual > Predicted 25th% Cut-off	Actual > Predicted 15th% Cut-off	Actual > Predicted 10th% Cut-off	Actual ES	p	Pred ES	d	p	Diff ES	d	p
Full Scale IQ	VC,MR,Age,Ed, Sex,Region, Eth	84.0	17.3	92.9	13.9	−8.9	7.7	62	59	53	108.3	10.3	109.1	8.8	−0.8	6.4	24	14	11	−2.36	<0.001	−1.84		<0.001	−1.27		<0.001
Full Scale IQ	VC,Age,Ed ,Sex,Eth	84.0	17.3	97.0	12.3	−13.0	9.5	75	59	47	108.3	10.3	109.1	8.1	−0.9	8.3	24	14	11	−2.36	<0.001	−1.50		<0.001	−1.47		<0.001
Full Scale IQ	MR,Age,Ed, Sex,Region	84.0	17.3	93.8	12.1	−9.8	10.3	66	56	53	108.3	10.3	109.1	7.6	−0.4	9.1	30	19	11	−2.36	<0.001	−2.01		<0.001	−1.04		<0.001
General Ability Index	VC,MR,Age,Ed, Sex,Eth	84.7	17.5	92.1	14.0	−7.4	10.2	61	36	36	108.8	12.2	108.8	9.4	0.1	5.5	24	16	11	−1.98	<0.001	−1.78		<0.001	−1.36		<0.01
General Ability Index	VC,Age,Ed, Sex,Eth	84.7	17.5	92.1	14.0	−7.4	10.2	67	58	52	108.8	12.2	107.0	9.4	1.8	8.0	22	11	3	−1.98	<0.001	−1.59	3	<0.01	−1.15		<0.001
General Ability Index	MR,Age,Ed,Sex, Region	84.7	17.5	94.5	14.3	−9.8	7.8	42	36	33	108.8	12.2	108.3	7.9	0.5	9.9	27	14	11	−1.98	<0.001	−1.75		<0.001	−1.05		<0.001
Verbal Comprehension Index	VC,Age,Ed, Sex,Eth	91.1	16.1	95.1	14.2	−4.1	5.4	54	46	36	109.1	12.1	108.3	9.8	0.8	4.8	11	0	0	−1.49	<0.001	−1.35		<0.001	−1.02		<0.001
Perceptual Reasoning Index	MR, Age, Ed, Sex	86.6	15.9	90.9	13.6	−4.3	9.5	57	30	24	106.5	13.4	106.1	9.1	0.4	8.6	24	16	8	−1.48	<0.001	−1.67		<0.001	−1.36		<0.01

Note: $n = 33$.

Copyright © 2009 NCS Pearson, Inc. All rights reserved.

low scores are atypical even for individuals with significant cognitive deficits. Specific cut-off scores are presented in the ACS manual.

Base rates of low scores (e.g., a score that is below the cut-off of the entire clinical sample at 25%, 15%, 10%, 5%, and 2% base rate) for the total ACS suboptimal effort clinical sample, moderate to severe TBI group, matched controls, low education controls, high education controls, and the entire WMS−IV standardization sample are presented in Table 10.21. When the 25th percentile cut-off in the clinical sample is applied, 48% of the TBI group and 68% of the low education group have one score at or below the cut-score, and 18% and 22% of have two scores that meet this criteria, respectively. Having three scores that meet the 25th percentile criterion is unusual in all of the samples (i.e., 3% and 11%, respectively). As such, using the 25th percentile cut-off score will produce high rates of false positives unless three or more low scores are required to classify suboptimal effort.

Applying the 15th percentile criterion, 36% of the TBI group and 43% of the low education group have at least one score at this cut-off. When a criterion of two scores at the 15th percentile cut-off is applied, only 9% of the TBI and 11% of the low education groups are classified as providing possible suboptimal effort. The false positive rate of 10% in the clinical sample is acceptable; however, clinicians must keep in mind that there will be some cases in which a patient may be incorrectly classified as providing suboptimal effort. The results for the 10th percentile cut-off are very similar to those reported for the 15% cut-off; although, fewer of the TBI group and low education control group are misidentified.

The most restrictive criteria are the 5th percentile and second percentile clinical cut-offs. In the low education control sample, 19% had one score at the 5th percentile and 11% had one score at the second percentile cut-off; however, the TBI group had substantially fewer cases having one score at these low cut-scores (9% and 6%, respectively). Having two scores at the 5th percentile or second percentile cut-score is very rare in matched controls, low education controls, the overall clinical group, and the TBI group. Any evaluation yielding multiple scores at this level needs to be carefully evaluated for possible response bias. The majority of TBI patients will not have any scores at 2−15% cut-off scores.

SOCIAL COGNITION

A subset of the moderate to severe TBI group was also administered the ACS Social Perception test (see Chapter 8 for a complete discussion of the Social Cognition tests). None of the patients were administered

TABLE 10.21   Base rates of low WAIS–IV/WMS–IV/ACS Effort Indicators in those with TBI Compared to the Overall Clinical Sample and the Normative Sample

Group of Interest	Percentages with Matching Number of Cut Scores at Cut-off				
	1	2	3	4	5
Number of Scores at 2% Cut-off					
Overall Clinical Sample	4	0	0	0	0
Traumatic Brain Injury	6	0	0	0	0
Matched Controls	3	0	0	0	0
Low Education Sample	11	3	3	3	0
High Education Sample	3	0	0	0	0
WMS–IV Normative Sample	1	0	0	0	0
Number of Scores at 5% Cut-off					
Overall Clinical Sample	9	2	0	0	0
Traumatic Brain Injury	9	3	0	0	0
Matched Controls	6	0	0	0	0
Low Education Sample	19	3	3	3	0
High Education Sample	3	0	0	0	0
WMS–IV Normative Sample	2	0	0	0	0
Number of Scores at 10% Cut-off					
Overall Clinical Sample	19	5	1	0	0
Traumatic Brain Injury	30	6	0	0	0
Matched Controls	16	3	0	0	0
Low Education Sample	27	3	3	3	0
High Education Sample	11	0	0	0	0
WMS–IV Normative Sample	7	1	0	0	0
Number of Scores at 15% Cut-off					
Overall Clinical Sample	22	7	2	0	0
Traumatic Brain Injury	36	9	0	0	0
Matched Controls	26	6	6	0	0
Low Education Sample	43	11	5	5	3
High Education Sample	11	0	0	0	0
WMS–IV Normative Sample	11	1	0	0	0

(Continued)

TABLE 10.21 (Continued)

Group of Interest	Percentages with Matching Number of Cut Scores at Cut-off				
	1	2	3	4	5
Number of Scores at 25% Cut-off					
Overall Clinical Sample	38	19	6	3	1
Traumatic Brain Injury	48	18	3	0	0
Matched Controls	30	6	6	3	3
Low Education Sample	68	22	11	8	3
High Education Sample	27	11	0	0	0
WMS–IV Normative Sample	23	7	2	0	0

Copyright 2009 Pearson, Inc. Reproduced with Permission, All rights reserved.

the Face Memory or Memory for Names tests, so those will not be discussed here. ACS Social Perception scores in the moderate to severe TBI group and matched controls are presented in Table 10.22. The WAIS–IV Comprehension subtest is included in these analyses because it is sometimes considered a measure of social cognition. In addition to the core Social Perception scores, the WAIS–IV GAI, VCI, and PRI versus Social Perception Total score contrast scaled scores are also presented. The contrast scores identify deficits in Social Perception after controlling for the effects of general suppression of cognitive abilities.

There were significantly lower ACS Social Perception scores in the TBI group compared to matched controls. In particular, the largest effect size was found for the Social Perception Total score. In the TBI group, 92% had a scaled score of eight or less, and 79% had a scaled score of seven or less compared to 27% and 15% of controls. The level of performance was consistent across the Social Perception measures indicating difficulty with basic labeling of facial expressions of emotion, identifying emotion from tone of voice and matching it to facial expressions, and utilizing multiple social cues including linguistic, body language, prosody, and facial expressions to interpret interactions between two people. The Prosody score also had a very large effect size indicating significant difficulties matching auditory and facial emotional cues.

The Comprehension subtest was significantly lower in the moderate to severe TBI group; however, the effect size was notably smaller than those observed for the Social Perception measures (albeit a large effect size). The Comprehension subtests is a complex verbal task requiring longer more elaborated response compared to the other WAIS–IV

TABLE 10.22 ACS Social Perception in Moderate to Severe TBI and Matched Controls

Score	Moderate to Severe TBI					Matched Control					Between Group Differences	
	Mean	SD	At or Below 25th %ile	At or Below 16th %ile	At or Below 9th %ile	Mean	SD	At or Below 25th %ile	At or Below 16th %ile	At or Below 9th %ile	ES	p
Social Perception Total	5.0	2.9	92	79	54	9.8	2.3	27	15	4	−2.07	<0.001
Affect Naming	5.5	3.1	79	75	58	9.7	2.4	35	19	12	−1.73	<0.001
Prosody	6.0	2.9	75	71	50	10.3	2.3	27	27	8	−1.90	<0.001
Pairs	5.8	3.4	83	78	65	10.8	3.4	28	16	12	−1.49	<0.001
GAI vs. Social Perception Contrast Score	6.5	2.5	81	71	43	10.1	2.4	23	12	4	−1.48	<0.001
VCI vs. Social Perception Contrast Score	6.0	2.9	86	81	48	10.0	2.6	27	15	4	−1.58	<0.001
PRI vs. Social Perception Contrast Score	6.2	2.8	88	75	46	10.2	2.7	23	8	4	−1.50	<0.001
Comprehension	7.7	2.5	74	44	35	10.3	3.0	27	15	12	−0.88	<0.01

Note: $n = 24$.
Copyright 2009 Pearson, Inc. Reproduced with Permission, All rights reserved.

verbal subtests and also requires some degree of cognitive flexibility (e.g., providing multiple, different responses to a single question). Its sensitivity to TBI may be related to these factors more than due to deficits in social reasoning.

The WAIS–IV GAI, VCI, and PRI versus Social Perception Total score were all significantly lower in the TBI group compared to the controls. These results indicate that social perception deficits are present beyond deficits in general cognitive functioning. Importantly, the WAIS–IV PRI versus Social Perception total score was significant and had a very large effect size of $d = -1.50$. Of the three WAIS–IV indexes used in the contrast scores, the PRI index is the most affected by brain injury. Therefore, it appears as if the difficulties with identifying facial expressions cannot be attributed to general problems in visual–perceptual abilities. Social Perception deficits, at least in this sample, appear to be a specific domain of cognitive impairment in moderate to severe TBI. Of all the tests administered of the WAIS–IV/WMS–IV/ACS, the lowest achieved score in TBI is the Social Perception total score (e.g., Verbal Paired Associates Delayed Free Recall is very close at a scaled score of 5.1) indicating that this cognitive domain is important in the assessment of the impact of moderate to severe TBI.

CASE STUDIES

Case Study 1

Mr. I. is a 20-year-old, Native-American man, who sustained a moderate TBI six months ago. He is currently enrolled in a local university, and he completed one full year prior to his injury. He skipped the Fall semester while recovering from his injury. He returned to school for the Spring semester, but he started having trouble completing his coursework and finishing his exams on time. He started the Spring semester with a 3.1 grade point average and he had previously been successful in all his courses. He is currently failing two courses and has low grades in two others. He has already dropped one class and is considering dropping out of school altogether. He was referred by the student educational resource center to the University affiliated medical school for evaluation of his cognitive functioning. The evaluation will help determine if accommodations can be made for completing tests and coursework.

The WAIS–IV/WMS–IV/ACS was administered as part of the evaluation. The results of the evaluation are presented in Table 10.23. Mr. I. has high average VCI and auditory WMI and average visual–perceptual skills (PRI). His PSI was unusually low. On the WMS–IV, his index

TABLE 10.23   WAIS−IV/WMS−IV/ACS Results for Mr. I.

WAIS−IV Index	Index/ Scaled Score	%ile	WMS−IV Index	Index/ Scaled Score	%ile
WAIS−IV Scores			**WMS−IV Scores**		
Verbal Comprehension	112	79	Auditory Memory	91	27
Perceptual Reasoning	96	39	Visual Memory	95	37
Working Memory Index	111	77	Visual Working Memory	91	27
Processing Speed	74	4	Immediate Memory	93	32
Full Scale IQ	99	47	Delayed Memory	90	25
WAIS−IV Subtests			**WMS−IV Subtest**		
Similarities	13	84	Logical Memory I	11	63
Vocabulary	11	63	Logical Memory II	9	37
Information	13	84	Logical Memory II Recognition	26	51−75
Block Design	7	16	Verbal Paired Associates I	6	9
Matrix Reasoning	13	84	Verbal Paired Associates II	7	16
Visual Puzzles	8	25	Verbal Paired Associates II Recognition	40	>75
Digit Span	10	50	Verbal Paired Associates Delayed Free Recall	5	5
Arithmetic	14	91	Designs I	9	37
Symbol Search	5	5	Designs II	8	25
Coding	5	5	Designs II Recognition	14	17−25
ACS Social Perception			Visual Reproduction I	10	50
Total	7	16	Visual Reproduction II	9	37
Affect Naming	7	16	Visual Reproduction II Recognition	6	26−50
Prosody	8	25	Spatial Addition	10	50
Pairs	6	9	Symbol Span	7	16
ACS TOPF plus Simple Demographics Scores					
TOPF	101	53	Predicted PSI	104	61
Predicted TOPF	102	55	Predicted FSIQ	105	63
Predicted VCI	105	63	Predicted IMI	102	52
Predicted PRI	105	63	Predicted DMI	101	53
Predicted WMI	105	63	Predicted VWMI	104	61

scores were all in the average range. His subtest scores ranged from unusually low to average.

The number of obtained low scores can be calculated by counting the number of index and subtests at or below the 25th% (index ≤90, SS < 8), 16th% (index ≤85, SS ≤7), 9th% (index ≤80, SS ≤6), 5th% (index ≤76, SS < 5), and 2nd% (index ≤70, SS ≤ 4). Mr. I. had three index scores at or below the 25th% cut-off; one score at or below the 16th%, 9th%, and 5th% cut-off; and no scores below the 2nd% cut-off. Chapter 2 provides tables to identify the base rates of low scores stratified by TOPF scores. Mr. I. has a TOPF predicted FSIQ score of 105 (i.e., simple demographics). Multivariate base rate analysis of Mr. I.'s WAIS–IV/WMS–IV index scores found two index scores ≤25th%, 1 score ≤16th%, 1 score ≤9th%, and one score ≤5th% cut-offs. The base rates of the number of low index scores that he obtained are 43.0%, 44.3%, 26.7%, 15.4% for the 25th%, 16th%, 9th%, and 5th% cut-offs for combined WAIS–IV/WMS–IV indexes (see Table A2.1). At the index level, most of the multivariate base rate data indicates that this is not an unusual cognitive profile, but having one score at or below the 5th percentile is unusual (i.e., base rate = 15.4%). At the subtest level, the number of obtained low scores are 8 (25th%), 6 (16th%), 3 (9th%), 2 (5th%) and 0 (2%). The multivariate base rates for these cut-offs are 28.0%, 22.5%, 28.8%, 21.1%, and 78.7% for his TOPF predicted FSIQ level (see Table A2.2). The multivariate base rates for the subtests are not unusual, indicating that the subtest profile does not have an atypical number of low scores. Considering the 10 primary subtest scores from the WMS–IV, he had three scores at or below the 16th percentile. This is common in healthy adults with TOPF-predicted average intelligence (base rate = 33.4%; see Table A2.18). Table A2.23 can be used in this case to examine how uncommon it is to obtain two processing speed scores ≤5th percentile. When considering three scores simultaneously, obtaining two scores ≤5th percentile is rare, occurring in only 1.9% of adults with TOPF estimated average intelligence. Of course, this base rate is not accurate for him because the Cancellation test was not given. However, it does give the clinician general information that having two very low scores in this domain is rare.

Chapter 3 provided tools for evaluating profile variability. The highest obtained index scores across both the WAIS–IV and WMS–IV was 112 (VCI). This highest score is in the average range (SS = 9). The lowest obtained index score of 74 is low average (SS = 7). These scores indicate that Mr. I. has cognitive abilities that are within the expected range, and that the overall profile is not suppressed. His lowest score is lower than expected but not very atypical. The highest versus lowest score of 38 points is in the low average range (SS = 7) indicating that at the extremes of cognitive performance there is more variability than is expected.

The general profile variability (index standard deviation = 10.91) was in the average range (SS = 8) indicating that cognitive skills are generally consistent with one another (compared to the normative sample). At the subtest level, the highest obtained subtest score of 14 is average (SS = 9) and the lowest score of 5 is also average (SS = 9). This indicates that the profile is not suppressed and that Mr. I. shows a normal range of strengths and weaknesses. The highest versus lowest score of 9 is average (SS = 9) and the standard deviation of subtest scores of 2.68 is also average. Mr. I. has a typical degree of cognitive variability among the subtests.

Chapter 5 discussed the estimation of premorbid cognitive functioning. Table 10.23 presents predicted scores using the TOPF and simple demographics method. The actual TOPF reading score was 101 and the predicted TOPF reading score was 102 indicating that the TOPF does not appear to have been affected by the brain injury. The VCI and WMI scores are higher than the predicted scores. All of the other index scores are significantly lower (p <0.05) than the predicted scores. While all these index scores are significantly lower than predicted, only the 30 point difference between actual and predicted PSI is unusual (base rate = 1%). All the other base rates range from 18% to 27.4%.

Chapter 7 reviewed the concept of suboptimal effort. Mr. I. achieved a score of 50 on the Word Choice subtest and the Reliable Digit Span score was 10. Table 10.23 provides data for the other embedded measures: Logical Memory II Recognition = 26, Verbal Paired Associated II Recognition = 40, and Visual Reproduction II Recognition = 6. None of these scores are flagged as unusually low compared at the 10% cut-off. These results indicate that there are no identifiable performance validity issues.

Chapter 8 presented information about the assessment of social cognition. The ACS Social Perception test was administered as part of this assessment. In the context of general verbal and visual–perceptual skills, the VCI versus Social Perception Total score (SS = 6), PRI versus Social Perception Test (SS = 7), and GAI versus Social Perception Total score (SS = 7) are below expected. Mr. I. may have difficulty reading social situations accurately.

The overall clinical profile indicates lower than expected processing speed. Additionally, social perception skills were a relative weakness compared to his intellectual abilities (VCI and PRI). Memory skills were not unusually low in the context of the whole cognitive profile; however, he does have some difficulties with verbal learning skills. The results are consistent with a mild degree of cognitive impairment. Based on the results of the evaluation, Mr. I. received additional time for testing and help with homework assignments. He also decided to reduce his course load to three classes and he is receiving counselling services to improve his social skills.

Case Study 2

Mr. Z. is a 22-year-old, white man, with an Associate's degree in Radiological Technology who sustained a severe TBI 18 months ago. Prior to his injury, he was employed full-time as a radiological technician with a local imaging center. Mr. Z. has been unable to return to work following his injury and he is being evaluated for a long-term disability claim.

The WAIS–IV/WMS–IV/ACS was administered as part of the evaluation. The results of the evaluation are presented in Table 10.24. Mr. Z. has unusually low-to-low average intellectual abilities. His WAIS–IV subtest scores range from extremely low to average. His WMS–IV index scores ranged from extremely low-to-low average. The WMS–IV subtest scores are in the extremely low-to-average range.

Multivariate base rate analysis of Mr. Z.'s WAIS–IV/WMS–IV index scores found 10 index scores $\leq$25th%, 7 scores $\leq$16th%, 5 $\leq$9th%, 5 $\leq$5th%, and 3 $\leq$2nd% cut-offs. Mr. Z. has a TOPF with simple demographics predicted FSIQ score of 95. The base rates of the low index scores in people with estimated average intelligence are 0.4%, 3.8%, 2.9%, 1.3%, and 1.5% for the 25th%, 16th%, 9th%, 5th%, and 2nd% cut-offs (see Table A2.1). At the index level, the multivariate base rate data indicates an atypical cognitive profile marked by significant cognitive deficits. At the subtest level, the number of obtained low scores are 18 (25th%), 12 (16th%), 10 (9th%), 7 (5th%) and 4 (2nd%). The multivariate base rates for these cut-offs are 1.0%, 4.0%, 2.1%, 2.3%, and 1.9% for people of TOPF estimated average intelligence (see Table A2.2). The multivariate base rates for the subtests are very unusual indicating that the subtest profile had a greater than expected number of low scores consistent with general cognitive impairment.

The highest obtained index scores across both the WAIS–IV and WMS–IV was 89 (VCI, WMI) which is uncommon in healthy adults (SS = 4). The lowest obtained index score of 67 is also uncommon (SS = 5). At the subtest level, the highest obtained subtest score of 11 is uncommon (SS = 6) and the lowest score of 3 is extremely uncommon (SS = 3). These scores indicate that this is a suppressed cognitive profile that does not show a normal level of cognitive strengths, and his cognitive weaknesses are well below expected levels.

Table 10.24 presents predicted scores using the TOPF and simple demographics method. The actual TOPF score was 85 and this is significantly lower than the predicted TOPF of 99. The degree of difference is

TABLE 10.24   WAIS–IV/WMS–IV/ACS Results for Mr. Z.

WAIS–IV Scores			WMS–IV Scores		
WAIS–IV Index	**Index/Scaled Score**	**%ile**	**WMS–IV Index**	**Index/Scaled Score**	**%ile**
Verbal Comprehension	89	23	Auditory Memory	67	1
Perceptual Reasoning	88	21	Visual Memory	81	10
Working Memory Index	89	23	Visual Working Memory	70	2
Processing Speed	76	5	Immediate Memory	69	2
Full-Scale IQ	82	12	Delayed Memory	72	3
WAIS–IV Subtests			**WMS–IV Subtest**		
Similarities	9	37	Logical Memory I	4	2
Vocabulary	7	16	Logical Memory II	5	5
Information	8	25	Logical Memory II Recognition	21	10–16
Block Design	6	9	Verbal Paired Associates I	4	2
Matrix Reasoning	11	63	Verbal Paired Associates II	5	5
Visual Puzzles	7	16	Verbal Paired Associates II Recognition	36	3–9
Digit Span	8	25	Verbal Paired Associates Delayed Free Recall	1	<1
Arithmetic	8	25	Designs I	8	25
Symbol Search	8	25	Designs II	8	25
Coding	3	1	Designs II Recognition	13	10–16
ACS Social Perception			Visual Reproduction I	5	5
Total	6	9	Visual Reproduction II	6	9
Affect Naming	7	16	Visual Reproduction II Recognition	5	17–25
Prosody	6	9	Spatial Addition	4	2
Pairs	2	<1	Symbol Span	6	9
			ACS TOPF Scores		
TOPF	85	16	Predicted PSI	96	39
Predicted TOPF	99	47	Predicted FSIQ	95	37
Predicted VCI	94	34	Predicted IMI	94	34
Predicted PRI	97	42	Predicted DMI	97	42
Predicted WMI	94	34	Predicted VWMI	97	42

unusual (base rate 2%). Therefore, the clinician should be cautious in using the TOPF as an estimate of premorbid ability because the reading score might have been lowered by his TBI. The VCI and WMI scores are not significantly different from the predicted scores. All of the other index scores are significantly lower ($p < 0.05$) than the predicted scores. The PRI actual versus predicted scores are significant but not unusual (base rate = 23.9%). For all other indexes, the discrepancy between the actual and predicted score is atypical with base rates ranging from 1.8% (VWMI) to 8.9% (FSIQ). These results indicate global intellectual and memory impairment with less effect on verbal intelligence and auditory working memory abilities. Given the unexpectedly low TOPF scores, verbal intellectual and working memory functioning were also likely affected by the injury.

Mr. Z. achieved a score of 49 on the Word Choice subtest and his Reliable Digit Span score was 9. Table 10.24 provides data for the other embedded measures: Logical Memory II Recognition = 21, Verbal Paired Associated II Recognition = 36, and Visual Reproduction II Recognition = 5. None of these scores is flagged as unusually low compared at the 10% cut-off. These results indicate that there are no identifiable performance validity issues.

The ACS Social Perception test was administered as part of this assessment. Compared to his intellectual abilities, the VCI versus Social Perception Total score (SS = 6), PRI versus Social Perception Test (SS = 7), and GAI versus Social Perception Total score (SS = 7) are below expected. Mr. Z. may have difficulty reading social situations accurately.

The results of the assessment indicate a general suppression of cognitive abilities. Mr. Z. shows a greater than expected number of low scores given his estimated premorbid ability, which is consistent with impairment in multiple cognitive domains. He also had multiple areas of cognition that were well below premorbid estimation of ability indicating significant difficulties with general cognitive functioning, processing speed, memory, and visual-working memory. Performance validity indicators were all within expected limits. Mr. Z. has moderate cognitive impairment associated with a severe TBI. Mr. Z. received long-term disability payments and continued to participate in rehabilitation and vocational training programs.

Case Study 3

Mr. S. is a 36-year-old white man with a university education who sustained a moderate TBI as a result of a fall from his roof (while cleaning the gutters). He was administered the WAIS–IV/WMS–IV/ACS approximately 8 months post injury. His age-adjusted and demographics-adjusted normative scores are presented in Table 10.25. Notice that his age-adjusted scores yield higher percentile ranks. This is because the age norms do not take into account his education. Compared to men his age, his VCI was superior, PRI was average, WMI was low average, and PSI was average. Compared to highly educated men his age, his VCI was average, his PRI and PSI were low average and his WMI was unusually low (4th percentile). A similar pattern can be seen on the subtest scores and on the WMS–IV scores. If a low score was defined as a T-score less than 40, he obtained low scores on Visual Puzzles (12th percentile), Digit Span (14th percentile), Arithmetic (1st percentile), Letter Number Sequencing (14th percentile), Coding (6th percentile), Symbol Span (14th percentile), and Verbal Paired Associates I (10th percentile).

The demographic norms printout from ACS provides comparisons between index scores. His Perceptual Reasoning Index was significantly lower (16 T points; directional base rate = 6.6%) than his VCI. His Working Memory Index (24 T points; directional base rate = 0.8%) and Processing Speed Index (13 T points; directional base rate = 13.9%) were also significantly lower than his VCI. His WMS–IV Auditory Memory Index was also significantly lower than his VCI (13 T points; directional base rate = 13.4%). On the WMS–IV, his Delayed Memory Index was significantly lower than his Immediate Memory Index (7 T points; directional base rate = 12.3%). These discrepancies are uncommon in healthy adults (as illustrated by the directional base rates).

He did not perform particularly well on the TOPF reading test (SS = 102, predicted reading score based on demographics = 111) for someone with a university degree. This could be longstanding, or his performance could have been attenuated by his TBI. Using the TOPF reading score combined with simple demographics method for estimating his pre-injury intellectual abilities, his VCI was significantly higher than predicted (12 points; BR = 8.2%) and his PRI (− 9 points; BR = 23.9%), WMI (− 17 points; BR = 5.5%), and WMS–IV Delayed Memory Index (− 12 points; BR = 20.7%) were all lower than predicted.

One interpretation of these results is that his VCI is simply a longstanding relative strength for him and the large uncommon discrepancies, therefore, are also longstanding. Given that: (a) he sustained a moderate TBI approximately eight months ago, (b) he and his wife have noticed that he has ongoing attention and short-term memory problems, (c) all five of his ACS effort indicators were normal (i.e., greater than the 25th percentile), and (d) he has low demographically adjusted subtest scores on multiple tests known to be affected by TBI, it is reasonable to assume that he has residual cognitive deficits from his TBI.

TABLE 10.25 WAIS–IV/WMS–IV scores for Mr. S.

WAIS–IV Indexes	Age-Adjusted			Demographic-Adjusted		
	Score	PR	Classification	Score	PR	Classification
Verbal Comprehension Index	120	91	Superior	56	73	Average
Perceptual Reasoning Index	98	45	Average	40	16	Low Average
Working Memory Index	89	23	Low Average	32	4	Unusually Low
Processing Speed Index	97	42	Average	43	24	Low Average
General Ability Index	110	75	High Average	48	42	Average
Full Scale IQ	103	58	Average	41	18	Low Average
Subtest Scores						
Vocabulary	14	91	Superior	57	76	High Average
Information	12	75	Average	47	38	Average
Similarities	15	95	Superior	62	89	High Average
Block Design	11	63	Average	45	31	Average
Visual Puzzles	8	25	Average	38	12	Low Average
Matrix Reasoning	10	50	Average	43	24	Low Average
Digit Span	9	37	Average	39	14	Low Average
Arithmetic	7	16	Low Average	28	1	Extremely Low
Letter Number Sequencing	9	37	Average	39	14	Low Average
Coding	7	16	Low Average	34	6	Unusually Low
Symbol Search	12	75	Average	53	62	Average
Cancellation	11	63	Average	52	58	Average
WMS–IV Indexes						
Auditory Memory Index	95	37	Average	43	24	Low Average
Visual Memory Index	96	39	Average	43	24	Low Average
Immediate Memory Index	102	55	Average	46	35	Average
Delayed Memory Index	90	25	Average	39	14	Low Average
Visual Working Memory Index	97	42	Average	42	21	Low Average
WMS–IV Subtests						
Spatial Addition	11	63	Average	47	38	Average
Symbol Span	8	25	Average	39	14	Low Average

(Continued)

TABLE 10.25   (Continued)

WAIS−IV Indexes	Age-Adjusted			Demographic-Adjusted		
	Score	PR	Classification	Score	PR	Classification
Logical Memory I	12	75	Average	54	66	Average
Logical Memory II	9	37	Average	44	27	Average
Verbal Paired Associates I	7	16	Low Average	37	10	Low Average
Verbal Paired Associates II	9	37	Average	44	27	Average
Verbal Paired Associates Word Recall	8	25	Average	—	—	—
Visual Reproduction I	10	50	Average	44	27	Average
Visual Reproduction II	6	9	Unusually Low	33	5	Unusually Low
Designs I	12	75	Average	54	66	Average
Designs-II	10	50	Average	48	42	Average

CONCLUSIONS

Moderate to severe TBI is associated with impairments in multiple cognitive domains. Patients with moderate to severe TBI performed worse than matched controls on most WAIS−IV and WMS−IV indexes and subtests. The most notable cognitive deficits in the TBI sample related to verbal learning, auditory mental manipulation, processing speed, and memory for visual details. The ACS Social Perception test also yielded very large effect sizes and was one of the lowest scores across all the tests administered. Patients with moderate to severe TBI had difficulties with identifying emotions from facial expression and tone of voice, and determining the nature of an interaction from social and linguistic cues.

The moderate to severe TBI group had a significantly greater number of low scores compared to matched controls. On variability measures, the TBI group had a generally suppressed cognitive profile. Contrary to clinical lore, increased variability in performance across the battery of tests was not common in patients with TBI. Both the TOPF and OPIE−IV effectively identified a decline in cognitive functioning from estimated premorbid levels; however, the OPIE−IV equations using Matrix Reasoning tended to yield lower estimates of premorbid functioning. The measures used to identify suboptimal effort are appropriate for use in those with TBI; they yielded small presumed false positive rates in the present sample.

KEY LEARNING

- Patients who have sustained a TBI can experience a range of cognitive outcomes from very mild decrements to severe cognitive impairment.
- The WAIS–IV is sensitive to the cognitive effects of moderate to severe TBI, particularly processing speed and auditory working memory.
- The WMS–IV is sensitive to memory impairments associated with moderate to severe TBI, particularly verbal learning and memory for visual details.
- Patients with TBI show a greater number of low WAIS–IV/ WMS–IV index and subtest scores compared to matched controls.
- Variability measures indicate that patients who have sustained a moderate to severe TBI have a suppressed cognitive profile that makes it difficult to identify significant cognitive variability. Variability in cognition does not appear to be a reliable diagnostic marker for cognitive impairment associated with TBI.
- Using demographic norms enables the examiner to identify cognitive deficits while controlling for the effects of background variables on test performance (such as high or low education).
- The TOPF is mildly affected by moderate to severe TBI which results in lower predicted premorbid scores for VCI and WMI, but not other WAIS–IV/WMS–IV indexes. The TOPF prediction equations are helpful for identifying decline in cognitive functioning associated with moderate to severe TBI.
- The OPIE–IV premorbid predictions equations are mildly to moderately impacted by TBI. Equations using Matrix Reasoning consistently underestimated premorbid ability in the present sample. Equations using Vocabulary yielded premorbid estimates similar to the TOPF and not significantly lower than matched controls. Additional research will help clarify the usefulness of the OPIE–IV in TBI.
- In a sample of moderate to severe TBI patients without external incentive for impairment, performance validity indicators identified only a small number of cases as having lower than expected scores in the range of possible suboptimal effort. The ACS effort indicators are useful for identifying possible suboptimal effort.
- The ACS Social Perception test is very sensitive to the effects of moderate to severe TBI. This subtest yielded one of the largest effect sizes between the TBI and control groups, and the lowest subtest level performance of any measure across the WAIS–IV/WMS–IV. The TBI group performed poorly on tasks of identifying emotion

from facial expressions, linking prosody to facial expression, and using multiple sources of social and linguistic information to interpret an interaction between people.

References

Anderson, C. V., & Bigler, E. D. (1995). Ventricular dilation, cortical atrophy, and neuropsychological outcome following traumatic brain injury. *Journal of Neuropsychiatry and Clinical Neurosciences, 7*(1), 42–48.

Ashman, T. A., Spielman, L. A., Hibbard, M. R., Silver, J. M., Chandna, T., & Gordon, W. A. (2004). Psychiatric challenges in the first six years after traumatic brain injury: cross-sequential analyses of Axis I disorders. *Archives of Physical Medicine and Rehabilitation, 85*(4 Suppl 2), S36–42.

Axelrod, B. N., Fichtenberg, N. L., Liethen, P. C., Czarnota, M. A., & Stucky, K. (2001). Performance characteristics of postacute traumatic brain injury patients on the WAIS–III and WMS–III. *The Clinical Neuropsychologist, 15*(4), 516–520.

Bigler, E. D., Kurth, S. M., Blatter, D., & Abildskov, T. J. (1992). Degenerative changes in traumatic brain injury: post-injury magnetic resonance identified ventricular expansion compared to pre-injury levels. *Brain Research Bulletin, 28*(4), 651–653.

Brooks, B. L., Holdnack, J. A., & Iverson, G. L. (2011). Advanced clinical interpretation of the WAIS–IV and WMS–IV: prevalence of low scores varies by level of intelligence and years of education. *Assessment, 18*(2), 156–167.

Bushnik, T., Englander, J., & Wright, J. (2008). The experience of fatigue in the first two years after moderate-to-severe traumatic brain injury: a preliminary report. *Journal of Head Trauma Rehabilitation, 23*(1), 17–24.

Clement, P. F., & Kennedy, J. E. (2003). Wechsler Adult Intelligence Scale-Third edition characteristics of a military traumatic brain injury sample. *Military Medicine, 168*(12), 1025–1028.

Curtis, K. L., Greve, K. W., & Bianchini, K. J. (2009). The Wechsler Adult Intelligence Scale–III and malingering in traumatic brain injury: classification accuracy in known groups. *Assessment, 16*(4), 401–414.

Dikmen, S., Bombardier, C. H., Machamer, J. E., Fann, J. R., & Temkin, N. R. (2004). Natural history of depression in traumatic brain injury. *Archives of Physical Medicine and Rehabilitation, 85*(9), 1457–1464.

Dikmen, S., Machamer, J., & Temkin, N. (2001). Mild head injury: facts and artifacts. *Journal of Clinical and Experimental Neuropsychology, 23*(6), 729–738.

Dikmen, S., Machamer, J. E., Powell, J. M., & Temkin, N. R. (2003). Outcome three to five years after moderate to severe traumatic brain injury. *Archives of Physical Medicine and Rehabilitation, 84*(10), 1449–1457.

Dikmen, S., Machamer, J. E., Winn, R., & Temkin, N. R. (1995). Neuropsychological outcome one-year post head injury. *Neuropsychology, 9*(1), 80–90.

Dikmen, S., McLean, A., Jr., Temkin, N. R., & Wyler, A. R. (1986). Neuropsychologic outcome at one-month postinjury. *Archives of Physical Medicine and Rehabilitation, 67*(8), 507–513.

Fisher, D. C., Ledbetter, M. F., Cohen, N. J., Marmor, D., & Tulsky, D. S. (2000). WAIS–III and WMS–III profiles of mildly to severely brain-injured patients. *Applied Neuropsychology, 7*(3), 126–132.

Flashman, L. A., & McAllister, T. W. (2002). Lack of awareness and its impact in traumatic brain injury. *NeuroRehabilitation, 17*(4), 285–296.

High, W. M., Jr., Briones-Galang, M., Clark, J. A., Gilkison, C., Mossberg, K. A., Zgaljardic, D. J., et al. (2010). Effect of growth hormone replacement therapy on cognition after traumatic brain injury. *Journal of Neurotrauma, 27*(9), 1565–1575.

Hillier, S. L., Sharpe, M. H., & Metzer, J. (1997). Outcomes five years post-traumatic brain injury (with further reference to neurophysical impairment and disability). *Brain Injury, 11*(9), 661–675.

Iverson, G. L. (2005). Outcome from mild traumatic brain injury. *Current Opinion in Psychiatry, 18*(3), 301–317.

Iverson, G. L., & Brooks, B. L. (2010). Improving accuracy for identifying cognitive impairment. In M. R. Schoenberg, & J. G. Scott (Eds.), *The black book of neuropsychology: A syndrome-based approach* (pp. 923–950). New York: Springer.

Iverson, G. L., Brooks, B. L., & Ashton, V. L. (2008). Cognitive impairment: Foundations for clinical and forensic practice. In M. P. Duckworth, T. Iezzi, & W. O'Donohue (Eds.), *Motor vehicle collisions: Medical, psychosocial, and legal consequences* (pp. 243–309). Amsterdam: Academic Press.

Iverson, G. L., Brooks, B. L., & Holdnack, J. A. (2008). Misdiagnosis of cognitive impairment in forensic neuropsychology. In R. L. Heilbronner (Ed.), *Neuropsychology in the Courtroom: Expert analysis of reports and testimony* (pp. 243–266). New York: Guilford Press.

Iverson, G. L., Brooks, B. L., & Holdnack, J. A. (2012). Evidence-based neuropsychological assessment following work-related injury. In S. S. Bush, & G. L. Iverson (Eds.), *Neuropsychological assessment of work-related injuries* (pp. 360–400). New York: Guilford Press.

Iverson, G. L., & Lange, R. T. (2011). Moderate-severe traumatic brain injury. In M. R. Schoenberg, & J. G. Scott (Eds.), *The black book of neuropsychology: A syndrome-based approach* (pp. 663–696). New York: Springer.

Iverson, G. L., & Lange, R. T. (2012). Traumatic brain injury in the workplace. In S. S. Bush, & G. L. Iverson (Eds.), *Neuropsychological assessment of work-related injuries* (pp. 9–67). New York: Guilford.

Johnstone, B., Vessell, R., Bounds, T., Hoskins, S., & Sherman, A. (2003). Predictors of success for state vocational rehabilitation clients with traumatic brain injury. *Archives of Physical Medicine and Rehabilitation, 84*(2), 161–167.

Jorge, R. E., Robinson, R. G., Moser, D., Tateno, A., Crespo-Facorro, B., & Arndt, S. (2004). Major depression following traumatic brain injury. *Archives of General Psychiatry, 61*(1), 42–50.

Jorge, R. E., Robinson, R. G., Starkstein, S. E., & Arndt, S. V. (1993). Depression and anxiety following traumatic brain injury. *Journal of Neuropsychiatry and Clinical Neurosciences, 5*(4), 369–374.

Kapoor, N., & Ciuffreda, K. J. (2005). Vision problems. In J. M. Silver., T. W. McAllister., & S. C. Yudofsky. (Eds.), *Textbook of traumatic brain injury* (pp. 405–415). Arlington, VA: American Psychiatric Publishing, Inc..

Kochanek, P. M., Clark, R. S. B., & Jenkins, L. W. (2007). TBI: Pathobiology. In N. D. Zasler, D. I. Katz, & R. D. Zafonte (Eds.), *Brain injury medicine: Principles and practice* (pp. 81–96). New York: Demos.

Langeluddecke, P. M., & Lucas, S. K. (2003). Wechsler Adult Intelligence Scale—Third Edition findings in relation to severity of brain injury in litigants. *The Clinical Neuropsychologist, 17*(2), 273–284.

Langeluddecke, P. M., & Lucas, S. K. (2005). WMS—III findings in litigants following moderate to extremely severe brain trauma. *Journal of Clinical and Experimental Neuropsychology, 27*(5), 576–590.

Lezak, M. D., Howieson, D. B., & Loring, D. W. (2004). *Neuropsychological assessment* (4th ed.). New York: Oxford University Press.

Mearns, J., & Lees-Haley, P. R. (1993). Discriminating neuropsychological sequelae of head injury from alcohol-abuse-induced deficits: a review and analysis. *Journal of Clinical Psychology*, *49*(5), 714–720.

O'Shanick, G. J., & O'Shanick, A. M. (2005). Personality disorders. In J. M. Silver., T. W. McAllister., & S. C. Yudofsky. (Eds.), *Textbook of traumatic brain injury* (pp. 245–258). Arlington, VA: American Psychiatric Publishing, Inc..

Olver, J. H., Ponsford, J. L., & Curran, C. A. (1996). Outcome following traumatic brain injury: a comparison between two and five years after injury. *Brain Injury*, *10*(11), 841–848.

Ord, J. S., Greve, K. W., & Bianchini, K. J. (2008). Using the Wechsler Memory Scale–III to detect malingering in mild traumatic brain injury. *The Clinical Neuropsychologist*, *22*(4), 689–704.

Padula, W., Wu, L., Vicci, V., Thomas, J., Nelson, C., Gottlieb, D., et al. (2007). Evaluating and treating visual dysfunction. In N. D. Zasler., D. I. Katz., & R. D. Zafonte. (Eds.), *Brain injury medicine* (pp. 511–528). New York, NY: Demos Medical Publishing, LLC.

Pearson (2009). *Advanced clinical solutions for the WAIS–IV/WMS–IV*. San Antonio, TX: Pearson Assessment.

Schretlen, D. J., & Shapiro, A. M. (2003). A quantitative review of the effects of traumatic brain injury on cognitive functioning. *International Review of Psychiatry*, *15*(4), 341–349.

Silver, J. M., Kramer, R., Greenwald, S., & Weissman, M. (2001). The association between head injuries and psychiatric disorders: Findings from the New Haven NIMH Epidemiologic Catchment Area Study. *Brain Injury*, *15*(11), 935–945.

Spikman, J. M., Timmerman, M. E., Zomeren van, A. H., & Deelman, B. G. (1999). Recovery versus retest effects in attention after closed head injury. *Journal of Clinical and Experimental Neuropsychology*, *21*(5), 585–605.

Thaxton, L. L., & Patel, A. R. (2007). Sleep disturbance: Epidemiology, assessment, and treatment. In N. D. Zasler., D. I. Katz., & R. D. Zafonte. (Eds.), *Brain injury medicine* (pp. 557–575). New York, NY: Demos Medical Publishing, LLC.

Psychological Corporation (1997). *WAIS–III/WMS–III Technical manual*. San Antonio, TX: Psychological Corporation.

Varney, N., Martzke, J., & Roberts, R. (1987). Major depression in patients with closed head injury. *Neuropsychology*, *1*(1), 7–8.

Warden, D. L., & Labbate, L. A. (2005). Post-traumatic stress disorder and other anxiety disorders. In J. M. Silver., T. W. McAllister., & S. C. Yudofsky. (Eds.), *Textbook of traumatic brain injury* (pp. 231–243). Arlington, VA: American Psychiatric Publishing, Inc..

Wechsler, D. (1997a). *Wechsler adult intelligence scale–third edition*. San Antonio, TX: Psychological Corporation.

Wechsler, D. (1997b). *Wechsler memory scale–third edition*. San Antonio, TX: The Psychological Corporation.

Wechsler, D. (2008). *Wechsler adult intelligence scale–fourth edition*. San Antonio, TX: Pearson.

Wechsler, D. (2009). *Wechsler memory scale–fourth edition*. San Antonio, TX: The Psychological Corporation.

West, L. K., Curtis, K. L., Greve, K. W., & Bianchini, K. J. (2011). Memory in traumatic brain injury: the effects of injury severity and effort on the Wechsler Memory Scale–III. *Journal of Neuropsychology*, *5*(Pt. 1), 114–125.

Whyte, J., Schuster, K., Polansky, M., Adams, J., & Coslett, H. B. (2000). Frequency and duration of inattentive behavior after traumatic brain injury: Effects of distraction, task, and practice. *Journal of the International Neuropsychological Society*, *6*(1), 1–11.

Zasler, N. D., Horn, L. J., Martelli, M. F., & Nicolson, K. (2007). Post-traumatic pain disorders: Medical assessment and management. In N. D. Zasler., D. I. Katz., & R. D. Zafonte. (Eds.), *Brain injury medicine* (pp. 697–721). New York, NY: Demos Medical Publishing, LLC.

Assessing Individual's with Psychiatric and Developmental Disorders

Gerald Goldstein*, Howard Oakes[†], David Lovejoy[†] and James A. Holdnack[‡]

*VA Pittsburgh Healthcare System, Pittsburgh, Pennsylvania, USA
[†]Hartford Hospital, West Hartford, CT, and The University of Connecticut School of Medicine, Farmington, Connecticut, USA [‡]Pearson Assessment, San Antonio, Texas, USA

INTRODUCTION

Psychological assessment of patients suffering from psychiatric and developmental disorders is one of the foundations of the practice of clinical psychology. Early standardized tests were designed to identify intellectual deficiency in children (Binet & Simon, 1916) and psychopathology in psychiatric patients (Hathaway & McKinley, 1940). In particular, the Wechsler Scales have a long history of research and clinical applications in evaluating patients with psychiatric and developmental disorders (see Goldstein & Saklofske, 2010, and Tulsky, Saklofske, & Ricker, 2003 for reviews). The WAIS–IV and WMS–IV development plan recognized the need for the tests to be useful and valid in individuals with psychiatric and developmental disorders. This is particularly evident with the inclusion of social cognition in the Advanced Clinical Solutions for the WAIS–IV and WMS–IV (ACS: Pearson, 2009). The clinical questions for these populations are quite varied and not only relate to the cognitive or

WAIS-IV, WMS-IV, and ACS.
DOI: http://dx.doi.org/10.1016/B978-0-12-386934-0.00011-0

© 2013 Elsevier Inc. All rights reserved.

psychological difficulties associated with specific disorders, but also to the purpose of the evaluation (e.g., disability determination, treatment planning, educational classification). The clinician must have knowledge of the disorder and of the requirements needed for the specific evaluation. In addition, the clinician must be aware of the tools available in the WAIS–IV, WMS–IV, and ACS, and their applicability to the patient's clinical presentation and to answer the appropriate questions required for the type of evaluation being performed.

In Chapters 9 and 10, cognitive deficits were described for disorders that primarily represent a change from a previously normal level of ability. The severity of the cognitive impairment in these conditions varies from mild (e.g., difficult to detect with cognitive tests) to profound (e.g., individuals with severely impaired cognitive functions and requiring constant supervision). Developmental disorders are chronic conditions in which impairments in cognitive functioning are present from early in the disorder; although, the manifestation and severity of these deficits may change over time. In psychiatric conditions, changes in thought processes occur after the onset of the disorder; however, it is not clear if cognitive impairments exist prior to the onset of psychiatric symptoms. Similar to brain injury and dementia patients, developmental and psychiatric conditions are associated with a range of cognitive impairments from mild (e.g., Attention Deficit Hyperactivity Disorder) to profound (e.g., moderate-severe intellectual deficiency). The sensitivity of the WAIS–IV, WMS–IV, and ACS to the cognitive difficulties associated with psychiatric and developmental disorders will vary with the severity of the impairments and the consistency with which the cognitive difficulties are expressed in patients with the disorder. Some of the challenges associated with detecting and differentiating mild cognitive impairments from patterns of normal variability are addressed in previous chapters.

ASSESSING INDIVIDUALS WITH PSYCHIATRIC DISORDERS

Cognitive testing of individuals with psychiatric and developmental disorders has numerous purposes that we will attempt to summarize in this chapter. Historically, intelligence tests were first used to evaluate educational potential of individuals with intellectual disability (then called mental retardation), but their use has expanded greatly since that time. The use of intelligence (IQ) tests is now ubiquitous, ranging from assessment of exceptionally high functioning, skilled individuals in work settings, to severely mentally and neurologically ill people. The application of intelligence tests to psychiatric patients probably began with the work of David Wechsler on the development of the Wechsler–Bellevue intelligence scales. Wechsler had specific interests in schizophrenia and dementia. Since that time, tests of intelligence and other cognitive abilities have been administered to individuals with schizophrenia, mood disturbance, neurodevelopmental disorders, and other cognitive disorders for numerous reasons, including those listed below.

- Evaluation of educational capacity, mainly in children and adolescents, and vocational capacity in adults.
- As part of a neuropsychological assessment to identify possible brain dysfunction associated with conditions that may be superimposed upon psychiatric or developmental disorders, such as brain trauma, stroke, or progressive dementia.
- To determine if a psychiatric disorder has an impact beyond normal changes in brain function associated with age. In children, the emphasis is on cognitive development, while in elderly individuals the focus is on cognitive deterioration.
- The Wechsler intelligence and memory scales are used in research to characterize the cognitive organization and structure of several mental illnesses. The goal of this research is identifying specific subtest scales that uniquely characterize individual disorders (e.g., is there a cognitive prototype of schizophrenia?).
- The Wechsler scales or individual subtests are used qualitatively or quantitatively to characterize thought disorder in schizophrenia. For instance, Goldstein and Scheerer (1941) used Block Design to identify concrete thinking. Other research using the Wechsler scales has examined various aspects of cognitive impairment in schizophrenia such as social cognition, attention, and working memory.
- In recent years there has been great interest in cognitive heterogeneity in various psychiatric disorders, notably schizophrenia, and efforts have been made to generate a viable subtype taxonomy. The Wechsler scales have been used extensively in the cluster analytic research that has taken place in several independent settings, with the specific goal of determining whether cluster analysis could identify subgroups of individuals with schizophrenia with unique cognitive profiles in level or pattern of performance. It is hoped that identifiable clusters will eventually be associated with differing neurobiological characteristics, perhaps involving structural brain differences or neurochemical variations.

This chapter will provide an overview of the normative data obtained from known clinical groups and interpretation strategies for the assessment of individuals with psychiatric disorders, specifically schizophrenia.

COGNITION IN SCHIZOPHRENIA

Schizophrenia is most prominently a disorder of thinking and is manifested by symptoms reflecting abnormal thought processes. These might include auditory hallucinations, false beliefs or delusions, disorganized or incoherent speech, and loss of social skills. All of the symptoms need not be present all of the time but their frequent appearance provides convincing evidence that the individual has the illness. It is thought that at the core of these varied symptoms is a profound impairment of thought processes that, while described in numerous ways, always assumes that there has been variability in contact with reality. This deficit or symptom has been conceptualized as an impairment of the abstract attitude, a deficit in logical reasoning, a loss of executive functioning, or a disability in conceptualizing. These higher-level cognitive deficits have been attributed by some researchers to deficits in more basic processes such as attention, speed of information processing and working memory, with vast literatures documenting these deficits in controlled studies.

There is an extensive research literature concerning cognition in schizophrenia. Historically, procedures drawn from the experimental psychology laboratory were used, notably reaction time experiments and studies of other basic processes such as attention, perceptual skills, and motor function. The early work of David Shakow and Joseph Zubin represent the major efforts in this area. This cognitive research continues, but in recent years neurobiological measures have been recorded during activity, notably electroencephalographic (EEG), generally in the form of evoked potentials, cerebral blood flow techniques, and various forms of neuroimaging, most recently functional MRI. These "activation" studies have greatly expanded our knowledge of the neuropathology of schizophrenia because they permitted study of various anatomic structural connections and systems while the brain was engaged in behavior-related activity, rather than in the resting state, which was previously the standard procedure for EEG or radiological study. In short, these studies revealed the significance of the dopaminergic system and the frontostriatal and temporolimbic systems in the development of schizophrenia.

Recently, an extensive effort was made to identify and organize the most sensitive cognitive indicators of schizophrenia. Two such organizations have been constructed, one for clinical cognitive tests, called Measurement and Treatment Research to Improve Cognition in Schizophrenia (MATRICS: Green et al., 2004) and one for experimental laboratory procedures, called Cognitive Neuroscience Treatment Research to Improve Cognition in Schizophrenia (CNTRICS: Carter & Barch, 2007).

Through a lengthy process, each of these organizations has recommended test batteries that consist of procedures thought by acknowledged experts in the field to be optimally sensitive to cognitive characteristics of schizophrenia. Both MATRICS and CNTRICS contain tests of various cognitive domains such as attention, memory, reasoning, visual and auditory organization, speed of information processing, and social cognition. Harvey and Keefe (1997) list a similar set of domains including various aspects of memory, attention, executive functions, processing speed, and verbal skills. It would appear that there is reasonably good consensus regarding the separable cognitive deficits found in individuals with schizophrenia.

Based on previously published research reviewed elsewhere (Goldstein & Saklofske, 2010), cognitive function in schizophrenia, as assessed by the Wechsler intelligence scales, is extremely heterogeneous with widely varying levels and patterns of ability. This cognitive heterogeneity is apparently not restricted to the Wechsler scales because numerous other studies have found it using many different cognitive tests (Palmer, Dawes, & Heaton, 2009). Studies have shown that many individuals with schizophrenia may retain average or above average levels of some abilities and global impairment is only present in some cases. It has been estimated that about 20% of individuals with schizophrenia produce normal level performances on numerous cognitive tests (Palmer et al., 1997). This finding has given rise to the concept of "Neuropsychologically Normal Schizophrenia" (Allen, Goldstein, & Warnick, 2003; Goldstein, Shemansky, & Allen, 2005; Palmer et al., 1997). This term has become exceptionally controversial with some critics suggesting there is no such thing, and its appearance varies with how one defines "normal." To some extent, this controversy appears to be based on an erroneous failure to distinguish between current functioning and deterioration. There is little question that there is cognitive deterioration in all individuals with schizophrenia (Bilder et al., 2006; Seidman, Buka, Goldstein, & Tsuang, 2006). By definition it is part of the illness, but the degree of deterioration may not always reach the point that cognitive function falls below the level of the general population. Thus, there appears to be a small subgroup of individuals with schizophrenia who, while they may have a history of deterioration, have not reached the point at which their cognitive abilities are at levels below those of the healthy population. It seems appropriate to use the term "neuropsychologically normal" in this sense, because such individuals may maintain general average or above average IQ and perform normally on various cognitive tests. Despite the heterogeneity, the organization of abilities as demonstrated by factor analysis is the same in people with schizophrenia as it is in normal individuals. That is, people with schizophrenia do not have idiosyncratic relationships among various abilities even when some or all of those abilities are significantly impaired.

Studies using the WAIS–R in schizophrenia have found: (a) that patients with a family history of schizophrenia performed in the borderline to low average range while those without a family history performed in the low average to average range (Wolitzky et al., 2006); (b) Verbal IQ (VIQ) scores are higher than Performance IQ (PIQ) scores in schizophrenia patients (Wolitzky et al., 2006); (c) subgroups of schizophrenia patients have intact intellectual functioning with average performance on all subtests except digit symbol, in contrast to a cognitively abnormal group with borderline to average scores (Goldstein et al., 2005); and (d) WAIS–R performance has been associated with total and regional brain size in schizophrenia (Toulopoulou et al., 2004). On the Wechsler Memory Scale-Revised (WMS–R), schizophrenia patients have lower scores on spatial and auditory working memory measures (Pirkola et al., 2005) and WMS–R performance is associated with total and regional brain size (Toulopoulou et al., 2004). Performance on the WMS logical memory subtest predicts level of independent functioning among schizophrenia patients (Fujii & Wylie, 2002).

The performance of schizophrenia patients on the WAIS–III and WMS–III was characterized by low average-to-average performance on the WAIS–III and borderline to low average performance on the WMS–III (Wechsler, 1997). On the WAIS–III, the highest index score was on VCI (93.3) and the lowest was on PSI (83.4). The WMS–III scores ranged from 79.1 for the Immediate Memory Index to 86.1 on the Auditory Delayed Recognition Index. Within the schizophrenia group, there was a significant degree of variability with scores ranging from impaired to above average (Wechsler, 1997). In samples where schizophrenia patients and controls are matched on WAIS–III FSIQ, the schizophrenia patients show a relative strength in VCI but relative deficits in WMS–III memory functioning (Wilk et al., 2005). Additionally, schizophrenia patients show low average performance on the WMS–III Family Pictures subtest that contains elements of verbal and spatial memory and social concepts (Gold, Poet, Wilk, & Buchanan, 2004). Performance on WAIS–III working memory skills predict social competence and work skills in individuals with schizophrenia (Bowie et al., 2008). WAIS–III and WMS–III subtests have been associated with global and regional brain size in schizophrenia (Antonova et al., 2005); although, other studies have found no relationship between WAIS–III and hippocampal volume (Nestor et al., 2007). Previous editions of the Wechsler scales have been found to be sensitive to cognitive deficits in schizophrenia and relate to brain morphology and functional outcomes.

In addition to intellectual and memory deficits, schizophrenia patients exhibit deficits in social perception. Affect recognition is significantly lower in schizophrenia patients compared to controls (Scholten, Aleman, Montagne, & Kahn, 2005). Schizophrenia patients perform significantly lower than matched controls on the ACS Social Perception test (prosody and pairs conditions; Kandalaft et al., 2012). Social perception deficits have been found to correlate with deficits in visual−perceptual processes and therefore may not exist independently from other cognitive limitations (Sergi & Green, 2002). However, deficits in facial affect recognition also correlate with amygdala volume (Namiki et al., 2007), suggesting that such deficits are related to abnormal brain morphology in schizophrenia. Research indicates that social perception is an important domain of cognitive functioning to assess when evaluating schizophrenia patients.

As part of the standardization of the WAIS−IV and WMS−IV a clinical validity study of 69 schizophrenia patients was conducted. The inclusion criterion included the following: ages 16−65; may be currently admitted to a medical hospital or psychiatric facility for treatment of schizophrenia; if taking medication, must be stabilized for at least 4 weeks prior to testing; meets DSM−IV−TR criteria for current diagnosis of schizophrenia by a qualified mental health professional (schizophrenia in remission was not an acceptable diagnosis); may have comorbid personality disorders; WAIS−IV GAI ≥ 70; and Texas Functional Living Scale Total Score >30 (TFLS: Cullum, Saine, & Weiner, 2009).

Table 11.1 describes the mean index and subtest scores for the schizophrenia special group and demographically matched controls (e.g., age, sex, education, and ethnicity) as well as the effect size for the between group differences. Using education-matched controls can result in attenuated effect sizes because schizophrenia can disrupt the patient's ability to complete their education. Notice that because people with schizophrenia, on average, attain lower levels of education than the general population, the matching process for healthy controls resulted in a sample that has intellectual scores in the lower bound of the average range (because the matched sample, too, had less education than the general population. Throughout this section, we compare the performance of the patients with schizophrenia to this matched sample and to the general population.

As can be seen, the effect sizes were significant across all index score comparisons with the largest effect seen on Verbal Comprehension and index scores that include verbal subtests. At the subtest level, Vocabulary, Similarities, and Coding produce the highest effect sizes.

TABLE 11.1 WAIS–IV Standard and New Index Scores and Subtests in Schizophrenia and Matched Controls

Score	Schizophrenia		Matched Control		Between Group Differences	
	Mean	SD	Mean	SD	ES	p
Verbal Comprehension Index	77.4	11.3	90.9	13.7	−0.99	<0.001
Perceptual Reasoning Index	81.7	10.8	91.3	14.9	−0.65	<0.001
Working Memory Index	83.0	11.7	93.0	14.8	−0.68	<0.001
Processing Speed Index	78.0	13.5	91.2	15.3	−0.87	<0.001
General Ability Index	77.5	12.2	90.9	15.5	−0.86	<0.001
Cognitive Proficiency Index	78.5	10.5	90.3	14.2	−0.83	<0.001
Full Scale IQ	76.3	10.3	89.8	14.3	−0.94	<0.001
Vocabulary	6.0	2.1	8.2	2.4	−0.96	<0.001
Similarities	5.8	2.2	8.5	2.7	−0.98	<0.001
Block Design	7.2	2.3	8.3	2.9	−0.36	<0.05
Matrix Reasoning	6.4	2.4	8.5	2.9	−0.75	<0.001
Visual Puzzles	7.1	2.4	8.8	3.2	−0.53	<0.01
Digit Span	7.4	2.4	9.1	3.2	−0.51	<0.01
Digit Span Forward	8.3	2.4	10.0	3.4	−0.51	<0.01
Digit Span Backward	8.0	2.0	9.1	2.8	−0.40	<0.05
Digit Span Sequencing	7.8	2.8	8.9	3.1	−0.38	<0.05
Arithmetic	6.5	2.2	8.5	2.9	−0.68	<0.001
Coding	5.6	2.6	8.2	2.8	−0.91	<0.001
Symbol Search	6.2	3.1	8.6	3.3	−0.70	<0.001

Note: Sample size for indexes = 55, for subtests 55–69. VCI, FSIQ, and GAI are pro-rated due to missing Information subtest.

Compared to matched controls, the schizophrenia group shows a cognitive deficit of about $\frac{1}{2}$ to 1 standard deviation across WAIS–IV measures. Compared to population norms, they perform $\frac{2}{3}$ to $1\frac{1}{2}$ standard deviations below the mean. These effects are consistent with those reported for general intellectual deficits observed on Wechsler scales in meta-analytic research (Reichenberg & Harvey, 2007).

The WMS–IV results are displayed in Table 11.2 and show a mix of significant and non-significant comparisons. At the index level, the largest effect was observed on the Quantitative Reasoning Index (ES = -0.97). Other large effects were observed for the General Memory, Immediate Memory, Delayed Memory, Combined Working Memory, Visual Working Memory, Auditory Immediate Memory, and Visual Delayed Recognition Indexes. This suggests a general deficit in memory and working memory functioning at a level similar to other cognitive functions. Effect sizes for memory indexes range from $\frac{3}{5}$ to $\frac{4}{5}$ standard deviations below the mean compared to controls. Compared to population norms, the effects are approximately 1 to $1\frac{1}{2}$ standard deviations below the mean, consistent with results from meta-analytic research (Reichenberg & Harvey, 2007). Working memory deficits were about $\frac{4}{5}$ to 1 standard deviation below the mean compared to controls and $1\frac{1}{3}$ standard deviations below population norms. Meta-analysis indicates an average effect size of about $\frac{1}{2}$ standard deviation below the mean (Lee & Park, 2005).

Among the WMS–IV subtests, Logical Memory I and II had the largest effect sizes. Several contrast scores were significantly different in the schizophrenia group compared to controls including Logical Memory II versus Delayed Recognition and Designs II Delayed Recall versus Recognition. Both of these scores indicate that recognition trials were somewhat lower than expected compared to delayed free recall. This indicates encoding problems rather than a retrieval deficit and reflects results observed at the index level (Retrieval Index = 82). Another interesting finding is that the schizophrenia sample did not show a high degree of forgetting; the Retention Index, the Immediate versus Delayed contrast score, and the subtest level immediate versus delayed contrast scores were not significantly different from controls. The only contrast score showing rapid forgetting in patients versus controls was the Designs Immediate versus Delayed Contrast Scaled Score ($p < 0.05$, ES = -0.49).

Table 11.3 presents cognitive variability data for the schizophrenia and matched control samples. Chapter 3 describes the interpretation of these measures in detail. The significant findings relate to the highest and lowest obtained scores on the WAIS–IV, WMS–IV, and the combined WAIS–IV/WMS–IV data. This result indicates a suppressed cognitive profile. A suppressed profile limits the amount of variability that

TABLE 11.2 WMS–IV Standard and New Index Scores and Subtest Scores in Schizophrenia and Matched Controls

Score	Schizophrenia		Matched Control		Between Group Differences	
	Mean	SD	Mean	SD	ES	p
General Memory Index	76.3	12.8	90.4	16.2	−0.87	<0.001
Immediate Memory Index	75.8	13.2	89.1	16.1	−0.82	<0.001
Delayed Memory Index	76.8	13.6	90.7	16.6	−0.83	<0.001
Immediate vs. Delayed Index	8.6	2.8	9.4	3.5	−0.23	>0.05
Auditory Memory Index	76.3	14.4	89.1	16.8	−0.76	<0.01
Auditory Immediate Index	75.9	14.5	89.0	16.4	−0.80	<0.01
Auditory Delayed Index	77.0	15.6	89.5	17.7	−0.70	<0.01
Auditory Delayed Recognition Index	79.9	18.0	90.8	16.7	−0.65	<0.05
Visual Memory Index	81.3	14.2	93.4	15.8	−0.76	<0.01
Visual Immediate Index	81.0	15.7	92.4	17.4	−0.65	<0.01
Visual Delayed Index	82.5	13.6	93.6	16.0	−0.70	<0.01
Visual Delayed Recognition Index	84.5	16.6	96.0	14.1	−0.81	<0.01
Designs Content Index	88.1	13.9	95.6	15.6	−0.48	>0.05
Designs Spatial Index	86.3	10.0	96.9	17.1	−0.62	<0.01
Retention Index	90.8	13.4	96.4	17.2	−0.33	>0.05
Retrieval Index	82.5	15.8	92.6	18.7	−0.54	<0.05

Visual Working Memory Index	80.2	12.8	93.5	16.2	−0.82	<0.01
Working Memory Index	80.8	9.0	93.7	15.5	−0.83	<0.001
Quantitative Reasoning Index	81.4	10.2	95.8	14.8	−0.97	<0.001
Logical Memory I	5.0	2.4	8.7	4.0	−0.93	<0.001
Logical Memory II	5.2	2.2	8.6	3.6	−0.94	<0.001
Logical Memory I vs. II	8.8	3.3	9.3	3.0	−0.15	>0.05
Logical Memory II vs. Rec	6.4	3.2	9.0	4.1	−0.64	<0.01
Verbal Paired Associates I	7.0	3.3	7.8	3.0	−0.27	>0.05
Verbal Paired Associates II	7.2	3.6	8.1	3.5	−0.28	>0.05
Verbal Paired Associates I vs. II	9.4	3.3	9.9	3.2	−0.17	>0.05
Verbal Paired Associates II vs. Rec	9.1	3.8	9.1	3.0	0.00	>0.05
Verbal Paired Associates II Free Recall	6.2	2.6	8.4	3.4	−0.65	<0.001
Verbal Paired Associates Trial A	7.4	3.1	8.5	2.9	−0.37	>0.05
Verbal Paired Associates Trial D	6.7	3.8	8.1	3.4	−0.42	>0.05
Verbal Paired Associates A vs. D	8.0	3.1	8.7	3.1	−0.25	>0.05
Verbal Paired Associates Total Intrusions	7.2	3.2	8.8	3.1	−0.51	>0.05
Verbal Paired Associates Easy Items	7.0	4.1	8.7	3.0	−0.55	>0.05
Verbal Paired Associates Hard Items	7.1	3.4	7.6	3.2	−0.16	>0.05
Visual Reproduction I	6.5	3.5	8.7	3.3	−0.67	<0.05

(Continued)

TABLE 11.2 (Continued)

Score	Schizophrenia		Matched Control		Between Group Differences	
	Mean	SD	Mean	SD	ES	p
Visual Reproduction II	7.2	3.0	8.2	3.5	−0.26	>0.05
Visual Reproduction I vs. II	9.1	2.8	8.6	3.0	0.19	>0.05
Visual Reproduction II vs. Rec	8.1	3.0	8.3	3.4	−0.07	>0.05
Designs I	7.2	2.8	8.7	3.3	−0.46	>0.05
Designs I Content	7.8	3.1	9.0	2.8	−0.41	>0.05
Designs I Spatial	7.5	2.2	9.2	3.4	−0.48	<0.05
Designs II	7.0	2.4	9.1	3.3	−0.65	<0.01
Designs II Content	7.7	2.4	9.1	3.6	−0.39	>0.05
Designs II Spatial	7.8	2.3	9.7	3.2	−0.59	<0.01
Designs I vs. II	8.5	2.5	10.1	3.3	−0.49	<0.05
Designs II vs. Recognition	7.8	2.3	9.7	3.2	−0.59	>0.05

Note: $n = 33$ for index and subtests.
Copyright © 2009 NCS Pearson, Inc. All rights reserved. Used with permission.

TABLE 11.3 WAIS–IV/WMS–IV Variability Measures in Schizophrenia and Matched Controls

Score	Schizophrenia		Matched Control		Between Group Differences	
	Mean	SD	Mean	SD	ES	p
WAIS–IV Subtest High vs. Low	11.3	3.2	10.6	3.1	0.25	>0.05
WAIS–IV Subtest Standard Deviation	11.3	3.5	10.6	3.3	0.20	>0.05
WAIS–IV Subtest Maximum Score	5.9	2.1	8.3	2.9	−0.80	<0.001
WAIS–IV Subtest Minimum Score	6.1	1.5	8.3	2.6	−0.86	<0.001
WAIS–IV Index High vs. Low	12.2	3.6	11.0	3.2	0.37	>0.05
WAIS–IV Index Standard Deviation	11.3	4.1	11.0	3.2	0.08	>0.05
WAIS–IV Index Maximum Score	5.6	1.6	8.1	2.6	−0.93	<0.001
WAIS–IV Index Minimum Score	6.3	1.9	8.4	2.7	−0.78	<0.001
WMS–IV Subtest High vs. Low	9.8	2.7	9.3	3.0	0.16	>0.05
WMS–IV Subtest Standard Deviation	9.7	3.1	9.5	3.1	0.06	>0.05
WMS–IV Subtest Maximum Score	6.1	2.8	8.9	3.5	−0.80	<0.001
WMS–IV Subtest Minimum Score	6.0	1.7	8.1	2.8	−0.77	<0.001
WMS–IV Index High vs. Low	9.9	2.7	10.0	2.6	−0.02	>0.05
WMS–IV Index Standard Deviation	10.0	2.7	9.8	2.5	0.09	>0.05
WMS–IV Index Maximum Score	5.5	2.5	8.3	3.2	−0.88	<0.001
WMS–IV Index Minimum Score	5.3	2.4	8.2	3.0	−0.97	<0.001

(*Continued*)

TABLE 11.3 (Continued)

Score	Schizophrenia		Matched Control		Between Group Differences	
	Mean	SD	Mean	SD	ES	p
WAIS–IV/WMS–IV Subtest High vs. Low	10.6	2.9	10.2	3.3	0.13	>0.05
WAIS–IV/WMS–IV Subtest Standard Deviation	10.1	2.9	9.9	3.4	0.07	>0.05
WAIS–IV/WMS–IV Subtest Maximum Score	6.0	2.4	8.6	3.1	−0.84	<0.001
WAIS–IV/WMS–IV Subtest Minimum Score	5.6	1.9	8.3	2.9	−0.93	<0.001
WAIS–IV/WMS–IV Index High vs. Low	10.5	2.7	10.6	3.0	−0.27	>0.05
WAIS–IV/WMS–IV Index Standard Deviation	10.0	2.9	10.3	3.1	−0.39	<0.05
WAIS–IV/WMS–IV Index Maximum Score	5.2	2.0	8.1	3.1	−0.74	<0.01
WAIS–IV/WMS–IV Index Minimum Score	5.2	2.2	8.2	2.7	−0.92	<0.001

Copyright © 2009 NCS Pearson, Inc. All rights reserved. Used with permission.

can be observed. None of the variability indicators, either highest versus lowest score or standard deviation of the indexes or subtests, are significantly different than controls. Because this is a suppressed profile, it is necessary to adjust the variability data by the highest achieved score. Table 11.4 presents variability data controlling for the highest achieved score.

These results show that within a specific battery, either the WAIS–IV or WMS–IV, the schizophrenia group does not show significant variability, even after controlling for the highest achieved score. However, the combined WAIS–IV and WMS–IV data are significantly more variable (i.e., a lower scaled score indicates more variability) in the clinical sample compared to controls. Variability exists between general cognitive functioning and memory; however, it is not possible to identify this variability unless the relatively low 'highest' score is taken into account.

In Chapter 4, it was proposed that adjusting scores by demographic variables (e.g., education, sex, and ethnicity) could yield better sensitivity and specificity for the WAIS–IV and WMS–IV in some clinical populations. Adjusting scores by education level presumes that education level has not been disrupted by the presenting illness. In the case of schizophrenia, some individuals are able to function well enough to obtain college degrees. However, in most cases the patient's education is disrupted by the disorder. Table 11.5 presents the effects of using demographic norms. Observe that the effect sizes between the schizophrenia and matched control groups are similar to those observed in the age only adjusted scores. This occurs because both groups are matched on the variables being adjusted (most notably, both are adjusting for lower educational attainment). However, compared to population norms with a mean of 50 (i.e., demographic norms are expressed as t-scores), the schizophrenia group performance is only about 0.6 to 1 standard deviation below the mean in contrast to the $2/3$ to $1^1/_2$ standard deviations below the mean observed when using age only adjusted scores. This occurs because the schizophrenia group is being compared to a population of individuals that have low educational attainment; the adjusted score would not reflect their ability to function in the general population. For this reason, demographic adjustments do not provide a better estimate of cognitive impairment in this population. The fact that demographically adjusted scores are still well below expected performance compared to matched controls and demographically similar population norms is consistent with research indicating that schizophrenia is associated with a decline in intellectual functioning from pre-morbid levels (Kremen, Seidman, Faraone, & Tsuang, 2001).

Table 11.6 provides descriptive statistics for multivariate base rates of low scores for the WAIS–IV, WMS–IV, and the combined

TABLE 11.4 WAIS–IV/WMS–IV Variability Measures Controlling for Maximum Subtest or Index Score in Schizophrenia and Matched Controls

Score	Schizophrenia		Matched Control		Between Group Differences	
	Mean	SD	Mean	SD	ES	p
WAIS–IV Subtest High vs. Low	9.0	3.3	9.4	3.2	−0.14	>0.05
WAIS–IV Subtest Standard Deviation	8.8	3.3	9.8	3.2	−0.33	>0.05
WAIS–IV Index High vs. Low	10.4	4.1	10.8	3.4	−0.12	>0.05
WAIS–IV Index Standard Deviation	9.6	4.7	10.2	3.3	−0.16	>0.05
WMS–IV Subtest High vs. Low	8.0	2.3	8.8	3.1	−0.25	>0.05
WMS–IV Subtest Standard Deviation	7.8	3.0	8.8	3.3	−0.32	>0.05
WMS–IV Index High vs. Low	8.3	3.0	9.2	2.2	−0.42	>0.05
WMS–IV Index Standard Deviation	9.1	2.1	9.1	2.1	0.00	>0.05
WAIS–IV/WMS–IV Subtest High vs. Low	7.6	2.4	8.9	3.1	−0.41	<0.05
WAIS–IV/WMS–IV Subtest Standard Deviation	7.5	2.8	8.8	3.0	−0.44	<0.01
WAIS–IV/WMS–IV Index High vs. Low	7.7	3.8	9.5	3.3	−0.54	<0.01
WAIS–IV/WMS–IV Index Standard Deviation	7.2	3.9	9.2	3.2	−0.63	<0.01

Copyright © 2009 NCS Pearson, Inc. All rights reserved. Used with permission.

WAIS–IV/WMS–IV in schizophrenia patients and controls. In this table, two cut-off scores are provided, the number of scores at or below one standard deviation and the number of scores at or below the fifth percentile. Because the matched controls have a relatively low education level, they tend to have multiple low scores just like the schizophrenia group. The patients had significantly more low scores on WAIS–IV subtests, WMS–IV indexes and subtests, and combined WAIS–IV/WMS–IV indexes and subtests. In general, even though the patients are matched on education level to controls, they have more scores below the specified cut-offs. The effect sizes were largest for WMS–IV subtests.

The ACS Social Perception test is particularly relevant to the assessment of patients with schizophrenia. Schizophrenia is associated with significant disruptions in social relatedness, which may relate to underlying deficits in processing social information. The Social Perception

TABLE 11.5 WAIS–IV Full Demographically Adjusted Standard Index Scores and Subtests in Schizophrenia and Matched Controls

Score	Schizophrenia		Matched Control		Between Group Differences	
	Mean	SD	Mean	SD	ES	p
Perceptual Reasoning Index	44.1	9.5	49.9	10.0	−0.58	<0.01
Working Memory Index	43.3	9.3	49.9	10.0	−0.66	<0.001
Processing Speed Index	40.7	10.8	49.6	9.3	−0.96	<0.001
Vocabulary	40.4	9.9	49.2	9.7	−0.90	<0.001
Similarities	40.6	8.3	49.5	10.4	−0.86	<0.001
Block Design	47.6	8.7	49.5	10.5	−0.18	>0.05
Matrix Reasoning	43.3	9.0	50.0	8.4	−0.79	<0.001
Visual Puzzles	45.1	10.4	50.5	11.3	−0.48	<0.01
Digit Span	45.7	9.2	50.4	10.6	−0.45	<0.01
Arithmetic	42.2	9.5	49.5	10.4	−0.70	<0.001
Coding	40.4	11.1	49.3	9.3	−0.96	<0.001
Symbol Search	42.0	11.2	50.0	10.3	−0.78	<0.001

Note: Sample size = 55.

Copyright © 2008 NCS Pearson, Inc. All rights reserved. Used with Permission.

TABLE 11.6 Descriptive Statistics and Base Rates of Low Scores in Schizophrenia and Matched Controls

| | Schizophrenia | | | | Matched Control | | | | Between Group Differences | | | |
| | At or below 1 SD | | At or below 5%ile | | At or below 1 SD | | At or below 5%ile | | At or below 1 SD | | At or below 5%ile | |
Score	Mean	SD	Mean	SD	Mean	SD	Mean	SD	ES	p	ES	p
WAIS–IV Index Low Scores	1.9	1.0	0.9	1.0	1.6	1.7	0.6	1.4	0.2	>0.05	0.2	>0.05
WAIS–IV Subtest Low Scores	6.0	1.8	2.8	2.1	3.6	3.0	1.3	2.2	0.8	<0.001	0.7	<0.01
WMS–IV Index Low Scores	3.5	1.8	2.4	1.9	1.6	1.8	0.7	1.4	1.1	<0.001	1.2	<0.001
WMS–IV Subtest Low Scores	6.6	2.6	3.8	2.2	3.8	3.0	1.5	2.1	0.9	<0.001	1.1	<0.001
WAIS–IV/WMS–IV Index Low Scores	5.4	2.1	3.3	2.2	3.2	3.0	1.3	2.4	0.8	<0.001	0.8	<0.001
WAIS–IV/WMS–IV Subtest Low Scores	12.6	3.6	6.6	3.5	7.3	5.3	2.9	3.9	1.0	<0.001	1.0	<0.001

Note: WMS–IV analysis includes visual working memory.

Copyright © 2008, 2009 NCS Pearson, Inc. All rights reserved. Used with Permission.

tests measure facial affect recognition, prosody recognition, and understanding body language and interactions between people. Table 11.7 presents results of the social perception test in schizophrenia patients versus matched controls. The schizophrenia patients performed significantly worse on all of the social perception measures. Their lowest score was observed on the Pairs portion of the test. In this section, the patient must interpret prosody in the context of two people interacting and determine if the tone of voice changed the meaning of what was said. The overall social perception score was significantly lower in patients than controls even after controlling for low overall visual–perceptual skills (e.g., PRI vs. Social Perception Total Score). Therefore, these deficits cannot wholly be understood as a general deficit in visual–perceptual skills. The effect sizes compared to matched controls indicate a social perception deficit of about $1/2$ to $4/5$ of a standard deviation; however, compared to the general population the social perception deficit is about 1 to $1^{1}/_{2}$ standard deviations below the mean.

Schizophrenia patients show diverse cognitive deficits compared to demographically matched controls. In the context of global cognitive deficits, this sample of patients has particularly low scores on Verbal Comprehension, Coding, Immediate and Delayed Memory, and Social Perception. Compared to controls, they show a suppressed cognitive profile with their highest and lowest scores being significantly lower than controls. They also have high rates of low scores (e.g., multivariate base rates). Even when controlling for their suppressed profile, they show consistently low performance on measures of intellectual functioning; however, memory and memory versus intellectual functioning measures show more variability when controlling for the overall suppression of their test performance. The effect of schizophrenia on cognitive functioning is a global lowering of most cognitive abilities, though the impact on specific aspects of memory functioning is more variable. As noted previously, the impact on overall cognitive functioning does not mean that all schizophrenia patients will perform in the impaired range on all cognitive tests. This is evident by mean performance for the entire group being in the borderline to low average range on most measures; therefore, nearly as many individuals will have scores above these mean scores as below it. That type of variability reflects the heterogeneity of cognition among patients diagnosed with schizophrenia.

Because of matters related to education, employment, and housing of individuals with severe mental illness, who no longer reside in institutional facilities for long periods of time, assessment of disability has become a highly significant matter. The Wechsler scales (among other cognitive tests) can provide useful information regarding placement and employment recommendations for these individuals. Because of the presence of cognitive heterogeneity among individuals with

TABLE 11.7 ACS Social Perception in Schizophrenia and Matched Controls

Score	Schizophrenia		Matched Control		Between Group Differences	
	Mean	SD	Mean	SD	ES	p
Social Perception Total	6.3	2.3	8.3	2.9	−0.66	<0.001
Affect Naming	7.4	2.8	9.2	3.3	−0.56	<0.01
Prosody	6.5	2.5	8.1	2.9	−0.58	<0.01
Pairs	5.6	2.2	8.0	3.1	−0.77	<0.001
Perceptual Reasoning Index	82.7	9.6	91.8	14.9	−0.61	<0.01
PRI versus Social Perception Contrast Score	8.0	2.1	9.0	2.6	−0.40	<0.05

Note: $n = 46$.

Copyright © 2009 NCS Pearson, Inc. All rights reserved. Used with Permission.

schizophrenia and other severe mental illnesses, individual cognitive evaluations are necessary for appropriate planning and placement.

ASPERGER'S AND AUTISM SPECTRUM DISORDERS

A full review of the empirical literature related to performance on the various Wechsler scales with individuals with autism spectrum disorders is beyond the scope of this chapter but several key findings and issues in this research are worth noting. First, this research has occurred in the context of evolving and not always empirically validated changes in the taxonomy of these disorders. With basic definitional variations of patient samples in the published research over time, there is a need for very careful considerations of both the positive and negative findings that have been reported. Disorders in the autism spectrum, including autism (AUT) and Asperger's syndrome (AS), are characterized by deficits in social interaction, but cognitive deficits, varying in severity, are more strongly associated with AUT than with AS. In addition, AUT is associated with impairment of verbal and nonverbal communication, stereotyped movements, repetitive activities, and resistance to change (APA, 2000). Even individuals with high-functioning autism (HFA), defined as having an intelligence quotient (IQ) of 70 or higher (Rutter & Schopler, 1987), typically demonstrate cognitive deficits.

Neuropsychological studies of children and adults with AUT are published in both the experimental cognitive and a psychometric literature. The psychometric literature, largely involving the various Wechsler scales, has provided substantial evidence of a characteristic profile marked by prominent variability in cognitive skills, with some impaired and some preserved abilities. On the Wechsler intelligence scales, both children and adults with HFA show better perceptual reasoning versus verbal skills, higher scores on Digit Span and Block Design compared with Comprehension (Goldstein & Saklofske, 2010), and an overall strength on the Block Design subtest (Gilchrist et al., 2001). Individuals with HFA typically perform worse on Comprehension than on other verbal subtests from the Wechsler Adult Intelligence Scale–Third Edition (WAIS–III) or Wechsler Intelligence Scale for Children–Third Edition (WISC–III: Mayes & Calhoun, 2003). Low scores are also found on the Picture Completion and Coding subtests (Goldstein & Saklofske, 2010). Cognitive skills in HFA have been described as strengths in short-term auditory memory, visual analysis, and visuomotor integration, with deficits in verbal reasoning, concept formation, inferential reasoning, and representational capacity (Lincoln, Courchesne, Kilman, Elmasian, & Allen, 1988).

Comparisons of intellectual function between individuals with HFA and AS have generally demonstrated higher ability levels in AS (Emerich, Creaghead, Grether, Murray, & Grasha, 2003; Ghaziuddin & Mountain-Kimchi, 2004; Hayashi, Kato, Igarashi, & Kashima, 2008; Rinehart, Bradshaw, Tonge, Bereton, & Bellgrove, 2002; Spek, Scholte, & van Berckelaer-Onnes, 2008) with some preliminary evidence of possibly associated differences in brain structure (Jou, Minshew, Keshavan, & Hardan, 2010). However, the evidence is not robust and is sometimes equivocal, creating controversy concerning whether AS is a distinct syndrome separate from HFA (Macintosh & Dissanayake, 2004). In addition to intellectual function, individuals with AUT spectrum disorders show deficits in the development of interpretation of affect, including face recognition and other aspects of emotional recognition (Golarai, Grill-Spector, & Reiss, 2006; Korkman, Kirk, & Kemp, 2007). Adolescents and adults with AUT have difficulties accurately identifying fearful, disgusted, happy (Humphreys, Minshew, Leonard, & Behrmann, 2007), and sad (Boraston, Blakemore, Chilvers, & Skuse, 2007) facial expressions. Additionally, they do not show normal brain activation in the amygdala and orbitofrontal regions in response to fearful faces but activate the cingulate and superior temporal lobes instead (Ashwin, Baron-Cohen, Wheelwright, O'Riordan, & Bullmore, 2007). Impaired processing of facial expressions of emotions is not attributable to general impairments in visual–perceptual processing (Humphreys et al., 2007). Deficits in emotion have also been reported for determining emotions from prosody (Hollander et al., 2007).

Holdnack, Goldstein and Drozdick (2011) compared adolescents and adults diagnosed with AUT and AS with a sample of matched controls on the WAIS–IV and ACS Social Perception Test. The individuals diagnosed with AUT performed significantly worse than both control and AS groups on all WAIS–IV indexes with large effects for VCI and PSI. The AS sample only differed from controls on PSI. On WAIS–IV subtests, the AUT group performed significantly worse than controls on all measures except Digit Span Forward and Matrix Reasoning. The AS group did not show significant differences from the control group on any WAIS–IV subtest measure. On the social perception test, the AUT group performed significantly worse than both AS and controls on the Prosody and Pairs condition but not the Affect Naming condition. The AS group did not differ from controls on any of the ACS Social Perception measures (Holdnack et al., 2011). In another study, Kandalaft et al. (2012) found strong convergent validity between the ACS Social Perception test and other measures of social cognition in a mixed sample of AS, schizophrenia patients, and controls. Further, the AS group was significantly different from controls on the ACS Social Perception Prosody items and at a lower level of significance on the

Affect Naming task (Kandalaft et al., 2012). Mean Social Perception scores of the AS sample in the Holdnack et al. (2011) study versus the Kandalaft et al. (2012) study were lower on all measures; however, the controls in the Holdnack et al. (2011) study also performed much lower than the controls in the Kandalaft et al. (2012) study, resulting in null findings in the Holdnack et al. (2011) research.

Asperger's Syndrome

The cognitive performance of individuals diagnosed with Asperger's Syndrome (AS) was compared to demographically matched controls. Table 11.8 presents WAIS–IV comparison data, including new index scores, between AS and matched control subjects. The AS group did not differ from matched controls on most WAIS–IV indexes. However, they did perform significantly worse on the Processing Speed and Cognitive Proficiency indexes with both having moderate effect sizes. At the subtest level, they had significantly lower scores on Coding, Symbol Search, Digit Span Forward, and Similarities. Based on the WAIS–IV results, individuals with AS do not show general intellectual deficits. Rather, some AS individuals may have subtle difficulties with basic attention, processing speed, and/or verbal reasoning. The effect sizes are too small for the WAIS–IV to be diagnostic of AS from healthy controls.

The AS group did not show significant cognitive difficulties as measured by the WAIS–IV. Table 11.9 presents results for AS versus matched controls on the WMS–IV. Of all the WMS–IV indexes, only the Visual Working Memory Index was significantly lower in the AS group versus controls. The WMS–IV subtests also showed few differences between the clinical and control samples. The AS group had significantly lower scores on Verbal Paired Associates I Easy Items, Designs II Content, and Symbol Span. Given the large number of comparisons, these significant findings may reflect chance outcomes; however, these could represent difficulties processing symbolic information or possibly some difficulties with basic attention affecting performance on these measures.

In general, AS individuals do not show cognitive deficits. Some individuals with AS may have cognitive difficulties but as a group these are relatively small. Given the small differences between highest and lowest index and subtest scores in the Asperger's group, it is unlikely that abnormal degrees of variability would be evident for individual cases. The highest and lowest obtained scores in the AS group were significantly different for WAIS–IV lowest index and scaled score. No differences were observed for highest obtained scores or WMS–IV highest

TABLE 11.8   WAIS–IV Standard and New Index Scores and Subtests in Asperger's Syndrome and Matched Controls

Score	Asperger's Syndrome		Matched Control		Between Group Differences	
	Mean	SD	Mean	SD	ES	p
Verbal Comprehension Index	104.3	16.4	105.7	12.3	−0.12	>0.05
Perceptual Reasoning Index	99.8	14.1	105.7	12.3	−0.48	>0.05
Working Memory Index	95.6	15.8	101.7	12.7	−0.47	>0.05
Processing Speed Index	89.0	13.9	98.4	14.3	−0.65	<0.01
General Ability Index	102.2	15.0	106.2	11.6	−0.34	>0.05
Cognitive Proficiency Index	91.1	13.0	99.9	14.0	−0.63	<0.01
Full Scale IQ	97.4	13.8	103.9	12.0	−0.54	<0.05
Vocabulary	10.9	3.2	10.8	2.6	0.04	>0.05
Similarities	10.0	2.7	11.5	2.8	−0.51	<0.05
Information	11.5	3.6	11.0	2.6	0.19	>0.05
Block Design	10.0	3.2	10.8	2.5	−0.31	>0.05
Matrix Reasoning	10.1	2.7	11.1	3.1	−0.33	>0.05
Visual Puzzles	9.9	3.3	10.8	2.8	−0.32	>0.05
Digit Span	9.1	3.0	10.2	2.6	−0.43	>0.05
Digit Span Forward	8.9	3.1	10.6	3.1	−0.57	<0.01
Digit Span Backward	9.6	2.7	10.3	2.7	−0.25	>0.05
Digit Span Sequencing	9.2	2.7	9.8	2.8	−0.22	>0.05
Arithmetic	9.4	3.4	10.4	2.8	−0.37	>0.05
Coding	7.4	2.6	9.4	2.9	−0.70	<0.01
Symbol Search	8.5	3.3	10.0	3.1	−0.49	<0.05

Note: $n = 42$.
Copyright © 2008 NCS Pearson, Inc. All rights reserved. Used with Permission.

and lowest obtained scores. The AS group does not have a suppressed profile but they do obtain low 'lowest' obtained scores compared to controls. Table 11.10 presents variability measures, controlling for highest obtained score from Chapter 3 to evaluate if there is significant intra-individual variability in AS versus healthy controls. No significant variability was observed for the WAIS–IV index and subtests. The AS group did show significant variability on the WMS–IV and the

TABLE 11.9 WMS–IV Standard and New Index Scores and Subtest Scores in Asperger's Syndrome and Matched Controls

Score	Asperger's Syndrome		Matched Control		Between Group Differences	
	Mean	SD	Mean	SD	ES	p
General Memory	95.2	19.2	100.0	13.7	−0.35	>0.05
Immediate Memory	95.9	19.4	100.3	13.1	−0.33	>0.05
Delayed Memory	96.4	18.4	101.0	14.4	−0.32	>0.05
Immediate vs. Delayed	10.6	3.8	10.3	2.5	0.10	>0.05
Auditory Memory	98.1	17.5	101.8	11.5	−0.32	>0.05
Auditory Immediate	98.2	18.2	101.8	10.7	−0.34	>0.05
Auditory Delayed	98.2	16.4	101.7	11.8	−0.30	>0.05
Auditory Delayed Recognition	95.6	15.8	99.8	15.2	−0.28	>0.05
Visual Memory	95.4	19.6	99.6	17.1	−0.25	>0.05
Visual Immediate	94.1	19.5	98.3	16.5	−0.25	>0.05
Visual Delayed	96.7	19.3	99.5	17.6	−0.16	>0.05
Visual Delayed Recognition	96.2	18.1	100.4	16.5	−0.25	>0.05
Designs Content Index	94.6	18.0	101.8	13.9	−0.52	>0.05
Designs Spatial Index	96.4	14.7	100.3	15.9	−0.24	>0.05
Retention Index	101.3	19.7	99.3	13.9	0.14	>0.05
Retrieval Index	98.7	17.5	100.9	11.9	−0.18	>0.05
Visual Working Memory Index	92.2	12.1	99.9	14.3	−0.53	<0.05
Working Memory	94.6	12.6	99.8	15.3	−0.34	>0.05
Quantitative Reasoning Index	97.9	14.1	102.8	16.2	−0.30	>0.05
Logical Memory I	9.9	3.5	10.7	2.6	−0.29	>0.05
Logical Memory II	9.6	2.8	10.4	2.9	−0.29	>0.05
Logical Memory I vs. II	9.7	3.0	9.9	2.8	−0.06	>0.05
Logical Memory II vs. Rec	10.5	2.3	10.8	3.0	−0.10	>0.05
Verbal Paired Associates I	9.6	3.7	10.0	1.9	−0.22	>0.05
Verbal Paired Associates II	9.9	3.7	10.2	2.2	−0.12	>0.05
Verbal Paired Associates I vs. II	10.4	2.8	10.0	2.5	0.16	>0.05
Verbal Paired Associates II vs. Rec	10.1	3.0	10.0	2.5	0.04	>0.05

(Continued)

TABLE 11.9 (Continued)

Score	Asperger's Syndrome		Matched Control		Between Group Differences	
	Mean	SD	Mean	SD	ES	p
Verbal Paired Associates II Free Recall	9.6	3.3	10.2	2.5	−0.26	>0.05
Verbal Paired Associates Trial A	9.6	3.5	9.9	2.3	−0.14	>0.05
Verbal Paired Associates Trial D	9.6	3.5	10.0	2.1	−0.19	>0.05
Verbal Paired Associates A vs. D	9.7	2.8	10.0	2.3	−0.13	>0.05
Verbal Paired Associates Total Intrusions	9.7	3.5	10.3	2.5	−0.21	>0.05
Verbal Paired Associates Easy Items	9.0	3.5	10.7	2.2	−0.74	<0.05
Verbal Paired Associates Hard Items	9.7	4.0	9.9	2.2	−0.07	>0.05
Visual Reproduction I	9.3	3.7	9.6	3.2	−0.08	>0.05
Visual Reproduction II	10.0	3.3	9.6	3.4	0.12	>0.05
Visual Reproduction I vs. II	10.5	3.7	9.8	3.1	0.22	>0.05
Visual Reproduction II vs. Rec	10.1	3.7	9.5	3.1	0.20	>0.05
Designs I	8.6	3.4	10.0	3.3	−0.41	>0.05
Designs I Content	9.3	3.4	10.2	2.8	−0.34	>0.05
Designs I Spatial	9.1	2.6	10.0	3.0	−0.29	>0.05
Designs II	8.9	3.4	10.2	3.2	−0.41	>0.05
Designs II Content	8.7	3.4	10.3	2.6	−0.61	<0.05
Designs II Spatial	9.6	3.1	10.1	3.1	−0.17	>0.05
Designs I vs. II	9.9	2.8	10.3	3.2	−0.11	>0.05
Designs II vs. Recognition	9.3	2.9	10.2	2.8	−0.32	>0.05
Spatial Addition	9.0	2.6	9.6	2.6	−0.26	>0.05
Symbol Span	8.4	2.5	10.2	3.0	−0.61	<0.01

Note: $n = 34$.

Copyright © 2009 NCS Pearson, Inc. All rights reserved. Used with Permission.

combined WAIS–IV/WMS–IV batteries compared to controls. These results indicate that some individuals with AS may have more intra-individual cognitive variability than controls.

In addition to mild deficits in processing speed, attention, and memory for symbolic information, individuals with AS show difficulties processing socially relevant information. Table 11.11 presents statistical comparisons of AS versus healthy controls on ACS Social Perception

TABLE 11.10 WAIS–IV/WMS–IV Variability Measures Controlling for Highest subtest or Index Score in Asperger's Syndrome and Matched Controls

Score	Asperger's Syndrome		Matched Control		Between Group Differences	
	Mean	SD	Mean	SD	ES	P
WAIS–IV Subtest High vs. Low	8.3	2.8	9.7	3.3	−0.42	>0.05
WAIS–IV Subtest Standard Deviation	8.1	3.1	9.6	3.3	−0.45	>0.05
WAIS–IV Index High vs. Low	9.5	4.1	10.0	3.6	−0.15	>0.05
WAIS–IV Index Standard Deviation	8.4	3.5	9.7	3.3	−0.38	>0.05
WMS–IV Subtest High vs. Low	9.1	2.4	10.4	2.9	−0.44	<0.05
WMS–IV Subtest Standard Deviation	9.3	2.6	10.6	3.1	−0.42	>0.05
WMS–IV Index High vs. Low	8.4	3.2	10.4	3.5	−0.56	<0.05
WMS–IV Index Standard Deviation	8.2	2.9	10.4	3.4	−0.67	<0.01
WAIS–IV/WMS–IV Subtest High vs. Low	8.2	2.9	10.1	3.2	−0.61	<0.05
WAIS–IV/WMS–IV Subtest Standard Deviation	8.5	3.5	10.2	3.2	−0.55	<0.05
WAIS–IV/WMS–IV Index High vs. Low	7.6	3.3	9.6	3.7	−0.53	<0.01
WAIS–IV/WMS–IV Index Standard Deviation	7.6	3.6	9.9	3.3	−0.71	<0.01

Copyright © 2009 NCS Pearson, Inc. All rights reserved. Used with Permission.

TABLE 11.11   ACS Social Perception in Asperger's Syndrome and Matched Controls

Score	Asperger's Syndrome		Matched Control		Between Group Differences	
	Mean	SD	Mean	SD	ES	p
Social Perception Total	8.2	3.0	10.6	3.0	−0.80	<0.01
Affect Naming	7.9	2.6	9.8	2.6	−0.75	<0.01
Prosody	9.0	3.2	10.6	2.9	−0.55	>0.05
Pairs	8.3	3.2	10.3	2.5	−0.82	<0.05
GAI vs. Social Perception Contrast Score	8.2	3.1	10.1	2.8	−0.71	<0.05
VCI vs. Social Perception Contrast Score	8.0	3.1	9.9	2.7	−0.70	<0.05
PRI vs. Social Perception Contrast Score	8.4	3.1	10.5	2.9	−0.70	<0.05
Comprehension	9.1	2.8	11.0	3.1	−0.61	<0.05

Note: $n = 28$.
Copyright © 2009 NCS Pearson, Inc. All rights reserved. Used with Permission.

and WAIS–IV Comprehension. These data have been reported elsewhere using a combined control matched to the AUT as well as the Asperger's sample and the education level of the controls was lower than the Asperger's sample education level (Holdnack et al., 2011). The controls used here are more precisely matched on education level of the AS sample. The AS group showed significantly lower scores on the Social Perception Total Score, Affect Naming, and Pairs measures. Affect Naming assesses the ability to identify and label facial expressions of emotion. The Pairs subtest requires the examinee to evaluate the interaction between two people using body language, affect recognition, prosody, and linguistic aspects of communication. The Social Perception Total score measures the ability to integrate verbal/auditory information with facial expressions. Low scores on social perception are not due to deficits in verbal or visual–perceptual skills, as evidenced by the Social Perception contrast scores. The AS group showed significantly lower performance on the WAIS–IV Comprehension subtest than controls. Comprehension requires the flexible use of language to describe aspects of social constructs. Although some of the effect sizes are large for ACS Social Perception, the degree of difference is not large enough to be a diagnostic indicator. Given mean scores near a scaled score of eight, most individuals with AS will achieve scores of eight or more, similar to healthy controls.

The overall results indicate that AS is associated with very mild deficits in cognitive functioning. In particular, they have difficulties with

TABLE 11.12 WAIS−IV Standard and New Index Scores and Subtests in Autism and Matched Controls

Score	Autism		Matched Control		Between Group Differences	
	Mean	SD	Mean	SD	ES	p
Verbal Comprehension Index	79.0	10.5	102.3	10.2	−2.28	<0.001
Perceptual Reasoning Index	87.6	15.7	100.9	15.1	−0.88	<0.01
Working Memory Index	82.7	15.3	99.3	15.1	−1.10	<0.001
Processing Speed Index	75.0	9.2	92.0	12.6	−1.35	<0.001
General Ability Index	81.0	11.8	101.8	11.9	−1.74	>0.001
Cognitive Proficiency Index	75.7	11.8	94.9	14.0	−1.38	<0.001
Full Scale IQ	77.6	11.5	99.0	12.6	−1.70	>0.001
Vocabulary	5.7	1.7	10.7	2.6	−1.93	<0.001
Similarities	6.3	2.5	10.0	1.9	−2.00	<0.001
Information	7.0	2.9	10.8	2.7	−1.40	<0.001
Block Design	7.5	2.8	10.2	3.3	−0.82	<0.01
Matrix Reasoning	8.7	3.4	9.3	2.9	−0.23	>0.05
Visual Puzzles	7.5	3.3	11.0	2.8	−1.26	<0.001
Digit Span	7.0	3.3	10.0	3.0	−1.01	<0.05
Digit Span Forward	7.4	3.2	9.9	2.7	−0.93	<0.01
Digit Span Backward	8.8	3.1	10.3	3.4	−0.45	>0.05
Digit Span Sequencing	6.8	3.7	9.8	2.9	−1.00	<0.05
Arithmetic	6.8	2.6	9.8	2.9	−1.00	<0.01
Coding	5.0	2.0	8.3	2.3	−1.37	<0.001
Symbol Search	5.6	2.0	8.9	2.8	−1.14	<0.001

Note: $n = 24$.

Copyright © 2009 NCS Pearson, Inc. All rights reserved. Used with Permission.

processing speed, and subtle difficulties with language functioning (e.g., reasoning and flexible use), registration in working memory for auditory and visual information, and ability to identify social information from facial expressions and body language. The AS group showed normal levels of highest obtained scores but a tendency to have a lowest obtained score below normal expectations. They have more variability in cognitive functioning controlling for their highest score. Most observed effect sizes are in the moderate range and are not large enough to use these measures for differential diagnosis. Rather, the cognitive tests enable the clinician to identify domains of cognitive weaknesses that could be affecting their academic, vocational, or social functioning.

Autism Spectrum Disorders

The cognitive performance of individuals diagnosed with Autism (AUT) was compared to demographically matched controls. Table 11.12 presents WAIS–IV comparison data, including new index scores, between AUT and matched control subjects. Unlike the AS group, AUT is associated with significant cognitive deficits. The WAIS–IV index results show very significant deficits on Verbal Comprehension with an effect size greater than two. Large effects were seen for Processing Speed, Working Memory, and Perceptual Reasoning. The overall results suggest a pattern of results with low but relatively spared visual–perceptual skills compared to verbal abilities. The AUT group performed significantly lower than controls on all subtest measures except Matrix Reasoning and Digit Span Backward. The largest effects were observed on Similarities, Vocabulary, Information, Coding, and Visual Puzzles. Consistent with the index level performance, the most significant deficits were observed on verbal measures. However, large effects occurred on mental construction tasks and visuomotor processing speed task. The effect sizes are significantly large enough to differentiate the AUT from healthy controls but not necessarily from other clinical groups.

The WMS–IV results are presented in Table 11.13. The AUT group was significantly lower on all WMS–IV indexes, including index level contrast scores, compared to matched controls. The largest effect sizes were on Visual Memory, Visual Immediate, General Memory, and Immediate Memory indexes, which were all near two. Both the Retention Index and the Immediate versus Delayed Memory Index Contrast Scaled Score were significantly lower in the AUT sample compared to controls, indicating greater than expected forgetting in the AUT sample. The significantly lower Retrieval Index in the AUT group indicates that recognition memory does not improve delayed memory functioning.

The WMS–IV subtests show a mix of significant and non-significant results. The largest effects were observed on Visual Reproduction I and II and Logical Memory I and II. Verbal Paired Associates was not significantly different between the AUT group and controls, except for the delayed free recall condition. The Designs subtest was also significantly

TABLE 11.13 WMS–IV Standard and New Index Scores and Subtest Scores in Autism and Matched Controls

	Autism		Matched Control		Between Group Differences	
Score	Mean	SD	Mean	SD	ES	p
General Memory	80.1	16.0	101.5	11.9	−1.81	<0.001
Immediate Memory	81.3	15.2	101.7	11.0	−1.85	<0.001
Delayed Memory	79.9	17.0	101.8	13.3	−1.64	<0.001
Immediate vs. Delayed	8.3	3.4	10.2	2.8	−0.71	>0.05
Auditory Memory	86.1	17.4	100.3	12.7	−1.12	<0.01
Auditory Immediate	87.0	18.0	100.0	12.7	−1.03	<0.05
Auditory Delayed	85.9	18.6	100.8	12.4	−1.19	<0.01
Auditory Delayed Recognition	83.7	15.2	102.0	14.7	−1.25	<0.001
Visual Memory	79.3	16.0	102.4	11.8	−1.97	<0.001
Visual Immediate	81.0	15.6	102.9	10.8	−2.03	<0.001
Visual Delayed	78.8	18.5	102.0	13.3	−1.75	<0.001
Visual Delayed Recognition	86.8	17.3	102.3	15.2	−1.02	<0.01
Designs Content Index	85.1	16.8	101.0	13.3	−1.20	<0.01
Designs Spatial Index	84.5	19.1	102.5	14.1	−1.28	<0.01
Retention Index	88.2	17.4	100.4	14.5	−0.85	<0.05
Retrieval Index	84.9	17.2	100.9	10.1	−1.59	<0.01
Visual Working Memory Index	82.2	18.6	101.5	14.6	−1.32	<0.01
Working Memory	81.4	17.3	100.7	16.5	−1.17	<0.01
Quantitative Reasoning Index	84.2	17.1	102.1	16.4	−1.10	<0.01
Logical Memory I	6.7	4.4	10.5	2.8	−1.38	<0.01
Logical Memory II	6.3	3.9	10.1	2.4	−1.59	<0.01
Logical Memory I vs. II	8.2	2.9	9.6	2.6	−0.52	>0.05
Logical Memory II vs. Rec	8.0	4.2	10.3	2.2	−1.06	<0.05
Verbal Paired Associates I	9.0	3.1	9.6	2.5	−0.25	>0.05

(Continued)

TABLE 11.13   (Continued)

Score	Autism		Matched Control		Between Group Differences	
	Mean	SD	Mean	SD	ES	p
Verbal Paired Associates II	9.0	3.7	10.1	2.5	−0.47	>0.05
Verbal Paired Associates I vs. II	9.4	4.4	10.7	3.0	−0.43	>0.05
Verbal Paired Associates II vs. Rec	9.7	2.3	9.5	2.1	0.09	>0.05
Verbal Paired Associates II Free Recall	7.2	3.7	10.3	2.9	−1.06	<0.001
Verbal Paired Associates Trial A	8.9	3.1	9.2	2.2	−0.13	>0.05
Verbal Paired Associates Trial D	9.0	3.3	10.2	2.5	−0.48	>0.05
Verbal Paired Associates A vs. D	9.2	3.7	10.7	2.3	−0.62	>0.05
Verbal Paired Associates Total Intrusions	7.9	3.6	9.8	3.3	−0.59	>0.05
Verbal Paired Associates Easy Items	8.6	3.1	10.1	2.2	−0.70	>0.05
Verbal Paired Associates Hard Items	9.0	3.5	9.5	2.7	−0.16	>0.05
Visual Reproduction I	6.4	3.6	10.8	2.3	−1.92	<0.001
Visual Reproduction II	6.3	3.1	10.2	2.6	−1.52	<0.001
Visual Reproduction I vs. II	8.1	3.5	9.7	2.7	−0.60	>0.05
Visual Reproduction II vs. Rec	6.9	2.7	10.2	2.7	−1.23	<0.001
Designs I	7.2	2.5	10.4	2.8	−1.13	<0.001
Designs I Content	7.4	2.7	10.2	2.6	−1.11	<0.01
Designs I Spatial	7.3	3.2	10.4	2.7	−1.12	<0.01
Designs II	7.1	3.7	10.4	2.9	−1.15	<0.01
Designs II Content	7.1	3.9	10.1	2.9	−1.05	<0.01
Designs II Spatial	7.4	4.3	10.5	2.9	−1.06	<0.05
Designs I vs. II	8.9	4.3	10.1	2.7	−0.44	>0.05

(*Continued*)

TABLE 11.13 (Continued)

Score	Autism		Matched Control		Between Group Differences	
	Mean	SD	Mean	SD	ES	p
Designs II vs. Recognition	7.7	3.2	10.3	3.1	−0.83	<0.05
Spatial Addition	7.2	4.0	10.0	2.6	−1.09	<0.05
Symbol Span	6.8	3.0	10.5	3.2	−1.16	<0.001

Note: $n = 19$.

Copyright © 2009 NCS Pearson, Inc. All rights reserved. Used with Permission.

lower in the AUT group versus controls for all measures except the Designs I versus II contrast score. The visual working memory subtests, Spatial Addition and Symbol Span, were both significantly lower in the AUT group. Memory difficulties in the AUT group cross visual and verbal modalities. Verbal repetition skills are relatively preserved while deficits in memory for complex verbal information are quite large. Visual Memory deficits were large in general but in particular when visual-construction skills are required as part of the memory measure. Both the verbal and visual memory scores may be exacerbated by the deficits in verbal skills and mental construction abilities observed on the WAIS–IV.

Both the WAIS–IV and the WMS–IV appear to have significant variability among subtest measures. Potentially, there is significant intra-individual cognitive variability associated with AUT. Table 11.14 presents the variability measures described in Chapter 3 for the AUT group versus healthy controls. The WAIS–IV index and subtest results are notable for the highest obtained score and lowest obtained score being significantly lower than controls. This indicates that the WAIS–IV profile is suppressed making it difficult to identify intra-individual variability. The WAIS–IV variability measures were not significantly different from controls. The same results were observed for WMS–IV indexes. The WMS–IV subtests, however, do not show a significantly lower 'highest' obtained score. The memory subtest scores are not suppressed and show significant variability for overall scatter (e.g., subtest standard deviation) and scatter at the extremes of performance (e.g., highest versus lowest score). Using the combined WAIS–IV/WMS–IV battery, the results show a very high degree of subtest variability but a suppressed profile for index scores.

Table 11.15 presents variability data controlling for the highest obtained score. When controlling for the highest obtained score, the AUT group shows a significant degree of variability on WAIS–IV

TABLE 11.14 WAIS–IV/WMS–IV Variability Measures in Autism and Matched Controls

Score	Autism		Matched Control		Between Group Differences	
	Mean	SD	Mean	SD	ES	p
WAIS–IV Subtest High vs. Low	9.5	3.4	9.9	2.7	−0.15	>0.05
WAIS–IV Subtest Standard Deviation	9.3	4.0	9.4	2.6	−0.07	>0.05
WAIS–IV Subtest Highest Score	7.0	2.9	9.5	2.5	−0.99	<0.05
WAIS–IV Subtest Lowest Score	5.8	1.4	9.5	2.4	−1.50	<0.01
WAIS–IV Index High vs. Low	9.5	3.7	9.8	3.4	−0.09	>0.05
WAIS–IV Index Standard Deviation	9.3	3.6	9.8	3.5	−0.14	>0.05
WAIS–IV Index Highest Score	6.5	2.6	9.9	2.8	−1.20	<0.05
WAIS–IV Index Lowest Score	5.5	1.9	9.8	2.8	−1.53	<0.01
WMS–IV Subtest High vs. Low	7.2	2.2	10.0	1.9	−1.47	<0.001
WMS–IV Subtest Standard Deviation	6.8	2.2	10.3	2.0	−1.72	<0.001
WMS–IV Subtest Highest Score	8.5	2.8	9.9	2.6	−0.55	>0.05
WMS–IV Subtest Lowest Score	5.7	2.4	10.0	2.6	−1.66	<0.05
WMS–IV Index High vs. Low	9.0	4.3	10.8	2.5	−0.71	>0.05
WMS–IV Index Standard Deviation	9.1	4.2	10.7	2.1	−0.76	>0.05
WMS–IV Index Highest Score	6.9	3.3	9.7	2.5	−1.11	<0.05
WMS–IV Index Lowest Score	5.7	3.6	10.2	2.7	−1.65	<0.001
WAIS–IV/WMS–IV Subtest High vs. Low	8.0	2.0	11.0	2.2	−1.35	<0.001
WAIS–IV/WMS–IV Subtest Standard Deviation	7.3	2.0	10.7	2.2	−1.51	<0.001
WAIS–IV/WMS–IV Subtest Highest Score	8.1	2.5	9.2	2.3	−0.49	>0.05
WAIS–IV/WMS–IV Subtest Lowest Score	5.5	2.3	10.3	2.8	−1.73	<0.001
WAIS–IV/WMS–IV Index High vs. Low	8.7	3.8	11.1	2.8	−0.27	>0.05
WAIS–IV/WMS–IV Index Standard Deviation	8.8	3.7	11.1	2.8	−0.39	>0.05
WAIS–IV/WMS–IV Index Highest Score	6.9	3.2	9.3	2.7	−0.74	<0.05
WAIS–IV/WMS–IV Index Lowest Score	5.1	2.8	10.1	3.0	−0.92	<0.001

Copyright © 2009 NCS Pearson, Inc. All rights reserved. Used with Permission.

TABLE 11.15   WAIS–IV/WMS–IV Variability Measures Controlling for Highest subtest or Index Score in Autism and Matched Controls

	Autism		Matched Control		Between Group Differences	
Score	Mean	SD	Mean	SD	ES	p
WAIS–IV Subtest High vs. Low	7.1	3.1	9.5	2.8	− 0.85	<0.01
WAIS–IV Subtest Standard Deviation	6.9	3.3	8.9	2.9	− 0.70	<0.05
WAIS–IV Index High vs. Low	8.4	4.2	10.1	3.5	− 0.48	>0.05
WAIS–IV Index Standard Deviation	7.7	3.6	9.5	3.3	− 0.54	>0.05
WMS–IV Subtest High vs. Low	6.1	2.1	10.1	2.0	− 1.99	<0.001
WMS–IV Subtest Standard Deviation	5.5	2.0	10.3	2.2	− 2.15	<0.001
WMS–IV Index High vs. Low	10.4	5.3	10.5	2.4	− 0.05	>0.05
WMS–IV Index Standard Deviation	7.7	4.2	10.8	2.4	− 1.26	<0.01
WAIS–IV/WMS–IV Subtest High vs. Low	5.9	2.0	10.5	2.3	− 1.98	<0.001
WAIS–IV/WMS–IV Subtest Standard Deviation	5.6	2.1	10.4	2.5	− 1.93	<0.001
WAIS–IV/WMS–IV Index High vs. Low	6.4	4.0	10.6	3.4	− 1.25	<0.01
WAIS–IV/WMS–IV Index Standard Deviation	6.8	3.5	10.9	2.9	− 1.40	<0.01

Copyright © 2009 NCS Pearson, Inc. All rights reserved. Used with Permission.

subtests but not indexes. Therefore, even though VCI and PRI appear to be quite discrepant at the group level, these scores will not appear to be discrepant on a case-by-case basis due to an overall suppression of the index scores. WMS–IV subtests show a very high degree of variability in the AUT group with effect sizes at or greater than two. However, WMS–IV index variability is significant only for overall variability rather than variability at the extremes of performance. The combined WAIS–IV/WMS–IV subtests also show a very high degree of variability with effect sizes near two. The index scores also show significant variability but not to the same degree as the subtests. These results illustrate that individuals with Autism have a high degree of cognitive variability when controlling for their relatively suppressed profile. The variability is particularly evident in memory functioning and combined intellectual and memory functioning.

In Chapter 2, the concept of multivariate base rates illustrated how healthy individuals obtain low scores on cognitive tests when considering performance across a battery of tests. Table 11.16 presents the

TABLE 11.16 Descriptive Statistics and Base Rates of Low Scores in Autism and Matched Controls

| Score | Autism | | | | Matched Control | | | | Between Group Differences | | | |
| | At or below 1 SD | | At or below 5%ile | | At or below 1 SD | | At or below 5%ile | | At or below 1 SD | | At or below 5%ile | |
	Mean	SD	Mean	SD	Mean	SD	Mean	SD	ES	p	ES	p
WAIS–IV Index Low Scores	3.2	1.6	2.0	1.8	0.6	1.1	0.3	0.8	2.3	<0.001	2.0	<0.001
WAIS–IV Subtest Low Scores	6.8	2.3	3.8	2.6	2.0	2.0	0.6	1.3	2.4	<0.001	2.4	<0.001
WMS–IV Index Low Scores	2.8	2.0	2.0	1.8	0.7	1.5	0.4	1.3	1.4	<0.001	1.2	<0.001
WMS–IV Subtest Low Scores	5.5	2.6	3.6	2.5	1.8	2.6	0.7	1.7	1.4	<0.001	1.7	<0.001
WAIS–IV/WMS–IV Index Low Scores	6.1	3.4	4.1	3.4	1.3	2.4	0.7	2.0	1.9	<0.001	1.7	<0.01
WAIS–IV/WMS–IV Subtest Low Scores	12.2	4.8	7.0	4.5	3.8	4.4	1.3	3.0	1.9	<0.001	1.9	<0.001

Copyright © 2009 NCS Pearson, Inc. All rights reserved. Used with Permission.

TABLE 11.17   ACS Social Perception Scores in Autism and Matched Controls

Score	Autism		Matched Control		Between Group Differences	
	Mean	SD	Mean	SD	ES	p
Social Perception Total	4.4	2.7	9.4	2.9	−1.72	<0.001
Affect Naming	6.4	4.1	9.5	3.1	−0.97	<0.05
Prosody	4.9	3.6	9.5	2.6	−1.79	<0.001
Pairs	4.9	3.4	9.6	2.6	−1.81	<0.001
GAI vs. Social Perception Contrast Score	6.4	2.6	9.1	2.4	−1.17	<0.01
VCI vs. Social Perception Contrast Score	5.9	3.1	9.1	2.8	−1.16	<0.01
PRI vs. Social Perception Contrast Score	5.8	2.7	9.5	2.1	−1.73	<0.001
Comprehension	5.0	2.1	10.3	2.9	−1.84	<0.001

Note: $n = 16$.

Copyright © 2009 NCS Pearson, Inc. All rights reserved. Used with Permission.

average number of low scores obtained by the AUT sample versus matched controls when a low score is defined as either at or below one standard deviation below the mean or at or below the fifth percentile. Multivariate base rates are usually applied to identify a change in cognitive functioning; however, these data demonstrate that individuals with chronic cognitive impairments will also exhibit a greater than expected number of low scores on cognitive tests. The AUT group has significantly more subtest and index scores at or below one standard deviation below the mean and at or below the fifth percentile than matched controls. The effect sizes are large, indicating significant cognitive impairment in intellectual and memory functioning.

The WAIS–IV and WMS–IV identified significant deficits in cognitive functioning, as well as areas of less impaired cognition. Deficits in social perception and interrelatedness are often associated with Autism. Table 11.17 presents AUT versus matched controls data on the ACS Social Perception Test. The AUT group had significantly lower scores on all Social Perception test measures compared to controls. Effect sizes were large for all measures including contrast scores. The significantly low contrast scores indicate that social perception deficits are present beyond the effects of low verbal and perceptual reasoning skills. In addition to low ACS scores, the AUT group had significantly lower scores on WAIS–IV Comprehension. This is consistent with other low verbal scores on the WAIS–IV, such that poor Comprehension scores do not necessarily represent social cognition deficits but general difficulties with using language to solve problems. The Social Perception tests did not have the largest effect sizes but they were the lowest subtest level scores obtained across all the batteries.

The AUT group displays a global suppression of cognitive functions that means that they typically do not have scores in the above average range. Rather, most of their scores will be average, below average, or unusually low. The exception to this finding would be some memory processes such as learning through repetition. When controlling for the lowering of most cognitive skills in AUT, a high degree of intra-individual variability in cognitive functioning, particularly memory functioning, is observed. These results suggest that AUT may be associated with some relatively persevered cognitive skills versus those that are quite impaired. The overall level of cognitive impairment in AUT is quite large as observed by effect sizes near or greater than two and high rates of low and very low scores. Diagnostically, it is possible to identify individuals with AUT from healthy controls using cognitive tests; however, the patterns of strengths and weaknesses would not be sufficient for differential diagnosis from other disorders. Rather, the cognitive tests are helpful in identifying cognitive strengths and weaknesses to help with treatment planning, remediation, and placement issues.

Although the observed cognitive strengths and weaknesses may not be sufficient for differential diagnosis, they provide insight into the profile of cognitive functions in AUT. There are clear and substantial deficits in cognitive skills that support effective interpersonal functioning. Global language difficulties, combined with difficulties identifying and integrating emotion recognition from facial expressions, tone of voice, and body language, severely hamper the capacity for social relatedness. Memory functioning is quite variable, which can be deceptive to people working with an individual with AUT. On one hand, they have intact ability to hear and repeat information but on the other, they forget more complex verbal information. Therefore, they can recall individual linguistic elements quite well but struggle with recalling integrated meaningful information. In the visual–perceptual domain, they appear to have intact ability to understand the relationship between visual details to solve problems, yet struggle with mental construction. Further, they have rather significant visual memory problems that are exacerbated when there is a visual-construction component to the recall. They are better at recognizing the individual pieces and parts compared to generating an integrated complex design. Assessment of individuals with AUT requires the use of multiple tools to gain a clear understanding of each person's unique strengths and weaknesses.

ASSESSING INDIVIDUALS WITH MAJOR PSYCHIATRIC OR DEVELOPMENTAL DISORDERS

Treatment Planning

Treatment planning has become an area of great concern in recent years for patients with severe mental illness. Typically, these patients are discharged to the community following a brief inpatient hospitalization and are followed as outpatients, generally stabilized on medication. Case management becomes a crucial matter with regard to preventing relapse and gaining optimal community adjustment. Programs involving educational and vocational rehabilitation, housing arrangements, working with families, hospital based or telephonic home care, supported employment, and medication monitoring are often implemented. Efforts are made to prevent or end the homelessness that some psychiatric patients experience following hospital discharge. It is beneficial to develop for each patient a treatment plan administered by a case manager to implement and maintain programs of this type.

The case manager may wish to use psychological testing to provide information pertinent to development of the plan. Important issues may include capacity for independent living, entry into educational or training programs, and exploration of vocational possibilities. Practical issues such as the individual's capacity to manage money and medication, shop, maintain some form of employment and a home, benefit from education or vocational rehabilitation and take care of personal health are typically areas of major concern. Serial psychological testing may be of value in assessing the individual's stability. In schizophrenia, relapse involving reoccurrence of clinical symptoms may have implications for cognitive function.

Intelligence testing is useful in the area of educational and vocational planning. Whether, for example, a patient who experienced an acute onset of schizophrenia, can return to school following stabilization and discharge from the hospital may be influenced by the level of intellectual functioning. While there are obviously numerous other considerations, the relevance of intellectual functioning in academic performance is well established. This consideration has become increasingly supportable since the research has appeared concerning cognitive heterogeneity, particularly in schizophrenia. It can no longer be assumed that individuals with schizophrenia are uniformly cognitively impaired, but rather they may have IQ levels essentially anywhere in the range of intelligence. Case management for the "neuropsychologically normal" cluster of individuals with schizophrenia may be a different matter from what is the case for significantly cognitively impaired individuals.

Of particular current interest is the use of supported employment in vocational rehabilitation and placement of patients with schizophrenia. A key feature of supported employment is the use of "job coaches" who are present with the patients in a work setting and provide advice and assistance regarding work performance. In a literature review, Kurtz (2011) showed that attention, memory, and problem solving abilities at job entry were most frequently linked to progress in this form of work therapy. Tan (2009), in a study of the relation between cognition and vocational functioning, made the following pertinent statement: *"Occupational therapists need to have a good understanding of the profile of cognitive problems among people with schizophrenia in order to tailor our intervention according to their cognitive strengths and difficulties* (Abstract)." McGurk et al. (2003) reported that the amounts of cognitive support and contact with employment specialists were predicted by executive, verbal learning, attention, and psychomotor speed abilities. There is substantial evidence supporting the use of evaluating cognitive function in vocational planning regarding supported work, and perhaps work in general.

Disability Evaluation

Clinicians frequently aid individuals with schizophrenia in applying for Social Security Disability. Similarly, individuals with severe developmental disabilities such as AUT often require disability assistance after they leave school supported services. Cognitive assessment is frequently included as part of the disability evaluation process to establish degree of functional impairment. This often includes both intellectual and memory functioning. However, formal assessment of suboptimal effort is not typically required of Social Security Disability evaluations; though, such testing is an important component of disability evaluations in other settings.

The goal of the disability evaluation from the psychologist's perspective is to obtain useful data that can in turn be used by government officials as part of the disability determination process. The Wechsler scales are frequently used for this purpose. Social Security Disability evaluations focus on current level of functioning and do not necessarily require assessment of premorbid functioning (which is often determined by education and occupation); unlike, in other types of private disability evaluations in which loss of functioning may be a critical component of the evaluation. In fact, the use of demographic normative adjustments as a means to identify loss in functioning from a premorbid level can work against some minority groups, and those with low educational attainment in the disability process (see Chapter 6).

Education Evaluations

Psychoeducational evaluations are required for appropriate special education classification and placement of individuals with disabilities. Although there has been a reduced emphasis on cognitive assessment with the advent of Response to Intervention (RTI) models for providing early intervention and remediation of learning problems, individuals classified as autistic should receive intensive cognitive assessment to identify strengths and weaknesses to inform educational intervention. Adolescents diagnosed with schizophrenia should also receive intensive evaluation of cognitive functions due to the high degree of variability of impairment in this group. While adolescents diagnosed with schizophrenia are served under the "emotionally disturbed" classification, the cognitive impairments may be more salient in evaluating their academic functioning.

The adolescent special education student requires educational planning beyond academic performance. During this time period, the educational planning must consider long-term outcomes and future placement. Vocational and employment training may be options considered for individuals with severely disabling conditions. Social skills and daily living skills training may also be considered for these individuals. Families of adolescents with severely disabled children need to understand the potential for the child to transition to supported living and vocational programs. As noted earlier in this chapter, cognitive functions, particularly memory and attention skills may be particularly relevant for succeeding in vocational and supported employment settings.

The adolescent with a significant psychiatric disorder requires coordination of services from multiple providers. The provision of psychiatric treatment, including medication and counseling services, are typically provided by external agencies, private or publically operated. Coordination of services between the school and providers of psychiatric care is critical for successful transition from higher levels of care (e.g., residential placement or inpatient hospitalization) to the less structured academic environment. Cognitive testing is critical in appropriately planning expectations for academic performance, potential social relatedness issues (e.g., bullying, isolation), and academic support services. The more comprehensive the assessment (e.g., not solely intellectual and academic functioning), the more tailored the educational planning can be. Level of stress, including academic and social pressures, will have a big impact on daily functioning in adolescents with psychiatric conditions.

CASE STUDIES

CASE STUDY 1

Below are scores of a 51-year-old African-American man, with an 11th grade education and a chronic history of schizophrenia. Mr. Y. was hospitalized after being picked up by police at a local library. The police were contacted when Mr. Y. would not leave the library. He had been wandering through the aisles talking loudly to himself, waving his arms in a threatening manner, and shouting at people who walked near him. Mr. Y. had apparently been homeless for the past 5 months following his discharge from the state hospital. He had not been taking his medication and did not follow-up with his outpatient treatment.

Mr. Y. returned to the state hospital for stabilization of his psychotic symptoms. During his hospitalization, he participated in a daily living skills training program and was evaluated for possible sheltered workshop placement or supported employment. Testing was completed to determine his capacity for participating in an employment setting and to determine if he would benefit from the training program. Additionally, the staff social worker was attempting to have Mr. Y.'s Social Security Disability reinstated. He had been receiving payments prior to his last hospitalization; however, his payments stopped when no address was provided for him to receive his check.

As part of the psychological assessment, the psychologist administered the WAIS–IV, WMS–IV, and ACS Social Perception test. The results from these measures are presented in Table 11.18. His performance on the WAIS–IV index scores reveals an overall Borderline range level of intellectual functioning. His highest obtained index score of 84 (PSI) and subtest scaled score of 10 are below normal (SS = 5 and 6, Chapter 3) indicating a suppressed intellectual profile. Even controlling for the low "highest" obtained index score; he does not show significant variability in his cognitive functioning. Mr. Y. functions intellectually in the borderline to low average range.

The WMS–IV results show memory functioning varying from extremely low to average. The highest obtained index and subtest scores of 90 (VMI) and 9 (DE I and VR I) are both atypically low (SS = 6 and 5, Chapter 3) indicating a suppressed memory profile. When the

TABLE 11.18   WAIS–IV/WMS–IV/Social Perception Scores for Mr. Y.

WAIS–IV Scores			WMS–IV Scores		
WAIS–IV Index	Scaled Score	%ile	WMS–IV Index	Scaled Score	%ile
Verbal Comprehension	81	10	Auditory Memory	53	0.1
Perceptual Reasoning	81	10	Visual Memory	90	25
Working Memory Index	80	9	Visual Working Memory	73	4
Processing Speed	84	14	Immediate Memory	70	2
Full Scale IQ	77	6	Delayed Memory	69	2
WAIS–IV Subtests			**WMS–IV Subtest**		
Similarities	7	37	Logical Memory I	2	<1
Vocabulary	10	84	Logical Memory II	4	2
Comprehension	3	50	Verbal Paired Associates I	2	<1
Block Design	6	9	Verbal Paired Associates II	2	<1
Matrix Reasoning	7	16	Designs I	9	37
Visual Puzzles	7	16	Designs II	8	25
Digit Span	8	25	Visual Reproduction I	9	37
Arithmetic	5	5	Visual Reproduction II	8	25
Symbol Search	10	50	Spatial Addition	7	16
Coding	4	2	Symbol Span	4	2
ACS Social Perception					
Total	7	16	Prosody	3	1
Affect Naming	12	75	Pairs	3	1

low highest scores are considered, the difference between the highest and lowest index (90 vs. 53, SS = 3) and subtest scores (9 vs. 2, SS = 7) are atypical (see Chapter 3). Memory functioning is quite variable and Mr. Y. shows a cognitive strength in his visual memory while auditory memory is quite impaired. Mr. Y. has difficulty remembering information even when it is repeated multiple times. Impairments in memory functioning may limit the type of work that Mr. Y. is capable of performing and the degree to which he will benefit from training programs.

The ACS Social Perception test results indicate variability in functioning in this domain. Overall his performance is in the low average range, consistent with his general cognitive abilities. He shows high average ability to identify facial expressions of emotion. When he is required to identify emotional content from tone of voice, his performance is extremely low. Furthermore, he shows extremely low ability to integrate linguistic, auditory and facial expressions of emotion, and body language to understand an interaction between two people. The more information required to interpret a social situation, the less accurate is his performance. His impairments in social perception could interfere with his ability to function in a supported employment setting.

The results of the assessment, combined with an analysis of his capacity for independent living, indicate rather significant problems with Mr. Y.'s capacity for semi-structured independent living. In addition, a significant alcohol abuse issue was identified that might further complicate his release from the hospital. Mr. Y. was kept in inpatient treatment for a longer than a typical stay. His social worker was able to find a structured outpatient living arrangement for Mr. Y. and his Social Security Disability was reinstated. Mr. Y.'s outpatient treatment team required consistent attendance for therapy and medication follow-up. His outpatient social worker arranged for Mr. Y. to participate in a sheltered workshop program three days a week. The long-term goal is for Mr. Y. to attain the capacity to live in a semi-structured, group home environment.

CASE STUDY 2

Mr. T. is a 17-year-old, white male special education student, who receives services through the statewide AUT intervention program. Mr. T. is a 10th grade student, placed in a self-contained classroom, at one of the school districts regional high schools. This is Mr. T.'s second year in the large high school. He adapted well in his first year but has experienced some behavioral issues in the early part of the 10th grade. In particular, he is significantly off-task in class and the teacher has difficulty redirecting him to his work. He occasionally has behavioral outbursts in which he yells and sometimes breaks objects. These episodes are infrequent but are quite disturbing to the classroom. A behavioral analysis was requested by the special education teacher to identify triggers for his emotional outbursts.

Behavioral assessment did not reveal specific environmental triggers but identified that Mr. T. has been preoccupied with his baseball card collection, which he carries with him in binders. He does not immediately act out when his cards are taken from him (e.g., due to inattention in class) but he does have an outburst within a day of having been reprimanded. Additionally, there is a new student in the classroom that appears to agitate Mr. T. making him edgy and irritated. Finally, Mr. T. has been struggling with his classroom performance in general and has not adjusted well to increased difficulty of his coursework.

The special education teacher and Mr. T.'s family met and decided that an updated psychoeducational evaluation should be completed. His last assessment was two years prior and showed generally border-line to low average intellectual functioning. A more comprehensive assessment was requested by the family to better understand why Mr. T. was struggling with his schoolwork and behavior this year. Mr. T. was referred to the AUT specialist in the schools state office. A compre-hensive assessment was completed with the purposes of educational and vocational evaluation. The WAIS–IV, WMS–IV, and ACS Social Perception test were administered as part of the evaluation. The results of those tests are presented in Table 11.19.

The WAIS–IV results indicate that Mr. T. shows a suppressed intel-lectual profile with his highest obtained index score of 92 and subtest score of 10 being in the low average range (e.g., SS = 6, Chapter 3). Controlling for his relatively low high scores, he shows some significant variability in cognitive functioning at the index level (SS = 7, Chapter 3) but not the subtest level (SS = 9, Chapter 3). His auditory working memory is a relative strength in this profile and processing speed is a weakness and the difference between the two scores is quite unusual (SS = 4, Chapter 3). Despite comments about Mr. T. appearing inatten-tive in class, he shows an average level ability to briefly focus his atten-tion. Problems in attention may be related to pre-occupation with highly desired objects rather than a cognitive limitation.

The WMS–IV scores range from extremely low (Auditory Memory Index = 47) to high average (Visual Working Memory = 117). The highest obtained subtest score of 14 is average (SS = 11, Chapter 3) and the highest obtained index score of 117 is in the upper bound of the average range (SS = 12, Chapter 3). Therefore, his memory profile is not considered suppressed and he shows a typical range of high scores. The discrepancy between his highest and lowest index scores of 70 points and highest and lowest subtest scales scores of 13 points are extremely unusual (SS = 1 and SS = 3, respectively). Intellectual functioning is generally suppressed but memory functioning is quite variable. In particular, Mr. T. has very good visual-working memory ability; however, auditory memory is very impaired even for simple information that is repeated multiple times. He is able to repeat infor-mation back if it can be held in working memory; however, when information exceeds working memory limits he is unable to remem-ber that information. Visual memory is less impaired, particularly for information that is related to multi-modal encoding (e.g., visual and motor).

TABLE 11.19   WAIS–IV/WMS–IV/Social Perception Scores for Mr. T.

WAIS–IV Scores			WMS–IV Scores		
WAIS–IV Index	**Scaled Score**	**%ile**	**WMS–IV Index**	**Scaled Score**	**%ile**
Verbal Comprehension	78	7	Auditory Memory	47	<.1
Perceptual Reasoning	88	21	Visual Memory	74	4
Working Memory Index	92	71	Visual Working Memory	117	87
Processing Speed	71	3	Immediate Memory	61	0.5
Full-Scale IQ	78	7	Delayed Memory	55	0.1
WAIS–IV Subtests			**WMS–IV Subtest**		
Similarities	6	9	Logical Memory I	2	<1
Vocabulary	6	9	Logical Memory II	2	<1
Comprehension	6	9	Verbal Paired Associates I	2	<1
Block Design	6	9	Verbal Paired Associates II	1	◁
Matrix Reasoning	10	50	Designs I	5	5
Visual Puzzles	8	25	Designs II	3	1
Digit Span	10	50	Visual Reproduction I	8	25
Arithmetic	7	16	Visual Reproduction II	7	16
Symbol Search	4	2	Spatial Addition	12	75
Coding	5	5	Symbol Span	14	91
ACS Social Perception					
Total	7	16	Prosody	9	37
Affect Naming	6	9	Pairs	1	◁

Social perception skills are variable. Mr. T.'s overall performance was in the low average range in his ability to identify emotions from facial expressions and to integrate auditory and facial emotion information. He had significant problems integrating auditory, linguistic, facial expressions, and body language to interpret interactions between two people. Mr. T. has had a significant amount of social skills training as part of the AUT program and in particular focusing on identifying emotions from expressions. Those skills are in the low average-to-average range; however, his ability to assess more dynamic aspects of social interaction in which multiple pieces of information must be simultaneously considered is extremely low. These results suggest that he may not interpret interactions with others accurately.

Based on the results of the cognitive assessment, academic evaluation, behavioral analysis, and teacher ratings the decision was made to change Mr. T.'s placement. It was recommended that he participate in a more vocationally oriented program with the goal of being able to obtain supported work after his graduation. The academic challenges of the vocational program are reduced and more pragmatic hands on work skills and interpersonal skills are the focus. The program specialist also worked with the vocational teachers to help them understand Mr. T.'s memory difficulties. This required a focus on very brief instructions and integrating visual, motor, and auditory modalities to improve recall. Also, Mr. T. was not allowed to bring his card collection to class anymore, but he was allowed to have them at school. He was given breaks and time to look at his cards when his behavior was appropriate and goal oriented.

CASE STUDY 3

Mr. B. is a 27-year-old, single, white man who has 12 years of education. Mr. B. currently works in a computer repair shop where he is a repair technician. Mr. B. has been employed for 6 months in his current position and performs his job well and is very knowledgeable about computers. While he performs his job well, he has difficulty relating to co-workers and customers and makes frequent inappropriate comments. Mr. B. is on the verge of losing his job because he has insulted and used profane language with customers. He has sought counseling as a means of appeasing his boss and as a good faith attempt to improve his control over his behavior.

Mr. B.'s counselor was struck by his odd presentation and atypical use of language. He perseverated on topics irrelevant to his current situation and was difficult to redirect. When he described his work situation, he took very little responsibility for his actions and really didn't understand why what he said was a problem. He reported no close interpersonal relationships and rarely had contact with his family. Apparently, he spends most of his time away from work playing computer games, fixing computers, and watching television. The counselor referred Mr. B. for a diagnostic evaluation for personality and cognitive testing because he was concerned that Mr. B. had more serious psychiatric or personality disorders than he was comfortable treating without more information.

Mr. B. was assessed by the psychologist in the same private practice as the counselor. The psychologist administered the WAIS–IV, WMS–IV, and ACS Social Perception test as part of the evaluation. The

TABLE 11.20   WAIS—IV/WMS—IV/Social Perception Scores for Mr. B.

WAIS—IV Scores			WMS—IV Scores		
WAIS—IV Index	Scaled Score	%ile	WMS—IV Index	Scaled Score	%ile
Verbal Comprehension	130	98	Auditory Memory	101	53
Perceptual Reasoning	129	97	Visual Memory	104	61
Working Memory Index	119	90	Visual Working Memory	115	84
Processing Speed	92	30	Immediate Memory	111	77
Full-Scale IQ	124	95	Delayed Memory	93	34
WAIS—IV Subtests			**WMS—IV Subtest**		
Similarities	14	91	Logical Memory I	11	63
Vocabulary	14	91	Logical Memory II	9	37
Comprehension	17	99	Verbal Paired Associates I	10	50
Block Design	14	91	Verbal Paired Associates II	11	63
Matrix Reasoning	14	91	Designs I	12	75
Visual Puzzles	17	99	Designs II	12	75
Digit Span	17	99	Visual Reproduction I	14	91
Arithmetic	10	50	Visual Reproduction II	5	5
Symbol Search	8	25	Spatial Addition	12	75
Coding	9	37	Symbol Span	13	84
			ACS Social Perception		
Total	8	25	Prosody	6	9
Affect Naming	12	75	Pairs	2	4

test results are presented in Table 11.20. The WAIS—IV results indicate that Mr. B. is currently functioning in the superior range of overall intellectual functioning. His highest obtained scores on WAIS—IV indexes and subtests are superior and his lowest obtained scores are in the average to high average range. The difference between his highest and lowest index scores (VCI 130 vs. PSI 92) is atypical (SS = 5, Chapter 3). The highest versus lowest subtest scores is also somewhat unusual (SS = 7, Chapter 3). Mr. B. shows significant variability in his cognitive functioning, with a pronounced weakness in processing speed. His processing speed score is still in the average range which should not be a disability for him but it may interfere with his ability to fully actualize his very high intellectual ability.

The WMS–IV data indicate that Mr. B. has high average working memory and immediate memory and average delayed recall. The highest and lowest WMS–IV scores are all in the average range. The highest versus lowest scores for indexes is average while the subtest difference of VR I (14) versus VR II (5) is somewhat atypical (SS = 7, Chapter 3). Like processing speed, delayed memory functioning is not disabling but may interfere with Mr. B.'s ability to effectively use his superior intellectual skills. The WMS–IV results are skewed by the one very poor performance on visual reproduction delayed; therefore, delayed memory functioning is not globally a problem for Mr. B.

The results of the ACS Social Perception test reveal a mix of abilities from extremely low to high average. The 10 point difference between highest and lowest scores would be considered atypical by WAIS–IV or WMS–IV standards (SS = 5 or 6, see Chapter 3). Mr. B. had average abilities in identifying and labeling emotions (75th percentile). His ability to integrate auditory and facial expressions of emotion is unusually low (9th percentile). His ability to use linguistic information, auditory, facial expressions and body language to interpret interaction between two people is extremely low. While Mr. B. may be able to describe how people are feeling, he has difficulty integrating more dynamic pieces of information that provide information about the relationship between two people. In comparison to his very high verbal and visual–perceptual reasoning abilities, his social perception skills are quite deficient and likely have a negative impact on his daily functioning.

The psychologist used symptom presentation and the results of the cognitive testing, background information, and personality testing to make a diagnosis of Asperger's Disorder. Of particular importance in the diagnosis were Mr. B.'s long-term history of impaired social relatedness, which had a negative impact on his academic success and interpersonal relationships, and a history of obsessive behavior. Mr. B. had the intellectual capacity to attend college but he underachieved in school and had consistent behavioral issues that interfered with his overall high school success. The results were communicated to the treating counselor and formal social skills training and on-going psychotherapy were implemented.

SUMMARY

Individuals with major psychiatric and developmental disorders have a variety of cognitive impairments that impact their daily functioning. Schizophrenia is associated with a general suppression of cognitive abilities of about $1/2$ to $1^1/_2$ standard deviations below the mean on most cognitive tasks. Individuals with schizophrenia do not show significant intra-individual variability within a specific cognitive domain (e.g., intellectual, memory, social perception). However, controlling for their overall suppressed profile, intra-individual variability across domains is observed (e.g., intellectual versus memory functioning). The variability among patients with schizophrenia is quite substantial, such that patients can have extremely low- to well above-average intellectual and memory functioning. Cognitive functioning in schizophrenia is associated with a number of important outcomes, including instrumental activities of daily living and the ability to benefit from work training programs. Assessment of cognitive skills is important for appropriate treatment planning.

Adolescents and adults diagnosed with Asperger's Syndrome show very mild deficits in cognitive functioning. Generally speaking, many individuals with Asperger's Syndrome will have completely psychometrically normal cognitive functions; the range of abilities being from low to superior. Subtle deficits in use of language (e.g., reasoning and flexibility), attention, and processing speed may be present in some individual's with AS. Although Asperger's Syndrome is associated with significant impairments in social relatedness, only mild deficits on measures of social perception are observed including naming of facial expressions of emotion and the ability to use multiple aspects of nonverbal and verbal information to understand the interaction between individuals. Cognitive assessment in AS focuses on identifying specific cognitive problems that may interfere with occupational, educational, and/or social functioning. Remediation of these problems through medication, individual therapy, and social skills training may result in improved daily functioning.

Autism is associated with very significant deficits in cognitive functioning. Specifically, impairments in language and social perception functions. Memory deficits can be quite severe when the information to be remembered is complex, either in visual or auditory modalities. However, memory functioning can also be a cognitive strength such as in rote memorization of simple auditory information. There is an overall suppression of their cognitive profile that may mask significant intra-individual variability in cognitive functioning. When accounting for the global suppression of cognitive functions, there is a high degree of intra-individual variability. The level of cognitive impairment generally falls in the 1 to 2 standard deviations below the population mean, which significantly interferes with their ability to function independently. Cognitive assessment is a very important component of comprehensive educational, vocational, and treatment planning for individuals with AUT.

KEY LEARNING

- Severe psychiatric conditions such as schizophrenia can be associated with significant impairment in cognitive functioning. Schizophrenia is associated with a general suppression of cognitive skills about $\frac{1}{2}$ to $1\frac{1}{2}$ standard deviations below the population mean.
- Schizophrenia is associated with consistent, rather than highly variable impairments in cognitive functioning; although, some intra-individual variability in memory functions can be observed. Among individuals with schizophrenia, there are broad individual differences in degree of cognitive impairment with some patients showing minimal deficits and others showing rather severe impairment.
- Cognitive testing is not used to diagnose schizophrenia. However, cognitive testing is critical in the comprehensive long-term care of individuals with this disorder. Level of cognitive functioning in schizophrenia predicts effectiveness of vocational and daily living skills training and employability. Many individuals with schizophrenia require government support through Social Security Disability and cognitive assessment is an important component of disability determinations in this disorder.
- Asperger's syndrome is associated with mild deficits in cognitive functioning. In fact, many individuals diagnosed with AS will have scores that are psychometrically within normal limits for all measured functions. As a group, individuals with AS show subtle deficits in language use (e.g., reasoning and flexibility), aspects of social perception (e.g., integrating multiple components of affect recognition, body language, and linguistic content), attention, and processing speed.
- Cognitive testing is not used to diagnose AS. However, the tests provide information regarding what cognitive deficits may be contributing to problems in daily functioning. Cognitive deficits may contribute to problems in work, educational, and social settings. Furthermore, subtle deficits in language use and social perception may interfere with social relatedness. Cognitive assessment may help with treatment and educational planning as well as recommendations for medication and individual therapy.
- Autism is associated with rather severe impairments in cognitive functioning. There is an overall suppression of cognitive functioning affecting most abilities. In the context of the overall suppression of all cognitive skills, there is clear variability with some areas of

cognition more impaired and others relatively preserved in some people. The degree of cognitive deficit is sufficient for cognitive tests to differentiate individuals with AUT from normal healthy controls. However, the strength of the profile variability is likely to be insufficient for differential diagnosis from other moderate to severely cognitively impairing disorders (e.g., intellectual disability, traumatic brain injury).

- Autism is associated with rather severe deficits in general language functioning and in aspects of social perception. Memory functioning is quite variable with recall of complex visual and auditory information significantly impaired, but rote learning of simple auditory information a cognitive strength. Degree of cognitive impairment is an important predictor for long-term educational and vocational outcomes. Therefore, cognitive assessment plays a critical role in educational, vocational, and treatment planning.

References

Allen, D. N., Goldstein, G., & Warnick, E. (2003). A consideration of neuropsychologically normal schizophrenia. *Journal of the International Neuropsychological Society, 9*(1), 56–63.

APA (2000). *Diagnostic and statistical manual of mental disorders* (4th ed., text rev.). Washington, DC: American Psychological Association.

Antonova, E., Kumari, V., Morris, R., Halari, R., Anilkumar, A., Mehrotra, R., et al. (2005). The relationship of structural alterations to cognitive deficits in schizophrenia: A voxel-based morphometry study. *Biological Psychiatry, 58*(6), 457–467.

Ashwin, C., Baron-Cohen, S., Wheelwright, S., O'Riordan, M., & Bullmore, E. T. (2007). Differential activation of the amygdala and the "social brain" during fearful face processing in Asperger syndrome. *Neuropsychologia, 45*(1), 2–14.

Binet, A., & Simon, T. (1916). *New methods for the diagnosis of intellectual level of subnormals.* (E. S. Kite, Trans.) Baltimore, MD: Williams & Wilkens Company. (Original work published 1905).

Bilder, R. M., Reiter, G., Bates, J., Lencz, T., Szeszko, P., Goldman, R. S., et al. (2006). Cognitive development in schizophrenia: Follow-back from the first episode. *Journal of Clinical and Experimental Neuropsychology, 28*(2), 270–282.

Boraston, Z., Blakemore, S. J., Chilvers, R., & Skuse, D. (2007). Impaired sadness recognition is linked to social interaction deficit in autism. *Neuropsychologia, 45*(7), 1501–1510.

Bowie, C. R., Leung, W. W., Reichenberg, A., McClure, M. M., Patterson, T. L., Heaton, R. K., et al. (2008). Predicting schizophrenia patients' real-world behavior with specific neuropsychological and functional capacity measures. *Biological Psychiatry, 63*(5), 505–511.

Carter, C. S., & Barch, D. M. (2007). Cognitive neuroscience-based approaches to measuring and improving treatment effects on cognition in schizophrenia: The CNTRICS initiative. *Schizophrenia Bulletin, 33*(5), 1131–1137.

Cullum, C. M., Saine, K., & Weiner, M. F. (2009). *Texas functional living scales.* San Antonio, TX: Pearson.

Emerich, D. M., Creaghead, N. A., Grether, S. M., Murray, D., & Grasha, C. (2003). The comprehension of humorous materials by adolescents with high-functioning autism and asperger's syndrome. *Journal of Autism and Developmental Disorders, 33*(3), 253–258.

Fujii, D. E., & Wylie, A. M. (2002). Neurocognition and community outcome in schizophrenia: Long-term predictive validity. *Schizophrenia Research, 59*(2), 219–223.

Ghaziuddin, M., & Mountain-Kimchi, K. (2004). Defining the intellectual profile of Asperger syndrome: Comparison with high functioning autism. *Journal of Autism and Developmental Disorders, 34*(3), 279–284.

Gilchrist, A., Green, J., Cox, A., Burton, D., Rutter, M., & le Couteur, A. (2001). Development and current functioning in adolescents with asperger syndrome: A comparative study. *Journal of Child Psychology and Psychiatry, 42*(2), 227–240.

Golarai, G., Grill-Spector, K., & Reiss, A. L. (2006). Autism and the development of face processing. *Clinical Neuroscience Research, 6*(3), 145–160.

Gold, J. M., Poet, M. S., Wilk, C. M., & Buchanan, R. W. (2004). The family pictures test as a measure of impaired feature binding in schizophrenia. *Journal of Clinical and Experimental Neuropsychology, 26*(4), 511–520.

Goldstein, G., & Saklofske, D. S. (2010). The Wechsler intelligence scales in the assessment of psychopathology. In L. G. Weiss, D. H. Saklofske, D. Coalson, & S. E. Raiford (Eds.), *WAIS–IV: Clinical use and interpretation: Scientist–practitioner perspectives.* San Diego: Academic Press.

Goldstein, G., Shemansky, W. J., & Allen, D. N. (2005). Cognitive function in schizoaffective disorder and clinical subtypes of schizophrenia. *Archives of Clinical Neuropsychology, 20*(2), 153–159.

Goldstein, K., & Scheerer, M. (1941). Abstract and concrete behavior. An experimental study with special tests. *Psychological Monographs, 53*(4), 141–151.

Green, M. F., Nuechterlein, K. H., Gold, J. M., Barch, D. M., Cohen, J., Essock, J., et al. (2004). Approaching a consensus cognitive battery for clinical trials in schizophrenia: The NIMH-Matrics conference to select cognitive domains and test criteria. *Biological Psychiatry, 56*(5), 301–307.

Harvey, P. D., & Keefe, R. S. E. (1997). Cognitive impairment in schizophrenia and implications of atypical neuroleptic treatment. *CNS Spectrum, 2*(1), 1–11.

Hathaway, S. R., & McKinley, J. C. (1940). A multiphasic personality schedule: I. Construction of the schedule. *Journal of Psychology, 10*(2), 249–254.

Hayashi, M., Kato, M., Igarashi, K., & Kashima, H. (2008). Superior fluid intelligence in children with Asperger's disorder. *Brain and Cognition, 66*(3), 306–310.

Holdnack, J. A., Goldstein, G., & Drozdick, L. W. (2011). Social Perception and WAIS–IV performance in adolescents and adults diagnosed with Asperger's syndrome and autism. *Assessment, 18*(2), 192–200.

Hollander, E., Bartz, J., Chaplin, W., Phillips, A., Sumner, J., Soorya, L., et al. (2007). Oxytocin increases retention of social cognition in autism. *Biological Psychiatry, 61*(4), 498–503.

Humphreys, K., Minshew, N., Leonard, G. L., & Behrmann, M. (2007). A fine-grained analysis of facial expression processing in high-functioning adolescents and adults with autism. *Neuropsychologia, 45*(4), 685–695.

Jou, R. J., Minshew, N. J., Keshavan, M. S., & Hardan, A. Y. (2010). Cortical gyrification in autistic and asperger disorders: A preliminary magnetic resonance imaging study. *Journal of Child Neurology, 25*(12), 1462–1467.

Kandalaft, M. R., Didehbani, N., Cullum, C. M., Krawczyk, D. C., Allen, T. T., Tamminga, C. A., et al. (2012). The Wechsler ACS social perception subtest: A preliminary comparison with other measures of social cognition. *Journal of Psychoeducational Assessment, 30*(5), 455–465.

Korkman, M., Kirk, U., & Kemp, S. (2007). *NEPSY–II* (2nd ed.). San Antonio, TX: Pearson.

Kremen, W. S., Seidman, L. J., Faraone, S. V., & Tsuang, M. T. (2001). Intelligence quotient and neuropsychological profiles in patients with schizophrenia and in normal volunteers. *Biological Psychiatry, 50*(6), 453–462.

Kurtz, M. M. (2011). Neurocognition as a predictor of response to evidence-based psychosocial interventions in schizophrenia: What is the state of the evidence?. *Clinical Psychological Revue, 31*(4), 663−672.

Lee, J., & Park, S. (2005). Working memory impairments in schizophrenia: A meta-analysis. *Journal of Abnormal Psychology, 114*(4), 599−611.

Lincoln, A. J., Courchesne, E., Kilman, B. A., Elmasian, R., & Allen, M. (1988). A study of intellectual abilities in high functioning people with autism. *Journal of Autism and Developmental Disorders, 18*(4), 505−524.

Macintosh, K. E., & Dissanayake, C. (2004). Annotation: The similarities and differences between autistic disorder and asperger's disorder: A review of the empirical evidence. *Journal of Child Psychology and Psychiatry, 45*(3), 421−434.

Mayes, S. D., & Calhoun, S. L. (2003). Analysis of WISC−III, Stanford−Binet−IV, and academic achievement test scores in children with Autism. *Journal of Autism and Developmental Disorders, 38*(3), 428−439.

McGurk, S. R., Mueser, K. T., Harvey, P. D., LaPuglia, R., & Marder, J. (2003). Cognitive and symptom predictors of work outcomes for clients with schizophrenia in supported employment. *Psychiatric Services, 54*(8), 1129−1135.

Namiki, C., Hirao, K., Yamada, M., Hanakawa, T., Fukuyama, H., Hayashi, T., et al. (2007). Impaired facial emotion recognition and reduced amygdalar volume in schizophrenia. *Psychiatry Research: Neuroimaging, 156*(1), 23−32.

Nestor, P. G., Kubicki, M., Kuroki, N., Gurrera, R. J., Niznikiewicz, M., Shenton, M. E., & McCarley, R. W. (2007). Episodic memory and neuroimaging of hippocampus and fornix in chronic schizophrenia. *Psychiatry Research: Neuroimaging, 55*(1), 21−28.

Palmer, B. W., Dawes, S. E., & Heaton, R. K. (2009). What do we know about neuropsychological aspects of schizophrenia? *Neuropsychological Review, 19*(3), 365−384.

Palmer, B. W., Heaton, R. K., Paulsen, J. S., Kuck, J., Braff, D., Harris, M. J., et al. (1997). Is it possible to be schizophrenic yet neuropsychologically normal? *Neuropsychology, 11*(3), 437−446.

Pearson (2009). *Advanced clinical solutions for WAIS−IV and WMS−IV*. San Antonio: Pearson Assessment.

Pirkola, T., Tuulio-Henriksson, A., Glahn, D., Kieseppä, T., Haukka, J., Kaprio, J., et al. (2005). Spatial working memory function in twins with schizophrenia and bipolar disorder. *Biological Psychiatry, 58*(12), 930−938.

Reichenberg, A., & Harvey, P. D. (2007). Neuropsychological impairments in schizophrenia: Integration of performance-based and brain imaging findings. *Psychological Bulletin, 133*(5), 833−858.

Rinehart, N. J., Bradshaw, J. L., Tonge, B. J., Bereton, A. V., & Bellgrove, M. A. (2002). A neurobehavioral examination of individuals with high-functioning autism and asperger's disorder using a fronto-striatal model of dysfunction. *Behavioral and Cognitive Neuroscience Review, 1*(2), 164−177.

Rutter, M., & Schopler, E. (1987). Autism and pervasive developmental disorders: Concepts and diagnostic issues. *Journal of Autism and Developmental Disorders, 17*(2), 159−186.

Scholten, M. R. M., Aleman, A., Montagne, B., & Kahn, R. S. (2005). Schizophrenia and processing of facial emotions: Sex matters. *Schizophrenia Research, 78*(1), 61−67.

Seidman, L. J., Buka, S. L., Goldstein, J. M., & Tsuang, M. T. (2006). Intellectual decline in schizophrenia: Evidence from a prospective birth cohort 28 year follow-up study. *Journal of Clinical and Experimental Neuropsychology, 28*(2), 225−242.

Sergi, M. J., & Green, M. F. (2002). Social perception and early visual processing in Schizophrenia. *Schizophrenia Research, 59*(2−3), 233−241.

Spek, A. A., Scholte, E. M., & van Berckelaer-Onnes, I. A. (2008). Brief report: The use of WAIS–III in adolescents and adults with HFA and Asperger syndrome. *Journal of Autism and Developmental Disorders, 38*(4), 782–787.

Tan, B. L. (2009). Profile of cognitive problems in schizophrenia and implications for vocational functioning. *Australian Occupational Therapy Journal, 56*(4), 220–228.

Toulopoulou, T., Grech, A., Morris, R. G., Schulze, K., McDonald, C., Chapple, B., et al. (2004). The relationship between volumetric brain changes and cognitive function: A family study on schizophrenia. *Biological Psychiatry, 56*(6), 447–453.

Tulsky, D. S., Saklofske, D. H., & Ricker, J. (2003). Historical overview of intelligence and memory: Factors influencing the Wechsler Scales. In D. S. Tulsky, D. H. Saklofske, G. J. Chelune, R. K. Heaton, R. J. Ivnik, & R. Bornstein, et al. *Clinical interpretation of the WAIS–III and WMS–III* (pp. 303–337). Burlington, MA: Academic Press.

Wechsler, D. (1997). *Wechsler memory scale–third edition.* San Antonio: Pearson.

Wilk, C. M., Gold, J. M., McMahon, R. P., Humber, K., Iannone, V. N., & Buchanan, R. W. (2005). No, it is not possible to be schizophrenic yet neuropsychologically normal. *Neuropsychology, 19*(6), 778–786.

Wolitzky, R., Goudsmit, N., Goetz, R. R., Printz, D., Gil, R., Harkavy-Friedman, J., et al. (2006). Etiological heterogeneity and intelligence test scores in patients with schizophrenia. *Journal of Clinical and Experimental Neuropsychology, 28*(2), 167–177.

Index